The Children's Culture Reader

The Children's Culture Reader

EDITED BY

Henry Jenkins

New York University Press

NEW YORK AND LONDON

NEW YORK UNIVERSITY PRESS
New York and London

Library of Congress Cataloging-in-Publication Data
The children's culture reader / edited by Henry Jenkins.
p. cm.
Includes bibliographical references and index.
ISBN 0-8147-4231-9 (cloth : alk. paper). — ISBN 0-8147-4232-7
(pbk. : alk. paper)
1. Children—Social conditions.   2. Children—United States—
Social conditions.   3. Children in popular culture.   4. Children in
popular culture—United States.   5. Mass media and children.
6. Mass media and children—United States.   7. Popular culture.
8. Popular culture—United States.   I. Jenkins, Henry, 1958–
HQ767.9.C4557   1999
305.23—dc21   98-24515
                              CIP

New York University Press books are printed on acid-free paper,
and their binding materials are chosen for strength and durability.

Manufactured in the United States of America

10 9 8 7 6 5

Contents

Acknowledgments   ix

Introduction: Childhood Innocence and Other
Modern Myths   1
Henry Jenkins

PART I: Childhood Innocence

1. From Immodesty to Innocence   41
   Philippe Ariès

2. The Case of Peter Pan: The Impossibility of
   Children's Fiction   58
   Jacqueline S. Rose

3. Children in the House: The Material Culture of
   Early Childhood   67
   Karin Calvert

4. From Useful to Useless: Moral Conflict over Child Labor   81
   Viviana A. Zelizer

5. The Making of Children's Culture   95
   Stephen Kline

6. Seducing the Innocent: Childhood and Television in
   Postwar America   110
   Lynn Spigel

7. Unlearning Black and White: Race, Media, and
   the Classroom   136
   Shari Goldin

8. The New Childhood: Home Alone As a Way of Life   159
   Joe L. Kincheloe

9. Child Abuse and the Unconscious in American
   Popular Culture   178
   Nancy Scheper-Hughes and Howard F. Stein

PART II: Childhood Sexuality

10.   Fun Morality: An Analysis of Recent American Child-
      Training Literature   199
      Martha Wolfenstein

11.   The Sensuous Child: Benjamin Spock and the
      Sexual Revolution   209
      Henry Jenkins

12.   How to Bring Your Kids Up Gay   231
      Eve Kosofsky Sedgwick

13.   Producing Erotic Children   241
      James R. Kincaid

14.   Popular Culture and the Eroticization of Little Girls   254
      Valerie Walkerdine

15.   Stealing Innocence: The Politics of Child Beauty Pageants   265
      Henry A. Giroux

16.   A Credit to Her Mother   283
      Annette Kuhn

PART III: Child's Play

17.   Children's Desires/Mothers' Dilemmas: The Social
      Contexts of Consumption   297
      Ellen Seiter

18.   Boys and Girls Together . . . But Mostly Apart   318
      Barrie Thorne

19.   Boy Culture   337
      E. Anthony Rotundo

20.   The Politics of Dollhood in Nineteenth-Century America   363
      Miriam Formanek-Brunell

21.   Older Heads on Younger Bodies   382
      Erica Rand

22.   Confections, Concoctions, and Conceptions   394
      Allison James

23.   Living in a World of Words   406
      Shelby Anne Wolf and Shirley Brice Heath

24.   The Tidy House   431
      Carolyn Steedman

PART IV: Sourcebook

Section A: Introduction 456

25. Reaching Juvenile Markets 459
   E. Evalyn Grumbine

26. Does Your "Research" Embrace the Boy of Today? 462
   Jess H. Wilson

27. "Selling" Food to Children 463
   The Mother's Own Book

Section B. The Family in Crisis 468

28. After the Family—What? 469
   John B. Watson

29. Against the Threat of Mother Love 470
   John B. Watson

Section C: Children at War 476

30. Children in Wartime: Parents' Questions 477
   Child Study Association of America

31. You Are Citizen Soldiers 480
   Angelo Patri

32. Raise Your Boy to Be a Soldier 483
   André Fontaine

Section D: Popular Culture and the Family 485

33. "Such Trivia As Comic Books" 486
   Frederic Wertham

34. The Play's the Thing 493
   Dorothy Walter Baruch

Section E: Freedom and Responsibility 496

35. New Parents for Old 497
   Sidonie Matsner Gruenberg

36. Families and the World Outside 499
   Elizabeth F. Boettiger

37. Time Bombs in Our Homes 501
   Mauree Applegate

38. Democratic and Autocratic Child Rearing 503
   Rudolf Dreikurs

Section F: The Permissive Family   507

39.   The Contemporary Mother and Father   508
       Lillian Jane Martin and Clare deGruchy

40.   The New Oedipal Drama of the Permissive Family   510
       Jules Henry

41.   The Modern Pediocracy   512
       Martha Weinman Lear

       Contributors   515
       Permissions   518
       Index   523

Acknowledgments

As scholars, we never fully escape the influence of our own autobiographies. So, in thanking the people who shaped our books, we are also, of course, always thanking the people who shaped us.

First, let me acknowledge Cynthia Jenkins, who has been questioning my assumptions about the nature of childhood since the day we met and who has collaborated with me in the grand experiment of raising our own son, Henry IV, a process that has really tested my theories and (on rare occasions) my patience. She remains both my biggest fan and my sharpest critic, and in both roles, she actively shapes every word that I write.

Second, let me acknowledge my son, Henry IV, who will be leaving home all too soon, but whose presence will always be felt in my thinking about childhood and children's culture. So much of the work I've written in the past sixteen years has taken shape around forms of popular culture he brought into my life, and so much of what I know about the difficulties and confusions of growing up in contemporary America was learned by helping him through both painful and rewarding moments of his life. Henry, I am proud of what you have become, a talented young writer, a passionate social critic, and a wonderful human being.

Third, let me thank my parents, H. G. and Lucile Jenkins, who have had the patience and wisdom not only to raise me but also to help me figure out how to raise my own son. Once, when I was just starting this parenting business, I called them, my arm deep within a box of Sugar Crisp cereal, trying to fish out the special prize, to thank them for all that I put them through growing up. Let me thank them again, publicly, and with less sugary fingers, for their patience, courage, and insight. My fascination with the permissive era of child-rearing reflects my attempt to understand better their generation and their hopes for my future. Apart from my general appreciation for their support, I owe a very specific debt to my in-laws, Jim and Ann Benson, who helped to tape the Republican and Democratic National Conventions for me.

I must also acknowledge the intellectual influences on this work, which certainly must start with Eric Zinner, who challenged me to put together such a collection and has shown shrewd editorial skills at every step in the process. This has been a wonderful experience. Shari Goldin has been an invaluable ally in pulling this collection together, and *The Children's Culture Reader* certainly benefits from her knowledge and resourcefulness as a scholar of children's media. I must also acknowledge the ever-watchful Jane Shattuc, who knows exactly when to tell me I've gone too far—or not far enough, as the case may be. I hope that I will never have to release a book upon the world without getting feedback from Jane. I am also in the debt of the students, graduate and undergraduate, who took my Reading Children's Fiction seminar in spring 1997, and helped me work through (and weed out) the materials for this collection; their questions and comments influenced my thinking on this project more than they probably realize. I would like to thank others who have shaped my thinking about childhood in recent years, including Ellen Seiter, Marsha Kinder, Lynn Spigel, Patricia Gillikin, Eithne Johnson, Eric Schaefer, Linda Dittmar, Kristine Brunovska Karnick, Peter Kramer, Brenda Laurel, Justine Cassell, Tara McPherson, Sherry Turkle, Amy Bruckman, Ruth Perry, Janet Murray, Janet Sonenberg, Eric Smoodin, David Thorburn, and countless others. I have also benefited from tough questions about my work on children and popular culture that have surfaced during my consulting work for Sega, Purple Moon, and Nickelodeon. Thanks also go to the MIT Class of 1942, who have helped to underwrite my research in recent years.

I would like to dedicate this book to the memory of the late Richard de-Cordova, a committed scholar of children's culture. I did not know Richard well. We met on only a few occasions, but we shared a similar passion for popular culture and a similar desire to understand more fully the historical evolution of our modern conception of children innocence. We once joked that Richard's study of childhood in the 1930s and 1940s would stand on many bookcases side by side with my proposed book on postwar children's culture and permissiveness. I took some comfort in the knowledge that he would fill in the gaps left by my own project as I struggled to resist the infinite regress that is the occupational hazard of historians. When he died, he was still at only the early stages of his research. I had hoped to reprint part of that work here, but it seems there are only loose piles of unsorted notes. My own book is still yet to be written. But, I know that I will feel a gap—an empty space on my mental bookshelf—where Richard's ideas and future books might have gone.

Introduction
Childhood Innocence and Other Modern Myths

Henry Jenkins

In the summer of 1996, the Democratic party held its presidential nominating convention in Chicago and the Republican Party held its convention in San Diego. Both gatherings focused as much on childhood and the family as on tax cuts or other traditional issues. The Republicans wanted to overcome the gender gap, and the Democrats wanted to show they still felt our pain after Clinton's support for devastating welfare cutbacks. Neither could resist the attractions of the innocent child. Both conventions offered classic stagings of parental concern.

Susan Molinari, congresswoman from Queens, presented the Republican keynote address, speaking as a misty-eyed and perky young "mom" about how her daughter's recent birth had refocused her political priorities. Network camera crews dutifully provided close-ups of her husband and her father hugging the newborn. After the speech, they brought the baby, Susan Ruby, to the podium for her mother to hold before the cheering crowds.

The cameras were equally obliging when the first lady, Hillary Clinton, addressed the Democratic convention several weeks later. Hillary and her handlers hoped to shift public attention from her controversial role in shaping health care policy onto her more traditional concern for America's children. When she spoke about the nation as a "family," the camera consistently showed the first daughter, Chelsea, as visible proof of Hillary and Bill's success as parents.

These close-ups of Susan Ruby and Chelsea rendered explicit the implicit politics of these occasions, giving us concrete images to anchor more abstract claims about childhood and the family. Both Susan and Hillary gained authority from their status as "moms" and both supported their agendas by referencing their children. While their political visions were dramatically different, the images of children they evoked and the rhetorical purposes they served were remarkably similar. Both Molinari and Clinton tapped into an established mythology of childhood innocence in the late twentieth century.

The myth of childhood innocence, as James Kincaid notes, "empties" the child of its own political agency, so that it may more perfectly fulfill the symbolic demands we make upon it. The innocent child wants nothing, desires nothing,

1

and demands nothing—except, perhaps, its own innocence. Kincaid critiques the idea that childhood innocence is something preexisting—an "eternal" condition—that must be "protected." Rather, childhood innocence is a cultural myth that must be "inculcated and enforced" upon children.[1]

This dominant conception of childhood innocence presumes that children exist in a space beyond, above, outside the political; we imagine them to be noncombatants whom we protect from the harsh realities of the adult world, including the mud splattering of partisan politics. Yet, in reality, almost every major political battle of the twentieth century has been fought on the backs of our children, from the economic reforms of the Progressive Era (which sought to protect immigrant children from the sweatshop owners) and the social readjustments of the civil rights era (which often circulated around the images of black and white children playing together) to contemporary anxieties about the digital revolution (which often depict the wide-eyed child as subject to the corruptions of cybersex and porn websites). The innocent child carries the rhetorical force of such arguments; we are constantly urged to take action to protect our children. Children also have suffered the material consequences of our decisions; children are the ones on the front lines of school integration, the ones who pay the price of welfare reform. We opportunistically evoke the figure of the innocent child as a "human shield" against criticism.

Until recently, cultural studies has said little about the politics of the child. Like everyone else, we have a lot invested in seeing childhood as banal and transparent, as without any concealed meanings of the sort that ideological critics might excavate, as without any political agency of the kinds that ethnographers of subcultures document, as without any sexuality that queer and feminist critics might investigate. Carey Bazalgette and David Buckingham identify a "division of labor" within academic research that subjects youth culture to intense sociological scrutiny while seeing childhood as a fit subject only for developmental psychology.[2] Children are understood as "asocial or perhaps, pre-social," resulting in an emphasis on their "inadequacies," "immaturity," and "irrationality," on their need for protection and nurturing. Because developmental psychology focuses on defining and encouraging "normative" development, it does not provide us tools for critiquing the cultural power invested in childhood innocence. Sociological critics focus on the "deviance" and "destructiveness" of youth cultures, their "irresponsibility," or the "rituals" of their subcultural "resistance." While we often celebrate the "resistant" behaviors of youth cultures as subversive, the "misbehavior" of children is almost never understood in similar terms.[3] This historic split has started to break down over the past five or six years, as more and more cultural scholars examine childhood.

This marginalization affects not only how we understand the child, its social agency, its cultural contexts, and its relations to powerful institutions but also how we understand adult politics, adult culture, and adult society, which often circle around the specter of the innocent child. *The Children's Culture Reader* is intended both to explore what the figure of the child means to adults and to offer a more complex account of children's own cultural lives.

Given the wealth of material about childhood that has emerged in sociology, anthropology, pedagogical theory, social and cultural history, women's studies, literary criticism, and media studies in recent years, it seems important to identify what this collection won't do. It will not be a collection of essays centered primarily on issues of motherhood, fatherhood, adult identities, pedagogy, schooling, advertising, media reform, mass marketing, computers, public policy, and the like, though all of these topics will be explored in so far as they impact contemporary and historical understandings of childhood. A surprising number of the essays written about children's media, children's literature, or education manage not to talk about children or childhood at all. The essays in *The Children's Culture Reader*, on the other hand, will be centrally about childhood, about how our culture defines what it means to be a child, how adult institutions impact on children's lives, and how children construct their cultural and social identities.

This book is intended not as a guidebook for media and social reformers, not as a series of attacks on the corrupting force of mass culture on children's lives. Rather, it will challenge some key assumptions behind those reform movements, rejecting the myth of childhood innocence in order to map the power relations between children and adults. This book avoids texts that see children primarily as victims in favor of works that recognize and respect their social and political agency.

Some may question the "political stakes" in studying the child, especially in moving beyond powerful old binarisms about adult corruption and victimized children. Such myths have survived because they are useful, useful for the Left as well as for conservative and patriarchal agendas. At a time when Republican crime bills would try children as adults and toss them into federal prisons or when we want to motivate state action against child abuse, images of innocent and victimized children are our most powerful weapon. Yet, the Right increasingly draws on a vocabulary of child protection as the bulwark of its campaign against multiculturalism, feminism, Internet expression, and queer politics. Any meaningful political response to this conservative agenda must reassess childhood innocence.

In this introductory essay, I outline work on children's culture across a range of disciplines and suggest some of this research's implications for thinking about contemporary cultural politics. In doing so, I identify what I see as three major strands in recent writings about childhood: (1) the examination of the meanings that children carry for adults; (2) historical research into our shifting understanding of the relations between children and adults; and (3) studies of children as cultural and social agents. Each of the next three sections of this introduction takes one of those strands as its central focus. In the closing section, I return to the question of the politics of childhood and outline some of the implications of this research.

Too often, our culture imagines childhood as a utopian space, separate from adult cares and worries, free from sexuality, outside social divisions, closer to nature and the primitive world, more fluid in its identity and its access to the realms of imagination, beyond historical change, more just, pure, and innocent, and in the end, waiting to be corrupted or protected by adults. Such a conception of the child dips freely in the politics of nostalgia. As Susan Stewart suggests, nostalgia is the desire to re-create something that has never existed before, to return to some place we've never been, and to reclaim a lost object we never possessed.[4] In short, nostalgia takes us to never-never land.

This book assumes that childhood is not timeless but, rather, subject to the same historical shifts and institutional factors that shape all human experience. Children's culture is not the result of purely top-down forces of ideological and institutional control, nor is it a free space of individual expression. Children's culture is a site of conflicting values, goals, and expectations. As Henry Giroux has argued:

> Children's culture is a sphere where entertainment, advocacy and pleasure meet to construct conceptions of what it means to be a child occupying a combination of gender, racial and class positions in society.[5]

Children, no less than adults, are active participants in that process of defining their identities, though they join those interactions from positions of unequal power. When children struggle to reclaim dignity in the face of a schoolyard taunt or confront inequalities in their parents' incomes, they are engaged with politics just as surely as adults are when they fight back against homophobia or join a labor union. Our grown-up fantasies of childhood as a simple space crumbles when we recognize the complexity of the forces shaping our children's lives and defining who they will be, how they will behave, and how they will understand their place in the world.

1. The "Fort" and the "Village": The Politics of Family Values

> The child was there waiting . . . defenseless and alluring, with no substance, no threatening history, no independent insistences. As a category created but not occupied, the child could be a repository of cultural needs or fears not adequately disposed of elsewhere. . . . The child carries for us things we somehow cannot carry for ourselves, sometimes anxieties we want to be divorced from and sometimes pleasures so great we would not, without the child, know how to contain them.
> —James Kincaid.[6]

In this section, I examine the convention speeches of Hillary Clinton and Susan Molinari as embodying different ideological strategies for mobilizing the figure of the innocent child. For Hillary Clinton, the child represents our "bridge to the twenty-first-century," the catalyst transforming uncontrollable change into meaningful progress. For Susan Molinari, the child represents our link to the past, carrying forth family tradition and "the American Dream" in a troubled world. For Clinton, the child is a figure of the utopian imagination, enabling her to conceive of a better world—a new "village"—that must be built in the present. For Molinari, the child is a figure of nostalgic remorse, whose violated innocence demands that parents "hold down the fort" against contemporary culture. But, both women, in Kincaid's sense, use their children to "carry things."[7] As Kincaid acknowledges, the very impermanence of childhood, its status as a transitional (and fragile) moment in our life cycle, enables many different symbolic uses: "Any meaning would stick but no meaning would stick for long."[8] Often, in our rhetoric, the child embodies change, its threat and its potential. The child, both literally and metaphorically, is always in the process of becoming something else. As Kincaid writes:

> If the child had a wicked heart from birth, that heart could be ripped out and a new one planted there in no time. If the child was ignorant, that wouldn't last long; if disobedient, there was always the whipping cure; if angelic, death would take him or, more likely, her; if loved or loving, that too would pass.[9]

Childhood—a temporary state—becomes an emblem for our anxieties about the passing of time, the destruction of historical formations, or conversely, a vehicle for our hopes for the future. The innocent child is caught somewhere over the rainbow—between nostalgia and utopian optimism, between the past and the future.

The American (Heterosexual) Dream

Within the Republican ideology of family values, the innocent child is most often figured in relation to the past, threatened by the prospect of unregulated change, endangered by modernity, and denied things previous generations took for granted. Molinari told how her grandfather had "bundled up a young son and left Italy in search of a dream," an "American dream," which "passed down" from generation to generation, until "a seat in a Queen's barbershop led to a seat in the U.S. Congress." Her "American dream" was, at core, the story of heterosexual courtship and reproduction: "find a job, marry your sweetheart, have children, buy a home and maybe start a business and in the process, always build a better life for your children." This "American" dream has become harder to achieve in the face of crippling taxes and other assaults upon the family. Far from an incidental detail, the child surfaces here both as a reward for living the right life and as a responsibility heterosexuals bear.

Barbara Ehrenreich's *The Hearts of Men* offers a somewhat more critical account of this 1950s-era version of the "American dream." Psychological discourse of the period made the reproductive imperative not only a social obligation but a test of maturation and sexual normality. Getting married and having children became one of those things "mature," "normal" adult men were expected to do; the failure to father was seen as evidence of maladjustment, immaturity, and often, homosexuality. Ehrenreich notes, "Fear of homosexuality kept heterosexual men in line as husbands and breadwinners; and, at the same time, the association with failure and immaturity made it almost impossible for homosexual men to assert a positive image of themselves."[10] If having children became proof of mature heterosexuality, then it is hardly surprising that the reverse—the prospect of homosexuals having access to children—was regarded as a horrifying contamination.

While Ehrenreich's book recounts the breakdown of this formulation over the past three decades of male-female relations, its persistence in Molinari's speech, and in Republican rhetoric more generally, suggests it is still a powerful tool for enforcing normative assumptions about gender roles and sexual identities. This commonsensical connection between heterosexuality and childhood innocence undergirds the exercise of homophobia in the late twentieth century. The idea that only heterosexuals can bear—or should raise—children shapes custody decisions that deny lesbian mothers access to their offspring. The shock that occurs when queerness and children's culture come together shaped the Southern Baptist Convention's choice of Disney as the target of its campaign against corporations that provide health insurance for domestic partners. The image of the crazed pedophile threatens the employment rights of gay teachers and led to a campaign to get Bert and Ernie banned from *Sesame Street* because of their "unnatural" relations. Molinari's version of the "American dream" represents a more benign version of these arguments, one that erases—rather than denounces—homosexuality as an aspect of American family life.

The Politics of Motherhood

For a moment, Molinari can't resist the tug of the myth of the innocent child as an agent of progress. The birth of her daughter, Molinari argues, makes her "think a little less about how the world is and a little more about the world you'll leave behind for your children." However, the conservative logic of her argument pulls her back toward the present as a decline from a past golden age, toward the "real pressures" that prevent modern moms and dads from achieving their parents' dreams. The modern world, she suggests, is a world that places our innocent children at risk: "Every morning they [parents] hesitate, at the kindergarten door, even if only for a moment, afraid to let go of that small hand clinging so tightly onto theirs." For a moment, Molinari hesitates, gesturing toward feminist protests against the unreasonable expectations placed on contemporary women, only to retreat toward a more traditional solution:

> I don't know a mom today who isn't stretched to her limits trying to hold down a job and trying to hold down the fort too. How many times have we said to ourselves that there just aren't enough hours in a day. . . . Well, the Republicans can't promise you any more hours in your day but we can help you spend more hours at home with your children.

The threat is transformed: it is no longer unequal gender relations, poverty, or unfair conditions of employment but the idea of working outside the home that renders working "moms" miserable. Her speech sees returning to the home as the natural desire of all women and depicts women's professional lives as an unwanted obligation that better tax policies would render unnecessary.

The figure of the defenseless child has been consistently mobilized in both support of and in opposition to American feminism. Because women have carried special responsibilities for bearing and caring for children, their attempts to enter political and economic life have often been framed in terms of possible impacts on children and the family. Fatherhood is one role among many for most men; historically, for many women, motherhood was the role that defined their social, economic, and political identity.[11] Early suffrage leaders represented their campaign for the vote in the late nineteenth and early twentieth centuries as a logical extension of their responsibilities as mothers to shield the home from the corruptions of the outside world. This maternal politics, or "domestic feminism," focused its attention on issues of alcoholism and prostitution and on the social conditions faced by the children of the urban poor. As one early suffrage leader explained, "The Age of Feminism is also the age of the child."[12] Yet, this maternal politics also restricted women's political voice to a narrow range of issues associated with children, home, and family.

Speaking as mothers gave the early feminists, who came mostly from the upper and middle classes, a vocabulary for linking their experiences, across class and racial divides, with those of other women. The revitalization of American feminism in the 1960s and 1970s often focused on issues of abortion, day care, child custody, and other family issues; middle-class women's entry into identity politics emerged from consciousness-raising strategies and the recognition that the "personal is the political." Women could gain economic autonomy only by shifting child-rearing burdens within the family and only by gaining greater control over the reproductive process. Decades later, Hillary Clinton evoked this rhetorical tradition of sisterly solidarity through motherhood when she told her convention audience, "I wish we could be sitting around a kitchen table, just us, talking about our hopes and fears for our children's futures."

This tradition of maternal feminism has given urgency to female politicians when they speak on behalf of children. Heather Hendershot has shown, for example, that Action for Children's Television gained attention from the press and from the Federal Communications Commission in the 1970s because it could speak as a group of "mothers from Newton"; ACT expressed impatience with the demands for traditional-media-effects research and spoke with "common sense" about the impact of media on their own children's lives.[13]

Yet, the heightened public discourse about maternalism has also provided a weapon for criticizing female politicians as "bad mothers" when they place too much attention on issues not directly linked to childhood or the family. Hillary Clinton was sharply criticized for the public roles she played in her husband's administration and for her flip remarks about not wanting to be reduced to "baking cookies." In her convention speech, she made fun of the need to reposition herself as a mother, joking that she might appear at the Democratic convention arm in arm with "Benti the child-saving gorilla from the Brookfield Zoo." Dan Quayle's 1992 attacks on Murphy Brown's status as an unwed mother became a major campaign issue.[14]

The figure of the absent mother, the neglectful mother, the mother who abandons her children for political and economic ambition always shadows the use of the maternal voice in American politics. Two of President Clinton's choices to become the first female attorney general of the United States were ultimately withdrawn because of public controversy surrounding their child-rearing arrangements, questions rarely if ever raised in considering the confirmation of male cabinet appointments. So, it is perhaps not surprising that when Molinari claimed common cause with other working mothers, it was in part to urge their return to the kitchen table. Less than a year after she delivered the keynote address at the Republican National Convention, Molinari herself resigned from the U.S. Congress to accept a job as a network anchorwoman, justifying her choice on the grounds that it would allow her to spend more time with her daughter.

The Suffering Father and the Unhappy Child

Republican formulations of the innocent child depict the home as "a fort" where mothers and fathers must protect their children from the chaos of modern life. Adopting characteristically military metaphors, former general Colin Powell spoke to the Republican convention about the need for families to remain strong in order to "withstand the assaults of contemporary life . . . resist the images of violence and vulgarity which flood into our lives every day . . . [and] defeat the scourge of drugs and crime and incivility that threaten us." This formulation of family values uses the figure of the innocent child to police boundaries between the family and the outside world. It often masks class and racial divisiveness, despite the presence of the African-American Colin Powell as a living symbol of Republican efforts toward becoming a "party of inclusion." This formulation, as Eric Freedman notes, also presupposes that the primary threat to our children comes from outside, while most cases of violence against children and most cases of "missing children" can be traced back to family members.[15] The Republican version of "family values," which sharpens our fears and anxieties about outside forces, lets the family itself off the hook.

One of the most memorable moments of the Republican convention involved the speech of a wheelchair-bound former policeman, crippled in the line of duty and now an advocate of tougher sentencing laws. He was attended by his young son, who stood behind him, one hand resting on his shoulder throughout the speech. With a slow and pained voice, he explained: "My son, Conner Mc-Donald, is nine years old and he has never seen his father move his arms or legs but when he puts his soft hands to his father's face I feel the promise of America and when he looks into my eyes I know that he can see the pride of America.

Few images more perfectly capture the melodramatic qualities of this "family values" politics. One of the moment's most striking aspects was its embodiment of male vulnerability and suffering. If conservative ideology has tended to hold women responsible for nurturing and raising the child, it sees the father as a breadwinner and as a bulwark protecting the family against the outside world. As Robert L. Griswold notes:

Men's virtual monopoly of breadwinning has been part and parcel of male dominance. The seventeenth-century patriarch has long since disappeared, but twentieth-century men have profited from their status as fathers. The linkage between fatherhood and breadwinning, for example, has helped legitimate men's monopoly of the most desirable jobs. . . . So, too, insurance policies, pension plans, retirement programs, tax codes, mortgage and credit policies, educational opportunities and many more practices have bolstered men's roles as providers.[16]

If women have found a politics based on motherhood a double-edged sword, justifying both their ability to speak in the public sphere and their continued restriction to the domestic sphere, men have found fatherhood a win-win situation, justifying their continued presence in public life, which, in turn, explains their negligible role in child rearing. While the charge of being a negligent mother can be directed against any woman entering politics, the "dead-beat dad," only now emerging as a political category, is treated as an aberration—a breakdown of the family-wage system. There is something unnatural, then, about this spectacle of a father who desperately wants to care for his son but is unable to do so.

The wounded father, who cannot wrap strong arms around his needful son, and the wide-eyed son, who struggles to maintain his belief in the "pride" of his nation, intensify our horror over the breakdown of law and order. As Mary Lynn Stevens Heininger notes, the discourse of childhood innocence has historically provided powerful tools for criticizing the "vicious, materialistic, and immoral qualities of American society."[17] The horrors of modernity are magnified through children's innocent eyes. Children serve as "soft and smiling foils to a more grim and grownup reality." Young Conner, his blond hair slicked down, his blue eyes shifting nervously, personifies suffering innocence and its rebuke against the adult order. At the same time, as Heininger notes, the figure of the "pristine" child has been an "indispensable element of American optimism": "It is precisely because the young are untainted that the nation can willingly vest in them its best hopes." The father feels "the promise of America" in his son's touch. The speech precariously balances the image of Conner as already damaged by a harsh world against the image of Conner (and his unblemished innocence) as potentially healing that world. As Heininger explains, "[B]ecause simplicity and innocence were considered to be children's most distinguishing characteristics, it followed that happiness should be their natural state."[18]

This ideologically powerful assumption allows us to direct anger against any social force that makes our children unhappy. As Kincaid argues, "[A]n unhappy child was and is unnatural, an indictment of somebody: parent, institution, nation."[19] The figure of the endangered child surfaced powerfully in campaigns for the Communications Decency Act, appearing as a hypnotized young face awash in the eerie glow of the computer terminal on the cover of *Time*, rendering arguments about the First Amendment beside the point.[20] As one letter to *Time* explained, "If we lose our kids to cyberporn, free speech won't matter."[21] The innocent child was to be protected at "all costs."

Throughout the 1996 presidential campaign, candidate Bob Dole consistently characterized liberal politics and countercultural "social experiments" in terms of the threats they posed to our children: "crime, drugs, illegitimacy, abortion, the abdication of duty and the abandonment of children." Higher taxes, Dole argued, meant a grandmother might be unable to call her grandchild or a parent might be unable to buy her child a book. Evoking the title of Hilary Clinton's best-selling book, Dole proclaimed:

> After the virtual devastation of the American family, the rock upon which this country was founded, we are told it takes the village—that is, the collective and thus the state—to raise a child . . . I am here to tell you. It doesn't take a village to raise a child—it takes a family.

Dole's slippage between the village, the collective, and the state is characteristic of a Republican rhetoric that reduces the problems of children to those confronted and solved by volunteerism and by individual families; Dole frames government action as the threat that makes children's lives miserable. Of course, many Republican solutions, such as the Communications Decency Act, depend upon the policing power of the village.

Democratic Family Values

Reworking conservative "family values" rhetoric—and thus "taking the issue off the table"—has been central to the "New Democrat" strategy of the Clinton administration. The 1992 Democratic Party convention was framed around rethinking the concept of the family to reflect the diverse ways Americans live in the 1990s. Clinton and the other "New Democrats" embraced a broader range of social units, including, at least briefly, the idea that gay and lesbian couples might constitute viable families. Clinton and Gore retooled ancient conceptions of the leader as a law-giving patriarch, adopting a postfeminist construction of the nurturing father watching over his children's bedside; images of Clinton marveling over Chelsea's birth or Gore attending his son, after a near-fatal accident, surfaced throughout speeches and campaign biographies. This kinder, gentler conception of the patriarch emerges from what Robert L. Griswold calls the discourse of "New Fatherhood" in postwar America. While historically fathers could gain power and authority from their public roles as breadwinners, they could now also get credit for their more private roles as educators and nurturers. Griswold sees this shift as a response to the expanded economic role of women in the workplace and to feminist critiques of the family but acknowledges that this new style of fatherhood often does not mean reciprocality of responsibilities. "Sensitive" male politicians can freely embrace the domestic sphere without becoming trapped there; Hillary Clinton's shifts between domestic and public sphere politics provoke controversy.

Hillary's law-review essays defending the concept of "children's rights" and her participation in Marian Edelman's Children's Defense Fund were ruthlessly attacked at the 1992 Republican convention by Marilyn Quayle and Barbara Bush as too "extremist" for a proper first lady.[22] Although she acknowledged in her writing that "the phrase 'children's rights' is a slogan in search of definition,"

Hillary Rodham presented a powerful case for reconsidering how the courts and other legal institutions dealt with children's issues. Sounding like many cultural critics of childhood innocence, Rodham wrote:

> No other group is so totally dependent for its well-being on choices made by others. Obviously this dependency can be explained to a significant degree by the physical, intellectual, and psychological incapacities of (some) children which render them weaker than (some) older persons. But the phenomenon must also be seen as part of the organization and ideology of the political system itself. Lacking even the basic power to vote, children are not able to exercise normal constituency powers, articulating self-interests to politicians and working towards specific goals.

She stressed the need of children to have a more powerful voice in custody disputes, insisted on an expanded conception of their rights to free expression, and argued for greater procedural protections for juveniles charged with criminal violations. Republican critics felt that her arguments depended on state authorities to protect children's interests even in the face of parental opposition and thus undermined the sovereignty of the family. Her book, *It Takes a Village*, reworked some of these earlier arguments, shifting from a discourse of children's rights to a language of parental responsibility. Her new approach to "family values" was consistent with the Clinton administration's endorsement of school uniforms, curfews, and the "V-Chip." Republican critics still found within the book's more banal prose signs of the state power central to her earlier formulations.

Forming the New Village

Lauren Berlant has argued that the Republican "family values" agenda involves a "downsizing" of the public sphere, a reduction of the role of politics in public life in favor of an exclusive focus on individual experience—on a politics of personal responsibilities and self-interest rather than one of the collective good.[23] The Clinton version of "family values" relocates the family within a revitalized public sphere. When Hillary speaks of the "village" and its responsibility for children, she evokes a middle ground between "the state" and the private, one consistent with her husband's unstable compromise between Republican pressures toward defederalization and traditional liberal conceptions of government activism. Hillary's village metaphor emerges from a politics of communitarianism, in which the community maintains a social contract to ensure the well-being of its members, a contract sometimes met by volunteerism and sometimes by government policy: "Home can—and should—be a bedrock for any child. Communities can—and should—provide the eyes and enforcement to watch over them, formally and informally. And our government can—and should—create and uphold the laws that set standards of safety for us all." Her book acknowledges the breakdown of traditional communities and the potential for new kinds of communities emerging in responses to changing technological and economic conditions. Rather than calling upon the community to preserve its traditional roles in protecting children, she calls a new community into being, one constituted through its mutual concern for children as much-needed agents of future progress. The village metaphor, with its evocation of the organic communities of small-town American life, depends upon the historic linkage of childhood innocence to pastoralism (an image that can be traced back to Rousseau and the Romantics.)

If the Republican formulation of family values pits the "collective" against the family, the Democratic version sees the individual and the community as vitally and positively linked. In her speech to the convention, Hillary Clinton evoked an image of a national community where "[r]ight now in our biggest cities and our smallest towns there are boys and girls being tucked gently into their beds and there are boys and girls who have no one to call Mom and Dad and no place to call home." What unites the haves and the have-nots, according to this account, is that all of us care about our children. Therefore, the needs of children must somehow be removed from the realm of the political and into a space of shared understanding and communal action, as we work together to create a "nation that does not just talk about family values but acts in ways that values family."

Her vision of a world where "we are all part of one family" depends on state actions (such as "dedicated teachers preparing their lessons for the new school year . . . or police officers working to help kids stay out of trouble") but also on individual action ("volunteers tutoring and coaching children . . . and of course, parents, first and foremost"). These community members work together against various threats: "gang leaders and drug pushers on the corners of their neighborhoods . . . a popular culture that glamorizes sex and violence, smoking and drinking." Their united efforts on behalf of childhood innocence become the basis for a utopian revitalization of the nation. This image of transformation is explicit in the final paragraph of her book:

> Nothing is more important to our shared future than the well-being of children. For children are at our core—not only as vulnerable beings in need of love and care but as a moral touchstone amidst the complexity and contentiousness of modern life. Just as it takes a village to raise a child, it takes children to raise up a village to become all it should be. The village we build with them in mind will be a better place for us all.[24]

For Clinton, it is not simply that children need the village but that the future of the village depends upon its shared commitments to children.

Race, Imperialism, and the Child

At a time when the Democratic Party was actively courting African Americans and Asian Americans for their votes and their campaign contributions, her choice of an African proverb, one widely used in Afrocentric pedagogy, as the book's title could not have been an accident. Hillary cites Marian Wright Edelman, the African-American woman who is the founder and head of the Children's Defense Fund as a mentor and friend. At the same time, she retreats from the explicit links Edelman draws between children's plight and racial politics. Edelman connects present-day struggles on behalf of children with the legacy of Martin Luther King's civil rights movement:

> We must put social and economic underpinnings beneath the millions of African-American, Asian American, Latino, White and Native American children left behind when the promise of the civil rights laws and the significant progress of the 1960s and 70s in alleviating poverty were eclipsed by the Vietnam War, economic recession, and changing national leadership priorities.[25]

Edelman had been sharply critical of Clinton's capitulation to the Republicans on welfare reform, a decision that she estimated would place five million more children into poverty.[26]

Edelman recognizes that suffering occurs most often to particular children, marked by racial and class differences, and Hillary engages in what Jacqueline Rose describes as the "impossible fiction" of the universalized child.[27] In our culture, the most persistent image of the innocent child is that of a white, blond-haired, blue-eyed boy, someone like Conner, and the markers of middle-classness, whiteness, and masculinity are read as standing for all children. *It Takes a Village* adopts a multicultural variant of this universalized child, depicting Hillary on the back cover surrounded by children of all different racial and ethnic backgrounds, all well dressed, all squeaky clean, all smiling. The implications of this "Family of Man"–style image are complex: the photograph envisions a utopian community united despite racial differences, and at the same time bleaches away Edelman's racial and class specificity.

For several generations, progressive civil rights policies, especially those surrounding school desegregation, have rested on the hope that children, born without prejudice, might escape racial boundaries. As Shari Goldin notes, school desegregation advocates promote the image of black and white children interacting freely together on the playgrounds and in the schoolrooms as the advanced guard for tomorrow's "color-blind" society.[28] Hillary Clinton depicts childhood as an escape from racial antagonism when she recalls the old hymn "Jesus Loves Me," which finds "all the children of the world, red, yellow, black, and white . . . precious in His sight." She wonders how "anyone who ever sang" this song "could dislike someone solely on for the color of their skin."[29] Her back-cover photo mimics classic pictures of Jesus "suffering the children."

At the same time, segregationists—from rural Alabama to South Boston—often posed school busing as a violation of childhood innocence, as a cynical bureaucratic "experiment" that turned children into "guinea pigs," "scapegoats," and "hostages" of a "liberal agenda." Racism, no less than the civil rights movement, has mobilized our hopes and fears for our children. Moreover, as Ashis Nandy has suggested, dominant ideologies of racism and colonialism have often mapped onto racial and cultural others the image of the child as "an inferior version of the adult—as a lovable, spontaneous, delicate being who is also simultaneously dependent, unreliable and wilful and thus, as a being who needs to be guided, protected and educated as a ward."[30] Such paternalism framed the official politics of colonial domination and the unofficial politics of racial bigotry;

white domination was presented as a rational (and benign) response to the "immaturity" of nonwhite peoples. Asian and African adults were often ascribed with the childlikeness of good "obedient" children or the childishness of bad "rebellious" children.

Common Ground

Both the Republican and Democratic formulations of "family values" cast popular culture as a social problem, roughly on the same level as crime and drugs. The same week that Congress passed welfare reform, President Clinton met with television executives to set up a ratings system and Bob Dole went to Hollywood to attack movie violence. Democratic senator Joseph Lieberman, who backed the welfare reform effort, has focused congressional attention on the problem of video-game violence, which he calls the "nightmare before Christmas." In each case, the attacks on popular culture shift attention away from material problems affecting children and onto the symbolic terrain.

Throughout the twentieth century, the myth of childhood innocence has helped to erect or preserve cultural hierarchies, dismissing popular culture in favor of middle-brow or high cultural works viewed more appropriate for children. As Lynn Spigel and I write, "By evoking the 'threat to children,' social reformers typically justified their own position as cultural custodians, linking (either implicitly or explicitly) anxieties about violence, sexuality and morality to mandates of good taste and artistic merit."[31] Within this protectionist rhetoric, taste distinctions get transformed into moral issues, with the desire to shelter children's "purity" providing a rationale for censorship and regulation. Once the innocent child has been evoked, it becomes difficult to pull back and examine these cultural issues from other perspectives, thus accounting for the bipartisan attacks against Hollywood.

Both the Republican and Democratic versions of family values presuppose the innocent child as requiring adult protection; they both speak for the child who is assumed to be incapable of speaking for herself. Young Conner remains mute as his father speaks of his own sufferings and those of his son. Three-month-old Susan Ruby was too young to talk, and the Clintons turned down Chelsea's request to speak at the convention, "protecting" her from the glare of the public spotlight.

Both the Republican and Democratic visions presume a clear separation between childhood and adulthood, with different rights and responsibilities ascribed to each phase of human development. The myth of childhood innocence depends upon our ability to locate such a break, as well as upon our sense of nostalgic loss when we cross irreversibly into adulthood. As the next section suggests, this particular conception of childhood innocence is of fairly recent historical origins. In the next section, I move beyond contemporary debates between Republicans and Democrats to frame the concept of childhood innocence in a larger historiographic context.

2. *The Historical Evolution of the Child*

> Members of any society carry within themselves a working definition of childhood, its nature, limitations and duration. They may not explicitly discuss this definition, write about it, or even consciously conceive of it as an issue, but they act upon their assumptions in all of their dealings with, fears for, and expectations of their children.
>
> —Karin Calvert[32]

Our modern conception of the innocent child presumes its universality across historical periods and across widely divergent cultures. The presocialized child exists in a state of nature. When we want to prove that something is so basic to human nature that it cannot be changed (the differences between the genders, for example), we point to its presence in our children. This universalized conception of the innocent child effaces gender, class, and racial differences, even if it holds those differences in place. This essentialized conception of the innocent child frees it of the taint of adult sexuality, even as we use it to police adult sexuality, and even as we use the threat of adult sexuality to regulate children's bodies. This decontextualized conception of the innocent child exists outside the culture, precisely so that we can use it to regulate cultural hierarchies, to separate the impure influence of popular culture from the sanctifying touch of high culture. This ahistorical conception of the innocent child is eternal, even as our political rhetoric poses childhood as constantly under threat and always on the verge of "disappearing" altogether. In short, the innocent child is a myth, in Roland Barthes's sense of the word, a figure that transforms culture into nature.

Like all myths, the innocent child has a history. In fact, one reason it can carry so many contradictory meanings is that our modern sense of the child is a palimpsest of ideas from different historical contexts—one part Romantic, one part Victorian, one part medieval, and one part modern. We do not so much discard old conceptions of the child as accrue additional meanings around what remains one of our most culturally potent signifiers. In this section, I do not trace a single lineage of the myth of the child, a task well beyond the scope of this essay. Rather, I outline how various historians have approached this question and examine the most prevalent meanings that have stuck to the semiotically adhesive child.

The Origins of Childhood

Philippe Ariès begins his book *Centuries of Childhood* with the startling statement that childhood—at least as we currently understand it—did not exist prior to the Middle Ages.[33] Childhood was not a cultural preoccupation, simply a brief phase of dependency passed over quickly and bearing little special importance. The category of enfant existed because few passed beyond this stage in an era of extraordinary mortality, but the category of child did not because those who could fend for themselves were treated as small adults. Children participated fully in all of the activities of the adult world, yet there seemed little need to separate them out as a social category.

As the conception of child as separate from adult took shape, however, it still did not bear connotations of innocence. As Ariès notes, sexual contact between children and adults, touching and stroking of the genitals, dirty jokes, sharing rooms and beds, and casual nudity, was taken for granted well into the ancien régime. Children were assumed to be closer to the body, less inhibited, and thus unlikely to be corrupted by adult knowledge.

The idea of the child as innocent first took shape, Ariès argues, within pedagogical literature, helping to justify a specialized body of knowledge centered on the education and inculcation of the young; this ideal rationalized the learned class's expanded social role and efforts to police the culture of the young. Other historians suggest alternative or supplementary explanations for this modern conception of the child. One key factor was the emergence of commercial capitalism and the rise of the middle classes; the child became central to the discussion of transfer of property and the rights of inheritance. The emerging bourgeois classes placed particular importance on the education and rearing of their sons as preparation for participation in the market economy. Out of the future-orientation of capitalism came a new focus on child rearing and pedagogy. Some subsequent historians, notably Lawrence Stone and Lloyd deMause, have pushed beyond Ariès's account to suggest that premodern parents had little attachment to their children, treating them with neglect and abuse. These claims have been sharply criticized by other historians as going well beyond available evidence.[34]

The importance of Ariès's research may not depend on whether he is correct on every particular; his book opened a space for examining the social construction of childhood as an ongoing historical process and for questioning dominant constructions of childhood innocence. As Ariès notes:

> The idea of childish innocence resulted in two kinds of attitude and behavior towards childhood: firstly, safeguarding it against pollution by life and particularly by the sexuality tolerated if not approved of among adults; and secondly, strengthening it by developing character and reason. We may see a contradiction here, for on the one hand childhood is preserved and on the other hand it is made older than its years.[35]

This contradiction runs through our modern conception of childhood innocence—we desire it and we want to help children to move beyond it. Or, to use Ariès's terms, we want to "coddle" the child and we want to "discipline" the child.

This emerging distinction between child and adult also played a central role in shaping and regulating adult behavior. In *The Civilizing Process*, Norbert Elias describes the gradual "refinement" of manners and etiquette as the upper classes adopted modes of behavior that separated them from the lower classes; the cultural transmission and imitation of those norms responded to the emerging middle class's desire for social betterment and political access.[36] In his account, rules of etiquette must first be explicitly expressed and consciously imitated but, subsequently, are internalized, becoming part of what defines us as human. However, since these norms must be acquired, they must be transmitted to children, who are initially perceived as operating outside the civilized order. The child behaved in ways that adults would not, and the adults were obligated to shape the child into conformity with social norms. According to Elias, the child comes of age in a context of fear and shame; shame is the process through which social norms are internalized. Elias sees our history since the Middle Ages in terms of increased restraint of the body and tighter regulation of emotions, necessary to facilitate participation in ever-more-complex spheres of social relations. However, more recent historians, such as John Kasson, have pointed to historical fluctuations during which society loosened or tightened its control over body and affect.[37] These fluctuations determine whether parents "discipline" or "coddle" children, whether they react to violations of adult norms with horror or amusement.

Drawing her evidence both from analysis of material culture and from popular discourse about childhood, Karin Calvert locates three distinct shifts in the cultural understanding and adult regulation of American childhood between 1600 and 1900. In the first phase, children led precarious lives confronting the harsh conditions of frontier settlement, subject to high infant mortality rates, "childhood illnesses, accidents, and a lack of sufficient nourishment." In such a culture, Calvert argues, childhood was experienced as "essentially a state of illness" or physical vulnerability: "Growing up meant growing strong and gaining sufficient autonomy to be able to take care of oneself."[38] Such a culture had little nostalgia for childhood, stressing the early acceptance of adult responsibilities. Child-rearing practices sought to "hasten" self-sufficiency.

Around the turn of the eighteenth century, attitudes shifted dramatically, with a "growing confidence in the rationality of nature."[39] If before parents saw themselves as protecting their children from natural threats, this new paradigm viewed excessive parental intervention as producing invalid children. Childhood was now perceived as a period of "robust health" during which "natural forces" took their course, allowing the young to grow into vital adulthood. Childhood was seen as a period of "freedom" before the anticipated constraints of adult civilization, and so parents valued the "childishness" of their children, their nonconformity to adult expectations.

In the third phase, from 1830 to 1900, adults did not simply take pleasure in childhood; they sought to prolong and shelter it as a special period of innocence from the adult world. As Calvert notes:

> Childhood was imbued with an almost sacred character. Children were pure and innocent beings, descended from heaven and unsullied by worldly corruption. The loss of this childish innocence was akin to the loss of virginity, and the inevitable loss of childhood itself was a kind of expulsion from the Garden of Eden.[40]

This new myth of childhood innocence served, in part, as the basis for criticism of modernity and the breakdown of traditional forms of family and community life.

Two Traditions: The "Free" Child and the "Disciplined" Child

As Calvert's account suggests, our recognition of a fundamental difference between children and adults did not predetermine what significance got attached to that difference. One strong tradition, as Jackson Lears has noted, envied children's close relations to nature and their freedom from adult constraints.[41] Romantic thinkers, such as William Blake or Jean-Jacques Rousseau, engaged in a "primitivist" celebration of children's "spontaneous feeling and intense experience." The child was emblematic of "freedom from social convention and utilitarian calculation." Adulthood was understood as corruption and formal education as an instrument that deforms the child's development. As Rousseau argued:

> Nature intends that children shall be children before they are men. If we insist on reversing this order we shall have fruit early indeed, but unripe and tasteless and liable to early decay. . . . Childhood has its own methods of seeing, thinking, and feeling. Nothing shows less sense than to try to substitute our own methods for these.[42]

Rousseau's *Emile* outlined an approach to education that linked learning to natural sensation and material consequences rather than adult instruction and regulation. Rousseau wanted to preserve children's pristine moral impulses, and especially to protect children's minds from the influence of books:

> The mind should be left undisturbed till its faculties have developed. . . . Therefore education of the earliest years should be merely negative. It consists, not in teaching virtue or truth, but in preserving the heart from vice and from the spirit of error. . . . Exercise his body, his limbs, his senses, his strength but keep his mind idle as long as you can. . . . Leave childhood to ripen in your children.[43]

The Romantics valued the child's easy access to the world of the imagination and sought to free themselves to engage with the world in a more childlike fashion.

Another tradition, grounded in puritan assumptions, focused on adult responsibility to constrain and "manage" the child, shaping development in line with community standards. According to Kincaid, the prevailing metaphors of Victorian child-rearing discourse emphasize the malleability of children's minds, their willingness and eagerness to submit to adults. Here children are not inherently evil—simply empty-headed—and thus appropriately disciplined and instructed by their elders:

> "Children's minds are like wax, readily receiving all impressions." (1880)

> "Like clay in the hands of the potter, they are waiting only to be molded." (1882)

> "There is a pliability in the young mind, as in the young twig; which renders it apt to take any shape into which circumstances may press it." (1818)[44]

These wax, clay, and botanical metaphors rationalize increased adult control over children's minds and bodies, often resulting in harsh punishment.

The persistence of these two contradictory strands—one celebrating childhood freedom from adult control, the other insisting on the necessity of adult restraint— helps to explain the ebb and flow between the authoritarian, discipline-centered approach and the permissive, child-centered approach. Yet, these contradictions can surface within the same thinker. Progressive Era child-rearing experts, such as William Buron Forbush or G. Stanley Hall, simultaneously celebrated childhood freedom and advocated increased adult intervention into children's play. Forbush might state, "[T]he infant is like the wild creature of the wood, and it is as cruel to confine the physical activities of young children as those of squirrels and swallows."[45] Hall might state, "Childhood is the paradise of the race from which adult life is a fall."[46] Yet, both promoted organized and supervised play activities, such as the Boy Scouts or the YMCA, and urged the development of classroom rituals intended to foster patriotism and religion. Drawing on social Darwinism, the young child was, in the words of one progressive reformer, "essentially a savage, with the interests of a savage, the body of a savage, and to no small extent, the soul of one."[47] Hall and his associates were remarkably literal minded in insisting that the child be pushed through the various stages of civilization—"from Rome to Reason"—in order to gain adulthood.[48]

The "Value" of Childhood

Hall's "Child Study Movement" responded to what economist Viviana A. Zelizer describes as a serious revaluation of the child within American culture.[49] In the agrarian cultures of the nineteenth century, children were expected to contribute labor to the family farm as soon as they were physically able. More children meant more income. Even in the immigrant families of turn-of-the-century New York, children contributed to the household economy. However, the rising middle classes directed increased public pressure against child labor, placing new emphasis upon the child's sentimental value and pitting the ideal of the untarnished "child of God" (and of Nature) against the horrors of working children. The sentimental conception of the child, Zelizer argues, compensated for the lost economic worth of child labor and quickly spread.[50] Children were to be shielded from participation in the economy, either in terms of productive labor or in terms of relations of consumption. Public attitudes toward adoption shifted, for example, from a culture that encouraged the "boarding out" of children as cheap labor to one that emphasized sentimental bonds between adoptive parent and child; the result was a decreased demand for older boy children (deemed economically productive) and an increased demand for babies and young girls (viewed as cute and cuddly). The death of children, no longer taken for granted, became a scandal that could be mobilized in reform campaigns.

With improvements in children's physical well-being, the primary focus of child rearing shifted toward concerns with psychological development, with cultural materials scrutinized for their potentially damaging effects upon children's mental health. Attacks on popular culture, for example, reflected this new psychological and sociological conception of the child. Media-reform campaigns started in the late nineteenth and early twentieth centuries with criticisms of series books, joke magazines, and the comics but soon spread to all commercial culture targeted at the young.[51] Joke magazines and comic strips, for example, were accused of destroying "all respect for law and authority," teaching "lawlessness," "cultivating a lack of reverence," and thereby "destroy[ing] the American homes of the future."[52]

Such attacks also reflected children's increasingly central role as consumers. Advertising aimed at children violated the "social contract" forged during this period of "sacredization." Madison Avenue, the critics charge, no longer viewed children as outside the sphere of economic life. However, as Stephen Kline suggests, the ideology of the "sacred" child also contained the roots of a consumerist ideology.[53] The marketing of consumer goods was coupled with parents' concerns for their children's well-being, ideals of sanitation or education, and improvements in domestic life. The child became a central salesperson for mass-marketed goods, with marketing researchers exploiting each new breakthrough in child psychology to reach this lucrative market more effectively.

The Permissive Paradigm

Writing in the 1950s, Martha Wolfenstein saw the shift from a culture of production (with its demands for discipline and regimentation) to a culture of consumption (with its expectations of a "fun morality") as a major force shaping child-rearing practices in the twentieth century.[54] The emergence of permissiveness in the postwar era, she argues, was partially a response to the expansion of the consumer marketplace and the prospect of suburban affluence. Permissive conceptions of the child embraced pleasure (especially erotic pleasure) as a positive motivation for exploration and learning. Bodily urges, seen as dangerous and threatening in early twentieth-century formulations, were now regarded as benign forces that could be "redirected" into more appropriate channels. Permissiveness represented an Americanization of Freudian psychoanalysis and its "discovery" of childhood sexuality. The association with childhood rendered these new (and foreign) ideas "innocent," allowing adults to rethink their own sexuality as well.[55]

At the same time, permissiveness represented an ideological response to the Second World War and public distaste for anything smacking of authoritarianism.[56] The mobilization of children as "citizen soldiers" during the war had led parents to rethink the distribution of power within the family in political terms.[57] In the postwar era, child-rearing experts promoted permissive approaches as more "democratic," as helping to prepare children for participation in the postwar era. Within this discourse, children's relations to their parents paralleled citizens' relations to the state; many child-rearing guides centered on discussions of domestic jurisprudence. The core ideology behind permissiveness can be traced back to progressive currents in American thought. Benjamin Spock, the most popular child-rearing expert of the immediate postwar period, drew insight from his political involvement in the Popular Front Movement; from anthropological discoveries of Margaret Mead, who stressed the more "liberated" approaches to children's sexuality found in various "primitive" cultures; and from emerging ideas about "social engineering" within American sociology and psychology.[58] Permissiveness's popularity in postwar America seems all the more ironic when read in relation to the militarization of American science and education, the Cold War, and McCarthyism. For some, the need to protect innocent children fostered public concern about the arms race and thus increased support for anticommunism at home and abroad. For others, the romantic conception of the free child as a utopian escape from adult regulation offered a way of coping with grown-up repression and conformity.

Postwar America was ripe for a new conception of parent-child relations; American women were having children at younger and younger ages; their dislocation from urban centers toward outlying suburbs separated them from their mothers and other traditional sources of child-rearing advice.[59] Spock's book guided their day-to-day practices; its mixture of "commonsense" and expert advice offered a security blanket for young and inexperienced parents.[60] This new approach to child rearing also helped to transform gender relations within the family, leading, as Robert Griswold notes, toward a reconceptualization of the father as playmate rather than patriarch,[61] and preparing for the revival of feminist politics in the 1960s.

At the same time, precisely because this shift in the power relations in the home meant a break with the way mothers and fathers had themselves been raised, young parents demanded more and more information, and thus permissiveness proved a highly productive cultural discourse. In the child-centered culture of postwar America, permissive themes and images surfaced everywhere, from advice manuals to magazine and television advertisements, from children's programming to adult novels.[62] Not surprisingly, the child became a potent political metaphor, with liberal critics characterizing Senator Joseph McCarthy as "Dennis the Menace" and Spiro Agnew suggesting that antiwar protestors should have been "spanked" more often when they were children. Similarly, political metaphors surface consistently in child-rearing guides, with a guilty conscience compared to the Gestapo or parental control to "brainwashing."

The mobilization of the image of the innocent child at the 1996 conventions reflected the continued breakdown of the permissive-era paradigm, which has been caught within the conservative backlash against the 1960s "counterculture." Republican ideology has tended to embrace a more discipline-centered approach, and Democratic ideology tends toward "authoritative parenting" as a middle position between permissive and authoritarian approaches.

Implications and Contradictions

This history of the innocent child presupposes some relationship between large-scale ideological shifts and localized practices. Our beliefs about childhood have some impact on our treatment of children, just as shifts in material practices, such as the responses to industrialization Zelizer documents, have some impact on our conceptual frameworks. However, historical traces of individual child-rearing practices are difficult to locate prior to the twentieth century. Historians of childhood depend upon adult records, most often upon records and advice from the learned classes, and thus they may accurately reflect only the experience of the middle class. Children left few direct traces of how they responded to adult expectations. Only in more recent eras does the historical record support a more dynamic account—one that sees competing interests between parents and children.

The actual business of living and parenting during these historical periods was no doubt much messier than our intellectual and social histories might suggest. In our own times, parents often find themselves muttering "my parents would never have let me get away with that," reflecting an internal conflict between their own experience of childhood and their idealized conceptions of how children should be raised. Many contemporary parents hold themselves accountable to the ideals of the permissive family culture of the 1950s and 1960. These ideals cannot be met within a changed economy that demands that both parents work outside the home or a changed social structure wherein more than half of American children have divorced parents. Faced with these uncertainties, parents, not surprisingly, are unable to maintain consistent ideology or a coherent style of parenting; instead, they respond to local conditions in confused and contradictory ways.

Recent scholarship also suggests that contemporary America may be a far less "child-centered" nation than it imagines. Joe Kincheloe locates a core "ambivalence" in American attitudes toward childhood, and Nancy Scheper-Hughes and Howard F. Stein describe a "pathological" culture in which "bad" children become scapegoats for our frustrations and guilt.[63] Often, Scheper-Hughes and Stein suggest, we focus on the individual child abuser as an aberration rather than acknowledge what our society exacts from its children. Their descriptions of abusive families, latchkey kids, and neglected children could not be further from the squeaky-clean and loving ideals of permissive child rearing—a nightmare culture that manifests itself most fully in black humor and horror movies.

A history of the ideology of childhood, then, is most convincing when it acknowledges the continued circulation of old conceptions and the emotional tug of previous practices; when it sees change in gradual rather than revolutionary terms; when it can account for the complex negotiations that occur during moments of cultural transition; and when it can acknowledge the gap between our best intentions and our worst impulses. Children's culture is shaped at the global level through powerful institutions and at the local level through individual families. Through these everyday practices, the myth of the innocent child gives way to the reality of children's experience.

3. *Children's Culture*

Parents and children negotiate all kinds of deals over television and toys. . . . The battle lines between public versus commercial television, educational videos and literary adaptations versus toy-based animated series, this video over that one, or one more hour of viewing versus one less are redrawn continually in parents' and children's daily lives.

—Ellen Seiter[64]

Many important contributions to the new scholarship about childhood have made the child disappear; cultural critics and historians have pulled the rug out from under our prevailing cultural myths to show us that the innocent child is often a figment of adult imaginations. Philippe Ariès taught us not only that childhood has a history but that there may have been a period before childhood existed. James Kincaid tells us that "what the child *is* matters less than what we *think* it is."[65] Jacqueline Rose suggests that behind the category of children's fiction, there exists only a fictional child—a projection of adult desire. Children's fiction, after all, is written by adults, illustrated by adults, edited by adults, marketed by adults, purchased by adults, and often read by adults, for children.[66] As Rose's analysis suggests, children's writers have a wide array of motives, some illicit, some benign, for their desire to "get close" to the child and to shape the child's thoughts and fantasies. The examination of children's fiction, then, starts by stripping away the fantasy child reader, or even the fantasy of "children of all ages," in order to locate and interpret the adult goals and desires that shape cultural production.

This displacement of the child from the center of our analysis was a necessary first step for critiquing the mythology of childhood innocence. Yet, such work often leaves children permanently out of the equation, offering no way to examine the social experience of actual children or to talk about the real-world consequences of these ideologies. Increasingly, the child emerges purely as a figment of pedophilic desire. Rose suggests that our desire to erase children's sexuality has less to do with adult needs to suppress or regulate children's bodies than with the desire to "hold off" our "panic" at the prospect of sexualities radically different from our own. At the same time, she sees the process of storytelling as one of "seduction"; adults tell tales to justify their prolonged closeness to the objects of their desire. Photography critic Carol Mavor has traced the complex desires that link Lewis Carroll's photographs of naked girls with his children's books; both reflect his urge to arrest young girls' development at the moment when they first "bud" while forestalling the inevitable approach of adult sexuality and death.[67]

Far from a perversion of the Victorian era, this fascination with the erotic child, James Kincaid argues, is utterly pervasive in our contemporary culture, surfacing in scandal-sheet headlines about molestation and murder, in Coppertone and Calvin Klein ads, and in popular films such as *Pretty Baby*.[68] Such images, he suggests, allow us to have our cake and eat it too—to be titillated by erotically charged images of children while clinging to their innocence of adult sexual knowledge. These interpretations reveal some of the fundamental hypocrisy surrounding childhood innocence in Victorian and contemporary culture. For writers like Kincaid and Mavor, pedophilia becomes a scandalous category, shocking us out of complacency and forcing us to examine the power dynamic between children and adults.

In evoking the shock of pedophilia, these critics are playing a dangerous game. Contemporary media scares about child molestation at day-care centers are the latest in a long series of attempts to use the ideology of the innocent child to force working women back in the home, especially when coupled with equally sensationalistic accounts of latchkey children and the horrors of video game/ television violence. No one is denying that child seduction and molestation can be real problems, but the overreporting of the most sensationalistic cases denies us any meaningful perspective for examining the actual incidence of such problems. These media campaigns leave working mothers feeling that there is no safe way to rear their children, short of providing them with the constant supervision demanded by child-rearing experts.

In such a culture, almost all representations that acknowledge children's sexuality are subject to legal sanctions. Courts and media reformers are taking legal actions against award-winning art films like *The Tin Drum*, the photographs of Robert Mapplethorpe, Sally Mann, and Jock Sturges, the class projects of a Harvard undergraduate, and hard-core pornography. Even Kincaid has been attacked in the British press for allegedly advocating pedophilia. Elementary schools in Wisconsin organized "secrets clubs" where children were encouraged to tell social workers about their parents' sexual and drug-use habits. There is no question that our culture proliferates eroticized images of children, yet there is also no question that our culture engages in a constant and indiscriminate witchhunt against anyone who shows too much interest in such images. Such hysteria makes it difficult for artists to question more-traditional modes of depicting children, for social critics to ask hard questions about sexuality, or for mothers and fathers to be certain which family photographs might become weapons in child custody battles. I am not denying the validity of cultural analysis that recognizes pedophilic impulses, yet there are serious dangers in reducing the question of adult power over children to erotic desire.

Strip away pedophilia and we are still left with questions about how contemporary scholarship might represent the power relations between children and adults. Many accounts of children's culture focus almost exclusively on the exercise of adult authority over children, leaving little space for thinking about children's own desires, fantasies, and agendas. For example, Stephen Kline denies children any role in the production of their own culture:

> What might be taken as children's culture has always been primarily a matter of culture produced for and urged upon children. . . . Childhood is a condition defined by powerlessness and dependence upon the adult community's directives and guidance. Culture is, after all, as the repository of social learning and socialization, the means by which societies preserve and strengthen their positions in the world.[69]

Children's culture is, within this formulation, something that happens to children. Children are not participants or contributors to that culture. However powerful it may seem as a criticism of the regulatory power of adult institutions, Kline's formulation rests on the familiar myth of the innocent and victimized child whom we must protect—the mute one whose voice we must assume.

Childhood Identities

Writing about our fascination with eroticized images of young girls, Valerie Walkerdine suggests that popular culture is often experienced as "the intrusion of adult sexuality into the sanitized space of childhood."[70] This model is too simple, she argues, since it denies children's own role in shaping and deploying these fantasies. As Walkerdine notes, such an account does not acknowledge, for example, the ways that working-class girls actively embrace elements from adult erotic representations as offering a fantasy of escape from limited social opportunities or restrictive adult authority. Walkerdine would find equally simplistic any account that celebrated the working-class girl's performance of erotic identities as "resistance to the position accorded her at school and in high culture," since this reading ascribes too much social autonomy to children. She describes popular culture as the site of contested and contradictory attempts to define the child. Children's culture is shaped both by adult desires and childhood fantasies, with material conditions determining whether or not we—as adults or as children—are able to enact our fantasies.

Walkerdine represents a larger scholarly tradition that examines the complex processes by which children acquire identities or internalize cultural norms. Annette Kuhn's *Family Secrets*, for example, uses close readings of family photographs to explore her own struggle with her mother to define personal memory.[71] Her autobiographical discussion becomes all the more poignant because, as a feminist, Kuhn recognizes the desperation behind her mother's attempt to project her own meanings onto her daughter:

> If a daughter figures for her mother as the abandoned, unloved, child that she, the mother, once was, and in some ways remains, how can mother and daughter disengage themselves from these identifications without harm, without forfeiture of love?[72]

In adopting the voice of the daughter, while acknowledging her mother's fears and fantasies, Kuhn reintroduces children's experiences into the discussion of "family values." Carolyn Steedman's *The Tidy House* explores how creative writing by young working-class girls reveals a pained recognition of their parents' ambivalence toward child rearing.[73] Steedman explains:

> They knew that their parents' situation was one of poverty, and that the presence of children only increased that poverty. . . . They knew that children were longed for, materially desired, but that their presence was irritation, regret and resentment. They knew that, in some clear and uncomplicated way, it would have been better had they never been born.[74]

Steedman reads the stories as the girls' "urgent" attempts to "understand what set of social beliefs had brought them into being."

This tradition of feminist analysis slides back and forth between psychological and sociological investigation, exploring the charged and unstable relations between mothers and daughters in order to rethink the social and psychic dynamics of the patriarchal family. Such analysis casts the child—whether understood through autobiographical introspection (*Family Secrets*) or textual analysis and ethnographic description (*The Tidy House*)—as an active participant in these family dramas; children's desires, hopes, fears, and fantasies are central to the process of constructing personal identities.

One limitation of our current research is that almost all such work has focused on issues of motherhood and femininity. This is not surprising, given women's primary responsibility for child rearing. However, we lack solid critical analysis of the relations between fathers and sons within these same critical terms; we need more work on the construction of masculinity through the rituals of boyhood. Feminism probably offers the best tools for initiating such a project, yet few male scholars have adopted its modes of analysis to confront their own formative experiences.

Children's Culture and Adult Institutions

These recent studies of childhood have generated a more complex picture of the power relations between children and adults. Parents, schoolteachers, church leaders, social reformers, the adult world in general, *are* powerfully invested in "fixing" children's identities. Eve Sedgwick has explored how parents' anxieties that their sons and daughters might grow up to be queer motivate the imposition of gender-specific behaviors on "tomboys" and "sissies."[75] Sedgwick reviews psychological literature and clinical practices that confuse gender identification and sexual preference, seeing inappropriate dress, play, and mannerism as early warning signs that a child has homosexual tendencies. Sedgwick challenges efforts by the mental health profession to "maximize the possibility of a heterosexual outcome," wondering who speaks for the rights of queer children.

Children *are* subject to powerful institutions that ascribe meanings onto their minds and bodies in order to maintain social control. Barrie Thorne suggests, for example, that teachers' needs to routinize their procedures and to break their classes into manageably scaled groups results in a constant reinforcement of the basic binaries between "boys and girls."[76] Children are more likely to play together across gender differences in their own neighborhoods, outside adult supervision, than within school cafeterias and playgrounds.

Children's culture *is* shaped by adult agendas and expectations, at least on the site of production and often at the moment of reception, and these materials leave lasting imprints on children's social and cultural development. Elizabeth Segel has examined how publishers, librarians, and educators shape children's access to different genres, resulting in gender divides in reading interests that carry into adult life. The separation of domestic-based stories for girls and adventure stories for boys reaffirm the gendering of the public and private spheres. Boys' books were often "chronicles of growth to manhood"; girls' books often "depicted a curbing of autonomy in adolescence."[77] The two forms of literature prepare girls and boys for their expected roles in adult society. However, these gender designations are not totally rigid in practice. Young girls often read boys' books for pleasure, and boys' books are more consistently taught in the classroom. On the other hand, boys typically have been reluctant to engage with books with female protagonists or feminine subject matter. Such an imbalance, Segel argues, extracts "a heavy cost in feminine self-esteem" and may be even "more restrictive of boys' . . . freedom to read." Ellen Seiter has extended Segel's analysis to the gendering of children's television. Feminists, she argues, may be well-meaning when they attack hyperfeminine programs like *My Little Pony* and *Strawberry Shortcake*, but their continued disparagement of the things girls like may contribute to— rather than help to rectify—girls' declining self-esteem.[78]

The Resistant Rituals of Childhood

Without denying the tremendous cultural power behind these adult efforts to control children's identity formation, scholarship on children's culture also acknowledges the ways children resist, transform, or redefine adult prerogatives, making their own uses of cultural materials and enacting their own fantasies through play. Miriam Formanek-Brunnel has researched the gender politics of doll play in the nineteenth century, indicating both the ways that dolls were valued by adults as a means of inculcating domestic skills in young girls and the ways that doll play might "subvert convention, mock maternalism, and undermine restrictions."[79] On the one hand, the gift of a doll was intended to encourage girls to sew and to rehearse other "domestic arts" expected of them as future wives and mothers; the fragility of china dolls required delicate movements and nurturing gestures. On the other hand, young girls often used the dolls to rehearse funerals and mourning rituals, expressing a core ambivalence about their future maternal roles, or played with them aggressively, chopping off their hair or driving nails through their bodies. Formanek-Brunnel suggests: "Girls in the process of constructing their own notion of girlhood engaged their parents in a pre-conscious political struggle to define, decide, and determine the meaning of dolls in their own lives and as representations of their own culture."[80]

Erica Rand's *Barbie's Queer Accessories* suggests such localized resistance continues in contemporary doll play.[81] Rand solicited and interpreted adults' memories of Barbie play, finding that these recollections often circle around unsanctioned and often erotically charged play. Many lesbians remembered transforming the fashion model into a "gender outlaw," drawing on their memories of childhood doll play to frame "dyke destiny" stories. Just as the myth of childhood innocence naturalizes heterosexual assumptions about appropriate gender roles, "dyke destiny" stories suggest the inevitability of queer sexual orientation by tracing its roots back to early childhood.[82] Rand encourages skepticism about such stories, examining the way that memory retrospectively rewrites the past to conform to our present-day identities. Rand sees a constant struggle within children's culture (and within adult memories of childhood) between moments of hegemonic incorporation and moments of resistance. The same girl or boy may sometimes conform and sometimes disobey.

Adult institutions and practices make "bids" on how children will understand themselves and the world around them, yet they can never be certain how children will take up and respond to those "bids." A growing literature depicts children as active creators who use the resources provided them by the adult world as raw materials for their play activities, their jokes, their drawings, and their own stories.[83] Shelby Ann Wolf and Shirley Brice Heath's *The Braid of Literature* offers a detailed description of Heath's own young daughters as readers, documenting the many ways they integrated favorite books into their lives. Children's books became reference points for explaining their own experiences. The girls often spoofed their language, characters, and situations.[84] They felt compelled not only to reread favorite stories but to enact them with their bodies. Such play represents a testing of alternative identities. Maintaining a fluid relationship to adult roles, children try things out through their play, seeing if they fit or make sense, and discarding them when they tire of them.

The Ket Aesthetic

Adult control over the cultural materials that enter children's lives certainly constrains the array of ideas and identities they can use in their play; adult restrictions on play activities limit this process of ideological exploration; yet, nothing can fully block oppositional meanings from entering children's lives. Alison James has explored how children's relations to cheap candies (which are called "kets" in British slang) suggest an oppositional aesthetic, one that challenges or reverses adult categories and carves out a kids-only culture.[85] Children embrace candies that provoke strange sensations (bubbling or crackling on their tongues), that incorporate unfamiliar taste combinations, that mimic things (rats, worms, and the like) adults refuse to eat, that embrace lurid or jarring colors, or that encourage playful and messy modes of consumption.

James describes "children's culture" as children's space for cultural expression using materials bought cheaply from the parent culture but viewed with adult disapproval. Her account could not differ more from Kline's conception of a children's culture produced and controlled by adults. The cheaper they are in price, the more cultural goods are likely to reflect children's own aesthetic and cultural sensibilities. Materials children can purchase with their allowances (such as candy, bubblegum cards, or comic books) are less likely to bear the heavy imprint of adult gatekeepers than high-cost items (books and videos) parents purchase as gifts.

This "ket" aesthetic can also be recognized within children's television programs, such as the "scream-real-loud" realm of *Pee-wee's Playhouse* or the slop-and-slime world of Nickelodeon's game shows, or in video games, which have often faced reformist pressures because of their use of scatological or gory imagery.[86] As Marsha Kinder has suggested, Nickelodeon's self-promotion has often encouraged an ethos of "generational conflict," stressing that parents "just don't get" its appeal to children: "adults are untrustworthy; they wear deodorant and ties; they shave under their arms, they watch the news and do other disgusting things."[87] Nickelodeon's self-presentation walks a thin line, using children's oppositional aesthetic to package shows (such as *Lassie*) that contain little parents would find offensive and creating programs (such as *Kids Court* or Linda Ellerbee's news specials) that almost—but usually not quite—embrace a politics of kid empowerment. Some of Nick's shows encourage children to cast a critical eye toward adult institutions, teach them to be skeptical readers of media images, encourage them to take more active roles in their communities (including leading fights for free expression within their schools) and take seriously their own goals for the nation's future (as in their *Kids Pick the President* campaign coverage). Nickelodeon's claims to be "the kids-only network" erects a sharp line between the realms of children and adults.

This approach contrasts sharply with the children's programs of the 1950s (such as *Howdy Doody* and *Winky Dink and You*), which Lynn Spigel has characterized as inviting a "dissolution of age categories."[88] Such programs, she argues, were "filled with liminal characters, characters that existed somewhere in between child and adult" and encouraged a playful transgression of age-appropriate expectations. Spigel points to their covert appeal to adult fantasies of escaping into the realm of childhood play free from the conformity and productivity expected of grown-ups in Eisenhower's America. The Nickelodeon programs such as *Double Dare* or *What Would You Do?*, on the other hand, stage contests between children and adults, invite children to judge their parents or to smack them with cream pies and douse them with green slime. They support children's recognition of a core antagonism with grown-ups, while positioning the network, its programs, and its spin-off products on the kid side of that divide.

This desire to create an autonomous cultural space for children's play is not new, nor does such freedom from adult control necessarily retard the child's inculcation into anticipated social roles. Children must break with their parents before they can enter into adult roles and responsibilities. Children's play has often been a space where they experimented with autonomy and self-mastery. E. Anthony Rotundo's analysis of "Boy Culture" in nineteenth-century America suggests its complex relationship to the adult world.[89] As industrialization led to a greater division of labor, forcing men to leave the home to work in the factories and leaving women in the domestic sphere to rear the young, the formation of masculine identities entered a new phase. Young boys sought an escape from maternal restraint, fleeing into a sphere of male action and adventure. Their play with other boys was clearly framed as oppositional to adults, taking the form of daring raids on privileged adult spaces, comic assaults on parental authority, or simply a rejection of maternal rules and restrictions. Through this play, boys acquired the aggression, competitiveness, daring, self-discipline, and physical mastery expected of those who would inhabit a culture of rugged individualism. The more rambunctious and irresponsible aspects of this culture would need to be tempered as the young males entered adult jobs and family relations, yet this rough-and tumble "boy culture" prepared them more fully for their future roles than the maternally sanctioned activities of the domestic sphere.

Embracing a politics of appropriation and resistance runs the risk of romanticizing child's play as the seeds of cultural revolution. I use the word *romanticizing* with precision here. In many ways, the celebration of children as "gender outlaws" or cultural rebels can be traced back to Rousseau's celebration of the "natural" and "spontaneous" child as embodying a freedom not yet subordinated to the demands of the civilized world. While this myth of the child certainly has advantages over the more-repressive image of the child as a blank slate or the multivalent image of the innocent child at risk, it is nevertheless a myth. Perhaps, there is no way for adults to speak of children without putting words in their mouths and turning them into symbols for our own use. However, Rotundo's analysis suggests one escape from this impasse: looking at the ways children's play represents a temporary space of freedom while it contributes actively to socialization and indoctrination into cultural values. Rotundo preserves the idea of children's social and cultural agency without assuming that they are outside the cultural formations or material conditions that shape all human interactions.

Conclusion: The Political Stakes of Children's Culture

Children are at the epicenter of the information revolution, ground zero of the digital world. . . . After centuries of regulation, sometimes benign, sometimes not, kids are moving out from under our pious control, finding one another via the great hive that is the net. . . . Children can for the first time reach past the suffocating boundaries of social convention, past their elders' rigid notions of what is good for them.
                                                                                    —Jon Katz[90]

The Children's Culture Reader seeks modes of cultural analysis that do not simply celebrate children's resistance to adult authority but provide children with the tools to realize their own political agendas or to participate in the production of their own culture. The challenge is to find models that account for the complexity of the interactions between children and adults, the mutuality and the opposition between their cultural agendas. Feminist analysis has taught us that politics works as much through the micropractices of everyday life as through large-scale institutions and that our struggle to define our identities in relations to other members of our families often determines how we understand our place in the world.

As I have been editing this collection, I have been continually asked to explain and justify the "political stakes" in reexamining children's culture. As this discussion has already suggested, I consider such questions misguided, both because they accept at face value the premise that childhood is a space largely "innocent" of adult political struggles and because they fail to recognize how foundational the figure of the innocent child is to almost all contemporary forms of politics. Issues involving children are often viewed as "soft" compared to "hard-core" issues like tax cuts, crime bills, and defense expenditures, a language that suggests historic divisions between a feminine domestic sphere and a masculine public sphere. Feminists have long campaigned for a reassessment of those priorities and a recognition of the political stakes in domestic life. Yet, the politics of the public sphere, no less than the politics of the domestic sphere, rests on the figure of the child, as we saw in the various evocations of childhood at the Republican and Democratic National Conventions. Often, the figure of the brutalized and victimized child gets mobilized in campaigns to build support for war; the figure of the dead child is the most powerful trope in the campaign for tougher sentencing of criminals. For example, the recent "Megan's Law," which requires public notification of the movement of convicted child molesters and other offenders into the community, will be forever associated with the memory of a specific child victim.

Moreover, without a politics of the family, without a progressive conception of children's culture, the Left lacks the ability literally and figuratively to reproduce itself. We need to be engaged in the process not only of critiquing traditional conceptions of the family but of imagining alternative ways that families might perform their responsibilities for the care and raising of the young. We need to think about our roles as parents, teachers, and citizens in ways that help us to prepare children to participate in the process of social change and political transformation. We need to embrace approaches to teaching and social policy that acknowledge children's cultural productivity and that provide them with the materials and skills they need to critique their place in the world. The Birmingham tradition of cultural studies helped us to question the labeling of youth cultures as "deviant" by adult standards, seeing in their "hooliganism" the signs of a subversive or resistant subculture. We still lack a similarly political vocabulary for examining moments when children buck adult demands. Instead, we frame such localized moments of resistance in moralistic categories of "naughtiness" or in developmental psychological terms as "testing limits." The need is to recognize that children's disobedience to teachers, for example, might originate in a context of economic or racial inequalities, might express something of the frustrations of coping with a world that devalues your interests and seeks to impose adult values onto your activities. If politics is ultimately about the distribution of power, then the power imbalance between children and adults remains, at heart, a profoundly political matter.

Herbert Kohl confronts these questions when he debates whether we should "burn *Babar*."[91] He invites us to question whether our recognition of noxious ideologies in traditional children's literature (such as *Babar*'s procolonialism agenda) compels us to banish them or whether we should encourage children to become critical readers locating and questioning the implicit assumptions they find in the culture around them. As Kohl writes:

> The challenge parents face is how to integrate encounters with stereotypes into their children's sensibility and help their children become critical of aspects of the culture that denigrate or humiliate them or anyone else. . . . Instead of prohibiting things

that tempt children, this means allowing them the freedom to explore things while trusting them to make sensible and humane judgements.[92]

Jon Katz confronts these challenges when he shifts the focus of debates about cyberspace away from the question of how we might protect our children from corrupting influences (whether through legal sanctions or filtering technology) and toward how we might empower children to contribute actively to the political culture of the net.[93] Katz argues that children, no less than adults, have "certain inalienable rights not conferred at the caprice of arbitrary authority," rights that include access to the materials of their culture and the technologies that enable more widespread communication as well as "the right to refuse to be force-fed other generations' values." Katz's polemical and suggestive essay points toward a reassessment of the role of education, away from a focus on the transmission of established cultural norms and toward the development of skills that enable children to question the society around them and to communicate their ideas, via new technologies, with others of their generations. He writes:

> Children need help in becoming civic-minded citizens of the digital age, figuring out how to use the machinery in the service of some broader social purposes. . . . But more than anything else, children need to have their culture affirmed. They need their parents, teachers, guardians and leaders to accept that there is a new political reality for children, and the constructs that governed their own lives and culture are no longer the only relevant or useful ones.[94]

Sally Mann confronts these challenges when she creates photographs of children that emphasize their fears, anxieties, and uncertainties, their everyday scrapes and bruises, and their sexuality rather than representing childhood as a wholesome utopia. At their best, Mann's photographs strip away the myth of childhood innocence to show the struggles of children to define themselves.

Linda Ellerbee confronts these challenges when she creates television programs that encourage children's awareness of real-world problems, such as the Los Angeles riots, and enable children to find their own critical voice to speak back against the adult world. She trusts children to confront realities from which other adults might shield them, offering them the facts needed to form their own opinions and the air time to discuss issues.

These critics, educators, and artists offer us models of a children's culture that is progressive in both its form and its content. They move beyond mythic innocence and toward a recognition and advocacy of children's cultural, social, and political agency. Such works do not ignore the fact that children suffer real material problems, including neglect, abuse, and poverty, and that there are times and places where adults must protect them from themselves and from the world. There are also times and places where we need to listen to our children and factor their needs, desires, and agendas into our own sense of the world and into the decisions that affect our children's lives. Children need adults to create the conditions through which they develop a political consciousness, to defend their access to the information they need to frame their own judgments, and to build the technologies that enable them to exchange their ideas with others of their generation. They need us to be more than guardians of the fort or protectors of the village, and we will not rise to those challenges as long as our actions are governed by familiar myths of the innocent child. The goal is not to erase the line between child and adult, which we must observe if we are both to protect and empower the young. The goal is to offer a fuller, more complex picture of children's culture that can enable more meaningful, realistic, and effective political change.

NOTES

1. James R. Kincaid, *Child-Loving: The Erotic Child and Victorian Culture* (New York: Routledge, 1992).

2. Cary Bazalgette and David Buckingham, "Introduction: The Invisible Audience," in Cary Bazalgette and David Buckingham, eds., *In Front of the Children: Screen Entertainment and Young Audiences* (London: BFI, 1995), p. 4.

3. For a good collection of key essays about youth cultures, see Sue Thornton, *The Subcultural Reader* (New York: Routledge, 1997).

4. Susan Stewart, *On Longing: Narratives of the Miniature, the Gigantic, the Souvenir, the Collection* (Durham: Duke University Press, 1993).

5. Henry A. Giroux, *Fugitive Cultures: Race, Violence and Youth* (New York: Routledge, 1996), p. 89.

6. James Kincaid, *Child-Loving* (New York: Routledge, 1992), pp. 78–79.

7. Convention rhetoric exaggerates dominant tendencies in American ideology, offering more differentiated versions of the party's positions than arise in everyday governmental actions. We listen to such speeches as an optimistic summation of ideals, which we share but do not fully believe can be realized. However, these ideals do translate into material practices, becoming the focus of specific policies or the crux of core political debates. These political statements are particularly vivid articulations of discourses about childhood that have a longer history.

8. Kincaid, *Child-Loving*, p. 78.

9. Ibid., p. 79.

10. Barbara Ehrenreich, *The Hearts of Men: American Dreams and the Flight from Commitment* (New York: Anchor, 1983), p. 26.

11. Lynn Spigel, "Seducing the Innocent: Childhood and Television in Postwar America," in this volume. See also, Barbara Ehrenreich and Deirdre English, *For Her Own Good: 150 Years of the Experts' Advice to Women* (Garden City, N.Y.: Anchor, 1978).

12. Quoted in Spigel, "Seducing the Innocent."

13. Heather Hendershot, *Endangering the Dangerous: The Regulation and Censorship of Children's Television* (Durham: Duke University Press, forthcoming).

14. John Fiske, *Media Matters: Everyday Culture and Political Change* (Minneapolis: University of Minnesota Press, 1994).

15. Eric Freedman, " 'Have You Seen This Child?': From Milk Cartoon to Mise-en-Abyme," in Henry Jenkins, Tara McPherson, and Jane Shattuc, eds., *Hop on Pop: The Politics and Pleasures of Popular Culture* (Durham: Duke University Press, 1998).

16. Robert L. Griswold, *Fatherhood in America* (New York: Basic Books, 1993), pp. 3–4.

17. Mary Lynn Stevens Heininger, "Children, Childhood and Change in America,

1820–1920," in Mary L. S. Heininger, Karin Calvert, Barbara Finkelstein, Kathy Vandell, Anne Scott MacLeod, and Harvey Green, eds., *A Century of Childhood, 1820–1920* (Rochester, N.Y.: Margaret Woodbury Strong Museum, 1984), p. 31.

18. Heininger, "Children, Childhood and Change," p. 16.

19. Kincaid, *Child-Loving*, p. 80.

20. Philip Elmer-Dewitt, "On a Screen Near You: Cyberporn," *Time*, July 2, 1995, pp. 39–45. For a fuller discussion of the role of "childhood innocence" in the Communications Decency Act debates, see Henry Jenkins, "Empowering Children in the Digital Age: Towards a Radical Media Pedagogy," *Radical Teacher* 50 (1997): 30–35.

21. Letter to the Editor, *Time*, July 24, 1995.

22. Hillary Rodham, "Children Under the Law," *Harvard Educational Review*, summer 1973, pp. 487–514.

23. Lauren Berlant, *The Queen of America Goes to Washington City: Essays on Sex and Citizenship* (Durham: Duke University Press, 1997).

24. Hillary Rodham Clinton, *It Takes a Village and Other Lessons* (New York: Simon & Schuster, 1996), p. 318.

25. Marian Wright Edelman, "An Unfinished Symphony" at http://www.sojourners.com/sojourners/950314.html.

26. For useful background on Edelman's Childrens Defense Fund, see its homepage at http://www.childrensdefense.org.

27. Jacqueline Rose, "The Case of Peter Pan," in this volume.

28. Shari Goldin, "Unlearning Black and White," in this volume.

29. Clinton, *It Takes a Village*, p. 176.

30. Ashis Nandy, "Reconstructing Childhood: A Critique of the Ideology of Adulthood," in *Traditions, Tyranny and Utopias: Essays in the Politics of Awareness* (Delhi: Oxford University Press, 1987).

31. Lynn Spigel and Henry Jenkins, "Same Bat Channel, Different Bat Times: Mass Culture and Popular Memory," in Roberta Pearson and William Uricchio, eds., *The Many Lives of The Batman: Critical Approaches to a Superhero and His Media* (New York: Routledge, 1991), p. 127.

32. Karin Calvert, *Children in the House: The Material Culture of Early Childhood, 1600–1900* (Boston: Northeastern University Press, 1992), p. 1.

33. Philippe Ariès, *Centuries of Childhood: A Social History of Family Life* (New York: Vintage Books, 1962).

34. For a thorough review of this whole research tradition, its strengths and its weaknesses, see Linda A. Pollock, *Forgotten Children: Parent-Child Relations from 1500 to 1900* (Cambridge: Cambridge University Press, 1983).

35. Philippe Ariès, "From Immodesty to Innocence," in this volume.

36. Norbert Elias, *The History of Manners* (New York: Urizen Books, 1978); Norbert Elias, *Power and Civility*, trans. Edmund Jephcott (New York: Pantheon Books, 1982).

37. John Kasson, *Rudeness and Civility: Manners in Nineteenth Century Urban America* (New York: Hill and Wang, 1990).

38. Calvert, *Children in the House*, p. 150.

39. Ibid., p. 152.

40. Ibid.

41. Jackson Lears, *No Place of Grace: Antimodernism and the Transformation of American Culture, 1880–1920* (New York: Pantheon, 1981), pp. 144–149.

42. Jean-Jacques Rousseau, "On Reasoning with Children," in Crane Brinton, ed., *The Portable Age of Reason Reader* (New York: Viking, 1956), p. 122.

43. Jean-Jacques Rousseau, *Emile*, trans. Barbara Foxley (New York: Dutton, 1963), pp. 57–58.

44. Kincaid, *Child-Loving*, pp. 90–91.

45. William Byron Forbush, *The Boy Problem* (1909), as quoted in Steven L. Schlossman, "G. Stanley Hall and The Boys' Club: Conservative Applications of Recapitulation Theory," *Journal of the History of the Behavior Sciences* 9, no. 2 (1973): 140–147.

46. Lears, *No Place of Grace*, p. 148.

47. J. Adams Puffer, *The Boy and His Gang* (1912), as quoted in Schlossman, "G. Stanley Hall," p. 144.

48. For a discussion of the cultural impact of Hall's ideas, see Richard DeCordova, "The Mickey in Macy's Window: Childhood, Consumerism, and Disney Animation," in Eric Smoodin, ed., *Disney Discourse: Producing the Magic Kingdom* (New York: AFI/Routledge, 1994), pp. 203–213.

49. Viviana A. Zelizer, *Pricing the Priceless Child: The Changing Social Value of Children* (Princeton: Princeton University Press, 1985).

50. Of course, this "sacredization" of the child is never absolute. Conservative attacks on "welfare mothers," for example, posit their reproduction as a "drain" on the American economy, denying their offspring the "sentimental value" that this ideology suggests is the birthright of all children. The discomfort provoked by such a blunt economic assessment of children's value may have contributed to the reframing of this issue in terms of teen pregnancy and the emotional readiness of "children to bear children." This new formulation is more closely aligned with an ideology of childhood innocence.

51. Mark I. West, *Children, Culture and Controversy* (Hamden, Conn.: Archon, 1988).

52. For a discussion of these issues, see Henry Jenkins, *What Made Pistachio Nuts? Early Sound Comedy and the Vaudeville Aesthetic* (New York: Columbia, University Press, 1991), pp. 42–43.

53. Stephen Kline, *Out of the Garden: Toys and Children's Culture in the Age of TV Marketing* (London: Verso, 1993).

54. Martha Wolfenstein, "Fun Morality," in this volume.

55. Henry Jenkins, "The Sensuous Child," in this volume.

56. See, for example, Henry Jenkins, " 'No Matter How Small': The Democratic Imagination of Dr. Seuss," in Jenkins, McPherson, and Shattuc, *Hop on Pop*.

57. For further discussion of the mobilization of children during the war, see Shari Goldin, "Patriotic Lessons: Radio, Childhood, and the Technological Imagination," working title, dissertation in progress, University of Wisconsin-Madison. William M. Tuttle, Jr., *"Daddy's Gone to War": The Second World War in the Lives of America's Children* (New York: Oxford University Press, 1993).

58. William Graebner, "The Unstable World of Benjamin Spock: Social Engineering in a Democratic Culture, 1917–1950," *Journal of American History* 167, no. 3 (spring 1980): 612–629.

59. For useful background on this period, see Elaine Tyler May, *Homeward Bound: American Families in the Cold War Era* (New York: Basic Books, 1990); Steven Mintz and Susan Kellog, *Domestic Revolutions: A Social History of American Family Life* (New York: Free Press, 1988); Arlene Skolnick, *Embattled Paradise: The American Family in an Age of Uncertainty* (New York: Basic Books, 1991); Joseph N. Hawes and N. Ray Hiner, eds., *American Childhood: A Research Guide and Historical Handbook* (Westport, Conn.: Greenwood Press, 1985).

60. Kenneth C. Davis, *Two-Bit Culture: The Paperbacking of America* (Boston: Houghton Mifflin, 1984).

61. Robert L. Griswold, *Fatherhood in America: A History* (New York: Basic Books, 1993).

62. See Henry Jenkins, " 'Her Suffering Aristocratic Majesty': The Sentimental Value of Lassie," in Marsha Kinder, ed., *Kids Media Culture* (Durham; Duke University Press, 1999). Henry Jenkins, "Dennis The Menace, The 'All American Handful' " in Lynn Spigel and Michael Curtin, eds., *The Revolution Wasn't Televised: Sixties Television and Social Change* (New York: AFI/Routledge, 1997), pp. 118–135. The cultural impact of permissive child-rearing doctrines is the focus of my current book project.

63. Joe Kinchcloe, "The New Childhood," in this volume.

64. Ellen Seiter, *Sold Separately: Parents and Children in Consumer Culture* (New Brunswick: Rutgers University Press, 1993), pp. 227–228.

65. Kincaid, *Child-Loving*, p. 62.

66. Jacqueline Rose, *The Case of Peter Pan: On the Impossibility of Children's Fiction* (London: Macmillan, 1984), pp. 1–2.

67. Carol Mavor, *Pleasures Taken: Performances of Sexuality and Loss in Victorian Photographs* (Durham: Duke University Press, 1995), p. 25.

68. James R. Kincaid, "Producing Erotic Children," in this volume.

69. Kline, *Out of the Garden*, p. 44.

70. Valerie Walkerdine, "Popular Culture and the Eroticization of Little Girls," in James Curran, David Morley, and Valerie Walkerdine, eds., *Cultural Studies and Communications* (London: Arnold, 1996), p. 325. See also Valerie Walkerdine, *Daddy's Little Girl* (Cambridge: Harvard University Press, 1997).

71. Annette Kuhn, *Family Secrets: Acts of Memory and Imagination* (London: Routledge, 1995).

72. Ibid., p. 49, and Annette Kuhn, "A Credit to Her Mother," in this volume.

73. Carolyn Steedman, *The Tidy House: Little Girls Writing* (London: Virago, 1984).

74. Carolyn Steedman, "The Tidy House," in this volume.

75. Eve Sedgwick, "How to Bring Your Kids Up Gay," in this volume.

76. Barrie Thorne, *Gender Play: Girls and Boys in School* (New Brunswick: Rutgers University Press, 1993). See selection from the book in this volume.

77. Elizabeth Segel, " 'As the Twig Is Bent . . . ': Gender and Childhood Reading," in Elizabeth A. Flynn and Patrocinio P. Schweickart, eds., *Gender and Reading: Essays on Readers, Texts, and Contexts* (Baltimore: Johns Hopkins University Press, 1986), p. 174.

78. Seiter, *Sold Separately*, pp. 145–171.

79. Miriam Formanek-Brunnel, *Made to Play House: Dolls and the Commercialization of American Girlhood, 1830–1930* (New Haven: Yale University Press, 1993), p. 8, and "The Politics of Dollhood in Nineteenth-Century America," in this volume.

80. Forman P K-Brunnel, "The Politics of Dollhood in Nineteenth-century America," in this volume.

81. Erica Rand, *Barbie's Queer Accessories* (Durham: Duke University Press, 1995) and "Older Heads on Younger Bodies," in this volume.

82. Elspeth Probyn has noted that this link between childhood experience and adult queerness has become a standard trope in novels by gay, lesbian, and bisexual authors. Elspeth Probyn, "Suspended Beginnings: Of Childhood and Nostalgia," in *Outside Belongings* (New York: Routledge, 1996), pp. 93–124.

83. Henry Jenkins, "Going Bonkers! Children, Play and Pee-Wee," in Constance Penley and Sharon Willis, eds., *Male Trouble* (Minneapolis: University of Minnesota Press, 1993), pp. 157–182; Robert Hodge and David Tripp, *Children and Television* (Stanford: Stanford University Press, 1986); Patricia Palmer, *The Lively Audience: A Study of Children Around the TV Set* (Sydney: Allen and Unwin, 1986).

84. Shelby Anne Wolf and Shirley Brice Heath, *The Braid of Literature: Children's Worlds of Reading* (Cambridge: Harvard University Press, 1992) and "Living in a World of Words," in this volume.

85. Alison James, "Confections, Concoctions and Conceptions," *Journal of the Anthropological Society of Oxford* 10, no. 2 (1979), and "Confections, Concoctions, and Conceptions" in this volume. See also Alison James, *Childhood Conceptions* (New York: Columbia University Press, 1996).

86. For discussions of *Pee-Wee's Playhouse*, see Constance Penley, "The Cabinet of Dr. Pee-Wee: Consumerism and Sexual Terror," Ian Balfour, "The Playhouse of the Signifier: Reading Pee-Wee Herman," Henry Jenkins, "Going Bonkers!: Children, Play and Pee-Wee," and Alexander Doty, "The Sissy Boy, The Fat Ladies, and the Dykes: Queerness and/as Gender in Pee-Wee's World," all in Penley and Willis, *Male Trouble*.

87. Marsha Kinder, "Home Alone in the 90s: Generational War and Transgenerational Address in American Movies, Television and Presidential Politics," in Bazalgette and Buckinghman, *In Front of the Children*, pp. 75–91.

88. Spigel, "Seducing the Innocent."

89. E. Anthony Rotundo, "Boy Culture," in *American Manhood: Transformations in Masculinity from the Revolution to the Modern Era* (New York: Basic Books, 1993), and "Boy Culture," in this volume.

90. Jon Katz, *Virtuous Reality* (New York: Random House, 1997), pp. 173–174.

91. Herb Kohl, "Should We Burn Babar? Questioning Power in Children's Literature," in *Should We Burn Babar? Essays on Children's Literature and the Power of Stories* (New York: New Press, 1995), pp. 3–29.

92. Ibid., p. 15.

93. Katz, *Virtuous Reality*. See also Don Tapscott, *Growing Up Digital: The Rise of the Net Generation* (New York: McGraw Hill, 1997).

94. Katz, *Virtuous Reality*, p. 197.

Childhood Innocence

Chapter One

From Immodesty to Innocence

Philippe Ariès

One of the unwritten laws of contemporary morality, the strictest and best respected of all, requires adults to avoid any reference, above all any humorous reference, to sexual matters in the presence of children. This notion was entirely foreign to the society of old. The modern reader of the diary in which Henri IV's physician, Heroard, recorded the details of the young Louis XIII's life is astonished by the liberties which people took with children, by the coarseness of the jokes they made, and by the indecency of gestures made in public which shocked nobody and which were regarded as perfectly natural.[1] No other document can give us a better idea of the non-existence of the modern idea of childhood at the beginning of the seventeenth century.

Louis XIII was not yet one year old: 'He laughed uproariously when his nanny waggled his cock with her fingers.' An amusing trick which the child soon copied. Calling a page, 'he shouted "Hey, there!" and pulled up his robe, showing him his cock.'

He was one year old: 'In high spirits,' notes Heroard, 'he made everybody kiss his cock.' This amused them all. Similarly everyone considered his behaviour towards two visitors, a certain de Bonières and his daughter, highly amusing: 'He laughed at him, lifted up his robe and showed him his cock, but even more so to his daughter, for then, holding it and giving his little laugh, he shook the whole of his body up and down.' They thought this so funny that the child took care to repeat a gesture which had been such a success; in the presence of a 'little lady', 'he lifted up his coat, and showed her his cock with such fervour that he was quite beside himself. He lay on his back to show it to her.'

When he was just over a year old he was engaged to the Infanta of Spain; his attendants explained to him what this meant, and he understood them fairly well. 'They asked him: "Where is the Infanta's darling?" He put his hand on his cock.'

During his first three years nobody showed any reluctance or saw any harm in jokingly touching the child's sexual parts. 'The Marquise [de Verneuil] often put her hand under his coat; he got his nanny to lay him on her bed where she played with him, putting her hand under his coat.' 'Mme de Verneuil wanted to play with him and took hold of his nipples; he pushed her away, saying: "Let go, let go, go away." He would not allow the Marquise to touch his nipples, because his nanny had told him: "Monsieur, never let anybody touch your nipples, or your cock, or they will cut it off." He remembered this.' Again: 'When he got up, he would not take his shirt and said: "Not my shirt, I want to give you all some milk from my cock." We held out our hands, and he pretended to give us all some milk, saying: "Pss, pss," and only then agreeing to take his shirt.'

It was a common joke, repeated time and again, to say to him; 'Monsieur, you haven't got a cock.' Then 'he replied: "Hey, here it is!"—laughing and lifting it up with one finger.' These jokes were not limited to the servants, or to brainless youths, or to women of easy virtue such as the King's mistress. The Queen, his mother, made the same sort of joke: 'The Queen, touching his cock, said: "Son, I am holding your spout." ' Even more astonishing is this passage: 'He was undressed and Madame too [his sister], and they were placed naked in bed with the King, where they kissed and twittered and gave great amusement to the King. The King asked him: "Son, where is the Infanta's bundle?" He showed it to him, saying: "There is no bone in it, Papa." Then, as it was slightly distended, he added: "There is now, there is sometimes." '

The Court was amused, in fact, to see his first erections: 'Waking up at eight o'clock, he called Mlle Bethouzay and said to her: "Zezai, my cock is like a drawbridge; see how it goes up and down." And he raised it and lowered it.'

By the age of four, 'he was taken to the Queen's apartments, where Mme de Guise showed him the Queen's bed and said to him: "Monsieur, this is where you were made." He replied: "With Mamma?" ' 'He asked his nanny's husband: "What is that?" "That," came the reply, "is one of my silk stockings." "And those?" [after the manner of parlour-game questions] "Those are my breeches." "What are they made of?" "Velvet." "And that?" "That is a cod-piece." "What is inside?" "I don't know, Monsieur." "Why, a cock. Who is it for?" "I don't know, Monsieur." "Why, for Madame Doundoun [his nanny]." '

'He stood between the legs of Mme de Montglat [his governess, a very dignified, highly respectable woman, who however did not seem to be put out—any more than Heroard was—by all these jokes which we would consider insufferable today]. The King said: "Look at Madame de Montglat's son: she has just given birth." He went straight away and stood between the Queen's legs.'

When he was between five and six, people stopped talking about his sexual parts, while he started talking more about other people's. Mlle Mercier, one of his chambermaids who had stayed up late the night before, was still in bed one morning, next to his bed (his servants, who were sometimes married, slept in his bedroom and do not appear to have allowed his presence to embarrass them). 'He played with her, toyed with her toes and the upper part of her legs, and told his nanny to go and get some birch twigs so that he could beat her, which he did ... His nanny asked him: "What have you seen of Mercier's?" He replied calmly: "I have seen her arse." "What else have you seen?" He replied calmly and without laughing that he had seen her private.' On another occasion, 'after playing with Mlle Mercier, he called me [Heroard] and told me that Mercier had a private as big as that (showing me his two fists) and that there was water inside.'

After 1608 this kind of joke disappeared: he had become a little man—attaining the fateful age of seven—and at this age he had to be taught decency in language and behaviour. When he was asked how children were born, he would reply, like Molière's Agnès, 'through the ear'. Mme de Montglat scolded him when he 'showed his cock to the little Ventelet girl.' And if, when he awoke in the morning, he was still put in Mme de Montglat's bed between her and her husband, Heroard waxed indignant and noted in the margin of his diary: *insignis impudentia*. The boy of ten was forced to behave with a modesty which nobody had thought of expecting of the boy of five. Education scarcely began before the age of seven; moreover, these tardy scruples of decency are to be attributed to the beginnings of a reformation of manners, a sign of the religious and moral restoration which took place in the seventeenth century. It was as if education was held to be of no value before the approach of manhood.

By the time he was fourteen, however, Louis XIII had nothing more to learn, for it was at the age of fourteen years two months that he was put almost by force into his wife's bed. After the ceremony he 'retired and had supper in bed at a quarter to seven. M. de Gramont and a few young lords told him some broad stories to encourage him. He asked for his slippers and put on his robe and went to the Queen's bedchamber at eight o'clock, where he was put to bed beside the Queen his wife, in the presence of the Queen his mother; at a quarter past ten he returned after sleeping for about an hour and performing twice, according to what he told us; he arrived with his cock all red.'

The marriage of a boy of fourteen was perhaps becoming something of a rare occurrence. The marriage of a girl of thirteen was still very common.

There is no reason to believe that the moral climate was any different in other families, whether of nobles or commoners; the practice of associating children with the sexual ribaldries of adults formed part of contemporary manners. In Pascal's family, Jacqueline Pascal at the age of twelve was writing a poem about the Queen's pregnancy.

Thomas Platter, in his memoirs of life as a medical student at the end of the sixteenth century, writes: 'I once met a child who played this trick [knotting a girl's aiguillette when she married, so that her husband became impotent] on his parents' maidservant. She begged him to break the spell by undoing the aiguillette. He agreed and the bridegroom, recovering his potency, was immediately cured.' Père de Dainville, the historian of the Society of Jesus and of humanist pedagogics, also writes: 'The respect due to children was then [in the sixteenth century] completely unknown. Everything was permitted in their presence: coarse language, scabrous actions and situations; they had heard everything and seen everything.[2]

This lack of reserve with regard to children surprises us: we raise our eyebrows at the outspoken talk but even more at the bold gestures, the physical contacts, about which it is easy to imagine what a modern psycho-analyst would say. The psycho-analyst would be wrong. The attitude to sex, and doubtless sex itself, varies according to environment, and consequently according to period and mentality. Nowadays the physical contacts described by Heroard would strike us as bordering on sexual perversion and nobody would dare to indulge in them publicly. This was not the case at the beginning of the seventeenth century. There is an engraving of 1511 depicting a holy family: St. Anne's behaviour strikes us as extremely odd—she is pushing the child's thighs apart as if she wanted to get at its privy parts and tickle them. It would be a mistake to see this as a piece of ribaldry.[3]

The practice of playing with children's privy parts formed part of a widespread tradition, which is still operative in Moslem circles. These have remained aloof not only from scientific progress but also from the great moral reformation, at first Christian, later secular, which disciplined eighteenth-century and particularly nineteenth-century society in England and France. Thus in Moslem society we find features which strike us as peculiar but which the worthy Heroard would not have found so surprising. Witness this passage from a novel entitled *The Statue of Salt*. The author is a Tunisian Jew, Albert Memmi, and his book is a curious document on traditional Tunisian society and the mentality of the young people who are semi-Westernized. The hero of the novel is describing a scene in the tram taking him to school in Tunis:

'In front of me were a Moslem and his son, a tiny little boy with a miniature tarboosh and henna on his hands; on my left a Djerban grocer on his way to market, with a basket between his legs and a pencil behind his ear. The Djerban, affected by the warmth and peace inside the tram, stirred in his seat. He smiled at the child, who smiled back with his eyes and looked at his father. The father, grateful and flattered, reassured him and smiled at the Djerban. "How old are you?" the grocer asked the child. "Two and a half," replied the father. "Has the cat got your tongue?" the grocer asked the child. "No," replied the father, "he hasn't been circumcised yet, but he will be soon." "Ah!" said the grocer. He had found something to talk about to the child. "Will you sell me your little animal?" "No!" said the child angrily. He obviously knew what the grocer meant, and the same offer had already been made to him. I too [the Jewish child] was familiar with this scene. I had taken part in it in my time, provoked by other people, with the same feelings of shame and desire, revulsion and inquisitive complicity. The child's eyes shone with the pleasure of incipient virility [a modern feeling, attributed to the child by the educated Memmi who is aware of recent discoveries as to early sexual awakening in children; in former times people believed that before puberty children had no sexual feelings] and also revulsion at this monstrous provocation. He looked at his father. His father smiled: *it was a permissible game* [our italics]. Our neighbours watched the *traditional scene* with complaisant approval. "I'll give you ten francs for it," said the Djerban. "No," said the child. "Come now, sell me your little . . ." the Djerban went on. "No! No!" "I'll give you fifty francs for it." "No!" "I'll go as high as I can: a thousand francs!" "No!" The Djerban assumed an expression of greediness. "And I'll throw in a bag of sweets as well!" "No! No!" "You still say no? That's your last word?" the Djerban shouted, pretending to be angry. "You still say no?" he repeated. ''No!'' Thereupon the grown-up threw himself upon the child, a terrible expression on his face, his hand brutally rummaging inside the child's fly. The child tried to fight him off with his fists. The father roared with laughter, the Djerban was convulsed with amusement, while our neighbours smiled broadly.'

This twentieth-century scene surely enables us to understand better the seventeenth century before the moral reformation. We should avoid anachronisms, such as the explanation by Mme de Sévigné's latest editor that the baroque excesses of her mother love were due to incest. All that was involved was a game whose scabrous nature we should beware of exaggerating: there was nothing more scabrous about it than there is about the racy stories men tell each other nowadays.

This semi-innocence, which strikes us as corrupt or naive, explains the popularity of the theme of the urinating child as from the fifteenth century. The theme is treated in the illustrations of books of hours and in church pictures. In the calendars in the Hennessy book of hours[4] and the Grimani breviary,[5] dating from the early sixteenth century, a winter month is represented by the snow-covered village; the door of one house is open, and the woman of the house can be seen spinning, the man warming himself by the fire; the child is in full view, urinating on to the snow in front of the door.

A Flemish 'Ecce homo' by P. Pietersz,[6] doubtless intended for a church, shows quite a few children in the crowd of onlookers: one mother is holding her child above the heads of the crowd so that he can have a better view. Some quick-witted boys are shinning up the doorposts. A child can be seen urinating, held by his mother. The magistrates of the High Court of Toulouse, when they heard Mass in the chapel in their own Palace of Justice, could have had their attention distracted by a similar scene. They had before them a great triptych depicting the story of John the Baptist.[7] On the centre volet the Baptist was shown preaching. There were children in the crowd; a woman was suckling her child; there was a boy up a tree; a little way away, facing the magistrates, a child was holding up his robe and urinating.

The frequency with which one finds children in crowd scenes, and the repetition of certain themes (the child being breast-fed, the child urinating) in the fifteenth and especially the sixteenth century, are clear signs of a new and special interest.

It is noteworthy too that at this time one scene of religious iconography recurs frequently: the Circumcision. This scene is depicted in almost surgical detail. It seems in fact that the Presentation of the Virgin in the Temple and the Circumcision were treated in the sixteenth and seventeenth centuries as festivals of childhood: the only religious festivals of childhood before the solemn celebration of the First Communion. In the parish church of Saint-Nicolas we can see an early seventeenth-century painting which comes from the Abbey of Saint-Martin-des-Champs. The scene of the Circumcision is surrounded by a crowd of children, some of them with their parents, others climbing the pillars to get a better view. For us, surely, there is something strange, almost shocking, about the choice of the Circumcision as a festival of childhood, depicted in the midst of children. Shocking for us, perhaps, but not for a present-day Moslem or for a man of the sixteenth or early seventeenth century.

Not only were children associated with an operation, admittedly of a religious nature, on the male sexual organ, but gestures and physical contacts were freely and publicly allowed which were forbidden as soon as the child reached the age of puberty, or in other words was practically adult. There were two reasons for this. In the first place the child under the age of puberty was believed to be unaware of or indifferent to sex. Thus gestures and allusions had no meaning for him; they became purely gratuitous and lost their sexual significance. Secondly, the idea did not yet exist that references to sexual matters, even when virtually devoid of dubious meanings, could soil childish innocence, either in fact or in the opinion people had of it: nobody thought that this innocence really existed.

Such at least was the general opinion: it was no longer that of the moralists and pedagogues, or at least of the better ones, innovators who found little support for their ideas. Their retrospective importance is due to the fact that in the long run they managed to win acceptance for their ideas—which are ours too.

This current of ideas can be traced back to the fifteenth century, a period when it was strong enough to bring about a change in the traditional discipline of the schools.[8] Gerson was then its principal representative. He expressed his ideas on the question with great clarity, showing himself to be an excellent observer, for his period, of childhood, and its sexual practices. This study of the sexual manners of childhood, and the importance which he attributed to them by devoting a treatise to them, *De confessione mollicei*,[9] reveal a novel attitude; this attitude can be compared to the indications we have already noted in iconography and dress as showing a new interest in childhood.

Gerson studies the sexual behavior of children for the benefit of confessors, to help the latter to arouse a feeling of guilt in the hearts of their little penitents (between ten and twelve years of age). He knows that masturbation and erection without ejaculation are general practices: if someone is questioned and denies all experience of masturbation then he is lying. For Gerson, this is a very serious matter. The *peccatum mollicei*, 'even if, because of the child's age, it has not been accompanied by pollution ... has taken away the child's virginity even more than if the child, at the same age, had gone with a woman'. What is more, it borders on sodomy. Gerson's judgment is closer to modern teaching, which regards masturbation as an inevitable stage of premature sexuality, than are the sarcastic remarks of the novelist Sorel, who sees it as the result of the scholastic confinement of the boarding-school.

The child, according to Gerson, does not feel any sense of guilt to begin with: '*Sentiunt ibi quemdam pruritum incognitum tum stat erectio* and they think that it is permissible that *se fricent ibi et se palpent et se tractent sicut in aliis locis dum pruritus inest.*' This is a consequence of original corruption: *ex corruptione naturae.* We are still a long way from the idea of childish innocence, but we are already quite close to an objective knowledge of the child's behavior, the originality of which is obvious in the light of what has been said above. How is childhood to be safe-guarded against this danger? By the confessor's advice, but also by changing the way in which children are brought up, by behaving differently towards them. One should speak decently to them, using only chaste expressions. One should see that when playing together they do not kiss each other, touch each other with their bare hands, or look at each other: *figerent oculi in eorum decore*. One should guard against any promiscuity between children and adults, at least in bed: *pueri capaces doli, puellae, juvenes* should not sleep in the same bed as older people, even of the same sex; cohabitation in the same bed was a widespread practice then in all classes of society. We have seen that it still existed at the end of the sixteenth century, even at the French court: Henri IV's frolics with his son, Louis XIII, brought to his bed together with his sister, justified Gerson's prudence of nearly two hundred years before. Gerson forbids people to touch each other *in nudo*, and warns his readers to beware '*a societaliatibus perversis ubi colloquia prava et gestus impudici fiunt in lecto absque dormitione.*'

Gerson returns to the topic in a sermon against lechery for the fourth Sunday of Advent: the child must prevent others from touching him or kissing him, and if he has failed to do so, he must report this in every instance in confession (this demand needs to be emphasized, because, generally speaking, people saw no harm in caresses). Later on, he suggests that it 'would be a good thing' to sepa-rate children at night—he recalls the case cited by St Jerome of a boy of nine who begot a child—but he does not dare to say more than 'it would be a good thing', for it was a general practice to put all the children of a family together when they were not sleeping with a valet, a maidservant or relatives.[10]

In the regulations which he drew up for the school of Notre-Dame-de-Paris he tries to isolate the children, to keep them under the constant supervision of the master. The singing master must not teach *cantilenas dissolutas impudicasque*, and the boys must report any of their classmates who is guilty of misbehavior or immodesty (punishable misdemeanours include speaking *gallicum*—instead of Latin—swearing, lying, cursing, dawdling in bed, missing the Hours, and chat-tering in church). A night-light must be kept burning in the dormitory: 'as much out of devotion to the image of Our Lady as for the natural functions, and so that they perform in the light the only acts which can and must be seen'. No child may change beds during the night: he must stay with the companion he has been given. *Conventicula, vel societates ad partem extra alias* are not allowed either by day or night. Every care is taken, in fact, to avoid special friendships and dangerous company, especially that of the servants: 'The servants must be forbidden to engage in any familiarity with the children, not expecting the clerks, the *capellani*, the church staff [there is a certain absence of trust here]: they must not speak to the children except when the Masters are present.' Children not on the foundation are not to be allowed to mix with the schoolboys, even to study with them (except by special permission of the Superior), 'so that our children do not contract bad habits from the example of others'.

This is all quite new: it must not be imagined that life in the school was really like this . . . Gerson was far ahead of the institutions of his time. His regulations

are interesting for the moral ideal which they reveal, which had not been formulated with such clarity before, and which was to become the ideal of the
Jesuits, of Port-Royal, of the Brothers of Christian Doctrine, and of all the moralists and strict pedagogues of the seventeenth century.

In the sixteenth century the pedagogues were more easygoing, for all that they
took care not to overstep certain bounds. We know this from books written for
the schoolboys, from which they learnt reading, writing, Latin vocabulary, and
finally etiquette; the treatises on etiquette and the conversations which, to make
the lesson more lifelike, involved several schoolboys or a schoolboy and a master.
These dialogues are excellent documents on school life. In Vivès's dialogues we
find certain passages which would not have been to Gerson's taste but which
were traditional: 'Which is the more shameful part: the part in front [note the
discreet euphemism] or the hole in the arse?' 'Both parts are extremely improper,
the behind because of its unpleasantness, and the other part because of lechery
and dishonour.'[11]

The coarsest jokes, as well as topics of anything but educational value, are to
be found in these dialogues. In Charles Hoole's English dialogues[12] we have a
number of quarrels: one takes place in a tavern—and taverns at that time were
far less respectable places than the modern public house. There is a lengthy
argument about which inn sells the best beer. However, even in Vivès, a certain
modesty is observed: 'The third finger is called the shameful one. Why?' 'The
master has said that he knows the reason, but that he does not want to give it
because it is dirty and unpleasant; however, do not press the matter, *for it is
unseemly for a child of good character to ask about such unpleasant things.*' This is quite
remarkable for the time. Broad talk was so natural that even later on the strictest
reformers would introduce into their sermons to children and students comparisons which would seem shocking today. Thus in 1653 we find the Jesuit Father
Lebrun exhorting the 'noble boarders of Clermont College' to avoid gluttony:
'They are fastidious about their food, *tanquam praegnantes mulierculae.*'[13]

But towards the end of the sixteenth century a much more obvious change
took place: certain pedagogues, whose ideas were to carry weight and who
would succeed in imposing their concepts and scruples on others, refused to
allow children to be given indecent books any longer. The idea originated of
providing expurgated editions of the classics for the use of children. This was a
very important stage, which may be regarded as marking the beginning of respect for childhood. This attitude was to be found among both Catholics and
Protestants, in France and England. Until then nobody had hesitated to give
children Terence to read, for he was a classic. The Jesuits removed him from their
curriculum.[14] In England the schools used an expurgated edition by Cornelius
Schonaeus, published in 1592 and reprinted in 1674—Brinsley recommends it in
his schoolmaster's manual.[15]

The French Protestant schools used Cordier's conversations (1564), which took
the place of the conversations of Erasmus, Vivès, Mosellanus, etc.[16] They reveal a
new decorum, a desire to avoid any word or expression which might be considered offensive or indecent. The most that is allowed is a joke about the uses of

paper—'schoolboy paper', 'envelope paper', 'blotting paper'—in a parlour game. Finally one boy gives up but the other guesses the answer: 'paper used for wiping your bottom in the privy'. An innocent concession to the traditional jokes. Cordier really could be 'put into anybody's hands'. In any case, his dialogues were used in conjunction with some religious dialogues by a certain S. Castellion.

Port-Royal in its turn produced a heavily expurgated edition of Terence: *Comedies of Terence made very decent while changing very little.*[17]

As for modesty of behavior, the Jesuit colleges introduced new precautions, duly recorded in the regulations, regarding the administration of corporal punishment. It was laid down that the breeches of the victims, *adolescentum*, were not to be removed, 'whatever the boy's rank or age'. Just enough of the skin was to be exposed as was necessary to inflict the punishment, but not more: *non amplius.*[18]

A great change in manners took place in the course of the seventeenth century. The least of the liberties permitted at the court of Henri IV would not have been allowed by Mme de Maintenon with the King's children, legitimate or illegitimate, any more than they would have been in the homes of the free-thinkers. It was no longer a case of a few isolated moralists like Gerson, but of a great movement which manifested itself on all sides, not only in a rich moral and pedagogic literature but also in devotional practices and a new religious iconography.

An essential concept had won acceptance: that of the innocence of childhood. It was already to be found in Montaigne, for all that he had few illusions about the chastity of young students: 'A hundred schoolboys have caught the pox before getting to Aristotle's lesson, *On Temperance.*[19] But he also tells an anecdote which reveals a different attitude: Albuquerque, 'in great danger of shipwreck, took a young boy on his shoulders, so that in their association in danger his *innocence* would serve him as a surety and a recommendation to obtain God's favour and bring him safely to land.'[20] A hundred years later, the idea of the innocence of childhood had become a commonplace. Witness the caption to an engraving by F. Guérard showing children's toys (dolls and drums): 'This is the age of innocence, to which we must all return in order to enjoy the happiness to come which is our hope on earth; the age when one can forgive anything, the age when hatred is unknown, when nothing can cause distress; the golden age of human life, the age which defies Hell, the age when life is easy and death holds no terrors, the age to which the heavens are open. Let tender and gentle respect be shown to these young plants of the Church. Heaven is full of anger for whosoever scandalizes them.'[21]

What a long way we have come to reach this point! It can be traced by means of an abundant literature, a few works of which we shall now examine.

L'Honineste garçon, described as 'the art of instructing the nobility in virtue, learning and all the exercises suitable to its rank', and published by M. de Grenaille of Chatauniers,[22] is a good example. The author had already written *L'Honneste fille*. The interest in education, in 'the institution of childhood', is worthy of note. The author knows that he is not the only writer on the subject and apologizes in his foreword: 'I do not believe that I am encroaching on M. Faret's province[23] in dealing with a subject on which he has only touched, and in speaking of the education of those whom he has depicted in their finished condition . . . Here I lead the Boy from early infancy as far as youth. I deal first with his birth and then with his education; I polish his mind and his manners at the same time; I instruct him in both religion and the proprieties, so that he shall be neither impious nor superstitious.' Treatises on etiquette were already in print which were simply manuals of *savoir-vivre*, books on good manners, and they continued to enjoy widespread favour until the early nineteenth century. In addition to these etiquette books which were meant for children, in the early seventeenth century a pedagogic literature for the use of parents and teachers came into being. Although it referred to Quintilian, Plutarch and Erasmus, it was something new. So new that M. de Grenaille feels called upon to defend himself against those who see the education of youth as a practical matter and not a subject for a book. 'There is Quintilian, and so on . . . but there is something else, and the subject has a special seriousness for a Christian . . . Since the Lord of Lords summons little innocents to Him, I do not believe that any of His subjects has the right to repulse them, nor that men should show reluctance to educate them, seeing that in doing so they are simply imitating the angels.' The comparison of angels with children was to become a common theme of edification. 'It is said that an angel in the shape of a child enlightened St Augustine, but on the other hand he took pleasure in communicating his wisdom to children, and in his works we find treatises intended for them as well as others for the greatest theologians.' He cites St Louis, who wrote a directive for his son. 'Cardinal Bellarmin wrote a catechism for children.' Richelieu, 'that great prince of the Church, gave instruction to the smallest as well as counsel to the greatest'. Montaigne too, whom one hardly expected to find in such good company, showed concern about bad teachers, especially pedants.

M. de Grenaille continues: 'It must not be imagined that when one speaks of childhood one is always speaking of something weak; on the contrary, I am going to show here that a condition which certain people consider contemptible is positively illustrious.' It was in fact at this time that people did talk of the weakness and imbecility of childhood. Hitherto they had tended to ignore childhood, as a transitional period soon finished with and of no importance. This stress laid on the contemptible side of childhood may have been a consequence of the classical spirit and its insistence on reason, but it was above all a reaction against the importance which the child had assumed in the family and the idea of the family. That feeling of irritation with childishness thus arose which is the modern reverse of the idea of childhood. With it went the contempt which that society of men of the open air and men of the world felt for the professor, the college regent, the 'pedant', at a time when the colleges were becoming more numerous and better attended, and when childhood was already beginning to remind adults of their schooldays. In reality, the antipathy to children shown by solemn or peevish spirits is evidence of the importance, in their eyes the excessive importance, which was attributed to childhood.

For the author of *L'Honneste garçon*, childhood is illustrious on account of Christ's childhood. This, he points out, was sometimes interpreted as a token of the humiliation accepted by Christ in adopting not only the human condition but the state of childhood: thereby putting himself on a lower level than the first Adam, according to St Bernard. On the other hand there are the holy children: the Holy Innocents, the child martyrs who refused to worship the idols, and the little Jew of St Gregory of Tours whose father tried to burn him in an oven because he had turned Christian. 'I can show too that in our own days the Faith has had its child martyrs as in past ages. The history of Japan tells of a little Louis who, at the age of twelve, showed greater courage than grown men.' A woman died at the same stake as Dom Carlo Spinola, together with 'her little child', which shows that 'God draws his praises from the mouths of children'. And the author piles up the examples afforded by the holy children of the two Testaments, adding a further example, drawn from French medieval history: 'I must not forget the courage of those French boys whose praises Nauclerus has sung, and who took the cross to the number of twenty thousand in the time of Pope Innocent III to go and deliver Jerusalem from the hands of the infidels.' The children's crusade.

We know that the children in the medieval verse-chronicles and romances of chivalry behaved like true knights, affording proof, in M. de Grenaille's eyes, of the courage and good sense of children. He cites the case of a child who appointed himself the champion of the Empress, the wife of the Emperor Conrad, against 'a famous gladiator'. 'Read in the romances of chivalry what the Rinaldos, the Tancreds and all those other knights are said to have done: legend does not attribute more to them in a single fight than true History grants that little Achilles.'

'After that, can anyone deny that the first age is comparable, indeed often preferable, to all the rest?' 'Who would dare to say that God favours older people more than children? He favours them on account of their innocence, which comes close to impeccability.' They have neither passions nor vices: 'Their lives seem to be most reasonable at a time when they seem least capable of using their reason.' Obviously there is no mention here of the *peccatum mollicei*, and in this respect the worthy nobleman of 1642 strikes the modern reader, familiar with psychoanalysis, as more old-fashioned than Gerson. The explanation is that the very idea of immodesty and sensuality in a child embarrasses M. de Grenaille, as being an argument used by those who consider childhood to be 'silly' and 'corrupt'.

This new attitude was to be found again at Port-Royal, exemplified first of all by Saint-Cyran. His Jansenist biographers all tell us of the lofty idea he had of childhood and of the respect due to children: 'He admired the Son of God, who, in the most august functions of His ministry, would not allow children to be prevented from coming to Him, who kissed and blessed them, who commanded us not to despise or neglect them, and who finally spoke of them in terms so favourable and so astonishing that they are capable of dumbfounding those who scandalize the little ones. Accordingly M. de Saint-Cyran always showed children a kindness which amounted to a sort of respect, in order to do honour to the innocence in them and the Holy Ghost which inhabits them.'[24] M. de Saint-Cyran was 'very enlightened' and 'far from approving these worldly maxims [contempt for pedagogues], and as he was aware of the importance of the care and education of youth, he regarded it in a totally different light. However disagreeable and humiliating people might find it, he none the less employed persons of merit for it who never felt that they had any right to complain.'

The result was the formation of that moral concept which insisted on the weakness of childhood rather than on what M. de Grenaille called its 'illustrious nature', but which associated its weakness with its innocence, the true reflection of divine purity, and which placed education in the front rank of man's obligations. It reacted at one and the same time against indifference towards childhood, against an excessively affectionate and selfish attitude which turned the child into a plaything for adults and encouraged his caprices, and against the reverse of this last feeling, the contempt of the man of reason. This concept dominates late seventeenth-century literature. This is what Coustel wrote in his rules for the education of children on the need to love children and to overcome the repugnance which they arouse in thinking men:[25] 'If one considers the child's exterior, which is nothing but weakness and infirmity of either body or mind, it cannot be denied that there is no apparent reason for holding it in high esteem. But one changes one's opinion if one looks into the future and acts in the light of Faith.' Beyond the child one will then be able to see 'the good magistrate', 'the good priest', 'the great lord'. But above all it must be remembered that children's souls, still possessed of their baptismal innocence, are the dwelling-place of Jesus Christ. 'God sets us an example by commanding Angels to accompany them on all their errands, without ever leaving them.'

That is why, according to Varet, 'the education of children is one of the most important things in the world.'[26] And Jacqueline Pascal, in the regulations for the little boarders of Port-Royal, writes: 'Looking after children is so important that we are bound to prefer that duty to all others when obedience imposes it on us, and what is more, to our personal pleasures, even if these are of a spiritual nature.'[27]

This is not a case of isolated observations but of a real doctrine—generally accepted by Jesuits as by Oratorians or Jansenists—which partly accounts for the profusion of educational institutions, colleges, little schools and special establishments, and the evolution of school life in the direction of stricter discipline.

A few general principles that were deduced from this doctrine were cited as commonplaces in the literature of the time. For example, children must never be left alone. This principle dated back to the fifteenth century and originated in monastic experience, but it was never really put into practice until the seventeenth century, by which time the logic of it was obvious to the public at large and not simply to a handful of monks and 'pedants'. 'As far as possible, all the apertures of the cage must be closed . . . A few bars will be left open to allow the child to live and to enjoy good health; this is what is done with nightingales to make them sing and with parrots to teach them to talk.'[28] This was done with a certain subtlety, for both the Jesuit colleges and the schools at Port-Royal had become increasingly familiar with child psychology. In the regulations for the children at Port-Royal we have Jacqueline Pascal writing: 'A close watch must be kept on the children, and they must never be left alone anywhere, whether they are ill or in good health.' But 'this constant supervision should be exercised gently and with a certain trustfulness calculated to make them think that one loves them, and that it is only to enjoy their company that one is with them. This makes them love this supervision rather than fear it.'[29]

This principle was absolutely universal, but it was carried out to the letter only in the Jesuit boarding-schools, in the schools at Port-Royal and in some private boarding-schools; in other words it affected only a small number of very rich children. The object was to avoid the promiscuity of the colleges, which for a long time had a bad reputation, though not as long in France—thanks to the Jesuits—as in England. Coustel writes: 'As soon as the young people set foot in that sort of place [the college], they rapidly lose that innocence, that simplicity, that modesty which hitherto made them so pleasing to God and to men.'[30] There was a general reluctance to entrust a child to a single tutor: the extreme sociability of manners was opposed to this solution. It was held that the child ought to get to know people and converse with them from an early age; this was very important, even more necessary than Latin. It was better 'to put five or six children with a good man or two in a private house', an idea which Erasmus had already put forward.

The second principle was that children must not be pampered and must be accustomed to strict discipline early in life: 'Do not tell me that they are only children and that one must be patient with them. For the effects of concupiscence appear only too clearly at this age.' This was a reaction against the 'coddling' of children under eight, and against the opinion that they were too small to make it worth-while finding fault with them. Courtin's manual of etiquette of 1671 explains at some length: 'These little people are allowed to amuse themselves without anyone troubling to see whether they are behaving well or badly; they are permitted to do as they please; nothing is forbidden them; they laugh when they ought to cry, they cry when they ought to laugh, they talk when they ought to be silent, and they are mute when good manners require them to reply. It is cruelty to allow them to go on living in this way. The parents say that when they are bigger they will be corrected. Would it not be better to deal with them in such a way that there was nothing to correct?'[31]

The third principle was modesty. At Port-Royal: 'As soon as they have retired for the night the girls' beds are faithfully inspected to see if they are lying with fitting modesty, and also to see if they are properly covered up in winter.'[32] A real propaganda campaign was launched to try to eradicate the age-old habit of sleeping several to a bed. The same advice was repeated all the way through the seventeenth century. We find it, for instance, in *La Civilité chrétienne* by St Jean-Baptiste de La Salle, which was first published in 1713: 'Above all, one must not, unless one is married [this is a reservation which nobody would dream of introducing nowadays into a book intended for children, but at that time books intended for children were not read only by children], go to bed in the presence of a person of the opposite sex, this being utterly contrary to prudence and decency. It is even less permissible for persons of different sexes to sleep in the same bed, even in the case of *very young children*, for it is not fitting for even persons of the same sex to sleep together. These are two things which St Francis of Sales especially recommended to Mme de Chantal with regard to children.' And: 'Parents must teach their children to conceal their bodies from one another when going to bed.'

The insistence on decency was to be found again in the matter of reading and conversation: 'Teach them to read books in which purity of language and wholesome subject-matter are combined.' 'When they start writing, do not allow them to be given examples full of unseemly expressions.'[33] We are a long way here from the outspoken talk of the child Louis XIII, which amused even the worthy Heroard. Naturally novel-reading, dancing and theatre-going were banned, and adults too were advised against indulging in these distractions. A close check was recommended on songs, an important and necessary precaution in a society where music was so popular: 'Take particular care to prevent your children from learning modern songs.'[34] But the old songs were not rated any more highly: 'Of the songs which are known everywhere and which are taught to children as soon as they start to talk . . . there are scarcely any which are not full of the most horrible slanders and calumnies, and which are not biting satires which spare neither the sacred persons of the sovereigns nor those of the magistrates, nor those of the most innocent and pious persons.' These songs were described as expressing 'dissolute passions' and as being 'full of indecent expressions'.[35]

St Jean-Baptiste de La Salle maintained this mistrust of entertainments:[36] 'It is no more seemly for a Christian to attend a puppet-show [than a theatrical performance].' 'A respectable person must regard entertainments of this sort with nothing but contempt . . . and parents must never allow their children to attend them.' Plays, balls, dances, and the 'more ordinary entertainments' provided by 'jugglers, mountebanks and tightrope walkers' were forbidden. Only educational games, that is to say, games which had been integrated in the educational system, were permitted; all other games were and remained suspect.

Another recommendation recurs frequently in this pedagogic literature, with its insistence on 'modesty': a warning not to leave children in the company of servants. This is a recommendation which went against an absolutely universal practice: 'Leave them as little as possible with servants, and especially with lackeys ['servants' had a wider significance then than it has now, and included what we would call companions]. These persons, in order to insinuate themselves into children's good graces, usually tell them nothing but nonsense and fill them with a love of gambling, amusement and vanity.'[37]

Again, in the eighteenth century, we have the future Cardinal de Bernis recalling his childhood—he was born in 1715: 'Nothing is more dangerous for the morals and perhaps also for the health than to leave children too long in the care of the servants.' '*People take liberties with a child which they would not risk with a young man.*'[38] This last sentence clearly refers to the mentality which we have analysed above in discussing the court of Henri IV and the scene between the Moslem boy and the Djerban in Tunis in the twentieth century. It still existed in the lower classes, but it was no longer tolerated in enlightened circles. The stress laid by the moralists on the need to separate children from the varied world of 'the servants' shows how well aware they were of the dangers presented by this promiscuity of children and servants (the servants themselves were often very young).

The fourth principle was simply another application of this insistence on decency and 'modesty': the old familiarity must be abandoned and its place taken by great moderation of manners and language, even in everyday life. This policy took the form of war on the use of the familiar *tu* form. In the little Jansenist college of Le Chesnay: 'They had been so accustomed to treat each other with respect that they never used the *tu* form of address, nor were they ever known to make the slightest remark which they might have considered likely to offend certain of their companions.'[39]

A 1671 manual of etiquette recognizes that good manners call for the *vous* form, but it has to make some concessions to the old French usage—this it does with a certain embarrassment: 'One normally says *vous*, and one must not say *tu* to anybody, unless it is to a little child and you are much older and it is customary for even the most polite and well-bred persons to speak thus. However, fathers with their children up to a certain age (in France until they are emancipated), masters with their pupils, and others in similar positions of authority, seem, according to common usage, to be allowed to say *tu* and *toi*. For close friends too, when they are conversing together, it is customary in certain places for them to say *tu* and *toi*; in other places people are more reserved and civilized.'[40]

Even in the little schools, where the children were younger, St Jean-Baptiste de La Salle forbade the masters to use the *tu* form of address: 'They must speak to the children with reserve, never saying *tu* or *toi*, which would be showing too much familiarity.' It is certain that under this pressure the use of *vous* became more widespread. From Colonel Gérard's memoirs one learns with surprise that at the end of the eighteenth century a couple of soldiers, one aged twenty-five and the other twenty-three, could actually say *vous* to one another. And Colonel Gérard himself could use the *vous* form without feeling ridiculous.

At Mme de Maintenon's Saint-Cyr, the young ladies were told to avoid 'saying *tu* and *toi*, and adopting manners contrary to the proprieties'.[41] 'One must never adapt oneself to children by means of childish language or manners; on the contrary, one must raise them to one's own level by always talking reasonably to them.'

Already, in the second half of the sixteenth century, the schoolboys in Cordier's dialogues were saying *vous* in the French text, whereas they naturally said *tu* in Latin.

In fact, the campaign for greater seriousness would triumph only in the nineteenth century, in spite of the contrary evolution of child welfare and more liberal, realistic pedagogics. An American professor of French, L. Wylie, who spent

his sabbatical year 1950—I in a village in the south of France, was astonished by
the seriousness with which the masters at the primary school treated their pupils,
and the parents, who were peasants, their children. The contrast with the American attitude struck him as enormous: 'Every step in the child's development
seems to depend on the development of what people call its *raison* . . . ' 'The child
is now considered to be *raisonnable*, and it is expected to remain *raisonnable*.'

This *raison*, this self-control and this seriousness, which are required of the
French child at an early age, while he is working for his certificate of study, and
which are no longer known in the United States, are the final result of the campaign launched at the end of the sixteenth century by monks and moralists. It
should be added that this state of mind is beginning to disappear from the French
town: it remains only in the country, where the American observer met it.

The idea of childish innocence resulted in two kinds of attitude and behaviour
towards childhood: firstly, safeguarding it against pollution by life, and particularly by the sexuality tolerated if not approved of among adults; and secondly,
strengthening it by developing character and reason. We may see a contradiction
here, for on the one hand childhood is preserved and on the other hand it is
made older than its years; but the contradiction exists only for us of the twentieth
century. The association of childhood with primitivism and irrationalism or pre-
logicism characterizes our contemporary concept of childhood. This concept
made its appearance in Rousseau, but it belongs to twentieth-century history. It
is only very recently that it passed from the theories of psychologists, pedagogues, psychiatrists and psycho-analysts into public opinion; it is this concept
which Professor Wylie used as a standard of comparison by which to gauge that
other attitude which he discovered in a village in the Vaucluse, and in which we
can recognize the survival of another concept of childhood, a different and older
concept, which was born in the fifteenth and sixteenth centuries and which became general and popular from the seventeenth century on. . . .

NOTES

1. Heroard, *Journal sur l'enfance et la jeunesse de Louis XIII.*
2. Père de Dainville, *La Naissance de l'humanisme moderne*, 1940, p. 261. Méchin, *Annales
du collège royal de Bourbon-Aix*, 2 vols, 1892.
3. Curjel, *H. Baldung-Grien*, plate XLVIII.
4. J. Destrée, *Les Heures de Notre-Dame dites de Hennessy*, 1895 and 1923.
5. S. de Vriès and Marpugo, *Le Bréviaire Grimani.*
6. H. Gerson, *Von Geertgen tot F. Hals*, 1950, vol. I, p. 95.
7. Musée des Augustins, Toulouse.
8. Cf. Part II, Chap. V.
9. Gerson, *De confessione mollicei, Opera*, 1706, vol. II, p. 309.
10. Ibid., *Doctrina pro pueris ecclesiae parisiensis, Opera*, 1706, vol. IV, p. 717.
11. Vivès, *Dialogues*, French translation, 1571.
12. Quoted in F. Watson, *The English Grammar Schools to 1660*, 1907, p. 112.
13. A. Schimberg, *Éducation morale dans les collèges de Jésuites*, 1913, p. 227.
14. Père de Dainville, op. cit.

15. F. Watson, op. cit.

16. M. Cordier, *Colloques*, 1586 edition.

17. By Pomponius and Trobatus.

18. Quoted by Père de Dainville, op. cit.

19. Montaigne, *Essais*, I, 26.

20. Ibid., I, 39.

21. F. Guérard, Cabinet des Estampes, Ee 3 a, pet. in-f°.

22. De Grenaille, *L'Honneste garçon*, 1642.

23. Faret, *L'Honnête homme*, 1630.

24. F. Cadet, *L'Éducation à Port-Royal*, 1887.

25. Coustel, *Règles de l'éducation des enfants*, 1687.

26. Varet, *De l'éducation chrétienne des enfants*, 1666.

27. Jacqueline Pascal, op. cit.

28. F. Cadet, op. cit.

29. J. Pascal, op. cit.

30. Coustel, op. cit.

31. *La Civilité nouvelle*, Basel, 1761.

32. J. Pascal, op. cit.

33. Varet, op. cit.

34. Varet, op. cit.

35. Ibid.

36. Jean-Baptiste de La Salle, *Les Règles de la bienséance et de la civilité chrétienne*. The first edition was published in 1713.

37. Varet, op. cit.

38. *Mémoires du Cardinal de Bernis*, 2 vols, 1878.

39. Regulations of Chesnay College, in Wallon de Beaupuis, *Suite des Vies des amis de Port-Royal*, 1751, vol. I, p. 175.

40. Cf. note 32.

41. T. Lavallée, *Histoire de la maison royale de Saint-Cyr*, 1862.

Chapter Two

The Case of Peter Pan
The Impossibility of Children's Fiction

Jacqueline S. Rose

Peter Pan offers us the child—for ever. It gives us the child, but it does not speak *to* the child. In fact so rarely has it spoken to the child throughout its history, that it led me to ask whether there might not be some relation between this all-too-perfect presence of the child and a set of problems, or evasions, in the very concept of children's fiction itself. Children's fiction rests on the idea that there is a child who is simply there to be addressed and that speaking to it might be simple. It is an idea whose innocent generality covers up a multitude of sins. This will attempt to trace the fantasy which lies behind the concept of children's fiction, and will base its case on *Peter Pan*.

Peter Pan stands in our culture as a monument to the impossibility of its own claims—that it represents the child, speaks to and for children, addresses them as a group which is knowable and exists for the book, much as the book (so the claim runs) exists for them. Where or how such a claim originates in the first place will be one of the questions asked here, but the question will be focused on *Peter Pan* in so far as *Peter Pan* is the text for children which has made that claim most boldly, and which most clearly reveals it as a fraud. *Peter Pan* has never, in any easy way, been a book for children at all, but the question this throws back to us is whether there can be any such thing.

Children's fiction is impossible, not in the sense that it cannot be written (that would be nonsense), but in that it hangs on an impossibility, one which it rarely ventures to speak. This is the impossible relation between adult and child. Children's fiction is clearly about that relation, but it has the remarkable characteristic of being about something which it hardly ever talks of. Children's fiction sets up a world in which the adult comes first (author, maker, giver) and the child comes after (reader, product, receiver), but where neither of them enter the space in between. To say that the child is inside the book—children's books are after all as often as not *about* children—is to fall straight into a trap. It is to confuse the adult's intention to get at the child with the child it portrays. If children's fiction builds an image of the child inside the book, it does so in order to secure the child who is outside the book, the one who does not come so easily within its grasp.

There is, in one sense, no body of literature which rests so openly on an acknowledged difference, a rupture almost, between writer and addressee. Children's fiction sets up the child as an outsider to its own process, and then aims, unashamedly, to take the child *in*.

None of this appears explicitly inside the book itself, which works precisely to the extent that any question of who is talking to whom, and why, is totally erased. We do see something of it in the expanding industry of children's book criticism, but mostly in the form of a disavowal—the best book for children is a book for adult *and* child, or else in the form of a moralism (another version of the same thing)—the best book is the book which does the child most good, that is, the book which secures the reader to its intent and can be absolutely sure of its effects.

Let it be said from the start that it will be no part of this chapter's contention that what is for the good of the child could somehow be better defined, that we could, if we shifted the terms of the discussion, determine what it is that the child really wants. It will not be an issue here of what the child wants, but of what the adult desires—desires in the very act of construing the child as the object of its speech. Children's fiction draws in the child, it secures, places and frames the child. How often has it been said recently that what is best about writing for children is that the writer can count absolutely on the child's willingness to enter into the book, and *live* the story? (Townsend, 1971, p. 13).

This is to describe children's fiction, quite deliberately, as something of a soliciting, a chase, or even a seduction. *Peter Pan* is certainly all of these. Recently we have been made at least partly aware of this, as J. M. Barrie's story has been told and retold, as the story of a man and five small boys, whom he picked up, stole and possessed (Dunbar, 1970; Birkin, 1978). Barrie eventually adopted the Llewellyn Davies boys around whom he built the story of *Peter Pan*, staking a claim to them which he had already acted out symbolically by drawing them into his tale. But in the case of *Peter Pan*, knowledge of this has taken longer to surface than it did, say, in the case of *Alice*, whose underworld journey was long ago traced to its author's fantasied seduction of a little girl. Charles Lutwidge Dodgson (*alias* Lewis Carroll) wrote his classic for children on condition that the child remain a little girl, held to him by the act of telling the tale. A sexual act which we can easily recognise now, despite (or because of) the innocence and youth of its object. But then, it is argued, Dodgson was a 'schizophrenic', both a mathematician and a writer for children (as if mathematics and verbal play were somehow incompatible), and the worst thing he did was take pictures of little girls (as if the visual image were not the ultimate fetish). *Alice* has been saved as a classic for children, and the question of what we mean by that *'for'*—the question of its more difficult implications—remains unasked.

In the case of *Peter Pan*, the problem is more delicate. Behind *Peter Pan* lies the desire of a man for a little boy (or boys), a fantasy or drama which has only recently caught the public eye. Thus just at the moment when we are accepting the presence of sexuality in children's fiction (which we believed—wrongly—that the Victorians had repressed (Marcus, 1966)), we are asked to recognise it in a form which violates not only the innocence of childhood, not just that of children's fiction, but what we like to think of as normal sexuality itself. There is nothing too disturbing about a man desiring little girls—it is, after all, the desire in which little girls are in the end expected to recognise themselves. And the fact has in any case been relegated to a contingent status as far as *Alice*'s position as a classic for children is concerned. But 'men and little boys' is something else, something in which our very idea of what constitutes normal sexuality is at stake. Children's fiction cannot, I will be arguing, be discussed without touching on this question, but it almost invariably is.

Suppose, therefore, that Peter Pan is a little boy who does not grow up, not because he doesn't want to, but because someone else prefers that he shouldn't. Suppose, therefore, that what is at stake in *Peter Pan* is the adult's desire for the child. I am not using 'desire' here in the sense of an act which is sought after or which must actually take place. It is not relevant, therefore, to insist that nothing ever happened, or that Barrie was innocent of any interest in sex (a point which is often made). I am using desire to refer to a form of investment by the adult in the child, and to the demand made by the adult on the child as the effect of that investment, a demand which fixes the child and then holds it in place. A turning to the child, or a circulating around the child—what is at stake here is not so much something which could be enacted as something which cannot be spoken.

The sexual act which underpins *Peter Pan* is neither act nor fantasy in the sense in which these are normally understood and wrongly opposed to each other. It is an act in which the child is used (and abused) to represent the whole problem of what sexuality is, or can be, and to hold that problem at bay. This is something which, we will see, surfaces constantly throughout the history of *Peter Pan*—it is part of the fabric of the work. But the fact is either not known, or else it is displaced (as with Carroll) onto Barrie himself, and then disavowed (Barrie as the innocent of all innocents).

To call *Peter Pan* a fantasy does not, therefore, absolve us of the sexual question. It focuses it more sharply. At the moment when Barrie was writing *Peter Pan*, Freud was making his most crucial (and in this context least known) discovery that sexuality works above all at the level of fantasy, and that what we take to be our sexual identity is always precarious and can never be assumed. Sexuality persists, for all of us, at the level of the unconscious precisely because it is a question which is never quite settled, a story which can never be brought to a close. Freud is known to have undermined the concept of childhood innocence, but his real challenge is easily lost if we see in the child merely a miniature version of what our sexuality eventually comes to be. The child is sexual, but its sexuality (bisexual, polymorphous, perverse) threatens our own at its very roots. Setting up the child as innocent is not, therefore, repressing its sexuality—it is above all holding off any possible challenge to our own.

The problem is not, therefore, J. M. Barrie's—it is ours. Ours to the extent that we are undoubtedly implicated in the status which *Peter Pan* has acquired as the ultimate fetish of childhood. All Barrie ever did was to write *Peter Pan*, and even that can be disputed. But it is we who have recognised *Peter Pan* ('recognised' in both senses of the term), and given it its status. *Peter Pan* has been almost unreservedly acclaimed as a children's classic for the greater part of this century. Its presence in our culture is in fact so diffused that most of the time we do not even notice it. We take it for granted as something which belongs to us and to children, without there being any need for us to ask the question of the relation between the two. Like all children's classics, *Peter Pan* is considered to speak for everyone—adult and child (which in itself neatly disposes of the whole issue of what we mean by fiction for children). The child and the adult are one at that point of pure identity which the best of children's books somehow manage to retrieve. Time and again in its history, *Peter Pan* has been set up as the very emblem of that purity and identity. But this, I would say, has only been possible (and desirable) because it reveals so crudely the travesty on which any such notion rests.

It is, therefore, no part of my intention to analyse Barrie, to try to produce a psychobiography which would diagnose the author so as to set *Peter Pan* free as a myth. *Peter Pan* is a myth, but its status as such rests on the very difficulty which most commentaries refuse to recognise, or else recognise in order to diagnose and remove. *Peter Pan* is a classic in which the problem of the relationship between adult and child is unmistakably at the heart of the matter.

Peter Pan was not originally intended for children. It first appeared inside a novel for adults, J. M. Barrie's *The Little White Bird* (Barrie, 1902), as a story told by the narrator to a little boy whom the narrator was trying to steal. In order for it to become a work for children, it was extracted from its source, transformed into a play, and sent out on its own. *Peter Pan* emerges, therefore, out of an unmistakable act of censorship. The book which it leaves behind is one of the most explicit accounts to date of what it might mean to write fiction for the child. *The Little White Bird* is the story of the difficulty of that process—the difficulty of the relation between adult and child, and a question about the sexuality of each. What is the sexuality of the narrator? What is the origin of the child? What is *going on* between them? Questions which are never quite answered in the book, but which provide the basis for the telling of *Peter Pan*. The rest of *Peter Pan*'s history can then be read as one long attempt to wipe out the residual signs of the disturbance out of which it was produced. *The Little White Bird* is an origin of sorts, but only in the sense that no origin is ever left behind, since it necessarily *persists*. *The Little White Bird* shows what cannot, or must not, be allowed to get into fiction for children, but the problems to which it so eloquently bears witness do not go away. They remain in such a way as to undermine, finally, any simple notion of children's fiction itself.

Thus the result of that first act of censorship was that *Peter Pan* was both never written and, paradoxically, has never ceased to be written. Barrie himself certainly couldn't manage it. He did not write the play until twenty-four years after its first production. The publication had nothing to do with children, since it was the only children's text in a volume of collected plays (this was the main publication although in the same year it was printed on its own). The story from *The Little White Bird* was eventually published separately, but it cannot be described as a book for children. It was released onto the fine art collector's market, at a time when a whole new market for children's books was developing, a market which it completely by-passed and to which it never belonged. Barrie persistently refused to write a narrative version of the play, and, when he did, it was a failure, almost incomprehensible, and later had to be completely rewritten along the lines of a new state educational policy on language in the early part of the century (Barrie, 1915). During this time Barrie authorised *Peter Pan* to a number of different writers, which means that its status as a classic for children depends at least as much on them as it does on Barrie himself. Barrie may well be the source of the play, but this constant dispersion of *Peter Pan* challenges any straightforward idea of origin or source. Above all it should caution us against the idea that things can simply be traced back to their beginning, since, in the case of *Peter Pan*, what followed is at least as important as what came before.

What has followed has been a total mystification of all these forms of difficulty and confusion. Barrie *is Peter Pan*, despite the fact that he could not write it. *Peter Pan* is a classic for children, despite the fact that they could not read it—either because it was too expensive, or because it was virtually impossible to read. Nowhere has it been recognised that there might be a problem of writing, of address, and of language, in the history of *Peter Pan*. *Peter Pan*'s dispersion—the fact that it is everywhere and nowhere at one and the same time—has been taken as the sign of its cultural value. Its own ethereal nature merely sanctions the eternal youth and innocence of the child it portrays, and for which it is most renowned.

The sexual disavowal is, therefore, a political disavowal. A disavowal of the material differences which are concealed behind the category of *all* children to which *Peter Pan* is meant to make its appeal. That *all* speaks volumes of a further set of evasions: not just why are we speaking to the child, and what is our investment in that process; but to which child are we speaking? For, as *Peter Pan* very clearly demonstrates, if we are talking to one group of children, then the chances are that we will not be speaking to another. More likely, the very idea of speaking to *all* children serves to close off a set of cultural divisions, divisions in which not only children, but we ourselves, are necessarily caught.

There is no children's book market which does not, on closer scrutiny, crumble under just such a set of divisions—of class, culture and literacy—divisions which undermine any generalised concept of the child. And there is no language for children which can be described independently of divisions in the institution of schooling, the institution out of which modern childhood has more or less been produced (Ariès, 1962). How language is spoken—both by and to the child—is subject to strictures which need to be located inside the institution where language is systematically taught. The clash between *Peter Pan's* status as a cultural myth and as a children's book is nowhere clearer than at the point of its confrontation with educational policy of the state.

When *Peter Pan* was written, educational policy on language was directed towards a rigorous separation of the forms of language to be taught in different sectors of the state schools. A whole new concept of 'synthetic' language was developed in the public elementary schools. It was a language to be based on the impressions of the visible world, as opposed to the classical and literary language which was simultaneously being taught in the secondary schools. This is a division which still affects the way in which we use language today, but it is rarely discussed in relation to children's writing. Recently there has been attention paid to class difference in children's books, but this has been posed exclusively in terms of values, to be identified and then avoided in subsequent children's books. *Peter Pan* is no exception to this, and it can certainly be assessed in this way. But when *Peter Pan* is rewritten in order for it to be accepted into the state schools, class difference can be seen to operate at a more fundamental level—that of the base components of the language which the child is actually allowed to speak.

This is an issue which relates to our understanding of literature as a whole— the fact that language has an institutional history which determines how it is written, spoken and understood. But it is a history which most literary criticism, in its concern to identify creativity and individual expression, makes every effort to ignore. In the case of children's fiction, however, the problem comes much closer, since the child belongs to the very institution through which language is being produced. The failure to discuss the importance of educational policy on language for children's writing is, therefore, the more conspicuous evasion.

The material and sexual aspects of *Peter Pan* have been the vanishing-points of its history. They are there, however, and they can be exposed. But what we have been given instead is a glorification of the child. This suggests not only a refusal to acknowledge difficulties and contradictions in relation to childhood; it implies that we *use* the image of the child to deny those same difficulties in relation to ourselves.

Peter Pan comes at the end of a long history, one which can be traced back to the beginnings of children's fiction. Literature for children first became an independent commercial venture in England in the mid-to late-eighteenth century, at a time when conceptualisation of childhood was dominated by the philosophical writings of Locke and Rousseau. This is a fact which is known, but its implications for thinking about children's fiction have not been fully recognised. It is assumed that children's fiction has grown away from this moment, whereas in fact children's fiction has constantly returned to this moment, repeated it, and reproduced its fundamental conception of the child. Children's fiction has never completely severed its links with a philosophy which sets up the child as a pure point of origin in relation to language, sexuality and the state.

The earliest children's writers took from Locke the idea of an education based on the child's direct and unproblematic access to objects of the real world, an education which would by-pass the imperfections of language (Newberry, 1944, 1756; Watts, 1741). They took from Rousseau the idea that it is sexuality which most totally sabotages the child's correct use of language and its exact knowledge of the world. One of the earliest extended narratives for children, Thomas Day's *The History of Sandford and Merton* (Day, 1783–9), was based directly on Rousseau's *Emile* (Rousseau (1762) 1763). It shared with Rousseau's tract a conviction that both sexuality and social inequality were realities that the child somehow be used to circumvent. The child is rendered innocent of all the contradictions which flaw our interaction with the world. Above all, for both Locke and Rousseau, the child can be seen, observed and known in exactly the same way as the world can be grasped by a rational understanding.

Children's fiction emerges, therefore, out of a conception of both the child and the world as knowable in a direct and unmediated way, a conception which places the innocence of the child and a primary state of language and/or culture in a close and mutually dependent relation. It is a conception which has affected children's writing and the way that we think about it to this day. We can see it, in differing forms, in such apparently diverse types of writing as the fairy tale and the adventure story for boys. Andrew Lang published his fairy tales in the nineteenth century as the uncontaminated record of our cultural infancy (Lang, 1899) to which, it was assumed, the child had a direct and privileged access (an idea whose purely mythical nature was pointed out by Tolkien long ago (Tolkien 1938) 1947)). And the boy's adventure story, which came into its own in the mid to late nineteenth century with writers such as Marryat, Kingston, Henty and Stevenson, was always part of an exploratory and colonialist venture which assumed that discovering or seeing the world was the same thing as controlling it. Both types of writing are present in *Peter Pan* which condenses a whole history of children's fiction into its form. They can also be seen in the works of Alan Garner who is considered by many to be one of the most innovatory writers today. But what I want to stress in both cases is the idea which they share of a primitive or lost state to which the child has special access. The child is, if you like, something of a pioneer who restores these worlds to us, and gives them back to us with a facility or directness which ensures that our own relationship to them is, finally, safe.

I am not, of course, talking here of the child's own experience of the book which, despite all the attempts which have been made, I consider more or less impossible to gauge. What I am describing is how these different forms of writing, in their long and continuing association with childhood, have been thought about *for* children. Again, Freud's concept of the unconscious can be seen as a challenge to this association, for it not only undermines our idea of sexuality; it equally questions the idea of mastery which lies behind the notion that the world is something to which we simply have access, or that language is something which we can control. And yet for all the apparent shifts in the way that childhood and children's writing is discussed, what always seems to return in the analysis, in one form or another, is this idea of mastery, which means by implication securing the child's rationality, its control of sexuality or of language (or both).

Thus, for example, even when a troubling of sexuality is recognised in the fairy tale (Bettelheim, 1976), it is something contained by the cohesion of the narrative, transcended on the path to reality, and resolved in the name of a psychological and sexual identity, which ensures in the end that we can master not only the world, but also ourselves. And although addressed to a very different context of children's writing, a similar demand can be seen in the recent appeal to the coherence of realist writing in children's fiction, against the disintegration of the adult novel form, which can lead such a well-known children's writer as John Rowe Townsend to say without inhibition 'I came to the child because I see in him the last refuge from a literature gone berserk and ready for suicide' (quoting Isaac Bashevis Singer, Townsend, 1971, p. 12).

Peter Pan was written at the time of Freud, and the status which it has been given seems to testify above all to our inability to recognise the dislocation which he operated on our conception of childhood. Not just in the sense of what childhood is supposed to be, but, more crucially, as a challenge to why, in terms of our own relationship to language and sexuality, we attempt to construct an image of the child at all.

What we constantly see in discussion of children's fiction is how the child can be used to hold off a panic, a threat to our assumption that language is something which can simply be organised and cohered, and that sexuality, while it cannot be removed, will eventually take on the forms in which we prefer to recognise and acknowledge each other. Childhood also serves as a term of universal social reference which conceals all the historical divisions and difficulties of which children, no less than ourselves, form a part.

There is no child behind the category 'children's fiction', other than the one which the category itself sets in place, the one which it needs to believe is there for its own purposes. These purposes are often perverse and mostly dishonest, not wilfully, but of necessity, given that addressing the child must touch on all of these difficulties, none of which it dares speak. *Peter Pan* is sometimes scoffed at today for the excessive and cloying nature of its innocence. It is in fact one of the most fragmented and troubled works in the history of children's fiction to date. *Peter Pan* is peculiar, and yet not peculiar, in so far as it recapitulates a whole history of children's fiction which has not yet come to an end. . . .

SOURCES

Aries, P. *Centuries of Childhood*, translated by Robert Baldick. London: Jonathan Cape, 1962.

Barrie. J. M. *The Little White Bird*. London: Hodder and Stoughton, 1902.

———. *Peter Pan and Wendy*. London: Henry Frowde, Hodder and Stoughton, 1915.

Bettelheim, B. *The Uses of Enchantment: The Meaning and Importance of Fairy Tales*. London: Thames and Hudson, 1976.

Birkin, A. *The Lost Boys*, a trilogy, BBC2 *Play of the Week*, 11, 18, 25 October, 1978.

Day, T. *The History of Standford and Merton*. London: Stockdale, 1783–89.

Dunbar, J. *J. M. Barrie, the Man behind the Image*. London: Collins, 1970.

Lang, A. *The Blue Fairy Book*. London: Longmans and Green, 1899.

Marcus, S. *The Other Victorians: A Study of Sexuality and Pornography in Mid-Nineteenth-Century England*. London: Weidenfeld and Nicolson, 1966.

Newberry, J. A. *A Little Lottery Book for Children*. London: Newberry, 1756.

———. *A Little Pretty Pocket Book*, (1944). Facsimile edition by M. F. Thwaite. London: Oxford University Press, 1966.

Rouseau, J. J. *Emile*, 1762. La Haye: Neaulme, 1762.

Tolkien, J. R. R. (1938) "On Fairy-Stories." in *Essays Presented to Charles Williams*. London: Oxford University Press, 1947.

Townsend, J. R. *A Sense of Story: Essays on Contemporary Writers for Children*. London: Longman, 1971.

Watts, I. *The Improvement of the Mind*. London: Buckland and Longman, 1741.

Chapter Three

Children in the House
The Material Culture of Early Childhood

Karin Calvert

Members of any society carry within themselves a working definition of child-hood, its nature, limitations, and duration. They may not explicitly discuss this definition, write about it, or even consciously conceive of it as an issue, but they act upon their assumptions in all of their dealings with, fears for, and expecta-tions of their children. Every culture defines what it means to be a child, how children should look and act, what is expected of them, and what is considered beyond their capabilities. Older children learn to adapt themselves to the perso-nas encouraged by their society, to be feminine or masculine, obedient or mis-chievous, innocent or worldly as their society expects of them. Very young children, however, lack the necessary perception and skills to conform.

Parents deal with the disparity between the individual infant and the cultural ideal in numerous ways. They adopt the convention that their child is everything they believe it should be. Today we tell ourselves and each other that any baby girl is dainty, pretty, and a little coquette and that any baby boy is strong, brave, and quite the little man. We see promising signs of intelligence or talent in all sorts of infant gestures. Parents also physically control infants to encourage de-sired behavior. Modern parents, for example, are more likely to cuddle and com-fort baby girls, and bounce and toss baby boys, to both affirm and encourage proper gender identification. Parents have further relied on clothing, furniture, and other material goods specifically designed to modify children's appearance or behavior to meet social and cultural expectations. For much of the twentieth century, for example, we have adhered to an amazingly rigid color code for infant clothing—pink (and recently lavender) for girls, blue for boys. The code goes much further. Only girls can wear ruffles on the shoulders of their overalls or lace edging on their play clothes; and while both baby boys and girls can wear their hair at a variety of lengths, only little girls can hold their hair in place with a barrette. In an age that stresses freedom, self-expression, and equality, such rigid and detailed rules seem quite curious, but they serve an important social function. Institutionalized sartorial differentiation informs everyone who comes in contact with a child of its gender, so that they will respond in socially accepted ways to this particular little person, thus reinforcing the gender role that will expected of it in the future. Pink and blue baby clothes become evidence of the importance of early gender identification in a society where so little seems certain. It tells us something about our present fears, preoccupations, and priorities. The objects used in the raising of children have changed dramatically over time, but they have always met more than the simple physical needs of the children. They have also met the parents' need to mold their infants into the accepted cultural image of the time.

The link between artifacts and cultural constructs makes the study of material culture an important method for gaining access to cultural beliefs and assumptions so basic that they are rarely verbalized and to social fears too emotionally laden for direct discussion. Some parents of the past did write down their views concerning proper upbringing and their own children's behavior.[1] A few contemporary physicians or other recognized authorities wrote about the mechanics of childrearing and the treatment of childhood illnesses. Most parents, however, took the ordinary details of caring for young children too much for granted to bother to write about them, if they wrote at all.

Children described the substance of their lives even less frequently. Those under the age of seven, the group of primary interest here, were usually both illiterate and inarticulate. The rare children who did write most often did so with explicit instructions concerning what to say ("be sure to tell Aunt Harriet how much you liked her present"), or under supervision, or with the knowledge that their letters, essays, and diaries might be read by other family members at any time. Ten-year-old Caroline Richards of Canandaigua, New York, for example, wrote that since her elders had the right to read her diary she dare not confide everything to it.[2] The right to the privacy of one's own thoughts is a quite recent acquisition in the history of childhood, and parents of the past expected to be able to read their children's diaries and correspondence. Very few children broke through the constraints of convention and parental control to record everything they really felt. Because examples of young people determined and able to speak their own minds are so rare, we are that much more charmed with the forthrightness of one Maryland girl who, in 1800, carefully cross-stitched onto her sampler, "Patty Polk did this and she hated every stitch she did in it. She loves to read much more."[3] If few adults and fewer children wrote about the methods and goals of common childrearing practices, many more left behind artifacts used for the task. The objects, as it were, became a physical trail by which to track cultural change.

From the cradle brought over on the *Mayflower* for little Peregrine White, parents availed themselves of leading strings, walking stools, swaddling clothes, skeleton suits, cribs, jumpers, dolls, rocking horses, pantaloons, perambulators, high chairs, bassinets, and crawling blankets in the day-to-day task of raising a child. Virtually no child-related objects have remained continuously in use in America, however. Rather, a few types of children's artifacts flourish for a time and then disappear, to be replaced by a new and quite different constellation of goods considered necessary to properly bring up a baby. An analysis of such artifact constellations can help uncover the nature of the everyday lives of children and the assumptions and concerns foremost in parents' minds at any one point in history. Such parental preoccupations, in turn, relate directly to the society's perception of the fundamental nature of children.

The little world parents create for their children reveals a great deal about the accepted place of children in the larger world. The key is to seek out the assumptions underlying the popularity of specific styles and forms of childrearing artifacts. For example, did the costume of a particular time accentuate gender differences or focus on distinctions of age? Did forms of furniture for infants encourage autonomy and efficacy or concentrate on comfort or protection? Were children's artifacts plain and functional, or elaborate and status bearing? Were particular rooms within the house reserved for the use of children, and if so where were they located, how were they furnished, and how much time did children spend there? When did a young person graduate from a strictly childish costume or room to adult dress and quarters? What toys, if any, were commonly available, and what gender or age restrictions were attached to particular toys? What was life really like for the children at a particular moment in American history, and how did those experiences shape their perception of life? How did parents use clothes, toys, and furniture to create, enforce, or encourage socially correct behavior in their very young children?

Any one object may be capable of numerous functions or meanings, only some of which are valid to a given society at a particular time. A doll, for example, can simply be a child's toy; but at times it has also been a religious image or magical fetish, fashion mannequin, effigy, educational tool, collectible, investment, or objet d'art. On the other hand, a single object might fulfill several different functions simultaneously. A seventeenth-century coral and bells, made of a shaft of red coral set in a silver handle and surrounded by tiny silver bells, served as a pretty rattle, a teether, a magical charm to ward off evil, an investment (as did any silver object), and a tangible symbol of the parents' wealth and status, all at the same time.

Similarly, an object may function on any or all of three distinct planes. It may have one or more technomic or practical uses, or uses accepted as practical by a society. The coral of the baby's rattle, for example, offered a smooth surface to relieve the discomfort of teething, and parents considered it a potent charm to protect children from the evil eye. An object may also have a sociotechnic role by which it facilitates the interactions or relationships between people or conveys information about the owner. The intrinsic value of the silver coral and bells announced the comfortable status of the infant and the family. Finally, an object can fulfill an ideotechnic function as part of a symbolic vocabulary expressing or affirming cultural beliefs and values.[4] In the case of our example, as one of the few toys made expressly for young children in the seventeenth century the coral and bells became a standard symbol or icon for infancy.

While objects can have multiple meanings for the society that uses them, constellations of objects, in this case things intended for use in raising young children, can share common meanings and can therefore point to common concerns and perceptions of reality. As basic cultural assumptions change over time, the artifacts associated with those assumptions lose their usefulness and disappear or undergo modification, and new forms are introduced to meet new needs. Most children's furniture of the seventeenth century was designed to stand babies up and propel them forward, whereas most nineteenth-century furniture was meant to hold infants down and contain them in one spot. The different intentions suggest very different attitudes toward the needs and best interests of the child. The interrelatedness of artifacts also means that when one object is abandoned, others become untenable. When American parents renounced restrictive swaddling for primarily social reasons, for example, they eventually abandoned cradles for the very practical reason that cradles could not effectively contain active, unbound infants.

Before the middle of the eighteenth century very few objects existed in Western culture expressly for the benefit of children, and such forms as did exist changed very little and very slowly over time. Then, with comparative suddenness between 1750 and 1850, a significant number of middle-class parents twice repudiated, abandoned, and replaced all of the popular forms of children's furniture, clothing, and playthings. Such a unique rejection and re-creation of the everyday artifacts of childrearing indicated profound change in society's perception of the nature of childhood and in attitudes toward children.

American children born before the middle of the eighteenth century enjoyed very few objects designed expressly for their use. Those artifacts that did exist—the cradle, swaddling clothes, standing stools, walking stools, and leading strings—forced the young child to lie straight, stand straight, or walk erect. This concern with uprightness, both in a physical and in a moral sense, was one of the crucial preoccupations of that era, since, among other things, it marked one of the major distinctions separating mankind from the rest of the animal kingdom. Very young children tottered precariously between upright humanity and the beasts of the field. By itself, nature in the seventeenth century seemed inadequate to the task of transforming infants into civilized and functioning adults. Parents, therefore, used specially designed artifacts to impose specific patterns of behavior on their offspring—to create at least the semblance of adult appearance and behavior—and to assimilate the child rapidly into adult society.

By the middle of the nineteenth century, the traditional forms of children's artifacts had disappeared, along with fears about the animalistic nature of children, to be replaced by completely new and different artifacts. The crib, high chair, swing, and perambulator all served as barriers between the child and the adult world. Their function was to contain, restrain, and isolate young children who had not yet mastered self-control or sufficient caution. In place of direct participation in the activities of adults, many nineteenth-century parents fabricated a separate world for their offspring filled with special artifacts, activities, and rituals that emphasized the perceived differences between children and adults. Accepting the era's sentimental image of childish sweetness and innocence, parents sought physical barriers to protect their children from physical injury, temptation, and worldly contamination.

In the two centuries following European settlement, the common perception in America of children changed profoundly, having first held to an exaggerated fear of their inborn deficiencies, then expecting considerable self-sufficiency, and then, after 1830, endowing young people with an almost celestial goodness. In each era, children's artifacts mediated between social expectations concerning the nature of childhood and the realities of childrearing; before 1750, they pushed children rapidly beyond the perceived perils of infancy, and by the nineteenth century they protected and prolonged the perceived joy and innocence of childhood. . . .

The evidence points to two periods of significant and widespread change before the beginning of the twentieth century. The first began about 1750 and gained momentum during the 1770s; the second occurred in the 1830s and 1840s. At each point the evidence indicates that virtually every aspect of the lives of young children changed. Old forms of dress disappeared to be replaced by radically new ones. Similarly, traditional furniture forms were rejected in favor of very different objects. Changes were made in where children slept, how they were cared for, what nicknames were popular, and what toys were available. A quantitative examination of nine hundred portraits of children, for example, charting the appearance of costume, toys, children's furniture, and representations of playfulness, indicated major shifts in the perception of young people and their roles occurring at about 1750 and 1830.[5] The findings were corroborated by changes in children's books, parental letters and journals, and childrearing manuals happening at about the same times. This does not mean that every parent abruptly dropped familiar methods of childrearing and embraced the new ideas. The process depended very much on where parents stood in their own family history (first-time parents have usually been more willing to try something new than parents who already have other children), on geographical location, since new ideas come first to urban populations, and on the whims and predilections of individual parents. The dates, therefore, remain only an approximate guideline indicating the point at which change in social patterns became evident. Older methods of childrearing continued among some families and communities long after they had been abandoned by others. The periods suggested here indicate only a significant change in childbearing practices in a substantial number of middle-class homes.

The normative methods of childbearing, and the attendant vision of the nature of children, were influential, but by no means universal. Many working-class and immigrant families in America continued into the twentieth century childrearing practices commonly abandoned here by 1750. This book sets out some of the concerns and assumptions held by the normative culture. Other studies are needed to examine the variety of childbearing methods actually practiced at any one time in America.

While this is an examination of child-related artifacts made or used in this country, there is little in the conclusions that is unique to America. For the most part, immigrants made the transatlantic journey bringing with them the social and cultural patterns of western Europe. Americans continued to purchase European-made goods, organize their living spaces in ways similar to their European counterparts, and read European books and newspapers. Lucy Larcom commented on the continued duality of identity still very much alive in the first half of the nineteenth century for a child growing up in New England:

> Our close relationship to Old England was sometimes a little misleading to us juveniles. The conditions of our life were entirely different, but we read her descriptive stories and sang her songs as if they were true for us too. One of the first things I learned to repeat—I think it was in the spelling book—began with the verse:
>
> > I thank the goodness and the grace
> > That on my birth has smiled,
> > And made me, in these latter days,
> > A Happy English child.[6]

Most of the changes that took place in the perception of the nature of childhood in America also occurred in Europe. Each nation or ethnic group there experienced change, but change at its own pace, reinterpreting general trends to accommodate local traditions. German parents lavished more toys and child-sized furniture on their children than did their English counterparts, for example, but clung to the custom of swaddling long after it had been abandoned elsewhere. Similarly, while American children of the nineteenth century remained a very real presence in the family, many English children gradually disappeared into the separate world of nursery, nanny, and boarding school. Although it is important to note those things that seem uniquely American in the development of the concept of childhood, the European theories, trends, books, fashions, and artifacts that made their way across the Atlantic and influenced American practices have been included here because they are as much a part of the American childrearing tradition as America is a part of Western culture.

The history of childhood has focused on two connected issues: first, whether Western culture had traditionally recognized a concept of childhood as inherently distinct from maturity; second, the nature of the emotional bond between parent and child. Philippe Ariès set the agenda for this debate in his highly influential book *Centuries of Childhood*, which first posited that the concept of childhood in the West did have a beginning and a consequent history. While Ariès drew most of his evidence from French sources, with occasional references to English society, he clearly saw his findings as applicable to all of Western culture. Ariès argues that medieval society did not recognize childhood as a distinct stage of human development with its own characteristics, needs, and limitations. Children were merely juvenile members of adult society. They participated in the same work as adults, wore the same styles of clothing, and enjoyed the same pastimes. Only in the seventeenth century, Ariès argues, did the concept of children as significantly different from, rather than merely smaller than, adults emerge. Once parents viewed their children as different from themselves, they began to limit children's access to adult activities and to offer more intense and specialized instruction and discipline. For Ariès, the seventeenth century was the great watershed, and the development of the concept of childhood has progressed apace ever since.[7]

Ariès bases many of his assumptions about medieval society on a lack of discernible distinctions between adults and children. Medieval children, for example, dressed like their parents and participated in many of the same activities as adults. Therefore, children were viewed as grown-ups in miniature. Unfortunately, the lack of manifest distinctions in any particular area is not evidence of a lack of recognized distinctions between different social groups. A society that has a special costume for children clearly sees them as in some way set apart from their elders, and has chosen to express that separateness visually. However, another society may have an equally well developed concept of the distinct nature of childhood, but not choose to give it sartorial expression. This should be very evident to a society in which members of both sexes, and persons of all ages and social classes, wear blue jeans and sneakers and yet remain very much aware of distinctions of age, class, and gender. That medieval children dressed like adults is not proof that there was no medieval concept of childhood. The absence of evidence is not evidence of absence.

Ariès argues that while some medieval parents had affection for their children, many were indifferent to their young. If the development of the notion of the specialness of children in the seventeenth century led to greater solicitude in their care, it also meant a significant loss of freedom, since special discipline and supervision were also seen as part of children's particular needs. Other scholars have been even more severe, viewing the history of childhood as a steady progress from a cold and brutal past to present enlightenment. Edward Shorter, in *The Making of the Modern Family*, argues that before the modern era parents were indifferent to their children at best. David Hunt, in *Parents and Children in History*, concentrates on Doctor Heroard's account of the upbringing of the future Louis XIII and extrapolates to the French population at large. If the infant Louis was treated as little more than a useful possession by the adults around him, Hunt reasons, how much worse must have been the lives of ordinary children. Lloyd deMause is by far the most pessimistic, describing a long, dark, and brutal story of the parent-child relationship. For him, the history of childhood is very nearly the history of child abuse. Only comparatively recently, deMause argues, has Western society developed a nurturing and loving environment for children.[8]

More recently, the absence of a notion of childhood has been challenged. Ross Beales, for example, cites convincing evidence that Puritans in seventeenth-century New England were well aware of developmental differences between infants, youths, and adults. Opposed to the view that most children were cruelly and callously treated before the modern era are scholars who have found evidence that parents in the past did love and care for their offspring. In *Inside the Great House*, Daniel Blake Smith examines letters written by Chesapeake planters and their wives in which they speak tenderly of their little children, fondly describing childish antics or accomplishments. Smith paints an uncompromisingly cheerful picture of life among the planter elite. There are no bad or neglectful parents here; even slavery is a positive element since it provides these privileged children early experience with command and enhances their self-confidence.[9]

A major revision of accepted thinking is Linda Pollock's *Forgotten Children*, which combines a thorough historiography of the subject with an examination of several hundred diaries from 1500 to 1900. She finds considerable evidence that parents in every century studied had affection for their children, recognized various stages of development, disciplined but did not abuse, and worried about their offspring's present and future well-being. From this Pollock concludes that "there have been very few changes in parental care and child life from the 16th to the 19th century in the home, apart from social changes and technological improvements."[10]

The history of childhood has often been bedeviled with a presentist point of view. Those who see considerable difference between the childhood of the past and the present see yesterday as bad and today as good; progress has been made. Those who find the hopes and feelings of parents much the same across time argue that child life has changed very little. Long frocks or dungarees, hornbooks or computers, the lives of children remain relatively constant in each successive generation. Neither position is wholly accurate.

There should be enough evidence that there have always been loving parents, neglectful parents, and abusive parents to put that issue to rest. Whether the proportionate numbers of each type change over time depends on whether one employs a modern, or contemporary, view of what is deemed proper and in the best interests of the child. The nature of childhood has been defined very differently in different eras. What is regarded as good or bad for children at any one time can change tremendously, and loving parents of one era can behave in ways diametrically opposed to the accepted practices of another time.

The issue, then, becomes not a question of whether parents loved their children but of how they treated the children they loved. A given parental attitude does not presuppose a single mode of behavior. The concept of childhood has changed dramatically over time, with changes in the social structure, cultural assumptions, and technological innovations leading one generation of parents to reject the childrearing patterns of its predecessors. The course of change was not so much a progression from traditional to modern (meaning from bad to good) as a succession of alternative approaches. Each succeeding stage in the history of childhood has had both positive and negative features. What children gained in one area of their lives, they usually lost in another.

Parents are individuals. Most of them feel affection for their children even in the most difficult of circumstances, though not necessarily all of the time or equally for all of their children. And some parents can be abusive under any circumstances. Instead of attempting to read the minds and hearts of parents, it may be more informative to look at the nature of children's experiences in past centuries. How were they cared for? What habits were stressed and which neglected? How did they spend their days, and where their nights? A few scholars have already given close scrutiny to the processes of family life. John Demos examined the Puritan family in seventeenth-century New England, trying to determine from physical evidence something of what it felt like to live in that society. Michael Zuckerman examined the diary of William Byrd of eighteenth-century Virginia to reconstruct Byrd's level and pattern of involvement with his family, slaves, neighbors, and peers. Each study produced a rich, complex, sometimes contradictory and untidy picture of actual family life.[11]

Regardless of which side of the debate scholars favored, they have treated the concept of childhood as a single entity in history. Most investigators have given little consideration to class differences affecting attitudes or methods of childrearing. In fact, the evidence presented in most studies on childhood has been culled from documents and artifacts produced by or for the middle and elite classes of America and the middle class and aristocracies of Europe. Those scholars who described a long, brutal past in Western childrearing practices have usually assumed conditions were even harsher for working-class children. Those who have contended that parents have always been affectionate and caring have cited evidence that poor parents felt guilt and regret over the privations their children suffered or the harsh work load they were forced to bear. But little work has been done on a separate in-depth investigation of the lives of poor children: a study of working-class or immigrant children is badly needed and has yet to be written.

My purpose is to get beyond the issues that have consumed much of the energy brought to the history of childhood in the last two decades, the issues of whether there was a concept of childhood in the past and whether parents felt affection for their little ones. I will assume that there was always some concept of childhood, although it may have been vastly different from the present one, and that many parents were genuinely fond of their offspring, though often in spite of, rather than because of, the accepted perception of children.

It is equally important that the middle class has had an influence in American society far beyond its real numbers. Working-class and immigrant parents tended to raise their children as they themselves had been raised, changing much more slowly and less radically; but they often did in fact change their childrearing methods over time, and those changes tended to follow the patterns established by the middle class. By the early twentieth century, photographs taken by Jacob Riis show tenements in New York City furnished with white metal cribs and wooden high chairs, objects only introduced into middle-class homes within the previous sixty years.

Even more neglected than class differences has been the significance of gender for concepts of childhood. Most scholars have simply mixed evidence about boys and girls or extrapolated from one to the other to produce a monolithic history of childhood for any given era. Scholars seem to assume that boys and girls were treated the same, loved (or neglected) to the same degree, and shared the same experiences of childhood. Ariès does acknowledge that childhood for French girls was very different from that of their brothers. In fact, while the primary thesis of *Centuries of Childhood* is that the concept of childhood was first recognized in the seventeenth century, making that the great watershed in the history of childhood, he rather casually mentions early on that, since virtually none of the changes he describes pertained to girls, then really only "boys were the first specialized children," and his conclusions would therefore be based on only their experiences. Since much of Ariès's argument focuses on the changing nature of the seventeenth-century French school system (from which girls were excluded), the book might better have been called *Centuries of Boyhood*. Similarly, Hunt focuses on the infancy of Louis XIII, generalizing to the public at large; but he is also studying the life of a young boy and extrapolating to children of both sexes. Would a baby girl, even a royal baby girl, have been given the same sort of childhood as Louis?[12]

In fact, life was often very different for boys and girls at any given time. Boys and girls in America were dressed differently, treated differently, given different amounts of time for play, work, and study, and taught to handle all three activities differently. The reality is that there has never been a single form of childhood in America, but two coexisting gender-specific paradigms. Any study of the history of childhood must be cognizant of the fact that gender is a crucial ingredient in a child's life experience and that change in the concept of childhood happened much more slowly and less decisively for girls than for boys.

In both a material and a grammatical sense, children have usually been regarded as objects. Traditionally, they were the possessions of their parents, to be dealt with as parents thought best. From the early years of colonization to the end of the nineteenth century, children were the recipients of discipline or largesse, care or neglect. Adults designed, produced, and purchased the material goods used by children, structured their time and their environment, and defined the recognized stages of development and the appropriate image and behavior for each stage. Any study devoted to children has as much to say about the adults who made the decisions, formed or accepted the cultural assumptions, purchased and used the material goods, and determined what it meant to be a child (and what it meant to be an adult) as it has to say about the children involved.

* * *

Parents do not merely raise their children; they define them. More precisely, they accept certain definitions concerning the nature and needs of children current in their culture, and then try their best to bring their youngsters into line with the accepted patterns. Parents dress their children to look the part expected of them and may favor clothing that encourages desired and restrains unacceptable behavior. They adopt furniture forms and childrearing devices to coerce or cajole their children into acting in ways deemed appropriate by accepted standards. As those standards change, old artifacts may be jettisoned in favor of new forms that better express the new perception of children or that produce newly desirable forms of behavior. Such major shifts in culturally accepted notions have occurred at least twice in America between the founding of the European colonies and the beginning of the twentieth century. The process was a long and gradual one, with some groups in society proceeding more slowly than others. However, rough periodization is possible, and the periods of change are characterized by a rejection of previously common forms of costume, furniture, toys, books, and other paraphernalia of childrearing. Such a change occurred around the last quarter of the eighteenth century and again in the second quarter of the nineteenth century. The result is a series of three very distinct approaches to childrearing among middle-class Americans before the beginning of the twentieth century.

Colonial children lived precarious lives. In the late seventeenth century, the New England divine Cotton Mather enjoyed the blessings of a large family. His first wife bore him ten children before her death at the age of thirty-six. His second wife gave him an additional six children before her death, while his third was past her childbearing years when she married Mather. He wrote with affection about his children in his journal, describing their antics, their progress with their studies and religious instruction, and his concerns for them. He also wrote of his grief and loss when any of his children died. Ten of them died before their fifth birthday—nine in their first year and one at the age of four. Three daughters and one son died while in their early twenties. Altogether, Cotton Mather saw fourteen of his sixteen children die before his own death at the age of sixty-four. Mather's family is not particularly demographically typical of colonial families in general; no one family could be. At the most, its size and his longevity were fairly common in seventeenth-century New England. It may, however, offer some insight into the mind-set of colonial parents. The first five years of life were by far the most vulnerable. Children died before, during, and soon after birth, and subsequently from childhood illnesses, accidents, and lack of sufficient nourishment. If a boy survived his first five years, he had a good chance of living to a healthy old age, barring accidents, of course—Mather's twenty-one-year-old son was lost at sea. Girls who survived infancy faced a second and much longer period of vulnerability when they reached their own childbearing years—Mather lost two wives and three daughters to the effects of pregnancy.[13]

Infancy represented such a precarious existence that parents regarded it as essentially a state of illness, rather the way pregnancy was understood in the first half of the twentieth century. Babies needed to be protected assiduously from light and drafts, dosed with medicines and tonics through their first few months, and then pushed beyond infancy as quickly as possible. Growing up meant growing strong and gaining sufficient autonomy to be able to take care of oneself.

Adults in the colonial period did not look back to their own youth, but forward to their prime in the fourth and fifth decades of life, before the decline into old age. Then, if all had gone well, they would enjoy the prestige, comfort, and security for which they had worked so hard throughout their youth. For women, life became decidedly easier once they passed their childbearing years and their children required less attention and began to offer more help. As David Hackett Fischer has pointed out in *Growing Old in America*, colonists admired the mature adult. Gentlemen cultivated a noticeable paunch and stocky figure and powdered their hair a fashionable gray. Mature men and women were honored, respected, and envied for the position they had attained. By comparison, the trials of youth held no charm, and infancy was best forgotten.[14]

Loving parents wanted to see their children out of the dangers and miseries of infancy and safely on their way to secure positions in the world. Furniture that would hasten the process—devices that got infants up and walking as quickly as possible—had great appeal. Autonomy and self-sufficiency were considered better for both the children themselves and their overworked parents.

Martha Custis bore four children and buried two before she married George Washington. Years later, she undertook to raise two young grandchildren. By then, however, the world had changed. In the decades around the turn of the eighteenth century, there was a growing confidence in the rationality of nature and in the ability of the young of any species, including our own, to grow into healthy adults if the natural process was not interfered with. Parents began to attribute infant deaths to too much, rather than too little, coddling. If children got sick, it was because their parents had weakened them by treating them as invalids. Mothers and fathers who embraced the new ideas rejected the confining devices of earlier generations, such as swaddling bands, standing stools, and tiny corsets. If infancy had formerly been viewed as a kind of illness, it came now to promise robust health. Children were best off unfettered, uncovered, and uncoddled. Light clothes, thin blankets, and cold baths would best ensure the health and happiness of the next generation.

Although the same sorts of changes were happening in England and in parts of Europe, youth took on special meaning in America. Americans of the Revolutionary era and of the new republic had become accustomed to a new political rhetoric in which America was the child colony or the young country, as opposed to the overbearing mother country and the old European monarchies distrusted as decadent and dying. The advantage lay with youth and vigor. Men's fashions matched the changing political climate. From the 1760s onward, the fashionable male silhouette slimmed to a youthful, athletic line as the clothes became more form fitting and the full skirt of the frock coat shrank back into narrow tails. Gradually, men gave up wigs and powder, appearing in their own natural hair. It is quite remarkable to view in chronological order the portraits of someone such as Thomas Jefferson, who had several painted over the course of his lifetime, and watch him get progressively younger as gray hair gives way to red. The new attitude toward youth could not help but to improve the image of youth and childhood. This is not to say that parents loved their children more, but that they found more to appreciate about the state their children were in. Childhood had its good points.

As childhood became more a period of essential preparation for life and less one of vulnerability, more the healthy natural state of freedom before the constraints of civilization, parents took greater delight in their children's childishness. Gradually, the duration of childhood increased. Instead of wishing their children through it, parents wanted their youngsters to get as much as possible out of their childhood years that they might be fully prepared for their roles as future citizens of the new country. Childhood had become a valued part of human development.

Godey's Lady's Magazine is filled with stories and poems, from the 1830s on, of a parent mourning the death of a small child and taking comfort in the fact that the little one has merely been called back to heaven, where it will be spared the harshness and wickedness of earthly life. Nineteenth-century Americans were preoccupied with the concept of loss. Mourning pictures, tragic love stories, and fears of the gradual decline of the human species were common fare. Childhood fit nicely into this romantic pattern; it was something bright and fleeting to be cherished while it lasted. Maturity, in the new schema, was a corrupting process from which no one emerged unscathed. It served to make childhood seem more precious, a time free of guilt, regret, or care. Parents tried to build a separate world for their children, far away from the harsher realities of the adult sphere.

At the same time, childhood was imbued with an almost sacred character. Children were pure and innocent beings, descended from heaven and unsullied by worldly corruption. The loss of this childish innocence was akin to the loss of virginity, and the inevitable loss of childhood itself was a kind of expulsion from the Garden of Eden.

It was the parents' duty to protect the happy innocence of their children, and they did so by isolating their offspring from adult society. Contact risked contamination. The separate nursery was a safe haven, and the newly available high chairs, jumpers, and prams imprisoned the innocent to protect them from the guilty. Freedom had become dangerous, but containment was possible and practical in the nineteenth-century middle-class world.

In the last half of the twentieth century, that is no longer the case. We have had to abandon the idea that children are best served by isolating them from the realities of the surrounding world so that they might remain carefree and innocent as long as possible. Such isolation is simply no longer possible. More akin to the views of their colonial counterparts, late twentieth-century parents see their youngsters surrounded by dangers from which there is no safe haven. In a world of latchkey children, illicit drugs, terrifying new illnesses, and the horrors of child molestation, innocence has become vulnerability. The uninformed child is the child at risk. The protected child is once again the child who can cope successfully in the adult world.

In an environment in which children need to be sophisticated and on their guard, it is not surprising that they no longer dress in clothes designed to stress their youth but, like their colonial predecessors, dress more often like little adults. Young people today wear jogging suits, bomber jackets, and miniature medical scrub suits, and they are eschewing childish forms of play at a far younger age than did their more sheltered Victorian counterparts. Perhaps the Victorian childhood will prove to be a fluke, a somewhat claustrophobic idyll in the more common pattern of integrating children into family and community life; or perhaps it is the postmodern childhood that is the aberration. It is still too early to tell.

Throughout our history, there were endless variations within and outside each model of a given society's concept of the nature of childhood. In every era there have been parents who did things quite differently. The real point is that the first dozen years of life can be and have been perceived and interpreted in radically different, even diametrically opposed, paradigms by different generations. Childhood is not an unchanging, natural phenomenon or a steady progression from a dismal past to an enlightened present. The question is not whether a given society at a given time had a concept of childhood, but rather what that concept was and the nature of its advantages and disadvantages. Infancy, with its very special needs, is an undeniable state of existence, and the maturation of the human being is a slow and gradual process continuing long after infancy ends; the concept of childhood, however, is very much a social invention, one reinvented by every society and age. It is the natural malleability of the young (or perhaps of the species) that enables children to make themselves into whatever is expected of them.

NOTES

1. Philip Greven, *The Protestant Temperamant: Patterns of Child-Rearing in Colonial Andover, Mass* (Ithaca, N.Y.: Cornell University Press, 1970).

2. Caroline Cowles Richards, *Village Life in America* (New York: Henry Holt & Co., 1913).

3. A photograph of Patty Polk's sampler is reproduced in Ethel S. Bottome and Eva J. Cove, *American Samplers* (Boston: Massachusetts Society of Colonial Dames of America, 1921).

4. Kenneth Ames, "Material Culture as Verbal Communication: A Historical Case Study," *Journal of American Culture* 3 (Winter 1980): 619–41.

5. Karin Calvert, "The Image of Childhood in America: 1670 to 1870" (master's thesis, 1979).

6. Lucy Larcom, *A New England Girlhood* (1889; reprint, Boston: Houghton Mifflin, 1924), p. 118.

7. Philippe Ariès, *Centuries of Childhood: A Social History of Family Life*, trans. Robert Baldick (New York: Vintage Books, 1962).

8. Edward Shorter, *The Meaning of the Modern Family* (London: William Collins, 1976); David Hunt, *Parents and Children in History: The Psychology of Family Life in Early Modern France.* (New York: Basic Books, 1970); and Lloyd deMause, ed., *The History of Childhood* (London: Souvenir Press, 1976).

9. Ross W. Beales, Jr., "In Search of the Historical Child: Miniature Adulthood and Youth in Colonial New England," *American Quarterly* 27 (1975): 379–98. Daniel Blake Smith, *Inside the Great House: Planter Family Life in Eighteenth-Century Chesapeake Society* (Charlottesville: University Press of Virginia, 1980).

10. Linda Pollack, *Forgotten Children: Parent-Child Relations from 1500 to 1900* (Cambridge: Cambridge University Press, 1983).

11. John Demos, *A Little Commonwealth: Family Life in Plymouth Colony* (New York: Oxford University Press, 1970) Michael Zuckerman, "An Amusement in This Silent Country: The Family Life of William Byrd," 1979.

12. Ariès, *Centuries of Childhood*, p. 58; David Hunt, *Parents and Children in History: The Psychology of Family Life in Early Modern France* (New York: Basic Books, 1970).

13. Cotton Mather, "Diary of Cotton Mather," *Massachusetts Historical Society Collections*, 7:8.

14. David Hackett Fischer, *Growing Old in America* (New York: Oxford University Press, 1977).

Chapter Four

From Useful to Useless
Moral Conflict over Child Labor

Viviana A. Zelizer

Where do we go from here—where?
—We remnants of the throng that started with us
Shall we keep on—
Or drop off on the way, as they have done?
They're earning money now, and make us feel
But useless children in comparison.
Why can't we, too, get into something real?
         —from "Eighth Grade," by F. B. W., 1923

The 1900 U.S. Census reported that one child out of every six between the ages of ten and fifteen was gainfully employed. It was an undercount: The total figure of 1,750,178 excluded many child laborers under ten as well as the children "helping out" their parents in sweatshops and on farms, before or after school hours. Ten years later, the official estimate of working children reached 1,990,225. But by 1930, the economic participation of children had dwindled dramatically. Census figures registered 667,118 laborers under fifteen years of age. The decline was particularly marked among younger children. Between 1900 and 1930, the number of children ten to thirteen years old in nonagricultural occupations alone decreased more than six fold, from 186,358 to under 30,000.[1]

The exclusion of children from the marketplace involved a difficult and prolonged battle lasting almost fifty years from the 1870s to the 1930s. It was partly an economic confrontation and partly a legal dispute, but it was also a profound "moral revolution."[2] Two groups with sharply conflicting views of childhood struggled to impose their definition of children's proper place in society. For child labor reformers, children's early labor was a violation of children's sentimental value. As one official of the National Child Labor Committee explained in 1914, a laboring child "is simply a producer, worth so much in dollars and cents, with no standard of value as a human being. . . . How do you calculate your standard of a child's value? . . . as something precious beyond all money standard."[3] On the other hand, opponents of child labor reform were just as vehement in their support of the productive child, "I say it is a tragic thing to contemplate if the Federal Government closes the doors of the factories and you send that little child back, empty-handed; that brave little boy that was looking forward to get money for his mother for something to eat."[4]

The child labor conflict is a key to understanding the profound transformation in the economic and sentimental value of children in the early twentieth century. The price of a useful wage-earning child was directly counterposed to the moral value of an economically useless but emotionally priceless child. In the process, a complex reassessment of children's economic roles took place. It was not just a matter of whether children should work or not. Even the most activist of child labor reformers were unwilling to condemn all types of child work, while their opponents were similarly reluctant to condone all child labor. Instead, their argument centered over conflicting and often ambiguous cultural definitions of what constituted acceptable work for children. New boundaries emerged, differentiating legitimate from illegitimate forms of economic participation by children.

It was not a simple process. As one perplexed contemporary observer noted: "To work or not to work—that is the question. But nobody agrees upon the answer. . . . Who among the controversialists is wrong? And just what is work anyway? When and where does it step across the dead line and become exploitation?"[5] Child work and child money were gradually redefined for the "sacred" twentieth-century child into primarily moral and instructional tools. While child labor laws regulated exclusively working-class children, the new rules for educational child work cut across classes, equally applicable to all "useless" children.

The Useful Child: From Family Asset to Social Problem

In recent studies, economists and historians have documented the vital significance of child labor for working-class families in the late nineteenth century. Using extensive national data from the 1880s and 1890s, Michael Haines concludes that child labor "appears to have been the main source of additional support for the late nineteenth-century urban family under economic stress."[6] In her analysis of U.S. Federal Population Census manuscripts for Philadelphia in 1880, Claudia Goldin found that Irish children contributed between 38 and 46 percent of the total family labor income in two-parent families; German children 33 to 35 percent, and the native-born 28 to 32 percent. Unlike the mid-twentieth century when married women entered the labor force, in the late nineteenth century a child, not a wife, was likely to become the family's secondary wage earner.

To use children as active participants in the household economy of the working class was not only economically indispensable but also a legitimate social practice. The middle class, with its own children in school, still wistfully admired the moral principle of early labor. As late as 1915, one observer recognized:

"There is among us a reaction to be noted from the . . . overindulgence of our children and a realization that perhaps more work and responsibility would do them good. . . ."[7] Even children's books and magazines, aimed at an educated middle-class audience, "hymned the joys of usefulness," praising the virtues of work, duty, and discipline to their young readers. The standard villain in these stories was an idle child.[8]

Child labor as a morally righteous institution was not a nineteenth-century invention. American children had always worked. In his classic study of family life in Plymouth Colony, John Demos suggests that by the time children turned six or eight, they were expected to assume the role of "little adults," engaged in useful tasks in their own homes, or apprenticed elsewhere.[9] Laws governing the poor in the seventeenth and eighteenth centuries similarly reflected prevalent Puritan views on the virtue of work by providing employment for dependent children.

Industrial work created different job opportunities for young children in the late eighteenth century. Employers welcomed their nimble "little fingers" for the "gigantic automatons of labor saving machinery."[10] Indeed, the first workers in the American spinning mill set up in Rhode Island by Samuel Slater in 1790, were nine children between the ages of seven and twelve. By 1820, young boys and girls constituted 55 percent of the operatives employed in Rhode Island's textile mills. An enthusiastic writer for *Nile's Register* eagerly anticipated the pecuniary payoffs of child labor for local economies: "If we suppose that before the establishment of these manufactories, there were two hundred children between seven and sixteen years of age, that contributed nothing towards their maintenance and that they are now employed, it makes an immediate difference of $13,500 a year to the value produced in the town!"[11]

Rapid industrialization multiplied job opportunities for children in the late nineteenth century. Official estimates show an increase of over a million child workers between 1870 and 1900. One-third of the work force in the newly developed southern textile mills, for instance, were children between the ages of ten and thirteen, and many even younger.[12] For working-class families, the employment of children was part of what historian John Modell calls a limited "defensive" mode of family cooperation, "an attempt to pool risks in what was experienced as a very uncertain world."[13] Particularly for nineteenth-century urban families dependent on daily wages, the unemployment, sickness, or death of the main family earner constituted a major threat. The middle-class father could afford to purchase financial protection from life insurance companies; as early as 1851, over $100 million of security was bought. Although cheaper industrial insurance became available to the working-class after the 1870s, it only provided limited burial coverage. Mutual aid groups and voluntary associations offered some institutional protection, yet Modell concludes that, for the working class, it was the "individual coresident family that, as budgetary unit, adapted in the face of uncertainty."[14]

The useful child, therefore, provided a unique economic buffer for the working-class family of the late nineteenth century. But by 1900, middle-class reformers began indicting children's economic cooperation as unjustified parental exploitation, and child labor emerged for the first time as a major social problem in the United States. The occasional attempts to regulate the work of children earlier in the century had been largely ineffective and unable to galvanize public opinion. Existing state laws were so lax and vague as to be unenforceable. In fact, they were not even intended to put children out of work. Instead, early child labor legislation was primarily concerned with assuring a minimum of education for working children. The pioneering Massachusetts statute of 1836, for instance, required three months' schooling for young factory laborers. As late as 1905, a *New York Times* editorial contested the "mistaken notion that the advocates for the restriction and regulation of child labor insist that children under fourteen everywhere shall not work at all and shall be compelled to attend school practically all the time." The true aim of the earlier movement was to determine "the amount of labor and the amount of schooling that would be reasonable." In fact, nineteenth-century child welfare organizations were more concerned with idle and vagrant children than with child laborers.[15]

Child labor only gradually achieved national visibility. In 1870, for the first time, the U.S. Census provided a separate count of adult and child workers. Bureaus of Labor Statistics were organized in ten states between 1869 and 1883, producing and distributing data on child workers. Child labor became an issue in the press. Poole's Index to Periodical Literature lists only four articles under child labor between 1897 and 1901. Between 1905 and 1909, according to the *Readers' Guide to Periodicals,* over 300 articles were published on child workers. Child labor rapidly established itself as a priority item in the political agenda of Progressive social reformers. Organizational growth was impressive. The first Child Labor Committee was formed in 1901; by 1910 there were twenty-five state and local committees in existence. A National Child Labor Committee was established in 1904. These groups sponsored and indefatigably publicized exposés of child labor conditions. Child Labor committees were assisted by the National Consumer's League, the General Federation of Women's Clubs, and the American Federation of Labor. The emerging Socialist Party also directed much attention to the issue of child labor. For instance, in 1903, Mother Jones, the well-known union organizer, led a dramatic "March of the Mill Children," from the Philadelphia area, through New Jersey and into New York, in order to expose the evils of child labor. By 1907, an article in Hearst's influential *Cosmopolitan* assured its readers that child labor would soon take its place "with all the institutions of evil memory—with bull baiting, witch-burning, and all other execrated customs of the past."[16]

Why did twentieth-century child labor lose its nineteenth-century good reputation? What explains the sudden vehemence and urgency to remove all children from the labor market? Most historical interpretations focus on the effect of structural, economic, and technological changes on child labor trends between the 1870s and 1930s. The success of industrial capitalism is assigned primary responsibility for putting children out of work and into schools to satisfy the growing demand for a skilled, educated labor force. Rising real incomes, on the other hand, explains the reduced need for children's wages. As the standard of living steadily improved between the late nineteenth century and the 1920s, child labor declined simply because families could afford to keep their children in school. Particularly important was the institutionalization of the family wage in the first two decades of the twentieth century, by which a male worker was expected to earn enough to forgo the labor of his wife and children. Stricter and better enforced compulsory education laws further accelerated the unemployment of children.[17]

In his analysis of changes in the youth labor market, Paul Osterman contends that children were "pushed out of industry" not only by the declining demand for unskilled labor but also by a simultaneous increase in its supply. The tide of turn-of-the-century immigrants were children's new competitors. For Osterman, compulsory school legislation was the result, not the cause, of a changing youth labor market: "Since firms no longer required the labor of children and adolescents, those pressing for longer compulsory schooling were able to succeed."[18] Joan Huber similarly points to a conflict of interest between age groups created by the new economic system. In an agrarian economy, as in the early stages of industrialization, the labor of "little work people" was a welcome alternative that freed men for agriculture. But by the turn of the century, the cheap labor of children threatened to depress adult wages.[19]

Demand for child laborers was further undermined by new technology. For example, in late nineteenth-century department stores, such as Macy's and Marshall Field's, one-third of the labor force was composed of cash girls or cash boys, young children busily involved in transporting money and goods between sales clerks, the wrapping desk, and the cashier. By 1905, the newly invented pneumatic tube and the adoption of cash registers had usurped most children's jobs.[20]

The issue of child labor, however, cannot be reduced to neat economic equations. If industrial technological developments combined with the increased supply of immigrant unskilled workers inevitably reduced the need for child laborers, why then was their exclusion from the work place such a complex and controversial process?

The Child Labor Controversy

The history of American child labor legislation is a chronicle of obstacles and defeats. At every step of the battle that lasted some fifty years, the sustained efforts of child labor reformers were blocked by an equally determined, vocal, and highly effective opposition. Until 1938, every major attempt to pass national regulation of child labor was defeated. The two groups were divided by conflicting economic interests and also by opposing legal philosophies. Yet, the emotional vigor of their battle revealed an additional, profound cultural schism. Proponents and opponents of child labor legislation became entangled in a moral dispute over the definition of children's economic and sentimental value.

Child labor legislation was first resisted on a state level. Although by 1899 twenty-eight states had some kind of legal protection for child workers, regulations were vague and enforcement lax. The typical child labor law, which only protected children in manufacturing and mining, often contained enough exceptions and loopholes to make it ineffective. For instance, poverty permits allowed young children to work if their earnings were necessary for self-support or to assist their widowed mothers or disabled fathers. As late as 1929, six states retained such an exemption. Legislative progress in the early twentieth century was further undermined by a lack of uniformity in state standards. Progressive states became increasingly reluctant to enact protective legislation that put them at a competitive disadvantage with states where employment of a cheap juvenile force was legal or else minimally regulated.[21]

The struggle for national regulation of child labor began inauspiciously in 1906 with Indiana Senator Albert Beveridge's dramatic but unsuccessful attempt in the U.S. Senate to create a federal law to end what he termed "child slavery." The threat of federal regulation only served to consolidate the opposition. In 1916, when Congress finally passed the first federal law banning the products of child labor from interstate and foreign commerce, opponents promptly challenged the new law in court, and two years later the bill was declared unconstitutional. A second federal law was passed in 1919, only to be again dismissed three years later by the Supreme Court as an unconstitutional invasion of state power.

The toughest battle began in 1924 after Congress approved a constitutional amendment introduced by reformers that would authorize Congress to regulate child labor. The campaign against state ratification of the amendment was staggering: "The country was swept with propaganda. It appeared in newspapers and magazine articles, editorials, and advertisements, in enormous quantities of printed leaflets, and in speeches, at meetings, and over the radio. The proposed child labor amendment was one of the most discussed political issues of the year."[22] The opposition effort succeeded; by the summer of 1925, only four states had ratified the amendment and thirty-four had rejected it. Briefly revived in 1933, the amendment again failed to secure sufficient state support. Effective federal regulation of child labor was only obtained after the Depression, first with the National Industrial Recovery Act and in 1938 with the Fair Labor Standards Act, which included a section on child labor.

What accounts for this catalog of obstacles? Why weren't child labor reformers able to easily dazzle legislatures or swiftly persuade the public with the justness of their cause? In large part, resistance to legislation was engineered by powerful interest groups. After all, in 1920 over 1 million children between the ages of ten and fifteen were still at work. From the start, southern cotton mill owners refused to forgo the profitable labor of their many child employees.[23] Child labor reform was often depicted as a dangerous northern conspiracy to destroy the recently expanded southern industry. Mill owners were eventually joined by farmers and other employers of children. Not surprisingly, the National Association of Manufacturers and the American Farm Bureau Federation were two leading forces against the 1924 constitutional amendment. A different type of opposition was

based on political and legal principle. In this case, the target was federal regulation. Conservative citizen organizations and even prominent individuals, including the presidents of Columbia University and Hunter College, actively crusaded
against the federal child labor amendment because it challenged states' rights.[24]

It would be inaccurate, however, to caricature the child labor dispute simply
as a struggle between humane reformers and greedy employers or to reduce it to
a technical dispute over the relative merits of state versus federal regulation. The
battle involved a much wider range of participants, from clergymen, educators,
and journalists to involved citizens, and included as well the parents of child
laborers. At issue was a profound cultural uncertainty and dissent over the
proper economic roles for children.

In Defense of the Useful Child

In a letter to the editor of the *Chicago News*, a Reverend Dunne of the Guardian
Angels' Italian Church bitterly criticized the 1903 Illinois child labor law as a
"curse instead of a blessing to those compelled to earn their bread by the sweat
of their brow." The priest ridiculed a law that transformed the noble assistance
of a working child into an illegal act: "He must not attempt to work; he must not
dare to earn his living honestly, because in his case . . . that is against the law."[25]
From the early skirmishes in state legislatures to the organized campaign against
the 1924 constitutional amendment, opponents of child labor legislation defended
the pragmatic and moral legitimacy of a useful child. As a controversial article in
the *Saturday Evening Post* asserted: "The work of the world has to be done; and
these children have their share . . . why should we . . . place the emphasis on . . .
prohibitions . . . We don't want to rear up a generation of nonworkers, what we
want is workers and more workers."[26] From this perspective, regulatory legislation introduced an unwelcome and dangerous "work prohibition": "The discipline, sense of duty and responsibility, . . . which come to a boy and girl, in home,
on the farm, in workshop, as the result of even hard work . . . is to be . . . prohibited."[27] The consequences would be dire: "If a child is not trained to useful work
before the age of eighteen, we shall have a nation of paupers and thieves." Child
labor, insisted its supporters, was safer than "child-idleness."[28]

Early labor was also nostalgically defended as the irreplaceable stepping stone
in the life course of American self-made men. The president of the Virginia Farm
Bureau, fondly recalling his early years as a child laborer, insisted on the need
"to leave to posterity the same chance that I enjoyed under our splendid form of
government."[29] Similarly upholding children's "privilege to work," a writer in
the *Woman Citizen* speculated if "Lincoln's character could ever have been developed under a system that forced him to do nothing more of drudgery than is
necessitated by playing on a ball team after school hours."[30] Overwork, concluded the article, was a preferable alternative to overcoddling. Child work was
even occasionally defended with theological arguments: ". . . The Savior has said,
'My Father worketh hitherto, and I work . . . May not the child follow the foot-

steps of the Savior . . . ?" If labor redeemed, regulatory laws served the interests of Hell, by making of idle young people the devil's "best workshop."[31]

For working-class families, the usefulness of their children was supported by need and custom. When parents were questioned as to why their children left school early to get to work, it was often "perplexing" for the mother to assign a reason for such an "absolutely natural proceeding—he's of an age to work, why shouldn't he?' " As one mother who employed her young children in homework told an investigator: "Everybody does it. Other people's children help—why not ours?"[32] Studies of immigrant families, in particular, demonstrate that the child was an unquestioned member of the family economic unit. For example, in her study of Canadian workers in the Amoskeag Mills of Manchester, New Hampshire, Tamara Hareven found that the "entire family economy as well as the family's work ethic was built on the assumption that children would contribute to the family's income from the earliest possible age."[33] While generally older boys were more likely to become wage-earners, boys under fourteen and girls were still expected to actively assist the family with housework, childcare, and any income obtained from odd jobs.[34]

Government reports occasionally provide glimpses of the legitimacy of child labor: A mother boasting that her baby—a boy of seven—could "make more money than any of them picking shrimp"; or an older sister apologizing for her seven-year-old brother who was unable to work in a shrimp cannery "because he couldn't reach the car to shuck."[35] Work was a socializer; it kept children busy and out of mischief. As the father of two children who worked at home wiring rosary beads explained: "Keep a kid at home, save shoe leather, make better manners."[36]

Child labor legislation threatened the economic world of the working class. In 1924, one commentator in the *New Republic* predicted the potential disruption of traditional family relationships: "The immemorial right of the parent to train his child in useful tasks . . . is destroyed. The obligation of the child to contribute . . . is destroyed. Parents may still set their children at work; children may still make themselves useful, but it will no longer be by right and obligation, but by default of legislation. . . ."[37] Many parents resented and resisted this intrusion. A 1909 investigation of cotton textile mills reported that "fathers and mothers vehemently declare that the State has no right to interfere if they wish to 'put their children to work,' and that it was only fair for the child to 'begin to pay back for its keep.' "[38] In New York canneries, Italian immigrants reportedly took a more aggressive stand. One study reports a quasi-riot against a canner who attempted to exclude young children from the sheds: "[He was] besieged by angry Italian women, one of whom bit his finger 'right through.' "[39] Parents routinely sabotaged regulatory legislation simply by lying about their child's age. It was an easy ploy, since until the 1920s many states required only a parental affidavit as proof of a child worker's age. For a small illegal fee, some notary publics were apparently quite willing to produce a false affidavit.[40]

Middle-class critics also opposed child labor legislation in the name of family autonomy. Prominent spokesmen such as Nicholas Murray Butler, president of

Columbia University, warned that "No American mother would favor the adoption of a constitutional amendment which would empower Congress to invade the rights of parents and to shape family life to its liking."[41] An assemblyman from Nevada put it more succinctly: "They have taken our women away from us by constitutional amendments; they have taken our liquor from us; and now they want to take our children."[42]

In Defense of the Useless Child

For reformers, the economic participation of children was an illegitimate and inexcusable "commercialization of child life."[43] As one New York City clergyman admonished his parishioners in 1925: "A man who defends the child labor that violates the personalities of children is not a Christian. . . ."[44] The world of childhood had to become entirely removed from the world of the market. Already in 1904, Dr. Felix Adler, first chairman of the National Child Labor Committee, insisted that ". . . whatever happens in the sacrifice of workers . . . children shall not be touched . . . childhood shall be sacred . . . commercialism shall not be allowed beyond this point."[45] If the sacred child was "industrially taboo," child labor was a profanation that reduced "the child of God [into] the chattel of Mammon."[46]

The persistence of child labor was attributed in part to a misguided economic system that put "prosperity above . . . the life of sacred childhood."[47] Employers were denounced as "greedy and brutal tyrants," for whom children were little more than a "wage-earning unit," or a profitable dividend.[48] Any professed support of child labor was dismissed as convenient rhetoric: "A prominent businessman who recently remarked that it is good for the children to work in industry is a hypocrite unless he puts his own children there."[49]

Reformers sympathized with the financial hardships of the working-class, yet, they rarely understood and seldom condoned working-class economic strategies. Instead, parents were depicted as suspect collaborators in the exploitation of their own children. "If fathers and mothers of working children could have their own way, would they be with the child labor reformer or against him?" was a question asked in *The American Child*, a publication of the National Child Labor Committee.[50] Others were more forthright in their indictment: "Those who are fighting for the rights of the children, almost invariably, find their stoutest foes in the fathers and mothers, who coin shameful dollars from the bodies and souls of their own flesh and blood." A child's contribution to the family economy was redefined as the mercenary exploitation of parents "who are determined that their children shall add to the family income, regardless of health, law, or any other consideration."[51] As early as 1873, Jacob Riis had declared that ". . . it requires a character of more disinterestedness . . . than we usually find among the laboring class to be able to forego present profit for the future benefit of the little one."[52] At the root of this harsh indictment was the profound unease of a segment of the middle class with working-class family life. The instrumental orientation toward children was denied all legitimacy: "... to permit a parent ... at his or her will to send a child out to work and repay himself for its maintenance from the earnings of its labor, or perhaps ... make money out of it seems ... nothing short of criminal."[53] Child labor, "by urging the duty of the child to its parents," obliterated the "far more binding and important obligation of the parent to the child."[54] This "defective" economic view of children was often attributed to the foreign values of immigrant parents, "who have no civilization, no decency, no anything but covetousness and who would with pleasure immolate their offspring on the shrine of the golden calf."[55] For such "vampire" progenitors, the child became an asset instead of remaining a "blessed incumbrance."[56]

Advocates of child labor legislation were determined to regulate not only factory hours but family feeling. They introduced a new cultural equation: If children were useful and produced money, they were not being properly loved. As a social worker visiting the canneries where Italian mothers worked alongside their children concluded: "Although they love their children, they do not love them in the right way."[57] A National Child Labor Committee leaflet warned that when family relations are materialistic, "It is rare to find a family governed by affection."[58] By excluding children from the "cash nexus," reformers promised to restore proper parental love among working-class families. "It is the new view of the child," wrote Edward T. Devine, editor of *Charities and the Commons*, a leading reform magazine, "that the child is worthy of the parent's sacrifice."[59]

Thus, the conflict over the propriety of child labor between 1870 and 1930 in the U.S. involved a profound cultural disagreement over the economic and sentimental value of young children. While opponents of child labor legislation hailed the economic usefulness of children, advocates of child labor legislation campaigned for their uselessness. For reformers, true parental love could only exist if the child was defined exclusively as an object of sentiment and not as an agent of production.

NOTES

1. For child labor statistics: See "Children in Gainful Occupations at the Fourteenth Census of the United States" (Washington: Government Printing Office, 1924); Grace Abbott, *The Child and The State* (Chicago: The University of Chicago Press, 1938) I: pp. 259–69; Raymond G. Fuller, "Child Labor," *International Encyclopedia of the Social Sciences* (1930): pp. 412–24.

2. A. J. McKelway, "The Awakening of the South Against Child Labor," *Proceedings of the Third Annual Conference on Child Labor* (New York: 1907), p. 17.

3. Josephine J. Eschenbrenner, "What Is a Child Worth?" National Child Labor Committee, No 236, p. 2.

4. Representative Sumners, cited in *The American Child* 6 (July, 1924):3.

5. Elizabeth Fraser, "Children and Work," *Saturday Evening Post* 197 (Apr. 4, 1925):145.

6. Michael R. Haines, "Poverty, Economic Stress, and the Family in a Late Nineteenth-Century American City: Whites in Philadelphia, 1880," in Theodore Hershberg, ed., *Philadelphia* (New York: Oxford University Press, 1981): p. 265; Claudia Goldin, "Family Strat-

egies and the Family Economy in the Late Nineteenth Century: The Role of Secondary Workers," ibid, p. 284.

7. Editorial, *Journal of Home Economics* 7(Aug. 1915):371.

8. Daniel T. Rodgers, *The Work Ethic in Industrial America 1850–1920* (Chicago: The University of Chicago Press, 1978), p. 131.

9. John Demos, *A Little Commonwealth* (New York: Oxford University Press, 1972), pp. 140–1. See also Edmund S. Morgan, *The Puritan Family* (New York: Harper & Row, 1966), p. 66.

10. *Report on Condition of Woman and Child Wage-Earners in the United States,* VI (Washington, D.C., 1910), p. 48.

11. Niles' Register, Oct. 5, 1816, cited by Edith Abbott, "A Study of the Early History of Child Labor in America," *American Journal of Sociology* 14 (July 1908): 25. See also *Report on Woman and Child Wage-Earners,* pp. 49, 52; Stanley Lebergott, *Manpower in Economic Growth* (New York: McGraw Hill, 1964), pp. 48–51; Robert H. Bremner, ed., *Children and Youth in America* (Cambridge, MA: Harvard University Press, 1971) I: pp. 145–148. On child labor in nineteenth century England and France, see Louise A. Tilly and Joan W. Scott, *Women, Work, & Family* (New York: Holt, Rinehart and Winston, 1978). Employment in the early American mills apparently was not restricted to the children of the poor, but included the "children of farmers, mechanics, and manufacturers, in good pecuniary circumstances." Bagnall, *Samuel Slater and the Early Development of the Cotton Manufactures in the United States* (1890), cited by Forest Chester Ensign, *Compulsory School Attendance and Child Labor,* Ph.D. diss., Columbia University, 1921.

12. Fuller, "Child Labor," *IESS,* p. 419; Bremner, ed., *Children and Youth in America* II, p. 601.

13. John Modell, "Changing Risks, Changing Adaptations: American Families in the Nineteenth and Twentieth Centuries," Allan J. Lichtman and John R. Challinor, eds. *Kin and Communities* (Washington, D.C.: Smithsonian Institution Press, 1979), p. 128. On the importance of the family as a work unit in the early stages of industrialization, see Neil J. Smelser, *Social Change and the Industrial Revolution* (Chicago: University of Chicago Press, 1959). Michael Anderson, *Family Structure in Nineteenth-Century Lancashire* (Cambridge: Cambridge University Press, 1971) and Tamara Hareven, *Family Time and Industrial Time* (Cambridge: Cambridge University Press, 1982) demonstrate the survival of the family as a work unit in the nineteenth and even twentieth centuries.

14. Ibid.

15. See "Child Labor and the Teachers," *New York Times,* July 8, 1905, p. 7, and Joseph M. Hawes, *Children in Urban Society* (New York: Oxford University Press, 1971).

16. Edwin Markham, "The Smoke of Sacrifice," *Cosmopolitan* 42 (Feb. 1907):397. See Philip S. Foner, *Women and the American Labor Movement* (New York: The Free Press, 1979), pp. 283–89. For a history of the National Child Labor Committee, see Walter I. Trattner, *Crusade for the Children* (Chicago: Quadrangle Books, 1970), and for an excellent account of child labor reform in New York State, Jeremy Felt, *Hostages of Fortune* (New York: Syracuse University Press, 1965).

17. On the effect of rising real income on the reduction of child labor, see Claudia Goldin, "Household and Market Production of Families in a Late Nineteenth Century American City," *Explorations in Economic History* 16 (1979):129. On the development of child labor and compulsory school legislation, see Ensign, *Compulsory School Attendance and Child Labor,* and Miriam E. Loughran, *The Historical Development of Child-Labor Legislation in the United States* (Washington, D.C.: Catholic University of America, 1921).

18. Paul Osterman, *Getting Started: The Youth Labor Market* (Cambridge, MA: The MIT Press, 1980), pp. 60–71. For additional economic explanations of the decline in child labor both in the United States and in nineteenth century England, see Allen R. Sanderson, "Child Labor Legislation and the Labor Force Participation of Children," *Journal of Economic History* 34(Mar.1974):298–99, and Clark Nardinelli, "Child Labor and the Factory Acts," *Journal of Economic History* (Dec., 1980): 739–53.

19. *Niles' Register* (June 7, 1817):226; Joan Huber, "Toward a Sociotechnological Theory of the Women's Movement," *Social Problems* 23 (Apr. 1976):371–88.

20. Osterman, *Getting Started*, pp. 56–59; Selwyn K. Troen, "The Discovery of the Adolescent by American Educational Reformers, 1900–1920," in Lawrence Stone, ed., *Schooling and Society* (Baltimore: Johns Hopkins University Press, 1976), pp. 239–51.

21. On early child labor legislation, see William F. Ogburn, *Progress and Uniformity in Child-Labor Legislation* Ph.D. diss. (New York: Columbia University, 1912); Loughran, *The Historical Development of Child Labor Legislation; Report On Condition of Woman and Child Wage-Earners in the United States* VI; Elizabeth H. Davidson, *Child Labor Legislation in the Southern Textile States* (Chapel Hill, NC: The University of North Carolina Press, 1939).

22. Elizabeth Sands Johnson, "Child Labor Legislation," in John R. Commons, ed., *History of Labor in The United States, 1896–1932* (New York: Macmillan, 1935), p. 446. For an excellent interpretation of the legislative aspects of the child labor controversy, see Stephen B. Wood, *Constitutional Politics in the Progressive Era* (Chicago: Chicago University Press, 1968) and Thomas George Karis, *Congressional Behavior at Constitutional Frontiers*, Ph.D. diss. (New York: Columbia University, 1951).

23. Davidson, *Child Labor Legislation*, p. 57.

24. The child labor amendment was also attacked as a Communist plot designed to nationalize American children. See Anne Kruesi Brown, "Opposition to the Child Labor Amendment Found in Trade Journals, Industrial Bulletins, And Other Publications for and By Business Men," M. A. diss. (Chicago, 1937); Katharine DuPre Lumpkin and Dorothy Wolff Douglas, *Child Workers in America* (New York: Robert McBride & Co., 1937), chapters 12, 13; "The Child Labor Amendment," *University of Texas Bulletin* No. 2529 (Aug. 1, 1925); Tom Ireland, *Child Labor* (New York: G. P. Putnam's Sons, 1937).

25. Reprinted in *Charities* 11(Aug. 8, 1903):130.

26. Fraser, "Children and Work," p. 146.

27. Iredell Meares, "Should the Nation Control Child Labor?" *Dearborn Independent*, Nov. 8, 1924. Reprinted in "The Child Labor Amendment," pp. 146,148.

28. Letter to the *New York Chamber of Commerce Bulletin* XVI, No.5 (Dec. 1924):50, cited in Brown, *Opposition to the Child Labor Amendment*, pp. 35–36.

29. Letter to the *Manufacturers Record*, LXXXVI, No.15(Oct. 9, 1924):91 cited in Brown *Opposition to the Child Labor Amendment*, p. 34.

30. Mrs. William Lowell Putnam, "Why the Amendment Is Dangerous," *The Woman Citizen* 9(Dec. 27, 1924):12; "The Twentieth Amendment," The Forum 73(Feb. 1925):281.

31. "What the Child Labor Amendment Means," in Abbott, *The Child and the State* I, p. 546; Lumpkin and Douglas, *Child Workers in America*, p. 219.

32. *Report on Condition of Woman and Child Wage-Earners* VII, p. 43; Mary Skinner, "Child Labor in New Jersey," U.S. Department of Labor, Children's Bureau Publication No.185 (Washington, D.C., 1928).

33. Tamara K. Hareven, "Family and Work Patterns of Immigrant Laborers in a Planned Industrial Town, 1900–1930," in Richard L. Ehrlich, ed., *Immigrants in Industrial*

America (Charlottesville: University Press of Virginia, 1977), p. 63. On the relative importance of class versus ethnicity in determining the use of child labor, see John Modell, "Patterns of Consumption, Acculturation, and Family Income Strategies in Late Nineteenth-Century America," in Tamara K. Hareven and Maris A. Vinovskis, *Family and Population in Nineteenth-Century America* (Princeton, NJ: Princeton University Press, 1978); Goldin, "Household and Market Production of Families"; and Miriam Cohen, "Changing Education Strategies Among Immigrant Generations: New York Italians in Comparative Perspective," *Journal of Social History* (Spring 1982):443–66. Until the 1920s, black children were less likely to be employed in the labor market than were immigrant children. See Elizabeth Pleck, "A Mother's Wages: Income Earning Among Married Italian and Black Women, 1896–1911," in Michael Gordon, ed., *The American Family in Social-Historical Perspective*, 2d ed. (New York: St. Martin's Press, 1978).

34. *Report On Condition of Woman and Child Wage-Earners* VII, p. 158; Goldin, "Household and Market Production," pp. 118–19.

35. Viola I. Paradise, "Child Labor and the Work of Mothers in Oyster and Shrimp Canning Communities on the Gulf Coast," U.S. Department of Labor, Children's Bureau Publication No.98 (Washington, D.C., 1922), pp. 11, 17.

36. "Industrial Homework of Children," U.S. Department of Labor, Children's Bureau Publication No.100 (Washington, D.C., 1924), p. 23.

37. "Child Labor, The Home and Liberty," *The New Republic* 41 (Dec. 3, 1924): 32.

38. *Report on Condition of Woman and Child Wage-Earners* I:p. 353.

39. Virginia Yans-McLaughlin, *Family and Community: Italian Immigrants in Buffalo, 1880–1930* (Ithaca, NY: Cornell University Press, 1971), p. 193.

40. Sands Johnson, "Child Labor Legislation," p. 429; Felt, *Hostages of Fortune* pp. 22–23.

41. *New York Times*, Dec. 7, 1924, p. 19.

42. Cited in *The American Child* (Apr. 1925):6. Strong Catholic opposition to the Child Labor Amendment was also partly based on the perceived threat to parental authority. See Rev. Vincent A. McQuade, *The American Catholic Attitude on Child Labor Since 1891* (Washington, D.C.: Catholic University of America, 1938).

43. J. W. Crabtree, "Dr. Pritchett, Dr. Butler and Child Labor," *School and Society* (Nov. 8, 1924):585. Opponents of child labor invoked a variety of different arguments, from the physical and moral hazards of early employment to the economic inefficiency of employing young children. My discussion focuses on those arguments between the 1870s and 1930s, which centered on the changing definition of children's economic and sentimental value.

44. Quoted in *New York Times*, Feb. 2, 1925, p. 21.

45. Quoted in "The Nation and Child Labor," *New York Times*, Apr. 24, 1904, p. 6.

46. Felix Adler, "Child Labor in the United States and Its Great Attendant Evils," *Annals of the American Academy of Political and Social Science* XXV(May 1905); Charles K. Gilbert, "The Church and Child Labor," in *The American Child* 9 (Aug. 1927):4.

47. A. J. McKelway, "The Evil of Child Labor" *Outlook* 85(Feb. 16, 1907):364.

48. Davidson, *Child Labor Legislation*, pp. 65–6; Elinor H. Stoy, "Child-Labor," *Arena* 36(Dec. 1906):586; "Education, Psychology, and Manufacturers," *The American Child* 8(Nov. 1926):2.

49. Quoted in *New York Times*, Feb. 2, 1925, p. 21.

50. "Potters' Clay," *The American Child* 8(Jan. 1926):3.

51. Marion Delcomyn, "Why Children Work," *Forum* 57(Mar. 1917):324–25.

52. Jacob Riis, "The Little Laborers of New York City," *Harper's New Monthly Magazine* XLVII(Aug. 1973):327.

53. Letter to the Editor, *New York Times*, Nov. 4, 1910, p. 8.

54. Alice L. Woodbridge, "Child Labor an Obstacle to Industrial Progress," *Arena* 10 (June 1894):158.

55. Editorial, *New York Times*, Dec. 17, 1902, p. 8.

56. Mrs. A. O. Granger, "The Work of the General Federation of Women's Clubs Against Child Labor," *Annals of the American Academy* 25(May 1905):104; A. J. McKelway, "The Leadership of the Child," ibid. 32(July 1908):21.

57. Quoted in Yans-McLaughlin, *Family and Community*, p. 190.

58. "The Cost of Child Labor," *National Child Labor Committee* 5(New York:1905):35.

59. Edward T. Devine, "The New View of the Child," *Annals of the American Academy* 32(July 1908):9. Reformers, however, recognized the need to subsidize nonworking children in families that could prove their financial need. In 1905, Child Labor Committees instituted a scholarship system in several cities to compensate needy families who kept a child in school, with a weekly payment equivalent to the child's forgone income. Apparently, most scholarships went to the children of widowed or deserted women.

Chapter Five

The Making of Children's Culture

Stephen Kline

> Because psychic structure must always be passed
> from generation to generation through the narrow
> funnel of childhood, a society's child-rearing practices
> are not just one item in a list of cultural traits. They
> are the very condition for the transmission and devel-
> opment of all other cultural elements, and place defi-
> nite limits on what can be achieved in all other
> spheres of history.[1]

Children's culture in the West has a complex history. Even the most cursory
mapping would require an overview of the succession of institutions—family,
law courts, church, school, media—that have had a stake in the matrix of socialization. This is because what might be taken for children's culture has always
been primarily a matter of culture produced for and urged upon children. This
appears to be as true of the hunting games or planting tales of preindustrial life
as of the street games and nursery-school songs of modern children. The earliest
stages of maturation have always been the period in which the young are most
intensely subjected to cultural forms designed for and directed at them. Childhood is a condition defined by powerlessness and dependence upon the adult
community's directives and guidance. Culture is, after all, as the repository of
social learning and socialization, the means by which societies preserve and
strengthen their position in the world.

The forms of children's cultural expression are therefore intimately bound up
with the changing alignments that define a community's social beliefs and practices of cultural transmission. Whether it is participation in medieval festivals, or
the nursery songs, riddles and stories of nineteenth-century childhood, or more
recent playground games and jokes, the seemingly autonomous expressions take
shape within a broader cultural framework. Medieval festivals needed to have
church sanction, nursery rhymes presumed both nurseries and books, and games
require both playgrounds and time to play. Children's culture is always highly
inflected with societal purpose.

This is not to say that young children on their own, in their games, humour, songs, stories and interactions, do not create and express themselves authentically. No doubt, wherever children gather together and interact among themselves, spontaneous acts of self-expression occur. Indeed, the momentum of contemporary trends in childrearing is towards granting greater freedom and encouragement to young children's leisure. Through language, art, play, music and peer interaction contemporary childrearing practice privileges children's cultural activities, including 'playfulness' itself. At first glance it appears that children's humour and play may be the two authentic (emancipatory) regions of their culture. Yet, as a Dutch study of the relationship between family practice and play concluded, even 'children's play seems to become more and more a product of the educational and cultural orientation of parents'.[2] The emphasis on play also makes the contemporary framework for socialization confusing, because the very idea of play cloaks the momentum of socialization in a hoped-for perception of autonomy and freedom.

In a series of interviews, a number of parents from the Toronto area responded to questions about priorities for their children's development. Some 78 per cent of them said learning to read and write was the top priority. A tie for second priority went to learning moral behaviour and interacting with peer social groups (52 per cent each), while the parents considered fitting in with society (44 per cent) and becoming imaginative and self-expressive (43 per cent) to be relatively less important. In other words, although parents recognize the importance of children's imagination and self-expression, that recognition exists within the context of a very directive concept of socializing purpose. Indeed, the results of this survey indicated some very confused and conflicted reasons for buying children toys and encouraging their 'free and expressive play'. Although the parents believed that these activities gave their children great pleasure, 38 per cent of the sample also expressed serious concerns about the way children play, especially with toys promoted on television. To some degree we must look back in history to find the roots of this conflicted attitude.

The Invention of Childhood

Modern society's fascination with children's culture and with the physical factors that shape children's maturation is possibly one of the most important inventions of the industrial era. As Edward Norbeck noted, 'It is still surprising for most of us to learn that various languages lack a generic term for play, and lack a concept of work and play in binary opposition.'[3] Our contemporary notions seem to be bound up in attitudes which link play and childhood. In early medieval life, however, children appear to have been more fully integrated into the daily flux of making and consuming, of getting along. They had no autonomy, separate status, privileges, special rights or forms of social comportment that were entirely their own.[4] Commenting on the parallel if somewhat miniaturized existence of the preindustrial child, historian J. H. Plumb notes:

There was no separate world of childhood. Children shared the same games with adults, the same toys, the same fairy stories. They lived their lives together, never apart. The coarse village festivals depicted by Breughel, showing men and women besotted with drink, groping for each other with unbridled lust, have children eating and drinking with the adults. Even, in the soberer pictures of wedding feasts and dances the children are enjoying themselves alongside their elders, doing the same things.[5]

In the medieval imagery of an organic and integrated social milieu there is no evidence of the existence of either special prerogatives for childhood or of children's culture. Children were expected to participate in the household economy almost as soon as they could walk. They worked more or less as servants. They toiled in the fields with their parents, helped to tend livestock, or picked and sorted wool. Children in the 'lower reaches of society', perhaps as young as five years old, were apprenticed off to learn a trade for terms of seven to nine years. In feudal society, children were defined through the property rights of their progenitors, and their activities were defined by the role of their families in society. The objects that children handled were no different from the cultural objects that adults had, and children's lives were essentially no different from those of adults. The whole community shared work and leisure as well as games, songs and tales.

The feudal worldview contrasts sharply with our own centuries-deep concern with children's rights, leisure and pleasure—a change in attitude most clearly expressed in the profusion of toys and specially designed objects that fill a typical child's own room.[6] But more importantly the change is rooted in a framework of legal and social structures that have crystallized children's rights and prerogatives, expanding upon legal definitions first articulated in England in the cruelty acts of 1889, which for the first time extended to children the same protection from abuse granted to animals under the earlier cruelty-to-animals legislation. It is only during the twentieth century that children's legislation began to extend and elaborate on children's property rights and apply new principles that cushioned children from the common law, including the controversial exemption from the adult criminal justice system on the grounds that due to developmental inadequacies children were 'incapable of a guilty mind'.[7]

The significance of this major revision to the conception of childhood has gone almost unnoticed by a historical gaze narrowly directed towards the cataclysmic social transformation that followed the mechanization of production. Children's lives began to be featured in fictional and social historical accounts of the early industrial period, notably in the novels and stories of Charles Dickens, often either as warnings about the brutality of industrialism or as indications of social progress achieved by the factory acts of the opening decades of the nineteenth century and the 'free' schooling acts of the later third. Indeed, these changing attitudes had first taken hold earlier, prodded by an active social movement that had its protective aspirations focused on removing children from the industrial environments that were oppressing adult working women and men.

During the early decades of the nineteenth century children as young as five worked alongside their parents in factories and mines, maintaining patterns of work continued from the feudal order. In England the factory acts of 1802, 1816, and especially 1833, began to challenge the assumption that children were simply the property of their progenitors and to restrict the abusive practices of industrial managers to use this cheap source of labour as they wished. Under the banner of protection, children were gradually excluded from the industrial world, helping to destroy the system of apprenticeship that had made the family an important locus for the transmission of skills and craft knowledge.

Until a small coterie of social historians, starting with Philippe Ariès, recently began to explore the issue, the sweeping changes in the conception of childhood and childrearing practice that occurred within the new framework of protection for children had rarely been carefully examined.[8] The related issues of family life and children's culture were largely ignored by the historians of the industrial era, who saw in the science, technology and the political economy more significant forces shaping social life. During the nineteenth century a powerful idea came to prevail as the dominant view of child development: that children are innocent beings in need of formation and learning, to be protected from the harsher realities of industrial society.

Historically, this was a radical idea, for within it we find the origins of a new, more self-conscious conception of children's culture. Throughout the nineteenth century the cultural matrix of socialization was changing dramatically. Children were being excluded more and more from the crucial arenas of life and the inherent conflicts and struggles that had shaped so much of the rest of history. They were similarly being denied the value and power such participation might bestow. In compensation they were granted rights of protection and a separate institutional space—the schools—which established the new agenda for their training. In that agenda, literacy and knowledge became the privileged objectives of socialization. This transition is critical, for it marks a period when the state was not only prescribing protective buffers for childhood but beginning to assert its own 'interest' in social communication with children.

As historian Lloyd DeMause has pointed out, the concern with children and the attendant conception of childhood were revised dramatically over the nineteenth century. The very idea of the family and schools as 'socializing' agencies— that is, as agents of conscious attempts to shape and mould children into civilized beings by orchestrating their learning and social experiences—gains its full force precisely during this intense period of upheaval. Interest in and concern with children's thought and experience permeate the second half of the nineteenth century. In the literature and popular writing of the period childhood became both a way of understanding the changes of industrialization and a fitting metaphor for growth and development.

DeMause's characterization of the Victorian approach to childrearing as becoming less concerned with dominating the child's will than with protecting children and guiding them in the proper paths, teaching them to conform through more conscious and civilized means, seems an apt description of this revised attitude.[9] The expression of such progressive ideas can be traced back to social thinkers such as John Locke and Jean-Jacques Rousseau, and even to earlier community traditions that highly prized and valued children in their own right. But it was the industrializing Victorians who took this new attitude seriously, who worked at undoing the feudal matrix of socialization with its strict definition of children based on the family's property rights.[10] In feudal society the family was not only the means of organizing working life; it was central to the transmission of property and power. The undoing of this concept of lineage was a precursor to the acceptance of children's rights. In this sense the child-labour laws and factory acts were aimed as much at limiting the rights of families who were pressuring children into work as at rejecting the cruel and abusive practices of the industrial workplace.[11]

The factory acts in Britain, however, do confirm that throughout the early industrial era childhood was increasingly seen as a stage of growth that in the long-term interests of civilized society had to be isolated and guarded from an abusive world. This implied a radical realignment not only in the rights and interests of those major agencies of socialization—the family, church and state—but also in the means and instruments of acculturation. Implicit in the new attitude towards childhood was a gradual drifting away from the notion of control towards an approach that sought to instil models of self-control in children. This attitude conceived of civilization as expanding its hold around a core of transmitted moral (Christian) precepts. Protection brought with it an equally important conception of the child as a separate social stratum, as an innocent in need of protection, and as an underdeveloped mind in need of nurturing, guidance and instruction.

During the eighteenth and nineteenth centuries, the church followed these principles, becoming increasingly engaged in organizing an alternative to home and factory, hoping minimally to expand the religious, moral and ideological training within children's learning experience. Arguing that education 'civilized' the naturally enthusiastic but underdeveloped child and infused everyday experience with moral rectitude, the churches became outspoken advocates and supporters of educationism and built church schools as the preferred venue for children's guidance. Schooling was also seen as a liberating and progressive element by early socialists, such as Robert Owen, who set up schooling for his millworkers' children. Schools were meant to inspire and create the basis of a more humane industrial order, an inspiration that similarly underwrote Friedrich Froebel's kindergarten, and later Rudolph Steiner's Waldorf schools and Maria Montessori's new system of education.

Through the activities of the schooling movement the issue of socialization became of increasing interest to the state. By 1871 the problem of educating children had become such an important social issue that the Free School Act made it compulsory for young children under the age of twelve to attend an institution of learning. The new mission for childhood was to become literate, numerate and well behaved. In accepting this mission, the school system was being built upon a less harsh vision of childhood: schools were to be a special world within which children could learn at a more leisurely pace, free from the demands and pressures of both parents and industrialists.

The Victorian state school and curriculum did not provide a children's paradise. Brutality was accepted and justified on the grounds that it was necessary to discipline the recalcitrant learner. Learning itself was defined and viewed as a very unliberating process of knowledge assimilation and repetition. Nor was the school completely without an industrial social purpose. The knowledge, skills and training offered children were praised widely as the training ground for the necessary attitudes, skills, knowledge and good work habits needed in both professional working and domestic life. Children were meant, as they progressed through the education system, to experience more fully the relations of production based on an industrial model: in the schools children encountered the 'educational' values of achievement, competition, authority, principled behaviour, obedience and reward and punishment in a significant way. The school curriculum featured these dimensions of social behaviour and moral growth as important dimensions of learning. For example, the London board schools included housewifery lessons that taught the science and practice of hygiene, home economics, and cookery as progressive innovations in girls' education.

The urgency of providing a truly engaging formative experience, including the social skills to participate in adult life, underscored much of the state's interest in schooling. It was at school, after all, that children would derive their first sense of their position in the broader social matrix of jobs, civic duty, social responsibility and moral choices. These liberating and democratizing possibilities for education were particularly taken up by twentieth-century educational theorists such as John Dewey in the United States and Susan Isaacs and Teddy O'Neil in England. The same underlying social perceptions were leading to a dramatic expansion of children's organizations, many of them focused on cultural activities, including games and other play activities. Sunday schools, scouting movements, camps, playgrounds, organized sporting groups, youth groups, and even pleasure parks, were mostly directed at the poor and working classes, whose idle hands and leisure were somewhat mistrusted. In play, games and sports activities a model providing a wholesome focus to the patterns of children's development was discovered. Play, it was argued, was not simple idleness but the 'work of childhood'—the moral equivalent of labour. Street children were ushered into the playground to have a taste of organized collective activity. Structured game play and organized sport were also highly recommended as ways of preparing children for a competitive society and of creating a location for class mingling and negotiation. Games for the young in which children pretended to be animals were recommended as providing models of appropriate childlike behaviour to the very unchildlike street children of the working class. It was upon these formative foundations of the nineteenth century that toys, sporting and play equipment, uniforms, and other accoutrements have been added as a now common part of so many children's lives.

This idea of free play was most particularly celebrated in Friedrich Froebel's notion of the kindergarten, which gained acceptance in the twentieth century as the most appropriate and widely accepted modality of early childhood socialization. Froebel's kindergarten—or children's garden—was not only a place of natural innocence but also a site that granted children *Spielraum*—room to play and mature according to their own dictates and schedules.[12] Helping children to enjoy learning became the concern of most educationists, social thinkers and psychologists, who in detailing children's underdevelopment and special needs implicitly backed the idea of a unique role for children's culture—a cultural environment that would support children's own developmental agendas.

The Rousseauean theme of innocence develops through the educational writings of the period and continues throughout the twentieth century. The favoured comparison is between childhood experience and the garden. Sometimes the metaphor is there to ascribe to children a state of prelapsarian grace and the originary state of Eden. At other times the allusion is to the neat, well-tutored, and ordered rows of a more familiar landscape benefiting from well-managed nurturance. The ambivalence of the metaphor did not not undermine the common emphasis on the need for new forms of social control and conformity, which within the emerging developmentalist approach could be achieved by recognizing and empathizing with children's needs, especially their needs for culture. The garden metaphor was particularly favoured by the writers and artists who furnished children's primary cultural artefact—the book.

Toys, pianos and sports equipment—and not the teacher's rod—were to become the privileged instruments of childhood enlightenment, delight and entertainment. Music, art, sports and dance lessons were expected activities for the properly civilized middle-class child. More broadly, an interest in the full spectrum of cultural development was being impressed on public institutions such as museums, art galleries, playgrounds and parks, places that became the mark of civic pride and achievement. From the narrow confines of literacy the garden of children's culture came to full flower.

The Commercialization of Childhood

During the closing decades of the nineteenth century, rapid industrialization was dramatically increasing the capacity of manufacturers to meet people's needs by supplying more goods. Much of the commentary on industrialization has focused on the changing relationship between capital, technology and labour within this process of social transformation, overlooking marketing's specific historical task in expanding the sale and distribution of these goods—that is, the insertion of manufactured goods into an ever wider sphere of human activity. Yet it was with a verve and energy equal to that of the engineers and designers that marketers sought new means of increasing the public's interest in buying the goods that the factories were producing. The motif of children's culture, which through the next century became ever more visible, emerged within the broad spectrum of the market's communication activity.

The neo-medieval art of the period gave vivid expression to the new sensibility of innocence and unassailable purity that grounded the Victorian perspective on childhood, and also lent itself to products. The cherub and fairy motifs long established in painting became part of the decorative frame and backdrop for goods. Indeed, this same imagery of childhood was featured in the poster art of the period and among the classics of turn-of-the-century advertising. The babe of the new century ventured optimistically on the sea of life, riding a wave of material goods or, fairy-like, bestowing the cornucopia of life. At the turn of the century this simple metaphor captured not so much the reality of industrial society as a sentiment of hope in an emergent order. In most turn-of-the-century advertising the child seems to symbolize not only the end to the rigidities of the past but also the promise of a gentler purer future. Within the world portrayed in advertising, personal growth, health and fulfilment were not incompatible with industrial progress and economic expansion.

The Victorian awakening to the preciousness of childhood helped ensure that children's goods would expand along with other markets. Childhood was being increasingly characterized by specific behavioral traits and products. The increasingly vivid image of a separate domain of childhood became standard in both the late Victorian arts and product appeals. Pears soap, for instance, focused on the images of childhood in its promotional efforts, equating cleanliness and spiritual purity. Pears commissioned the famous Pre-Raphaelite painter Millais to design one of its display ads, with memorable effect. Other advertisers followed suit, making the Victorian cult of cleanliness part of the essence of good parenting. But implicit in the soap manufacturer's invocations was a new sense of childhood: the young were no longer viewed as simply miniaturized replicas of adults.

Many families across the social spectrum—not just the wealthy—were benefiting from the rapid mechanization of production and the increasing availability of manufactured goods. The shift of focus towards youth helped ensure that children shared the industrial largesse. Along with soap, other products—shoes, clothes, foods, medicines for children—were being produced in greater abundance than ever before and distributed in rural as well as urban communities. Families now had additional resources available to purchase products in the market rather than having to make them within the household or buy them from local artisans. The ability to provide more adequately for the family became recognized as a touchstone of progress itself. One prominent example was the gentle expression of anxiety about the ill child, which in the context of advertising became a powerful reason for buying manufactured medicines.

The child's health was a bearer of another message locating childhood in a grander organic unit. As T. Jackson Lears was to point out, in response to the rationality and mechanization implicit in progressivism, a contrapuntal theme was being voiced in the nineteenth-century organs of popular culture. Ads were stressing a 'therapeutic' ethos with an emphasis on well-being, self-help and betterment:

A characteristic therapeutic strategy domestic responsibilities with nostalgia for a pristine, natural state. 'Mothers do you not know that children crave natural food until you pervert their taste by the use of unnatural food?' a Shredded Wheat advertisement asked in 1903. Unnatural food develops unnatural and therefore wrong propensities and desires in children.[13]

Food and health always play an important role in family life, and specialized breakfast foods and medication were among the first brand goods to become associated with the theme of children's natural innocence and their unique nutritional and health needs.

The rounded and pliant images of the child convey these organic qualities. Pictures of both contented and suffering children began to decorate the packages and displays for an ever-increasing circle of products. Advertising repeatedly articulated the need for parents to become aware of the unique needs, vulnerabilities and sensitivities of their child. Most particularly, this idea was expressed through a madonna-and-child motif: the concerned mother and the frail and innocent child were coupled in the image of a bond rooted in a deep emotional concern for the child's well-being. Indeed, the theme of anxiety about children accompanied one of promise and innocence in the imagery of turn-of-the-century advertising. Advertisers found in the nurturing instincts of mothers a useful thematic warp into which they could weave their products complete with the evolving protectionist sentiments.

The increasing awareness of the domain of children's goods was also witnessed in the new and often elaborate department stores, which began to feature children's sections. Children's goods infiltrated the catalogues and display advertising of these early pioneers of merchandising. The department store established its place as purveyor to the whole family by bringing forth in one place a greater range of goods required for family life. This pattern of marketing continues today, with 65 per cent of the volume of children's wear still purchased in department stores. Stocked with a variety of general-purpose provisions for the family, the department stores thrived by responding to parents' perceived sense that family well-being was a matter judged across the whole spectrum of consumption and care.

Meanwhile, the educational interest in child development and welfare encouraged manufacturers and producers to consider a distinctive children's array of goods. Some of the new products of the period were even designed differently to strengthen their association with the new attitudes and activities that had arisen in children's culture. For example, during the nineteenth century clothes were being more extensively designed and styled for children's use: pinafores, knickerbockers and smocks, sailor suits and short trousers. In paintings and illustrations, too, clothing helped to signal the child's new station in life. Similarly, new items of furniture—for example, high chairs and chairs, school desks, and chairs that made children sit more erectly at the table—were among the design innovations at the end of the period.

A historian of design, Adrian Forty, writes:

Only at the very end of the century were there entire ranges of nursery furniture that were different from those for adults, not only in scale but also in form and appearance. Some of these new articles, such as the purpose-designed toy cupboards, specially filled children's needs, some offered the advantage of being hygienic and easy to clean, while others were decorated with pictures of animals or with colours that were particularly appropriate for children.[14]

Forty quotes the 1914 Heal's nursery furniture catalogue, which gives the reasoning behind the changes in design:

> Formerly the children, even in the families of the well-to-do, were relegated to an attic or some room not thought sufficiently good for any other purpose. . . . Now the nursery is carefully chosen, well lighted and well planned . . . suitable to the needs of the occupants, and in every way a fit training ground, both physical and moral for the young. Children are admittedly very susceptible to their environment, therefore, how important it is to surround them with things at once beautiful and useful.[15]

The special designs made children stand out from the social continuum. In his painting *Bubbles* which appeared in a famous Pears poster, Sir John Everett Millais had presented a boy caught in a reverie, dressed in clothing befitting not only his station in life but also his youthful position in the social spectrum. The uniforms of school, the neckerchiefs of scouts and the caps favoured by youth-activity groups helped to create a cultural stylization that levelled children but clearly demarked childhood. Children are much easier to recognize in the art and photography of the twentieth century for this very reason: a separate clothing style and, implicitly, a unique place in society were created for them. Together, the new designs, catalogues, advertising and consumer-magazine stories and advisories of the turn of the century jointly contributed to a new sense that children were at the hub of the domestic scene.

The stylization and voice in early consumer-magazine advertising were directed to parents. The advertising duplicated the content of much of the popular writing in women's magazines and books, which devoted increasing attention to advisories on childrearing practice and discussions of children's well-being. In the advertising of the period this 'advisory voice' was woven into many product appeals. It was, after all, the mother's attention that was being targeted by advertisers. It was the mother's concerns that were being discussed: health, ease of preparation, building strong bodies, gentle on the system. These were appeals designed to connect with the maternal anxieties and values being more broadly discussed. There is no doubt that the parent was supposed to buy the product. There are only a few examples in the advertising of the period of goods marketed to children directly: an occasional bicycle or train set. The merchandisers had little interest in motivating or addressing children themselves.

Symbols of Domesticity

Among the ads for general domestic goods after the turn of the century was a new motif which pictured the modern family as a unit. This was not the stern and forbidding autocratic patriarchy that psychiatry described as the roots of repression, but a more engaging image of family life—a vision of the household as a cultural sanctuary from industrial life. The image was increasingly repeated in the advertisements of the 1920s and 1930s for food, cars, houses, furniture, appliances and a variety of other products. As advertising historian Roland Marchand comments:

> If the view from the office window defined the dominant fantasy of man's domain in the world of work, another visual cliche—the family circle—expressed the special qualities of the domain that he shared with his wife and children at home. During the nineteenth century . . . the notions of work and home had become dichotomized. The home came to represent a sheltered haven to which men escaped to find surcease from the harsh world of competition, ambition, and cold calculation. More than ever, the concept of the family circle, with its nuances of closure and intimate bonding, suggested a protective clustering—like the circling of the settlers' wagons—in defense of qualities utterly distinct from those that prevailed outside.[16]

Stuart Ewen sees another parable in advertising's fascination with the family and home life. He argues that the emerging image of a modern nuclear family was not simply a reflection of broader social changes taking place in industrial society (for example, urbanization, mobility, population growth) but was more precisely connected to the conscious attempts by industrialists to solve the problems emerging with the maturation of industrial society. Industrialists during the 1920s, Ewen points out, were beginning to recognize that the family's home life, and with it the child's earliest experience, were growing beyond the family's grasp:

> On the one side stood the corrupting and masculine world of business; on the other, a home ruled by the father and kept moral and virtuous by the mother. Where the home and community had once attempted to comprise a totality of social existence, and patriarchy had been its 'legal code,' Victorianism elevated the patriarchal home into a spiritual sanctuary against the realities of the productive sphere.[17]

Ewen's reflections on the history of commercial culture see in industries a renewed interest in the social dynamics of the household and a rethinking of the problems of industrial overproduction. During the 1920s and 1930s, industrialists began to think seriously about the function of the family, and in particular of women, as a consuming unit. The family made its contribution in the form of the demand for goods rather than in terms of labour and its potential for labour. Youth became an element in visualizing the promise of consumption as a wholesome preoccupation of life:

> In the opening decades of the twentieth century, the symbolic role of youth was central to business thought. The fact that childhood was increasingly a period of

consuming goods and services made youth a powerful tool in the ideological framework of business. Beyond the transformation of the period of childhood and adolescence into a period of consumption, youth was also a broad cultural symbol of
renewal, of honesty, and of criticism against injustice—the young have always provided a recurrent rejection of the ancient virtues of the 'establishment'.[18]

Advertising therefore began to configure its discussion of the benefits and uses
of manufactured goods within a continuum of domestic consumption that featured the child as central in the dynamics of the household.

Ewen's comments help show why women's work, portrayed in advertising as
the labour of consumption, was continuously denied significance and validity
until merchandisers began to reveal to industrialists the real dynamics of the
marketplace. Given the belief in men's industrial work as the only valid form of
labour, the nonwaged work of the household, including childrearing, was
granted only marginal notice among social historians—at least until feminist
theory refocused attention on the social significance of the household as a place
of labour. Ewen's study suggests the importance of the merchandisers' increasing
attention to the domestic scene. The marketplace is a meeting ground between
producers and consumers: the expansion of production depends upon the expansion of consumption: yet the social dynamics of consumption are defined in and
by the family unit—not the factory.

It is odd, therefore, that in the social commentary and advice that emerges
around the topic of childrearing, so little attention has been given to children's
place in the framework of consumption. In twentieth-century advertising the
imagery of childhood became vital in the tapestry of the consuming family—as
a motivation for adequate provisioning, as an indicator of family pride and virtue, and as an easily understood symbol of the long-term benefits of continued
economic prosperity. In an age of anxieties about social progress, advertising's
images of family solidarity provided some comfort. As Roland Marchand points
out:

> This visual cliche was no social mirror; rather, it was a reassuring pictorial conven-
> tion. . . . When father, mother, and child in an advertising tableau stood gazing off
> into the distance with their backs turned directly or obliquely toward the reader, it
> could mean only one thing. In the language of visual cliches they were looking into
> the future.[19]

The future, though lacking in detail, was filled with hope and promise—for
which children were often the visual clue.

Although the present became more troubled during the war years of the 1940s,
advertising did not lose sight of this promised future. Even in the depth of those
years, the images of war's end indicated that in her airplane factory Rosie the
Riveter still dreamed of the infinitely clean and modern domestic vistas of consumption. The kitchen, the hub of domestic labour and familial warmth, was to
be transformed by the very technology and enterprise that was helping to win
the war.

Indirectly, the advertisements for a remodelled domesticity in the first half of the twentieth century also provide a glimpse of the impact of the emerging philosophy of developmentalism on the conception of childrearing. In advertising's version of modern domesticity, appropriate clothing and the central positioning of the child on the floor clearly demarcate a status that stresses the legitimacy of childish aspirations and pastimes. Some of the ads convey directly the need to recognize children's own playful and imaginary approaches to goods. In others, the presence of books, toys, wagons, special furniture, games and learning equipment, along with school bags, playground equipment, sports equipment and other pastimes all imply the expanding sphere of children's cultural products.[20] These product lines were starting to consolidate in the marketplace a conception of children's goods which compounded the perception of the autonomy of childhood.

The carefully constructed commercial scenes of these advertisements reflect the importance that parents attached to finding the right vehicles and objects to encourage their children's development. Few of the ads depict adults unreservedly impressing their ideas and will upon the child. Most of them, rather, convey the sense that the common tools of childhood—the ball, the doll, the bicycle— are essential to good parenting. The moral force of the presentation of these objects is that parents who cannot provide them are in some ways inadequate.

The toy has a special significance among the symbols of children's cultural requirements. The ball or wooden train serves as a useful reference point in the scheme of domesticated consumption, because it connotes a different aspect of utility. Roland Barthes notes that the toy is a cultural signifier conveying not only the common preoccupations of children with play but also their changing experience of things.[21] The toy is a symbol of a world distinct from the processes and social relations of work. It is the possibility of a youngster's isolation and buffering from a harsh industrial reality that lies at the centre of these representations of childhood preoccupations. The child with toys is a symbol of the pleasures of consumerism, of the new objects primarily designed for leisure and fantasy. Play is a childhood labour whose essence is a mental transformation—the distancing from daily experience and the re-creation of self in an imaginary world. The toy is therefore an effective symbol of a simpler form of gratification steeped in pleasure alone and not in the rational adjudication of a product's attributes, benefits and construction.

In addition, toys are fitting symbols of economic progress because they direct consumers to the rewards of leisure and relaxation. The re-created atmosphere of domestic consumption takes its emotional cues and mood from the absence of labour implied by a playful child. The advertising of the 1920s ascribes to the family unit a new self-confidence and softer structure of feeling. For example, Roland Marchand notes how:

'Soft focus' defined the family circle tableau almost as readily as its specific content. Nostalgic in mood . . . the soft focus atmosphere suggested harmony and tenderness . . . the artist recognizing the moral ambience of the scene he was invading, washed an affectionate, rosy mist over the scene. It was the family circle, rather than the home itself, that laid claim to the soft focus treatment. . . . The addition of a child, connoting family, increased the likelihood of a soft focus treatment. The addition of the father completed the circle, more or less assuring that the scene would fall into one of the sentimentalized categories of leave-taking, homecoming, sharing of a meal, or evening leisure in the living room.[22]

During the 1930s the hues of family sentimentality were intensified, and the imagery of youthful play became increasingly crystallized as a symbol of the benefits of modernization.

Industrialists, notes Stuart Ewen, reconceptualized the family within the framework of their business interests by favouring a depiction of the household economy as an exemplar of the progressive democratic consumerism:

> To businessmen, the reconstituted family would be one which maintained its repro-
> ductive function, but which had abandoned the dogma of parental authority, except
> in-so-far as that authority could be controlled and provide a conduit to the process
> of goods consumption.[23]

Yet the imagery of domestic consumption was not an entirely placid affair. The image of the happily playing child had to assert itself against the traditional backdrop of industry and patriarchy. The tensions in the family often presented in allegory the contradictions experienced in the progressive period. In this respect much of the consumer advertising directed to women takes on an educational tone, instructing mothers on the values and practices implicit in new approaches to childrearing and contrasting these with the premodern values of unthinking autocratic paternalism. Sometimes a woman (generously armed with information provided by advertisers) is arrayed in argument with the old-fashioned forces of patriarchy. Sparing the rod can be justified, however, when another solution found in the market solves the problem. A rather typical ad shows a scene of family disputation centred on the failure of the father to understand the modern means of childrearing. Children were often caught at the middle of a tug of war, and an interest in children's needs turned out to be a metaphor for the struggles to establish a market democracy.

A corresponding tone of anxiety pervades much of the advertising of the 1930s, which overtly recognized the significance of a child's changing stature within the family. Much of the anxiety concerned parents' ways of relating to children, of controlling and directing their abundant energies, imagination and creativity. Sometimes mothers fretted over their lack of control of their children's well-being; sometimes experts intruded into the scene to help resolve this sense of insecurity; and sometimes parents disputed the appropriate ways to deal with the troubled moments of childrearing. These scenes seem to speak of a more fundamental unsettledness that went beyond the disputes over childrearing practice.

NOTES

1. Lloyd DeMause, 'The Evolution of Childhood', in Lloyd DeMause, ed., *The History of Childhood*, New York, Harper & Row, 1974, p. 3.

2. Van der Kooij, Rimmert and Wilma Slaats-van den Hurk, 'Relations between Parental Opinions and Attitudes about Child Rearing and Play', *Play and Culture*, 4, 1991, p. 120.

3. Norbeck, Edward, 'The Study of Play—Johan Huizinga and Modern Anthropology', in David Lancy and B. Allan Tindall, *The Study of Play: Problems and Prospects*, New York, Leisure Press, 1977, p. 17.

4. Ariès, Philippe, *Centuries of Childhood: A Social History of Family Life*, New York, Alfred Knopf, 1962.

5. Quoted in Tucker, M. J., 'The Child as Beginning and End: Fifteenth and Sixteenth Century English Childhood', in DeMause, *The History of Childhood*, p. 251.

6. Rheingold, H. and K. V. Cook, 'The Content of Boys' and Girls' Rooms as an Index of Parents' Behavior', *Child Development*, 46, 1975, pp. 459–63.

7. Adams, Paul, Leila Berg, Nan Berger, Michael Duane, A. S. Neil and Robert Ollendorff, *Children's Rights: Towards the Liberation of the Child*, Wellingborough, Elek Books, 1971.

8. See Ariès, *Centuries of Childhood*; DeMause, ed., *The History of Childhood*; Pollock, Linda A., *Forgotten Children: Parent—child Relations from 1500 to 1900*. New York, Cambridge University Press, 1983; Jordan, Thomas, *Victorian Childhood: Themes and Variations*, Albany, State University of New York Press, 1987.

9. DeMause, 'The Evolution of Childhood', p. 52.

10. Marc Bloch, *Feudal Society*, Chicago: University of Chicago Press, 1961, pp. 134–42.

11. Adams, Paul, 'The Infant, the Family and Society', in Adams et al., eds, pp. 51–90.

12. Rubin, K., 'Introduction' and 'Early Play Theories Revisited: Contributions to Contemporary Research and Theory', in Pepler, D. and K. Rubin, eds, *The Play of Children: Current Theory and Research*, Basel and New York, Krager, 1982.

13. Jackson Lears, T., 'From Salvation to Self-Realization: Advertising and the Therapeutic Roots of the Consumer Culture 1880–1930', in Richard Fox and T. J. Lears, eds, *The Culture of Consumption*, New York, Pantheon, 1983, p. 23.

14. Adrian Forty, *Objects of Desire*, London, Pantheon Books, 1986, pp. 68–70.

15. Ibid., p. 72.

16. Marchand, Roland, *Advertising the American Dream: Making Way for Modernity, 1920–1940*, Berkeley, University of California Press, 1985, p. 248.

17. Ewen, Stuart, *Captains of Consciousness*, New York, McGraw-Hill, 1976, p. 126.

18. Ibid., p. 139.

19. Marchand, *Advertising*, pp. 254–5.

20. Snyder, Richard, 'Trends in the Sporting Goods Market', in M. Marie Hart, ed., *Sport in the Socio-cultural Process*, Dubuque, Wm. C. Brown, 1972, pp. 423–44.

21. Barthes, Roland, *Mythologies*, London, Paladin, 1973.

22. Marchand, *Advertising*, 248–9.

23. Ewen *Captains*, p. 139.

Chapter Six

Seducing the Innocent
Childhood and Television in Postwar America

Lynn Spigel

In August 1991, Pee-wee Herman moved out of his kidvid playhouse into the pornhouse of the nightly news when a mug shot of the children's idol revealed him to be a fully grown man, a man arrested for exposing himself in an adult movie theater. In true Pee-wee style, the arrest sparked a series of nervous reactions. Psychologists appeared on local newscasts, advising parents on ways to tell children about their TV play-pal, offering tips on how to make youngsters understand the scandal of Pee-wee's adult desires. All grown up and seemingly all washed up, Pee-wee was axed from the CBS lineup, and Pee-wee dolls and paraphernalia were removed from the shelves of the local Toys R Us.

Pee-wee is a perfect example of what Jacqueline Rose has called the "impossibility" of childhood. As Rose argues in her work on *Peter Pan*, the child is a cultural construct, a pleasing image that adults need in order to sustain their own identities. Childhood is the difference against which adults define themselves. It is a time of innocence, a time that refers back to a fantasy world where the painful realities and social constraints of adult culture no longer exist. Childhood has less to do with what children experience (since they too are subject to the evils of our social world) than with what adults want to believe.[1] In this regard, the problem with Pee-wee is not so much his indecent exposure, but the fact that he exposes the fantasy of childhood itself. Pee-wee, as a liminal figure somewhere between boy and man, is always on the verge of revealing the fact that children are not the pleasing projection of an adult imagination. He is always threatening to disrupt adult identities by deconstructing the myth of childhood innocence.

The Pee-wee panic is the most recent skirmish in an older battle to define and preserve childhood on television. Since the medium's rise in the late 1940s, educators, citizen groups, the clergy, and other social organizations have attacked television for its unwholesome effects on children. Graphic violence, suggestive sexuality, and bad behavior of the Bart Simpson kind are continually seen as threats to youngsters, threats that need to be researched and controlled. But, rather than examine television's effects on children per se, I want to look at the *image* of the child that television, and the debates around it, have constructed. In order to do so, I will return to the years following World War II, when television was first defined as a "family" medium. In particular, I want to explore the efforts in that period to make distinctions between adult and children's entertainment, and the need, among the adult population, to keep those distinctions intact. Critics in the popular press established a set of taste standards and reception practices for children's programs that were predicated on middle-class ideals for child rearing, ideals that stressed the need to maintain power hierarchies between generations and to keep children innocent of adult secrets. But even if the advice literature suggested such controls and regulations, the actual children's television programs that emerged in this period played with the culturally prescribed distinctions between adults and children. Drawing upon the fantasy figures of children's literature, puppet shows, the circus, movies, and radio programs, these television shows engaged the hearts of children (and often adults as well) by presenting a topsy-turvy world where the lines between young and old were blurred and literally re-presented by clowns, fairies, and cowboys who functioned as modern-day Peter Pans. Indeed, as we shall see, the narrative pleasure these programs offered was based in large part on the transgression of generational roles that were idealized in the child-rearing advice literature of the period.

Presumed Innocent: Childhood and Cultural Power

After World War II, the American public was deluged with images of nuclear family bliss. The ravages of war, it was suggested, could in part be assuaged through the protection of a stable home, a home far removed from the horrors experienced in previous decades. Films such as *It's a Wonderful Life* (Frank Capra, 1947) showed how family values could insulate individuals from economic hardships and compensate for wartime sacrifices, encouraging Americans to return to the "basics"—Mom, Dad, and the kids.[2] Advertisements for luxury goods told women to leave their wartime jobs and return home, where they could rekindle romance and purchase their share of washing machines and electric blenders. Meanwhile, in social reality, people were marrying at record rates, and the baby boom, which began during the war and lasted through 1964, created a nation of children who became a new symbol of hope.[3] Children, after all, were innocent; they did not know what their parents knew; they hadn't lived through the hardships of the Great Depression and the war, nor did they bear the blame.

The concept of childhood innocence—and the investment in youth as a symbolic future—was, of course, not a new invention. Since the early centuries of industrialization, children have been conceptualized as blank slates upon whom parents "write" their culture.[4] In the American context, this tabula rasa conception of the child gained new force and meanings with the transition from an agrarian to an industrialized society that took place over the course of the nineteenth century. While the agrarian child had been a worker in the farm economy, in the industrial society children were no longer crucial to the family income. This was particularly true for white middle-class households, where the family income was high enough to sustain a comfortable life without the contribution of a child's wages. Stripped of immediate ties to the family economy, the white middle-class child emerged as a new sociological category in whom the middle-class adult culture invested new hopes and dreams. By the turn of the century, with falling birthrates and advances in medical science that decreased infant mortality, parents placed increased focus on individual children, regarding them as distinct personalities who needed guidance and moral support. At the same time, the exploitation of child laborers (who came largely from black, immigrant, and working-class families) created a common cause for "child-saving" movements that attempted to combat child abuse by proposing wide-reaching reforms for children of all classes and races.

While this focus on children had humanitarian goals, the particular battles fought over childhood were linked to power struggles in the adult culture. At the core of this concentration on children was a battle between women and men for cultural, social, and political authority. Especially in middle-class households, the focus on children was linked to women's role in the new economy. Like the child's, the woman's place in patriarchal industrial culture was in the home, and her confinement to the domestic sphere was legitimated by the idea that women were morally obliged to be the caretakers and nurturers for their children. The sentimentalization of the mother-child bond worked to secure the middle-class woman's exclusion from the public sphere. Importantly, however, many women at the time perceived the mother role as an empowering one, and for this reason numerous women turned to mothering as an avenue for increased dominion and prestige.

The "mothers' movement," which took institutional form as the National Congress of Mothers in 1897, gave a public voice to women's issues. Although for some this movement was a complicit embrace of women's domestic confinement, for others it served as a venue for expressing what we might now call "feminist" values. At a time when "genteel" women were expected to leave matters of civic governance to men, women activists justified their interests in the suffrage struggle and other social reforms by invoking the more acceptable female concerns of motherhood and child welfare. "The Age of Feminism," one spokeswoman claimed, "is also the age of the child."[5] As this woman must have understood, the child had become a key to power in the public world. The child, after all, was a link to the future. In a world where Darwin's theories of evolution were taking hold, the child became a vehicle for changing the course of history, for bettering the world through imparting one's goals upon a new generation.

Just as women saw the child as a means to their own social power, men began to turn to children as a way to reinvent their authority in the alienating conditions of the industrial world. According to Margaret Marsh, a sentimental vision of childhood was at the core of the "male domesticity" that gained force at the turn of the century. Faced with white-collar desk jobs and increasing feelings of anonymity in the urban world, men were advised to turn toward their homes—and particularly their children—to regain a sense of authority and prestige. Camping trips, family games, and other child-rearing activities promised to refortify men's diminishing power in public life.[6] Again, at the heart of this endeavor was the notion that children were innocent creatures who needed guidance into a world that they would help transform.

This image of children—as both innocents and arbiters of progress—was not only at the center of power struggles at home; it also served to legitimate the institutional power of scientists, policy-makers, and media experts who turned their attention to chidren's welfare. Policy reform movements of the Progressive Era fashioned an image of the child as the means to modernization: as a new generation, children linked the past with the future, tradition with progress. As such, the child was no longer simply the responsibility of the private family, but also a prime concern of public agencies. In 1912, the federal government gave official credence to this logic by establishing the Children's Bureau as an official administration for overseeing the care of the young. The twentieth century thus emerged as the "century of the child," an era in which children became discrete individuals who, with the proper socialization, would carry the nation into the future.[7]

While social reforms and public institutions were based on humanitarian efforts, they often worked to diminish the regional, class, ethnic, and racial diversity of family life by disseminating an American "norm" based largely on white, middle-class values and life experiences. By 1915, the emphasis on creating standards for child rearing changed from reform per se to scientific investigation of what constituted the "normal" child, and such investigations became the basis for further social policy.[8] In both its reform and investigatory modes, the child-saving movement was a bedrock for a new organization of childhood experiences: the rise of public schools and decline of child labor ensured that the "normal" child would be an individual educated according to the standards of the dominant class, race, and sex (that is, according to white, patriarchal, middle-class curricula). In addition, the child-saving movement set out to regulate children's play: the rise of municipal playgrounds and national organizations such as the Boy Scouts (1910) and Girl Scouts (1912) helped institutionalize ideas about what constituted children's appropriate use of leisure time.

This normalization of childhood experience and formation of standards for child development were promoted by a stream of media experts who disseminated professional advice. In their book on the history of expert advice to women, Barbara Ehrenreich and Deirdre English have shown how the original goals of the mothers' movement were co-opted by a stream of professional scientists who spoke through the venues of women's media to teach women how to raise their young.[9] Rather than finding increased authority through child rearing, women were repositioned as consumers of information that only scientists and institutions of higher education could produce.

By the 1920s, then, child rearing was no longer seen as a natural instinct of the mother; rather, it was a professional skill that women had to learn by heeding the wisdom of (mostly male) professionals. Women were confronted with a host of scientific advice from "experts" who spoke to them through such popular venues as women's magazines and radio shows. At the heart of this advice was the idea that children were pliable, innocent creatures who needed to be guided by adults. It was the adult's responsibility to generate moral values in the young by guarding the gates to knowledge. By doling out adult secrets only at the proper stages in child development, parents could ensure that children would carry the torch of progress for future generations. A mistake in this regard, the experts warned, could prove fatal—not only for the individual child, but for the moral character of the entire nation. And it is in the context of this moral discourse on knowledge and cultural power that the debates on television should be viewed.

Television and the Gates to Knowledge

As the above brief sketch suggests, childhood is something that adults attempt to maintain through various systems of governance, surveillance, and prescriptive science. And while the protection of children appears to be a consequence of "natural" instinct, the way in which our social system goes about this task is also a function of particular material conditions, ideological concerns, and struggles over social and political power. Childhood, then, historically has been an unstable category, one that must be regulated and controlled constantly. Childhood—or at least the image of the innocent youth to which this category refers—can exist only through a certain disciplinary power that, as Michel Foucault has shown, operates to regulate knowledge.[10] Adulthood brings with it authority, and even more a civic duty, to control the dissemination of information about the world. And childhood—as a moment of purity and innocence—exists only so long as the young are protected from certain types of knowledge.

Given this, it is not surprising that mass media typically have been viewed with trepidation by the adult culture. Be it the 1920s movie matinee or the contemporary video game, mass media have been seen as a threatening force that circulates forbidden secrets to children, and that does so in ways that parents and even the state cannot fully control. Worse still, parents may not even know how and where their children have acquired this information. With the mass, commercial dissemination of ideas, the parent is, so to speak, left out of the mediation loop, and the child becomes the direct addressee of the message. Perhaps for this reason, the history of children's involvement with mass media has been marked by a deep concern on the part of adult groups to monitor their entertainment and survey their pleasure. From Anthony Comstock's crusade against dime novels to the more liberal approach of matinee mothers who chaperoned children at the movies, the adult culture has continually tried to filter the knowledge that mass media transmit to the young.[11]

After World War II, this legacy of child saving, and the skepticism about mass media that it presupposed, was taken to its logical extreme when local, state, and federal governments focused with unparalleled concern on the figure of the "juvenile delinquent." Although it is by no means certain that actual incidents of juvenile crimes multiplied after the war, it is clear that law enforcement agencies began to police criminal youth in more rigorous ways.[12] In the late 1940s, the federal government established the Continuing Committee on the Prevention and Control of Delinquency, and law enforcers began to count instances of youth crimes more thoroughly than ever before. It was also at this time that the Senate took a profound interest in juvenile delinquency, and in 1952, under the auspices of Senator Estes Kefauver, began a series of investigations that continued into the 1960s. Meanwhile, women's magazines and child psychologists such as Dr. Benjamin Spock (whose *Common Sense Book of Baby and Childcare* was first published in 1946) advised mothers how to prevent their children from becoming antisocial and emotionally impaired. Although it is hard to determine how many parents actually followed the experts' advice, the popularity of this literature (for example, by 1952 Spock's book had sold more than four million copies), attests to the fact that people were eager to hear what the experts had to say.[13]

Juvenile delinquency was blamed primarily on two separate but related causes—a bad family life and mass media.[14] According to the popular wisdom, the splintering of families during the war left children vulnerable to outside forces that encouraged the development of immoral habits and criminal behavior. Experts argued that the rise in juvenile crimes during the war was largely caused by working mothers who did not properly devote their energies to their young. Thus, as in the past, the mother-child bond served to justify the idea that women's place was in the home. Indeed, at a time when the female labor force was being told to relinquish their jobs to returning GIs, the mass media (and the scientific experts who spoke through these venues) promoted a romantic ideal of motherhood that must have helped to encourage middle-class women to spend the lion's share of their energies on domestic concerns. Then, too, men were told to invest more concern in family life. Like the male domesticity at the turn of the century, this postwar version of the child-centered family provided men with a conduit to power that promised to compensate for their increasing loss of authority in the bureaucratic corporate world. Magazines such as *Esquire* and *Popular Science* told men to take renewed interest in all facets of family life, particularly those that involved family fun and leisure (as opposed to the actual work women performed as housekeepers and mothers). Whether the advice was aimed at men or women, the child emerged as a terrain on which to assert adult power, and the parent in turn relied on the experts' wisdom. Failure to follow this advice could result in "problem" children or, worse still, criminals.

In the advice literature of the period, mass media became a central focus of concern as the experts told parents how to control and regulate media in ways that promoted family values. As a domestic medium that brought the outside world directly into the home, television was at once ally and enemy. Television was often considered to have beneficial effects because it would bring the family together for recreation. In 1952, when the House of Representatives held hearings on the content of radio and television programs, government officials speculated that television was a necessity for family bliss. Representative Joseph Byrson from South Carolina admitted:

My two younger children spent much of their time watching the neighbor's television. In a year or two, when my youngest son had graduated from a local junior high school, he wanted to go away to school. I believe, if I had purchased a television set at that time, he would have finished high school here in Washington.[15]

Similar sentiments were expressed in audience research of the day. In *The Age of Television* (1956), Leo Bogart summarized a wide range of audience studies that showed many Americans believed television would revive domestic life. Drawing upon these findings, Bogart concluded that social scientific surveys "agree completely that television has had the effect of keeping the family at home more than formerly."[16] The respondents in studies around the country testified to the particular ways that television enhanced their family life. In a 1950 study of families from Evanston, Illinois, one parent claimed that television "has given the children a happier home where they can laugh," while another admitted, "My two 16-year-olds like to stay home now. I'm so glad, as I would not know where they were otherwise."[17]

Popular magazines publicized, and perhaps encouraged, such sentiments by advising parents on ways to use television as a tool for family cohesion. In 1948, *Parents Magazine* (which generally took a favorable attitude toward television) published the advice of April Ella Codel, who claimed that television repaired the damage radio had done in her home:

> Our family is rather closely knit, anyhow, yet with practically every room having a radio, it was not uncommon for all to scatter to enjoy particular programs. With the one television set, our family is brought together as a unit for a while after dinner.

The following year, another author for *Parents Magazine* claimed, "All the mothers I have talked to are enthusiastic about television for their children. Certainly it has brought back the family circle in the living room." And in 1955 *Better Homes and Gardens* published a readership survey in which parents praised television's ability to unify the family.[18]

Even while critics praised television as a source of domestic unity and benevolent socialization, they also worried about its harmful effects, particularly its dissemination of debased knowledge and its related encouragement of passive minds and bodies. In 1951, *Better Homes and Gardens* complained that the medium's "synthetic entertainment" produced a child who was "glued to television."[19] Worse still, this new addiction would reverse good habits of hygiene, nutrition, and decorum, causing physical, mental, and social disorders. A cartoon in a 1950 issue of *Ladies' Home Journal* suggests a typical scenario. The magazine showed a little girl slumped on an ottoman and suffering from a new disease called "telebugeye." According to the caption, the child was a "pale, weak, stupid looking creature" who grew "bugeyed" from sitting and watching television for too long.[20] Perhaps responding to these concerns, advertisements for television sets depicted children spectators in scenes that associated television with the "higher arts," and some even implied that children would cultivate artistic talents by watching television. In 1951, General Electric showed a little girl, dressed in a tutu, imitating an on-screen ballerina, while Truetone showed a little boy learning to play the saxophone by watching a professional horn player on television.[21]

As the popular wisdom often suggested, the child's passive addiction to television might itself lead to the opposite effect of increased aggression. According to this logic, television decreased children's intellectual abilities, leaving them vulnerable to its unsavory content. The discussions followed in the wake of critical and social scientific theories of the 1930s and 1940s that suggested mass media inject ideas and behavior into passive individuals. The popular press circulated stories about a six-year-old who asked his father for real bullets because his sister didn't die when he shot her with his toy gun, a seven-year-old who put ground glass in the family's lamb stew, a nine-year-old who proposed killing his teacher with a box of poison chocolates, an eleven-year-old who shot his television set with his B.B. gun, a thirteen-year-old who stabbed her mother with a kitchen knife, and a sixteen-year-old babysitter who strangled a sleeping child to death—all, of course, after witnessing similar murders on television.[22] In reaction to the popular furor, as early as 1950, the Television Broadcasters' Association hired a public relations firm to write protelevision press releases that emphasized the more positive types of programming television had to offer.[23] But, as I have shown elsewhere, the controversies grew more heated as grass-roots groups and government officials battled to censor the airwaves.[24] Even after the National Association of Broadcasters adopted its code in 1952 (a code that included a whole section on children), the debates continued.[25] In that same year, Representative Ezekiel Gathings of Arkansas spearheaded a House investigation of radio and television programs that presented studies demonstrating television's negative influence on youth.[26] By 1954, Estes Kefauver's Senate subcommittee hearings on juvenile delinquency were investigating television's relationship to the perceived increase in youth crimes, focusing particularly on the "ideas that spring into the living room for the entertainment of the youth of America, which have to do with crime and with horror, sadism, and sex."[27] In the face of such criticism, parental control over children's use of this new medium and the knowledge it disseminated emerged as a number-one concern.

Mastering the Child

The anxieties about television's effects on youth were connected to more general fears about its disruption of generational roles, particularly with regard to power struggles over what constituted proper children's entertainment. At the 1952 House hearings, for example, government officials expressed their discomfort with programming that they found offensive, but that delighted the hearts of children. When describing *You Asked for It* (a half-hour variety format premised on viewers' requests to see various acts), Ezekiel Gathings claimed that while most of the program was "wholesome . . . something like a vaudeville show," he could not abide one act that featured "a grass-skirted young lady and a thinly clad gentleman dancing the hoochie-coochie. They danced to a very lively tune and shook the shimmy. . . . My children saw that, and I could not get it turned off to save my life."[28] This problem of controlling children's program choices was voiced more generally by popular critics, who warned that television might disrupt family unity by inverting the power dynamics between children and adults. According to this logic, the television image had usurped the authority previously held by parents. As television critic John Crosby claimed, "You tell little Oscar to trot off to bed, and you will probably find yourself embroiled in argument. But if Milton Berle tells him to go to bed, off he goes."[29]

Women's magazines published articles and cartoons showing how parents might lose dominion over TV-addicted children who refused to eat dinner, go to bed, contribute to family conversations, finish their chores, or do their homework.[30] In 1950, *New York Times* critic Jack Gould wrote, "Mealtime is an event out of the ordinary for the television parent; for the child it may just be out." In that same year, a cartoon in *Better Homes and Gardens* showed parents seated at the dining room table while their children sat in the living room, glued to the television set. Speaking from the point of view of the exasperated mother, the caption read, "All right, that does it! Harry, call up the television store and tell them to send a truck right over!"[31]

Television's potential inversion of power relationships between child and adult gave way to humorous speculations about the ways in which adults themselves were becoming more like children. In numerous popular comedies of the period, parents—especially fathers—were shown to regress to a childlike state after watching too much television. In a 1955 episode of *The Adventures of Ozzie and Harriet* titled "The Pajama Game," Ozzie Nelson and his sons, Ricky and David, are shown seated before the TV set. The boys are able to do complicated algebra formulas while watching television, and they maintain their general capabilities for industrious behavior. Ozzie, on the other hand, becomes mesmerized by television, and after his wife Harriet has already gone to bed, he decides to read a novelization of the movie he had been watching on television most of the night. The next morning, Ozzie is in a stupor, unable to wake up on schedule. The episode thus humorously inverts the popular fear that television would interfere with children's activities. Now it is the father who is unable to use the new medium in a responsible, adult way.

In 1954, *Fireside Theatre*, a filmed anthology drama series, evoked a similar theme in an episode titled "The Grass Is Greener." Based on the simple life of a farm family, the program begins with the purchase of a television set, a purchase that the father, Bruce, adamantly opposes. Going against Bruce's wishes, his wife, Irene, makes use of the local retailer's credit plan and has a television set installed in her home. When Bruce returns home for the evening, he finds himself oddly displaced by the new center of interest as his family sits enthralled by a TV western. When he attempts to get their attention, his son hushes him with a dismissive "Shh," after which the family resumes its fascination with the television program. Not only does Bruce lose control over his youngsters, but in the next scene, he actually regresses to the behavior of his children when he too finds himself enthralled by a TV western, slumped in an easy chair, passively addicted to the new medium.

The most explicit and humorous case of infantilization took place in the first episode of *The Honeymooners*, "TV or Not TV" (1955), when Alice and Ralph Kramden chip in with neighbor Ed Norton to buy a television set. Ralph and Norton become classic couch potatoes, sprawled before the set and enthralled by mindless entertainment. Midway into the teleplay, Ralph sits before the TV set with a smorgasbord of snacks, ready to tune in to a movie. But Norton has other ideas; he wants to watch the children's serial *Captain Video*. Norton takes out his Captain Video helmet and begins reciting the club member pledge, promising Captain Video to obey his mommy and daddy and drink milk after every meal. In case the sense of male regression is not yet clear enough, at the end of the episode Alice scolds the men, saying, "Stop acting like babies and try to grow up a little." Finally, Ralph and Norton fall asleep before the set and Alice tucks them in for the night covering them with a blanket and shaking her head with motherly condescension.

While the infantilized fathers that such television programs portrayed might have been hyperbolic, they spoke to a more general set of anxieties about television's inversion of the power dynamics between adults and children. Summarizing parents' attitudes toward television, Leo Bogart claimed, "There is a feeling, never stated in so many words, that the set had a power of its own to control the destinies and viewing habits of the audience, and that what it 'does' to parents and children alike is somehow beyond the bounds of any individual set-owner's power of control."[32] In this context, popular media offered solace by showing parents how they could reclaim power in their own homes—if not over the medium, then at least over their children. Television opened up a whole array of disciplinary measures that parents might exert over their youngsters.[33]

Indeed, the bulk of discussions about children and television were offered in the context of mastery. If the machine could control the child, then so could the parent. Here, the language of common sense provided some reassurance by reminding parents that it was they, after all, who were in command. As Jack Gould wrote in 1949, "It takes a human hand to turn on a television set."[34] But for parents who needed a bit more than just the soothing words of a popular sage, the media ushered in specialists from a wide range of fields; child psychologists, educators, psychiatrists, and broadcasters recommended ways to stave off the evils of the new medium.

At the heart of the advice on children and television was a marked desire to keep childhood as a period distinct from adulthood. Critics of the medium feared that television might abolish such distinctions by making children privy to adult secrets. In 1951, television critic Robert Lewis Shayon claimed, "Television is the shortest cut yet devised, the most accessible backdoor to the grownup world."[35] More generally, the issue of accessibility became the primary cause for alarm. Television's immediate availability in the home threatened to abolish childhood by giving children equal access to the ideas and values circulated in the adult culture. In 1950, Phyllis Cerf, the wife of the publisher of *Parents Magazine*, claimed that "television, like candy, is wonderful, provided you don't have too much of it. You can run out of candy, or carefully place it out of your children's reach, but television, once it has come into your home, can go on and on."[36] If Cerf addressed the problem of accessibility mostly through fears about the quantity of television that children consumed, others also worried about the quality of messages that it distributed to old and young alike. Television, it was often suggested, failed to discriminate among its audiences; it addressed all family members with the same message. As *Parents Magazine* claimed in 1952:

> A large part of what children see and hear is intended mainly for adult eyes and ears. Of the things that are intended for children, many are unsuitable or questionable. Some people see no problems or dangers in this. "TV keeps the children from underfoot," they say. Or "TV keeps Billy off the streets. It's a built-in baby sitter." But other adults are concerned. "It's not healthy. All day long it's machine guns, murder and gangs. You can't tell me children don't get dangerous ideas from TV."[37]

As such statements imply, television increased parental dilemmas because it undermined their dominion over the kinds of knowledge that their children might acquire.

In the wake of such criticism, popular media advised parents how to protect their young by filtering out television's undesirable elements. One method of purification came in the form of disciplining the child's use of television by establishing a schedule. Drawing on cognitive and behavioralist theories of childhood that had been popular since the 1920s, and mixing these with the liberal approach of Dr. Spock, the experts recommended ways for parents to instill healthy viewing habits in their children, advising methods of punishment and reward that would reinforce particular viewing routines that adults deemed appropriate for youngsters.

But even if children adopted "healthy" viewing habits and routines, they still might see programs unsuited for innocent eyes, particularly in the early 1950s, when crime, mystery, and sexually suggestive programs often appeared during early prime-time hours. Thus, experts advised parents on how to establish a canon of wholesome programs. A readership survey in *Better Homes and Gardens* indicated that some parents had, in fact, set standards for appropriate and inappropriate entertainment:

> Forty percent of all the parents answering do not approve of some of the programs their children would like to see—chiefly crime, violent mystery or horror, western, and "emotional" programs. . . .
>
> About one-fourth of the parents insist on their children viewing special events on TV. In this category they mention parades, children shows, educational programs, great artists, and theater productions.[38]

In many ways this canon of good and bad TV recalled Victorian notions of ideal family recreation. Overly exciting stimuli threatened to corrupt the child, while educational and morally uplifting programs were socially sanctioned. In the years to come, magazines such as *Reader's Digest* and *Saturday Review* internalized this canon of wholesome and culturally enriching programs, particularly giving their seal of approval to educational fare such as *Ding Dong School* and *Captain Kangaroo*. In all cases, critical judgments were based on adult standards. Indeed, this hierarchy of television programs is symptomatic of the more general efforts to establish an economy of pleasure for children spectators that suited adult concepts of appropriate children's entertainment.

The idea that fun should promote industrious behavior rather than passive reflection was paramount in critical discussions. According to a 1954 article in *Parents Magazine*, the best shows are " 'programs designed for children with understanding of their growth and development, and which give, if possible, some opportunity for participation.' "[39] With this assumption in mind, *Parents Magazine* commended programs with drawing and essay contests, claiming that they promoted active forms of play:

> The idea of the drawing program—what used to be called "Chalk Talks" in the old Chatauqua days—promises to become very popular on television. WJZ-TV and its affiliates show *Cartoon Teletales*, with one artist drawing illustrations for stories told by his companion. On WABD New York's *Small Fry Club*, and WTMJ Milwaukee's *Children's Corner*, drawings sent in by children are shown on the screen. And on WCBS-TV there is a program which shows real television originality and inspires creative activity by the young audience: *Scrapbook, Jr. Edition*; among its features is a cartoon strip beginning a new adventure story, and the children are asked to write in their ideas for an ending; then the winning conclusion is drawn by the artist in another cartoon strip show the following week.[40]

Such programs acted as a Band-Aid cure for the deeper political and economic demands of commercial broadcasting's one-way communication structure. But, while television critics frequently argued that children's shows should encourage participatory forms of play, they never demanded that adult programming should elicit these active forms of reception. Perhaps in this sense, adults wished to protect their young from the undemocratic aspects of their one-way commercial broadcast system, even while they accepted that system as the dominant forum for communication.

The critical expectations for children's television voiced in magazines like *Parents* tell us more about adult taste standards than they do about what children actually found pleasurable. Indeed, adults seem to have watched the shows supposedly aimed at children. Since children's shows were often scheduled during late afternoon and early evening hours, adults would have ample occasion to view these programs. *Kukla, Fran and Ollie*, for example, had a strong appeal for grownups, so much so that when NBC attempted to split it into two fifteen-minute shows in 1951, the network was, in the words of one executive, "swamped" with audience mail from angry adults. Robert G. Pilkington, an insurance underwriter, wrote to the network, complaining:

> I have read with interest your general letter sent to me among others in answer to the protests regarding Kukla, Fran and Ollie [sic]. . . .
> The biggest reason for the change is obviously the greater revenue that can be

derived from two 15-minute shows, combined with the lack of sponsorship on many stations. Which leads me to inquire, what is the matter with your Sales Department? Regardless of the popular conception that radio and television is directed to the 12-year-old mentality, there is a large enough segment of your viewing audience appreciative of the KFO type show and buying its sponsors' products to warrant a sales effort in its direction. After one program, I went out, simply in appreciation, and immediately bought some of the goods advertised.

Who ever got the idea that Kukla, Fran, and Ollie is a juvenile show? It's an adult program, pure and simple, and contains too many subtleties to be successful completely except with that mind. Maybe your salesmen and sponsors overlooked that little detail.[41]

Mr. Pilkington's acknowledgment of his enjoyment of a children's show is vivid testimony to the paradox at the heart of television's attempts to make distinctions between adults' and children's narrative pleasures. While cultural ideals may have dictated that those pleasures be kept apart, in practice the situation was never so clearcut. Adults seemed to enjoy what children should have liked, and children seemed to like the very things that adults deemed inappropriate juvenile entertainment.

Perhaps for this reason, the impartation of adult tastes onto children became the number-one goal in the popular media of the time. As Serafina Bathrick has argued, *Parents Magazine* showed mothers how to be "TV guides" who helped their children develop the right sensibilities.[42] In 1954, for example, the magazine claimed:

> We can only hope to cultivate good taste in our children by developing good taste in ourselves and helping our children to be sure to see the programs that are good programs.... Parents can accomplish a lot by pointing out sequences of bad taste, by reacting themselves to elements of bad taste, by appreciating aloud or indirectly programs which are in good taste.... as one expert put it, "Children cannot be protected, in life, from exposure to unwholesome influences, but they can be taught how to recognize and deal with them when they are exposed."[43]

Thus, according to the popular wisdom, by elevating children's taste standards, parents could better regulate the undesirable elements of mass culture. Even if they could not control entirely their children's access to the kinds of messages circulated by television, they could, at least, ensure that children internalized their parents' sensibilities toward program content. Revealingly in this regard, an audience study conducted in Columbus, Ohio, reported that parents found it particularly important to regulate the program choices of pre-and grade-schoolers, but high school students received less parental supervision because "their program tastes apparently are considerably closer to those of their parents."[44]

This preoccupation with the establishment of taste standards reflected a class bias. Summarizing numerous social scientific studies, Leo Bogart claimed that it was mainly the middle class who feared television's influence on children and that while "people of higher social position, income and education are more critical of existing fare in radio, television and the movies ... those at the lower end of the social scale are more ready to accept what is available." But even if he believed that discriminating taste was a function of class difference, Bogart internalized the elitist preoccupation with canon formation, lending professional credence to the idea that adults should restrict their children's viewing to what they deemed "respectable" culture. As he suggested:

> If television cannot really be blamed for turning children into criminals or neurotics, this does not imply that it is a wholly healthful influence on the growing child. A much more serious charge is that television, in the worst aspects of its content, helps to perpetuate moral, cultural and social values which are not in accord with the highest ideals of an enlightened democracy. The cowboy film, the detective thriller and the soap opera, so often identified by critics as the epitome of American mass culture, probably do not represent the heritage which Americans at large want to transmit to posterity.[45]

Thus, while Bogart noted that working-class parents did not find a need to discriminate among programs, and that the formation of critical standards was mainly a middle-class pursuit, he nevertheless decided that television programs would not please the value systems of "Americans at large." Here, as elsewhere, the notion of an enlightened democracy served to justify the hegemony or bourgeois tastes and the imparting of those tastes onto children of all classes.

For their part, children often seemed to have different ideas. Like Senator Gathings's youngsters who wanted to watch dancers do the "hootchie coochie," children respondents in audience studies often claimed to prefer programs their parents found unwholesome, especially science fiction serials and westerns. Surveys also indicated that children often liked to watch programs aimed at adults and that "parents were often reluctant to admit that their children watched adult shows regularly."[46] Milton Berle's *Texaco Star Theater* (which was famous for its inclusion of "off-color" cabaert humor) became so popular with children that Berle adopted the persona of Uncle Miltie, pandering to parents by telling his juvenile audience to obey their elders and go straight to bed when the program ended.[47] But other programs were unable to bridge the generation gap. When, for example, CBS aired the mystery anthology *Suspense*, affiliates across the country received letters from concerned parents who wanted the program taken off the air. Attempting to please its adult constituency, one Oklahoma station was caught in the cross fire between parents and children. When the station announced it would not air "horror story" programs before the bedtime hour of 9:00 p.m., it received a letter with the words "We protest!" signed by twenty-two children.[48]

The Children's Hour

If the adult culture attempted to distinguish children's entertainment from adult shows, the actual children's programming that emerged in this period was based largely on the dissolution of age categories. Children's programs were filled with liminal characters, characters that existed somewhere in between child and adult, as the shows played with the cultural concepts of childhood that circulated at the time. Indeed, the pleasure encouraged by these programs was rooted in the transgression of taboos and regulations found in the advice literature aimed at adults.

In the TV playhouse, adults functioned for the sole purpose of fulfilling the child's wish. If in everyday life adults represented rules, knowledge, and the threat of punishment, on television they represented mayhem, entertainment, and prizes. On *Howdy Doody* (1947–60, NBC), host Buffalo Bob was ambiguously a grownup and a *cowboy*, who, like Peter Pan, had not abandoned the land of make-believe. Indeed, children's programs had their own never-never lands— impossible places like "Doodyville," places that mocked the confines of real domestic space.[49] Then, too, children's shows set aside the mundane nature of real time by presenting children with the marvelous antics of "Howdy Doody time," a time in which youngsters need not do their homework, go to bed, or wash behind their ears. In fact, *Howdy Doody* began with a cartoon depiction of a cuckoo clock—literally going cuckoo—as the hands span feverishly around the dial, signaling the temporary abandonment of the normal schedule for the next thirty minutes of fantastic clowns and puppets.

Johnny Jupiter (1953–54, DuMont and NBC) similarly transported children from the confines of their living room into a magical world. Johnny was a puppet who lived on Jupiter with his pals Reject the Robot and Major Domo. At their outerspace television station, Johnny, Reject, and Major Domo were contacted by earthling Ernest Duckweather, a teenage techno-nerd who invented a magic television set on which he spoke with his Jupiterian pals. Ernest was a 1950s Peewee, a liminal figure who straddled the categories of child and adult. And like Pee-wee (although without the campy wink), Ernest suffered from a case of arrested sexual development, underscored in numerous episodes by his disinterest in the advances of his boss's daughter. Johnny, like other children's hosts, played with the fantasy of childhood itself, presenting himself as a half boy/half man who defended himself against the constraints and cares of the grownup world.

By blurring the boundaries between adult and child identities, such programs presented a ripe environment through which to address children as consumers. As both authority figures and wish fulfillment, the casts of clowns and cowboys promised children a peek at toys and sweets behind their mothers' backs. The children's show was a candy store populated by dream parents who pandered forbidden products. Even more important, these programs taught children the art of persuasion, advising them how to tell their parents about the wondrous items advertised on the show. In a 1958 episode of *Howdy Doody*, for example, Buffalo Bob chats about Hostess Cupcakes with Howdy, who marvels at the delicious creamy centers. Bob then directly addresses the children at home, telling them to "make sure to tell your mom to put a package of Hostess Cupcakes in your lunch box when you go to school, or ask her to buy some as a special reward sometime during the week." In this imaginary transaction between Buffalo Bob and the child audience, the parent becomes a functionary through which the child accomplishes consumer goals. Children are taught how to influence their parents' product choices, and in the process the child's narrative pleasure is inextricably intertwined with the pleasure of consumption.

Winky Dink and You, (1953–57, CBS), a cult classic of 1950s TV, took this consumer logic to its extreme by making the program completely dependent upon the product it advertised. Winky was a flatly drawn Tinkerbell-like cartoon character who cohosted the show with the real-life Jack Barry. Although by current standards extremely low-tech in nature, the program was premised on an interactive use of television technology. *Winky Dink* offered children the possibility of drawing on the television set through the purchase of a special Winky Dink kit, complete with rub-off crayons, an erasing cloth, and the all-important "magic window," a piece of tinted plastic that, when sufficiently rubbed by the child's hands, stuck to the television screen. With this apparatus in place, the child could draw along to the animation on the screen, perhaps filling in features on cartoon characters' faces or completing story narratives by drawing in the necessary scenery and props. In a 1953 episode, Jack Barry showed children how the whole thing worked by picking up a remote feed from the home of Helen, a little girl in Pittsburgh, Pennsylvania. Helen demonstrated how the kit worked, and Barry reminded children (and no doubt their parents as well) of the prosocial skills that would be learned on the show. After Helen erected her plastic screen, Barry told the children at home to "share your Winky Dink kits" by evenly dividing the crayons. And, at a time when television was considered a major cause of eyestrain, Barry told the audience to "notice how that plastic is lightly tinted. That makes it much easier to watch our television show, even for your parents." The consumer message of the show was thus tempered with the rhetoric of public service. In the middle commercial, this mixture of commercialism and goodwill was drawn out in a long speech delivered by Barry, who looked directly into the camera to address the children at home:

> I tell you what, if you had your Winky Dink kits and played along with us, well, there's no reason for any of us to miss all the fun. It's so easy to get your Winky Dink kits. And, you know something, the fun starts as soon as you get your kit. Of course, you can watch the program without a kit, but you can't really be a part of the program without 'em. And you can't have the fun that the other boys and girls who have their Winky Dink kits do have. Now, I know you're just used to watching television shows and you just sit back and watch all the other shows, but not this show. This show you really get a chance to be a part of 'cause it's different. You get a chance at home to play right along with us, and what you at home draw actually becomes part of the program. But to be a part of the show, you must have one of our Winky Dink kits [Barry holds up the kit and describes its contents].

Thus, the product pitch worked by drawing on the popular fears that television made children passive. Like the "chalk talks" applauded by *Parents Magazine*, *Winky Dink* encouraged participation from children, but participation came at a price. Buying the Winky Dink kit, the ad suggested, would ensure that children took an active part in the communication process, and with this prosocial message intact, Barry went on to pander to the child audience in the most crass and unabashed way. Still holding up the kit, he exclaimed:

Now boys and girls you *must* have this kit, and here's how you get it. Mark down the addr.·ss, will you? To get this Winky Dink kit for yourself or for your friends, you send fifty cents [Barry holds up a sign with fifty cents boldy printed on it]. Boys and girls, send fifty cents, got that? Fifty cents, with your name and address [Barry holds up a sign that says to print your name and address] and send it to Winky Dink, Box 5, New York 19, New York [Barry holds up a sign with the address]. Now, I do hope you'll all get your Winky Dink kit right away because you really can't have as much fun as if you have a kit.

Programs such as *Howdy Doody* and *Winky Dink* were products of a world in which the age limits of consumption were shifting, a world in which parents had less and less control over the kinds of objects children would desire and potentially own. Just as Jack Barry saw little need to worry where children would possibly get the fifty cents needed to purchase his kit, other industrialists were increasingly appealing directly to children, assuming that they would either buy products on their own or use their powers of persuasion to coax parents into purchasing them. In the postwar years, teenagers, who often held after school jobs, became a viable market for low-ticket consumer items such as clothing, makeup, and records.[50] And even in the case of high-ticket items—especially household commodities—advertisers discovered that tapping into the new consumer power of children and teens was also a way to urge adults to buy more. An editor of *Home Furnishings* (the furniture retailers' trade journal) claimed, "The younger generation from one to twenty influences the entire home furnishings industry."[51]

Children especially were considered to have "nagging" power in family purchases of television sets. Surveys indicated that families with children tended to buy televisions more than childless couples did. Television manufacturers quickly assimilated the new findings into their sales techniques. As early as 1948, the industry trade journal *Advertising and Selling* reported that the manager of public relations and advertising at the manufacturing company Stromberg-Carlson, "quoted a survey . . . indicating that children not only exert a tremendous amount of influence in the selection and purchase of television receivers but that they are, in fact, television's most enthusiastic audience."[52] Basing their advertisements on such surveys, manufacturers and retailers formulated strategies by which to convince parents to buy products for the sake of their children. In 1950, the American Television Dealers and Manufacturers ran nationwide newspaper advertisements that played on parental guilt. The first ad in the series had a headline that read, "Your daughter won't ever tell you the humiliation she's felt in begging those precious hours of television from a neighbor." Forlorn children were pictured on top of the layout, and parents were shown how television could raise their youngsters' spirits. This particular case is especially interesting because it shows that there are indeed limits to which advertisers can go before a certain degree of sales resistance takes place. Outraged by the advertisement, parents, educators, and clergymen complained to their newspapers about its manipulative tone. In addition, the Family Service Association of America called it a "cruel pressure to apply against millions of parents" who could not afford television sets.[53]

Not surprisingly, the area of consumerism remains one of the most heatedly debated in the discourse on television and youth. Commercials induct the child into the market, and market values appear to be in direct opposition to conceptions of childhood innocence.[54] Yet, once again, while adults historically have argued against the commercialization of children's television, they too have been seduced by its consumer fantasies. Indeed, since the 1950s, children's programs have found ways to draw adults into the joys of spending money by offering them a ticket for a nostalgic return to a childhood dreamland of make-believe.

The appearance of *The Mickey Mouse Club* in the 1955 fall season is an emblematic example. This show and its 1954 predecessor, *Disneyland*, were created as one big advertisement for Walt Disney's theme park in Anaheim, California. Despite the blatant commercialism of *Disneyland*, it won a Peabody Award for its educational value and an Emmy for best adventure series, and was among the top ten programs in the ratings. Not surprisingly, the program's success paved the way for a new surge of sponsor interest in other children's fare. In its first season, *The Mickey Mouse Club* was similarly successful, although some television critics were initially wary of its Disney product endorsements and its overabundance of commercials (critic Jack Gould was outraged that the premier episode had about twenty ads, one of which cut off a Pluto cartoon).[55] Still, its syrupy dose of prosocial themes—respect for elders, family values, courage—must have tempered adult fears about the commercial aspects of the show.[56]

Like other children's programs, *The Mickey Mouse Club* contained a set of liminal characters that played with culturally prescribed generational roles. The opening credits began with Mickey Mouse himself, who then introduced the Mouseketeers, an odd blend of children—from toddlers to teens—and grown-ups Roy and Jimmy, who dressed just like the children in mouse ears and T-shirts. And like *Howdy Doody*, *The Mickey Mouse Club* existed in a kind of never-never land. But it took the concept one step further by promising children that its never-never land could in fact become a virtual reality, a real place where children might venture—that is, if they could persuade their parents to take them to Southern California. Of course, as with other Disney products, the theme park was predicated on the pleasure of playing with the culturally prescribed distinctions between child and adult. Disneyland was a place where adults could rediscover the joys of youth in fantasy replicas of narrative spaces (like Frontierland, Fantasyland, and Tomorrowland), which they once traversed in storybooks and movies. The roller coasters and teacup rides offered adults the chance to shake up their conceptions of normal time and space, to look at the world from the perspective of childhood exhilaration and curiosity. Indeed, the fact that Disneyland was promoted as a place of family amusement reminds us that the liminality of children's entertainment is often just as appealing to adults as it is to children. Moreover, as the biggest tourist attraction of the 1950s, Disneyland was dramatic proof that despite the arguments against it, children's commercial entertainment could be marketed as wholesome fun for the entire family.[57]

The End of the Innocence?

The controversy that surrounded children's television in the 1950s, and the assumption that children's viewing pleasures should be monitored by adults, continued into the next decades with increased force. In 1961, one of the first and most influential book-length studies of the subject, *Television in the Lives of Our Children*, reported that by the sixth grade children spent almost as much time watching television as they did in school. Moreover, authors Wilbur Schramm, Jack Lyle, and Edwin B. Parker speculated that television might contribute to "premature aging" by encouraging American youth to grow up too fast. The boundaries between children and adults might blur, particularly because, as the authors noted, children often watched programs that were made for an adult audience.[58]

As the 1960s came to a close, critics who grew up in the turmoil of the new youth movement began to blame television for the perceived generation gap between themselves and their parents. In his 1973 book *No Peace, No Place: Excavations along the Generational Fault*, Jeff Greenfield claimed that television threatened to abolish childhood innocence because it allowed youngsters to "eavesdrop" on adult secrets. Similarly, in *Looking Back: A Chronicle of Growing Up Old in the Sixties*, Joyce Maynard said that television played a major role in her premature sophistication.[59] And more recently, in *No Sense of Place*, Joshua Meyrowitz has claimed that television contributes to a "blurring of childhood and adulthood." According to Meyrowitz, television not only exposes "many adult secrets to children," it also "reveals the 'secret of secrecy.'" For example, Meyrowitz argues that by broadcasting warnings about programs that children are not supposed to see, television lets young viewers know exactly what is being forbidden. Television, in other words, makes children privy to the fact that adults are hiding knowledge from them.[60]

While debates about children and television continue to base themselves around the ideal of childhood innocence, the industrial producers of children's culture have learned more sophisticated ways to tap into children's enjoyment of entertainment that adults deem inappropriate. The 1950s debates over comics and television did not destroy the popularity of magazines such as *Mad*, nor did they diminish the next generation's penchant for the perverse pleasures of Ugly Stickers and Wacky Packs. The recent merchandising of "Toxic High" stickers, a set of Topps trading cards based on the perverse, violent, and authority-bucking antics at a typical high school, is a case in point. Cartoonist Mark Newgarden (also the brains behind the popular Garbage Pail Kids) admits gleefully, "We did a focus test where we showed it to kids behind one of those two-way mirrors, and the kids went wild for it. And then we showed it to their mothers, and their mothers were aghast."[61] As this "tasteless test" suggests, the strength of a child's toy is now predictable in part by the degree to which the parent disapproves.

Broadcast television has emerged, perhaps, as a more "protected" arena. At the time of this writing, the reform group Action for Children's Television (ACT) has discontinued its two-decade attempt to raise children's program standards. According to the organization's founder, Peggy Charin, ACT's work has been accomplished with the recent passing of the Children's Television Act, which mandates broadcasters' responsibility to young viewers. Ironically, however, these gains come at a time when more and more children are finding their entertainment outside the auspices of broadcast television. Now, cable television, VCRs, and Nintendo games offer youngsters alternative venues for pleasure, venues about which critics are more and more anxious.[62] And, as in the 1950s, such anxieties revolve around the central problem of keeping childhood separate from adulthood. In an episode of *The Simpsons*, for example, precocious son Bart is shown charging his school pals twenty-five cents to watch the Playboy channel on cable TV, while in another episode he beats his father Homer at a video game, to the degree that Homer is reduced to a child, yelling and screaming because he can't score points.

Like the child-saving movement in the early part of this century, the anxieties about children as victims of television and the urge to reform the commercial nature and degrading content of electronic media often have humanitarian goals. But, as in the past, this humanitarian urge is no more than a Band-Aid cure for the public's larger disempowerment and alienation from the channels of expression in our country. In fact, since the inception of television as a privately controlled commercial medium, the American public has rarely argued against its basic corporate structure. Little was said about the fact that television technology (with its inherent capability for two-way communication) was being developed as a one-way medium used mostly for the financial gain of major corporations.[63] Instead, the only widespread challenge to commercialization of the airwaves has taken place in the name of the child. The child in this configuration becomes an alibi and a conduit for larger issues regarding the commercialization of communication and the price tags attached to free speech on our country's mass media. The discourse of victimization that surrounds the child viewer might, in this sense, usefully be renamed and reinvestigated as a discourse of power through which adults express their own disenfranchisement from our nation's dominant mode of communication.

NOTES

1. Jacqueline Rose, *The Case of Peter Pan: The Impossibility of Children's Fiction* (London: Macmillan, 1984).

2. It should be noted that many films of this period—particularly film noir and family melodrama—depicted dysfunctional families, showing, for instance, how infidelity, missing parents, overprotective mothers, or henpecked fathers could cause destruction for

child and parent alike. See, for example, *Rebel without a Cause* (Nicholas Raye, 1955) or *Mildred Pierce* (Michael Curtiz, 1945).

3. In the early 1950s, the median marriage age ranged between twenty and twenty-one; the average family started having children in the beginning of the second year of marriage and had three to four children. For birthrates, see Rochelle Gatlin, *American Women since 1945* (Jackson: University Press of Mississippi, 1987), 51, 55, 61; Susan M. Hartmann, *American Women in the 1940s: The Home Front and Beyond* (Boston: Twayne, 1982), 25, 91, 170, 213; Glenna Matthews, *"Just a Housewife": The Rise and Fall of Domesticity in America* (New York: Oxford University Press, 1987), 265; Elaine Tyler May, *Homeward Bound: American Families in the Cold War Era* (New York: Basic Books, 1988), 7, 136–37. On marriage and divorce rates, see Hartmann, *American Women in the 1940s*, 163–65; Gatlin, *American Women since 1945*, 51; and Tyler May, *Homeward Bound*, 6–8, 21, 59, 117, 185.

4. For a detailed study of the social construction of childhood, see Philippe Aries, *Centuries of Childhood: A Social History of Family Life*, trans. Robert Baldick (New York: Vintage, 1962).

5. Beatrice Hale, cited in Barbara Ehrenreich and Deirdre English, *For Her Own Good: 150 Years of the Experts' Advice to Women* (Garden City, N.Y.: Anchor, 1978), 194. Also see Ehrenreich and English's description of the mothers' movement, 192–96.

6. See Margaret Marsh, *Suburban Lives* (New Brunswick, N.J.: Rutgers University Press, 1990) and her article "Suburban Men and Masculine Domesticity, 1870–1915," *American Quarterly* 40 (June 1988): 70–83.

7. The phrase "century of the child" was used to describe the twentieth century's child-centeredness in Arthur W. Calhoun, *Social History of the American Family*, vol. 3, *Since the Civil War* (Cleveland: Arthur H. Clark, 1919), 131.

8. For a good overview of child saving in the early decades of the twentieth century, see Hamilton Cravens, "Child-Saving in the Age of Professionalism, 1915–1930," in *American Childhood: A Research Guide and Historical Handbook*, ed. Joseph M. Hawes and N. Ray Hiner (Westport, Conn.: Greenwood, 1985), 415–88.

9. Ehrenreich and English, *For Her Own Good*, 183–211.

10. The links between power and the regularization of knowledge through discourse runs throughout Foucault's body of research and methodological works. For a series of interviews with Foucault about these broad interests, see Michel Foucault, *Power/Knowledge: Selected Interviews and Other Writings 1972–1977*, ed. Colin Gordon, trans. Colin Gordon et al. (New York: Pantheon, 1977).

11. For more on this, see Mark West, *Children, Culture and Controversy* (Hamden, Conn.: Archon, 1988); Richard deCordova, "Ethnography and Exhibition: The Child Audience, the Hays Office and Saturday Matinees," *Camera Obscura* 23 (May 1990): 91–107.

12. For more on this and other aspects of the public concern over juvenile delinquents, see James Gilbert, *A Cycle of Outrage: America's Reaction to the Juvenile Delinquent in the 1950s* (New York: Oxford University Press, 1986). Gilbert shows that while public officials, educators, psychologists, and other "experts" increasingly focused on criminal youth, "the incidence of juvenile crime does not appear to have increased enormously during this period." Gilbert goes on to show that crime statistics were imprecise and, since the definition of juvenile crime and the policing of it had changed over the course of the century, it is difficult to prove that the postwar period actually witnessed a substantial rise in teenage crimes. Given this, Gilbert argues that the perception of juvenile delinquency in the 1950s was based less on reality than on the way crime was labeled and reported, as well as the general worries about the future direction of American society (pp. 66–71).

13. For more on Spock's popularity and influence, see Charles E. Strickland and Andrew M. Ambrose, "The Changing Worlds of Children, 1945–1963," in *American Childhood: A Research Guide and Historical Handbook*, ed. Joseph M. Hawes and N. Ray Hiner (Westport, Conn.: Greenwood, 1985), 538–44. Strickland and Ambrose also point out that while it is impossible to say exactly how many parents actually practiced Spock's teachings, anthropological and psychological studies conducted during the period suggest that many parents, particularly of the middle class, did opt for the more permissive methods of child rearing that Spock advised.

14. For more on how juvenile delinquency was blamed on mass media (especially music and film), see Gilbert, *A Cycle of Outrage*, 143–95.

15. House Interstate and Foreign Commerce Committee, *Hearings before a Subcommittee of the Committee on Interstate and Foreign Commerce: Investigation of Radio and Television Programs*, 82nd Cong., 2d Sess., H. Res. 278 (Washington, D.C.: U.S. Government Printing Office, June 3, 1952), 23. The hearings reconvened on June 4, 5, and 26, 1952; September 16, 17, 23, 24, 25, and 26, 1952; and December 3, 4, and 5, 1952.

16. Leo Bogart, *The Age of Television: A Study of Viewing Habits and the Impact of Television on American Life* (New York: Frederick Ungar, 1958[1956]), 101. As a cautionary note, I would suggest that in his attempt to present a global, synthetic picture of the television audience, Bogart often smooths over the contradictions in the studies he presents. This attempt at global synthesis goes hand in hand with Bogart's view that the television audience is a homogeneous mass and that television programming further erases distinctions. He writes, "The levelling of social differences is part of the standardization of tastes and interests to which the mass media give expression, and to which they also contribute. The ubiquitous TV antenna is a symbol of people seeking—and getting—the identical message" (p. 5). Through this logic of mass mentalities, Bogart often comes to conclusions that oversimplify the heterogeneity of audience responses in the studies he presents.

17. Paul Witty, "Children's, Parents' and Teachers' Reactions to Television," *Elementary English* 27 (October 1950): 8, cited in Bogart, *The Age of Television*, 264.

18. Ella April Codel, "Television Has Changed Our Lives," *Parents Magazine*, December 1948, 64; Henrietta Battle, "Television and Your Child," *Parents Magazine*, November 1949, 58; *Better Homes and Gardens*, October 1955, 209.

19. William Porter, "Is Your Child *Glued* to TV, Radio, Movies, or Comics?" *Better Homes and Gardens*, October 1951, 125.

20. *Ladies' Home Journal*, April 1950, 237. For a similar cartoon, see *Ladies' Home Journal*, December 1955, 164.

21. *House Beautiful*, June 1951, 8; *Life*, November 26, 1951, 11.

22. For these examples, see "Bang! You're Dead," *Newsweek*, March 21, 1955, 35; Norman Cousins, "The Time Trap," *Saturday Review of Literature*, December 24, 1949, 20; Don Wharton, "Let's Get Rid of Tele-Violence," *Parents Magazine*, April 1956, 93.

23. Edward M. Brecher, "TV, Your Children, and Your Grandchildren," *Consumer Reports*, May 1950, 231.

24. For more on early censorship campaigns, see Lynn Spigel, *Make Room for TV: Television and the Family Ideal in Postwar America* (Chicago: University of Chicago Press, 1992).

25. The networks also tried to police themselves. As early as 1948, NBC executives considered problems of standards and practices in television. *NBC Standards and Practices Bulletin — No. 7: A Report on Television Program Editing and Policy Control*, November 1948, NBC Records, Box 157, Folder 7, Wisconsin Center Historical Archives, State Historical Society, Madison. In 1951, NBC became the first network to establish standards for chil-

dren's shows, crime shows, mention of sex on programs, proper costuming, and so on. See *NBC Code*, 1951, NBC Records, Box 163, Folder 1, Wisconsin Center Historical Archives, State Historical Society, Madison. For a general explanation of the code, see "Catholic Council Plans TV Legion," 63.

26. House Interstate and Foreign Commerce Committee, *Hearings*.

27. Chairman Senator Robert C. Hendrickson, cited in Committee on the Judiciary United States Senate, *Hearings before the Subcommittee to Investigate Juvenile Delinquency: Juvenile Delinquency (Television Programs)*, 83rd Cong., 2d Sess., S. Res. 89 (Washington, D.C.: U.S. Government Printing Office, June 5, 1954), 1. The committee reconvened on October 19 and 20, 1954, and also met on April 6 and 7, 1955, to continue the debates.

28. House Interstate and Foreign Commerce Committee, *Hearings*, 10–11.

29. John Crosby, "Parents Arise! You Have Nothing to Lose but Your Sanity," in *Out of the Blue! A Book about Radio and Television* (New York: Simon & Schuster, 1952), 115. For more on television's threat to parental power, and particularly its threat to patriarchal dominion, see my book, *Make Room for TV*, and my chapter, "TV In the Family Circle: The Popular Reception of a New Medium," in *Logics of Television: Essays in Cultural Criticism*, ed. Patricia Mellencamp (Bloomington: Indiana University Press, 1990), 73–97.

30. As Ellen Wartella and Sharon Mazzarella have observed, early social scientific studies suggested that children were not simply using television in place of other media; instead, television was colonizing children's leisure time more than any other mass cultural form ever had. Social scientists found this "reorganization hypothesis" to be particularly important because it meant that television was changing the nature of children's lives, taking them away from schoolwork, household duties, family conversations, and creative play. Ellen Wartella and Sharon Mazzarella, "A Historical Comparison of Children's Use of Leisure Time," in *For Fun and Profit: The Transformation of Leisure into Consumption*, ed. Richard Butsch (Philadelphia: Temple University Press, 1990), 183–85. This reorganization hypothesis was also at the core of early studies conducted by school boards around the country, which showed that television was reducing the amount of time children spent on homework. For early school board activities, see, for example, "TV Also Alarms Cleve. Educators," *Variety*, March 22, 1950, 29; "Students Read, Sleep Less," *Variety*, April 5, 1950, 38.

31. Jack Gould, "TV Daddy and Video Mama: A Dirge," *New York Times Magazine*, May 14, 1950; 56; *Better Homes and Gardens*, September 1950, 56. Audience research showed that people claimed television was disrupting mealtimes and other traditional occasions for family interaction. See Eleanor E. MacCoby, "Television: Its Impact on School Children," *Public Opinion Quarterly* 15 (Fall 1951), 428–30, 438; Bogart, *The Age of Television*, 261.

32. Bogart, *The Age of Television*, 268.

33. In the context of Dr. Spock's popularity, discipline was often a tricky matter. One of the central theses in that book was that parents should avoid conflict to ensure that their home created a democratic environment where children felt they too had a say in family matters. In this regard, much of the disciplinary advice centered on finding ways for different family members to coexist harmoniously with television—even in the face of family squabbles over program choices and viewing duration. As I detail elsewhere, much of the expert advice on television focused on ways to avoid conflict. For example, home magazines showed women how to divide domestic space so that family members of all sexes and generations could watch television separately, without interfering with the activities of others. See chapter 2 in my book, *Make Room for TV*, and my article, "Television in the Family Circle."

34. Jack Gould, "What Is Television Doing to Us?" *New York Times Magazine*, June 12, 1949, 7. *Popular Science*, March 1955, took the logic of human agency to its literal extreme, presenting a "lock-and-key" TV that "won't work until Mama sees fit and turns it on with her key" (p. 110).

35. Robert Lewis Shayon, *Television and Our Children* (New York: Longmans Green, 1951), 37.

36. Cited in "What Shall We Do About Television? A Symposium," *Parents Magazine*, December 1950, 37.

37. Paul Witty and Harry Bricket, "Your Child and TV," *Parents Magazine*, December 1952, 37.

38. *Better Homes and Gardens*, October 1955, 202.

39. Robert M. Goldenson, "Television and Our Children—The Experts Speak Up," *Parents Magazine*, December 1954, 76.

40. Dorothy L. McFadden, "Television Comes to Our Children," *Parents Magazine*, January 1949, 74.

41. Robert G. Pilkington, letter to Sylvester L. Weaver, December 17, 1951, NBC Records, Wisconsin Center Historical Archives, State Historical Society, Madison.

42. Serafina K. Bathrick, "Mother as TV Guide," in *From Receiver to Remote Control*, ed. Matthew Geller (New York: New Museum of Contemporary Art: 1990), 23–30.

43. Goldenson, "Television and Our Children," 78.

44. Freda Postle Koch, *Children's Television Habits in the Columbus, Ohio, Area*, Television Committee, Franklin County, Ohio Section, White House Conference on Children and Youth, 1952, cited and summarized in Bogart, *The Age of Television*, 262. Specifically, the study reported that 42 percent of kindergarteners to second graders, 47 percent of fourth through eighth graders, and 26 percent of high school students said that they disagreed with parents on program choices. According to Bogart, however, the bulk of children in this study said that parents primarily established schedules for children, rather than restricting content per se (p. 263).

45. Bogart, *The Age of Television*, 289. In the 1954 Kefauver hearings, similar findings about the relationship between social class and parents' attitudes toward television were made part of the official record. See Committee on the Judiciary United States Senate, *Hearings*, 21–23.

46. The Reverend Everett C. Parker, summarizing findings from the Information Service, Central Department of Research and Survey, National Council of the Churches of Christ in the United States of America, *Parents, Children, and Television: The First Television Generation* (New York: n.p., 1954); reprinted and summarized in Committee on the Judiciary United States Senate, *Hearings*, 28. The surveys included in Bogart's account include a 1955 study from the *New York Herald Tribune* that studied 1,200 schoolchildren; a 1952 and 1955 study by the American Research Bureau of children ages six to sixteen; H. H. Remmars, R. E. Horton and R. E. Mainer, *Attitudes of High School Students toward Certain Aspects of Television* (Indiana: Purdue University, 1953). These are all summarized in Bogart, *The Age of Television*, 252–56. Also see the *Better Homes and Gardens* survey cited above and also summarized in Bogart.

47. For example, in 1952, the American Research Bureau observed that by the age of seven, one child in four had stayed up to watch Berle. Bogart, *The Age of Television*, 254.

48. "Kids Not Kidding," *Variety*, March 29, 1950, 33.

49. In his ethnographic study of children who watch *Pee-wee's Playhouse*, Henry Jenkins shows how similar aspects of contemporary programming might appeal to child viewers.

He claims that the ambiguity about Pee-wee's status as boy and man as well as the program's disruption of rule-governed behavior allow young viewers to work through anxieties about the day-to-day power hierarchies between children and adults as well as their own anxieties about becoming adults. See Henry Jenkins, " 'Going Bonkers!': Children, Play, and Pee-wee," *Camera Obscura* 17 (May 1988): 169–93.

50. For an overview of the rise of teenage consumer culture in the postwar period, see Thomas Doherty, *Teenagers and Teenpics: The Juvenilization of American Movies in the 1950s* (Boston: Unwin Hyman, 1988), 42–61.

51. Sylvia O'Neill, "Are You Guilty of Juvenile Delinquency?" *Home Furnishings* August 1954, 14.

52. "Video's Juvenile Audience," *Advertising and Selling*, August 1948, 99.

53. "Television Tempest," *Newsweek*, November 27, 1950, 62.

54. For two scholarly articles on the commercialization of contemporary children's culture, see Stephen Kline, "Limits to the Imagination: Marketing and Children's Culture," in *Cultural Politics in Contemporary America*, ed. Ian Angus and Sut Jhally (New York: Routledge, 1989), 299–316; Tom Englehart, "The Strawberry Shortcake Strategy," in *Watching Television*, ed. Todd Gitlin (New York: Pantheon, 1987), 74–108.

55. For a discussion of the success of *Disneyland*, see William Melody, *Children's Television: The Economics of Exploitation* (New Haven, Conn.: Yale University Press, 1973), 41; for a discussion of critical responses to the premier episode, (including Gould's), see Jerry Bowles, *Forever Hold Your Banner High! The Story of the Mickey Mouse Club and What Happened to the Mouseketeers* (Garden City, N.Y.: Doubleday, 1973), 16–17. *The Mickey Mouse Club* went off the air in 1957 and returned in syndication in 1962. Although its ratings did fall in 1956, its cancellation probably had more to do with disputes between Disney and ABC. See Bowles, 23–24.

56. In *Forever Hold Your Banner High!*, Jerry Bowles claims that "part of the show's impact had to do with its really not being a children's show at all but, rather, a show that featured children playing roles of little adults. All the values the show taught—reliability, reverence, bravery, loyalty, good behavior, the ickky-sticky grown-up stuff of romantic love—are things adults think kids like to be taught" (p. 21).

57. Disney's success with targeting a dual audience of children and adults was to become major marketing strategy by the next decade. Prime-time programs such as *The Flintstones* and *Batman* self-consciously aimed to attract different age levels by building in a range of interpretive possibilities. *Batman*, for example, was targeted to appeal as "camp" for adults and as action-adventure fantasy for children. For more on this, see Lynn Spigel and Henry Jenkins, "Same Bat Channel/Different Bat Times: Mass Culture and Popular Memory," in *The Many Lives of the Batman: Critical Approaches to a Superhero and His Media*, ed. William Uricchio and Roberta Pearson (New York: Routledge, 1991), 117–48.

58. Wilbur Schramm, Jack Lyle, and Edwin B. Parker, *Television in the Lives of Our Children* (Stanford, Calif.: Stanford University Press, 1961), 156. The authors based this speculation on numerous social scientific studies that also suggested television was making children grow up too fast.

59. Jeff Greenfield, *No Peace, No Place: Excavations along the Generational Fault* (Garden City, N.Y.: Doubleday, 1973), 114–16; Joyce Maynard, *Looking Back: A Chronicle of Growing Up Old in the Sixties* (Garden City, N.Y.: Doubleday, 1973), 51–52. Both of these books are cited in Strickland and Ambrose, "The Changing Worlds of Children," 560.

60. Joshua Meyrowitz, *No Sense of Place: The Impact of Electronic Media on Social Behavior* (New York: Oxford University Press, 1985), 247.

61. Mark Newgarden, cited in Bill Forman, "Sticker Shock," *Creem*, May 1992, 28.

62. A 1988 Nickelodian press release, "Kids Spend $15.8 Billion Annually," underscores the popularity of new technologies such as cable, VCRs, and personal computers with the younger generation. Some 72 percent of American children say they will subscribe to cable TV as adults, and among those already receiving cable in their homes, 85 percent say they will subscribe as adults. Among the 73 percent of American children in households that own VCRs, almost half (43 percent) report watching videotapes "every day or almost every day." And the press release reported that 24 percent of the nation's children own personal computers. These data were compiled by the Nickelodian/Yankelovich Youth Monitor. See the Children's Television clipping file, Doheny Cinema-Television Library, University of Southern California. In his recent book on video games, Eugene F. Provenzo, Jr., reports that video games took off in the late 1980s. For example, two years after its introduction in 1986, Nintendo had sold about 11 million units, and in 1990 alone it sold 7.2 million units. More generally, by February 1989, "16 of the 20 top selling toys in the country were video games or video-game related." See Eugene F. Provenzo, Jr., *Video Kids: Making Sense of Nintendo* (Cambridge: Harvard University Press, 1991), 8, 12. For more recent analysis of video games and children, see Marsha Kinder, *Playing with Power: In Movies, Television and Video Games* (Berkeley: University of California Press, 1991). For a general discussion of the children's marketplace in contemporary culture, see Kline, "Limits to the Imagination."

63. Although television's corporate structure was not heavily contested, there were heated debates about the commercial uses of radio broadcasting in the 1920s, and there were also alternative visions. See Robert W. McChesney, "conflict, not consensus: The Debate over Broadcast Communication Policy, 1930–1935" in Robert W. McChesney (ed.) *Ruthless Criticism* (Minneapolis; University of Minnesota Press, 1993), pp. 22–258.

Chapter Seven

Unlearning Black and White
Race, Media, and the Classroom

Shari Goldin

I have a dream that one day, down in Alabama . . .
little black boys and black girls will be able to join
hands with little white boys and white girls as sisters
and brothers. I have a dream today!
—Martin Luther King, 1963

King's words epitomize the ideals of the civil rights era—pacifism, equality, and cooperation—a dream of blacks and whites working together in harmony. Central to King's "I have a Dream" speech of 1963 is the hope that one day all children "will be able to join hands" as part of the larger family of man. The speech conflates an ideology of childhood innocence and a utopian fantasy that casts children as the bearers of cultural transformation.

Utopian images of children holding hands can be contrasted with the more dystopian accounts of children that circulate within our popular memory of the period, such as children waiting for the school bus early in the morning anticipating a long and tedious journey that will take them away from their homes and neighborhoods to an unfamiliar community, or images of federal troops escorting black youths into supposedly integrated schools in 1957 Little Rock, Arkansas. The juxtaposition of these contradictory images suggests the central role of the child within civil rights era discourse; the child both embodied the victimization experienced in a contemporary racist society and represented the vehicle for a more just society in the future. As James Kincaid has argued, children represent a "repository of cultural needs or fears not adequately disposed of elsewhere."[1] "Holding hands"—a joyous physical bond between white and black children—suggested the shared sense of freedom achieved through integration; the alternative—children standing alone, being called names—powerfully expressed adult fears of unfairness and inequality. However, the image of black and white children standing together suggests yet another role: a shared victimhood of all children to racist society and to continued adult attempts to "orient" children in certain directions, using them as tropes for political justification and as sops for popular sentiment.

Years later, Vincent Harding, who was a close participant in King's campaign and a significant historian of the civil rights movement, recounted how children played a central role in creating a new political consciousness within the black community. He recounts how black children and parents were "thrust into the center arena of the struggle," and families were put in the position where they had to explain what was happening to their children:

> From those praying sessions in the kitchens in the morning with aunts, uncles, deacons and many "mommas," to every step of the hard-fought yardage to the school door, to all the questions and tears and anger that children brought back home, the black family and its community were fully engaged. Parents had to answer a thousand questions from their children about the white gauntlets they had run, and the savagery and fear which they had seen. Preachers had to say something about the threats, the bombs, the state troopers. Someone had to explain to the children (and to themselves) why all this was going on in America the Beautiful. And in the course of this process of acting and reflecting a new political conscious began to develop, starting with the children.[2]

Harding's words describe situations confronted by many across the black community and by many whites who found themselves questioned about their own roles within a racist society. The child—in the home and in the school—had become one of the major focuses of the civil rights movement.

Delivered almost a decade after the 1954 *Brown v. Board of Education of Topeka, Kansas* decision, King's speech can be understood within the context of successes and disappointments that marked the unrealized dream of integrated education. As King spoke, the successes seemed promising. New educational movements promoted curricular changes; policy decisions led to the development of federal programs that targeted young children; the creation of alternative open learning spaces provided signs that all children would be able to learn together unencumbered by racial biases; and the process of integration—at least in the South— seemed to be occurring more smoothly. Yet attempts to desegregate were still met with widespread opposition: state governments provided social and legal reasons for the continuation of segregation; protests and riots over busing questioned the negative social and physical effects of moving children to different locations for schooling; and white flight—the movement of whites from cities to suburbs—threatened to segregate communities further. Despite these barriers, the image and dream of the integrated classroom remained the primary apparatus for social change. Within the mainstream media and within assimilationist discourse, the message was apparent: integrated education and schooling of children was to become the central vehicle for moving the populace from a racist to a race-free society.

Television, during the civil rights era, embraced the classroom as one of the major images for exploring the politics of social transformation. Fictional programs such as *Mr. Novak, The Mod Squad, Mr. Peepers,* and *Room 222,* and documentaries, such as *The Eye of the Storm,* CBS's Reports Black America series, and

Frederick Wiseman's *High School* among others, appropriated the classroom as both a backdrop and a vehicle for exploring race. The media's adoption of the classroom situated television as a place of instruction. Through observing actual and fictional classrooms, viewers theoretically could learn about the process of cultural transformation. In addition, televising the classroom provided viewers with an inside perspective on the educational process, one normally closed to outside observation by adults, and offered a way to evaluate America's progress toward a race-blind society.[3]

Media images of the classroom reinforced what Shanti Kumer and Ellen Seiter refer to as the "will to orient" children, "the cultural conflict between the reality of orienting knowledge in an enlightened civic society, and the fantasy of securing an idealized essence of savage, innocent beauty."[4] Pedagogical practice often reflects adult needs to guide or shape children's development toward the acquisition of the kinds of feelings and identities deemed best for them and for society. The "will to orient" reflects the projection of adults' needs and expectations onto children, who are presumed incapable of meaningful resistance. Within this "orientalist" discourse, the child is placed on a pedestal and yet is forced to submit to adult authorities, celebrated as free and—it is hoped—"civilized" through adult institutions, imagined as innocent and yet taught adult knowledge. In integrationist discourse, there emerged an inherent tension between the fantasy of children's innocence transcending adult racism and the anticipated role of teacher and educational apparatus as policing children's actions and shaping their identities. One side of the equation assumed that black and white children would become friends if they were only left alone, yet adult needs to regulate the classroom and shape child development meant that children could, would, and should never be "left alone."

According to Chris Jenks, children are often perceived as unformed and undeveloped, yet they are always in the process of development and socialization.[5] The child is, on the one hand, seen as embodying innocence and purity, and yet, on the other hand, we all know that the child changes and grows. Reflecting those contradictory perceptions, the classroom becomes both a place in which to capture and preserve the innocence of childhood and also a place that allows for development and growth. Thus, in terms of integration, the classroom provided a site for learning and unlearning difference. It provided a place to observe and evaluate change, and a place to reflect upon children's play and symbolic innocence in light of new legal policies. The media accounts immediately following the beginnings of legally mandated school integration depicted young black and white children playing together on playground or eating lunch together, images demonstrating to researchers, teachers, and the public that children "naturally" play together regardless of the color of their skin. However, if the classroom was a place for child development and instruction, for growth, understanding, and learning, it also was a place that captured and immobilized children, setting them up as subjects—cherished victims—of social change.

In this essay, I concentrate mainly on a twenty-year period in the larger history of the civil rights movement, from the *Brown v. Board of Education* decision to roughly the mid-seventies, in order to discuss how the image of the child and the idea of the classroom provide an integrative "solution," but one that also reveals contradictory responses to the civil rights movement and the proposed mechanisms for confronting racial injustice. The schoolhouse became a central place for learning not only new and old curriculum but also new and old values. Media images of the integrated classroom illustrated the idealism and equality assumed by a picture-perfect liberal pluralist agenda, but these same media images have been criticized for erasing racial difference and for promoting a "standard" white method—a criticism that bell hooks might argue supports a "white supremacist meta narrative."[6] Throughout this essay, I plan to juxtapose images of the classroom in educational and political discourse with images of classrooms on television. I will demonstrate how the image of integrated and nonintegrated classrooms signified new attempts to make sense of America's changing education policy and of different factions within the civil rights movement. Looking at media representations of the classroom can help us to understand better the investment we make in these racially coded images of the child, images that retain political resonance in contemporary cultural debates.

Contradictions abound. White liberal discourse spoke of the desire to expand freedom and equality while advocating policies based on forced busing. Educators struggled with the contradictions between the "open classroom" model, embraced by many integrated schools encouraging free interaction and expression, and the more Afro-centric teaching methods that deployed disciplinary procedures associated with traditional schoolrooms. Prevailing metaphors, which reference the classroom as a laboratory for social experimentation, ran against a presumed need to protect and shelter children. Many educators placed importance on learning and unlearning racism through developing a fuller understanding of history, while teachers were often unable or unwilling to examine the historical context(s) that shaped the classroom itself. Media images promoted an antiracist agenda, yet reflected the blindnesses of dominant institutions to minority needs and interests—a perfect example of what John Fiske calls "nonracist racism."[7] Although the intent was to combat racism, the power to produce and narrativize these images of racial equality remained in the hands of white producers who only imperfectly understood the political debates within the black community.

Unlearning History

In the years immediately following the *Brown v. Board of Education* decision, news magazines made the school and the classrooms a focal point for discussing the civil rights agenda, often constructing images that juxtaposed white and black students and teachers. One photograph in the September 24, 1954, issue of *U.S. News and World Report* depicted a young black student and young white student, standing side by side, right hands crossed over their hearts, reciting the Pledge of Allegiance to the flag.[8] The image captures the contradictions and ideals surrounding the end of segregation in the South: both children are following national laws and reinforcing the authority of the federal government. Together, the two children embody the ideal of "one nation . . . , with . . . justice for all"; they are symbols of the nation's hopes for successful integration. Another *U.S. News and World Report* article, from 1955, similarly juxtaposed two images, one a photograph depicting a white teacher teaching black students, the other a black teacher teaching white students.[9] These pictures of young children and teachers calmly going about the process of establishing new norms based on familiar behaviors and rituals provided a tranquil and hopeful image of what an integrated society might look like, but other images helped to drive home the divisions within the national fabric. Often these more utopian images of race-blind children appeared alongside pictures of youths, mostly high school students, standing outside their schools, being escorted by federal troops. In one image, picketers (including mothers of white students) stand on a curb outside a local high school jeering at black children—just one example of a local community where the ending of legalized segregation was met with opposition.[10] Many school officials in states previously mandating segregation approached the situation as though if they "held out long enough, things would go back to normal."[11]

The *Brown* decision reversed the 1896 *Plessy v. Ferguson* ruling of 1896. Passed in the midst of the reconstruction of the South following the Civil War, the *Plessy* decision declared that schools could be "separate but equal." White and black schools could supposedly operate independently from each other because each group would be better educated if its members were segregated and provided with "equal" resources. The *Plessy* decision was framed in terms of good intentions, holding that the provision of equal resources and equal opportunities for both white and black students could ideally ensure that neither group would feel inadequate or challenged by the other. However, the ruling only emphasized racial inequality, reinforcing Jim Crow laws that were passed after the Civil War —a period prior to the development of public schools, when white children would typically attend private schools and black children were, for the most part, illiterate. Despite the fact that black children could now attend public schools, Jim Crow segregation continued, demonstrating to anyone who cares to look at the faulty reasoning behind the *Plessy* decision that the morality behind "separate-but-equal" was a pretense that disguised the stigmatization that went along with unequal access to public facilities.[12] The role of education was particularly problematic, for education is often seen as the "great equalizer." However, under *Plessy*, white schools received preferential treatment and benefited from a much higher economic investment in facilities while schools for black students were ill-equipped, lacking even the most basic necessities—running water and safe sanitary conditions. And black children often had to endure hardships, such as traveling long distances to blacks-only schools despite the fact that there were schools closer to their homes.

As decades passed, social science research increasingly identified social and psychological effects of segregated classrooms upon children's development.[13] In an influential study, Frederick Werthem concluded that children, regardless of race, associated segregation with punishment—a factor that affected children's self-esteem and academic performance. Black children, he said, felt insecure in segregated classrooms because they did not have the chance to be themselves. Negative effects were also felt by white children: "In some of the white children we found a subtle though definite tendency to identify themselves unconsciously with the Negro children."[14] Conversely, the segregation of schools compounded the racial prejudices the white children encountered in their homes and communities.

Not all states had legalized segregation at the time of the *Brown* decision. In 1952, a year after the initial suit was filed, seventeen states had laws requiring public schools to be segregated; four states permitted segregation; eighteen states had segregation as a local option; and only nine states prohibited segregation—at least formally. In Kansas, where the lawsuit was brought, a provision authorized segregation in high schools, but there was no such provision in regard to elementary schools. The action challenged the local school board's policy of segregation at the elementary-school level, challenging the fallacy of "separate but equal" facilities, and insisting that children had a right to go to schools close to their neighborhoods.[15]

Proving that segregation had negative effects upon children was an important part of the *Brown* case, as well as of other cases against segregation. The expert testimony of social scientists who had researched the effects of segregation was a key factor. Numerous witnesses focused on motivational factors, arguing that social expectations can influence what students are able to learn and thus the lowered expectations of segregated schools stunted black children's ability to achieve their full potential.[16] Many of the experts referred to visual identification tests that sought to demonstrate how children saw their place in the world. In the 1951 *Briggs* case in North Carolina, for example, black psychologist Kenneth Clark referred to his experiments that used colored dolls to test children's awareness of and attitude toward their race. Black children showed "an unmistakable preference for the white doll and a rejection of the brown doll," suggesting a negative evaluation of their own racial background.[17] Clark also asked children to choose a crayon that best represented their own skin color, and later examined their artworks for clues into their self-perception. Similar visual identification tests were also used by Marian J. Radke and Helen G. Trager, who asked children in Philadelphia to identify living conditions, and by Robert Coles, who studied children's coloring and drawing samples in a therapeutic context to evaluate black and white children's adjustment to desegregation.[18]

The public attention paid to these social scientific and psychological "experiments" was significant. A growing number of school segregation cases were decided on the basis of not only legal reasoning but also expert testimony. The courts saw social science research as central to defining what was best for children. The final words of the Supreme Court's ruling in the 1954 *Brown* case reflected this social scientific discourse: "To separate [Negro children] from oth-

142 SHARI GOLDIN

ers of similar age and qualifications solely because of their race generates a feeling of inferiority as to their status in the community that may affect their hearts and minds in a way unlikely ever to be undone."[19] Children's innocence became the place where integration could start; not having lived through the divisive previous decades, children were not contaminated by adult prejudices. They represented the best hope that America could break with the past and begin to fulfill its ideals of "liberty and justice for all." As schools made plans for accommodating the change, news magazines closely monitored community response, hoping to capture a glimpse of children in the process of learning and socializing together. Many wondered how integrated schools would affect other aspects of life in a still largely segregated society.

Relearning Race

The process of desegregating the schools went slowly, despite a ruling made the following year mandating that integration take place "with all deliberate speed." Harold Engstrom, the president of the Little Rock School Board during the 1957 Little Rock crisis, noted that calling for a change to occur with "all deliberate speed" helped perpetuate the idea that the government did not expect desegregation to occur immediately. Contrary to its explicit purpose, the 1955 ruling gave school boards more room (as well as time) to delay and debate integration policies rather than put them into action.[20] Individual states and school boards attempted to stall desegregation as long as possible. Some states passed laws allowing students to choose the schools they wanted to attend; the underlying assumption was that students would not go to schools where they felt unwanted. Other states threatened to close public schools rather than integrate them. In Mississippi, for example, state officials threatened that they would make all public schools private; the government would then subsidize private education through tuition or grants.[21]

New concerns arose in the southern black communities, which had functioned within a system of segregation since the Civil War. In light of the integration rulings, some black businesses and professionals worried about their survival in the changing social structure because worked and prospered within a community where there were only black lawyers, black doctors, black schools, and black-run stores. Many feared they would be driven into bankruptcy if they had to compete with whites. Teachers in black schools, in particular, were concerned that desegregation might jeopardize their jobs.[22] Yet there was also a sign of relief and success resounding in the black community, as many southern blacks saw *Brown* as a sign that the government was behind them in their struggle for justice.[23]

Many white parents expressed concern that their children's education would be compromised, citing findings released after the initial years of integration that black students were likely to be below the educational level of white students.[24] Rumors and news reports that black students often had behavioral problems in the new liberal environments prompted (white) parental worries that the general atmosphere of the schools would likely be changed as a result of integration. Behavioral problems among certain black students were attributed to the change from a more-discipline-schools, where overcrowding had forced teachers to spend more time maintaining order than teaching. The behavioral problems among black students could be blamed on any number of factors, including a prior system of segregation that put added burdens on black teachers as well as overcrowded schools that allowed students to move ahead without having mastered materials. Although the problems were a product of segregation, they were often used as arguments against integration; black students were blamed for holding white students back.[25]

In contrast to the South's experience, northern school districts were almost immune from criticism in the period immediately following the desegregation ruling. However, by the early sixties, when southern states integration attempts were going more smoothly, turmoil was erupting in northern cities over *de facto segregation*, a form of segregation based not on laws but on housing segregation, and the informal attempts to keep blacks and whites in separate residential arrangements.[26] School officials in northern cities such as Chicago and Boston rebutted the claims being made, arguing that unlike the South, the North had never been segregated.[27] Black mothers in Boston saw things differently and argued the unconstitutionality of de facto segregation, a battle that led to the Massachusetts Board of Education's 1964 requirement that school districts tally their students by race. More than a 50 percent nonwhite student body in any one school was considered unbalanced. A subsequent new law was regarded as "a model of civil rights legislation" because it provided a way to monitor the balance between blacks and whites.[28] Like many other cities, New York City attempted to integrate children through the costly enterprise of restructuring schools districts and busing children from one location to another. Busing was frequently met by resistance, primarily from white parents, who in 1964 boycotted the schools, objecting to the busing of their children to poorer and often "unsafe" neighborhoods for the purpose of obtaining a better racial balance.[29]

By the midsixties, in the wake of rising urban violence, both black and white groups questioned the viability of integration. Urban violence, particularly in northern cities, revealed deep divisions between the races and conflicting opinions within the black community. A 1964 issue of U.S. *News and World Report* reprinted an article from 1958 that had compared desegregation to Prohibition, predicting that desegregation would fail. People, the author asserted, were not going to change their fundamental attitudes. They just wanted to "get along" according to traditional patterns. The "noble experiment" of "forcing Negroes into white schools will not gain acceptance: it will further aggravate the situation."[30] Indeed, the rising tide of violence and discontent during that time provoked white nostalgia for the earlier system of segregation.

The challenges to integrationist discourse in those years were also attributed to the release of the controversial Moynihan Report in 1965. "The Negro Family: The Case for national Action," was written by Daniel Patrick Moynihan for the U.S. Department of Labor. Initially, it was presented as a working paper at a conference for professionals and civil rights workers and was written in the hope of changing the social welfare system and encouraging government intervention. However, the report drew sharp criticism from black activists, who argued that it blamed the black family rather than the social conditions that were the real cause of poverty in America. This report, a continuation of the Johnson administration's "War on Poverty," described the "cyclical" nature of poverty, a situation in which impoverished people and groups found themselves unable to escape.[31]

The controversy arose over the claim that the "social pathology" of the black culture was rooted in the matriarchal structure of the black family, one that often "reversed roles of husband and wife." According to the report, "Negro females were better educated." Girls, studies had found, were more likely to become honor students, have higher achievement, and were more likely to have white-collar or professional jobs than black males, who were often employed in blue-collar jobs. The report also found more broken families within black communities. Growing up in a family without a male figure was likely to have a negative effect on children—especially boys—who were likely to fail, have lower IQ's, and have a propensity toward delinquency—because they did not have male role models.[32]

The focus on the family in the Moynihan Report provoked protest and argument within the black community.[33] Black nationalist groups resented Moynihan's assertions that there was something inherently wrong with the black family structure because the characterization took the blame off whites and erased a history of oppression. The report also treated the white family structure as the implicit norm against which alternative cultural traditions would be evaluated. The final section referred to school integration, stating that in the South only one child in nine went to school with white children, and that in the North, neighborhoods and schools were becoming more segregated. The resulting family and community, the report said, was "a tangle of pathology."

Black nationalist movements turned away from the assimilationism implicit within an ideal of integration.[34] Instead, they placed priority on recognizing, defending, and celebrating black identity, insisting that black children should be educated within the black community.[35] At the center of this debate was the figure of the child, its needs and the purpose of its education. Should education be administered according to an assimilationist model that sought to lessen racial differences, taking the child further from his or her community? Or should education for black children teach black community values and affirm a sense of black identity? Should children be protected and sheltered from racism so that they could transcend it or should they be taught awareness of racism so that they could consciously combat it?

Both blacks and whites expressed a general distrust of the schools, albeit for different reasons. They were concerned about a loss of parental and community control over children's development of core values. The government program, Head Start, might well have played into this concern; it was one more way that government could provide for children in ways that parents could not. Two different goals for education can be identified in these instances. The integrationalist idea saw the ideal classroom as a place to transcend the limitations of one's surroundings. In the words of John Dewey: "Each individual gets an opportunity to escape from the limitations of the social group in which he was born, and to come into living contact with a broader environment."[36] If desegregation was going to work, children were going to have to learn to think about race in terms very different than their parents' generation, and this reeducation effort demanded some distance between the school and the family. In contrast, W. E. B. Du Bois's words from 1935 evoke the necessity for blacks to link education with their community, and in turn to create its own forms of education: "American Negroes have, because of their history, group experiences and memories, a distinct entity, whose spirit and reaction demand a certain type of education for its development."[37] Du Bois's ideas had resurfaced within black nationalist discourse, as African-American leaders argued for the development of a strong and self-sufficient black community separate from the white community. Such arguments implicitly and often explicitly criticized assimilationist discourse as erasing racial difference and isolating children from their own people. Instead, blacks advocated the creation of separate, community-run schools for black children to learn, and practice, a new black identity. If the integrationist project sought to protect children from a consciousness of racism, so that their innocence could transcend adult prejudices, the community-schools movement sought to prepare children to confront and overcome the harsh realities of a racist society.

Mediating: Learning and Unlearning

Could there be a medium between these two extremes? Television documentaries and fictional programming in the late sixties and early seventies offered a glimpse of these two positions, often mediating between them within the nonviolent space of the classroom. The plethora in the late 1960s of documentaries based on themes of race relations were a response to the findings of the National Advisory Commission on Civil Disorders, which President Lyndon Johnson had asked to analyze the causes of urban violence. The commission, headed by Governor Otto Kerner of Illinois, concluded in what became known as the Kerner Report that the country was moving toward apartheid and that "white institutions" were the cause of the black protest. Government officials meet with network executives to persuade them to cover black concerns, and the summer of 1968 saw a television focus on black issues. The programming reflected both a heightened awareness of the black experience and an underlying sense of white guilt over America's charged race relations.[38] The second episode in ABC's *Black America* series, the most well known, made the "classroom" its central location. Thus, almost a decade and a half after the initial *Brown* decision, the classroom was once again chosen as a key location for teaching Americans how to think about race.

Black History: Lost, Stolen, or Strayed

In "Black History: Lost, Stolen, or Strayed," producer Perry Wolff appropriated the space of the classroom and the rhetorical strategy of instruction to inform viewers about the stereotypical representation of blacks in popular culture.[39] Whites, the documentary suggests, had traditionally presented a version of history that met their own needs and fantasies but that significantly distorted the image of blacks in America. The film features the space of the classroom as a central location for discussion and contemplation, and for demonstrating ways that American children were being taught to overcome racial biases, often developing an understanding of historical and contemporary race relations far beyond that of adults. Bill Cosby is the narrator, interpreter, and informer who provides a "lesson" for members of the audience. Using children's drawings, film texts, and an inside view of the black ghetto, not to mention occasional lighthearted jokes and earnest narration, the film demonstrates how misconceptions shape the way people (especially children) feel about themselves. Speaking from the classroom setting, Cosby provides his students in the television audience with an up-to-date view of a world, one being reshaped through the transformation occurring in classrooms across the nation.

The film contrasts two types of educational settings: a successfully integrated fourth-grade classroom, which is seen at the beginning of the film and provides a background for Cosby's lesson, and a storefront school, seen at the end in a news report format that demonstrates an alternative type of education designed to prepare black preschoolers for entrance into segregated schools. In the first part of the film, black and white students are shown working together in groups at clustered desks and then singing along with the teacher. Their interaction and play provide the background sound throughout much of Cosby's narration, a calming reminder that integration works. The integrated classroom is an environment that enables the learning or relearning of history.

In the makeshift classroom small children peer across large tables and sit at attention in chairs much too big for their bodies. Their teacher verbally drills them as preparation for their entrance into the city schools. The inquisition-type procedure readies the children to assert their newly constructed "Afro-American" identities proudly and to reject more colloquial labeling, such as "Negro" or "Colored," which reflects the history of racism.[40]

Churchville: Stand up, young man. Are you a Negro?
Travis: No.
Churchville: Are you a flunky?
Travis: No.
Churchville: What are you?
Travis: I'm black and beautiful.
Churchville: And what else are you? Are you a boy?
Travis: No.
Churchville: What are you?

Travis: I'm a man.

Churchville: What kind of man?

Travis: A black and beautiful man.

Churchville: But what kind—are you an old man or a young man?

Travis: Young man.

Churchville: All right. Suppose I tell you something wrong. Travis, are you going to do it?

Travis: Yes.

Churchville: You're going to do something if I tell you when it's wrong?

Travis: Yes.

Churchville: Have a seat young man.[41]

This approach appears harsh and militant, particularly because it is directed toward a young child. Yet the comic ending of this scene, where the child says that he will do something wrong, reveals the unexpected downfalls of children responding without full awareness of what they have said. Whether the children in the storefront classroom actually are resisting, however, is questionable. They have obviously been taught what to say, and thus adult voices and adult anxieties (and a history of black oppression, of which the children have little or no knowledge) are projected onto the child. The depiction raises questions: Does the image of children fighting for their rights, their "freedom," reflect the black power movement's desire to train children to defend themselves? Or, is the movement using children as devices for larger political goals?

Churchville's inquiry counters a long history of the use of terms or expressions that communicated to blacks the necessity and appropriateness of deference to white authorities. One question and response in particular, is laden with historical significance—and a certain irony in this context: Churchville's question, "Are you a boy?" and the youngster's reply, "No, I'm a man," speaks to the sardonic use of "boy" in white master/black slave relationships. Thus, while white society traditionally treated blacks as children, the Afro-centric reaction was to turn African-American boys into men, at least verbally. The child's claim to manhood speaks to his resistance to being treated today as fellow blacks have been in the past. It also suggests the trajectory of a young child who will probably be put into situations in which he will be forced to grow up quickly.

Cosby's comment at the close of the segment, "It's kind of like brainwashing. Or is it? Can you blame us for overcompensating?" expresses the film's ambivalence about the most effective way to teach awareness of race. The two sides can be contrasted: the storefront school teaches children defense mechanisms premised on understanding power relations; the pedagogical methods of the integrated classroom encourage the exploration of the self through drawing exercises and working in multiracial groups in a race-blind context that preserves the children's innocence. The storefront classroom, seen here as new approach to education, ironically uses traditional pedagogical methods—drill and response, a focus on the teacher, and memorization. The integrated classroom, on the other hand, presents learning in an "open-school" setting, one where students work alongside their teacher and can function independently as well. The discipline and respect for authority promoted by the storefront classroom, while protective and orderly, is also construed as domineering and oppressive in comparison to integrated schools and their characteristically more open approach. The film's image of the young black child whose lips quiver and who is on the edge of tears when he hesitates to speak, lingers in one's memory.

Does the militant technique hurt the children? Is it a necessary evil? Kinkaid's notion of our "tragic romance" with children comes to mind. "The child," Kinkaid writes, "enters into discourse as an article for inquiry and concern, as a visible image of expansion and degeneration, of happiness and play, misery and exploitation, of the future and the past, of faith and death, of the existence of class lines and their dissolution."[42] The television image that lingers raises core questions about this application of traditional teaching methods and its lasting effects, inviting us to wonder, with Cosby, whether the child educated in the freedom-school movement is a willing participant. Yet, Cosby's concluding remarks about compensating for a history of racism, suggests this style of education may be necessary for preparing black children to deal with social practices that negatively impact their lives.

The two black adult males in the film also present a contrasting view of a divided black community. Although Cosby is not the teacher but a visitor to the classroom, he is offered as an expert on race because of his unstated affiliation with black community. Cosby is a black man who has gained recognition from both black and white viewers through his successful career as a stand-up comic (whose routines often centered around the common problems experienced by children) and as a costar (with Robert Culp) of *I Spy*, a television drama that ran from 1965 through 1968, in which he played a secret agent protecting U.S. interests around the globe. The program was widely recognized for its depiction of a partnership that cut across racial lines and for its portrayal of the Cosby character as well educated and intellectually gifted. Far from an image of black discontent, Cosby was a role model for black acceptance into white society, for improving race relations through bridging old divisions, and for working within the system as a dedicated civic spokesman. If the film's message about the need to reclaim black history and question old stereotypes might prove challenging to white America, its spokesman did not. The other black man in the film, John Churchville, is a study in opposites. His overall appearance, complete with glasses, starched white shirt, and narrow tie, echoes the iconography surrounding Malcolm X. His gestures and emphatic voice convey a sense of urgency, suggesting the necessity for the black community to rise to its own defense. Yet he appears to connect with the children, and the call-and-response exercise is set up a game in which he warms up (and the children warm up) if they answer correctly.

Churchville and Cosby thus offer different conceptions of the kind of educators needed to bring about social and cultural transformation. Both black men have somehow regained the self-esteem that many feared black boys had lost and they have positions of authority. And both men are shown devoting at least some portion of their lives to teaching and connecting with children. As black men who have "made it" they become potential role models.

Room 222

Another image of the black male teacher surfaced on fictional television. *Room 222*'s Pete Dixon is a high school history teacher who inspires youths of different ethnicities to learn and grow together, turning his classroom into a forum where they can openly discuss their responses to contemporary social issues. Dixon, as the show's father figure, combines sensitivity to his students' distinctive needs, with an awareness of the historic position of minorities. He negotiates the politics of the school, offering links between students and teachers and between school and community.

The ABC comedy drama, which ran from 1969 until 1973, is set in suburban Los Angeles, in mythical Walt Whitman High School, appropriately named after the poet whose works are known for their focus on democracy, freedom, equality, individuality, and patriotism. The school serves as a literal oasis, where the space of the classroom and the layout of campus encourage an open forum for students and teachers to gather. Its opening credits, which depict students of many races arriving at school, accompanied by a jaunty but tranquil sound track, offer an image of racial harmony that contrasts quite drastically with newspaper images and television news reports of black youths needing federal protection in order to walk into a school building. Dixon's classroom models the way students can utilize the freedoms and equality being advocated by the era's various social movements, including the civil rights movement, the black freedom movement, the women's movement, and the gay liberation movement. *Room 222* provides a location for confronting and challenging authority and for testing limits, a different version of the laboratory. Television viewers had a chance to observe this new kind of classroom in action, as students learned to question old ways of thinking and to stand up for their own needs.

The youths in the series become emblematic for the counterculture, despite the fact that the student body is far from counter within the "school culture," which recognizes, accepts, and channels rebellion, and—most important—offers students (and teachers) a chance to learn from their mistakes and successes. Within this permissive atmosphere, Dixon serves as role model, confidant, and inspiration for students and the faculty alike. He provides the liberal center for the school, employing untraditional teaching methods and approaching historical subjects with new perspectives; his teaching draws equally upon his understood (though rarely openly acknowledge) black perspective, his understanding of youth politics, and his goodwill as a dedicated and caring teacher. The series celebrates the learning process, allowing both the fictional students and the television viewers to explore the social changes occurring around them, situations that test the community's ability to work together and the students' willingness to work with authority figures. Episode after episode, the series explores controversial subjects ranging from racial difference to flag burning, as Dixon encouraged the reconsideration of American history, say, the Sacco and Vanzetti case, or promotes debate about Lincoln's contradictory stances on slavery.

In the 1971 episode, "The Lincoln Story," Dixon deals with the Civil War from the perspective of blacks at the time. A school administrator happens to witness students fiercely arguing the issues, and one criticizes Lincoln for saying, in effect, that he was not in favor of bringing about social or political equality of black and white races. Outraged, the administrator questions Dixon's decision to remain aloof. Dixon responds that if he were to intervene in the "free-flowing discussion", the discussion and learning might cease. Curricular changes were thus being reinforced and complemented by the social and intellectual environment in the school. The school and education in this way became the idealized solution to the larger problems confronting American society, a place for learning about issues and for learning new ways of living together as a democratic community.[43]

Room 222 incorporated the ideals of integration and cultural assimilation while imagining the classroom as a part of the larger community, a part that bridges the gap between learning space and "the real world." The high school students are at an age when they are finding their own space and gravitating toward their future public roles—a factor that distinguishes them from the images of children in the classroom. But the representation of the school as a community where learning occurs across racial, cultural, and generational differences suggests the transformative power of education. In the world of *Room 222* the classroom/ laboratory is occasionally thrown into disarray, but the community works to self-correct.

Eye of the Storm—*Testing Racism*

Another example of television's mediating potential, *Eye of the Storm*, also explores the process of learning and unlearning race, and presents a third-grade class in Iowa as the "eye," the laboratory of an experiment of prejudice. Here, the walls of the classroom are not quite as flexible, and the younger students are less apt to assert themselves against adult authorities. The goal of the documentary and the experiment is to convey to white children what discrimination feels like.

The film *Eye of the Storm* makes explicit the links between the classroom and the laboratory, depicting a controversial "experiment"—a classroom simulation— designed to subject white children to racist feelings and practices. Children are turned into both perpetrators and victims of racism, and their classroom becomes a fishbowl for observing and documenting their responses. Teacher Jane Elliott developed the two-day exercise in 1968 after the assassination of Martin Luther King, Jr., as a way of dramatizing to her all-white class the significance of King's role in society and to demonstrate the social conditions that motivated his struggle.

In the film, Elliot introduces the exercise to her students as a role-playing game. Because they don't have different skin colors, the children will be separated by eye color. The children eagerly participate in this play with identity. Elliott asks the children to rearrange their seats so that blue-eyed children sit in the front of the room; brown-eyed children in the back. The children are apparently content with how they are divided, recognizing strong bonds with other members of their same-eye-color groups. Elliott gives the brown-eyed children paper collars to call further attention to the difference between the groups.[44]

Once the children are seated, Elliott outlines a code of conduct that knowledgeable viewers will associate with the Jim Crow laws of the segregated South. Students who have brown eyes are not allowed to use the drinking fountain. Students with brown eyes have to stand at the back of the line. During the class lessons when Elliott calls on the blue-eyed children, she gives subtle positive feedback regardless of whether answers are right or wrong. When her calls on the brown-eyed children elicit incorrect answers, she makes these children feel inadequate individually and collectively by attributing the answers and, on other occasions, wrongful behaviors to the fact of brown-eyedness.

As the day unfolds, the blue-eyed children continue to get favorable treatment, and the brown-eyed children are, in effect, disregarded or insulted The impact of this differential treatment moves beyond the teacher's watchful eye. When the brown-eyed students cluster in a corner in the schoolyard (which suggests they are not feeling good about themselves), the blue-eyed children ridicule the disenfranchised group by calling them "Brown eyes!"

On the second day, the treatment is reversed: the brown-eyed children sit in the front of the class and are given affirmation by the teacher. At the end of the day, Elliott allows the children to take off their paper collars, and they vehemently tear their "ID's." into small pieces or stomp on them.

The exercise is powerful and resonates with its participants and viewers. The dramatic shifts in the children's attitude over a relatively short time period suggest the effects of physical and racial coding that had been identified by social scientists in the 1950s: children respond quickly to how they are treated by adult authorities. In this case, the teacher's treatment determines their self-esteem or their submissiveness.

The experiment has proved controversial because of the ways it brings into conflict our expectation that a teacher would protect her student from emotional hurt and psychological harm and our recognition that the experiment depends on re-creating some of the devastating effects of racism so that white children will understand what it feels like to be a victim. The "Brown Eyes/Blue Eyes" experiment could even be described as a betrayal of children's innocence and a violation of adult responsibilities. At the same time the experiment has been held up as a model for effectively teaching racism, and it is used widely throughout the world.[45]

What is surprising and glaringly apparent, however, is not just that these are helpless children being subjected to a harsh experiment, but that they demonstrate complex behaviors and attitudes. The savage meanness displayed when the dominant group taunts the subordinate group contrasts with the equally horrifying passivity of the "inferior" children, who don't stand up for themselves and instead just "take it." One wonders if these behaviors are exaggerated only because they take place within the confines of a role-playing exercise, where both the children and teacher know that the treatment is only temporary. To teach about racism in a segregated classroom, the teacher must manufacture differences and then encourage the children to act upon those differences. In this context, certain behaviors might also be exaggerated or downplayed for the camera. (The children never directly acknowledge its presence, but Elliott does talk to the camera, providing a link to the world beyond the classroom.) However exaggerated the behaviors and attitudes may seem, they closely mirror those historically experienced whenever groups of people are singled out on the basis of physical characteristics or social, ethnic, and religious differences, from the Nazi Holocaust to the treatment blacks receive in a segregated culture. Although the division of students on the basis of eye color may seem initially fanciful, it is not historically innocent, recalling the Nazis' identification of a "pure" Aryan race marked by blond hair and blue eyes in contrast to the darker attributes generally associated with Jews, Gypsies, and other denigrated groups, which were read as markers of a less-pure or "polluted" race.

How might we understand the powerful image of school children stomping on the collars that in the experiment had identified their inferior status? Does this action allow us to maintain our romantic conception of the inherently good child who is horrified by the introduction of race and inequality into the classroom and thus naturally destroys the markers of cultural difference? The meanness revealed throughout the day contradicts our myths of childhood innocence, inviting us to read the children as "little devils." Psychological discourse might read the treatment of the collars as symptomatic of a self-destructive impulse: if a child defaces signs of his or her identity, it means not feeling good about himself or herself. Might we see this moment as emblematic of the ways that the introduction of adult knowingness about racism destroys children, corrupting their innocence and denying them the ability to act as children? Or, might we see the children as defacing the exercise, expressing anger and frustration at being manipulated by their teacher? *Eye of the Storm* invites us to read the classroom space as both symptomatically confining—in its issuance of exercises and its conducting of social experiments—and as potentially progressive, a space to rehearse, reflect upon, and move beyond the negative practices of real-world racism.

The Iowa classroom experiment can be compared with the example of the storefront school in *Black History, Lost, Strayed or Stolen*. Both sets of pedagogical practices depend upon the intensification of feelings associated with racism in order to teach students how to react to real-world practices. Both amplify children's anxieties so that adults may study children's reactions to see whether the children fight back, are mean, or cower and accepts abuse. Both teachers assume that children must be taught about racism before they can combat it. And both must construct a simulation of difference within a segregated environment—the abusive teacher in *Black History* standing in for jeering white racists; the inferior "brown-eyed" students in *Eye of the Storm* substituting for the absent blacks. Neither school preserves the ideal of childhood innocence that was once so central to the project of school integration. Both point to situations of adult intervention, a shaping of the conditions of the classroom in order to "orient" the child toward desired behaviors and attitudes rather than simply to observe and document the "natural" or "spontaneous" behavior of children in the face of racial difference. These experimental teaching methods veer dramatically away from other depictions the media offered as America waited breathlessly to see what would happen after integration: images of black and white children playing or saying the Pledge of Allegiance together. Adults did not simply want to wait to see what would happen as black and white children entered the same classroom; they felt a need to shape the outcome, to reintroduce racism in the name of combating it, to reorient the child in order to preserve its innocence.

Other Spaces/Other Times — Re-conceptualizing Learning and Unlearning

In all of these media depictions, the classroom becomes a place for observing children confronting race. By the midseventies, national priorities had shifted. A conservative backlash had promoted a more "back-to-basics" approach that sought to isolate the classroom from social change and to focus on teaching children timeless skills, the "three R's."[46] On television, the classroom was displaced by other spaces where children might learn about social and cultural norms, the street in *Sesame Street*, the junkyard and playground in *Fat Albert*. These new spaces offered forms of learning that were not so formal, not so overtly institutionalized, and not so directly shaped by the adult "will to orient."

The site of the classroom, however, remains a central location in contemporary debates about race, especially during a period when we are "rethinking integration" and reconsidering affirmative action. More than forty years after the *Brown* decision, the appropriateness of desegregation remains the subject of controversy. On a national level, President Clinton revisited the Little Rock, Arkansas, schoolhouse where black school children faced boos and jeers as they sought to make good the promise of integrated education, while his administration pondered the dismantling of civil-rights-era protections against racial discrimination. In many state and local school districts, students are being offered new forms of "school choice," which ironically mirror the tactics initially embraced by southern schools in response to the threat of desegregation. Educators and parents ponder why high school students tend to self-segregate on the basis of race, even when they sat and played together in elementary school. Some point to these images of black and white self-segregation as evidence of a failure of integration, wondering whether any progress has been made since *Brown* and if all the school busing was worth the fuss and bother. Others argue that self-segregation is part of a developmental process, that adolescents have a need to connect with their own community in order to affirm their developing sense of identity.[47] Once again, the question seems to be whether the ideal is a fully integrated society in which racial differences are effaced or one in which black students maintain stronger ties to their community and to their cultural heritage.

These same contradictory impulses surface when we turn from efforts at school integration to ongoing debates surrounding the introduction of multicultural curriculums. Educators debate whether there are significant differences in the educational needs of black and white students.[48] Once again, the issue of black history and black culture must be faced, as well as the concern about whether the classroom should shield children from the experience of racism or teach them to confront and challenge its history, its institutions, and its practices. The logic of integration assumed no differences in what black and white students need in the classroom, but several decades of identity politics suggests otherwise.

Many of these issues came to light in the national debate that followed the December 1996 decision of the Oakland, California School Board to include ebonics, a combination of African languages and standard English ("Black English"), in the curriculum. Proponents asserted that learning ebonics would give black students an advantage in learning standard English. Teaching ebonics would allow teachers to impart the historical richness of African-American expression, offering a link between black children and their cultural history.[49] Others, including black leaders such as Jesse Jackson, Marian Wright Edelman, and Maya Angelou, protested that teaching ebonics to black children would deny them access to the professional skills needed to compete for jobs within an integrated culture. The issue sparked popular debates as well, and although the controversy was short-lived, it served as a reminder of the contradictory impulses that have always shaped the politics surrounding school integration. By giving ebonics second-language status, alongside French or Spanish, educators advocating ebonics once offer recognition to African-American culture and define it as something other than "American." A gesture toward racial inclusion was at the same time a statement of racial exclusion.

Focusing on what was "good for children," on what should be valued within the classroom, gave many a chance to debate what was "good for America" and what should be valued—or even what belonged—within our culture. The ideals of liberal pluralism and integrationism, themselves grounded in racial blindness and insensitivity to cultural difference, seem increasingly dated and problematic. At the same time, many are worried that even the most token gestures toward equality and acceptance are disappearing, that the lines between black and white America are policed as fiercely today as ever before. Some are arguing that integration was a temporary process, no longer necessary in order to achieve equal treatment; others suggest that integration never achieved its original goals and that we continue to live in an unequal society.

Not surprisingly, these debates are most often played out around the child, staged through the classroom, which remains the primary testing ground of strategies for social and cultural transformation. We still look toward our children's faces for signs of hate or signs of hope, and yet we still also seek to "orient" both black and white children to conform to our political agendas for the future. The media still bring us images of the classroom to illustrate both utopian and dystopian discourses surrounding the child, to document how children interact with one another when they are outside adult control, and to study how children's minds are being formed and re-formed in response to shifting social agendas. Within many of these representations, there is an anticipation that invidious difference will be overcome and true diversity will be welcome. There is a hope that children—young children in particular—will provide answers to our social problems, for their undeveloped minds may somehow escape the history of racism, oppression, and discrimination. We still cling to the promise that "one day little black boys and black girls . . . will join hands."

NOTES

1. James R. Kincaid, *Child-Loving: The Erotic Child and Victorian Culture* (New York and London: Routledge, 1992), p. 78.

2. Vincent Harding, "The Black Wedge in America: Struggle, Crisis and Hope, 1955–1975," *Black Scholar*, December 1975, p. 35.

3. The media's "race blindness" is often a result of antiracist intent, according to John Fiske, *Media Matters* (Minneapolis: University of Minnesota Press, 1994). Fiske refers to Stuart Hall's distinction between overt racism and "inferential racism," emphasizing that inferential racism is likely to be hidden and therefore more dangerous because it is used by liberals with antiracist intent. Although Fiske does not refer specifically to children, he uses the distinctions between childhood and adulthood metaphorically in discussing minority and majority. Fiske also makes reference to the use of the word *minority* as it is used in progressive or liberal discourse for the purpose of arguing for antiracist intent, where the use of the word *minor* calls attention to that which is childlike, or as Fiske puts it, "not quite fully adult." He compares this with the word *majority*, which implies, he says, social maturity or adulthood, thus suggesting that inferential racism works on the minority in a way similar to the ways adults work upon the image of the child. See also Stuart Hall, "The Whites of Their Eyes: Racist Ideologies and the Media," in *The Media Reader*, ed. Manual Alvarado and John Thompson (London: British Film Institute, 1990), pp. 8–23.

4. Ellen Seiter and Shanti Kumer, "In the Name of the Child: 'Will to Orient,' " *International Journal of Cultural Studies*, forthcoming.

5. Chris Jenks, *Childhood (Key Concepts)* (London: Routledge, 1996).

6. bell hooks, *Black Looks: Race and Representation* (Boston: South End Press, 1992).

7. Fiske, *Media Matters*, p. 37.

8. "When Negroes Go to School with Whites," *U.S. News and World Report*, September 24, 1954, pp. 24–28.

9. "Do Mixed Schools Really Work?" *U.S. News and World Report*, June 10, 1955, p. 20.

10. See, for instance, "Mixed Schools—Trouble Starts," *U.S. News and World Report*, October 8, 1954, pp. 40–42. "This Year's Mixed Schools:—Trouble in North, Calm in South," *U.S. News and World Report*, September 28, 1964, pp. 77–78.

11. See, for instance, "The South Digs in to Fight Mixed Schools," *U.S. News and World Report*, September 7, 1956, pp. 25–27. "Third Year—Few Schools Mixed," *U.S. News and World Report*, August 31, 1956, pp. 51–52.

12. Richard Kluger, *Simple Justice* (New York: Vintage Books, 1975), p. 713. Robert Fredrick Burk, *The Eisenhower Administration* (Knoxville: University of Tennessee Press, 1984), pp. 132–133.

13. Kluger, *Simple Justice*.

14. Ibid., p. 443. Frederic Werthem, "Psychological Effects of School Segregation," *American Journal of Psychotherapy* 6 (January 1952): 94–103.

15. "Segregation Issue: What's It All About?" *U.S. News and World Report*, December 26, 1952. pp. 55–57.

16. Kluger, *Simple Justice,* chap. 17.

17. Ibid., pp. 317–318.

18. Ibid., Chap. 14. Robert Coles, "When I Draw the Lord He'll Be a Real Big Man," *Atlantic* May 1966, pp. 69–72.

19. *Brown v. Board of Education of Topeka, Kansas,* 347 U.S. 483 (1954).

20. Henry Hampton and Steve Fayer, *Voices of Freedom: An Oral History of the Civil Rights Movement from the 1950s through the 1980s* (New York: Bantam Books, 1990), p. 37.

21. "Time & the Schools," *Time,* September 27, 1964, p. 60. "The South Digs in to Fight Mixed Schools," 10 *U.S. News and World Report,* September 7, 1956, pp. 25–27. "The Real State of School Integration," *Newsweek,* September 17, 1956, pp. 68–70. "Guns and Bayonets" Cannot Promote Education," *U.S. News and World Report,* October 5, 1956, pp. 100–104.

22. "Negro Teachers for the North?" *U.S. News and World Report,* August 1954, pp. 35–36.

23. Harding, "The Black Wedge in America," p. 30.

24. "Do Mixed Schools Lower Classroom Standards?" *U.S. News and World Report,* February 3, 1956, pp. 38–40.

25. Secondary sources referring to concerns about black community and integration argue that blacks were also divided on the issue of integrated schools because there was concern about possible unfair treatment toward black children. John Davis, a lawyer arguing to defend the constitutionality of segregated schools, presented versions of this opinion before the Supreme Court in the *Brown* case. Davis referred to Gunnar Myrdal's *An American Dilemma* to suggest this opinion. See Kluger, *Simple Justice,* pp. 545–546.

26. "This Year's Mixed Schools: Trouble in North, Calm in South," *U.S. News & World Report,* September 28, 1964, pp. 77–78.

27. "Big City Schoolmaster," *Time,* September 15, 1961. Chicago's General Superintendent of Schools Benjamin C. Willis ignored racial differences and requests made by black students to attend white schools on the grounds that children should go to schools where they live, and "we treat children as children." J. Anthony Lukas, *Common Ground: A Turbulent Decade in the Lives of Three American Families* (New York: Vintage, 1985). Lukas describes Louise Day Hicks, chairwomen of the Boston School Board during the early and midsixties, as a public figure who was caught within the politics of the time between white and black. She is quoted as saying, "I never think of people as Negro or white." "Boycotts and other actions have drawn a color line in our schools that never existed before" (p. 128).

28. Jotte Chancy and Brenda Franklin, "Report from Boston: The Struggle for Desegregation," *Black Scholar,* December 1975. p. 20.

29. "This Year's Mixed Schools," pp. 77–78.

30. Deets Pickett, "Another 'Noble Experiment'?" *U.S. News & World Report,* May 11, 1964, p. 120. Reprinted from *U.S. News & World Report,* October 17, 1958, and *Washington Evening Star,* October 8, 1958. For another example of this perspective, see T. R. Waring, "The Southern Case Against Desegregation," *Harper's,* January 1956 reprinted in Horace Knowles, ed., *Treasury of Great Writers: Collected from Harper's Magazine* (New York: Wing's

Books, 1995), pp. 144–156. Waring's purpose is to "try to put before the open-minded readers of this magazine the point of view of the Southerner—whom the rest of the United States apparently cannot believe to be open-minded at all on the subject of race." For a viewpoint that advocates desegregation, see William Faulkner, "On Fear—The South in Labor," June 1956, *Harper's*, also reprinted in Knowles *Treasury of Great Writers*, pp. 157–167. Faulkner writes that "southern white man's shame" stems from his fear that the southern whites will lose economic power through integration, an idea that is not conducive to ideals of freedom. The Mississippian argues that there appeared to be irreconcilable differences between the government and the South. Faulkner directs his article to southern leaders, urging them to deal with the region's shame, to teach blacks about equality, to "practice" freedom in their interactions with minorities, and not to "becloud the issues with the bugaboo of miscegenation." Practicing freedom and equality, he declares, will help Americans fight against inimical political or social forces that challenge American national identity.

31. Herbert Gans "The Negro Family: Reflections on the Moynihan Report," *Commonweal* 47 (October 15, 1965): 47–51. Response to Gans's article: "Negro Family Life," *Commonweal* 47 (November 26, 1965): 229–230.

32. Daniel Patrick Moynihan, *The Negro Family: The Case for National Action* (Washington, D.C.: U.S. Department of Labor, Office of Planning and Research, March 1965).

33. Criticism of black matriarchy and Moynihan's conception of the family was also leveled by black feminists. See Bonnie Thornton Dill, "The Dialectics of Black Womanhood," in *Feminism and Methodology*, ed. Sandra Harding Bloomington: Indiana University Press, 1984), pp. 97–108.

34. Lerone Bennett, Jr., *The Negro Mood* (New York: Ballantine Books, 1964).

35. Sandra Harding, ed., *Feminism and Methodology* (Bloomington: Indiana University Press, 1984), p. 39.

36. Dewey, quoted in Kluger, *Simple Justice*, p. 319.

37. W. E. B. Du Bois, "Does the Negro Need Separate Schools?" *Journal of Negro Education*, 1935, as quoted in Benjamin Foster, Jr., "The Case of Vouchers," *Black Scholar*, May-June 1973.

38. J. Fred MacDonald, *Blacks and White TV: Afro-Americans in Television since 1948* (Chicago: Nelson-Hall, 1983).

39. "Black History: Lost, Stolen, or Strayed," produced by Andrew A. Rooney and Vern Diamond, written by Perry Wolff and Andrew A. Rooney, *CBS Reports: Of Black America*; executive producer, Perry Wolff. The program aired July 2, 1968, 10:00 P.M., EST, and was rebroadcast on July 24. It was one part of a seven-part series during the 1968 summer season.

40. Much has been written about the changing terminology *Black, Afro* or *African American, Negro, Colored*. In this essay I use the colloquial *black*, recognizing the historical importance of words like *Negro*, which is generally regarded negatively at present and was controversial during the sixties.

41. From the script *Black History: Lost, Stolen, or Strayed*, CBS Reports: Wisconsin State Historical Society. Perry Wolff Additions, M91-044, Box 12, Folder 3.

42. Kincaid, *Child-Loving*, p. 83.

43. "The Lincoln Story," an episode produced and directed by Gene Reynolds for the series *Room 222*, 1970–71.

44. *Eye of the Storm*, produced by ABC TV News, 1971.

45. Variations on the "Blue Eye/Brown" simulation have been used in exercises for

both adults and children. Elliot continues to conduct workshops in the United States and throughout Europe.

46. Ben Brodinsky, "Back to the Basics: The Movement and Its Meaning," *Phi Delta Kappan*, March 1977.

Joan Baum, "The Politics of Back to Basics," *Change Magazine* 8, no. 10, as quoted in Fred Schultz, ed., *Readings in Education 78/79*, annual ed. (Guilford, Conn.: Dushkin, 1978), pp. 58–63, 70–73.

47. John Yemma, "On Campus, the Trend Toward Self-Segregation," *Boston Globe*, September 15, 1997, p. A8. See Beverly Daniel Tatum, *'Why Are All the Black Kids Sitting Together in the Cafeteria?': And Other Conversations about Race* (New York: Basic Books, 1997).

48. Janice E. Hale-Benson, *Black Children: Their Roots, Culture, and Learning Styles* (Baltimore: Johns Hopkins University Press, 1986).

49. The ebonics question is not a new one. Educators debated whether or not Black English should be incorporated into the curriculum throughout the civil rights era. The debate often revolves around two opposing camps, those focusing on the educational needs of children and those focusing on American national identity. Geneva Smitherman, "White English in Blackface, or, Who Do I Be?" *Black Scholar*, May–June, 1973, pp. 32–38.

Chapter Eight

The New Childhood
Home Alone As a Way of Life

Joe L. Kincheloe

Home Alone (1990) and *Home Alone 2: Lost in New York* (1992) revolve around Kevin McAlister's (Macaulay Culkin) attempts to find his family after (1) being left behind on a family Christmas trip to Paris; and (2) being separated from his family on a Christmas trip to Miami. Wildly successful, the two movies portray the trials and tribulations of Kevin's attempts to take care of himself while his parents try to rejoin him. In the process of using these plots to set up a variety of comedic stunts and sight gags, the movies inadvertently allude to a sea of troubles relating to children and family life in the late twentieth century. As we watch the films, an entire set of conflicts and contradictions revolving around the lives of contemporary children begin to emerge. In this way *Home Alone* 1 and 2 take on a social importance unimagined by producers, directors, and screenplay writers. In this essay I will use the family dynamics of the *Home Alone* movies as a means of exposing the social forces that have altered Western childhood over the last couple of decades. In both films a central but unspoken theme involves the hurt and pain that accompany children and their families in postmodern America.

A Generation of Kids Left Home Alone

Childrearing is a victim of the late twentieth century. With divorces and two working parents, fathers and mothers are around children for less of the day. As parents are still at work in the afternoon when children get home from school, children are given latchkeys and expected to take care of themselves. Thus, we have seen generations of "home aloners"—kids that in large part have had to raise themselves. The last thirty years have witnessed a change in family structure that must be taken seriously by parents, educators, and cultural workers of all stripes. Since the early 1960s the divorce rate as well as the percentage of children living with one parent has tripled. Only one-half of today's children have parents who are married to each other. By the twenty-first century only one-third of U.S. children will have such parents. Among children under six years old, one in four lives in poverty. The stress that comes from the economic changes of the last twenty years has undermined the stability of the family. Family incomes have stagnated, as costs of middle class existence (home owner-ship, health care, and higher education) have skyrocketed. Since the late 1960s the amount of time parents spend with their children has dropped from an av-erage of thirty hours per week to seventeen (Lipsky and Abrams 1994; Galston 1991). Increasingly left to fend for themselves, contemporary children have turned to TV and video games to help pass their time alone.

Any study of contemporary children must analyze the social conditions that shape family life. Rarely do mainstream social commentators make reference to the fact that the American standard of living peaked in 1973, creating a subse-quent declining economic climate that demanded mothers work. While the ef-fects of international competition, declining productivity, and the corporate reluctance to reinvent the workplace all contributed to a depressed economy, not all recent family problems can be ascribed to the declining post-Fordist economy. The decline of the public space and the growth of cynicism have undermined the nation's ability to formulate creative solutions to family dysfunction. The 1970s and 1980s, for example, while witnessing the birth and growth of a family values movement, also represented an era that consistently privileged individual grati-fication over the needs of the community (Paul 1994; Coontz 1992). Such an impulse justified the privatistic retreat from public social involvement that has been institutionalized in the 1990s as part of a larger right-wing celebration of self-reliance and efficient government. Unfortunately, it is often our children who must foot the cost of this perverse abrogation of democratic citizenship.

One scene in *Home Alone* particularly highlights the decline of the public space in postmodern America. While Kevin's parents attempt to arrange a flight from Paris to their home in Chicago, the rest of the family watches *It's a Wonderful Life* dubbed into French on TV. This positioning of movie within a movie confronts viewers with the distance between the America of Jimmy Stewart's George Bailey and Macaulay Culkin's Kevin McAlister. Kevin has no community, no neighbors to call for help—he is on his own in his "private space." George Bailey had a score of neighbors to help bail him out of his financial plight and to help him fight the capitalists' efforts to destroy the community. Kevin is not just home alone—he is socially alone as well. But such realizations are not present in the conscious mind of the movie makers. On the surface the McAlisters live in a desirable community and are a perfect family. Like millions of other late twenti-eth century families, they are physically together but culturally and emotionally fragmented. Plugged into their various "market segments" of entertainment me-dia, they retreat into their "virtual isolation booths."

Like millions of other kids Kevin feels isolated in such an existence—isolation leads to powerlessness, hopelessness, and boredom. How could kids with every-thing handed to them, adults ask, become so alienated from their parents, schools, and communities? The answer to this question involves on some level the pervasive violation of childhood innocence. Popular culture via TV promised our children a *Brady Bunch* family circus, but they had to settle for alienated and isolated homes. The continuing popularity of *The Brady Bunch* is testimony to the mind-set of American children—*The Brady Bunch* with its family values and two engaged parents seemed to provide what our children found lacking in their own homes. This melancholy nostalgia for suburban family bliss indicates a yearning for a lost childhood. All those hours home alone have taken their toll (James 1990; Rapping 1994; Ferguson 1994).

The Unwanted

Although *Home Alone* 1 and 2 work hard to deny it, they are about a child unwanted by his family—as are many other films of the 1980s and early 1990s. The comedic forms of the movies supposedly render the unwanted theme harmless, in the process revealing contemporary views of parenting and the abandonment of children. In one particular scene in the first *Home Alone* Kevin's mother (Catherine O'Hara) pays for abandoning her son by riding home to Chicago through midwestern snow storms in a truck carrying a polka band leader (John Candy) and his band. In one dialogue mother and band leader engage in a confessional on bad parenting and child abandonment:

Mother: "I'm a bad parent."
Band Leader: "No, you're not. You're beating yourself up. . . . You want to see bad parents. We're [band] on the road 48 to 49 weeks out of the year. We hardly see our families. Joe over there, gosh, he forgets his kids' names half the time. Ziggy over there hasn't even met his kid. Eddie, let's just hope none of them [his children] write a book about him."
Mother: "Have you ever gone on vacation and left your child home?"
Band Leader: "No, but I did leave one at a funeral parlor once. Yeah, it was terrible. I was all distraught and everything. The wife and I, we left the little tyke there in the funeral parlor all day, ALL DAY. We went back at night when we came to our senses and there he was. Apparently, he was there alone all day with the corpse. He was O.K. You know, after six or seven weeks he came around and started talking again. But he's O.K. They get over it. Kids are resilient like that."
Mother: "Maybe we shouldn't talk about it."
Band Leader: "You brought it up."

So comfortable are marketers with the theme of abandonment that promos on the home video of *Home Alone 2: Lost in New York* present a "Home Alone Christmas Album." Commodifying child abandonment, promoters urge viewers to "begin a tradition in your house." Something is happening in these movies and the promotions that surround them that is not generally understood by the larger society. By the early 1990s social neglect of children had become so commonplace that it could be presented as a comedic motif without raising too many eyebrows. There was a time when childhood accorded protected status—but that time is growing obsolete, as safety nets disintegrate and child supports crumble. Now, as children are left to fend for themselves, few public institutions exist to address their needs.

In *Home Alone* 1 and 2 not only is Kevin left to take care of himself, but when his parents and family are on screen they treat him with disdain and cruelty. In one scene Kevin's uncle unjustifiably calls him a "little jerk." After understandably asking why he always gets "treated like scum," Kevin is banished to the attic upon which he proclaims for his generation: "families suck." These early experiences set up the comedic bread and butter of *Home Alone*: Kevin's transference of his anger toward his family to burglars Marv (Daniel Stern) and Harry (Joe Pesci) and his subsequent torture of them. *Home Alone* 1 and 2 are not the only movies of the era that address child abandonment and child revenge. In horror-thrillers *Halloween* and *Friday the 13th* the only individuals spared from violence are those who give time to and care for children. Those who neglect children must ultimately pay with their lives. As neglected social rejects, children are relegated to the margins of society. It is not surprising, therefore, that in *Home Alone* 2 Kevin forges an alliance with a homeless pigeon lady who lives in Central Park—after all they are both social castoffs. Together they learn to deal with their cultural status.

The American Ambivalence Toward Children

After World War II Americans began to realize that childhood was becoming a phase of life distinctly separate from adulthood. This distinction was most evident in the youth culture beginning to take shape in the 1950s; it was this youth culture that convinced parents that they were losing the ability to shape the culture in which their children lived. As a result, they were losing control of their sons and daughters. This fear has informed the academic study of youth in the last half of the twentieth century, often focusing attention on children as "the problem." Too often refusing to question the dominant culture and values of the adult world and the tacit assumptions of the field of childhood studies itself, mainstream scholars have often viewed conflict between children and parents as dysfunctional. Childhood "experts" and the mainstream education establishment have often insisted in this academic context that children need to be instructed to follow directions. This functionalist orientation assumes that the order and stability of environments must be maintained (Paul 1994; Lewis 1992; Griffin 1993; Polakow 1992). This, of course, ensures that institutions such as schools become unable to accommodate change, as they regress into a state of "equilibrium," that is, rigidity.

The virtual ubiquity of parent-child alienation and conflict is rarely perceived at the individual level of human interaction as a social phenomenon. When such conflicting dynamics occur in almost all parent-child relations, it is not likely that fault rests solely with individual parents and individual children. As we said before, something larger is happening here. It seems as if individual children cannot help but judge parents for their inconsistencies and shortcomings. On the other hand, parents cannot help but resent their judgment and strike back with equal venom (Ventura 1994). Adults must understand the social nature of this familial phenomenon and based on this recognition attempt to transcend the demand for order inscribed into their consciousness by the larger culture. Indeed, Americans don't understand their children or the dynamics of children's culture. Kids understand that adults just don't get it, as they listen and watch adults express and act on their misunderstandings of the differences between generational experiences and mind-sets. Schools are perceived by children as virtually hopeless—indeed, they are institutionally grounded on a dismissal of these differences. Little has changed since the 1960s when Kenneth Keniston wrote that adult misunderstanding of youth contributed to the conclusion reached by many children: American mainstream culture offers us little to live for (Lewis 1992).

Understanding this adult-child alienation, children slowly begin to withdraw into their own culture. Culkin's Kevin has absolutely no need for adults, as he shops (with newspaper coupons even), takes care of the house, and defends himself against robbers all by himself. This is quite typical for the films of John Hughes, whose children and teenagers rule in a world where youth culture is the only one that matters. Parents in these films are notoriously absent either at work or on vacation; their advice is antiquated, consisting generally of pompous pronouncements about subjects they obviously know nothing about. Typical of the genre is *The Breakfast Club*, which revolves around the stupidity of parents and adult authority. While it is a flagrant attempt by Hughes to commodify and exploit youth culture, the film does point out the width and depth of the chasm that separates kids and adults (Rapping 1994). Children's culture, of course, takes shape in shadows far away from the adult gaze—as well it should. The point here is that it behooves parents, teachers, social workers, and other cultural workers who are interested in the welfare of children to understand the social dynamics that shape children and their culture in the final years of the twentieth century. When parents intensify their anxiety about the threat of postmodern kinderculture (Kincheloe and Steinberg 1996) and strike out against it, they simply widen the chasm between themselves and their children. In this situation, the assertion of parental control becomes simply an end in itself, having little to do with the needs of children.

As adults in the 1950s and early 1960s began to understand the power of children's culture and the separations between childhood and adulthood it represented, parental and educator anxiety levels reached new highs. Adult fears that the kids were out of control expressed themselves in a variety of ways, none more interesting than in two British films of the early 1960s, *Village of the Damned* and its sequel, *Children of the Damned*. *Village of the Damned* is based on an invasion by an intergalactic sperm that impregnates earth women to produce a new race of mutant children who mature quickly and are capable of reading adult minds. Reflecting adult anxieties of the era concerning the growing partition between childhood and adulthood, the movie offers a "solution" to the youth problem. Though it is embraced with great difficulty, adults in *Children of the*

Damned ultimately decide that they must kill their children. Understanding that child murder by necessity is suicidal in that it involves killing a part of oneself, parents sacrifice themselves in order to eradicate the iniquity their children embody. The youth rebellions of the mid-and late sixties that followed *Children of the Damned* would serve to raise the emotional ante expressed in the movie's fantasized infanticide.

The adult hostility toward children is omnipresent in *Home Alone* 1 and 2, but such issues are consistently hidden from overt recognition. Previous films—*The Other, The Exorcist, The Bad Seed, Firestarter, It's Alive*—recognized adult hostility but projected it onto evil children as a means of concealing it. The abundance of these evil children films points to a social tendency of parents to view their children as alien intruders. This child-based xenophobia positions children as foreigners whose presence marks the end of the family's configuration as a couple (Paul 1994). Old routines are undermined and new demands must be met, as the child's power as manipulator is experienced by harried adults. Such familial dynamics set the scene for the postmodern child custody case where lawyers, judges, and parents decide who *has* to take the kids.

Commercial children's culture understands what parents and educators don't—children and adolescents are wracked by desire that demands stimulation and often gets out of hand. We see its manifestation in children and children's culture with the constant struggle to escape boredom. Of course, most adults view this childhood desire as a monstrous quality to be squashed by any means necessary even if it requires the stupidification of young people in the process. In the *Home Alone* movies Kevin constantly feels as if he has done something terribly wrong, as if he were a bad kid. In *Home Alone 2: Lost in New York* Kevin prays to the Rockefeller Square Christmas tree: "I need to see my mother, I need to tell her I'm sorry." Exactly for what he should be sorry, no one is quite sure. One can only conclude that he is sorry for being a child, for intruding on the smooth operation of the family, of being goaded by his monstrous desire.

If we equate children with that which is monstrous, it is not a long jump to the position that the manipulative aliens are evil. In *The Bad Seed*, a successful novel, play, and movie of the mid-1950s, Rhoda is an eight-year-old murderess endowed with a greed for material things—childhood desire run amuck. As the first work that explored this homicidal dimension of childhood, *The Bad Seed* equates youth with absolute malignancy—concealed at first in an innocent package. As Rhoda's landlady says of her: "She never gets anything dirty. She is a good child, a perfect child. She saves her money and keeps her room clean." The appearance of evil so close to goodness and innocence made the child monster that much more horrible. Children who are so evil (or at least so capable of it) in a perverted sense justify child abuse. By 1990 this image of the bad child would be used for comic effect in *Problem Child* and *Problem Child 2* a year later. The way adults in the *Problem Child* movie reacted to the problem child is revealing:

> *School principal:* "Being a principal's great 'cause I hate kids. I have to deal with the weenies."

School teacher to principal after he brings problem child to her class as a new student: "O God, another one. How many kids are they going to make me teach?"

Lawanda, the owner of the bank: "What's this thing [referring to problem child]? This kid's a nightmare. . . . Kids are like bum legs. You don't shoot the patient, you cut off the leg."

Problem child's Grandfather to father: "You little psycho—you're an evil boy. You got to learn to respect your elders."

Lawanda: "Listen you little monster. I'm going to marry your father and send you to boarding school in Baghdad."

School principal: "You rotten kids should be locked in cages."

Lawanda: "I hate children. They ruin everything. If I had enough power I'd wipe them off the face of the earth."

Child murderer Susan Smith never stated it this clearly and unambiguously.

Whenever the problem child seeks to subvert the order of the status quo, viewers are alerted to what is coming by George Throughgood's blues guitar riff from "Bad to the Bone." Such innate "badness" cannot be indulged. As with the neo-folk wisdom in 1990s America that criminals cannot be rehabilitated, there is no hope for the growth and development of the problem child. *Home Alone's* Kevin, who is certainly capable of "badness" and sadistic torture, is still struggling with parental forgiveness; the problem child is beyond all that. Parental and educational authority is concerned simply with control; the issue is naked power—there is no need for ameliorative window dressing in this *realpolitik* for children. In this context kindness becomes the cause of juvenile delinquency, child advocacy the response of dupes and bleeding heart fools. Movie audiences want to see the problem child punished, if not physically attacked. Not too far from such sentiments looms child abuse.

In John Carpenter's *Halloween* the camera shows the audience an unidentified murderer's point of view of a middle American suburban house occupied by two teenagers making love in an upstairs bedroom. As we watch from the murderer's eyes, he picks up a carving knife in the kitchen, observes the teenage boy leave the house, and walks back up the stairs to the bedroom where the teenage girl is now in bed alone. Looking directly into the gaze of the camera the girl expresses her annoyance with an obviously familiar character wielding the knife. At this point the hand carrying the knife stabs the girl to death, principally focusing the attack on her bare breasts. It is only after the murder that we are granted a reverse angle shot of the killer, who is a six-year-old boy. By 1978 when *Halloween* was made, movie commentators made little of the age of the murderer (Paul 1994). So accustomed was the American audience to the "innate" evil potential of children that movie makers perceived no need to explain the etymology of the child's violent behavior. By the end of the 1970s headlines such as "Killer Kids" and newspaper copy such as "Who are our children? One day they are innocent. The next, they may try to blow your head off" (Vogel 1994, p. 57) had made an impact. No more assumptions of innocence, no surprises. A new era had emerged.

The Blame Game

Clusters of issues come together as we consider the role of mothers and fathers in the family wars of the late twentieth century. The battle to ascribe blame for family dysfunction in general, and childhood pathology in particular, plays out on a variety of landscapes: politics, religion, and popular culture. On the political terrain, the 1990s have witnessed the Dan Quayle-Murphy Brown showdown over single mothers as parents, while on the religious battleground right-wing Christian fundamentalists have fingered feminism as the catalyst for mothers' neglect of their children. The analysis of this blame game as expressed in popular culture offers some unique insights.

In *Home Alone* 1 and 2 Kevin's mother has internalized the right-wing blame of women for the neglect (abandonment) of Kevin in particular and family pathology in general. Though they are uncomfortable with a negative maternal figure, the screenplay writers of *Home Alone* 1 and 2 leave no doubt as to who's to blame. Banished to the attic because he has been *perceived* as a nuisance, Kevin is (justifiably) hurt and angry.

> *Kevin:* "Everyone in this family hates me."
> *Mother:* "Then maybe you should ask Santa for a new family."
> *Kevin:* "I don't want a new family. I don't want any family. Families suck."
> *Mother:* "Just stay up there. I don't want to see you again for the rest of the night."
> *Kevin:* "I don't want to see you again for the rest of my whole life. And I don't want to see anyone else, either."
> *Mother:* "I hope you don't mean that. You'd be pretty sad if you woke up tomorrow morning and you didn't have a family."
> *Kevin:* "No, I wouldn't."
> *Mother:* "Then say it again. Maybe it'll happen."
> *Kevin:* "I hope I never see any of you again."

The mother here is the provocateur, the one who plants the ideas that emerge as Kevin's wishes. Insensitive to his emotional hurt, she induces him to request a new family, she is the first to speak of not wanting to see him, she is the one who dares Kevin to tempt fate by wishing away his family (Paul 1994). There is little doubt left by the *Home Alone* movies that child care is the mother's responsibility. John Heard's father character is virtually a non entity. He is disinterested in, condescending and hostile to Kevin. He knows (along with the audience) that he is not responsible for Kevin's abandonment even though he was present during the entire episode. He has no reason to gnash his teeth or rend his garment in displays of penitence—this is the domain of the mother. And pay she does with her polka band trip in the first *Home Alone* and her frenzied running the nighttime streets of New York calling for her son in *Home Alone* 2. In an era when child abuse and child murder by mothers occupy national headlines, Kevin's mother's request for forgiveness may signify a much larger guilt. The right-wing male's blame of women for the ills of the family, however, is grotesquely perverse, implying, as it does, that battalions of strong but tender men are struggling with their wives to let them take charge of child-rearing—not hardly (Rapping 1994).

Feminist research and analysis of child abuse and domestic violence have subverted the happy depiction of family life as a safe heaven far removed from pathologies emanating from internal power inequities. As such scholarship documented the ways that family life has oppressed women and children, pro-family conservative groups responded by calling for a reassertion of patriarchal control in the home. Women, they argued, should return to child-rearing. Some conservatives have even maintained that women who don't adequately perform these "maternal" chores should have their children taken away and placed in orphanages. The most optimistic estimates place the number of children who would be institutionalized under this plan at over one million—the costs of such care would run over 36 billion dollars (Griffin 1993; Morganthau et al. 1994). The male backlash to the assertive feminist critique has only begun with its depiction of women's political organization as the rise of a dangerous special interest group. Protectors of male power are waging an effective public relations battle: any campaign that is able to deflect blame for family failure from absent and often abusive fathers to mothers possesses a superior penchant for persuasion and little concern for truth.

Home Alone displays these gender dynamics in its complete refusal to implicate the father in the abandonment. Upon learning that Kevin is not in Paris with the family, his mother exclaims, "What kind of mother am I?" The lack of affect on the part of the adult males of the family, Kevin's father and his uncle, is perplexing. The careful viewer can only conclude that they neither like nor care about the eight-year-old. An explanation of the father's dismissiveness is never provided. All the viewer can discern is that the father and the uncle seem to be fighting for their manhood, expressing it perhaps in their resistance to the "breadwinner-loser" male character who forfeits his "male energy" in his domestication and subsequent acceptance of fidelity in marriage, dedication to job, and devotion to children (Lewis 1992). Such a male figure was ridiculed by beatniks as square, by *Playboy* devotees as sexually timid, and by hippies as tediously straight. The search for a hip male identity along with a healthy dose of irresponsibility has undermined the family as a stable and loving environment. Indeed, to "do the right thing" in regard to one's family as a man is to lose status among one's fellow men.

An examination of adult male behavior in families indicates that many men are desperately concerned with peer group status. For example, men on average pay pitifully inadequate child support to their former spouses, if they pay it at all. Only half of women awarded child support ever receive what they are owed, another quarter receive partial payments, and the remaining quarter get nothing at all (Galston 1991). This ambiguous role of the father in the family highlighted by the indifferent father of *Home Alone* is addressed in a more overtly oedipal manner in other movies of the last couple of decades (Paul 1994). *The Shining*, for example, retrieves that which has always been repressed in Western culture, a father's hostility toward his own son, and builds an entire plot around it. Danny, the child protagonist in *The Shining*, develops the psychic power to see beyond the limits of time and space after his father (Jack Nicholson) in an alcoholic stupor broke Danny's arm. Danny's power, his shining, is expressed through his imaginary friend, Tony, who lives in Danny's mouth. Tony exists to help Danny cope with his violent and abusive father. Danny's presence and growth remind his father of his emasculation, his stultification by the family. The father's solution to his problem—the attempted ax murder of his wife and child—allows for none of the *Home Alone* ambiguity; the movie jumps headfirst into the maelstrom of the conflict between virile masculinity and the demands of domesticity.

As the screen image of the crazed ax-wielding Jack Nicholson fades into a blurred image of *Jurassic Park* (1993), the continuity of the child hating adult male remains intact. Even in this "child-friendly" Spielberg-produced dino-drama, the paleontologist (Sam Neill) holds such an extreme hatred of children that he won't ride in the same car with them. At one point in the film in response to a prepubescent boy's sarcastic question about the power of dinosaurs, Neill evokes the image of the violent Nicholson circling and threatening the child with the ominous claw of a velociraptor. The difference between *Jurassic Park* and *The Shining*, however, involves Neill's moment of epiphany; when the children are endangered by the dinosaurs, Neill sheds his hatred and like a good father risks mutilation and death to save their lives. As in the *Home Alone* movies, the issue of the father's hatred is buried in a happy McAlister family celebrating Christmas in a frenetic present-opening ritual. The demand for family values in the 1980s and 1990s had changed the cultural landscape: family values must triumph; adult men must be depicted as ultimately devoted to their children; the feminists' portrayal of the "bad father" must not be reinforced.

And as if the Ambiguity Wasn't Bad Enough, Some Kids Matter More Than Others

It doesn't take long to discern that with the class dynamics of the 1990s, poor children in America don't matter as much as upper-middle-class children, that is, privileged children like the ones portrayed in the *Home Alone* movies. The frequent assertion that America is not a class society, uttered so confidently by mainstream politicians and educators, holds profound psychological and political consequences. This class silence undermines the well-to-do's understanding that they were granted a head start, while paralyzing the less successful with a feeling of personal inferiority. On the political level as it sustains the fiction, the belief reifies the status quo: when the poor are convinced that their plight is self-produced, the larger society is released from any responsibility (Rubin 1994).

An overt class silence pervades *Home Alone* 1 and 2. Even newspaper reviewers referred to the upper-middle class, white, and Protestant "bleached and sanitized" microcosm of the two movies (Koch 1990). The McAlisters are very wealthy, living in their enormous brick colonial in a generic Chicago suburb filled with extravagant furnishings and conveniences. Indeed, they are an obnoxious and loathsome crew, but being so privileged they believe they can act any way they want. The filmmakers go out of their way to make sure viewers know that the family deserves its money—as father McAlister (John Heard) drinks from crystal in first class on the plane to Paris, he alludes to his hard work and humble origins. The message is clear—the American dream is attainable for those willing to put in the effort. The McAlisters deserve their good fortune.

Into this restricted world of affluent WASPs Harry and Marv (two small-time robbers with an attitude) make their appearance as the only poor people and the only non-WASPs in the two movies. Harry (Joe Pesci) and Marv (Daniel Stern) are quickly positioned as "the other" in both screenplays: they speak in specific lower socioeconomic class accents; obviously ethnic, Pesci exaggerates his working-class Italian accent, and just so we are not confused Stern signifies his Jewishness with a curiously gratuitous "Happy Hanukkah" reference as he steals money from a toy store; they are ignorant and uneducated—Pesci makes specific reference to the fact he never completed the sixth grade; they hold an irrational hatred of the affluent, their "crime-signature" involves flooding affluent homes after each robbery (they are known as the "wet bandits"). These class-and ethnic-specific traits set Marv and Harry apart to such a degree that the audience can unambiguously enjoy their torture at the hands of Kevin.

Home Alone 1 and 2 pull their weight in the larger social effort to erase class as a dynamic in late twentieth century American life. Under interrogation the movies confess their class complicity, as evidenced through the "otherization" of Marv and Harry. Compare Marv and Harry with Mr. Duncan, the toy store owner who appears in *Home Alone* 2. Imbued with the sweetness and generosity of Joseph the angel in *It's a Wonderful Life*, Duncan is the most charming character in the *Home Alone* movies. After the McAlisters' reunification in *Home Alone* 2, he showers them with scores of presents. His only motivation for being in business is that he loves children and wants to see their happy faces when they open presents from his store. His loving smiles prove that capitalism cares and the status quo is just. He deserves every penny of his profits just as much as Marv and Harry deserve their torment. Such characterization gently dovetails with the dominant political impulses of the moment, marked by a callous acceptance of poverty, child poverty in particular, in the midst of plenty.

Over 12.6 million children live below the poverty line, making one out of every five American children poor. Too often unaware of even the existence of such class realities, Americans and their institutions are far removed from the insidious effects of such poverty. Poor children too infrequently escape the effects of living with parents scarred by their sense of shortcoming, of having to negotiate movie and TV images of the poor and working class as dangerous and oafish caricatures (as in *Home Alone* 1 and 2), and of confronting teachers and social workers who hold lower expectations for them than their middle and upper-middle class peers. A key feature of the class dynamic in *Home Alone* 1 and 2 involves the public reaction to the McAlisters' child abandonment episodes as "good fun," as opposed to the real-life home alone cases that keep surfacing in the 1990s. When Kevin's parents report his having been left alone in New York to the police after they reach their vacation destination in Miami, it's no big deal. Even when they admit that abandoning the child has become "a family tradition," no one is excited—after all, the McAlisters are upper class, well-to-do people. Almost daily, parents (especially single mothers) who leave their young children home alone for sometimes just a few hours are arrested and forced to relinquish their child/children to foster care. With child care often costing 200 to 400 dollars a month, poor mothers are placed into virtually impossible circumstances (Seligman 1993). The society's refusal to address poor and single mothers' need for child care has contributed to the feminization of poverty (Polakow 1992). *Home Alone* 1 and 2 indicate the double standard that dominates the American view of the rich and the poor and the mean-spirited class bias of some expressions of popular culture in this conservative age.

The Postmodern Childhood

Within *Home Alone* 1 and 2's bizarre mix of child abandonment, child-parent alienation, children caught in the crossfire of gender wars, crass class bias, and comedy resides something profound about the role of children in contemporary American culture. The movies could have been made only in a culture that had experienced a profound shift in the social role of children. For all individuals who have a stake in understanding children—parents, teachers, social workers, family counselors, and so forth . . . —knowledge of these changing conditions becomes a necessity. A no-growth economy has mandated that all adults in the family must work outside the home; because of such needs, children find themselves saddled with daily duties ranging from house cleaning, baby-sitting, and grocery shopping to cooking, laundry, and organizing carpools. With the "family values" agenda of right-wing movements of the 1900s threatening to eviscerate the governmental support of poor and middle-class families, the economic problem of children look to get worse before they get better.

The new era of childhood, the postmodern childhood, cannot escape the influence of the postmodern condition with its electronic media saturation. Such a media omnipresence produces a hyperreality that repositions the real as something no longer simply given but artificially reproduced as real. Thus, media-produced models replace the real—simulated TV kids on sit-coms replace real life children as models of childhood. In this same media-driven postmodern condition a cultural implosion takes place, ripping apart boundaries between information and entertainment as well as images and politics. As media push the infinite proliferation of meaning, boundaries between childhood and adulthood fade as children and adults negotiate the same mediascape and struggle with the same impediments to meaning making. Children become "adultified" and adults become "childified" (Aronowitz and Giroux 1991; Best and Kellner 1991). Boundaries between adulthood and childhood blur to the point that a clearly defined, "traditional," innocent childhood becomes an object of nostalgia—a sure sign that it no longer exists in any unproblematic form (Lipsky and Abrams 1994; Postman 1994).

There is nothing child-like about a daily routine of child care, cooking, and shopping. In *Home Alone* 1 and 2 Kevin is almost completely adult-like in meeting the demands of survival on his own. He checks into hotels, uses credit cards, buys pizzas, and grocery shops (even with coupons), all as a part of a day's work. He needs no adult-figure; he can take complete care of himself. In the postmodern childhood being home alone is an everyday reality. Children now know what only adults used to know: postmodern children are sexually knowledgeable and often sexually experienced; they understand and many have experimented with drugs and alcohol; and new studies show they often experience the same pressures as single working mothers, as they strive to manage the stresses of school, work at home, and interpersonal family dynamics. When the cultural dynamics of hyperreality collide with post babyboom demographics and the economic decline of the early 1970s, 1980s, and 1990s, the world changes (Lipsky and Abrams 1994). The daily life of media-produced family models such as the Cleavers from *Leave it to Beaver* is convulsed. June must get a job and Wally and Beaver must take care of the house. No longer can Beaver and his friends Larry and Whitey leisurely play on the streets of Mayfield after school. Anyway, it's dangerous—Mayfield is not as safe as it used to be.

Children under twelve of the mid-1990s belong to a generation only half the size of the baby boomers. As a result, children as a group garner less attention in 1996 than in 1966 and exert a correspondingly diminished voice in the society's social and political conversation. In such a context, youth issues are not as important as they once were. Add to this a declining economy complicated by rising expectations. As American manufacturing jobs have disappeared and dead-end service jobs have expanded, advertising continues to promote higher and higher consumer desire. Frustration levels among children and teenagers rise as a direct result of this socioeconomic contradiction. Given the centrality of TV in the lives of this postmodern home alone generation, the awareness of the desirability of children's consumer goods becomes a central aspect of their lives. Consumer desire, however, is only one aspect of the effect of TV and other electronic media on American children. TV is where children find out about American culture. Indeed, one doesn't have to be a movie critic to know how often Hollywood has drawn on the TV-taught-me-all-I-know theme. In *The Man Who Fell to Earth*, David Bowie as an alien learns all about earth culture from TV; in *Being There* Peter Sellers as idiot-savant Chauncey Gardner knows nothing about the world but what he has learned on TV. The movie ends with Chauncey on his way to a possible presidential candidacy—life imitates art? The robot in *Short Circuit*, the mermaid in *Splash*, the aliens in *Explorers*, and the Neanderthal in *Encino Man* all are completely socialized by TV (Lipsky and Abrams 1994).

What does the repeated invocation of this theme say to observers of childhood? With the evolution of TV as a medium that attempts to more or less represent reality, children have gained an adult-like (not necessarily an informed) view of the world in only a few years of TV watching. Traditional notions of childhood as a time of sequential learning about the world don't work in a hyperreality saturated with sophisticated but power-driven views of reality. When a hotel porter asks Kevin McAlister in *Home Alone 2* if he knows how the TV in his hotel room works, Kevin replies "I'm ten years old, TV's my life." The point is well taken, and as a consciousness dominating, full disclosure medium TV provides everyone—sixty-year-old adults to eight-year-old children with the same data. As postmodern children gain unrestricted knowledge about things once kept secret from non-adults, the mystique of adults as revered keepers of secrets about the world begins to disintegrate. No longer do the elders know more than children about the experience of youth—given the social/technological changes they often know less, for example, about video games, computers, TV programs, and so forth. . . . Thus, the authority of adulthood is undermined, as kids' generational experience takes on a character of its own.

The social impact of such a phenomenon is profound on many levels. A subversive kinderculture is created where kids through their attention to child-targeted programming and commercials know something that mom and dad don't. This corporate-directed kinderculture provides kids with a body of knowledge adults don't possess, while their access to adult themes on TV at least makes them conversant with marital, sexual, business-related, criminal, violent, and other traditionally restricted issues (Kincheloe and Steinberg 1996). When combined with observations of families collapsing, the dynamics of the struggle of a single mother to support her family, parents involved in the "singles" scene, and post-divorce imposition of adult-like chores, children's TV experience provides a full-scale immersion into grown-up culture.

In the context of childhood education the postmodern experience of being a kid represents a cultural earthquake. The curriculum of the third grade is determined not only by what vocabulary and concepts are "developmentally appropriate" but by what content is judged to be commensurate with third grade experience in the lived world (Lipsky and Abrams 1994; Postman 1994). Hyperreality explodes traditional notions of curriculum development—third graders can discuss the relationship between women's self-image and the nature of their sexual behavior. While parental groups debate the value of sex education in the public schools, their children are at home watching a TV docudrama depicting a gang rape of a new inmate in the federal penitentiary. When teachers and the culture of school treats such children as if they know nothing of the adult world, the kids come to find school hopelessly archaic, out of touch with the times. This is why the postmodern subversive kinderculture always views school with a knowing wink and a smirk—how quaint school must look to our postmodern children.

There is nothing easy about the new childhood. Indeed, many teenagers and young adults speak of their stress and fatigue originating in childhood. If one has judged the responsibilities of adulthood since the age of seven, physical and psychological manifestations of stress and fatigue during one's adolescence should surprise no one. Adolescent suicide did not exist as a category during the "old childhood"—by 1980 it was second only to accidents as the leading cause of death of teenagers. By the 1990s, 400,000 young people were attempting suicide yearly and youth suicide was being described in the academic literature as an epidemic (Gaines 1990). The covenant between children and adults has been broken by parental and clerical child abuse and the pathological behavior of other caretakers. Too often children of the late twentieth century have callously been deposited in inadequate child care institutions administered on the basis of cost-efficiency concerns not on a larger commitment to the welfare of children. The tendency to segregate by age is well established in late twentieth century America, and unless steps are taken to reverse the trend more generational alienation and antagonism will result (Gaines 1994; Polakow 1992).

In the context of this child segregation cultural pathologies manifest themselves. Excluded from active participation in the social order, children find themselves both segregated and overregulated by institutional forms of social control. The overregulators pose as experts on child raising, child development, child morality, and early childhood education with their psychodiscourse on the rigid phases of child development and the strict parameters of normality. In the name of "proper child rearing techniques" experts tap into the larger ideology of personnel management that adjusts individuals to the demands of an orderly society. Like all strategies of personnel management mainstream child psychology masks its emphasis on control. Intimidated by the scientific language of the experts, parents lose faith in their own instincts and surrender control to the authority figure on *Sally*. Play gives way to skill development, as structure permeates all aspects of the child's life. While middle-and upper-middle-class children suffer from the hyper-structure of skill-development, poor children labeled "at risk" are medicated and drilled in the misguided effort to reduce chaos and disorder in their lives. In the name of order the experience of poor children is further bureaucratized (Seiter 1993; Polakow 1992).

The Worldliness of Postmodern Childhood: The Wise Ass As Prototype

The *Home Alone* movies can be understood only in the context of the postmodern childhood. Kevin McAlister is a worldly child—light-years separate Kevin from Chip, Ernie, and Robbie Douglas on *My Three Sons* of the late 1950s and early 1960s. As a black comedy for children, *Home Alone* struck an emotional chord with movie watchers that made it one of the most popular and profitable films of all time. Kevin, as kiddie-*noir* hero, is a smart-kid with an attitude; Macauley Culkin's ability to portray that character turned him into an overnight celebrity— a role model for the pre-pubescent wise ass.

Kevin as postmodern wise ass could not tolerate children from the 1940s and 1950s with their simple-minded "the policeman is our friend" view of the world. Bizarre in their innocence, such children are viewed by postmodern kids as anti-matter reflections of themselves without responsibilities or cynicism. "What would we talk about?" Kevin might ask of a meeting with such kids. Unless

Kevin had watched old movies or lived near a separatist group such as the Amish, he would have never seen such unworldly children. Almost every child depicted on TV in the contemporary era—Alex Keaton on *Family Ties*, Michele in *Full House*, Lisa and Bart Simpson on *The Simpsons*, Rudi on *The Cosby Show*— is worldly and wise. Bart Simpson may be an underachiever, but only in school— a place he finds boring, confining, and based on a childhood that no longer exists. Bart is not childish, the school is. The smart ass child à la Culkin and Bart Simpson is the symbol for contemporary childhood. Imagine Bart's reaction to a "Yes, Virginia, there is a Santa Claus" adult monologue: "Right, daddy-o, now eat my shorts."

The wise ass is the hero of the subversive kinderculture. The appeal of *Home Alone* 1 and 2 is connected to this insurgent response to middle-class propriety with its assumption of child helplessness and its worship of achievement. Child and adult are pitted against one another with the child as the sympathetic char-acter. In the case of *Home Alone* 1 and 2 no one could feel much sympathy for Kevin's parents with their lack of empathy for Kevin's position in the family and their lack of attention to his needs. Kevin's behavior is an act of righteous resis-tance to this unjust status quo. Like his kindred spirits, Bart Simpson, and Beavis and Butthead, Kevin thrives on disorder—a chaos that undermines the social order constructed around bourgeois stability. As Beavis and Butthead might put it, order "sucks" disorder is "cool." The subversive kinderculture of the post-modern childhood thrives on this disorder.

Indeed, one of the subtexts running through both *Home Alone* movies involves the humorous juxtaposition of comments of family members concerning poor, helpless little Kevin with the visual depiction of Kevin happy and in control of the disorder of his solitude. The appeal of the film revolves around Kevin's ability to tell his parents: "Even in the middle of all this exciting chaos, I don't need you." The self-sufficient, boy-hero of the postmodern era—what a movie-marketing bonanza. He shows no remorse on learning that his parents have left him home alone: (with eyebrows raised Kevin speaks to the audience) "I made my family disappear." Compare this postmodern reaction to parent-child sepa-ration to Dorothy's in *The Wizard of Oz*—Judy Garland's *raison d'être* is getting back home to Kansas. Kevin is self-actualized, living out the childhood fantasy of life without parental encumberment. Since he "can't trust anybody in his fam-ily," Kevin decides he would rather vacation alone than with "such a group of creeps." As a bellman scoops ice cream for him in his posh New York hotel room, it is obvious that Kevin's intuitions are correct. "*This* is a vacation," he sighs.

Confronting the Intensity of Youth in a Postmodern Childhood

As parties interested in the status of contemporary childhood, we ask, what does the popularity of the *Home Alone* movies tells us about the inner-lives of children and their attempt to understand their relationship with the adult world? For a generation of home aloners Culkin's Kevin is a character with whom they can identify, as he negotiates the cultural obstacles they also have had to confront. He offers them a sense of hope, a feeling that there is something heroic in their daily struggle. Once again, the corporate marketers are one step ahead of the rest of us, as they recognize the changing nature of childhood and colonize the psychological ramifications such changes produce. In retrospect it seems so easy: to canonize a child who is left home alone for Christmas is to flatter every postmodern child in the audience. Kevin's predicament validates a generation's lived experience, transforming them from unwanted children into pre-teen Ninja warriors. If nothing else, *Home Alone* is a rite-of-passage story about a boy home alone, endangered, besieged who emerges victorious and transformed (Koch 1990). "I'm no wimp," he proclaims as he marches off to battle, "I'm the man of the house."

In a postmodern era where children have already seen everything, have watched the media sell laundry detergent by exploiting a mother's love for her children, it is no surprise that kids of the 1990s experience difficulty with emotional investment. As a result the interpersonal affect of postmodern children tends to be minimal—everything is kept at a distance and treated ironically (Grossberg 1994). Kevin offers such children both something in which to invest, and a sense that their desire for real experience is not pathological. This childhood and adolescent desire for extremes, for intense sensation is typically viewed by the adult world as dangerous and misguided. Indeed, the very purpose of certain forms of traditional schooling and child rearing has been to tame such feelings. This visceral energy of the young—so central to Kevin in *Home Alone* and so enticing to young moviegoers—lays the foundation for a progressive postmodern childrearing and childhood education. Too often adults who are "in charge" of children forget the nature and power of this visceral energy/life force of young people. In their adult amnesia they fail to connect with the force and, as a result, relinquish the possibility of guiding it or being replenished by it. They often blame rock music, MTV videos, video games, communists, or Satanists for creating the energy, forgetting that historically-mediated forms of it have expressed themselves from ancient hunter-gatherer societies to modern and postmodern ones (Ventura 1994; Rodriguez 1994).

The suppression of childhood desire in the postmodern North American culture at the end of the twentieth century undermines our civic, psychological, and intellectual growth. The very qualities adults fear most in the our children—their passion, visceral energy, and life force—can be used as the basis for a postmodern childhood education. In a sense the genie is out of the bottle and there is no way to get her or him back in. As the communication revolution has opened adult esoterica to children, we find there is no turning back. The endless debates over movie and record ratings are futile exercises; the question now revolves around: how do we provide children the type of emotional and intellectual supports that help them balance the interaction between their visceral energy and their newfound insights? Just as traditional forms of teaching and childhood curricular arrangements are passé given the "new times," forms of discipline and control strategies are obsolete. Can kids who hold Kevin's knowledge of the world in general and the anxieties and tribulations of adulthood in particular be domesticated and controlled (not to mention the question of *should* they . . .) in the same ways as children of a different era of childhood were? Custodial schooling is no longer adequate for children of the 1990s—indeed, it was never adequate for children no matter what the era.

Education for domestication assumes that the information a child encounters can be regulated and sequentially ordered (Polakow 1992; Gaines 1990). Much schooling and child rearing is still based on such an archaic assumption, resulting in strategies that negate children's exploration, invention, and play. Indeed, the purpose of many of these strategies is to prevent the integration of acquired information from a variety of sources into the cognitive and emotional structures of an evolving personhood, that is, growth itself. Thus, childrearing insufficiently prepares children for adulthood or even postmodern childhood, as it ignores the world that surrounds children and shapes their lives. The lessons to be excavated from this quick analysis of the *Home Alone* movies are sobering in their urgency. The state of the family at the end of the twentieth century and the inability of the public conversation about it to transcend the most trivial forms of platitudes to the value of the family in our "national character" is distressing. An effort to examine the nature of kinderculture and the forces that shape it simply does not exist in the surreal image-based politics of the present era. The ambivalent adult relationship with children is a suppressed feature of the cultural landscape, rarely, if ever, addressed in even the professional schooling of child welfare professionals, child psychologists, or elementary educators. These silences must end.

REFERENCES

Aronowitz, S. and H. Giroux. 1991. *Post-modern Education: Politics, Culture, and Social Criticism.* Minneapolis: University of Minnesota Press.

Best, S. and D. Kellner. 1991. *Postmodern Theory: Critical Interrogations.* New York: The Guilford Press.

Coontz, S. 1992. *The Way We Never Were: American Families and the Nostalgia Trap.* New York: Basic Books.

Ferguson, S. 1994. "The Comfort of Being Sad." *Utne Reader* 64 (July/August): 60–61.

Gaines, D. 1994. "Border Crossing in the USA." Pp. 227–234 in *Microphone Fiends: Youth Music, Youth Culture,* edited by A. Ross and T. Rose. New York: Routledge.

———. *Teenage Wasteland: Suburbia's Dead End Kids.* New York: Harper Perennial.

Gaines, D. (1990). *Teenage Wasteland: Suburbia's Dead End Kids.* New York: Harper Perennial.

Galston, W. 1991. "Home Alone: What Our Policymakers Should Know About Our Children." *The New Republic,* (December 2): 40–44.

Griffin, C. 1993. *Representation of Youth: The Study of Youth and Adolescence in Britain and America.* Cambridge, MA: Polity Press.

Grossberg, L. 1994. "Is Anybody Listening? Does Anybody Care? On the State of Rock."

Pp. 41–58 in *Microphone Fiends: Youth Music, Youth Culture*, edited by A. Ross and T. Rose. New York: Routledge.

James, C. 1990. "Scrooge Pens the Screenplay." *New York Times*, December 23.

Kincheloe, J. and Steinberg, S. 1996. *Kinderculture: The Corporate Construction of Childhood*. Boulder, CO: Westview Press.

Koch, J. 1990. "Home Alone Hits Home with a Powerful, Disturbing Pop-culture Potion." *The Boston Globe*, December, 27.

Lewis, J. 1992. *The Road to Romance and Ruin: Teen Films and Youth Culture*. New York: Routledge.

Lipsky, D. and A. Abrams. 1994. *Late Bloomers, Coming of Age in Today's America: The Right Place at the Wrong Time*. New York: Times Books.

Morganthau, T. et al. 1994. "The Orphanage." *Newsweek*, 124(24): 28–32.

Paul, W. 1994. *Laughing Screaming: Modern Hollywood Horror and Comedy*. New York: Columbia University Press.

Polakow, V. 1992. *The Erosion of Childhood*. Chicago: University of Chicago Press.

Postman, N. 1994. *The Disappearance of Childhood*. New York: Vintage Books.

Rapping, E. 1994. *Media-tions: Forays into the Culture and Gender Wars*. Boston: South End Press.

Rodriguez, L. 1994. "Rekindling the Warrior." *Utne Reader*, 64 (July/August): 58–59.

Rubin, L. 1994. *Families on the Faultline: America's Working Class Speaks About the Family, the Economy, Race, and Ethnicity*. New York: HarperCollins.

Seiter, E. 1993. *Sold Separately: Parents and Children in Consumer Culture*. New Brunswick, NJ: Rutgers University Press.

Seligman, K. 1993. "Poor Kids Often Home Alone." *San Francisco Examiner*, August 1.

Ventura, M. 1994. "The Age of Endarkenment." *Utne Reader* 64 (July/August): 63–366.

Vogel, J. 1994. "Throw Away the Key." *Utne Reader*, 64 (July/August): 56–60.

Chapter Nine

Child Abuse and the Unconscious in American Popular Culture

Nancy Scheper-Hughes and Howard F. Stein

The "Discovery" of Child Abuse

During the 1960s child abuse and neglect, long grappled with as a vexing and chronic social problem by generations of child welfare and social workers, was suddenly "discovered" and expropriated by a more powerful profession: medicine. When C. Henry Kempe and his associates (1962) at Colorado General Hospital created a new diagnostic entity—the "Battered Child Syndrome"—the American public finally sat up and took notice.[1]

With the mantle of medical legitimacy now thrown over the old problem of child maltreatment, the nation mobilized in a frontal attack on assaultive parents. Into this newly created social space appeared: state reporting laws,[2] new sources of federal funding, programs, and professionals. The National Center for the Treatment and Prevention of Child Abuse was established in 1974, and a whole research industry flourished with specialized journals, research centers, national and international societies and conferences all focused upon child abuse and neglect. National incidence studies, begun in the 1970s, reported sharp increases annually in the reports of maltreatment. Between 1976 and 1981, the total number of reports documented nationwide has more than doubled (the American Humane Society 1983). Social and behavioral scientists rushed in, often with premature causal explanations based on retrospective studies of poorly defined abusers and abused.[3] Research instruments and procedures were designed and implemented for the early detection of "high risk" parents (i.e. *mothers*) at public hospitals. Welfare patients, especially single mothers, were observed throughout labor, delivery, and the hours postpartum for signs of inadequate attachment to their newborns (see Kempe and Kempe 1978: 62–63). Based on inferences from this brief period of observation, "problem" mothers were targeted for early intervention programs that included home visits by nurses, clinical social workers, and child welfare workers.

Not surprisingly, the "discovery" of child abuse and the consequent development of interventional strategies also resulted in a proliferation of child abuse experts—researchers, educators, clinicians, therapists, and social workers—occupying newly created positions as members of child trauma teams in hospitals, on child abuse "hot lines", as facilitators in self-help "parenting" and stress management groups, and in emergency shelters and treatment programs for the abused. Child Abuse Prevention (CAP) workers visited schools, clinics, and day care programs in order to alert teachers, doctors and child care professionals to the covert signs (i.e. the distress and agitation) thought to be symptomatic of "sexually abused" children. In addition, they hold classes to educate even young toddlers, with the use of "anatomically correct" puppets and dolls, about the difference between "good" and "bad" touches by parents and other adult caretakers.[4] This was said to be part of the process of "empowering" children.

Meanwhile, the media (newspapers, television, radio, films, popular books) played an important role in sensitizing the American public to some of the more bizarre and sadistic examples of child maltreatment. The magazine stories and "docu-dramas" broadcast into homes across the nation created a social climate and consensus that allowed for a very dramatic increase in public interventions in the private lives of citizens.

On one level it appeared that we, as a nation, were finally coming to terms with the ways in which children were being used by their parents as receptacles in which to discard the worst remnants of their own childhoods. On another level, however, there is a note of hysteria in the protest and the outrage, somewhat out of proportion to the extent of, and long history of, the problem of child abuse. It seems that we need to raise another question: Why now? Why did it take so long to bring to consciousness and to respond to the problem? Why did public awareness await the *medicalization* of abuse?

This essay is an attempt to answer these questions, and to explain the "choice" of child abuse as a key (or master) social problem of our times by applying a critical analysis to aspects of the cultural "collective unconscious". In taking a psycho-historical approach to the problem of child maltreatment we are not going to concern ourselves with the issue of whether there is, in fact, more abuse now than in earlier decades or other historical periods. Anthropologists, demographers, social-and psycho-historians have amply documented that children have been killed, exposed, beaten, exploited, severely neglected, and sexually molested throughout the ethnographic and historical records (see deMause 1974, 1982; Hippler 1978; Stein 1978, 1980; Korbin 1981; Shorter 1975; Stone 1977; Scheper-Hughes 1979, 1984; Hausfater and Hrdy 1984). As for the present time, good (i.e. valid, reliable) statistics that could support or deny the allegations of an "epidemic" or a "rising tide" of child abuse are lacking. Child Protective Service Agencies get only the cases that a community will allow it to receive. Meanwhile there is little professional agreement on the definitions of child abuse, neglect, sexual exploitation (see Giovanni and Becerra 1979) and on what, in fact, constitutes the "Best Interests of the Child" (see Goldstein, Freud, and Solnit 1973).

Here we are concerned with exploring the contemporary meanings and functions of child maltreatment in terms of the unconscious role it seems to play in

American life at the present moment. We are attempting what Foucault and his associates call a "history of the present". In taking a strong social constructionist stance, however, we do not mean to imply that child maltreatment is a figment of the imagination, nor do we mean to underestimate its lethal effects on the health and wellbeing of American children. Along with child welfare professionals we, too, would like to see the cycle of family pathology that contributes to child abuse and neglect broken. But we also know that even the most benevolent and altruistic of motives can sometimes disguise unconscious aggressive and hostile impulses against the poorer and more vulnerable segments of society that most often deviate from dominant patterns of social life and cultural mores (see Gaylin, Glasser, Marcus, and Rothman 1978; Pivan and Cloward 1971; Geiser 1973; Prescott 1981). We can see this quite clearly in the Moral Majority rhetoric on women who choose to have abortions, and in the vilification of alleged child abusers in the media, and in public intervention programs, and in the courts.

We suggest that the choice of child abuse as an official social problem, and the timing of its occurrence (1960s–1980s) cannot be explained solely in terms of the phenomenon of child maltreatment itself. Rather, the emergence of child abuse as a key social problem concerns, in part, its functions as a generative metaphor, serving to displace other collective unconscious anxieties and contradictions in American society. Specifically, the attention to individual cases of child abuse "out there" masks the complicity (and collective responsibility) in the implementation of local, national, and international policies that are placing our nation's and, indeed, the world's children at great risk. National "guilt" about these hostile policies are displaced by identifying the "real" abusers as those poor and unfortunate wretches who beat or molest their own children. In this light, the identified, individualized, and *punished* child abusers function as one of our society's official symptom bearers for what is, in fact, a normative pathology. It conceals that extent to which we are an abusive society.[5]

As we approach it here, the social problem of "child abuse" has three distinct aspects which are often merged in practice: (1) child abuse as a description of adult behavior toward children with a value judgment about that behavior; (2) the cultural fantasy—or projective—use to which actual child abuse is put; (3) the acting out of a group fantasy of child abuse through social policies that place children at real risk, thereby actualizing or making real the fantasy. We wish to emphasize that fantasy, here, refers to the unconscious, non-rational influences on thought and decision-making—influences which are out of control precisely to the degree that they are inaccessible to conscious awareness except as mediated by symbol or expressed in action. Often, the occurrence of disturbing or disruptive phenomena in society is both explained and blamed on relatively powerless or marginalized social groups. New England had its witches; late Ottoman Turkey its Armenians; Nazi Germany its Jews, Catholics, and homosexuals. In short, blaming, scapegoating, and stereotyping are frequently involved in the identification, labeling, and proposed solutions to, social problems. Here we will argue that child abuse as a modern social problem is highly contaminated with similar unconscious agendas, a few of which we will try to bring to light in the following pages.

Group Violence and the Timing of Sacrifice

We are compelled to argue, somewhat counter-intuitively and against our wishes, that the current outrage against child abusers and the wish to rescue young victims from their adult assailants is an expression of contemporary political culture and is continuous with a larger cultural trend. This cultural trend is expressed in the election into public office of those who have instituted a Draconian social policy toward poor and otherwise vulnerable minorities, including abusive adults and abused children.

Throughout President Reagan's terms of office, beginning in 1980, the progressive social and economic programs put into place during the 1930s through the 1960s with their preferential options for the poor, the unemployed, and minorities (i.e. the Roosevelt, Kennedy, and Johnson programs) were gradually dismantled. Reagan's administration ushered in a new era of belligerent conservatism, and health, social welfare, and educational programs suffered their greatest cuts in the last half century. As a consequence, the vulnerable segments of the population (including mothers and infants, children and adolescents) constituted part of an internal sacrifice.

An understanding of the unconscious dynamic of what deMause calls the present "Time of Sacrifice" (1984: 79) in American popular culture, helps to account for the apparent paradox that *the time of greatest public outcry against child abuse is also the time of the widespread, official planning of sacrifice of children in public policy.* Americans, while giving their consent to abusive social policies, simultaneously expressed renewed horror against child abuse, and exercise a grim moralism toward individuals suspected of harming their children and toward women who have abortions. The 1960s and the early 1970s that were an era of self-indulgence and pleasure-seeking (see Lasch 1978) have given way to the era of dour moralism and punishment in the late 1970s and 1980s. This has contributed to the economic conservatism, and to the victim-blaming that has only exacerbated the problems of the poor. From his analysis of the unconscious content of themes in political speeches and in the media, deMause has argued that during the 1980s,

> in accordance with the basic family drama in our unconscious reality, in the deaths of real children. . . . when cuts were proposed for Aid to Families with Dependent Children, school lunches, child care, food programs, food stamps, child abuse programs and dozens of other government activities directly affecting the welfare and lives of children, few spoke up, and those few who did were puzzled by the impotence of their cries (1984:79). . . . article after article was written during the winter of 1981–2 on the rise in infant mortality in areas hardest hit by budget cutbacks and unemployment, on the over one million additional children on the poverty rolls, or

> the six million children who had lost health coverage . . . of the half million children
> who lost health services because of the closing by the government of 239 community
> health centers. . . . *What had happened to the guilt?* (1984:80)

The answer, deMause suggests, is that we have displaced the guilt onto selected
"criminal" scapegoats so that righteous anger is spent in punishing these "bad"
individuals, rather than in providing jobs and health care and social welfare
programs that could reduce "poor peoples' crimes" (including domestic violence), and thereby increase the survivability of minority infants and babies. In
so doing Americans ignore and deny the institutionalized forms of child abuse
which they are supporting in public elections, local and national. What is being
repudiated, as well, is a whole century of insight which western culture had
gained from the psychoanalytic revolution, including a denial of unconscious
motivation in adults *and* in children, and in their actions, thoughts and behaviors
toward each other. This has resulted in a ruthless punitiveness toward "sleazy"
child abusers and child molesters, unrelieved by compassion and understanding.
We have, then, a classic case of victim-blaming. "The more children Reagan
sacrificed," writes Lloyd deMause, "the more local newspapers discovered . . .
'an epidemic of child abuse sweeping the city' [*New York Post*, October 5, 1981,
p. 3] (1981: 82).

Contributing to, and informing, the new social conservatism is the resurgence
of social Darwinism. This has various facets, a few of which bear directly on
public attitudes toward child abuse and child abusers. There is, for example, the
renewed interest in the 'natural' and the biological dimensions of human behavior, and a consequent belief that society should, insofar as possible, model itself
after certain biological imperatives. Motherhood and 'maternal sentiments' are
seen as universal, natural attributes, and those who depart from contemporary,
middle class interpretations of *proper* maternal behavior are seen as 'un-natural'
as well as 'un-fit' mothers. As Schreir, chief child psychiatrist at Children's Hospital in Oakland, has pointed out with reference to national anxiety about child
maltreatment, and sexual abuse in particular:

> Some of the reactions to child sexual abuse is fueled by anxieties created in other
> social arenas. Many people are threatened by the increased number of women work-
> ing, children in day care, abortion rights, and the so-called 'sexual liberation' of the
> past two decades. Some see the sexual abuse of children as an out-growth of these
> changes. The ideological and political battles that surround these issues are growing
> more intense. (1985: 59)

In other words, the anxiety about child abuse is, in part, the displaced expression
of anxiety about the many changes our society has undergone with respect to sex
roles, sexuality and family life. There is a growing tendency to question the
wisdom of these changes and to attribute social problems to them. There is a fear
that we, as a nation, have moved too far and too fast in refashioning the family,
and that the 'epidemics' of child abuse and incest are the unfortunate, but somewhat predictable, consequences.

Another aspect of the new social Darwinism that bears on our attitude toward the poor and the vulnerable is the current focus on individual and group 'fitness'. Stein and others have documented the burgeoning of the "fitness" and "wellness" movements of the 1970s and 1980s (see Stein 1982a, 1982b, 1982c; Crawford 1977, 1980, 1985; Pollitt 1982; Whorton 1982) which have been interpreted as having as much to do with a "toughening up" of the national fibre and 'stock' as with promoting health. In attitude and ideology the wellness movement articulates a Darwinist ethos: those individuals or vulnerable social groups that will not or cannot "shape up" will simply lose and drop out of the future. Health and fitness are increasingly defined as an *achieved* rather than as an *ascribed* status, one involving free will and choice, conforming to competitive notions of the *self-made* man or woman. Fat, weak, or unhealthy individuals are morally culpable: they obviously did not eat well, care for themselves properly, or exercise sufficiently. The weak, the poor, and the sick have made that "choice" for themselves, and have only themselves to blame. In all, health and fitness have become new commodities in the bustling, impersonal marketplace of American society, and commodities, as usual, more accessible to some segments and classes than to others. Smugness about one's fiscal and, now, physical fitness are joined with an appalling lack of compassion toward vulnerable and twice stigmatized social groups.

The ethos of personal fitness and toughness expressed in the "self-health" and wellness movements of the 1970s and 1980s is also found in a heightened militancy as the new conservatism comes to bear on public policy. The larger cultural trend includes an internal sacrifice that is itself part of a larger, and largely unconscious, preparation for war and toward a readiness for the sacrifice of the young, especially young pubescent males (see Biesel 1985; M. Coleman 1984; deMause 1984; Stein 1982b). Americans acting "as if" preparing to go to war—expressed in the fitness movement and in a fascination with war games, toys, and dress—can weep sentimentally over the fetuses of the unborn while *readying to arm their own children for combat in a war that will spell the end to all life and all generativity*. (See Daube 1983.)

The American national mood—one which underlies various cultural expressions of pugnacity and a lust for violence—is exemplified in the 1984 Olympic nationalistic fervor and celebration of physical superiority; the "heroism" of Bernhard Goetz, the subway vigilante who brutally shot his teenage assailants in cold blood in New York City in late 1984; in the cyclical popularity of G.I. Joe dolls, paraphernalia, and breakfast cereal; the popularity in young women's fashion of shaved and short hair, neutered dress, and shoulder-padded jackets, emphasizing a more muscular, "aggressive" and "masculine" body image; the on-again, off-again popularity of army surplus, khaki fatigues, and camouflage dress among youth and adolescents. It is within this popular culture emphasizing toughness and militarism that the outrage against child abuse is taking place.

Part of the tragic dynamic of this current strengthening of the national fibre is that it is purchased by the weakening of the already frail and vulnerable, as if the latter must always be singled out and sacrificed in order that the social body and the body politic feel strong and renewed once again. Rationalized by the presumed moral superiority of 'wellness' and 'strength', one need not flinch nor suffer twinges of social conscience at the neglect, if not abuse, of the weak. The burden of guilt is projected onto the classes of "bad" people who are kept in constant public view in the media and under the surveillance of police, teachers, doctors, therapists, and social workers.

It is into this arena that child abuse is introduced as a cultural morality play. The sense of tragedy, of unwitting collusion by family and community members, the many unconscious forces in child victim and adult abuser alike—these are all banished from the lived-out drama. In this way, the field is cleared for the "abusers" (who, God knows, are real enough) to come to bear the entire burden of the public's displaced guilty conscience about the institutionalized abuse of the weak, the young, and the vulnerable to which they, too, are party. There are also suggestions of the projection of a fantasy—the wish to abuse, to hurt, to torture the weak and vulnerable that is concealed in the aggressive tracking down of the "evil" perpetrators of the "crime." In seeing abusers and molesters hunted down and severely punished, members of the social mainstream are able to experience a symbolic sacrifice and thus feel themselves cleansed, stabilized, and whole. The collective fantasy-use of the American child abuse drama is akin to the projections of political and religious "conspiracy theories": e.g. what *we* wish to do, and what *we* feel guilty for having done (or "thought in our hearts" about doing), we accuse *others* of doing. Within the drama of played out role expectations, labeling, and counter-labeling the accused often act out their crimes at *our* own behest and in *our* behalf. Accused and accuser are needed to complete the task, to play out the drama.

Violence, Rebirth and Child Sacrifice

Summing up over a decade of psychohistorical research by David Beisel, Lloyd deMause, Henry Ebel, Stephen Ryan, Casper Schmidt, and Howard Stein, as well as others, Beisel writes:

> Understanding how and why groups regress to earlier ways of thinking and feeling has become a major task for psychohistorians. Much is now known about that process . . . Accompanying . . . primitive fantasies of sacrifice, suicide, and wishes for death are longing for rebirth. Whatever the psychobiological foundations of fantasies of birth and rebirth might be, no one can deny their widespread existence in history. There is solid evidence that birth and rebirth fantasies cluster at a particular time in a group's life. They appear whenever group regression has reached the point at which its members' aggressive impulses are bubbling to the surface and the group is feeling the need to act them out. (1984: 135)

The rebirth is always effected through violence, during which one kills off the bad parts of oneself (those one feels to be the unlovable parts) and revives or restores the good parts (so that one feels cleansed and therefore lovable again). In a paper entitled "Nuclear Politics in the 1980's," Coleman writes that child sacrifice existed in many cultures. In Carthage, where whole cemetaries of sacrificed children exist, "their own parents offered them and fondled their children just before they were killed so that they might not be sacrificed in tears" [Tertullian 1984: 31]. A more modern way of sacrificing children is spending money for useless, redundant nuclear weapons while there is a "Sharp Rise in Poor Children" [The *New York Times*, 4/29/83, p. A12], and we see headlines telling us "Hunger a Severe Problem" [The *New York Times*, 3/11/84, p. 46]. (Coleman 1984: 126)

Under the fantasy of the political sacrifice and rescue of children, it is the "bad" (i.e. impulsive, lazy, aggressive, sexual) children who are being disciplined and purged (to a great extent representing the young members of already stigmatized and therefore suspect and vulnerable ethnic, racial and class minorities), and it is the "good" (i.e. the innocent, a-sexual) children who are understood as being rescued. The splitting into two "kinds" of children corresponds, of course, to the idealized and devalued portions of the adult's own self-image. Likewise we can detect a splitting between two "types" of adults. There are the "bad" adults who abuse or molest their innocent children. These tend to cluster in the poorer and marginalized social groups and classes. One thinks of the grossly stereotyped images of the incest-prone Appalachian hillbillies, or the brutal and abusive alcoholic working class Irish father, or the sexually active and maternally immature and neglectful Black teenage mother that one sees portrayed in media dramatizations of child abuse. Conversely, there are the "good" adults, especially the investigative reporter, the dedicated child welfare worker, the tough District Attorney who are the champions of children's rights, and who are portrayed as rescuing and redeeming victimized children. These are the "Child Savers" (see Prescott 1981), the new American "culture-heroes."

To use a dramaturgical metaphor these four distinct psychological "types" constitute the players on the cultural stage: the larger dramaturgical context— the audience, director, script, etc.—is occupied by the wider mainstream culture, including the official policy makers whose elected job it is to crystallize group fantasies into doctrine.

Unconscious Factors in Child Abuse

It is surprising how often people who seek analytic treatment for hysteria or an obsessional neurosis confess to having indulged in the phantasy: 'A child is being beaten,' (Freud 1919)

Several books published between 1979 and 1984 (among them: Finkelhor 1979; Rush 1980; Herman 1981; Masson 1984) collectively built a case for psychiatry's denial of the reality of child abuse, especially the sexual abuse of young girls. They suggest that the timing of the recent 'discovery' of child abuse has to do with the uncovering of the 'truth' of allegations of abuse and sexual molestation. Jeffrey Masson's *Assault on Truth*, the most celebrated of the attacks on psychoanalysis from this perspective, contends that Freud was unable, or chose to ignore the actual occurrence of sexual assault in the life histories of his female patients in preference for the analysis of the unconscious reworking of early events. It is not our intent in this chapter to argue with the feminist analyses of Freud's unconscious (including his own apparent inability to deal with *real* individual and family aggression/violence), nor even less to deny the valid point that has been made in these writings. Rather, we wish to suggest another dimension of unconscious defenses at work in the national obsession with child abuse and rescue: the national collective unconscious fear/wish that a "child is being beaten" "a girl is being molested" (Chase 1975). We will explore, through themes in popular and political culture, what happens when the actual occurrence of child abuse coincides with group fantasy.

Hollywood has, of late, produced a genre of science fiction films that portray big, bad, corrupt adults who harm, and sometimes kill, childlike, innocent creatures. In the film, *Close Encounters of the Third Kind*, benign aliens from space are the heroes: infantile, neotonous, fetus-like creatures who communicate with simple souls (the pure of heart) through a lilting melody, a lullabye. Likewise in Spielberg's vastly popular film *E.T.: The Extra-Terrestial*, good and wise children do battle with an uncomprehending adult world. Adults and children are pitted against one another, with adults representing a society corrupted by materialism and an alienating technology. But these films have their counterpart in other films depicting children as evil, satanic, and seductive, such as: *Rosemary's Baby, The Bad Seed, The Omen*, and *The Exorcist*. Again we have the splitting of good and evil images.

In all there is a rejection of moral subtlety or ambiguity, and a wish for decisive action, a simple definition of the problem, and clean solutions. The popular fantasy is enacted in the characters of Indiana Jones, Crocodile Dundee, the survivalist hero of *Mosquito Coast*, Rocky, Rambo, the heroes of *Star Wars*, and so on, where the will to immediate action is the key. As Erikson noted (1959: 28), in times of cultural crisis, the American public endeavors to set things right by wiping the moral slate clean.

A second theme in American popular culture concerns ambivalence toward reproduction and generativity, played out in the dialectical fantasy between rescue and adoption versus murder and infanticidal themes. On the one hand we have the adoption and rescue impulse expressed in the Save-the-Child organizations, as well as in the movement to adopt Third World children, especially Southeast Asian and Central American children whose lives, families, and homes have been disrupted, in large part, by North American aggression and militarism. While school lunch programs and food stamps are cut in American cities, while infant mortality in Detroit and Oakland equals that of some Third World countries, we have an outpouring of sympathy and famine relief aid for mothers and children in Africa. Again, guilt and displacement of guilt, always at a safe distance.

A darker, more obsessive side of the adoption/rescue/infanticide fantasy can also be witnessed in the "Cabbage Patch" doll mania that swept the nation in the early 1980s (Beisel 1984). The Cabbage Patch dolls, fetus-like in appearance, are advertized as abandoned (can we think they are possibly aborted?) infants in search of good homes and the "right kind" of parents. The dolls are extravagantly expensive to adopt, so that poorer families can shelter a cabbage patch kid only at a great personal sacrifice. The dependent dolls come with "authentic" adoption papers and with a proper name. During the 1985 Christmas season a new line of orphaned dolls was introduced—a "Rice Paddy Baby," described as a "squeezable Asian doll that comes with a British passport and a voice that coos: 'I want to immigrate. Will you sponsor me?' " (*Newsweek Magazine*, 12/16/85: 49). From the 1983 Christmas season through Christmas 1986 these Cabbage Patch type dolls have been highly sought after, even fought over, in department stores throughout the United States in an altogether appalling display of consumer fetishism and bad taste on the part of the public. While Asian baby dolls were evidentially highly prized, others were not. In New York City, for example, during the 1985 pre-Christmas "rush" on Cabbage Patch dolls, the only ones still available the week before Christmas at May's Department store in Queens, New York were either damaged or black.

A journalist, writing for the North Carolina *Independent* in 1985 concluded the following:

> Life's real facts are that adoptable babies usually come out of somebody's sorrow. And we know that there are a lot of real orphans out there in the world: in Lebanon, Vietnam, Nicaragua, and in El Salvador. And some of them are half-American. . . . Some of us deal with this good-heartedly by posting a monthly check to Foster Parents. . . . It's even cheaper and easier to buy our kid a Cabbage Patch orphan. [We feel better] . . . and Coleco collects the cash, a lot of cash. (Collier 1985)

A distorted and misplaced altruism (and some real confusion) contributed to a massive give-away of Cabbage Patch dolls to the children of America's poor, sick, and needy during the Christmas season of 1985, sponsored by *Woman's Day* magazine. One thousand dolls were distributed to children beset by a multitude of domestic tragedies. The following excerpts from letters to *Woman's Day* concerning the Cabbage Patch give-away are illustrative of the social blindness of the kind-hearted donors:

> The doll will go to one of the patients at Kaiser Foundation Hospital who has been diagnosed as having approximately one year to live. . . .
>
> [Another] child reaping the benefit is an eight year old girl from a one-parent home with a handicapped brother. Her mother walked off and left the children when the girl was two years old. The father is unemployed.
>
> . . . A ten-year old member of our church, whose Dad had a heart problem and is unable to work will receive a [Cabbage Patch] doll for Christmas. (Garbarini and Pascoe 1985)

What we have here is the adoption of dolls for some of the United States' own dispensable and "throw-away" children, those for whom government support and many social services have been greatly attenuated.

Cabbage Patch dolls are serious business, occupying a special niche in American popular culture. The reverse side of the dolls' lovability and their innocence and of the adult's wish to extend solicitous care and protection through the fantasy of rescue and adoption barely disguised fantasies of abuse, mutilation, cannibalism, and infanticide. Commenting on the national mood in the 1980s, Lloyd deMause commented:

> Sometimes our cannibalistic wishes come close to breaking through into consciousness in their most regressed form—that of eating babies—as we, through such popular comedians as Johnny Carson, made jokes on TV about how much fun it would be to hack up, boil, and eat Cabbage Patch dolls, which children that Christmas had taken to adopting by the millions. (1984: 160–161)

A contemporary form of child sacrifice is the spending of money for genocidal and redundant nuclear weapons while there is a sharp rise in the numbers of poor, disadvantaged, malnourished, and illiterate children in the United States. . . .

Sadistic, infanticidal jokes and commentary directed against the Cabbage Patch dolls has entered into popular discourse. During a TV talk show interview, for example, a rock music star complained that her Mexican-American maid refused to enter or clean the daughter's room because she was afraid of the girl's Cabbage Patch doll. The maid said that the doll was "evil". One of our neighbors told of having bought her daughter a Cabbage Patch doll for Christmas which turned out to be damaged, its arm was torn. The woman wrote to the manufacturer asking for a replacement for the expensive doll. The company responded by issuing the mother *and* her daughter a death certificate for the original doll, and promised that a search was under way to locate a more acceptable adoptive baby doll. One can only imagine the barely suppressed hostility toward children that was involved in the toy manufacturer's death certificate fantasy. The incident is reminiscent of the penultimate bad taste of the cyclically popular and in vogue "dead baby jokes" which Alan Dundes (1979) has linked to cycles in the national anxiety about and obsessive fascination with, abortion. . . .

Infanticidal fantasies lead guiltily to counter-phobic fantasies of rescue that are played out in the responses to harm wrought to real children by our own domestic and international policies. We set up rescue missions to undo the damage to those we have placed in jeopardy in the first place.

To reiterate our thesis: the children who are being championed and—albeit few—rescued are seen as the victims of child abusers who are viewed more as criminals to be punished than as tragic, sometimes pitiful characters who need compassion if they are to be helped to change. Child abusers, then, serve as a delegate group (Sterlin 1974) to embody the disavowed evil impulses of mainstream America, while children serve as a delegate group both to embody projected innocence (especially sexual innocence) of childhood, and to serve as group sacrifices. Child abuse, of course, began as a fact, and not as the product of a group fantasy. However, as it has become fueled by unconscious wishes, projections of endangerment and rescue, it has become inseparable from the collective unconscious which has used child abuse toward its own collective ends. If there is a prevalent fantasy that "a child is being abused", "a girl is being molested", then whatever the actual incidence or prevalence of such occurrence, we must also address and understand the combined fear *and wish* that such occurrences take place. In his epochal paper 'A Child Is Being Beaten': A Contribution to the Study of the Origin of Sexual Perversions" (1919), a quote from which opens this section, Freud was talking about neurotic patients' sado-masochistic fantasies about child-beating. Here we are talking about what happens when the actual occurrence of child maltreatment coincides with a group fantasy/obsession.

Probably the most disheartening aspect of the de-responsibilitization for child abuse and neglect in this country is the search-and-destroy mission directed at the "bad" parents (especially mothers) who are held individually responsible for the maltreatment of children. We might point, for example, to the vigorous medical-legal campaign to uncover sexual abuse presently being waged in the courts, in schools, and in doctors' offices throughout the country. This campaign has lead to such institutionalized and professionalized forms of sexual abuse as the suggestion to introduce vaginal inspection of little girls by pediatricians during routine medical exams (Krugman 1986) and the often inappropriate use of ana-tomically correct (SAC) dolls in clinics, social welfare offices, and nursery schools with preschool aged children for the purposes of sexual abuse "screening" (see White, Strom, and Santilli 1985). Due to the number of false allegations of sexual abuse resulting from the indiscriminate use of such experimental and highly questionable investigative measures several class action suits on behalf of the falsely accused are currently in litigation (see L. Coleman 1986; Dolan 1984; Goodwin, Sahd, and Rada 1978; Green, n.d.). Among their claims are violations of civil rights, the poor scientific status of the criteria in use for verifying suspected cases of sexual abuse, and the eroticization of children by aggressive and suggestive questioning, and use of the SAC dolls by poorly trained police, social workers, teachers, nurses, and doctors. In short, the "child saver" investigators are themselves suspect of playing out a child molestation fantasy. In all, the national focus and obsession with physical and sexual violence toward children serves to divert attention away from the more endemic and more life-threatening problem of child *neglect*.

The Neglect of Child Neglect As a Social Problem

To date, national attention and public outrage and response has been directed, almost exclusively, at those "criminal" or "psychopathological" parents who either batter, sexually molest, or otherwise physically abuse their children. However, recent surveys and analyses of national child abuse reporting indicate quite clearly that child battering and sexual molestation are neither the most frequent, nor the most potentially fatal assaults against children. The American Humane Society's analysis (1983) of all officially reported child maltreatment cases in the United States for 1981 indicated that physical injury accounted for less than one-third of all reported cases of child maltreatment for 1979 through 1982, and for approximately 34% of all fatalities (American Humane Society 1983: 12). Sexual abuse accounts for 7% of all reported cases of child maltreatment and for no fatalities. The greatest threat to child well-being and survival in our society today is from neglect, which is broadly defined in child welfare discourse as the "deprivation of necessities", or, in other words, poverty. The intentionality of the "neglectful" parent (usually the mother) is not necessarily taken into account, and even a loving and well-intentioned, but poor, parent raising her child in a sub-standard environment of poor housing, insufficient food, inadequate clothing, education and medical care can be reported for child neglect (see Stack 1984). By far the most pervasive, costly, intractable, and potentially fatal risk to American children today is that of child neglect, not child abuse. Neglect accounts for 60% of all child abuse reporting and for 56% of all related fatalities. Yet, child neglect has been ignored by the media, and in the national hysteria about child maltreatment. This, too, must be accounted for.

In its final section on the policy implications of the Humane Society's analysis of official report statistics, the report includes:

> A significant issue is that the majority of children (60 percent) seen by CPS [the Child Protective Service] were reported as experiencing deprivation of necessities, or neglect. It is commonly thought that neglect is less 'serious' than other forms of maltreatment. Consequently, at a time when CPS agencies are being forced to limit their responses to cases perceived as the most serious, *neglect cases are likely to be among the first ones screened out*. This poses a serious dilemma. It is clear that in its present form the CPS cannot accommodate all children reported as maltreated, so perhaps it is necessary to screen cases out. However, it was neglect that was the most frequently indicated type of maltreatment for fatalities. . . . [The findings also] support the notion that there is a strong association between the stresses of poverty and the inability to adequately care for children. The problem is that the CPS system is neither equipped nor intended to alleviate poverty. . . . The reporting data revealed that the predominant service type was casework counselling; specific support services were indicated much less frequently. (1983:23)

Finally, the report concludes with the injunction that, in general, the focus of child welfare policies in this country be "broadened to incorporate the reality of poverty" (ibid.). We could not agree more fully with this assessment. The point, relevant to our particular analysis, is that the "choice" of child abuse as a master social problem of our times, also includes a strong "choice" for only certain forms of child abuse—battering and sexual abuse—and a *selective inattention* to other forms—specifically, poverty-related neglect. This selective inattention is a consequence of the need to deny the role of our punitive public policies in contributing to the "feminization of poverty", and to the problem of childhood mortality in our inner city, minority neighborhoods. Far less anxiety-provoking is to continue our pursuit of the "bad", out-of-control, assaultive parents. This "choice" in the popular construction of the real problem of child maltreatment was brought home to one of us (NS-H) who was recently interviewed for a televised news series examining child abuse and neglect in California. A taped half-hour interview was reduced to a five-minute segment that comprised a response to the reporter's incessant questioning about child molestation. Clearly, the much longer discussion of child neglect and poverty in California (and the childhood mortality rate in Oakland) were neither sufficiently "sexy" nor *violent* enough for popular consumption. Moreover, who is there to blame, who is there to punish when a child goes to bed hungry? (While we *know* who to blame and punish—or think that we do—when a child has been beaten, or a young girl molested).

Conclusion

What George Devereux spoke of as a "vicious cycle of pathology" (1980:19) can be seen in the social psychological dynamics and drama of the child abuse problem. As the actual abuse of children is more defined as a social and medical problem, public outrage has led to an increasingly punitive policy toward identified abusers. This, in turn, leads to a diminished sense of social relatedness and responsibility for the problem, and to further reductions in social and economic support for parents with vulnerable and dependent children. This leads to increased stress, and frequently to increased abuse and neglect in those families at greater risk, who are seen as intrinsically bad. Hence, at least some of the child maltreatment that is observed, diagnosed, and treated is actually *created*, and those forms of institutionalized maltreatment reproduced in our social policies and enacted in our popular culture, remain below consciousness, and therefore unrecognized and untreated. If we are to avoid this tangle of absurdities, it is essential to un-mask the contradictions in our behavior. At that time, and not before, we will be prepared to solve, rather than use, the problems of child abuse.

NOTES

1. A similar process of "medicalization" is now occurring with the attempt to create a new diagnostic category for sexual abuse: the "Child Sexual Abuse Accommodation Syndrome" (Summit 1983) and the "Sexually Abused Child's Disorder" (Corwin 1985). The essential diagnostic features of the latter include a child's displays of age-inappropriate *"awareness* of differentiated sexual behaviors as demonstrated by *specific knowledge*, emotional or behavioral reactions to direct questions about parts of the body" (1985:8). In other words if a child displays "age-inappropriate" *knowledge* about sexual anatomy and function s/he might be suspect as a victim of sexual molestation. The fact that classes and ethnic groups, rural v. urban children differ with respect to such cultural information is nowhere recognized in this diagnostic check-list for clinicians.

2. To date (1985), forty-two states have centralized registers for reports of child abuse and neglect. The information kept in these files varies, however, as do state rules on sealing, destruction, and access to, and confidentiality of, these records (Federal Register 1985:32771).

3. For a critique of a portion of this literature, see Cicchetti and Aber 1980.

4. While directing a team field research project on professional and community definitions of child abuse and neglect in Taos County, New Mexico in the summer of 1985 (see

ScheperHughes 1987), one of us learned that a Sexual Abuse Prevention worker gained permission to hold a workshop on sexual abuse with Pueblo Indian children attending a community Head Start program. Using the Colorado format, children there were told to distinguish "bad" touches as "anywhere the bathing suit covers the body," despite the fact that these children do not use bathing suits in their ritual ablutions in the stream that runs through the Pueblo community. Moreover, anxiety was raised by the suggestion that co-sleeping with parents and cross-sex siblings is "not good", although these celebrated "apartment-dwellers" have lived for more than a thousand years in preferred domestic arrangements of close physical intimacy that includes co-sleeping of parents and childrens and of siblings.

5. Precisely how, and how subtly, this occurs can be discerned from the following "microanalysis": A number of medical colleagues are ardent child advocates (e.g., "The worst sin is to harm a child"; "I can't imagine why someone would abuse their child."). They work zealously in their clinics, hospitals and community agencies to ensure that abused children are identified, taken to shelters if necessary, receive proper treatment, and that the parents are reported to child welfare. Many of these same clinicians, however, have in recent years developed a caustic humor toward poor and welfare patients and their families, accept or wish to accept in their practices only paying or third-party insured patients, express a diminished sense of personal responsibility toward patients while heightening their sense of biomedical responsibility toward them, and in their humor about abusive parents reveal a vindictiveness toward them without much tempering compassion (i.e., identifying wholly with the child as victim). Questioning the need for AFDC, food stamps, WIC, subsidized school lunches, etc., they often seem to wish upon others the deprivation they once had, or perhaps feel they themselves deserve.

REFERENCES

American Humane Society
  1976–80 Highlights of Official Child Neglect. . . . Denver: A.H.S.
  1983 Highlights of Official Child Neglect and Abuse Reporting. Denver: A.H.S.
Beisel, David R.
  1984 Thoughts on the Cabbage Patch Kids. The Journal of Psychohistory 12(1):133–142.
  1985 The Vietnam War: A Beginning Psychohistory. The Journal of Psychohistory 12(3):
  371–393.
Cantwell, H.
  1983 Vaginal Inspection as It Relates to Young Girls. Child Abuse and Neglect 7:171–
  176.
Chase, Naomi
  1975 A Child Is Being Beaten. New York: McGraw-Hill.
Cicchetti, Dante and Lawrence Aber
  1980 Abused Children—Abusive Parents: An Overstated Case? Harvard Educational
  Review 50(2):244–255.
Coleman, Lee
  1986 False Allegations of Child Sex Abuse: Have the Experts Been Caught With Their
  Pants Down? Forum (January–February): 12–20.
Coleman, Mary
  1984 Nuclear Politics in the 1980s. The Journal of Psychohistory 12(1):121–132.

Collier, Carol
  1985 Toys That Bear Watching: The Cabbage Patch Conspiracy. The Independent, December 6–19: 2.
Corwin, David L.
  1985 Sexually Abused Child's Disorder. Draft #3, October 14. Children's Hospital, Oakland, California.
Crawford, Robert
  1977 'You Are Dangerous to Your Health': The Ideology and Politics of Victim-Blaming. International Journal of Health Services 7: 663–680.
  1980 Healthism and the Medicalization of Everyday Life. International Journal of Health Services 10: 365–388.
  1985 A Cultural Account of 'Health'—Self-Control, Release, and the Social Body. In J. McKinlay, ed. Issues in the Political Economy of Health Care. New York: Methuen.
Daube, David
  1983 Black Hole. Unpublished manuscript. Boalt Hall, School of Law, University of California, Berkeley.
deMause, Lloyd
  1974 The History of Childhood. New York: The Psychohistory Press.
  1982 Foundations of Psychohistory. New York: Creative Roots
  1984 Reagan's America. New York: Creative Roots
Devereux, George
  1980 Basic Problems of Ethno-Psychiatry. Chicago: University of Chicago Press.
Dolan, M.
  1984 Molest: False Allegations on the Increase. Los Angeles Times July 16, Part 1, p. 1.
Dundes, Alan
  1979 The Dead Baby Joke Cycle. Western Folklore 38(3): 145–157.
Edgerton, Robert
  1981 Foreword. In Jill Korbin, ed. Child Abuse and Neglect: Cross-Cultural Perspectives. Berkeley: University of California Press.
Erikson, Erik
  1959 Identity and the Life Cycle: Selected Papers by Erik H. Erikson. New York: International Universities Press.
Federal Register
  1985 Office of Human Development Services: "Child Abuse and Neglect Prevention and Treatment Proposed Research Priorities for Fiscal Year 1986," vol. 50, no. 157: 32769–32771.
Finkelhor, David
  1979 Sexually Victimized Children. New York: Free Press.
Freud, Sigmund
  1959 (1919) "A Child Is Being Beaten": A Contribution to the Study of the Origin of Sexual Perversions. The Complete Freud 17. London: Hogarth Press.
Garbarini, Alice and Elizabeth Jean Pascoe
  1985 Does Anybody Out There Care? Yes! Woman's Day, December 3: 52, 56.
Gaylin, Willard, Ira Glasser, Steven Marcus, and David Rothman
  1978 Doing Good: The Limits of Benevolence. New York: Pantheon.
Geiser, Robert
  1973 The Illusion of Caring. Boston: Beacon.
Giovanni, Jeanne and Rosina Becerra
  1979 Defining Child Abuse. New York: Free Press.

Goldstein, Joseph, Anna Freud, and Albert Solnit
    1973 Beyond the Best Interests of the Child. New York: Free Press.
Goodwin, J., D. Sahd, and R. Rada
    1978 Incest Hoax: False Accusations, False Denials. Bulletin of the American Academy
    of Psychiatry and the Law 6(3): 269–276.
Green, Arthur H.
    n.d. Did He or Didn't He? True and False Allegations of Sexual Abuse in Child Cus-
    tody Disputes. Unpublished paper available from the author at the Presbyterian Hos-
    pital, BH 616–622 West 168th Street, New York, New York 10032
Hausfater, Glenn and Sarah Blaffer Hrdy
    1984 Infanticide: Comparative and Evolutionary Perspectives. New York: Aldine.
Hefler, Ray E. and C. Henry Kempe
    1978 Child Abuse and Neglect: The Family and the Community. Cambridge, Mass.:
    Ballinger.
Herman, Judith
    1981 Father/Daughter Incest. Cambridge: Harvard University Press.
Hippler, Arthur E.
    1978 A Culture and Personality Perspective of the Yolngu of Northeastern Arnhem
    Land.
    Part I: Early Specialization. The Journal of Psychological Anthropology 1(2): 221–244.
Kempe, C. Henry, et al.
    1962 "The Battered Child Syndrome," Journal of the American Medical Association
    181:17–24.
Kempe, Ruth and C. Henry Kempe
    1978 Child Abuse. Cambridge: Harvard University Press.
Korbin, Jill
    1981 Child Abuse and Neglect. Berkeley: University of California Press.
Krugman, Richard D.
    1986 Recognition of Sexual Abuse in Children. Pediatrics in Review 8(1): 2–7.
Lasch, Christopher
    1978 Haven in a Heartless World: The Family Besieged. New York: Basic Books.
Masson, Jeffrey
    1984 The Assault on Truth: Freud's Suppression of the Seduction Theory. New York:
    Farrar, Straus and Giroux.
Pivan, Frances and Richard Cloward
    1971 Regulating the Poor. New York: Vintage.
Pollitt, Katha
    1982 The Politically Correct Body. Mother Jones (May): 66–67.
Prescott, Peter S.
    1981 The Child Savers. New York: Knopf.
Rush, Florence
    1980 The Best Kept Secret: The Sexual Abuse of Children. New York: Prentice-Hall.
Ryan, William
    1971 Blaming the Victim. New York: Vintage.
Scheper-Hughes, Nancy
    1979 'Breeding Breaks Out in the Eye of the Cat': Sex Roles, Birth Order and the Irish
    'Double-Bind'. Journal of Comparative Family Studies, 10(2): 207–226.
    1984 Infant Mortality and Infant Care: Cultural and Economic Constraints on Nurturing
    in Northeast Brazil. Social Science and Medicine 19(5): 535–546.

1987 The Best of Two Worlds, the Worst of Two Worlds: Reflections on Culture and Fieldwork Among the Rural Irish and Pueblo Indians. Comparative Studies in Society and History 29(1) (January).

Schreier, Herbert
1985 Child Sex Abuse Laws Too Rigid? Open Forum, San Francisco Chronicle, October 24:59.

Shorter, Edward
1975 The Making of the Modern Family. New York: Basic Books.

Stack, Carol
1984 Cultural Perspectives on Child Welfare. New York University Review of Law and Social Change.

Stein, Howard F.
1978 Judaism and the Group-Fantasy of Martyrdom: The Psychodynamic Paradox of Survival Through Persecution. The Journal of Psychohistory 6(2): 151–210.
1980 An Ethno-Historic Study of Slovak-American Identity. New York: Arno Press/ New York Times Press.
1982a 'Health' and 'Wellness' as Euphemism: The Cultural Context of Draconian Health Policy. Continuing Education for the Family Physician 16(3): 33–43.
1982b Neo-Darwinism and Survival Through Fitness. The Journal of Psychohistory 10(2): 163–187.
1982c Wellness as Illusion. Delaware Medical Journal 54(11): 637–641.

Sterlin, Helm
1974 Separating Parents and Adolescents: A Perspective on Running Away, Schizophrenia, and Waywardness. New York: Times Books.

Stone, Lawrence
1977 The Family, Sex, and Marriage in England, 1500–1800. New York: Harper and Row.

Summit, Roland C.
1983 The Child Sexual Abuse Accommodation Syndrome. Child Abuse and Neglect 7: 177–193.

Tertullian
1984 Quoted in "Child Sacrifice in Carthage—Religious Rite or Population Control?" Biblical Archeological Review 10(1).

White, Susan, Gerald Strom, and Gail Santilli
1985 Clinical Protocol For Interviewing Preschoolers With Sexually Anatomically Correct Dolls. Available from the senior author at the Department of Psychiatry, Case Western Reserve University, Cleveland, Ohio 44109.

Whorton, James
1982 Crusaders for Fitness: The History of American Health Reformers. Princeton: Princeton University Press.

Part II

Childhood Sexuality

Chapter Ten

Fun Morality
An Analysis of Recent American Child-Training Literature

Martha Wolfenstein

A recent development in American culture is the emergence of what we may call "fun morality." Here fun, from having been suspect, if not taboo, has tended to become obligatory. Instead of feeling guilty for having too much fun, one is inclined to feel ashamed if one does not have enough. Boundaries formerly maintained between play and work break down. Amusements infiltrate into the sphere of work, while, in play, self-estimates of achievement become prominent. This development appears to be at marked variance with an older, Puritan ethic, although, as we shall see, the two are related.

The emergence of fun morality may be observed in the ideas about child training of the last forty years. In these one finds a changing conception of human impulses and an altered evaluation of play and fun which express the transformation of moral outlook. These changing ideas about child training may be regarded as part of a larger set of adult attitudes current in contemporary American culture. Thus I shall interpret the development which appears in the child-training literature as exemplifying a significant moral trend of our times.

The ideas on child training which I shall present are taken from the publications of the United States Department of Labor Children's Bureau. These publications probably express at any given time a major body of specialized opinion in the field, though how far they are representative would have to be determined by further study of other publications. In taking these publications as indicative of certain changing attitudes, I leave undetermined to what extent these attitudes are diffused among parents and also to what extent parents' actual behavior with their children conforms to these ideas. Both these topics would require further research.

The innovations in child-training ideas of the past few decades may readily be related to developments in psychological research and theory (notably behaviorism, Gesell's norms of motor development, and psychoanalysis). However, the occurrence and particularly the diffusion of certain psychological ideas at certain periods are probably related to the larger cultural context. A careful study of the ways in which psychological theories have been adapted for parent guidance and other pedagogical purposes would show that a decided selection is made from among the range of available theories, some points being overstressed, others omitted, and so on.

The *Infant Care* bulletin of the Children's Bureau, the changing contents of which I shall analyze, was first issued in 1914. The various editions fall into three main groupings: 1914 and 1921, 1929 and 1938, 1942 and 1945 (i.e., the most drastic revisions occurred in 1929 and 1942).[1] For the present purpose I shall mainly contrast the two ends of the series, comparing the 1914 edition with those of 1942 and 1945 (the two latter are practically identical) and skipping over the middle period. Thus I shall attempt to highlight the extent of the change rather than to detail the intermediate stages (which in any case show some complicated discontinuities).

As the infant embodies unmodified impulses, the conception of his nature is a useful index of the way in which the impulsive side of human nature generally is regarded. The conception of the child's basic impulses has undergone an extreme transformation from 1914 to the 1940's. At the earlier date, the infant appeared to be endowed with strong and dangerous impulses. These were notably autoerotic, masturbatory, and thumb-sucking. The child is described as "rebelling fiercely" if these impulses are interfered with.[2] The impulses "easily grow beyond control"[3] and are harmful in the extreme: "children are sometimes wrecked for life."[4] The baby may achieve the dangerous pleasures to which his nature disposes him by his own movements or may be seduced into them by being given pacifiers to suck or having his genitals stroked by the nurse.[5] The mother must be ceaselessly vigilant; she must wage a relentless battle against the child's sinful nature. She is told that masturbation "must be eradicated . . . treatment consists in mechanical restraints." The child should have his feet tied to opposite sides of the crib so that he cannot rub his thighs together; his nightgown sleeves should be pinned to the bed so that he cannot touch himself.[6] Similarly for thumb-sucking, "the sleeve may be pinned or sewed down over the fingers of the offending hand for several days and nights," or a patent cuff may be used which holds the elbow stiff.[7] The mother's zeal against thumb-sucking is assumed to be so great that she is reminded to allow the child to have his hands free some of the time so that he may develop legitimate manual skills; "but with the approach of sleeping time the hand must be covered."[8] The image of the child at this period is that he is centripetal, tending to get pleasure from his own body. Thus he must be bound down with arms and legs spread out to prevent self-stimulation.

In contrast to this we find in 1942–45 that the baby has been transformed into almost complete harmlessness. The intense and concentrated impulses of the past have disappeared. Drives toward erotic pleasure (and also toward domination, which was stressed in 1929–38) have become weak and incidental. Instead, we find impulses of a much more diffuse and moderate character. The baby is interested in exploring his world. If he happens to put his thumb in his mouth or to touch his genitals, these are merely incidents, and unimportant ones at that, in his over-all exploratory progress. The erogenous zones do not have the focal attraction which they did in 1914, and the baby easily passes beyond them to other areas of presumably equal interest. "The baby will not spend much time handling his genitals if he has other interesting things to do."[9] This infant explorer is centrifugal as the earlier erotic infant was centripetal. Everything amuses him, nothing is excessively exciting.

The mother in this recent period is told how to regard autoerotic incidents: "Babies want to handle and investigate everything that they can see and reach. When a baby discovers his genital organs he will play with them. . . . A wise mother will not be concerned about this."[10] As against the older method of tying the child hand and foot, the mother is now told: "See that he has a toy to play with and he will not need to use his body as a plaything."[11] The genitals are merely a resource which the child is thrown back on if he does not have a toy. Similarly with thumb-sucking: "A baby explores everything within his reach. He looks at a new object, feels it, squeezes it, and almost always puts it in his mouth."[12] Thus again what was formerly a "fierce" pleasure has become an unimportant incident in the exploration of the world. Where formerly the mother was to exercise a ceaseless vigilance, removing the thumb from the child's mouth as often as he put it in, now she is told not to make a fuss. "As he grows older, other interests will take the place of sucking."[13] (Incidentally, this unconcerned attitude toward thumb-sucking is a relatively late development. The 1938 edition still had an illustration of a stiff cuff which could be put on the infant at night to prevent his bending his elbow to get his fingers to his mouth. The attitude toward masturbation relaxed earlier, diversion having already been substituted for mechanical restraints in 1929).

This changing conception of the nature of impulses bears on the question: Is what the baby likes good for him? The opposition between the pleasant and the good is deeply grounded in older American morals (as in many other ascetic moral codes). There are strong doubts as to whether what is enjoyable is not wicked or deleterious. In recent years, however, there has been a marked effort to overcome this dichotomy, to say that what is pleasant is also good for you. The writers on child training reflect the changing ideas on this issue.

In the early period there is a clear-cut distinction between what the baby "needs," his legitimate requirements, whatever is essential to his health and well-being, on the one hand, and what the baby "wants," his illegitimate pleasure strivings, on the other. This is illustrated, for instance, in the question of whether to pick the baby up when he cries. In 1914 it was essential to determine whether he really needed something or whether he only wanted something. Crying is listed as a bad habit. This is qualified with the remark that the baby has no other way of expressing his "needs"; if he is expressing a need, the mother should respond. "But when the baby cries simply because he has learned from experience that this brings him what he wants, it is one of the worst habits he can learn." If the baby cries, "the mother may suspect illness, pain, hunger or thirst." These represent needs. If checking on all these shows they are not present, "the baby probably wants to be taken up, walked with, played with," etc. "After the baby's needs have been fully satisfied, he should be put down and allowed to cry."[14] (This position remained substantially unchanged up to 1942.)

In 1942–45, wants and needs are explicitly equated. "A baby sometimes cries because he wants a little more attention. He probably needs a little extra attention under some circumstances just as he sometimes needs a little extra food and water. Babies want attention; they probably need plenty of it."[15] What the baby wants for pleasure has thus become as legitimate a demand as what he needs for his physical wellbeing and is to be treated in the same way.[16]

The question of whether the baby wants things which are not good for him also occurs in connection with feeding. The baby's appetite was very little relied on to regulate the quantity of food he took in the early period. Overfeeding was regarded as a constant danger; the baby would never know when he had enough. This is in keeping with the general image of the baby at this time as a creature of insatiable impulses. In contrast to this, we find in the recent period that "the baby's appetite usually regulates successfully the amount of food he takes."[17] Thus again impulses appear as benevolent rather than dangerous.

Formerly, giving in to impulse was the way to encourage its growing beyond control. The baby who was picked up when he cried, held and rocked when he wanted it, soon grew into a tyrant.[18] This has now been strikingly reversed. Adequate early indulgence is seen as the way to make the baby less demanding as he grows older.[19] Thus we get the opposite of the old maxim "Give the devil the little finger, and he'll take the whole hand." It is now "Give him the whole hand, and he'll take only the little finger."

The attitude toward play is related to the conception of impulses and the belief about the good and the pleasant. Where impulses are dangerous and the good and pleasant are opposed, play is suspect. Thus in 1914, playing with the baby was regarded as dangerous; it produced unwholesome pleasure and ruined the baby's nerves. Any playful handling of the baby was titillating, excessively exciting, deleterious. Play carried the overtones of feared erotic excitement. As we noted, this was the period of an intensive masturbation taboo, and there were explicit apprehensions that the baby might be seduced into masturbation by an immoral nurse who might play with his genitals.

The mother of 1914 was told: "The rule that parents should not play with the baby may seem hard, but it is without doubt a safe one. A young, delicate and nervous baby needs rest and quiet, and however robust the child much of the play that is indulged in is more or less harmful. It is a great pleasure to hear the baby laugh and crow in apparent delight, but often the means used to produce the laughter, such as tickling, punching, or tossing, makes him irritable and restless. It is a regrettable fact that the few minutes' play that the father has when he gets home at night . . . may result in nervous disturbance of the baby and upset his regular habits."[20] It is relevant to note that at this time "playthings . . . such as rocking horses, swings, teeter boards, and the like" are cited in connection with masturbation, as means by which "this habit is learned."[21] The dangerousness of play is related to that of the ever present sensual impulses which must be constantly guarded against. (In 1929–38, play becomes less taboo, but must be strictly confined to certain times of the day. In this period the impulse to dominate replaces erotic impulses as the main hazard in the child's nature, and the corresponding danger is that he may get the mother to play with him whenever he likes.)

In the recent period, play becomes associated with harmless and healthful motor and exploratory activities. It assumes the aspect of diffuse innocuousness which the child's impulse life now presents. Play is derived from the baby's developing motor activities, which are now increasingly stressed. "A baby needs to be able to move all parts of his body. He needs to exercise. . . . At a very early age the baby moves his arms and legs aimlessly. . . . As he gets older and stronger and his movements become more vigorous and he is better able to control them he begins to play."[22] Thus play has been successfully dissociated from unhealthy excitement and nervous debilitation and has become associated with muscular development, necessary exercise, strength, and control. This is in keeping with the changed conception of the baby, in which motor activities rather than libidinal urges are stressed. For the baby who is concerned with exploring his world rather than with sucking and masturbating, play becomes safe and good.

Play is now to be fused with all the activities of life. "Play and singing make both mother and baby enjoy the routine of life."[23] This mingling of play with necessary routines is consonant with the view that the good and pleasant coincide. Also, as the mother is urged to make play an aspect of every activity, play assumes a new obligatory quality. Mothers are told that "a mother usually enjoys entering into her baby's play. Both of them enjoy the little games that mothers and babies have always played from time immemorial." (This harking back to time immemorial is a way of skipping over the more recent past.) "Daily tasks can be done with a little play and singing thrown in."[24] Thus it is now not adequate for the mother to perform efficiently the necessary routines for her baby; she must also see that these are fun for both of them. It seems difficult here for anything to become permissible without becoming compulsory. Play, having ceased to be wicked, having become harmless and good, now becomes a new duty.

In keeping with the changed evaluation of impulses and play, the conception of parenthood has altered. In the earlier period the mother's character was one of strong moral devotion. There were frequent references to her "self-control," "wisdom," "strength," "persistence," and "unlimited patience." The mothers who read these bulletins might either take pride in having such virtues or feel called upon to aspire to them. The writers supposed that some mothers might even go to excess in their devoted self-denial. Thus the mothers were told that, for their own health and thus for the baby's good, they should not stay bound to the crib-side without respite, but should have some pleasant, although not too exhausting, recreation.[25] The mother at this time is pictured as denying her own impulses just as severely as she does those of her child. Just as she had to be told to let the baby's hands free occasionally (not to overdo the fight against thumb-sucking), so she must be counseled to allow herself an intermission from duty.

(In the 1929–38 period parenthood became predominantly a matter of know-how. The parents had to use the right technique to impose routines and to keep the child from dominating them.)

In the most recent period parenthood becomes a major source of enjoyment for both parents (the father having come much more into the picture than he was earlier). The parents are promised that having children will keep them together, keep them young, and give them fun and happiness. As we have seen, enjoyment, fun, and play now permeate all activities with the child. "Babies—and usually their mothers—enjoy breast feeding"; nursing brings "joy and happiness" to the mother. At bath time the baby "delights" his parents, and so on.[26]

The characterization of parenthood in terms of fun and enjoyment may be intended as an inducement to parents in whose scheme of values these are presumed to be priorities. But also it may express a new imperative: You ought to enjoy your child. When a mother is told that most mothers enjoy nursing, she may wonder what is wrong with her in case she does not. Her self-evaluation can no longer be based entirely on whether she is doing the right and necessary things but becomes involved with nuances of feeling which are not under voluntary control. Fun has become not only permissible but required, and this requirement has a special quality different from the obligations of the older morality.

I should now like to speculate on the connection between the attitudes revealed in this child-training literature and a wider range of attitudes in American culture today. The extent of diffusion with respect to class, region, etc., of the attitudes I shall discuss would be a topic for further research.

The changing attitudes toward impulse and restraint, the changing treatment of play, the changing evaluation of fun which we have found in the child-training literature, would seem to have many counterparts in other areas of adult life. Play, amusement, fun, have become increasingly divested of puritanical associations of wickedness. Where formerly there was felt to be the danger that, in seeking fun, one might be carried away into the depths of wickedness, today there is a recognizable fear that one may not be able to let go sufficiently, that one may not have enough fun. In the recent past there has been an increased tendency to attempt by drinking to reduce constraint sufficiently so that we can have fun. Harold Lasswell has defined the superego as that part of the personality which is soluble in alcohol. From having dreaded impulses and being worried about whether conscience was adequate to cope with them, we have come round to finding conscience a nuisance and worrying about the adequacy of our impulses.

Not having fun is not merely an occasion for regret but involves a loss of self-esteem. I ask myself: What is wrong with me that I am not having fun? To admit that one did not have fun when one was expected to arouses feelings of shame. Where formerly it might have been thought that a young woman who went out a great deal might be doing wrong, currently we would wonder what is wrong with a girl who is not going out. Fun and play have assumed a new obligatory aspect. While gratification of forbidden impulses traditionally aroused guilt, failure to have fun currently occasions lowered self-esteem. One is likely to feel inadequate, impotent, and also unwanted. One fears the pity of one's contemporaries rather than, as formerly, possible condemnation by moral authorities. In our book, *Movies: A Psychological Study,*[27] Nathan Leites and I referred to this new obligatoriness of pleasure as "fun morality" as distinguished from the older "goodness morality," which stressed interference with impulses. We noted a particular type of current American film heroine, the masculine-feminine girl, whose major merit consists in making the achievement of fun not too effortful. She initiates the flirtation, keeps it casual, makes it clear that she does not require excessive intensity from the man. At the same time she supports his self-esteem by implying that she never doubts his resources for having fun, however cool or abstracted he may seem. She affords a relief from the pressures of fun morality.

David Riesman, in *The Lonely Crowd,*[28] has observed how extensively work and play have become fused in business and professional life. Activities formerly sharply isolated from work, such as entertainment, have become part of business relations. Aspects of the personality, such as pleasingness or likability, formerly regarded as irrelevant to work efficiency, have been increasingly called into play in working life. Relations with work associates have become less and less sharply distinguishable from relations outside working hours. Thus there has been a mutual penetration of work and play. Work tends to be permeated with behavior formerly confined to after work hours. Play, conversely, tends to be measured by standards of achievement previously applicable only to work. One asks one's self not only in personal relations but now also at work: Did they like me? Did I make a good impression? And at play, no less than at work, one asks: Am I doing as well as I should?

In the past when work and play were more sharply isolated, virtue was associated with the one and the danger of sin with the other. Impulse gratification presented possibilities of intense excitement as well as of wickedness. Today we have attained a high degree of tolerance of impulses, which at the same time no longer seem capable of producing such intense excitement as formerly. Is it because we have come to realize that the devil does not exist that we are able to fuse play and fun with business, child care, and so on? Or have we developed (without conscious calculation) a new kind of defense against impulses? This defense would consist in diffusion, ceasing to keep gratification deep, intense, and isolated, but allowing it to permeate thinly through all activities, to achieve by a mixture a further mitigation. Thus we would have preserved unacknowledged and unrecognized the tradition of puritanism. We do not pride ourselves on being good, and we secretly worry about not having enough fun. But the submerged superego works better than we know, interspersing play in small doses with work and applying a norm of achievement to play. Instead of the image of the baby who has fierce pleasures of autoeroticism and the dangerous titillation of rare moments of play, we get the infant who explores his world, every part of whose extent is interesting but none intensely exciting, and who may have a bit of harmless play thrown in with every phase of the day's routine. We get the

adult whose work is permeated with personal relations and entertainment requirements, the impact of which is far from intensely pleasurable, and whose
playtime is haunted by self-doubts about his capacity for having as much fun as
he should.

I should like to add a further instance which epitomizes this tendency to fuse
work and fun, manifestly to make work more agreeable, but in effect probably
reducing the impact of fun. Recently a ten-year-old boy showed me one of his
schoolbooks. It had the title *Range Riders* and showed on the cover a cowboy on
a galloping horse. The subtitle was *Adventures in Numbers*—it was an arithmetic
book. The problems involved cowboys, horses, and so on. The traditional image
of the American schoolboy has been that he sits with a large textbook propped
up in front of him, a book representing the hard and tedious lessons which he
wants to evade. And inside the textbook he conceals a book of Wild West stories,
detective stories, or the like, which he is avidly reading. These two books have
now been fused into one. I do not know whether this succeeds in making the
arithmetic more interesting. But I have a suspicion that it makes the cowboys less
exciting.

After I had made the analysis of child-training literature presented in the fore-
going pages, a new edition of the *Infant Care* bulletin appeared, in the fall of 1951.
This new bulletin contains some points which are worth remarking. While it
perpetuates many of the tendencies of the 1942–45 editions, it also shows some
changes. Fun morality remains prominent. The new parents are told that they are
making a good start if they can enjoy their baby.[29] The child should learn that
mother and father are "two people who enjoy each other."[30] Introducing the baby
to solid foods will be "fun" and "amusing" for the mother, and the baby will
"enjoy the new experience more if you are having a good time."[31] The mother
should arrange the baby's bath so that it will be "the pleasant time it should be.
. . . If you feel hurried, bath time won't be the fun for either of you that it should
be."[32]

The difficulty of achieving fun, which, as we have observed, tends currently
to worry adults, is now ascribed to the infant as well (following the general
tendency to see the infant as the model of impulse life). The infant now may
suffer from boredom. And this has become the main reason for autoerotic activities. The baby may suck his thumb out of "loneliness or boredom."[33] He may
rock or bang his head because of "boredom."[34] In toilet training the baby, the
mother must take care that it does not become a "hateful bore" for him.[35] Masturbation is mentioned only in the section on toilet training: "sometimes a baby
handles his genitals when he is on the toilet, or at other times when he is undressed."[36] While it is not said explicitly that he does this out of boredom, we
might infer it on an analogy with thumb-sucking, rocking, and head-banging,
since we are told that the baby may also get bored on the toilet. Thus the auto-
erotic activities which were first derived from fierce impulses, later from less
intense exploratory tendencies, now arise as an escape from boredom. The dwindling of impulsive intensity has proceeded further than before.

The exploratory impulse of the baby continues to be stressed. We have interpreted this as an attempt to conceive the child's impulsive endowment in harmless terms. But the puritanical condemnation of impulses seems to be catching up with this displacement. Bounds must now be set to the baby's exploration. "We know that if we leave him free to creep everywhere he'd get into trouble." Thus we must "set a limit" for the baby "while he explores."[37]

There are still more striking signs that the belief in the dangerousness of impulses is breaking through the defenses that have been erected against it. In 1942–45 the view was advanced that the early gratification of the baby's demands led to the subsequent moderation of demands. There is now a conflict on this point. In some areas the precept is maintained, notably in relation to sucking and food preferences.[38] But in respect to the impulse to dominate, it has been reversed. The apprehension of the twenties that the baby may get the upper hand if his parents give in to him reappears. The baby may get the parents "at his mercy by unreasonable demands for attention."[39] Although the baby's need for companionship and for being held when he cries is stressed,[40] the mother is also warned: "If you get in the habit of picking your baby up every time he whimpers, you may do more harm than good." The gratified demand is apt to grow rather than to subside. The mother "may find her baby getting more and more demanding."[41]

Thus the conflict about facing and accepting human impulses is far from solved. On the one hand, the attempt to dilute and diffuse impulses seems to lead to doubts about adequate impulsive intensity, boredom, and the difficulty of achieving fun. On the other hand, the anxiety that impulses in one form or another will tend to grow beyond control has not been successfully warded off.

NOTES

1. My analysis is based on the six editions indicated. I was unable to obtain those of 1926 and 1940.

2. *Infant Care* (1914), p. 58.

3. Ibid., p. 62.

4. Ibid.

5. Ibid.

6. Ibid.

7. Ibid., p. 61.

8. Ibid.

9. Ibid. (1942), p. 60.

10. Ibid.

11. Ibid.

12. Ibid., pp. 59–60.

13. Ibid.

14. Ibid. (1914), pp. 60–61.

15. Ibid. (1945), p. 52.

16. In a recent television advertisement, Angelo Patri is quoted as saying: "Youngsters today need television for their morale as much as they need fresh air and sunshine for their health."

17. *Infant Care* (1945), p. 95.
18. Ibid. (1914), pp. 60–61.
19. Ibid. (1945), p. 30.
20. Ibid. (1914), pp. 59–60.
21. Ibid., p. 62.
22. Ibid. (1942), p. 41.
23. Ibid.
24. Ibid.
25. Ibid. (1914), p. 34.
26. Ibid. (1945), pp. 1, 29, 38, 62.
27. Wolfenstein and Leites, 1950.
28. Riesman, 1950.
29. *Infant Care* (1951), p. 3.
30. Ibid., p. 1.
31. Ibid., p. 32.
32. Ibid., p. 64.
33. Ibid., p. 57.
34. Ibid., p. 56.
35. Ibid., p. 87.
36. Ibid.
37. Ibid., p. 76.
38. Ibid., pp. 47, 57.
39. Ibid., p. 55.
40. Ibid., p. 53.
41. Ibid., p. 42.

REFERENCES

Children's Bureau, Department of Labor. *Infant Care*. 1914–51. Washington, D.C.: Government Printing Office.

Reisman, David. 1950. *The Lonely Crowd*. New Haven: Yale University Press.

Wolfenstein, Martha, and Leites, Nathan. 1950. *Movies: A Psychological Study*. Glencoe, Ill.: Free Press.

Chapter Eleven

The Sensuous Child
Benjamin Spock and the Sexual Revolution

Henry Jenkins

> I was, actually, a little uncomfortable about it. But I'd
> seen how relaxed Anna was about it all, and I didn't
> want to screw that up or anything. So I tried to seem
> natural, not cover up or anything. But then she said,
> "Can I touch it?" . . . I honestly didn't think about it
> for more than a second. I just said sure. And, um, she
> did. She . . . held it for a second. . . . I started to get an
> erection. And I said, "that's enough, Molly," and I
> turned away. I put the towel on. . . . To tell the truth,
> I was embarrassed. And I thought I'd handled it O.K.
> or as well as anyone could've.
>
> —Sue Miller, *The Good Mother*

Sue Miller's best-selling novel, *The Good Mother*, centers on the problem of rec-
onciling adult sexuality with the demands of motherhood.[1] The book's protagonist, Anna, a recently divorced mother, experiences an intense sexual awakening
with her new lover, Leo, an erotic experience that inevitably affects her relations
to her daughter, Molly. The girl's "seemingly complete comfort with Leo was
like a benediction on all aspects of the relationship, even the sexual."[2] The two
adults are comfortable with both their erotic and parental roles, displaying casual
domestic nudity, allowing the young girl to enter the bathroom when they are
bathing, even acting nonchalantly when the she accidentally stumbles onto them
making love. Their relationship sours, however, when Anna's vindictive former
husband accuses them of "sexual irregularities" and seeks to regain custody of
Molly. The two lovers are crushed by the social work and legal establishments
that question them about every aspect of their relationship and pathologize what
they have experienced as a natural and uninhibited sensuality. Repeatedly, they
explain and justify their choices as parents, their desire not to inhibit the child's
own sexual development, their hopes to have their erotic relations become

a natural part of family life. However, they encounter few people, not even their own lawyer, who can see such sexual openness as part of being a "good mother."

They should have consulted Doctor Spock!

What gives this contemporary maternal melodrama its power is the degree to which *The Good Mother* reflects America's shifting understandings of the erotic relations within the family. On one level, there is something absolutely normal about the sexual experiences Miller describes, many of which could have come directly from the pages of child-rearing guides from the immediate postwar period. On another level, such frankness and openness ran directly counter to growing public hysteria about sexual molestation and incest, which had, by the early 1980s, charged all forms of sexual exchange between children and adults.

Confronted with the fact that Leo has allowed Molly to touch his penis, their lawyer asks, "So you might say you misunderstood the rules." Leo responds angrily, "I thought I understood them."[3] What Leo didn't understand was that the rules were changing. In this essay, I want to look more closely at the social context that led, for a short while, toward a loosening of the "rules" governing sexual contact between children and adults, a changing understanding of children's erotic life and its place within the home.

In the 1960s, a spate of books appeared with titles like *The Sensuous Man* and *The Sensuous Woman*. Nobody published a book called *The Sensuous Child*. Yet, the title seems an appropriate description of the utopian erotic fantasies that underlay permissive child-rearing books. The recognition of children's sexuality as a positive, rather than as a negative, force led to a close examination of how parents should respond to and facilitate children's erotic awakenings. Children, so often, in our culture become the bearers of our own utopian fantasies for a better world. In this case, the world that was being envisioned was a world without erotic inhibitions, a world that was open to sexual pleasure and free from guilt and negative self-images.

By looking closely at children, their bodies and their desires, permissiveness developed an ideology about sexuality that helped to prepare the way for the sexual revolution of the 1960s. First, sex was rendered "wholesome," natural, biologically necessary, and in the process, old superstitions and moral prohibitions were pushed aside. Second, sex was striped of its ties to procreation, with the child's masturbatory exploration of its own body and its pursuit of pleasure assuming positive values in and of themselves. Third, healthy sensuality extended to the entire body and not simply the genitals. The child's polymorphous eroticism was to be retained in adult life as a new and more vivid form of sexual experience. Fourth, pleasure was seen as beneficial, necessary, and the body was depicted as knowing its own needs. The body doesn't lie; if it feels good, it can't be bad. Fifth, all aspects of life, especially learning and creativity, assumed an erotic dimension, as practices of redirection and sublimation transformed sexual energies into other kinds of activities, and the desire to explore the world was understood as primarily sensual in origins. We know through our senses, and as a result, we should awaken our senses to the broadest possible range of experiences. Sexual frustration and perversion were seen as resulting from boredom and understimulation. Sixth, sexual openness within the domestic sphere was viewed as positive, including some "healthy" interplay between parents and children, yet sex was, by its design, a private act, which should be performed behind closed doors and held in check by public expectations. Morally charged concepts, such as "sin" or "guilt," were gradually displaced by socially directed concepts, such as "privacy" and "propriety." Most of these conceptions of eroticism would become core tenets of the self-help books or liberation literature of the sexual revolution; they would become the common wisdom of a generation that sought to expand the place of recreational sex within American life and to prolong the period of childhood sexual experimentation into a richer, fuller erotic life as adults.

Historians of adult sexuality characterize the immediate post–World War II period in terms of erotic containment, contrasting it with post–World War I moral shifts or the 1960s sexual revolution. While researchers are starting to explore the ways that World War II created a new "urgency" in the erotic relations between men and women, paving the way for extramarital and premarital relations,[4] they have tended to depict the late 1940s and 1950s as frigid and frustrated. One recent history of American sexuality explains: "Sexual experimentation appeared lost in a maze of suburban housing developments as a new generation took on family responsibilities and raised more children than their parents had. The erotic seemed to disappear under a wave of innocent domesticity."[5] Within such an account, parenting is perceived as oppositional to eroticism, as a sublimation or repression of sexual desire. The presupposition is that sexual experimentation occurs primarily outside marriage, not that shifts in sexual desire and expression might originate within the family. Of course, such accounts leave us with that awkward question: If adult erotic life was so dull, where did all the babies come from?

The writers of these accounts have even less to say about the sexuality of children. Our prevailing conception of childhood innocence excludes children from the realm of adult sexuality. As James R. Kincaid notes, the modern division between adult and child is defined along such lines: "The child is that species which is free of sexual feeling or response; the adult is that species which has crossed over into sexuality."[6] Yet, as Kincaid suggests, such distinctions are hard to maintain. Children remain both subjects and objects of desire. Children display an inconvenient degree of sexual curiosity and sensual pleasure. Children are central to the erotic dynamics of families and, often, become the vehicles for parents' erotic fantasies and desires. Just as Kincaid argues that the Victorians' sentimentalized conception of the innocent child was vitally linked with pedophilic impulses, permissive discourse offered a new conception of the sensuous child, which posed awkward questions about adult sexuality. In constructing a new model of children's sexuality, postwar parents opened new erotic prospects for adults.

This essay will trace this shifting conception of children's minds and bodies through a close examination of pre-and postwar child-rearing guides. Specifically, I want to explore how conceptions of childhood sensuality and bodily pleasure emerge as positive forces in the postwar literature. I will be especially interested in the ways that the desire to "liberate" children from inhibitions was seen as forcing adults to be more open about their sexuality and more accepting of their own bodies. At the same time, in stressing how child-rearing guides spoke to and justified adult erotic interests, we need also to recognize the tremendous anxieties and uncertainties that surrounded this transformation in our social construction of childhood. Parents were being asked to rear their children according to principles dramatically different from those followed by their own parents. As child-study expert Eda J. LeShan wrote, "Sometimes, because what we have tried to do is strange and new, we take ourselves too seriously and try much too hard. In trying to help their children to be less frightened of their feelings, parents often become more afraid of their own feelings!"[7] Imagining change was one thing; living with that change was something else.

Regulating the Body: The Prewar Paradigm

Writing in 1951, Martha Wolfenstein identified what she saw as a "changing conception of human impulses" within dominant child-rearing practices.[8] Newer conceptions of childhood embraced "fun morality," an acceptance of sensation, pleasure, spontaneity as an important part of how humans grow and learn. She saw these new child-rearing practices as standing in stark contrast to the more discipline-centered approach of prewar authorities. Erotic impulses, seen as dangerous and overpowering in prewar discourse, were reconceptualized as benign, natural, and even necessary for children's intellectual growth. The prewar paradigm saw the relations between parents and children primarily in terms of discipline and authority; the postwar model saw parent-child relations increasingly in terms of pleasure and play. The prewar paradigm, grounded in behaviorism, stressed the importance of forming habits of behavior necessary for productive life; the postwar paradigm, grounded in Freudianism and most often labeled "permissiveness," sought to limit inhibitions upon basic impulses and desires. Wolfenstein saw these shifts as linked both to changing understandings of child psychology and to larger social shifts from a culture of production toward a culture of consumption. The prewar model prepared children for the workplace within a society of scarcity, the postwar model prepared them to become pleasure-seeking consumers within a prosperous new economy. The adult world was working hard to overcome inhibitions on their children's ability to seek and achieve pleasure.

The dominant prewar experts owed strong allegiances to behaviourist psychology and to Progressive Era ideologies. Behaviorism bracketed off questions of interior mental life as ultimately not open to scientific examination, focusing instead on understanding external behaviors. According to John Watson, who was both a leader in behaviorism and the best-selling child-care expert of the period, humans possessed no instincts, except the fear of loud noises and the fear of being dropped. Asserting that children are "made, not born," Watson saw

parents as being similar to blacksmiths in their shaping of their children's malle-
able minds into "instruments" appropriate for the modern world:

> The fabricator of metal takes his heated mass, places it upon the anvil and begins to
> shape it according to patterns of his own. . . . So inevitably do we begin at birth to
> shape the emotional life of our children. . . . How few human instruments have ever
> been perfectly shaped to fit the environments in which they must function![9]

Watson's primary metaphors are those of the industrial (or in this case, the preindustrial) age, centering on the construction and processing of "raw materials"
(i.e., children's minds and bodies) into finished products. The goal of his *Psychological Care of Infant and Child* was to make this process more "scientific" by
bringing emotional life under "control."

As practiced by Watson, behaviorism had strong antisensual and antisenti-
mental underpinnings, depicting the body as requiring constant discipline. Watson hoped to develop "impartial" children with few emotional attachments and
limited erotic interests. Following his advice, middle-class mothers moved from
breast-feeding toward bottle-feeding, seeing a carefully calculated formula as
offering better nutrition, while showing little interest in the potential loss of the
affective bond between mother and child.[10] Parents were urged not to play with
their children, since even a few minutes' play could cause "nervous distur-
bances" or "disruptions of regular habits." To avoid such overexcitemant and
disruption, the outward display of affection was to be minimized: "Treat them
as though they were young adults. Dress them, bathe them with care and circumspection. Let your behavior always be objective and kindly firm. Never hug and
kiss them, never let them sit on your lap. . . . Shake hands with them in the
morning."[11] Discipline, control, regularity were essential. By feeding the child on
a regular schedule, putting it to bed and picking it up according to the clock,
toilet training it at the appropriate age, parents would instill in their infant good
"habits" that would carry into the work world. As Ellen Richards urged, "Let
the furrows be plowed deeply enough while the brain cells are plastic, then
human energies will be the right result."[12]

Watson and his disciples saw childrearing primarily in terms of preparation
for the demands of an increasingly regimented adult world. For Watson, the
ideal child is silent and obedient, one "who never cries unless struck by a pin . . .
who quickly learns to overcome small difficulties in his environment without
running to mother, father, nurse or other adults. . . . [W]ho eats what is set before
him and asks no questions for conscience sake."[13] Such a child should be autonomous and stoic, "as free as possible of sensitivities to people . . . independent of
the family."[14]

Developing good habits required that parental authority be absolute and un-
wavering, that discipline be systematic and strict. Ada Hart Arlitt's *The Child from
One to Six* (1930) warned that the child "will not know that there are laws that
govern the universe unless he knows that there are laws that govern the home."[15]
The home was to be regulated not by "mother love" but by the "kitchen time-
piece." Parents, Arlitt insisted, should "cut down the number of times that one

speaks to the child. Speak only when necessary then expect to be obeyed." The signs of adult authority were to be overt and unmistakable; the separation between the child's sphere and the parents' sphere was rigidly enforced. Children were to be taught a proper relation to hierarchy and authority so they could become workers on the assembly line or employees in the emerging American corporations.

The danger of "spoiling the child" was ever present and often irreversible. Watson argued that "invalidism" was a direct product of too much nurturing and fondling of children.[16] The ideal of a tightly regulated mind and body could be maintained only if more unruly impulses were checked. Mother's love was "an instrument which may inflict a never healing wound, a wound which may make infancy unhappy, adolescence a nightmare, an instrument which may wreck your adult son or daughter's vocational future and their chances for marital happiness."[17]

Almost all aspects of daily life posed dangers of sexual excitement or sensual stimulation. Watson insisted, for example, that the bath "should be a serious but not gloomy occasion," objecting to the "useless and foolish" practice of putting toys in the tub: "The object of the bath is to get the child clean and not to entertain it."[18] He warned against too much time spent cleaning the "sex organs" since "any continued handling of them may start masturbation on the child's part."[19] Watson advocated allowing a child to take a stuffed toy to bed since it will be "less tempted to explore its own body" but urged that this practice be abandoned at an early age, since it also posed dangers.[20] As the child is put to sleep, the parents should check to see "that his hands are placed outside the cover (if he is not a thumb sucker, inside if he is.)"[21] Watson's uncertainty reflects the fact that thumb sucking posed almost the same dangers as masturbation. For one thing, "the child with its mobile hands gathers germs everywhere" and thus falls victim to disease.[22] The persistent thumb sucker, Watson felt, "doesn't conquer his world. He becomes an 'exclusive,' an auto-erotic."[23] Hands should be bound and constrained at night, if necessary, to stop negative habits from forming.

Watson advocated an even more aggressive campaign against masturbation:

> Almost from birth watchfulness begins. . . . Clothing should not be tight or too warm. Covers should not be too heavy or too numerous. Their hands should be watched. Persistent tree climbing, the popular sport of sliding down the banister— the earlier dangling astride the father's leg—are all forms of activity that must be scrutinized somewhat.[24]

Subsequently, the campaign extends to verbal instruction specifying the harmful nature of masturbation. Watson reports his horror about a youngster who told him, "Why can't I play with it—it is mine."[25] Such personal pleasures were antithetical to Watson's desire to accommodate the child to larger social responsibilities. Assuming that marital life precluded autoeroticism, parents were to inform their children emphatically that "father or mother does not do this."[26] As with thumb sucking, such sexual interests were seen as demanding "time and energy for doing and learning other things which will help you get along in life."[27] However, the most serious harm of masturbation, in Watson's view, was that *"if it is persisted in too long and practiced too often it may make heterosexual adjustment difficult or impossible"* (emphasis in original). Ever vigilant against environmental factors that might lead to homosexuality, Watson argued that participation in the Boy Scouts or the YMCA was "unwise and dangerous" because such exclusive and unhealthy involvement in homosocial relations might also contribute to homosexuality.[28]

Exploring the Body: The Postwar Paradigm

Postwar parents, on the other hand, saw children's groping fingers as evidence of an innate curiosity about the world, a desire to explore their immediate environment. Constraint of erotic impulses, far from necessary, was potentially harmful to the child's natural development. *Parents* magazine warned, "[M]uch of the actual socializing process is a throttling of the child's spontaneity and a stifling of his creativity," a deformation of mental development likened to "brainwashing."[29] Parents were to relinquish traditional authority in order for children to develop autonomy and self-worth. Many parental restrictions ran directly counter to the child's pleasures (and by extension, their needs). As one child-rearing expert writes:

> Noises fascinate a child. He can't understand why yells, crashes and thumps disturb grownups. He loves to explore but there are a disheartening number of things he may not touch. . . . Dirt is pleasant and mud feels good when it is squished between the fingers or toes. Parents don't always see it that way, especially when the stuff gets tracked into the kitchen.[30]

Parents were urged to accommodate these impulses as much as possible, since it was through such activities that children learn about the world around them. Learning was motivated by sensual pleasure and experimentation: "The tiny child wants to touch, feel, and taste everything which he can reach. This is his way of learning. Yet, so often mother follows him around turning aside his interest and his curiosity with 'Don't touch that,' 'Don't put that in your mouth.' "[31] Here, two classic permissive themes come together: first, a core faith in the body as driven toward pleasure and knowledge (with little distinction drawn between the two); second, the fear of cutting off that natural growth and exploration through adult restrictions. While the prewar model sought to master children's nature, children's bodies were now viewed as largely self-regulating.

The child's mind was to be free to develop without adult inhibitions, fears, or anxieties. In one *Parents* magazine article, mothers were urged to allow their children to splash in the bathtub or even paint the bathroom floors and walls with water: "As for the floor, let the youngster help mop it up. It's less important than his healthy emotional development."[32] Spock adopts a similar stance toward playing in the dirt:

> A small child wants to do a lot of things that get him dirty, and they are good for him, too. He loves to dig in earth and sand and wade in mud puddles, splash in water in the washstand. He wants to roll in the grass, squeeze mud in his hands. When he has chances to do these delightful things, it enriches his spirit, makes him a warmer person, just the way beautiful music or falling in love improves an adult. The small child who is always sternly warned against getting his clothes dirty or making a mess, and who takes it to heart, will be cramped. If he becomes really timid about dirt, it will make him too cautious in other ways, also, and keep him from developing into the free, warm, life-loving person he was meant to be.[33]

If the prewar writers had treated children's minds as clay, which could be shaped and modeled by a strong hand, the postwar model saw children's minds as ripe fruit, which could be bruised and mangled by too much manipulation. Guilt, once introduced, could be a powerfully destructive force. The idea of spoiling a child through too much physical attention, on the other hand, was seen as the baggage of prewar puritanism.

The threat of childhood diseases and the problems of hygiene that dominated prewar accounts gave way to a new focus on psychological health and social development. The parent's attention to mental health was as important as its focus on the infant's bodily development. Spock explains: "Every baby needs to be smiled at, talked to, played with, fondled—gently and lovingly—just as much as he needs vitamins and calories, and the baby who doesn't get any loving will grow up cold and unresponsive."[34] Moralistic concerns about "overstimulation" were displaced by advice that stressed the importance of early and frequent physical contact and stimulation for mental health and social development.

New research pointed to psychological harms resulting from sensory depravation. Children denied physical contact could suffer from marasmus, literally "wasting away," an ailment that some doctors claimed resulted in "more than half of the deaths of babies" in the first year of life.[35] Drawing on such research, Margaret A. Ribble's *The Rights of Infants* (1943) stressed the "vital importance" of parents respecting and even encouraging children's "sensuousness," with bodily pleasure seen as evidence of a healthy and well-cared-for child. Ribble writes:

> Nature seems to have a purpose in this earliest biological endowment of pleasure, for it gives the child a sense of the goodness of his physical self. It puts the first stamp on the rightness of physical pleasure, which is one of the basic roads to happiness. The child's body is the tool which introduces him to life, and he must feel that it is a good tool. His mental self and his awareness develop hand in hand with the physical. . . . Erotic feeling is diffuse in a baby, but it is not misplaced and does not imply something evil which must be weeded out.[36]

Almost every aspect of child development is erotically charged in her account, including sucking the mother's breast, rocking in the crib, or taking a bath. In that sense, she resembles Watson except for one vital difference—she embraces the sensuality he sought to eradicate. The physical development of the child is both motivated by and helps to facilitate masturbatory impulses:

> His tiny fingers soon begin to explore his own body with evident satisfaction, wandering at times into the navel and genital regions. Baby boys are known to have

erections from the time of birth. A one-year old likes to be naked, to have admiring audiences when he is bathing and being dressed, he likes to snuggle into bed with his parents.[37]

Such impulses are safe and healthy, according to Ribble, though she sees some danger that parents may overrespond to children's erotic impulses.

The problems arise less from children's sexuality, which is pure and natural, than from adult sexuality, which often seems incapable of marking proper boundaries:

> The difficulty lies in those parents who themselves are frustrated or lonely in their personal lives and get too much satisfaction from continuous or exaggerated fondling of the child. If they are not aware of the latent eroticism of the infant they can easily overstimulate him, making him more demanding and creating tensions and anxiety.[38]

"Healthy" parents, on the other hand, can help the child overcome an undue fixation on one part of the body. A "baby who sucks to excess" can be "helped by diverting a part of this tension from the mouth zone to the skin by means of oil rubs, frequent bathing, and gentle massage."[39] Mirroring advice that Masters and Johnson, and other sexologists were offering for resolving adult "sexual problems," Ribble calls upon the mother to become a sensuality facilitator, ensuring that the child develops an erotically diffused relationship with its body. Such physical contact between mother and child is "an important stimulus to sensory growth and awareness," continuing the relationship forged in the womb when "the child was like an organ of the mother's body."[40] Ribble sees a full-body eroticism as an ideal embodiment of the sensual potential of childhood; premature genital fixation involves a closing of stimulation that may ultimately stunt mental growth.

Within the highly charged discourse of permissive child rearing, almost all of the child's activities have an underlying eroticism. As Haim G. Ginott writes:

> Though not in an adult way, the infant's enjoyment of his body and its functions is sexual in nature. . . . He handles his limbs and delights in being touched, tickled, and cuddled. These early touchings and strokings are part of his sex education. Through them he learns to receive love.[41]

Self-exploration as a natural aspect of sexual awakening should not only be tolerated by parents; it should be facilitated, rendered safe and sanitary. Ginott acknowledged that the anal phase posed particularly vexing problems for parents, who do not share the child's fascination with the "sight, smell and touching of feces."[42] Parents, however, were urged to overcome their own discomfort in order not to pass inhibitions onto their children: "Special care must be taken not to infect him with disgust towards his body and its products. Harsh and hasty measures may make the child feel that his body and *all* of its functions are something to dread, rather than to enjoy."[43] Like many permissive writers, Ginott found the solution to this dilemma through sublimation and redirection, the seeking of "acceptable substitute ways" to "enjoy forbidden pleasures," such as playing with sand, mud, paint, clay and water.[44] Once again, it seems, that in order to prevent sex from feeling dirty, permissive writers made dirt sexy.

Consistently, Ginott and the other permissive writers operate on the assumption that children's sexuality is more liberated and uninhibited than the sexuality of their parents, who often are depicted as suffering tremendous anxieties and phobias about bodily contact. He writes, "When a little girl discovers her clitoris and confides in her mother that it is her 'best-feeling place,' it takes both faith and diplomacy not to cry out, 'don't touch.' "[45] Yet, within this new understanding of children's sexuality, direct genital stimulation, far from a problem, is read as a sign of normal sexual development because "her most pleasurable sensations now come from the genitals rather than from the anus or the mouth."[46]

Benjamin Spock urges parents to simply ignore children's first masturbatory experiences:

> It's better not to give him the idea that he is bad, or that his genital is bad. You want him to go on having a wholesome, natural feeling about his entire body. If he is scared about any part of himself, it draws his attention to it, gets it on his mind, and may have bad results later.[47]

Parental restraints or interventions can stifle the growth of creativity and sensuality, can cause the child to develop negative attitudes toward itself or its body. In Spock's account, one can see signs of the domestic isolation experienced by suburban mothers, perhaps even the sense of loss from being shoved out of wartime jobs and into full-time maternalism: "A worrisome mother is completely wrapped up in her baby. She has no outside interests or pleasures, doesn't keep up her friendships. She just hovers over the child." However, Spock's sympathies lie with the child, who becomes an unwilling vehicle for the mother's excess energies and desires: "He seems to absorb some of his mother's tenseness and uneasiness."[48]

The permissive household was organized around the child, with the mother taught to read the child's body (its cries, its excrement, its complexion, its gestures) for signs of desires that were to be facilitated and accommodated. The child's body told the child when it needed to eat, when it needed to rest, and when it was ready to go potty. Spock cites a study by Dr. Clara Davis that demonstrated that children left to choose their own foods would gravitate toward a well-balanced diet. Discussing this study, Spock appeals to a belief that children, like primitive man, like other animal species, has "some instinctive knowledge of what is good for him," knowledge residing in bodily impulses and sensations.[49] Spock rejected the Watsonian notion that good habits can be conveyed through drill or regimentation:

> His bowels . . . will move according to their own healthy pattern, which may or may not be regular. . . . He will develop his own pattern of sleep, according to his own needs. . . . The desire to get along with other people happily and considerately develops within him as part of the unfolding of his nature, provided he grows up with loving, self-respecting parents. . . . You can't drill these into a child from the outside in a hundred years.[50]

As far as possible, the permissive parent was to accommodate the home to the child's "creative" and exploratory impulses.

Where this is not possible, the child should be taught to sublimate aggressive, destructive, or autoerotic impulses toward some more acceptable outlet. The postwar model saw desire as polydirectional and multifocused; erotic impulses can be projected onto a range of possible objects. As Spock writes, "[T]he year old baby is so eager to find out about the whole world that he isn't particular where he begins or where he stops."[51] Crib toys are recommended for parents concerned about their children's autoeroticism; masturbation or thumb sucking, the experts suggest, are often a sign of boredom.

Many factors led to this shifting conception of children's sexuality and psychology. The advent of permissiveness was closely linked to the popularization of Freud, with Spock translating psychoanalytic categories, such as the anal phase, into pragmatic advice on how to toilet train your child. Freud's work had encouraged a wider acceptance of children's sexuality and its importance for their development. One of Spock's primary accomplishments was to introduce Freudian concepts as "common sense" while avoiding the confusing and off-putting Freudian vocabulary. Spock's everyday language made these often foreign sounding concepts comfortable and familiar, even for a Cold War America charged with xenophobia and anti-intellectualism. Postwar parents, aware of the neurosis caused by various forms of repression, sought to raise children free of inhibitions, to ensure children's smooth passage through successive stages of sexual development so they could avoid unnatural fixations.

The child-rearing literature is full of advice, for example, on how to cope with the oedipal phase and its attending traumas. Fitzhugh Dodson writes:

> In a home where the sexual atmosphere is open and healthy and sexual organs are taken casually, a little boy's fears that something might happen to his genitals by way of punishment will soon subside. As a matter of fact, a little boy generally takes considerable pride in his penis and loves to show it off to his parents and peers. If a mother is able to be relaxed about such things herself, she will probably be able to enjoy the naive manner in which a little boy will show off his newfound masculine characteristics.[52]

Mothers might be given concrete advice about how to help a young girl overcome pangs of penis envy: "A mother may help a little girl build up her confidence and self-esteem by explaining to her that while only boys and men have a penis, she has something that boys do not have: a uterus."[53] Through frank talk and sexual openness, the parents could help children deal with gender difference and feel more comfortable with their bodies. Sexual openness and comfort were depicted consistently as something parents owed to their children, so the task rapidly became not only to avoid repressing the child's growing sexuality but to overcome parental inhibitions.

The emergence of this ideal of the sensuous child also reflected the popularization of anthropological discoveries about alternative constructions of sexuality. Margaret Mead's work on the Samoans, in particular, offered postwar America an image of a less sexually repressed society, one free of shameful taboos and accepting of erotic experimentation.[54] Mead's descriptions of a culture that dealt matter-of-factly with casual nudity, social masturbation, and sex play (both heterosexual and homosexual) titillated middle America, challenging it to rethink its own taboos, restrictions, and complaints. Consistently, postwar child-rearing experts use the defamiliarizing potential of anthropological observation to contest puritanism and to urge parents to accept natural bodily urges. In his discussion of masturbation, Spock refers to "lands where childhood masturbation is not disapproved of by anyone" as a contrast to American society, where "many people consider genital play in childhood wrong, and almost everybody objects to seeing it in public."[55]

Often, as this anthropological literature was adopted by child-rearing experts, children became "noble savages" whose natural wisdom and sensuality needed to be protected from the corruptions of adult civilizations. Spock describes children as recapitulating the evolution of human cultures, starting as a single-cell organism, working through lower animal forms within the womb, and then slowly learning to walk, talk, communicate, and participate within the culture. As Spock writes, "[H]e's following the whole history of the human race."[56] If Spock saw children's intellectual development as natural and historically inevitable, he nevertheless romanticizes the closer relation between man and nature within the more "primitive" stages of human evolution. Spock, for example, appeals to the organicism of "primitive" cultures to justify his advocacy of feeding on demand:

> It will help you to realize how natural a flexible schedule is if you stop and think of a mother, far away in an 'uncivilized' land, who has never heard of a schedule, or a pediatrician, or a cow. Her baby starts to cry with hunger. This attracts her attention and makes her feel like putting him to breast. He nurses until he is satisfied, then falls asleep. . . . The rhythm of the baby's digestive system is what sets the schedule. The mother follows her instinct without any hesitation.[57]

Just as Spock saw the child as more knowing about its needs than were the parents, Spock saw the "primitive" culture as having a more comfortable relationship to the body, unmarred by civilized society's constraints. Mead, herself, went back and forth between examining the child-rearing practices of non-Western cultures and commenting on her own culture, offering advice to parents through the pages of mass-market magazines.

Between Parent and Child: Making the Home Safe for Sex

A "sex quiz" published in *Escapade* in the mid-1960s and intended to assess adult comfort with a range of erotic activities asked the sticky question, "Would you allow your children (or other people's children) to witness you performing oral sex?" This question was seen as a decisive measure of sexual liberation, with those who could answer it positively, viewed as "the new, new generation of emancipated parents."[58] The quiz pushed well beyond the limits of what even the most radical advocates of permissiveness in the 1950s would have seen as necessary or appropriate. Spock, after all, still maintained the Freudian concern about children witnessing the "primal scene" and for that reason, advocated that children from an early age sleep in separate rooms from their parents'.[59] Yet, Spock also acknowledged that parents often felt pressures to overcome their own erotic anxieties in order to create a comfortable climate for children's growing sexual awareness. The permissive writers were gently prodding adults to embrace more liberated attitudes toward erotic life. In that sense, adults were performing sexuality for their offspring, perhaps even for "other people's children."

Most of the child-care writers found themselves negotiating between extremes in their advice, offering counsel to parents who had conservative ideas about sex, nudity, and the body and to parents who had embraced "more liberated" attitudes toward child sexuality. Spock's discussion of masturbation, for example, deals with a range of differing parental views and values, while pushing toward as much tolerance as the parents could comfortably embrace. First, there are the "enlightened" parents "who are well aware of the medical view that no physical or emotional harm results from genital play itself in a well adjusted child."[60] These parents "can matter-of-factly say something to the effect that this is not considered polite in public, just as urinating in public is not considered polite." For Spock, the central issue isn't whether or not to masturbate (since this is something all children do) but whether the child should do so in public settings: "It doesn't help a child to bring him up thinking it's all right to offend the sensibilities of the community." Spock responds to conflicting social attitudes by restricting sexual expression to private space, where individual choice reigns, while insisting that collective values must determine public behavior.

On the other hand, Spock addresses parents "whose religion definitely disapproves of genital play or whose upbringing makes them distinctly uncomfortable when they see it in their children." These parents will want to discourage all forms of masturbation "in a considerate way." The parents' sensibilities (which Spock has isolated from any medical or psychological validity) must be respected because "they can't be good parents in other respects if they are uncomfortable with their children in one respect." Moral reasons are clearly secondary to the issue of maintaining a "comfortable" domestic environment, in avoiding stress and tension within the family. In these cases, however, the psychological climate surrounding the regulation of bodily pleasure is important. Spock wants to keep the focus on sexual acts, not on sexual identities:

> When parents prohibit running in the street, it's usually done in a manner which clearly shows that it is the act which is disapproved. But sometimes when parents are disturbed by an act which has moral implications . . . their anxiety may prompt them to land on the child with such a vigorous condemnation of *him*—as a person— that he doubts his own goodness and fears his parents will stop loving him altogether.

Ultimately, Spock felt, sexual desires are stronger than social prohibitions. Children should not be made to live in fear of their own transgressive appetites: "Even very obedient small children will yield to temptation again on a few occasions (just as almost all adolescents do), which would then result in an increase in the sense of dread or unworthiness."

This need to address multiple sets of family values suggests that American society was undergoing a transition in its sexual attitudes. The core issue became not whether or not sex was good (since it clearly carries positive values within this formulation) but how individual sexual expression can be negotiated in relation to dominant community values. Sexual desires are too powerful to repress fully, but they can, apparently, be closeted. However, the goal is to avoid conflict about sexuality within the family and within the community and to avoid heaping too much guilt on the child for urges that cannot be fully regulated. Even the most liberated parent, however, may be "quite surprised to find how anxiously they react when they unexpectedly find their child involved in it." It is precisely these latent, inbred inhibitions parents were trying to cure in their children by creating a domestic environment where sexuality was experienced as "wholesome" and "natural."

When American sociologists interviewed parents in the late 1950s, they located many different strategies for confronting parental discomfort about infantile masturbation. First, parents sought to prevent stimulation that encouraged children to touch themselves. For some parents, this was as simple as altering basic consumer choices, such as buying a larger size of shorts (advice echoing Watson's concern that children's dress encouraged self-examination). For other parents, permissive-era strategies of redirection and sublimation proved useful. For the most part, the parents avoided direct reference to the act itself, since they felt to "make an issue of it" would give the child "food for thought" and encourage increased awareness of genitals. As one parent suggested, "I think it is very important for them to hardly realize any difference between different parts of their body."[61] Others borrowed sanctions appropriate to other contexts and applied them to the problem, suggesting children might catch colds if they went without clothing or could hurt themselves if they handled "tender regions" too often. One mother hit the masturbating child with an all-purpose question of the era, "Do you want me to get a Band-aid to put on it?"[62] Echoing Watson's prewar concerns, some parents did express fears that too much childhood masturbation would result in sexual perversion. As one mother explained, "If they (boys) aren't stopped, as they grow older, I think they'd be more girl than boy, to tell you the truth."[63] The recurring concern was that the child would be unable to abandon masturbation for mature heterosexual relations or that a preoccupation with his or her own genitals would lead to same-sex attractions.

Spock's treatment of parental nudity offers another vivid example of the ways the experts negotiated around contradictory adult attitudes. On the one hand, Spock expressed concern that some parents, interested in exhibiting "healthy" sexual attitudes, felt too strong an urge to display their own bodies: "Some of those who were most impatient of modesty deliberately practiced some degree of nudity at home, feeling that they were conscientiously aiding their children's education."[64] Spock warned that parental nudity might disturb children rather than comfort them, if it had the "wrong spirit behind it." The important thing, Spock argued, was not "the number of minutes and the number of inches of body exposure" but "parent's general attitude towards nudity, towards sex and towards their children." Gently, cautiously, Spock raised the specter that parents might achieve erotic gratifications in their relations with children: "Some people have a greater-than-average urge to make the opposite sex look at them by means of clothes or the lack of them. . . . Some of them, without realizing it, may enjoy showing off a bit too much to their children." Young children might be confused or "puzzled" by looking at their parents' genitals, prematurely sparking castration anxiety or oedipal rivalries. Young boys, he warned, often feel rivalry with their fathers about penis size, a trait he saw as pervading masculine culture.

At the other extreme were parents who were too self-consciously struggling to overcome their own inhibitions and as such, passed that tension onto their children. As Spock explains, "[A] modest parent trying to be a nudist for a child's education can't help being an embarrassed nudist and this is more likely to trouble than to help the child." If parents have no obligation to perform erotic displays for their children, they do have an obligation not to overreact to the child's own nudism and exhibitionism: "[I]t's not necessary or wholesome for a parent who is discovered by the child, accidentally, in the bathroom or undressed to scream or act as if the child had committed a crime. Overemphasizing the 'badness' of nudity only produces morbid shame and sometimes, morbid curiosity." Here, as elsewhere in permissive discourse, the challenge was to accommodate the child's urges and impulses rather than to impose adult standards or inflict grownup inhibitions.

What comes through powerfully in Spock is the fact that children's sexuality takes shape within the context of adult sexuality and often gets caught within adult erotic urges, rivalries, and inhibitions. What Spock didn't tell us, however, is that adult sexuality is also taking shape in relation to children's sexuality, that mothers and fathers were responding to this changing definition of children's erotic urges and using them to justify a fuller range of erotic expression for themselves. Parental obligations were paving the way for sexual liberation.

Selma H. Frailberg's *The Magic Years*, another popular child-rearing guide of the late 1950s, voices the questions many parents must have confronted:

> If a child is curious about the way in which his mother's or father's body is made, should he be given opportunities to see the parent nude, to satisfy his curiosity directly by looking? . . . If we restrict the child's curiosity, if we interfere with these manifestations of sexuality, won't the child feel that there must be something secret and shameful about such things?[65]

Frailberg recounts a daughter's seduction of her father, with the daughter cast as "open in her curiosity" and "persistent" in her demands for adult display, and the father is described as uncomfortable in responding to such requests, eager to preserve his own privacy, and "uncertain" about the appropriate response. Frailberg recounts a stereotypical incident:

> She asked repeatedly to visit her father in the bathroom, showed her interest in her father's penis and recently had asked to touch it. Should he permit it? His wife felt that if this action satisfied the child's curiosity, it should be allowed.

Here, we return to the situation described in *The Good Mother*. In a society where debates about incest and child abuse are conducted in every newspaper and talk show, one naturally wants to question whose desires are being expressed through this narrative, who is seducing whom in this story. Yet, reading the story in this contemporary fashion denies children's own sexual desires and interests. In this permissive context, those desires are assumed to be "pure" and "healthy," helping to justify the erotic tensions charging this exchange between father and daughter. That both husband and wife are capable of considering such an action points toward the comfort about child sexuality found in these guides. Children's sexuality has been safely domesticated, accommodated to the family space, even if it still poses lingering questions about what role adults should play in its development. The challenge becomes how to deal with a potentially embarrassing situation without simultaneously stunting the daughter's erotic growth and development. In a classic example of permissive redirecting of erotic desires, Frailberg advocates substituting open discussions and even illustrations in books for direct exposure to the father's body. Through such means, "we have denied her the privilege of intimacy with her father, but we have not denied her the right to be curious and to ask questions." Here, sex information can become the means of controlling direct sexual activity. It is precisely by setting limits that such books are able to express such transgressive desires in the first place.

Wild in the Streets

The new openness toward the body was presenting problems not addressed by prewar experts. As *Your Child Is a Person* (1965) explains, "Children used to be brought up not to touch or even look at certain parts of their bodies. Now their parents bathe, pat and admire them—in whole and in part, naked as well as clothed."[66] The problem for these writers was that children needed to be taught the appropriate spaces where sexual expression could occur: "Permissiveness in private . . . is not the same as permissiveness in public."[67] Parents who do not caution their children against public masturbation, for example, risk "exposing the child to public scolding, ridicule and even ostracism" and thereby cause "the very confusion and anxiety modern sex education hopes to avoid."[68] If the permissive home was to be made safe for children's sexuality, it was important that sexuality be contained within the home.

How, for example, should parents respond to their children's sex play?[69] Sex play between children, Spock argues, can be wholesome: "They are interested in each others' bodies, have the desire occasionally to see and touch them." The primary danger, once again, is that a mature sexuality may corrupt the purity of these initial erotic urges: "Some children are upset and worried by what is done and said, especially if there is an older child, with an unwholesome attitude, leading them on." What should be avoided, however, would be too direct an intervention by adults into the situation: "Parents should not become suspicious snoopers or make accusations."

The Gesell Institute at Yale similarly argues that children should not be "blamed" for their mutual sex play, since such experimentation "just naturally occurs if several children are left together unsupervised, with nothing better to do."[70] Rather, the parent should act to interrupt and redirect these erotic impulses into more acceptable objects without displaying shock or displeasure toward what they have witnessed.

For Lee Salk, the central distinction was between heterosexual sex play and same-sex interactions. In the case of heterosexual contact between two children, Salk suggests "react as you would to excessive masturbation, but don't be surprised if, in spite of your attitude, your child continues his sexual expression." In many ways, creating an aura of the forbidden about such contact "may intensify your child's pleasure and perhaps encourage the idea that sexual pleasure, sexual activity and sexual stimulation have some special significance in life." Same-sex contact, on the other hand, posed a much more serious challenge because the ultimate goal was to generate a more liberated and pleasurable *heterosexuality*, not to broaden the range of acceptable erotic expressions. Even at the risk of trauma or inhibition, children were turned away from homoerotic-erotic contact, though even here, the origins of the desire are treated as free from negative adult connotations:

> A child's first experience involving intense sexual satisfaction can have a marked influence on his ultimate sexual adaptation. . . . All things being equal, if your child finds satisfaction with the same sex in his initial activities, there is a tendency to repeat the experience and the particular type of activity becomes usual. In short, if you want to avoid the possible hazards of a homosexual adjustment, take a more relaxed view of heterosexual experiences and a more disapproving stance towards sexual stimulation that involves members of the same sex.

Writing in the early 1970s, at the end of the permissive era, Salk is more overt about the homophobic dimensions of permissive discourse, yet similar fears surface in many child-care guides, which often included detailed discussions about handling sissy boys and tomboys, and how to direct children toward gender-appropriate modes of behavior and desire. Homosexuality and transgender conduct were often seen as responses to inappropriate situations and influences on child development, not as originating within the child itself. The "wholesome" sexuality of the child was presumed to be primarily heterosexual, though as this discussion suggests, the child probably had not developed strong inhibitions against homoerotic contacts.[71]

The issue of sex play was further complicated by contradictory adult standards. Within a suburban neighborhood, parents were unlikely to agree about what constituted the appropriate response, yet the problem became a community interest as soon as it involved children from more than one family. As one sociological study reported:

> Mothers are not entirely free agents in the matter of controlling such behavior. Any mother who does not enforce this rule for her children is subject to considerable pressure from other mothers. . . . If one child persistently behaved in a manner which the other mothers disapproved, the other children were told not to play with him. Knowing that her child would be ostracized if he did not conform to neighborhood standards, a mother might teach him that he had to conform to those neighborhood standards even if his own family disagreed with them.[72]

Parents often contacted one another by telephone, reporting incidents of sex play and encouraging adoption of a response appropriate to prevailing community standards. Most of the mothers adopted "an unwritten rule that one mother must not punish another mother's child" and as a result, the problem was reported to parents for future action. Suburban America policed erotic life to ensure that liberatory impulses did not spill over into the streets, and to teach children the importance of fitting their sexual desires within dominant social patterns. If the impulse toward erotic expression originates within the child (which then influences the parent's behavior toward more openness and acceptance of sexual feelings), then the impulse toward restraint and regulation comes from outside the family, from within the community that reserved the right to override parents who went beyond its norms. As one mother told the researchers:

> I explain to him that we have to live in the group, and we have to have the respect of the group, and unless he accepts some of those things—which I always explain are ridiculous to me but we still have to observe some of the amenities—they will not get along well, and they will not be happy.[73]

The regulation of sexuality was shifting from moral prohibitions (which were now seen as superstitious and unscientific) toward social pressures (which were to be respected and observed within an other-directed society). This conflict between public morality and personal sexual expression would frame the battles around erotic life in the 1960s and 1970s.

Conclusion

By the early 1970s, these uncertainties and contradictions would eventually lead to a strong backlash against permissiveness, a return to more "traditional" forms of discipline and greater restraints on children's erotic expression. The perceived need to reestablish parental authority might be suggested by contrasting the titles of such permissive works as *Stop Annoying Your Children, Your Child Makes Sense, Keep Them Human,* and *Democracy in the Home* to postpermissive titles such as *How to Survive Parenthood, Raising a Responsible Child, Dare to Discipline,* and *Par-*

ents Deserve to Know. Conservatives such as Norman Vincent Peale, Spiro Agnew, or Columbia University Vice President David Truman linked the "instant gratification" of permissiveness to the moral decay and social unrest of America's youth.[74] Agnew characterized antiwar protestors as "spoiled brats who never had a good spanking" and cited Spock as the primary negative influence on an entire generation of middle-class sons and daughters. Spock sought to rebut such charges. While he embraced the antiwar movement and expressed hope that its "idealism" might have been shaped by his advice, he denied ever advocating total license or "instant gratification."[75] Spock consistently placed checks on erotic life and individual impulse, yet at the same time he and the other permissive writers loosened restraints that dominated the previous era.

The 1960s sexual revolution pushed beyond the limits carefully put into place by the permissive writers. Spock and others had seen their goal as healthy, comfortable sensuality within heterosexual marriage. The breakdown of the family through divorce, the introduction of sexual experimentation outside marriage, and the limited acceptance of homosexuality shocked many such writers, who viewed these developments as going contrary to the goal of improved American family life. Writing in 1969, Spock saw the promiscuous sexual relations of contemporary college students to be "a mechanical, loveless matter," with students finding in one another what earlier adolescents had been content to discover through masturbation.[76] College students "permit themselves to go far in physical intimacy but unconsciously resist yielding to a tender, idealistic love for these same partners." The students he had helped to nurture were pulled by "contradictory impulses"—"the insistent glandular pressure, the growing curiosity, the compulsion to learn how to make out" on the one hand and a sense of stepping outside social norms, "uneasiness about losing self-respect," and an instinctive "desire, strong or faint, to reserve intimacy for the beloved." Just as children's bodies knew what they needed, these adolescent bodies knew what they were doing was wrong.

Utopian sexual fantasies, desires, and hopes were not simply the product of the baby-boom generation's rebellion against their parents. They were fantasies that postwar parents had for and about their children. Recognizing that their own puritanical upbringings had restricted their ability to give and receive bodily pleasure, they sought a more liberatory world for their children. In doing so, they used their children to open erotic spaces for expression within their suburban homes and within their marriages. These parents did not so much desire their children's bodies (as would be implied by a traditional conception of pedophilia); they desired their children's desires. They desired the prospect of "wholesome," uninhibited, pleasure-driven sexuality. Yet, they also feared it. They feared it in themselves and in their children. Those contradictions surface repeatedly as Spock and other writers seek to calm (and yet acknowledge) parental fears and to guide readers toward a more progressive approach.

For a generation having more children and at an earlier age than any other in the twentieth century, being a parent was not a retreat from erotic life but the means by which they came to understand their own erotic feelings and impulses.

Themselves the product of a period when child-rearing advice sought to regulate and regiment bodily impulses, they sought to protect and facilitate children's sexual desires. At the same time, they sought to redirect those desires into what were viewed as "normal" heterosexual marriages, into socially sanctioned forms of sexuality. Sexuality was held in check by public opinion, not morality or fear. The shift of public opinion, the loss of social checks on erotic expression in the 1960s, led to a backlash against permissive understandings of children's sexuality and a new definition of what constituted a "good mother."

NOTES

1. Sue Miller, *The Good Mother* (New York: Harper and Row, 1986), p. 177.

2. Ibid., p. 124.

3. Ibid., p. 178.

4. John Costello, *Virtue under Fire: How World War II Changed Our Social and Sexual Attitudes* (New York: Fromm, 1987).

5. John D'Emilio and Estelle B. Freedman, *Intimate Matters: A History of Sexuality in America* (New York: Harper and Row, 1988), p. 242.

6. James R. Kincaid, *Child-Loving: The Erotic Child and Victorian Culture* (New York: Routledge, 1992), pp. 6–7.

7. Eda J. LeShan, *How to Survive Parenthood* (New York: Random House, 1965), p. 15.

8. Martha Wolfenstein, "Fun Morality: An Analysis of Recent American Child-Training Literature," in Margaret Mead and Martha Wolfenstein, eds., *Childhood in Contemporary Cultures* (Chicago: University of Chicago Press, 1955), p. 168.

9. John B. Watson, *Psychological Care of Infant and Child* (New York: Norton, 1928), pp. 46–47.

10. See Shari L. Thurer, *The Myths of Motherhood: How Culture Reinvents the Good Mother* (New York: Penguin, 1994). See also Dan Beekman, *The Mechanical Baby: A Popular History of the Theory and Practice of Childraising* (Westport, Conn.: L. Hill, 1977); Barbara Ehrenreich and Deirdre English, *For Her Own Good: 150 Years of the Experts' Advice to Women* (New York: Anchor, 1978); Nancy Pottishman Weiss, "Mother, the Invention of Necessity," in N. Ray Hiner and Joseph M. Hawes, eds., *Growing Up in America: Children in Historical Perspective* (Chicago: University of Illinois Press, 1985), pp. 283–303.

11. Watson, *Psychological Care of Infant and Child*, pp. 81–82.

12. Ellen Richards, *Euthenics: The Science of Controllable Environments* (Boston: Whitcomb and Burrows, 1912), pp. 82–83.

13. Watson, *Psychological Care of Infant and Child*, pp. 9–10.

14. Ibid., p. 186.

15. Ada Hart Arlitt, *The Child from One to Six* (New York: McGraw-Hill, 1930), as cited in Beekman, *The Mechanical Baby*, p. 138.

16. Watson, *Psychological Care of Infant and Child*, pp. 76–77.

17. Ibid., p. 87.

18. Ibid., pp. 114–115.

19. Ibid.

20. Ibid., p. 119.

21. Ibid., p. 120.

22. Ibid., p. 135.

23. Ibid., p. 136.

24. Ibid., pp. 174–175.

25. Ibid., p. 175.

26. Ibid., p. 176.

27. Ibid., p. 177.

28. "The boy brought up only or mainly with boys is very likely to want club life and to be with men all his days. He may marry, but home gives him very little stimulation. His wife and children see little of him. This forms a poor basis for marriage. And this is only the least alarming of the possible pictures. The boy so brought up may shy away completely from marriage and turn to men for a sex outlet. This is called *homosexuality*. Exactly the same is true for women. Our whole social fabric is woven so as to make all women slightly homosexual. Girls hold hands, kiss, embrace, sleep together, etc. Mothers think this is a natural kind of relationship." Ibid., pp. 178–179.

29. Marvin R. Weisbord, "Let's *Not* Stifle Our Children's Creativity," *Parents*, October 1961, p. 106. The "brainwashing" metaphor carried particular weight in the Cold War context because of concerns that American POWs may have been "brainwashed" in North Korea.

30. Constance J. Foster, "Why Children Misbehave," in Phyllis B. Katz, ed., *The Child Care Guide and Family Advisor* (New York: Parents' Institute, 1960), p. 247.

31. Gladys Gardner Jenkins, "Watch Your Child's Mental Growth," in Katz *The Child Care Guide*, p. 144.

32. Robert M. Goldenson and Constance J. Foster, "Water Play," in Katz, *The Child Care Guide*, p. 197.

33. Benjamin Spock, *The Common Sense Book of Baby and Child Care* (New York: Duell, Sloan and Pearce, 1945), pp. 263–264.

34. Ibid., pp. 19–20.

35. Margaret A. Ribble, *The Rights of Infants* (New York: Columbia University Press, 1943), p. 11.

36. Ibid., p. 59.

37. Ibid., p. 60.

38. Ibid.

39. Ibid., p. 61.

40. Ibid.

41. Haim G. Ginott, *Between Parent and Child: New Solutions to Old Problems* (New York: Macmillan, 1965), p. 148.

42. Ibid., pp. 149–150.

43. Ibid.

44. Ibid.

45. Ibid., p. 151.

46. Ibid.

47. Spock, *The Common Sense Book of Baby and Child Care*, p. 300.

48. Ibid., p. 103.

49. Ibid., pp. 217–219.

50. Ibid., p. 20.

51. Ibid., p. 204.

52. Fitzhugh Dodson, *How to Parent* (New York: New American Library, 1970), p. 176.

53. Ibid.

54. Margaret Mead, *Coming of Age in Samoa* (New York: American Museum of Natural History, 1928). For present purposes, I am uninterested in whether Mead's account accu-

rately reflects actual Samoan practices, a subject of ongoing debate among anthropologists. It was the popularization of her account that was influential on how child-rearing experts thought about alternatives to American sexual norms.

55. Spock, *The Common Sense Book of Baby and Child Care*, pp. 300–304.

56. Ibid., p. 145.

57. Ibid., p. 26.

58. Laurence Schwab, "Sex Quiz: Is Your Vintage '69?" *Escapade* [circa 1968], p. 11.

59. Spock, *The Common Sense Book of Baby and Child Care*, p. 101. "Another trouble is that the young child may be upset by the parent's intercourse, which he misunderstands and which frightens him."

60. Benjamin Spock, "Dealing with Worries and Sexual Interests," in *Dr. Spock Talks with Mothers* (New York: Crest, 1961), pp. 169–170. All quotations in next two paragraphs are taken from this passage.

61. Robert R. Sears, Eleanor E. Maccoby, and Harry Levin, *Patterns of Child Rearing* (Evanston, Ill.: Row, Peterson, 1957), p. 189.

62. Ibid., p. 188.

63. Ibid., p. 200.

64. This quotation, other quotations in this paragraph, and the quotations in the next paragraph are from Benjamin Spock, "The Question of Nudity," in *Dr. Spock Talks about Problems of Parents* (New York: Crest, 1962), pp. 141–147.

65. This quotation and all others in the paragraph come from Selma H. Frailberg, *The Magic Years* (New York: Charles Scribner's Sons, 1959), pp. 216–217.

66. Stella Chess, Alexander Thomas, and Herbert G. Birch, *Your Child Is a Person* (New York: Viking, 1965), pp. 106–107.

67. Ibid.

68. Ibid.

69. Spock, *The Common Sense Book of Baby and Child Care*, p. 301.

70. Frances L. Ilg and Louise Bates Ames, *Child Behavior* (New York: Harper and Row, 1955), p. 190. "Try to realize that it may be better for the child to show too much rather than too little interest in sex" p. 193.

71. Lee Salk, *What Every Child Would Like His Parents to Know* (New York: Warner, 1972), p. 97.

72. Sears, Maccoby, and Levin, *Patterns of Child Rearing*, pp. 205–206.

73. Ibid., p. 206.

74. Ehrenreich and English, *For Her Own Good*, pp. 261–263.

75. Benjamin Spock and Mary Morgan, *Spock on Spock: A Memoir of Growing Up with the Century* (New York: Pantheon, 1985), pp. 206–207.

76. Benjamin Spock, *Decent and Indecent: Our Personal and Political memoir* (New York: McCall, 1969) pp. 76–83.

Chapter Twelve

How to Bring Your Kids Up Gay

Eve Kosofsky Sedgwick

In the summer of 1989, the United States Department of Health and Human Services released a study entitled *Report of the Secretary's Task Force on Youth Suicide*. Written in response to the apparently burgeoning epidemic of suicides and suicide attempts by children and adolescents in the United States, the 110-page report contained a section analyzing the situation of gay and lesbian youth. It concluded that because "gay youth face a hostile and condemning environment, verbal and physical abuse, and rejection and isolation from families and peers," young gays and lesbians are two to three times more likely than other young people to attempt and to commit suicide. The report recommends, modestly enough, an "end [to] discrimination against youths on the basis of such characteristics as . . . sexual orientation."

On October 13, 1989, Dr. Louis W. Sullivan, Secretary of the Department of Health and Human Services, repudiated this section of the report—impugning not its accuracy, but, it seems, its very existence. In a written statement Sullivan said, "[T]he views expressed in the paper entitled 'Gay Male and Lesbian Youth Suicide' do not in any way represent my personal beliefs or the policy of this Department. I am strongly committed to advancing traditional family values. . . . In my opinion, the views expressed in the paper run contrary to that aim."[1]

It's always open season on gay kids. What professor who cares for her students' survival and dignity can fail to be impressed and frightened by the unaccustomed, perhaps impossible responsibilities that devolve on faculty as a result of the homophobia uniformly enjoined on, for example, teachers in the primary and secondary levels of public school—who are subject to being fired, not only for being visibly gay, but, whatever their sexuality, for providing any intimation that homosexual desires, identities, cultures, adults, children, or adolescents have a right to expression or existence?

And where, in all this, is psychoanalysis? Where are the "helping professions"? In this discussion of institutions, I mean to ask not about Freud and the possibly spacious affordances of the mother-texts, but about psychoanalysis and psychiatry as they are functioning in the United States today.[2] I am especially interested in revisionist psychoanalysis, including ego-psychology, and in developments following on the American Psychiatric Association's much-publicized

1973 decision to drop the pathologizing diagnosis of homosexuality from its next Diagnostic and Statistical Manual (DSM-III). What is likely to be the fate of children brought under the influence of psychoanalysis and psychiatry today, post-DSM-III, on account of anxieties about their sexuality?

The monographic literature on the subject is, to begin with, as far as I can tell, exclusively about boys. A representative example of this revisionist, ego-based psychoanalytic theory would be Richard C. Friedman's *Male Homosexuality: A Contemporary Psychoanalytic Perspective*, published by Yale in 1988.[3] (A sort of companion-volume, though by a nonpsychoanalyst psychiatrist, is Richard Green's *The "Sissy Boy Syndrome" and the Development of Homosexuality* [1987], also from Yale.)[4] Friedman's book, which lavishly acknowledges his wife and children, is strongly marked by his sympathetic involvement with the 1973 de-pathologizing movement. It contains several visibly admiring histories of gay men, many of them encountered in nontherapeutic contexts. These include "Luke, a forty-five-year-old career army officer and a life-long exclusively homosexual man" (152); and Tim, who was "burly, strong, and could work side by side with anyone at the most strenuous jobs": "gregarious and likeable," "an excellent athlete," Tim was "captain of [his high-school] wrestling team and editor of the school newspaper" (206–7). Bob, another "well-integrated individual," "had regular sexual activity with a few different partners but never cruised or visited gay bars or baths. He did not belong to a gay organization. As an adult, Bob had had a stable, productive work history. He had loyal, caring, durable friendships with both men and women" (92–93). Friedman also, by way of comparison, gives an example of a *hetero*sexual man with what he considers a highly integrated personality, who happens to be a combat jet pilot: "Fit and trim, in his late twenties, he had the quietly commanding style of an effective decision maker" (86).[5]

Is a pattern emerging? Revisionist analysts seem prepared to like some gay men, but the healthy homosexual is (a) one who is already grown up and (b) acts masculine. In fact Friedman correlates, in so many words, adult gay male effeminacy with "global character pathology" and what he calls "the lower part of the psychostructural spectrum" (93). In the obligatory paragraphs of his book concerning "the question of when behavioral deviation from a defined norm should be considered psychopathology," Friedman makes explicit that while "clinical concepts are often somewhat imprecise and admittedly fail to do justice to the rich variability of human behavior," a certain baseline concept of pathology will be maintained in his study; and that baseline will be drawn in a very particular place. "The distinction between nonconformists and people with psychopathology is usually clear enough during childhood. Extremely and chronically effeminate boys, for example, should be understood as falling into the latter category" (32–33).

"For example," "extremely and chronically effeminate boys"—this is the abject that haunts revisionist psychoanalysis. The same DSM-III that, published in 1980, was the first that did not contain an entry for "homosexuality," was also the first that *did* contain a new diagnosis, numbered (for insurance purposes)

302.60: "Gender Identity Disorder of Childhood." Nominally gender-neutral, this diagnosis is actually highly differential between boys and girls: a girl gets this pathologizing label only in the rare case of asserting that she actually is anatomically male (e.g., "that she has, or will grow, a penis"); while a boy can be treated for Gender Identity Disorder of Childhood if he merely asserts "that it would be better not to have a penis"—*or*, alternatively, if he displays a "preoccupation with female stereotypical activities as manifested by a preference for either cross-dressing or simulating female attire, or by a compelling desire to participate in the games and pastimes of girls."[6] While the decision to remove "homosexuality" from DSM-III was highly polemicized and public, accomplished only under intense pressure from gay activists outside the profession, the addition to DSM-III of the "Gender Identity Disorder of Childhood" appears to have attracted no outside attention at all—nor even to have been perceived as part of the same conceptual shift.[7] Indeed, the gay movement has never been quick to attend to issues concerning effeminate boys. There is a discreditable reason for this in the marginal or stigmatized position to which even adult men who are effeminate have often been relegated in the movement.[8] A more understandable reason than effeminophobia, however, is the conceptual need of the gay movement to interrupt a long tradition of viewing gender and sexuality as continuous and collapsible categories—a tradition of assuming that anyone, male or female, who desires a man must by definition be feminine; and that anyone, male or female, who desires a woman must by the same token be masculine. That one woman, *as a woman*, might desire another; that one man, *as a man*, might desire another: the indispensable need to make these powerful, subversive assertions has seemed, perhaps, to require a relative deemphasis of the links between gay adults and gender-nonconforming children. To begin to theorize gender and sexuality as distinct though intimately entangled axes of analysis has been, indeed, a great advance of recent lesbian and gay thought.

There is a danger, however, that that advance may leave the effeminate boy once more in the position of the haunting abject—this time the haunting abject of gay thought itself. This is an especially horrifying thought if—as many studies launched from many different theoretical and political positions have suggested— for any given adult gay man, wherever he may be at present on a scale of self-perceived or socially ascribed masculinity (ranging from extremely masculine to extremely feminine), the likelihood is disproportionately high that he will have a childhood history of self-perceived effeminacy, femininity, or nonmasculinity.[9] In this case the eclipse of the effeminate boy from adult gay discourse would represent more than a damaging theoretical gap; it would represent a node of annihilating homophobic, gynephobic, and pedophobic hatred internalized and made central to gay-affirmative analysis. The effeminate boy would come to function as the open secret of many politicized adult gay men.

One of the most interesting aspects—and by interesting I mean cautionary— of the new psychoanalytic developments is that they are based on *precisely* the theoretical move of distinguishing gender from sexuality. This is how it happens that the *de*pathologization of an atypical sexual object-choice can be yoked to the *new* pathologization of an atypical gender identification. Integrating the gender-constructivist research of, for example, John Money and Robert Stoller, research that many have taken (though perhaps wrongly) as having potential for feminist uses, this work posits the very early consolidation of something called Core Gender Identity—one's basal sense of being male or female—as a separate stage prior to, even conceivably independent of, any crystallization of sexual fantasy or sexual object-choice. Gender Disorder of Childhood is seen as a pathology involving the Core Gender Identity (failure to develop a CGI consistent with one's biological sex); sexual object-choice, on the other hand, is unbundled from this Core Gender Identity through a reasonably space-making series of two-phase narrative moves. Under the pressure, ironically, of having to show how gay adults whom he considers well-integrated personalities do sometimes evolve from children seen as the very definition of psychopathology, Friedman unpacks several developmental steps that have often otherwise been seen as rigidly unitary.[10]

One serious problem with this way of distinguishing between gender and sexuality is that, while denaturalizing sexual object-choice, it radically *re*naturalizes gender. All ego-psychology is prone, in the first place, to structuring developmental narrative around a none-too-dialectical trope of progressive *consolidation* of self. To place a very early core-gender determinant (however little biologized it may be) at the very center of that process of consolidation seems to mean, essentially, that for a nontranssexual person with a penis, nothing can ever be assimilated to the self through this process of consolidation unless it can be assimilated *as masculinity*. For even the most feminine-self-identified boys, Friedman uses the phrases "sense of masculine self-regard" (245), "masculine competency" (20), and "self-evaluation as appropriately masculine" (244) as synonyms for any self-esteem and, ultimately, for any *self*. As he describes the interactive process that leads to any ego-consolidation in a boy:

> Boys measure themselves in relation to others whom they estimate to be similar. [For Friedman, this means only men and other boys.] Similarity of self-assessment depends on consensual validation. The others must agree that the boy is and will remain similar to them. The boy must also view both groups of males (peers and older men) as appropriate for idealization. Not only must he be like them in some ways, he must want to be like them in others. They in turn must want him to be like them. Unconsciously, they must have the capacity to identify with him. This naturally occurring [!] fit between the male social world and the boy's inner object world is the juvenile phase-specific counterpoint to the preoedipal child's relationship with the mother. (237)

The reason effeminate boys turn out gay, according to this account, is that other men don't validate them as masculine. There is a persistent, wistful fantasy in this book: "One cannot help but wonder how these [prehomosexual boys] would have developed if the males they idealized had had a more flexible and abstract sense of masculine competency" (20). For Friedman, the increasing flexibility in what kinds of attributes or activities *can* be processed as masculine, with increasing maturity, seems fully to account for the fact that so many "gender-disturbed" (pathologically effeminate) little boys manage to grow up into "healthy" (masculine) men, albeit after the phase where their sexuality has differentiated as gay.

Or rather, it *almost* fully accounts for it. There is a residue of mystery, resurfacing at several points in the book, about why most gay men turn out so resilient—about how they even survive—given the profound initial deficit of "masculine self-regard" characteristic of many proto-gay childhoods, and the late and relatively superficial remediation of it that comes with increasing maturity. Given that "the virulence and chronicity of [social] stress [against it] puts homosexuality in a unique position in the human behavioral repertoire," how does one account for "the fact that severe, persistent morbidity does not occur more frequently" among gay adolescents (205)? Friedman essentially throws up his hands at these moments. "A number of possible explanations arise, but one seems particularly likely to me: namely, that homosexuality is associated with some psychological mechanism, not understood or even studied to date, that protects the individual from diverse psychiatric disorders" (236). It "might include mechanisms influencing ego resiliency, growth potential, and the capacity to form intimate relationships" (205). And "it is possible that, for reasons that have not yet been well described, [gender-disturbed boys'] mechanisms for coping with anguish and adversity are unusually effective" (201).

These are huge blank spaces to be left in what purports to be a developmental account of proto-gay children. But given that ego-syntonic consolidation for a boy can come only in the form of masculinity, given that masculinity can be conferred only by men (20), and given that femininity, in a person with a penis, can represent nothing but deficit and disorder, the one explanation that could *never* be broached is that these mysterious skills of survival, filiation, and resistance could derive from a secure identification with the resource-richness of a mother. Mothers, indeed, have nothing to contribute to this process of masculine validation, and women are reduced in the light of its urgency to a null set: any involvement in it by a woman is overinvolvement; any protectiveness is overprotectiveness; and, for instance, mothers "proud of their sons' nonviolent qualities" are manifesting unmistakable "family pathology" (193).

For both Friedman and Green, then, the first, imperative developmental task of a male child or his parents and caretakers is to get a properly male Core Gender Identity in place, as a basis for further and perhaps more flexible explorations of what it may be to *be* masculine—that is, for a male person, to be *human*. Friedman is rather equivocal about whether this masculine CGI necessarily entails any particular content, or whether it is an almost purely formal, preconditional differentiation that, once firmly in place, can cover an almost infinite range of behaviors and attitudes. He certainly does not see a necessary connection between masculinity and any scapegoating of male homosexuality; since ego-psychology treats the development of male heterosexuality as nonproblematical after adolescence, as not involving the suppression of any homosexual or bisexual possibility (263–67), and therefore as completely unimplicated with homosexual panic (178), it seems merely an unfortunate, perhaps rectifiable misunderstanding that for a proto-gay child to identify "masculinely" might involve his identification with his own erasure.

The renaturalization and enforcement of gender assignment are not the worst news about the new psychiatry of gay acceptance, however. The worst is that it not only fails to offer, but seems conceptually incapable of offering, even the slightest resistance to the wish endemic in the culture surrounding and supporting it: the wish that gay people *not exist*. There are many people in the worlds we inhabit, and these psychiatrists are unmistakably among them, who have a strong interest in the dignified treatment of any gay people who may happen already to exist. But the number of persons or institutions by whom the existence of gay people is treated as a precious desideratum, a needed condition of life, is small. The presiding asymmetry of value assignment between hetero and homo goes unchallenged everywhere: advice on how to help your kids turn out gay, not to mention your students, your parishioners, your therapy clients, or your military subordinates, is less ubiquitous than you might think. On the other hand, the scope of institutions whose programmatic undertaking is to prevent the development of gay people is unimaginably large. There is no major institutionalized discourse that offers a firm resistance to that undertaking: in the United States, at any rate, most sites of the state, the military, education, law, penal institutions, the church, medicine, and mass culture enforce it all but unquestioningly, and with little hesitation at even the recourse to invasive violence.

The books cited above, and the associated therapeutic strategies and institutions, are not about invasive violence. What they are about is a train of squalid lies. The overarching lie is that they are predicated on anything but the therapists' disavowed desire for a nongay outcome. Friedman, for instance, speculates wistfully that—with proper therapeutic intervention—the sexual orientation of one gay man whom he describes as quite healthy might conceivably (not have *been changed* but) "have shifted *on its own*" (Friedman's italics): a speculation, he artlessly remarks, "not value-laden with regard to sexual orientation" (212). Green's book, composed largely of interview transcripts, is a tissue of his lies to children about their parents' motives for bringing them in for therapy. (It was "not to prevent you from becoming homosexual," he tells one young man who had been subjected to behavior modification, "it was because you were unhappy" [318]; but later on the very same page, he unself-consciously confirms to his trusted reader that "parents of sons who entered therapy were . . . worried that the cross-gender behavior portended problems with later sexuality.") He encourages predominantly gay young men to "reassure" their parents that they are "bisexual" ("Tell him just enough so he feels better" [207]), and to consider favorably the option of marrying and keeping their wives in the dark about their sexual activities (205). He lies to himself and to us in encouraging patients to lie to him. For instance, in a series of interviews with Kyle, the boy subjected to behavioral therapy, Green reports him as saying that he is unusually withdrawn—"I suppose I've been overly sensitive when guys look at me or something ever since I can remember, you know, after my mom told me why I have to go to

UCLA because they were afraid I'd turn into a homosexual" (307); as saying that homosexuality "is pretty bad, and I don't think they should be around to influence children. . . . I don't think they should be hurt by society or anything like that—especially in New York. You have them who are into leather and stuff like that. I mean, I think that is really sick, and I think that maybe they should be put away" (307); as saying that he wants to commit violence on men who look at him (307); and as saying that if he had a child like himself, he "would take him where he would be helped" (317). The very image of serene self-acceptance?

Green's summary:

> Opponents of therapy have argued that intervention underscores the child's "deviance," renders him ashamed of who he is, and makes him suppress his "true self." Data on psychological tests do not support this contention; nor does the content of clinical interviews. The boys look back favorably on treatment. They would endorse such intervention if they were the father of a "feminine" boy. Their reason is to reduce childhood conflict and social stigma. Therapy with these boys appeared to accomplish this. (319)

Consistent with this, Green is obscenely eager to convince parents that their hatred and rage at their effeminate sons really is only a desire to protect them from peer-group cruelty—even when the parents name *their own* feelings as hatred and rage (391–92). Even when fully one-quarter of parents of gay sons are *so* interested in protecting them from social cruelty that, when the boys fail to change, their parents kick them out on the street, Green is withering about mothers who display any tolerance of their sons' cross-gender behavior (373–75). In fact, his bottom-line identifications as a clinician actually seem to lie with the enforcing peer group: he refers approvingly at one point to "therapy, be it formal (delivered by paid professionals) or informal (delivered by the peer group and the larger society via teasing and sex-role standards)" (388).

Referring blandly on one page to "psychological intervention directed at increasing [effeminate boys'] comfort with being male" (259), Friedman says much more candidly on the next page: "[T]he rights of parents to oversee the development of children is a long-established principle. Who is to dictate that parents may not try to raise their children in a manner that maximizes the possibility of a heterosexual outcome?" (260). Who indeed—if the members of this profession can't stop seeing the prevention of gay people as an ethical use of their skills?

Even outside of the mental health professions and within more authentically gay-affirmative discourses, the theoretical space for supporting gay development is, as I've pointed out in the introduction to *Epistemology of the Closet*, narrow. Constructivist arguments have tended to keep hands off the experience of gay and protogay kids. For gay and gay-loving people, even though the space of cultural malleability is the only conceivable theater for our effective politics, every step of this constructivist nature/culture argument holds danger: the danger of the difficulty of intervening in the seemingly natural trajectory from identifying a place of cultural malleability, to inventing an ethical or therapeutic mandate for cultural manipulation, to the overarching, hygienic Western fantasy of a world without any more homosexuals in it.

That's one set of dangers, and it is as against them, as I've argued, that essentialist and biologizing understandings of sexual identity accrue a certain gravity. Conceptualizing an unalterably *homosexual body* seems to offer resistance to the social-engineering momentum apparently built into every one of the human sciences of the West, and that resistance can reassure profoundly. At the same time, however, in the postmodern era it is becoming increasingly problematical to assume that grounding an identity in biology or "essential nature" is a stable way of insulating it from societal interference. If anything, the gestalt of assumptions that undergird nature/nurture debates may be in process of direct reversal. Increasingly it is the conjecture that a particular trait is genetically or biologically based, *not* that it is "only cultural," that seems to trigger an estrus of manipulative fantasy in the technological institutions of the culture. A relative depressiveness about the efficacy of social-engineering techniques, a high mania about biological control: the Cartesian bipolar psychosis that always underlay the nature/nurture debates has switched its polar assignments without surrendering a bit of its hold over the collective life. And in this unstable context, the dependence on a specified *homosexual body* to offer resistance to any gay-eradicating momentum is tremblingly vulnerable. AIDS, although it is used to proffer every single day to the news-consuming public the crystallized vision of a world after the homosexual, could never by itself bring about such a world. What whets these fantasies more dangerously, because more blandly, is the presentation, often in ostensibly or authentically gay-affirmative contexts, of biologically based "explanations" for deviant behavior that are absolutely invariably couched in terms of "excess," "deficiency," or "imbalance"—whether in the hormones, in the genetic material, or, as is currently fashionable, in the fetal endocrine environment. If I had ever, in any medium, seen any researcher or popularizer refer even once to any supposed gay-producing circumstance as the *proper* hormone balance, or the *conducive* endocrine environment, for gay generation, I would be less chilled by the breezes of all this technological confidence. As things are, a medicalized dream of the prevention of gay bodies seems to be the less visible, far more respectable underside of the AIDS-fueled public dream of their extirpation.

In this unstable balance of assumptions between nature and culture, at any rate, under the overarching, relatively unchallenged aegis of a culture's desire that gay people *not be*, there is no unthreatened, unthreatening theoretical home for a concept of gay and lesbian origins. What the books I have been discussing, and the institutions to which they are attached, demonstrate is that the wish for the dignified treatment of already gay people is necessarily destined to turn into either trivializing apologetics or, much worse, a silkily camouflaged complicity in oppression—in the absence of a strong, explicit, *erotically invested* affirmation of some people's felt desire or need that there be gay people in the immediate world.

NOTES

This essay was originally written for a panel on psychoanalysis and homosexuality at the Modern Language Association conference, December 1989. Several paragraphs of it are adapted from what became the introduction to my *Epistemology of the Closet* (Berkeley and Los Angeles: University of California Press, 1990). Jack Cameron pointed me in the direction of these texts; Cindy Patton fortified my resistance to them; and Jonathan Goldberg helped me articulate the argument made here. The motivation for this essay, and some of its approaches, are immensely indebted to several other friends, as well—most particularly to conversations over a long period with Michael Moon.

1. This information comes from reports in the *New York Native*, 23 September 1989, 9–10; 13 November 1989, 14; 27 November 1989, 7.

2. A particularly illuminating overview of psychoanalytic approaches to male homosexuality is available in Kenneth Lewes, *The Psychoanalytic Theory of Male Homosexuality* (New York: Simon and Schuster, 1988; New York: Penguin/NAL/Meridian, 1989).

3. Richard C. Friedman, *Male Homosexuality: A Contemporary Psychoanalytic Perspective* (New Haven: Yale University Press, 1988).

4. Richard Green, *The "Sissy Boy Syndrome" and the Development of Homosexuality* (New Haven: Yale University Press, 1987).

5. It is worth noting that the gay men Friedman admires always have completely discretionary control over everyone else's knowledge of their sexuality; there is no sense that others may have their own intuitions that they are gay; no sense of physical effeminacy; no visible participation in gay (physical, cultural, sartorial) semiotics or community. For many contemporary gay people, such an existence would be impossible; for a great many, it would seem starvingly impoverished in terms of culture, community, and meaning.

6. American Psychiatric Association Staff, *Diagnostic and Statistical Manual of Mental Disorders*, 3d ed. (Washington, D.C.: American Psychiatric Association, 1980), 265–66.

7. The exception to this generalization is Lawrence Mass, whose *Dialogues of the Sexual Revolution*, vol. 1: *Homosexuality and Sexuality* (New York: Harrington Park Press, 1990), collects a decade's worth of interviews with psychiatrists and sex researchers, originally conducted for and published in the gay press. In these often illuminating interviews, a number of Mass's questions are asked under the premise that "American psychiatry is simply engaged in a long, subtle process of reconceptualizing homosexuality as a mental illness with another name—the 'gender identity disorder of childhood' " (214).

8. That relegation may be diminishing as, in many places, "queer" politics comes to overlap and/or compete with "gay" politics. Part of what I understand to be the exciting charge of the very word "queer" is that it embraces, instead of repudiating, what have for many of us been formative childhood experiences of difference and stigmatization.

9. For descriptions of this literature, see Friedman, *Male Homosexuality*, 33–48; and Green, *"Sissy Boy Syndrome,"* 370–90. The most credible of these studies from a gay-affirmative standpoint would be A. P. Bell, M. S. Weinberg, and S. K. Hammersmith, *Sexual Preference: Its Development in Men and Women* (Bloomington: Indiana University Press, 1981), which concludes: "Childhood Gender Nonconformity turned out to be more strongly connected to adult homosexuality than was any other variable in the study" (80).

10. Priding himself on his interdisciplinarity, moreover, Friedman is much taken with recent neuroendocrinological work suggesting that prenatal stress on the mother may affect structuration of the fetal brain in such a way that hormonal cues to the child as late

as adolescence may be processed differentially. His treatment of these data as data is neither very responsible (e.g., problematical results that point only to "hypothetical differences" in one chapter [p. 24] have been silently upgraded to positive "knowledge" two chapters later [p. 51]) nor very impartial (e.g., the conditions hypothesized as conductive to gay development are invariably referred to as *inadequate* androgenization [14], a *deficit* [15], etc.). But his infatuation with this model does have two useful effects. First, it seems to generate by direct analogy this further series of two-phase narratives about psychic development, narratives that discriminate between the circumstances under which a particular psychic structure is *organized* and those under which it is *activated*, that may turn out to enable some new sinuosities for other, more gay-embracing and pluralist projects of developmental narration. (This analogical process is made explicit on 241–45.) And, second, it goes a long way toward detotalizing, demystifying, and narrativizing in a recognizable way any reader's sense of the threat (the promise?) presented by a supposed neurobiological vision of the already gay male body.

Chapter Thirteen

Producing Erotic Children

James R. Kincaid

This essay is divided into eleven parts, eleven being a prime number. The eleven parts are not equal in length or weight, and they do not carry the same importance; nonetheless, they are exactly symmetrical and harmonious.

These are the parts:

1. Ellie Nesler's Son
2. Michael Jackson
3. McMartin-Menendez
4. The Coppertone Child Home Alone
5. Questions We Love to Ask
6. My Thesis
7. Resisting the Obvious
8. Recovered Memory
9. Scandal—That's What We Need
10. Me
11. You

1. Ellie Nesler's Son

Ellie Nesler's son is named Willy, Willy Nesler. He is now about thirteen years old, living, I think, in Jamestown, California, where, in 1993, in April, he was in a courtroom waiting to testify in the preliminary hearing of one Daniel Driver, accused of seven counts of child-molesting. The papers say Willy Nesler was one of the alleged victims; they also say that, according to his mother, he was vomiting wildly the morning he was scheduled to tell his story. Anyway, before he got the chance to speak, his mother took control, silencing her boy and the accused forever. When Daniel Driver looked at that mother with what she took to be a smirk, Ellie, goaded beyond her limits, bolted from the courtroom, filched a .22 semiautomatic from her sister's purse, charged back in, and plugged the guarded and manacled Driver in the head and neck five times at close range, proclaiming, "Maybe I'm not God, but I'll tell you what: I'm the closest damn thing to it."[1] I mention Willy Nesler because at this point he becomes invisible, silent and empty, a vacancy at the center of the story—filled up and written on by his mother, and the press, and the nation's outrage, our own included. Willy Nesler becomes our principal citizen, the empty and violated child, whose story we need so badly we take it into ourselves. No one wants Willy Nesler testifying, taking on substance: the erotic child is mute, under our control. Once the accused is out of the way, and the child is rendered speechless and helpless, we can proceed to our usual business: the righteous, guilt-free constructions of violent pornographic fantasies about child sexuality.

In this case, Willy Nesler's mother thrusts herself between us and the speaking child, blocking his words just in time, and giving us the screen we need. In the scores of accounts I read of the trial, Willy appears only as "Ellie's boy," "Nes-ler's son."[2] Ellie Nesler herself forms the displaced, disowned, and finally dis-carded projection we can use for a while to contemplate with impunity her thoroughly sexualized boy. For a moment, Ellie grabs the headlines, becomes a vigilante June Cleaver, the American Mom of the fifties, reborn snarling, protect-ing her chick. Defense funds spring up, fueled by spaghetti suppers; school-children are forced to write thank-you notes; T-shirts and bumper stickers scream, "Nice Shootin' Ellie"; *Hard Copy* and Charles Kuralt descend on James-town. All this so we can do as we like with our image of Willy Nesler. We can sentimentalize him erotically, as a townsperson does by saying, "His little soul died the day he was molested."[3] or we can indulge in the full-scale fantasies scripted by Ellie's attorney, who asked the jury to "pick a child you know and look at their innocence and sweetness," and then imagine it being violated.[4]

This does not last very long. For a while, Ellie gave us a story so compelling in its gothic simplicities that it was irresistible: drive a stake through the heart of the pedophile and bourgeois America will be safe, along with our illusions about childhood, the family, sexuality, and our own rectitude. But Ellie's story never sold. The crowds of media talent that drew into Jamestown from Los Angeles and New York, like vultures to road kill, fled even more quickly. All of a sudden, Ellie was abandoned—left to fend for herself in the trial and reduced to claiming that she was insane at the time of the killing. In a last-ditch, double-barreled bid for sympathy, she claimed that she had been molested herself as a child, and also that she had a fatal disease; but the insanity defense failed, and nobody cared by then whether Ellie had cancer or not, or even whether those she named—her father's poker buddies and a state senator[5]—had sexually abused her.

What had happened was that Ellie turned out to be complicated, not the sim-ple heroine we needed for gothic, but a woman with a history, a history we did not want. She had a minor criminal record; she had taken drugs, perhaps on the morning of the shooting; she had threatened to kill Daniel Driver months earlier. We no longer had the clean-cut simplicity that would allow us the screen of outrage between us and our object of interest, which had never been Ellie or Driver but Willy Nesler, the breached, silent child. Without the screen story, we were left to face the music ourselves, or go and find other stories. Since the stories are not hard to find, we hesitated not a second in getting out of Jamestown and leaving Ellie to her sentencing—ten years—while we hustled to locate more guiltfree eroticism.

2. *Michael Jackson's Driveway*

In the joke, Michael Jackson's driveway is as erotic as our construction of Willy Nesler. The joke is this: How do you know Michael Jackson is having a party? By all the Big Wheels parked in his driveway. The other Michael Jackson joke has him visiting O. J. Simpson and offering to look after the children, should things go badly for Simpson. It's the same joke. Simpson's children, Willy Nesler, the drivers of all those Big Wheels: they take their parts in the narratives we manufacture, the narratives of innocence protected and pure, that is, lost and sullied. It does not matter much what line we take on the issues we can pretend these cases contain. Issues are there simply to give us, as they say, deniability, psychic deniability.

Take the fun in being outraged with Michael Jackson as boy-lover, and telling our friends how outraged we are. And not just with Jackson either, but with the failure of others to be as loving to children as we are: "Can you imagine anyone letting a son sleep with that man?" Actually, imagining is what we are all good at; otherwise such stories would not find ready listeners such as me and you. Had Michael Jackson not existed, we would have been forced to invent him, which is, of course, what we did.

Or take the way we can use the Jackson story to blow off steam about "the media," as if "the media" were an independent agent, an outsider whose desires and energies are foisted on us against our will. "The media," then, becomes a little like "the pedophile," a handy fabrication and focus for our passions that we can abuse and pretend to disown.

The hounding of Michael Jackson is a spectacular case in point. Michael Jackson, to whose music we have sent our children and our soft drink companies with record piles of dollars, is superchild and now super–child-molester. Michael Jordan would have done as well, or Barney. Jackson as a construction of our eroticism and our guilt, of our lavish, capitalist fantasies and generosities, and our frightened, repression-driven paranoia: he can hardly be said to exist outside our needs. Once he was a child himself, and it is commonly said that he still is; but we can make him play the part of the *guilty* child, absolving us from guilt. Jackson is reduced to his bed and his relationships, to the "sharing" of that bed. That's all he is, as he and dozens of boys (including our star boy, Culkin) pose for our collective scrapbooks. Even Jackson's first marriage was openly construed as a reason for getting not Lisa Marie but her children into that bed.

Not mentioned in my eleven-point outline, and offered as an undeserved bonus: Woody Allen forms a more troubled, sophisticated version of this cultural drama. His story and his role shift before our eyes, as he bounces from child to child (younger and younger all the time), from villain to victim, from comedian to ogre. Allen becomes, like Oscar Wilde, the repository of a fair number of hatreds—of artists, Jews, New Yorkers, cosmopolitans generally, short guys, red-heads, Knicks fans—but primarily he becomes (as in Chaucer's "Prioress's Tale") the monster who threatens the child, and thus gives us exactly what we want.

3. *McMartin-Menendez*

The McMartin trial, dealing with allegations of child-molesting and ritual Satanic abuse at a Southern California preschool, began with charges in the summer of 1983 and did not end until the summer of 1990, the trial itself running, with one short break, from April 1987 until July 1990. This, the longest criminal trial in American history, ended mostly with acquittals, along with some deadlocks and inconsequential declarations of mistrials, all signaling that we had other specta-cles to attend to, and could finally let this one go. Along the way, though, we had provided ourselves with seven rich years of titillating narratives about ani-mal sacrifice and demonic possession, about games of Tickle and Naked Movie Star, about Raymond Buckey's underwear and his collection of *Playboy* maga-zines, about children and sex.

Menendez is McMartin II, an artful variation on what has become our favorite public entertainment: staged dramas of child-molesting, masked as exercises in justice. Lyle Menendez, who has been compared to Judy Garland and Montgom-ery Clift as a "great neurotic actor,"[6] testifies, with a tough-guy sob we have all become attached to, "He raped me." Not only that—he testifies the very next day that he had, as an eight-year-old, molested his fellow defendant, Erik, then six, with a tooth-brush. "I'm sorry," Lyle said to his brother, right there in the courtroom, not omitting the sob.

According to most spectators, Erik is not so gifted, despite his acting ambi-tions, and really pours out too many details without anything like his brother's mastery of narrative pace and flow. Erik talks, all in a rush, about the taste of his father's semen, sweetened with cinnamon; he speaks of his mother squeezing blisters on his penis; he mentions categories of incestuous activities and the names each had—Knees, Nice, Rough, and Sex—respectively oral, hand, needles and tacks, and anal. He is in too much of a bustle to add flourishes from bad novels: his father lighting candles and slowly placing them about the room before saying to the boy, like an X-rated Vincent Price, "One last fuck before I kill you." Still, even Erik manages to do the job. One alternate juror on the Donahue show confesses, "Phil . . . it was sickening. . . . I could *visualize* this pedophile father—he's down the hall in the bedroom, he is sodomizing his six-year-old child."[7]

What is being visualized so clearly is a child, a figure in this drama so impor-tant that it seems to replace the actual bodies of the grownup and athletically bulky Lyle and Erik. Both are referred to, not only by their attorneys but by many of our deputies in the press, as children, kids, boys, sometimes prefixed by "little." It is this image of the child that we are paying for in the trial, and we use the besweatered young men as transparent agencies, peering back through them to the child within, down the hall in the bedroom.

4. *The Coppertone Child Home Alone*

But what about Macaulay Culkin? What about the adorable child? The adorable child is not our only child-species, as Lyle and Erik demonstrate, but adoration is still dear to our erotic centering of the child. The vacantly androgynous Culkin on the beach, his swimming trunks being pulled down behind cutely by a cute little dog: that's the national pinup.[8] I grant you that Culkin is fast losing his hold on this role, and his ability to present himself to us with no face and no body, as a blankness we can fill in. Still, the desire that once rushed into his emptiness lingers on, and he is still the ghost of a cultural wish-fulfillment dream to find the perfectly evacuated child, isolated and suitably domesticated, at home in bourgeois familiarity. The film *Home Alone* covers its own appeals just barely, using Three-Stooges comedy, and loading the child with sadistic potency in the make-believe layering of "fun" that allows us to enjoy the erotic formulations without beginning to acknowledge them: the child alone, defenseless, needing us. The sequel is a lot less smooth about all this, coarsening itself to the point of having Culkin make comments about seeing naked butts, and forcing him to jump into a swimming pool with a suit so many sizes too big that it peels off when he hits the water—surprise, surprise.

As Culkin reluctantly acquires a body of his own, and thus fades from our fantasies, others are found to take his place, in films like *The Client* or *The Little Rascals*, where adorable children inherit Culkin's position, one he took over in turn from a long line of culturally mandated cuties: Ricky Schroeder, Henry Thomas, Jay North, Tatum O'Neal, Jodie Foster, Brooke Shields, Mark Lester, Shirley Temple, Freddie Bartholomew, and on into the night.

Last year's Clint Eastwood film, *A Perfect World*, offers a darker, less obviously "cute" version of Culkin: a small boy played by T. J. Lowther, in a role which is actually given some substance, thus reducing his potential as a target for our usual erotic adoring. All the same, he plays out explicitly a variety of our most distressing and titillating narratives about child sexuality, in scenes that either reproduce or parody (depending on one's position) the child as object of sexual attention. He spends the first half of the movie in his briefs, and the last half in a Halloween costume that gets torn so as, again, to expose his underpants. At one point, the vicious convict, commenting on the boy's "cute underwears," inserts his hand into them to examine the penis, pronouncing it "puny." Later the good convict (Kevin Costner), sensing that the boy is reluctant to undress before him, and learning that it is all because he is ashamed of his "puny" penis, says, "Let me see it," takes a long look, and tells him it's OK, thus reassuring us that our own voyeurism here is also absolutely OK. The film works over again the erotic pedagogical territory tromped on in *The Earthing, Treasure Island, Searching for*

Bobbie Fisher, Kidnapped, Redneck, Willy Wonka, The Man Without a Face, The Champ, Shane, and *The Client.*

5. Questions We Love to Ask

But first: questions we don't love to ask. Let us take the stories of Ellie Nesler, Menendez, Woody Allen, Michael Jackson, the day-care trial du jour, and ask about the source, the nature, and the size of the pleasures we take from such stories. What are these stories, where do they come from, and why do we tell them with such relish? What kind of relish is it? Why do we want to hear these feverish tales about the sexuality of children, and why do we listen to them so eagerly? What is it about the child and its eroticism that so magnetizes us? In short, Why do we tell the stories we tell? Why do we need to hear them? Those are plain sorts of questions; but we don't often attend to them. We prefer others:

1. How can we spot the pedophiles and get rid of them?
2. Meanwhile, how can we protect our children?
3. How can we induce our children to tell us the truth, and all of it, about their sexual lives?
4. How can we get the courts to believe children who say they have been sexually molested?
5. How can we get the courts to believe adults who suddenly remember they were sexually molested as children?
6. How can we get ourselves to believe others when they say they remember being sexually molested years ago?
7. How can we know if maybe some people are not making these things up, misremembering?
8. How can we know if bumbling parents, cops, and (especially) therapists are not implanting false memories?

Though some of these questions seem to take revenge on other questions, they all have one thing in common: they demand the same answer, "We can't."

I think that is why both the standard and the backlash stories are so popular: they have about them an urgency and a self-flattering righteous oomph. Asking them, I can get the feeling that I care very much, and that I am really on the right side in these vital issues of our time. Even better, these open-ended, unanswerable questions generate variations on themselves, and allow us to keep them going, circulating them among ourselves without ever experiencing fatigue, never getting enough of what they are offering.

And what they are offering is a nicely protected way of talking about the subject of child sexuality. I do not deny that we are also talking about detection and danger. Certainly we care about the poor, hurt children. But we care also about maintaining the particular erotic vision of children that is putting them in this position in the first place.

6. My Thesis

You have already beat me to it, but here it is anyway, blunt and persuasive. My argument is that erotic children are manufactured—in the sense that we produce them in our cultural factories, the ones that make meanings for us. They tell us what "the child" is, and also what "the erotic" *is*. I argue that for the last two hundred years or so, they have confused us, have failed to distinguish the two categories, have allowed them dangerously to overlap. And the result of all that is the examples I've mentioned to this point. All these are public spectacles of child eroticism, an eroticism that can be flaunted and also screened, exploited and denied, enjoyed and cast off, made central and made criminal.

This new thing, the post-Romantic child, has been deployed as, among other things, a political and philosophical agent, a weapon used to assault substance and substitute in its place a set of negative inversions: innocence, purity, emptiness. Childhood in our culture has come to be largely a coordinate set of *have nots*: the child is that which *does not have*. Its liberty, however much prized, is a negative attribute, as is its innocence and purity. Moreover, all these, throughout the nineteenth century, became more and more firmly attached to what was characterized as sexually desirable, innocence in particular becoming a fulcrum for the nineteenth and twentieth century's ambiguous construction of sexuality and sexual behavior. Innocence was what came to you in heaven, or in marriage, as a kind of prize. Innocence was that which we have been trained to adore and covet, to preserve and despoil, to speak of in hushed tones and in bawdy songs.

The same goes for purity, of course, another empty figure that allows the admirer to read just about anything he likes into that vacancy, including a flattering image of his very self. The construction of the modern "child" is very largely an evacuation, the ruthless sending out of eviction notices. Correspondingly, the instructions we receive on what to regard as sexually arousing tell us to look for (and often create) this emptiness, to discover the erotic in that which is most susceptible to inscription, the blank page. On that page we can write what we like, write it and then long for it, love it, have it. Children are defined, and longed for, according to what *they* do not have.

Bodies are made to conform to this set of cultural demands. Heathcliff and Cathy (aged twelve) are symbols of titanic passion; Shirley Temple was enticing until puberty, when she instantly became a Republican frump; Rick Schroeder lost our interest when he stopped calling himself "Ricky"; Macaulay Culkin teeters on the brink of unerotic oblivion; Tom Sawyer's later adventures do not interest us. Baby-smooth skin is capable of making us pant with desire, while unsmooth, or contoured skin is not: Is this because flatness is innately more titillating than texture, or because flatness signifies nothing at all and thus does not interfere with our projections? In the same way, desirable faces must be blank, washed out of color, eyes big and round and expressionless, hair blond or colorless altogether, waists, hips, feet, and minds small. The physical makeup of the child has been translated into mainstream images of the sexually and mate-rially alluring. We are told to look like children, if we can and for as long as we can, to pine for that look. (These cultural directives equating the erotic with eternal youth operate, perhaps, with special ferocity on women, but not only on women: think of Tom Cruise, Marky Mark, John Kennedy Jr., Matthew Broder-ick, Prince Charles, David Letterman, Jimmy Connors, Tom Brokaw, Mick Jagger, Jack Nicholson, George Burns—all cute little boys forever.)

It is worth noting that these various narratives of the child not only focus and allow desire, but also erase various social and political complications, performing essential cultural work that is not simply erotic. By formulating the image of the alluring child as inevitably bleached, bourgeois, and androgynous, these stories mystify material reality, and render nearly invisible, certainly irrelevant, ques-tions we might raise about race, class, and even gender. Such categories are scrubbed away in this state, laved and snuggled into the grade-A homogeneity we might call Shirley Shroeder Culkin/Macaulay Ricky Temple. When poor chil-dren are allowed, as they sometimes are, to play this part, they are elevated (helped) into the class above them; boys and girls leave gender markers behind and meld together; children of color find themselves blanched to ungodly sallow-ness, Moby-Dicked, we might say. In all our stories, there is but one erotic child, and his name is Purity: neither rich nor poor, neither male nor female, neither black nor brown (yellow and red being out of the question). These swirling tales of desire allow nothing that would distract us from the primary fantasy.

In any case, the major point and dilemma is that we are instructed to crave that which is forbidden, a crisis we face by not facing it, by becoming hysterical, and by writing a kind of pious pornography, a self-righteous doublespeak that demands both lavish public spectacle and constant guilt-denying projections onto scapegoats. Child-molesting becomes the virus that nourishes us, that empty point of ignorance about which we are most knowing. It is the semiotic short-hand that explains everything, that tells us to look no further: having been on either side of the child-molesting scene defines us completely. Lawyers know this, as do politicians and storytellers. In *Forrest Gump* for instance, as in a hun-dred other recent narratives, the fact that the heroine was abused by her father, who was also drunk and lower-class, explains to our full satisfaction why she is suicidal, drug-infested, looking for love in all the wrong places, and willing to settle for the dim-witted hero.

It is not a pretty landscape we have constructed, nor one with clearly marked exits. We think we know a great deal about this subject of child-molesting; we are told that many things connected with it are obvious. But it is possible that this obviousness is the glue that cements the double bind.

7. Resisting the Obvious

So we might try to avoid the stupefyingly obvious: common and natural assump-tions that seem to be continuous with the problem of child-molesting. We might even resist the most compelling ritual gesture of all: acknowledging that, of course, sexual child abuse does exist, and exists on a very large scale. We need not deny it; we just do not want to begin the discussion in the territory left to us once we offer that disclaimer. I suspect that this disclaimer is a vital part of the discourse that eroticizes the child, and keeps us blind to what we are doing. It forces the discussion into channels of diagnosis and cure, mandates certain assumptions about what is and is not important, allows us to see some things, and blinds us to others. It traps us into offering one more set of tips on how to determine whether or not child-molesting "happened." But what if we explored another set of happenings: what is happening to us and to our children as we tell our customary stories of the child and of sexuality?

It is not rewarding to keep acknowledging that "molestation happens." One notices that every debunker of every salacious popular myth (even brilliant debunkers like Elizabeth Loftus and Paul McHugh) begins by saying, in effect, "Now, don't misunderstand me; I know that millions of children are sexually abused." I think we need to fly past that net. That we are compelled to say that molestation happens is an insistence that it must. Where would we be without it? Its material presence is guaranteed by our usual stories, stories of displacement and denial, stories that act to keep alive the images that guarantee the molesting itself or at least our belief in it. Now, it is true that the stories themselves are based on a cultural inheritance that is very deep and complex. I do not claim that if we outlawed the stories, then the attraction to children would end. Censorship would not help us. It is just that the molesting and the stories protesting the molesting walk the same beat. When we seek to adjust the protesting stories by saying "Yeah, but let's take recovered memory out of the plot," we do nothing to disrupt the circuitry, only to further remove from investigation its generating sources. Why do we talk about sex with children as if it were an isolated physical catastrophe, divorced from our talk? Maybe the child-molesting problem is married to the way we think about "the child-molesting problem."

8. Recovered Memory

But haven't we already recognized our position, and aren't we moving even now to correct it? The pendulum is swinging, we might say, and we now are starting to see that things are more complicated than we supposed, that not absolutely everyone mentioned in connection with child-molesting may be guilty. We are now willing to grant that there are neurotics out there, and misrememberers, and clumsy therapists, and even liars. In our zeal, we may have falsely convicted some and driven others to suicide; we may have been so eager to hear children make accusations that we were not critical enough of what they were saying; we may even have implanted those accusations by being so insistent; we may have victimized ourselves, some of us, by asking ourselves to remember molesting scenes of years ago, asking in such an expectant way that we remembered in detail things that never happened.

We like to think we see all this now, with a clarity that is perhaps not unflinching, but growing in sharpness and focus. And the result of this creditable advance, we suppose, is that we have abandoned the old, melodramatic, gothic way of seeing intergenerational sex, the simple plot wherein there were grotesque villains, easy to spot, attacking a pure, uncomplicated virtue.

Or *maybe* all this complicating in reference to the dubiousness of recovered memory and of children's testimony about sexual issues is really just a matter of keeping the talk going by slightly rejiggling the terms. Maybe it's not so much a complication as a reversal, a way of maintaining the same structure of titillating talk and effective self-protection. Turning the accuser into the accused, swapping villain and victim, does not, when you look at it, seem like that much of a change. Demonizing Freud and psychoanalysis can be done without a paradigm leap. It is still a gothic melodrama, filled with self-protective name-calling. The game stays as it was; we all just switch sides: the accused now deserves sympathy and the accuser condemnation. But the primary discourse stays. In fact, these new twists are so intriguing they demand even more talk, serving the same old needs.

9. Scandal — That's What We Need

Scandal: the Oxford English Dictionary (OED) says it is, at root, a trap; it is believed to be from the IndoGermanic *skand*, to spring or leap. Early on, "scandal" meant to cause perplexity of conscience, to hinder the reception of faith or obedience to Divine Law, to present a stumbling block. Ignoring all the alternate meanings given by the OED, let us settle on this cluster. Scandal is a trap sprung on the main bullies of any culture: faith, law, and submission to them. Scandal is the enemy of cultural hegemony; it is the offense that frees us from piety; it is the gross material fact that thumbs its nose at all metaphysical policemen. We are drawn to scandal by a hope to trip up the cultural censors, by a dream of escaping culture or transforming it. Compliance, we sense, will get us nowhere, great as the rewards for compliance may be. Let me prove all this to everyone's satisfaction.

Take the most banal of all scandals, political scandal—and ask yourself what draws you to it. Why are the erotic doings of, say, Bill Clinton so much more interesting than his policies? Not, let me suggest, because he is himself erotic; like most politicians, where he is, eros is not. Most of us would do a great deal to avoid imagining the actual doings of Clinton's body. Let me assume, then, that what draws us to scandal is the energy and promise of scandal itself, not the particulars of any one scandal. It is the offense that matters, that holds out promise, that gives us hope.

10. Me

I caused a scandal myself, but it was a comic miniscandal, altogether insufficient for the job I have in mind. Still, how would you like it if you got a review, a prominent review, by an Oxford don in the *London Times* (albeit *The Sunday Times*) and the best thing in that review was the following: "It is astonishing that a Professor of English could be so poorly informed." The review goes on to call my book, *Child-Loving: The Erotic Child and Victorian Culture*,[9] "fatally flawed," but that amounts almost to praise compared to the allegation that, although I do not exactly "recommended the practice or admit to it myself," being annoyingly "evasive" on what I really do in my spare time, the book I have written makes it clear that I am "a passionate champion of pedophilia."[10] In a separate article in the same edition, *The Sunday Times* said: "Kincaid's theories support those of the infamous Paedophile Information Exchange, or PIE," banned in Britain several years ago for allegedly dealing in child pornography. To cement the connection between me and PIE, *The Sunday Times* contacted Lord Bernard Braine, Tory MP for Castle Point and crusader for sexual decency, who said he was sending a copy of my book to the Home Secretary so he could ban it. "I simply cannot believe," said Lord Braine, "a reputable publisher could consider printing a book with such views. For any rational human being to give currency to what the vast majority of people regard as the vilest crime possible is deeply shocking." This article was headlined, "Anger over US don's support for paedophiles."[11]

This was nothing compared to the coverage in *The Daily Mail*, which was more forthright in its headline: "Paedophile Book 'Should Be Banned'." *The Daily Mail* said my book portrays pedophiles as "kindly people who cause no ill-effects"; and they sought out Lord Braine again, who says, "We have enough social problems in this country without encouraging publications of this kind." Ann Winterton, Conservative MP for Congleton, agreed—"I am appalled that this book is being published in Britain"—and so does Dame Jill Knight, Tory MP for Edgbaston: "It is crucial for the normal development of children that their innocence be preserved." *The Daily Mail* also quoted some experts in the field as saying that "Child sexual abuse can have very damaging effects," suggesting, I guess, that I was the passionate champion of the reverse view. Michael Hames, head of Scotland Yard's Obscene Publications Squad, gave the judicious overview: "People will be rightly outraged. This book won't offend against the law, but it will give comfort to paedophiles."[12]

11. *You*

But my book only tapped, predictably, a small feeder line of outrage, and caused hardly more than a belch. For the truly scandalous, I look to you readers, the leaders of our profession. The OED tells us that being scandalous means being willing to take on big-time opprobrium, and that takes big shoulders, and many of them. The only way, though, to rewrite the script is, I think, first to jar loose the present one, to drain its power by drawing it into the trap that scandal can set and then spring.

Disgrace can do that, can revise the narrative, perhaps into one kinder to us and to children as well. For one thing is clear: our present gothic scapegoating stories, our stories of denial and projected desire, are doing few of us any good. Perhaps we can write ourselves into the plot directly, give up our immunity. We might then be anxious to find narratives other than the gothic, to cast about for other genres so we can avoid playing the monster part. Such alternate genres, I think, would be mixed, modulated, abandoning, for instance, stark essentialist notions of sexuality and sexual behavior in favor of the idea of a range of erotic feelings even within and toward children. Such scandalous narratives, finally, might see more calmly the way children and eroticism have been constructed for us, and might help us decide that the problems involved in facing these things are much smaller than those that come down on us when we evade them. We know that a child's memory is developed not simply from data but from learning a canonical narrative; we know that what we are and have been comes to us from narrative; we know that what we are and have been comes to us from narrative forms that take on so much authority they start looking like nature. We suspect that events themselves are complicit with the narrative authority that forms and licenses them. Why not snub the authority and change the stories? We might find that, all along, we have been afraid of the wrong things. We might even find stories that are not fueled by fear.

But none of this is going to happen without a fuss, without a most distressing and ignominious set of scandals—which is where you come in.

NOTES

1. *Los Angeles Times*, July 23, 1993, p. A26.

2. It was not until *Redbook* published Beverly Lowry's account of the imprisoned Ellie Nesler's struggle with cancer, "Should Ellie Nesler Go Free?" (August, 1994, pp. 82–85, 114–117), that Willy's name surfaced. It is possible, of course, that his name was withheld from the newspaper accounts out of consideration for his age (though this is by no means a universal practice); but such erasures still have the effect of eroticizing the emptiness. They also fold the child into the adult, as a possession or an extension: "Ellie's boy" is really a part of Ellie (Ellie's foot), a function of Ellie (Ellie's job), and an object (Ellie's afghan).

3. Frankie Tinkle, "mother of three" and lifelong resident, as quoted in the *San Francisco Chronicle*, August 13, 1993, p. A17.

4. Tony Serra, San Francisco attorney and Nesler's lawyer, quoted in the *San Francisco Chronicle*, August 12, 1993, p. A18.

5. According to the *Los Angeles Times* (September 10, 1993, p. A32), Nesler blurted out this accusation during the sanity phase of her trial, charging that psychiatrists covered up for a probation officer she says molested her when she was fourteen, the cover-up being arranged, she yelled, "because he's a state senator." She named no names, but State Sen. Patrick Johnston issued a statement acknowledging that he had been Nesler's probation officer and denying the allegation.

6. Dominick Dunne, "Menendez Justice," *Vanity Fair* (March, 1994), p. 111. Other details are drawn from this article, from television news coverage and Court TV, and from newspaper accounts running in the *Los Angeles Times*.

7. Transcript from *The Donahue Show*, February 2, 1994, p. 9; concerning the statements of Ms. Judy Zamos, identified as "Jury Alternate in Lyle's Trial."

8. Interestingly (I guess), a prominent child actor, Culkin's costar in *The Good Son* and his rival for the big bucks, Elijah Wood, serves as the model for a Coppertone kid in Rob Reiner's *North*. The child is used in a scene as the model for a tourist billboard, where his trunks are pulled down repeatedly by a dog, causing Wood to protest, repeatedly, about having his "crack," "the most private crevice on my body," shown. Nonetheless, shown it is, albeit as a representation (graphic).

9. Published by Routledge, 1992.

10. John Carey, "The Age of Innocents," *Sunday Times* (London), March 7, 1993, "Features," pp. 9–11.

11. James Dalrymple, *Sunday Times* (London), March 7, 1993, n.p.

12. Edward Verity, "Paedophile Book 'Should Be Banned'," *The Daily Mail* (London), March 8, 1994, n.p.

Chapter Fourteen

Popular Culture and the Eroticization of Little Girls

Valerie Walkerdine

If studies of popular culture have largely ignored young children and studies of girls are limited to teenagers, the topic of popular portrayals of little girls as eroticized—little girls and sexuality—is an issue which touches on a number of very difficult, and often taboo areas. Feminism has had little to say about little girls, except through studies of socialization and sex-role stereotyping. With regard to sexuality, almost all attention has been focused on adult women. Little girls enter debates about women's memories of their own girlhood in the main: discussions of little girls' fantasies of sex with their fathers or adult men; as in Freud's Dora case, the debate surrounding Masson's claim that Freud had suppressed the evidence that many of his female patients had been sexually abused as children; and of course, the discourse of abuse itself. The topic of little girls and sexuality has come to be seen, then, as being about the problem of the sexual abuse of innocent and vulnerable girls by bad adult men, or conversely, less politically correct but no less present, the idea of little girls as little seductresses, who in the words of one judge in a child abuse case are 'no angel[s]'. I want to open up a set of issues that I believe are occluded by such debates. That is, in short, the ubiquitous eroticization of little girls in the popular media and the just as ubiquitous ignorance and denial of this phenomenon.

Childhood Innocence and Little Lolitas

Janie is six. In the classroom she sits almost silently well behaved, the epitome of the hard-working girl, so often scorned as uninteresting in the educational literature on girls' attainment (Walkerdine 1989). She says very little and appears to be constantly aware of being watched and herself watches the model that she presents to her teacher and classmates, as well as to myself, seated in a corner of the classroom, making an audio recording. She always presents immaculate work and is used to getting very high marks. She asks to go to the toilet and leaves the classroom. As she is wearing a radio microphone I hear her cross the hall in which a class is doing music and movement to a radio programme: the teacher tells them to pretend to be bunnies. She leaves the hall and enters the silence of the toilets and in there, alone, she sings loudly to herself. I imagine her swaying in front of the mirror. The song that she sings is one on the lips of many of the girls at the time I was making the recordings: Toni Basil's 'Oh Mickey'.

'Oh Mickey' is a song sung by a woman dressed as a teenager. In the promotional video for the song she wears a cheerleader's outfit, complete with very short skirt and is surrounded by large, butch-looking women cheerleaders who conspire to make her look both smaller and more feminine. 'Oh Mickey, you're so fine, you're so fine, you blow my mind', she sings. 'Give it to me, give it to me, any way you can, give it to me, give it to me, I'll take it like a man.' What does it mean for a six-year-old girl to sing these highly erotic lyrics? It could be argued that what we have here is the intrusion of adult sexuality into the innocent world of childhood. Or indeed, that because she is only six, such lyrics do not count because she is incapable of understanding them. I shall explore the issue of childhood innocence in more detail, and rather than attempting to dismiss the issue of the meaning of the lyrics as irrelevant, I shall try to place these meanings in the overall study of little girls and sexuality. In moving out of the public and highly supervised space of the classroom, where she is a 'good, well-behaved girl', to the private space of the toilets she enters a quite different discursive space, the space of the little Lolita, the sexual little girl, who cannot be revealed to the cosy sanitized classroom. She shifts in this move from innocent to sexual, from virgin to whore, from child to little woman, from good to bad. Is this one more place of the corruption of the young through imitation (*pace* the literature on children, television and violence for example)? Or do we have to try to tell a different kind of story, one that differs quite markedly from those previous stories of little girls and tries to intervene into the ponderous silence within feminism and cultural studies.

Children and the Popular

Cultural studies has had almost nothing to say about young children. Its agenda has been concerned primarily with male and later female youth. It is not surprising that this should have been so, given the concern of such work with the issue of resistance: if teenage girls had to struggle to gain a place (McRobbie 1980), tiny tots certainly come low in the resistance stakes! However, media studies by comparison, together with developmental and social psychology as well as education, have been fairly obsessed with children's viewing of television, especially with respect to sex and violence, though these disciplines have had nothing to say about children's consumption and engagement with other forms and aspects of popular culture. I shall return to the issue of television by examining the case of a moral panic in the 1980s about the Channel 4 series *Minipops*. But, I want to begin by examining some central issues about conceptions of childhood.

I want to explore some of the 'gazes' at the little girl, the ways that she is inscribed in a number of competing discourses. In this essay I will concentrate on the figure of the little girl as an object of psycho-pedagogic discourse and as the eroticized child-woman of popular culture. I have written extensively elsewhere about psychology and education's production of 'the child' as what Foucault has termed a 'fiction functioning in truth' (Walkerdine 1984, 1988, 1989, 1992, 1993). I have argued that 'the nature of the child' is not discovered but produced in regimes of truth created in those very practices which proclaim the child in all his naturalness. I write 'his' advisedly, because a central plank of my argument has been that although this child is taken to be gender-neutral, actually he is always figured as a boy, a boy who is playful, creative, naughty, rule-breaking, rational. The figure of the girl, by contrast, suggests an unnatural pathology: she works to the child's play, she follows rules to his breaking of them, she is good, well behaved and irrational. Femininity becomes the Other of rational childhood. If she is everything that the child is not supposed to be, it follows that her presence, where it displays the above attributes may be considered to demonstrate a pathological development, an improper childhood, a danger or threat to what is normal and natural. However, attempts (and they are legion) to transform her into the model playful child often come up against a set of discursive barriers: a playful and assertive girl may be understood as forward, uppity, over-mature, too precocious (in one study a primary teacher called such a ten-year-old girl a 'madam': see Walkerdine 1989). Empirically then, 'girls' like 'children' are not discovered in a natural state. What is found to be the case by teachers, parents and others is the result of complex processes of subjectification (Henriques et al. 1984). Yet, while this model of girlhood is at once pathologized, it is also needed: the good and hard-working girl who follows the rules prefigures the nurturant mother figure, who uses her irrationality to safeguard rationality, to allow it to develop (Walkerdine and Lucey 1989). Consider then the threat to the natural child posed by the eroticized child, the little Lolita, the girl who presents as a little woman, but not of the nurturant kind, but the seductress, the unsanitized whore to the good girl's virgin. It is my contention that popular culture lets this figure into the sanitized space of natural childhood, a space from which it must be guarded and kept at all costs. What is being kept out and what safe inside this fictional space?

The discourses of natural childhood build upon a model of naturally occurring rationality, itself echoing the idea of childhood as an unsullied and innocent state, free from the interference of adults. The very cognitivism of most models of childhood as they have been incorporated into educational practices, leaves both emotionality and sexuality to one side. Although Freud posited a notion of childhood sexuality which has been very pervasive, it was rather concepts like repression and the problems of adult interference in development which became incorporated into educational practices rather than any notion of sexuality in children as a given or natural phenomenon. Indeed, it is precisely the idea that sexuality is an adult notion which sullies the safe innocence of a childhood free to emerge inside the primary classroom, which is most important. Adult sexuality interferes with the uniqueness of childhood, its stages of development. Popular culture then, in so far as it presents the intrusion of adult sexuality into the sanitized space of childhood, is understood as very harmful.

Visually these positions can be distinguished by a number of gazes at the little girl. Psychopedagogic images are presented in two ways: the fly-on-the-wall documentary photograph in which the young girl is seen always engaged in some educational activity and is never shown looking at the camera, and the cartoon-type book illustration in which she appears as a smiley-faced rounded (but certainly not curvy) unisex figure. If we begin to explore popular images of little girls they present a stark contrast. I do not have room in this piece to explore this issue in detail, but simply let me make reference to newspaper and magazine fashion shots, recent television advertisements, for example for Volkswagen cars, Yoplait yoghurt and Kodak Gold film. All present the highly eroticized alluring little girl, often (at least in all three TV ads) with fair hair and ringlets, usually made up and with a look which seductively returns the gaze of the camera. Indeed, such shots bear far more similarity with images taken from child pornography than they do with psychoeducational images. However, the popular advertisement and fashion images are ubiquitous: they are an everyday part of our culture and have certainly not been equated with child pornography.

It would not be difficult to make out a case that such images are the soft porn of child pornography and that they exploit childhood by introducing adult sexuality into childhood innocence. In that sense then, they could be understood as the precursor to child sexual abuse in the way that pornography has been understood by some feminists as the precursor to rape. However, I feel that such an interpretation is over-simplistic. The eroticization of little girls is a complex phenomenon, in which a certain aspect of feminine sexuality and childhood sexuality is understood as corrupting of an innocent state. The blame is laid both at the door of abusive and therefore pathological and bad men who enter and sully the terrain of childhood innocence; and of course conversely, with the little Lolitas who lead men on. But popular images of little girls as alluring and seductive, at once innocent and highly erotic, are contained in the most respectable and mundane of locations: broadsheet newspapers, women's magazines, television adverts. The phenomenon that we are talking about therefore has to be far more pervasive than a rotten apple, pathological and bad abusive men approach. This is not about a few perverts, but about the complex construction of the highly contradictory gaze at little girls, one which places them as at once threatening and sustaining rationality, little virgins that might be whores, to be protected yet to be constantly alluring. The complexity of this phenomenon, in terms of both the cultural production of little girls as these ambivalent objects and the way in which little girls themselves as well as adults live this complexity, how it produces their subjectivity, has not begun to be explored.

I want to point to a number of ways in which this issue can be fruitfully examined (all of which are developed in Walkerdine, 1997).

Eroticized Femininity and the Working-Class Girl

Let us return to Janie and her clandestine singing. I have been at some pains to point out that Janie presents to the public world of the classroom the face of hard-working diligent femininity, which, while pathologized, is still desired. She reserves the less acceptable face of femininity for more private spaces. I imagine her dancing as she sings in front of the mirror: this act can be understood as an acting out, a fantasizing of the possibility of being someone or something else. I want to draw attention to the contradictions in the way in which the eroticized child-woman is a position presented publicly for the little girl to enter, but which is simultaneously treated as a position which removes childhood innocence, allows entry of the whore and makes the girl vulnerable to abuse. The entry of popular culture into the educational and family life of the little girl is therefore to be viewed with suspicion, as a threat posed by the lowering of standards, of the intrusion of the low against the superior high culture. It is the consumption of popular culture which is taken as making the little working-class girl understood as potentially more at risk of being victim and perpetrator (as has similarly been propounded in relation to young boys and violence, *pace* the James Bulger murder). Janie's fantasy dirties the sanitary space of the classroom. But what is Janie's fantasy, and at the intersection of which complex fantasies is she inscribed? I want to explore some of the popular fictions about the little working-class girl and to present the way in which the eroticization presents for her the possibility of a different and better life, of which she is often presented as the carrier. The keeping at bay of sexuality as intruding upon innocent childhood is in sharp contrast to this.

There have been a number of cinematic depictions of young girls as capable of producing a transformation in their own and others' lives, from Judy Garland in *The Wizard of Oz*, through Shirley Temple, *Gigi, My Fair Lady* to (orphan) *Annie. Annie.* . . . In the majority of these films the transformation effected relates to class and to money through the intervention of a lovable little girl. Charles Eckert (1991) argued that Shirley Temple was often portrayed as an orphan in the Depression whose role was to soften the hearts of the wealthy so that they would identify her as one of the poor, not dirty and radical, but lovable, to become the object of charity through their donations. In a similar way, Annie is presented as an orphan for whom being working class is the isolation of a poor little girl, with no home, no parents, no community. She too has to soften the heart of the armaments millionaire, Daddy Warbucks, making him soften at the edges, as well as finding herself happiness through dint of her own lovable personality. It is by this means that she secures for herself a future in a wealthy family, which she creates, by bringing Daddy Warbucks and his secretary Grace together. By concentrating on these two characters alone it is possible to envisage that the little working-class girl is the object of massive projections. She is a figure of immense transformative power, who can make the rich love, thereby solving huge social and political problems; and she can immeasurably improve her own life in the process.[1] At the same time she presents the face of a class turned underclass, ragged, disorganized, orphaned, for whom there is only one way out: embourgeoisement. Thus, she becomes the epitome of the feminized, and therefore emasculated, less threatening, proletariat. In addition to this, Graham Greene pointed to something unmentioned in the tales of innocent allure: the sexual coquettishness of Shirley Temple. His pointing to her paedophilic eroticization led to the closure of the magazine *Night and Day* of which he was editor, after it was sued for libel in 1936.

What does the current figure of the eroticized little girl hold? What fantasies are projected on to her and how do these fantasies interact with the fantasy scenarios little working-class girls create for themselves and their lives? I have explored aspects of the life of one such little girl elsewhere (Walkerdine 1993 and 1997).

If she is simultaneously holding so much that is understood as both good and bad, no wonder actual little girls might find their situation overwhelming. It would be easy to classify Janie and other girls' private eroticization as resistance to the position accorded to her at school and in high culture, but I hope that I have demonstrated that this would be hopelessly simplistic.

Fantasies of Seduction

Let us see then what psychoanalysis has had to say about seduction and the eroticization of little girls. It is easy to pinpoint Freud's seduction theory and his account of an auto-erotic childhood sexuality. We might also point to the place of the critiques of the seduction theory in the accusation that psychoanalysis had ignored child abuse; the raising of the spectre of abuse as a widespread phenomenon; and the recent attacks on therapists for producing 'false memories' of abuses that never happened in their clients. In this sense then, the issue of little girls and sexuality can be seen to be a minefield of claim and counter-claim focusing on the issue of fantasy, memory and reality. If one wants, therefore, to examine sexuality and little girls as a cultural phenomenon, one is confronted by a denial of cultural processes: either little girls have a sexuality which is derived from their fantasies of seduction by their fathers or they are innocent of sexuality, which is imposed upon them from the outside by pathological or evil men who seduce, abuse and rape them. Culturally, we are left with a stark choice: sexuality in little girls is natural, universal and inevitable; or, a kind of Laura Mulvey–type male gaze is at work in which the little girl is produced as object of an adult male gaze. She has no fantasies of her own and in the Lacanian sense, we could say that 'the little girl does not exist except as symptom and myth of the masculine imaginary'. Or, in the mould of the Women Against Violence Against Women approach of 'porn is the theory, rape is the practice', we might conclude that 'popular representations of eroticized little girls is the theory and child sexual abuse is the practice'. Girls' fantasies prove a problem in all these accounts, because only Freud credited them with any of their own, although Freud made it clear that, like others working on psychopathology at the time, feminine sexuality was the central enigma. Indeed his main question was 'what does the woman, the little girl, want?' A question to which Jacqueline Rose in her introduction to Lacanian writing on feminine sexuality (1985) asserts that 'all answers, including the mother are false: she simply wants'. So little girls have a desire without an object, a desire that must float in space, unable to find an object, indeed to be colonized by masculine fantasies, which create female desire in its own image. Of course, Laura Mulvey's original 1974 work on the male cinematic gaze has been much revised and criticized (e.g. *Screen* 1992). But the position has somewhat polarized, with critics for and against psychoanalysis, with those opposing psychoanalysis pointing to its universalizing tendencies and dredging up the concept of 'social fantasy'. However, what is not clear in these criticisms is how the critics would engage with the intersection of the social and the psychic. It is all very well to oppose psychoanalysis but cultural processes do not all happen in a rational, conscious world. How then to do justice to the psychological aspects of this issue without reductionism?

Let us return to the psychoanalytic arguments about sexuality. Laplanche and Pontalis (1985) discuss seduction in terms of 'seduction into the fantasies of the parents'. Those fantasies can be understood in terms of the complex intertwining of parental histories and the regimes of truth, the cultural fantasies which circulate in the social. This may sound like a theory of socialization, but socialization implies the learning of roles and the taking on of stereotypes. What we have here is a complex interweaving of the many kinds of fantasy, both 'social' in the terms of Geraghty (1991) and others; and psychic, as phantasy in the classic psychoanalytic sense. Lacan, of course, argued that the symbolic system carried social fantasies which were psychic in origin, an argument he made by recourse to structuralist principles, from de Saussure and Lévi-Strauss. However, it is possible to understand the complexity in terms which conceive of the psychic/social relation as produced not in a historical and universal categories, but in historically specific regimes of meaning and truth (Henriques et al. 1984).

However, what Freud did argue for was what he called a 'childhood sexuality'. What he meant was that the bodily sensations experienced by the baby could be very pleasurable, but this pleasure was, of course, always crosscut by pain, a presence marked by the absence of the care-giver, usually the mother. In this context little children could learn in an omnipotent way that they too could give these pleasurable sensations to themselves, just as they learnt, according to Freud's famous example of the cotton-reel game, that in fantasy they could control the presence and absence of the mother. So, for Freud there is no *tabula rasa*, no innocent child. The child's first senses of pleasure are already marked by the phantasies inherent in the presence and absence of the Other. However, as Laplanche and Pontalis point out, the infantile sexuality, marked by an 'infantile language of tenderness', is cross-cut by the introduction of an adult 'language', the language of passion. 'This is the language of desire, necessarily marked by prohibition, a language of guilt and hatred, including the sense of orgastic pleasure' (Laplanche and Pontalis 1985: 15). How far does this view take us down the road of sorting out the problems associated with childhood innocence etc. models?

The model suggests that there are two kinds of sexuality: an infant one about bodily pleasures and an adult one which imposes a series of other meanings upon those pleasures. We should note here, therefore, that Laplanche and Pontalis do go as far as implying that not all of the fantasy is on the side of the child, but that the parents impose some of their own. The sexuality would then develop in terms of the admixture of the two, in all its psychic complexity. Let me illustrate that briefly by making reference to a previous study of mine (Walkerdine 1985) in which I discussed my own father's nickname for me, Tinky, short for Tinkerbell, which I was reminded of by a father, Mr. Cole's nickname for his six-year-old daughter, Joanne, as Dodo. I argued that Tinky and Dodo were fathers' fantasies about their daughters: a fairy with diminutive size but incredible powers on the one hand and a preserved baby name (Dodo, as a childish mispronunciation of JoJo) on the other. But a dodo is also an extinct bird, or for Mr Cole, that aspect of extinction which is preserved in his fantasy relationship with his daughter: a baby. Joanne is no longer a baby; babyhood, like the dodo has gone, but it is preserved in the fantasy of Mr Cole's special nickname for his daughter, and in so designating her, he structures the relationship between them: she remains his baby. In the case of my own father's fantasy, Tinky signified for me the most potent aspect of my specialness for him. I associated it with a photograph of myself aged three winning a local fancy-dress competition, dressed as a bluebell fairy. This is where I won and 'won him over': my fairy charms reciprocated his fantasy of me, designating me 'his girl' and fuelling my Oedipal fantasies.

I am trying to demonstrate that those fantasies are not one-sided, neither on the side of the parent, nor the little girl, but, as the Tinky example illustrates, the 'language of adult desire' is entirely cultural. Tinkerbell and bluebell fairies are cultural phenomena which can be examined in terms of their semiotics and their historical emergence, as well as their production and consumption. My father did not *invent* Tinkerbell or the Bluebell Fairy. Rather he used what were available cultural fantasies to name something about his deep and complex feelings for his daughter. In return, I, his daughter, took those fantasies to my heart and my unconscious, making them my own. Now, of course it could be argued that this sails very close to Laura Mulvey's original position, following Lacan, that woman (the little girl) does not exist (or have fantasies which originate with her) except as symptom and myth of male fantasy. But I am attempting to demonstrate that a position which suggests that fantasies come only from the adult male is far too simplistic. My father might have imposed Tinkerbell on me but my own feelings for my father had their own role to play.

I want to argue that the culture carries these adult fantasies, creates vehicles for them. It carries the transformation of this into a projection on to children of the adult language of desire. In this view the little seductress is a complex phenomenon, which carries adult sexual desire but which hooks into the equally complex fantasies carried by the little girl herself. The idea of a sanitized natural childhood in which such things are kept at bay, having no place in childhood in this model, becomes not the guarantor of the safety of children from the perversity of adult desires for them, but a huge defence against the acknowledgement of those, dangerous, desires on the part of adults. In this analysis, 'child protection' begins to look more like adult protection.

It is here then that I want to make a distinction between seduction and abuse. Fantasies of Tinky and Dodo were enticing, seductive, but they were not abuse. To argue that they were is to make something very simplistic out of something immensely complex.

As long as seduction is subsumed under a discourse of abuse, issues of 'seduction into the fantasies of the parents' are hidden under a view which suggests that adult sexual fantasies about children are held only by perverts, who can be kept at bay by keeping children safe and childhood innocent. But if childhood innocence is really an adult defence, adult fantasies about children and the eroticization of little girls is not a problem about a minority of perverts from whom the normal general public should be protected. It is about massive fantasies carried in the culture, which are equally massively defended against by other cultural practices, in the form of the psychopedagogic and social welfare practices incorporating discourses of childhood innocence. This is not to suggest that children are not to be protected. Far from it. Rather, my argument is that a central issue of adult sexual projections on to children is not being addressed.

Ann Scott (1989) sees seductiveness as a form of parental intrusion, in which children are seduced into the fantasies of their parents. We could add here, and into the fantasies of the culture. Such fantasies in this model are about unresolved adult sexuality and eroticism, for example, desire for the mother marked by prohibition, projected on to little girls: doubly prohibited and therefore doubly exciting. The popular cultural place which admits the possibility that little girls can be sexual little women provides a place where adult projections meet the possibility for little girls of being Other than the rational child or the nurturant quasi-mother, where they can be bad. It can then be a space of immense power for little girls and certainly a space in which they can be exploited, but it is not abuse.

So the issue of fantasy and the eroticization of little girls within popular culture becomes a complex phenomenon in which cultural fantasies, fantasies of the parents and little girls' Oedipal fantasies mix and are given a cultural form which shapes them. Laplanche and Pontalis (1985) argue that fantasy is the setting for desire, 'but as for knowing who is responsible for the setting, it is not enough for the psychoanalyst to rely on the resources of his [sic] science, nor on the support of myth. He [sic] must become a philosopher!' (p. 17).

In post-structuralist terms this would take us into the domain of the production of knowledges about children and the production of the ethical subject. I want to explore lastly this latter connection by suggesting several courses of action and to examine the issue (briefly) through a specific example of a 'moral panic' about popular culture and the eroticization of children.

Minipops

I want to end this essay by looking at the case of *Minipops*, a series transmitted on Channel 4 television in 1983. The series presented young children, boys and girls, white and black, singing current pop songs, dressed up and heavily made up. This series became the object of what was described as a moral panic. The stated intention of the director was to present a showcase of new talent, the idea having come from his daughter, who liked to dress up and sing pop songs at home. The furor caused by the programmes was entirely voiced by the middle classes. The broadsheet papers demanded the axing of the series on the grounds that it presented a sexuality which spoiled and intruded into an innocent childhood. One critic wrote of 'lashings of lipstick on mini mouths'. By contrast, the tabloids loved the series. For them, the programmes represented a chance for young children to be talent-spotted, to find fame. There was no mention of the erosion of innocence. Why this difference? It would be easy to imagine that the tabloids were more exploitative, less concerned with issues of sexual exploitation so rampant in their own pages, with the broadsheets as upholders of everything that is morally good. However, I think that this conclusion would be erroneous. While I deal with this argument in more detail elsewhere (Walkerdine, 1997), let me point out here that I have argued that the eroticized little girl presents a fantasy of otherness to the little working-class girl. She is inscribed as one who can make a transformation, which is also a self-transformation, which is also a seductive allure. It is not surprising, therefore, that the tabloid discourse is about talent, discovery, fame: all the elements of the necessary transformation from rags to riches, from flower-girl to princess, so to speak. Such a transformation is necessarily no part of middle-class discourse, fantasy and aspiration. Rather, childhood for the middle class is a state to be preserved free from economic intrusion, producing the possibility of the rational and playful child who will become a rational, educated professional, a member of the 'new middle class'.

I would argue, then, that the examination of the complex cultural phenomenon which I have outlined would require analyses at all of the levels that I have signalled. Each without the other would be reductive.

Seduction and the eroticization of little girls are complex cultural phenomena. I have tried to demonstrate that the place of the little working-class girl is important because her seductiveness has an important role to play in terms of both a social and personal transformation, a transformation which is glimpsed in the fantasies of fame embodied in series like *Minipops*. The figure of the little working-class girl then simultaneously 'holds' the transformation of an emasculated working class into both lovable citizens and the fear against which the fantasy defends. This is the little Lolita: the whore, the contagion of the masses which will endanger the safety of the bourgeois order. On the other hand, child protection—as the outlawing of perversion and a keeping of a safe space of innocent childhood—can also be viewed as class-specific, and indeed the fantasy of the safe space which has not been invaded by the evil masses.

I have tried to place an understanding of unconscious processes inside of all of this. Because, as I hope that I have demonstrated, psychic processes form a central component of how social and cultural fantasies work. Some may argue that my recourse to psychoanalysis presents such psychic processes as universal and inevitable, but I have tried to show how the social and the psychic merge together to form particular fantasies at a specific moment. This is only a very small beginning that may help to sort out how we might approach a hugely important topic which has been badly neglected in cultural and feminist theory.

NOTE

1. My previous work on girls' comics (Walkerdine 1985) pointed to very similar fictions occurring in comic stories directed at young working-class girls.

REFERENCES

Eckert, C., 1991: 'Shirley Temple and the House of Rockefeller', in C. Gledhill (ed.) *Stardom*. London: Routeledge.

Geraghty, C., 1991: *Women and Soap Opera*. Oxford: Polity Press.

Henriques, J., Hollway, W., Urwin, C., Venn, C. and Walkerdine, V., 1984: *Changing the Subject: Psychology, Social Regulation and Subjectivity*. London: Methuen.

LaPlanche, J. and Pontalis, J.-B., 1985: 'Fantasy and the Origins of Sexuality', in V. Burgin, J. Donald and C. Kaplan (eds.) *Formations of Fantasy*. London: Routledge.

McRobbie, A., 1980: 'Settling accounts with subcultures', *Screen Education*, 34: pp. 37–50.

Rose, J., 1985: 'Introduction', in J. Lacan and the Ecole Freudienne *Feminine Sexuality*, London: Macmillan.

Scott, A., 1989: 'Seduction and Child Abuse', *Feminist Review*, 31:pp. 6–16.

Screen, 1992: *The Sexual Subject*, London: Routledge.

Walkerdine, V., 1984: 'Developmental Psychology and the Child Centered Pedagogy'. In J. Henriques et al. *Changing the Subject: Psychology, Social Regulation and Subjectivity*. London: Methuen.

Walkerdine, V., 1985: 'Video Replay', in V. Burgin, J. Donald and C. Kaplan (eds.) *Formations of Fantasy*. London: Routledge.

Walkerdine, V., 1988: *The Mastery of Reason*, London: Routledge.

Walkerdine, V., 1989: *Counting Girls Out*, London: Virago.

Walkerdine, V., 1992: 'Reasoning in a Post-modern Age', paper presented at Fifth International Conference on Thinking. Australia: Townsville.

Walkerdine, V., 1993: 'Beyond Developmentalism', *Theory and Psychology*, 3 (4): pp. 451–69.

Walkerdine, V., 1997: *Daddy's Girl: Young Girls and Popular Culture*. London: Macmillan.

Walkerdine, V. and Lucey, H., 1989: *Democracy in the Kitchen: Regulating Mothers and Socialising Daughters*. London: Virago.

Chapter Fifteen

Stealing Innocence
The Politics of Child Beauty Pageants

Henry A. Giroux

Only in a climate of denial could hysteria over satanic rituals at daycare centers coexist with a failure to grasp the full extent of child abuse. (More than 8.5 million women and men are survivors.) Only in a culture that represses the evidence of the senses could child pageantry grow into a $5 billion dollar industry without anyone noticing. Only in a nation of promiscuous puritans could it be a good career move to equip a six-year-old with bedroom eyes.[1]

The Disappearing Child and the Politics of Innocence

Constructed within the myth of innocence, children are often portrayed as inhabiting a world that is untainted, magical, and utterly protected from the harshness of adult life. Innocence in this scenario not only erases the complexities of childhood and the range of experiences different children encounter but also offers an excuse for adults to ignore responsibility for how children are firmly connected to and shaped by social and cultural institutions run largely by adults. Innocence makes children invisible except as projections of adult fantasies—fantasies that allow adults to believe that children do not suffer from adult greed, recklessness, and perversions of will and spirit, and that adults are, in the final analysis, unaccountable.[2]

If innocence distinguishes children from adults, the discourse of the disappearing child depicts childhood as threatened with the potential collapse of that distinction. For example, in cultural critic Neil Postman's thoroughly modernist view of the world, the electronic media, especially television, present a threat to the existence of children and the civilized culture bequeathed to the West by the Enlightenment.[3] Not only does the very character of television—with its fast paced format, sound-bite worldview information overload, and fragmented structure—undermine the possibility for children to engage in critical thinking, television expel images of the child from its programming by both "adultifing" the child and promoting the rise of the "childfied" adult.[4] Postman is quick to extend his thesis to other spheres and notes, for example, the disappearance of children's clothing and games, the entry of children into professional sports, and the increasing willingness of the criminal justice system to treat children as miniature adults. Postman's lament represents less a concern with preserving childhood innocence than with bemoaning the threat passed by popular culture to the traditions of high culture and to a restricted notion of literacy and citizenship training. The loss of childhood innocence in this scenario refers to the passing of a historical and political period during which children could be contained and socialized under the watchful tutelage of dominant regulatory institutions such as the family, school, and church.

The specter of the child as an endangered species has also been appropriated by politicians, including President Clinton, eager to establish themselves as protectors of childhood innocence. In their rush to implement new social and economic policies, they hold up children as both the inspiration and prime beneficiaries of their reforms. Lacking opportunities to vote, mobilize, or register their opinions, young children become an easy target and a ready referent in the discourse of moral uplift and social legitimation. Children also become pawns and victims. Far from benefiting children, many of the programs and government reforms proposed by Clinton and enacted by the Republican-led Congress represent what Senator Edward Kennedy has called "legislative child abuse."[5] In this case, protecting the innocence of children has a direct connection with the disappearing child, though not in the sense predicted by Postman. The "draconian" cuts in social welfare, it is estimated, will result in eleven million families losing income under the new welfare bill, including more than eight million families with children. Moreover, it is predicted that the new welfare reform measure will be responsible for moving "2.6 million people, including 1.1 million children, into poverty."[6] In this instance, children are indeed disappearing—right into the hole of poverty, suffering, and despair.[7]

Backing from the program's original concerns with the welfare of all children, politicians are showing little interest in the welfare of kids who are poor and nonwhite. Under these circumstances, talk of innocence and the disappearance of childhood advances a conservative political agenda. Within this conservative notion of "family values," white and middle-class children are viewed as most deserving of the material resources and cultural goods of the larger society.[8] In this selective appropriation, the everyday experience of childhood is held hostage to the realities and the disingenuous rhetoric of power politics.

As the rhetoric of child welfare enters the public consciousness, innocence is increasingly being redeployed to rearticulate which specific children are deserving of entitlements and adult protection. Shot through with political and ideological values, innocence is not merely selective about which children are endangered and need to be protected, it also is used to signal who and what constitutes a threat to children.

As politicians, the popular press, and media increasingly deploy the child as a moral yardstick, adults find it more difficult to elide responsibility for what they do to kids. Consequently, childhood innocence appears both threatened and threatening. According to popular wisdom, the enemies of children are not to be found in the halls of Congress, in the poisonous advertisements that commodify and sexualize young children, or even in the endless media bashing that blames children for all of society's ills.[9] On the contrary, the biggest threat to children is to be found in the child molesters, pedophiles, abductors, and others who prey on children in the most obscene ways imaginable. In this instance, the discourse of childhood innocence does more than serve the needs of political opportunism, it also provides the basis for moral panics. Both conservatives and liberals have fed off the frenzy of fear arising from a decade of revelations of alleged child abuse. Starting with the 1987 McMartin preschool case, fear-inspired legislation has sought to protect children from pedophiles, child molesters, predatory priests and teachers, and anyone else who might be labeled as a sexual deviant who might pose a threat to the innocent child.[10] In this scenario child abuse is explained through reference to the individual pathology of the molester and pedophile. The fear and anger child abuse arouses is so great that the Supreme Court is willing to suspend certain constitutional liberties in order to keep sexual predators in prison even after they finish serving their sentences.[11]

The issue of widespread child abuse has done more than inspire a national fear of child molesters. We must move beyond the language of individual pathology to examine the more substantive issue of how society is treating its children and how society has failed to provide resources necessary to ensure children's security, safety and well-being. The most disturbing threat to innocence may be child abuse, but this abuse can not be ascribed to sexual predators. Such abuse reflects a broader set of political, economic, and social factors. To understand this abuse requires us to probe deeply into the cultural formations that see children as a menacing enemy or as a market to be exploited. The social investment in children's innocence may be at the center of political rhetoric in the halls of Congress, but there are other forces in American society that aggressively breed a hatred and disregard for children, especially those already marginalized because of their class, race, gender, or noncitizen status.

When Debra McMahon, a vice-president for Mercer Management Consulting, gleefully asserts that "kids are the most pure consumers you could have. . . . They tend to interpret your ad literally. They are infinitely open," she is focusing on innocence as a weakness that permits manipulating children into consumers. McMahon barely raises an eyebrow about the ethical implications of such an act.[12] Innocence in this instance becomes powerlessness.

In what follows, I want to argue that the central threat to childhood innocence lies not in the figure of the pedophile or sexual predator but can be found in the diminishing public spheres available for children to experience themselves as critical agents. As cities become increasingly ghettoized because of the ravaging effects of deindustrialization, the loss of revenue, and white flight, children are left with fewer services to fulfill their needs and desires. As the public schools are abandoned or surrendered to the dictates of the market, children increasingly find themselves isolated from the community and no longer the recipients of compassion. As the state is hollowed out and only the most brutal state apparatuses remain intact, children have fewer opportunities to protect themselves from an adult world that offers them dwindling resources, dead-end jobs, and diminished hopes for the future.[13] At the same time, children are increasingly subjected to exploitation, sexualization, commodification, and commercialization.[14]

JonBenet, Race, and the Perils of Home

While the concept of innocence may incite adults to proclaim publicly their support for future generations, such talk masks harsh social realities and the growing impoverishment of children's lives. Of course, there are often flash points that signal that children are in danger and allow us to identify actual threats to their innocence. Conservatives, for example, have focused on the dangers to children presented by rap music, cinematic violence, and drugs; they have launched an attack on Hollywood films, the fashion world, single teen moms, and what they call the cultural elite. But rarely do conservatives and the dominant press locate the ongoing threats to children within dominant economic, political, and cultural institutions. Poverty, racism, sexism, and the dismantling of the welfare state do great harm to children, and some of the effects of these social conditions either do not get reported in the press or if they do, prompt little public discussion and self-examination.

One recent exception can be found in the case of JonBenet Ramsey, the six-year-old who was found strangled in her wealthy parents' Boulder, Colorado, home the day after Christmas, 1996. Throughout the first half of 1997, the press displayed a fixation on the case. Major media networks, newspapers, and tabloids besieged the public with images of JonBenet, dubbed as the slain little beauty queen, posing coquettishly in a tight dress, wearing bright-red lipstick, her hair a highlighted blonde. The JonBenet Ramsey case revealed once again that the media gravitate toward victims that fit the dominant culture's image of itself. Children who are white, blond, and middle class are not only invested with more humanity, they become emblematic of the social order, while abused children who "don't fit the image of purity defiled are banished from the public eye."[15]

Consider the case of a nine-year-old, African-American child, labeled in the press as Girl X. Girl X was raped, beaten, blinded, and dumped in a stairwell in the rundown Cabrini Green Housing Project in Chicago. The brutal murder aroused a great deal of publicity in Chicago, but not as much as the JonBenet Ramsey investigation. The case was virtually ignored by the national media. Girl X was treated as a nonentity because of her race and poverty. Innocence is primarily applied to children who are white and middle class, often tucked away in urban townhouses and the safe sanctuaries of segregated suburban America.

Innocence also mystifies the sexualization and commodification of young girls who are being taught to satisfy the desires of the adult gaze. The child becomes the principal incitement to adult desire, but the pedagogical and commercial practices at work in such a construction remain unexamined because they take place within acceptable cultural forms such as children's beauty pageants. Jon-Benet's murder jolted the public because it shatters the assumption that the primary threat to innocence lies outside the family. The death of the young beauty queen raises serious questions about those forces at work in children's everyday lives that deny them the possibility to enter adulthood without encountering violence, intimidation, and abuse along the way.

The beauty pageant is an exemplary site for examining how the discourse of innocence mystifies the appropriation, sexualization, and commodification of children's bodies. In pursuing this argument, I will examine how the culture of child beauty pageants constitutes a pedagogical site where children learn about pleasure, desire, and the roles they might assume in an adult society. I also will examine how such pageants are rationalized, how they are upheld by commercial and ideological structures and how they are reproduced, reinforced, and sustained in related spheres such as advertising and fashion photography, which also play an important role in marketing children as objects of pleasure and desire. I hope to challenge the innocence ascribed to such rituals. I don't mean to suggest that all child beauty pageants engage in a form of child abuse. Pageants vary both in the way they are constructed and how they interact with local and national audiences. But as sites of representation, identity formation, consumption, and regulation, these events interact with other cultural institutions engaged in the production and regulation of youth, the packaging of desire, and the sexualized body.

Beauty Pageants and the Shock of the Real

Reality sometimes defies the ideological and institutional forces that attempt to keep it at bay. This seems to have been the case during the blitz of media coverage following the brutal murder of six-year-old JonBenet Ramsey. On one level, JonBenet's case attracted national attention because it fed into the frenzy and moral panic Americans are experiencing over the threat of child abuse—fueled by horrific crimes like the kidnap and murder of Polly Klaas in California. Similarly, it resonated with the highly charged campaigns by various legislators and citizen groups urging the death penalty for sex offenders such as Jesse Timmendequas, the child molester who killed seven-year-old Megan Kanka. On another level, the case provided another high-profile example of a child succeeding at the make-believe game of becoming an adult. Not unlike Jessica Dubroff, the seven-year-old would-be Amelia Earhart who, while attempting to be the youngest pilot to cross the United States, died tragically in a plane crash, JonBenet Ramsey also projected the aura of a child with the uncanny ability to present herself as an adult. But if the boundary between innocence and impurity, child and adult, became blurred in both cases, JonBenet's notoriety as an object of public fascination revealed a dark and seamy element in the culture.

Night after night the major television networks aired videotapes of little JonBenet Ramsey wearing tight off-the-shoulder dresses, bright-red lipstick, and curled, teased, and bleached blond hair pulling a feathered Mardi Gras mask almost seductively across her eyes as she sashayed down a runway. Playing the role of an alluring sex kitten, JonBenet's image belied the assumption that the voyeuristic fascination with the sexualized child was confined to the margins of society—inhabited largely by freaks and psychopaths.

The JonBenet Ramsey case revealed not only how regressive notions of femininity and beauty are redeployed in this conservative era to fashion the fragile identities of young girls but also how easily adults will project their own fantasies onto children, even if it means selling them on the beauty block. With the recent attention generated by celebrities such as Roseanne and Oprah Winfrey, the general public has come to recognize that child abuse often takes place at home and that the conception of the child molester as strictly an outsider has become less credible. The image of the home as a safe space for children was also made problematic as it became clear that the Ramsey family imposed their own strange fantasies on their daughter and in doing so denied her an identity suitable for a six-year-old. Instead, they introduced her to a child beauty pageant culture that blurred the boundary between child and adult.

Images of six-year-olds cosmetically transformed into sultry, Lolita-like waifs are difficult to watch. Such images challenge our culture's claims to decency and respect for children. Whereas young women often bear the blame for the often violent consequences associated with this eroticized costuming, the JonBenet Ramsey affair makes it difficult to blame kids for this objectification and commodification. The usual demonization of kids which holds them responsible for society's ills, breaks down in this case as adults find it more difficult to elide responsibility for what they do to children—their own and others.[16] Painted up like a miniature Pamela Anderson, JonBenet's image implies a breakdown of adults' sacred responsibility for protecting childhood innocence. Children can no longer expect "protection . . . consistency and some sort of dignity from adults."[17]

The JonBenet Ramsey case prompted an unusual debate in the national press. Lacking the theoretical tools or political will to analyze the institutional and ideological forces that generate such disregard for children, the media focused on what was often termed the "the strange subculture of child beauty pageants," and more often than not suggested that the abuse children suffered in such pageants was due to overbearing mothers trying to control their daughters' lives. If young girls are unavailable for scapegoating, their mothers apparently make up for the loss. Rarely did the media raise the larger issue of how young girls are being educated to function within a limited notion of public life or how such a regressive education for young girls was the norm rather than the exception.

The traditional moral guardians of children's culture who would censor rap lyrics, remove "dangerous" videos and CDs from public circulation, boycott Disney for progay and lesbian labor practices, and empty school libraries of many of their classic texts have had little to say about the sexualization of young children in children's beauty pageants, a social form as American as apple pie. Amidst the silence by conservatives and the family-values crowd, liberal and progressive reporters began to raise some important questions. For example, CBS anchorman Dan Rather criticized the television networks for running the Jon-Benet tapes on the air, asserting that they amounted to nothing less than kiddy porn. Frank Rich wrote a courageous piece in the *New York Times* in which he argued that the "strange world of kids' pageantry" is not a 'subculture'—it's our culture. But as long as we call it a subculture, it can remain a problem for somebody else."[18] Richard Goldstein followed up Rich's insights with a three-part series in the *Village Voice* in which he argued that the marketing of the sexual child has a long history in the United States and that the JonBenet case "brings to the surface both our horror at how effectively a child can be constructed as a sexual being and our guilt at the pleasure we take in such a sight."[19] For Goldstein, the JonBenet case challenges the American public to confront the actual nature of child abuse, which is all too often a part of family life and further legitimated by our culture's attempts to capitalize on children for adult pleasure and economic gain.

All of these critiques raise valid concerns about the role of child beauty pageants and how they produce culturally specific notions of beauty, pleasure, and femininity that degrade children. Such criticism also prompted a debate about the nature of adult needs and desires that push kids into pageants. In what follows, I want to examine these issues in detail by focusing on the scope and popularity of child beauty pageants, what they attempt to teach young girls, and the broader commercial forces that sustain them. I also want to locate the phenomenon of child beauty pageants within a broader and related set of cultural practices, including the rise of the teenage model in the world of high fashion.

Beauty and the Beast: A Genealogy of Child Beauty Pageants

Ted Cohen, president of World Pageants, Inc., which publishes an international directory of pageants, estimates that the pageantry industry is a billion-dollar-a-year industry, and includes sponsors such as Procter and Gamble, Black Velvet, and Hawaiian Tropics.[20] It is estimated that more than 3,000 pageants a year are held in the United States involving more than 100,000 children under the age of twelve.[21] In some cases, children as young as eight months old are entered in pageants. California, Florida, and New York hold the most pageants, and the overall number in the United States appears to be growing, even though many, especially at the national level, charge contestants between $250 and $800 to enter.[22]

Pageants are a lucrative business. Promoters market pleasure and rake in big dividends, with some making as much as $100,000 on each event. In addition, child beauty pageants have produced an offshoot of support industries, "including costume designers, grooming consultants, interview coaches, photographers, and publishers,"[23] not to mention the cosmetics, weight-reduction, and other "beauty aid industries." Trade magazines such as *Pageant Life*, which has a circulation of sixty thousand, offer their readers images and advertisements celebrating ideals of femininity, glamour, and beauty, reshaping young girls in the image of adult drives and desires. In some cases, parents invest big money for makeup artists, hair stylists, and coaches to teach prepubescent kids particular modeling styles and tornado spins.[24] One story that appeared in *Life* magazine in 1994 featured Blaire, an eleven-year-old, as a seasoned beauty pageant performer. Blaire won more contests when her mom and dad hired Tony, a voice coach and makeup artist, at forty dollars an hour, to redesign her completely. When Blaire's father was asked why he was so involved with entering Blaire in child beauty pageants, he answered: "I am a plastic surgeon only from the neck up. I enjoy the beauty of the face. No doubt that's why I am so involved with Blaire."[25] The article reported that "Bruce is captivated by his daughter's beauty but prefers it enhanced: He apologizes to strangers when she is not wearing makeup. Some parents have accused Bruce of enhancing Blaire's looks with surgery."[26] Blaire indicates that she loves pageants, which are her only interest. The article ends by pointing out that Blaire lacks a child's spontaneity and then conjectures that she "shows so little offstage emotion because she's so busy editing herself with adults."[27]

Blaire's case may appear to some as a caricature of pageant life, replete with stereotypical parents who push their kids too hard and impose their own interests and desires on children too small to refuse. But the popular literature on child beauty pageants is full of such stories. For instance, there are endless examples in the media of little girls caked with makeup, adorned with dyed, coiffured helmetlike hair, performing childish burlesquelike routines under the direction of overbearing parents.[28] There appears to be little concern on the part of many of these parents about the possible negative consequences of dressing their children up in provocative clothing, capping their teeth, putting fake eyelashes on them, and having them perform before audiences in a manner that suggests a sexuality well beyond their years.

The popular literature that supports the child beauty pageant culture lacks any recognition that "sexualized images of little girls may have a dangerous implications in a world where 450,000 American children were reported as victims of sexual abuse in 1993."[29] Trade magazines such as *Pageant Life* and *Babette's Pageant and Talent Gazette* are filled with ads sponsored by companies such as Hawaiian Tropic in which toddlers strike suggestive poses. The age span represented in full-page spreads of contest finalists often runs from two years old to twenty-four. All of the entrants are defined by the same aesthetic. The makeup, pose, smile, and hair styles of the six-year-olds are no different from those of the much older contestants. All of the images depict the same cool estrangement and sexual allure. In addition, the magazines are filled with ads addressing prepubescent youth that hawk pageant clothes from designers such as "Hollywood Babe" and "Little Starlet Fashions"—with many ads invoking the warning "Don't be

Left Behind."[30] All the prepubescent children portrayed in the magazines I examined between 1992 and 1997 are dressed suggestively, wear shocking-red lipstick, and have teased hair, and with few exceptions are white. Success stories for the younger age set (four-to eight-8 year-olds) consistently focused on the thrill of competition, winning titles, and the successful modeling careers of the pageant winners.

Parents and sponsors who participate in these pageants often respond to public criticisms by arguing that the press overreacted to JonBenet Ramsey's death and unfairly implicated the beauty pageant in her murder. Others legitimate the child beauty pageant culture as a productive route to get their children into lucrative careers such as modeling, or to win college scholarships, financial awards, and other prizes. The most frequently used rationale is that pageants build self-esteem in children, "help them to overcome shyness, and [teach them how] to grow up."[31] One pageant director in Murrieta, California refuted the criticism that pageants are detrimental for young girls. "many young girls look at pageants as a protracted game of dress up, something most young girls love."[32] Another pageant participant, Pam Griffin, whose daughter trained JonBenet Ramsey, remarked that "more girls are trying pageants after seeing how much fun JonBenet had."[33] *Vogue* reporter Ellen Mark concluded that most kids who participate in beauty pageants end up as success stories. The reason for their success, according to Mark, is that "pageants made them feel special. . . . Little girls like to look pretty."[34]

Appropriating the discourse of liberal feminism, this argument is often associated with attributes affirming self-direction, autonomy, and a strong competitive spirit. But such arguments define self-esteem within a very narrow standard of autonomy. Self-esteem in this context means embracing rather than critically challenging a gender code that rewards little girls for their looks, submissiveness, and sex appeal. The broader culture, through television, music, magazines, and advertising, consistently bombards young girls with a sexualized ideal of femininity "from which all threatening elements have been purged."[35] Self-esteem often becomes a euphemism for self-hatred, rigid gender roles, and powerlessness.

There is a certain irony in appropriating the language of self-esteem in defending child beauty pageants, especially since the latter provide young children with standards of beauty that only one of forty thousand young women will actually meet. Must we ask what's wrong with young girls wanting to become fashion models (a.k.a Kate Mosses) who increasingly look as if they will never grow up, and for whom beauty is not only defined by the male gaze but appears to be one of the few requisites to enter "into the privileged male world."[36] Naomi Wolf is right in arguing that the problem with linking standardized notions of sexualized beauty to self-esteem is that it doesn't present young girls or adult woman with many choices, especially when sexual pleasure and self-determination are held hostage to notions of femininity which make it difficult for women to grow up and express themselves in public spaces.[37] Moreover, the glamorization of the waif-child as the fashion icon of beauty reflects the nymphet fantasy of a patriarchal society where "men impose their authority on women and children alike."[38]

Once again, little is said about what children are actually learning in pageants, how a child might see herself and mediate her relationship to society when her sense of self-worth is defined largely through a notion of beauty that is one-dimensional and demeaning. Nor does there seem to be much self-reflection on the part of parents and other pageant participators in allowing children to be sponsored by corporations. What a young girl learns in this case is that the identities of the young girls who enter the pageants become meaningful only when tied to the logic of the market—that "in order to enter [the] contest she must represent someone other than herself."[39]

Unlike pageants that took place ten or fifteen years ago, pageants now offer bigger prizes and are backed by corporate sponsors, especially the national pageants. Moreover, as the commercial interests and level of investment in such pageants has risen, so has the competitive nature of the pageants. V. J. LaCour, publisher of *Pageant Life* magazine and a firm supporter of child beauty pageants, thinks that many parents have resorted to makeup and other "extreme" measures because "the parents are trying to get a competitive edge."[40] In some cases, parents resort to measures mentally punitive and physically cruel to get their kids to perform "properly." Lois Miller, owner of the Star Talent Management in Allentown, Pennsylvania, reports that she has "seen parents who have pinched their children for messing up their dress or not looking appropriate or not wiggling enough or not throwing kisses."[41] Parents often respond to such criticisms by asserting that their kids are doing exactly what they want to do and enjoy being in the pageants. This argument becomes strained when parents enter children who are as young as eight months old, or when parents decide, as reported in *Money* magazine, that their four-year-old child needed a talent agent in order to make the right connections.

Sixty Minutes aired a segment on child beauty pageants on May 18, 1997, in the aftermath of the JonBenet Ramsey controversy. The premise of the segment, announced by Morley Safer at its beginning, was to explore if "child beauty pageants exploit children to satisfy ambitions of parents, mothers." To provide a historical perspective on such pageants, *Sixty Minutes* aired cuts from child beauty pageants that had been seen on the program in 1977 and then presented videotaped shots of JonBenet and other children performing in a recent pageant. The contrast was informative. The children in the 1977 pageants wore little-girl dresses, ribbons in their hair, and embodied a kind of childlike innocence as they displayed their little-girl talents—singing, tap dancing, and baton twirling. In the JonBenet pageant shots, the contestants did not look like little girls but, rather, like coquettish, young women whose talents were reduced to their ability to move suggestively across the stage. Clearly, as Safer indicated, "By today's beauty pageant standards, innocence seems to have vanished." To prove his point, he then asked one of the stage mothers who had appeared in the 1977 program what she thought of today's pageants. She responded that she recently went to a child beauty pageant and "walked in the door and walked out. It was disgusting to see the beaded dresses and blown up hair on kids." *Sixty Minutes'* take on child beauty pageants was critical, yet it failed to consider the broader social practices, representations, and relations of power that provide the context for such pageants. Nor did it analyze the increased popularity of the pageants as part of a growing backlash against feminism in the media, culture, and fashion industries, and in conservative economic and political establishments.[42] Safer placed the responsibility for such abuse squarely on the shoulders of overly ambitious and exploitative mothers.

But the backlash against feminism has not stopped more informed criticisms from emerging. For example, some child psychologists argue that the intense competition at pageants, along with the nomadic lifestyle of traveling from one hotel to another when school is not in session, makes it difficult for young children to make friends and increases their problems in their social interactions with other children. Other child specialists argue that it is as developmentally inappropriate to "teach a 6 year old to pose like a 20 year old model as it is to allow her to drive [and] drink alcohol."[43] Of course, there is also the stress of the competition and the danger of undermining children's self-confidence, especially when they lose, if the message they receive is that how they look is the most important aspect of who they are.

Renowned psychologist David Elkind argues that parents used to be concerned with the ethical behavior of children. A decade ago, when children got home from school their parents asked them if they had been good. Now parents are fearful that their children will be losers because of the new economic realities of downsizing and deindustrialization. Marly Harris writes that the "massive restructuring of the economy creates a winner-take-all society in which parents believe that if kids don't end up as one of the few winners they will join the ranks of the many losers."[44] The question children get when they come home in the nineties is no longer "Have you been good?" but "Did you win?"

Another criticism is that the money spent on child pageants by parents, up to $10,000 per child a year in some cases, could be invested in more productive ways such as a savings plan to alleviate the cost of a college education. Not only are children objectified by the child beauty pageant, they are given only limited opportunities to develop and express themselves.

In spite of such criticisms, child beauty pageants are enormously popular in the United States, and their popularity is growing.[45] In part, such popularity can be explained by the pageants' potential to make money for promoters, but there is more to the story. Child beauty contests also represent places where the rituals of small-town America combine with the ideology of mass-consumer culture. Pageants with titles such as "Miss Catfish Queen," "Miss Baby Poultry Princess," and "The Snake Charmer Queen," suggest that such rituals are easily adapted to "local meanings and familiar symbols, values, and aesthetics—those relevant to the producers, performers, and consumers of the contest."[46] Such rituals are easy to put on, are advertised as a legitimate form of family entertainment, resonate powerfully with dominant Western models of femininity, beauty, and culture, and help reproduce particular notions of citizenship and national identity. As

American as apple pie, child beauty pageants are often embraced as good, clean entertainment and defended for their civic value. Moreover, while adult beauty contests such as the annual Miss America pageant have been the object of enormous amounts of feminist criticism,[47] few critics have focused on child beauty pageants as a serious object of cultural analysis.[48]

Beyond the Politics of Child Abuse

Any attempt to challenge the sexist practices and abuses at work in child beauty pageants must begin with the recognition that the pageants represent more than trivial entertainment. Not only do they occupy a reputable public space in which preadolescent girls are offered particular subject positions and identities, they also suggest the degree to which viable public spheres are diminishing for children. As public funding decreases, support services dry up, and extracurricular activities are eliminated from schools, young people find few public spheres of experience which are not already part of the commodity culture. As market relations expand their control over public space, corporations increasingly teach children to become consuming subjects, offering limited opportunities to develop their full range of intellectual and emotional capacities and become critical citizens.

Many progressives are well aware that the struggle over culture is tantamount to the struggle over meaning and identity. Any viable cultural politics must also locate specific cultural texts within wider semiotic, material, and social relations of power that shape everyday life. Understood in these terms, child beauty pageants become an important object of critical analysis for a number of reasons. First, the conservative and rigid gender roles that are legitimated at many child beauty pageants must be analyzed in terms of the specific ideologies they construct for children, and in terms of how these ideologies surface elsewhere in the culture. The values and dominant motifs that shape beauty pageants gain their meaning and appeal precisely because they find expression in related cultural spheres. For instance, the ideologies at work in beauty pageants circulate in advertising campaigns such as those used by Calvin Klein that represent the ideal modern American female as young, anorexic, sexually alluring, and available. The processes at work in the sexualization and commodification of young children are not altogether different from the ways in which the bodies and body parts of young girls are used to sell commodities. Innocence as a trope for doing what is best for children is appropriated by beauty pageants in the name of dominant family values. Practices that might be seen in other contexts as abusive to children are defined within the beauty pageant culture as good, clean, family entertainment.

In advertisements for Calvin Klein's Obsession or his more recent jean ads, innocence becomes a fractured sign and is used unapologetically to construct enticing images of childlike purity and to transform children into the objects of voyeuristic adult desire. The impulse to children can be seen in the rise of models such as Kate Moss who portray women as waifs—sticklike, expressionless, and blank-eyed.[49] Or in the celebrityhood granted to teenage models and film stars such as Ivanka Trump and Liv Tyler, who are left wondering in their waning teen years if they are too old to have a career. In those culture industries, a woman's beauty and desirability are illusive and short-lived. What connects the beauty pageants to the world of advertising and fashion modeling is that young girls are being taught to become little women, while in the adult society women are being taught to assume the identities of powerless, childlike waifs. Lolita grows up only to retreat into her youth as a model for what it means to be a woman.[50]

As an ethical referent, innocence humanizes the child and makes a claim on adults to provide them with security and protection. But innocence gains its meaning from a complex set of semiotic, material, and social registers. And the reality of what is happening to children in cultural spheres as seemingly unrelated as child beauty pageants and the world of advertising and fashion modeling suggests how vulnerable children actually are to misogyny, sexism, racism, and violence. Innocence needs to be understood as subject to diverse appropriations; its effects can be both positive and devastating for children. If innocence is to become a useful category for social analysis, the term must be understood politically and ethically in terms of the ways in which it is represented and used within everyday life and the ways it is shaped through language, representations, and the technologies of power. We need to address why, how, and under what conditions the marketing of children's bodies permeates diverse levels of society. We need to to uncover not only the political and ideological interests and relations of power at work in such processes but also the actual ways such cultural practices influence how children and adults learn about themselves and their relationship to others.

Innocence can be both a mystifying ideology and a vehicle for commercial profit. In the first instance, *innocence* is a highly charged term and can be deployed through moral panics against pedophiles and sexual perverts. Such a restricted notion of child abuse fails to examine how exploitation operates through the most seemingly benign of cultural spheres such as the beauty pageant. Under such circumstances, the beauty pageant is not only ignored as a serious object of social analysis, it is dismissed as simply a subculture. Innocence in this case protects a particular notion of family values that is class specific and racially coded. Moreover, it offers no language for understanding how the conditions under which children learn in specific sites, such as the beauty pageant, resonate and gain legitimacy through their connection to other cultural sites.

In the second instance, innocence falls prey to the logic of the market and the successful operations of consumerism as children provide the sexualized bait to market goods and advertisements circulate images and representations that tread close to pornography. In this scenario, children's sense of play and social development are transformed through marketing strategies and forms of consumer education that limit their imaginations, identities, and sense of possibility while simultaneously providing through the electronic media a "kind of entertainment that subtly influence[s] the way we see [children], ourselves, and our communities."[51]

Concerned educators, parents, and activists must challenge and counter such representations, ideologies, and social practices as part of a cultural politics that makes issues of pedagogy and power central to its project.[52] This means expanding our understanding of how pedagogy is played out on the bodies of the young children involved in pageants and how this pedagogical practice resonates with what children are taught in other cultural spheres. Essential to such a challenge is the political necessity for educators and other cultural workers to pressure schools and other educational sites to treat popular culture as a serious object of analysis in the curriculum so children and adults can learn how to demystify such images and to become cultural producers capable of creating new forms of representations that honor and critically engage their own traditions and experiences. Educators need to provide students with texts, resources, and performative strategies that allow them to inhabit and experiment with a complex range of subject positions. Developing pedagogical practices and theoretical discourses that address how the operations of power work in sites such as beauty pageants requires teaching students and adults how to organize social movements at the local and national levels to pressure and boycott companies that engage in abusive practices toward children. Underlying this merging of the political and the pedagogical is the overt "political" goal of "enabling people to act more strategically in ways that may change their context for the better"[53] and the "pedagogical" goal of finding ways for diverse groups to work together to transform popular public spheres into educational sites that address social problems through democratic, rather than merely market, considerations.

In short, the socialization of children must be addressed within a larger discourse about citizenship and democracy, one that resists what Theodor Adorno calls the "obscene merger of aesthetics and reality."[54] Adorno advocates the refutation of those ideologies and social practices that attempt to subordinate forms of identity fundamental to public life to an economy of bodies and pleasures that is all surface and spectacle. Such a discourse questions not only the conditions under which children learn, but also the material and institutional relations of power. The integrity of public life is essential for all children to learn, so as to be critical participants in the shaping of their lives and the larger social order.

Democracy is in the throes of a major crisis. Surely, if democracy is to carry us forward into the next century, it will be based on a commitment to improving the lives of children. Such improvements can not emerge from the degrading logic of a market that treats their bodies like a commodity and their futures as a trade-off for capital accumulation. On the contrary, critical educators and other progressives need to create a cultural vision along with strategies of understanding, representation, and transformation informed by "the rhetoric of political, civic, and economic citizenship."[55] The challenge to take up that commitment has never been so urgent.

NOTES

1. Richard Goldstein, "The Killer Inside Me: Shirley Temple Meets the Demon Dad," *Village Voice*, June 24, 1997, p. 48.

2. For an insightful analysis of the myth of innocence, see Marina Warner, *Six Myths of Our Time* (New York: Vintage, 1995); especially chap. 3, "Little Angels, Little Monsters: Keeping Childhood Innocent," pp. 43–62. Of course, the concept of childhood innocence as a historical invention as has been pointed out by a number of theorists. See, for example, Philip Ariès, *Centuries of Childhood* (Harmondsworth: Penguin, 1979); Lloyd deMause, ed., *The Evolution of Childhood* (New York: Psychohistory Press, 1974).

3. Neil Postman, *The Disappearance of Childhood* (New York: Vintage, 1982, 1994).

4. Ibid., chap. 8, "The Disappearing Child," pp. 120–142. The notion that television and popular culture represent the main threat to childhood innocence is central to the conservative call for censorship, limiting sex education in the schools, restricting AIDS education, redefining the home as the most important source of moral education, and the "Gumping" of American history, in which the sixties are often seen as the source of the country's current social ills. The quintessential expression of this position can be found in the speeches, press releases, and writings of former secretary of education and "drug czar" William Bennett. It can also be found in legislation supported by groups such as the Christian Coalition, especially the Parental Rights and Responsibilities Act of 1995. Examples of the conservative position on child abuse, the loss of innocence, and the "poisonous" effects of popular culture abound in the popular press. See, for example, Jeff Stryker, "The Age of Innocence Isn't What It Once Was," *New York Times*, July 13, 1997, p. E3.

5. Senator Kennedy cited in Peter Edelman, "The Worst Thing Bill Clinton Has Done," *Atlantic Monthly*, March 1997, p. 45.

6. Ibid., p. 46.

7. For specific statistics on the state of youth in the United States, see Children's Defense Fund, *The State of America's Children Yearbook, 1997* (Washington, D.C.: Children's Defense Fund, 1997); Ruth Sidel, *Keeping Women and Children Last* (New York: Penguin, 1996).

8. For an analysis of the ideological underpinnings of the right wing's family-values crusade, see Judith Stacey, "The New Family Values Crusaders," *Nation*, July 25/August 1, 1994, pp. 119–122; Judith Stacey, *In the Name of the Family: Rethinking Family Values in the Postmodern Age* (Boston: Beacon Press, 1996).

9. For an analysis of the widespread assault currently being waged against children, see Henry A. Giroux, *Channel Surfing: Race Talk and the Destruction of Today's Youth* (New York: St. Martin's Press, 1997); Mike A. Males, *The Scapegoat Generation: America's War On Adolescents* (Monroe, Maine: Common Courage Press, 1996); Charles R. Acland, *Youth, Murder, Spectacle: The Cultural Politics of "Youth in Crisis"* (Boulder: Westview Press, 1995); Holly Sklar, "Young and Guilty by Stereotype," Z, July/August 1993, pp. 52–61; Deena Weinstein, "Expendable Youth: The Rise and Fall of Youth Culture," in Jonathan S. Epstein, ed., *Adolescents and Their Music* (New York: Garland, 1994), pp. 67–83. See also various articles in Andrew Ross and Tricia Rose, eds., *Microphone Fiends* (New York: Routledge, 1994).

10. For a brilliant analysis of how the image of the sexual predator is used to preclude from public discussion the wide range of social factors at work in causing child abuse, see James R. Kincaid, *Child-Loving: The Erotic Child and Victorian Culture* (New York: Routledge, 1992).

11. For an analysis of the Supreme Court's decision, see Linda Greenhouse, "Likely Repeaters May Stay Confined," *New York Times,* June 24, 1997, p. A19.

12. Cited in Larry Armstrong, "Hey Kid, Buy This," *Business Week,* June 30, 1997, p. 66.

13. The concept of the hollow state comes from Stanley Aronowitz, *The Death and Birth of American Radicalism* (New York: Routledge, 1996).

14. The literature on advertising and the marketing of children's desires is too extensive to cite, but one of the best examples is Stephen Kline, *Out of the Garden: Toys, TV, and Children's Culture in the Age of Marketing* (London: Verso Press, 1993).

15. Richard Goldstein, "The Girl in the Fun Bubble: The Mystery of JonBenet," *Village Voice,* June 10, 1997, p. 41.

16. For a sustained treatment of the current assault on children, especially those who are poor and nonwhite, and live in the cities, see Henry A. Giroux, *Fugitive Cultures* (New York: Routledge, 1996).

17. Annie Gottlieb, "First Person Sexual," *Nation,* June 9, 1997, p. 26.

18. Frank Rich, "Let Me Entertain You," *New York Times,* January 18, 1997, sec. 1, p. 23.

19. Goldstein, "The Girl in the Fun Bubble."

20. Cited in Karen de Witt, "All Dolled Up," *New York Times,* January 12, 1997, sec. 4, p. 4.

21. While the statistics on child beauty pageants vary, a number of sources cite figures similar to the ones I cite here. See, for example, Rich, "Let Me Entertain You"; Ellen Mark, "Pretty Babies," *Vogue,* June 1997, p. 240; Beverly Stoeltje, "The Snake Charmer Queen Ritual Competition, and Signification in American Festival," in Colleen Ballerino, Richard Wilk, and Beverly Stoeltje, eds., *Beauty Queens* (New York: Routledge, 1996), p. 13.

22. Cited in Pat Jordan, "The Curious Childhood of an 11-Year-Old," *Life,* April 1994, p. 38.

23. Mark, "Pretty Babies," p. 240.

24. Linda Caillouet echoes a point made by many academics and journalists across the country: "Pageants have changed over the past 30 years. Grade-schoolers are wearing makeup, modeling swim wear and sashaying down runways. . . . Today's little girls' parents often invest big money in coaches to teach the children the pro-am modeling style and tornado spins. They pay for makeup artists and hair stylists to accompany the children to pageant's. Some of the kids use tanning beds. Seven-year olds have reportedly worn false teeth, false eyelashes, and colored contact lenses." Cited in Linda Caillouet, "Slaying Has Child Pageants on Defensive," *Arkansas Democrat-Gazette,* April 14, 1997, p. 1A.

25. Jordan, "The Curious Childhood of an 11-Year-Old," p. 62.

26. Ibid.

27. Ibid., p. 68.

28. One of the most disturbing examples of this can be found in the *Sixty Minutes* footage used in its analysis of child beauty pageants aired on May 18, 1997. Also see the BBC documentary series *Under the Sun,* which aired "Painted Babies" on January 31, 1996. This was an equally disturbing portrait of child beauty pageants.

29. Michael F. Jacobson and Laurie Ann Mazur, *Marketing Madness* (Boulder: Westview Press, 1995), p. 79.

30. Cited in ad for Debbrah's: Nation's Top Pageant Designers, *Pageant Life* 4, no.3 (winter 1996): 26.

31. Elliot Zaren, "Eyebrows Lift at Child Strutting in Sexy Dresses, Makeup," *Tampa Tribune,* January 14, 1997, p. 4.

32. Cited in Jodi Duckett, "In the Eyes of the Beholder: Child Beauty Pageants Get Mixed Reviews," *Morning Call*, Allentown, PA, April 6, 1997, p. E1.

33. Ibid.

34. Mark, "Pretty Babies," p. 283.

35. Susan Bordo, *Unbearable Weight: Feminism, Western Culture, and the Body* (Berkeley: University of California Press, 1993), p. 162.

36. Ibid., p. 179.

37. Naomi Wolf, *The Beauty Myth* (New York: Anchor Books, 1992).

38. Richard Goldstein, "Nymph Mania: Honoring Innocence in the Breach," *Village Voice*, June 17, 1997, p. 71. This is not to suggest that women and children don't mediate and resist such domination as much as to make clear the determinate relations of power that lie behind the resurrection of the nymphet in the culture.

39. Stoeltje, "The Snake Charmer Queen Ritual Competition," p. 23.

40. Cited in Caillouet, "Slaying Has Child Pageants on Defensive," p. 1A.

41. Cited in Duckett, "In the Eyes of the Beholder," p. E1.

42. See, for example, Susan Faludi, *Backlash: The Undeclared War Against American Women* (New York: Anchor Books, 1991).

43. This paragraph relies heavily on comments by pediatric psychologists cited in Rebecca A. Eder, Ann Digirolamo, and Suzanne Thompson, "Is Winning a Pageant Worth a Lost Childhood?" *St. Louis Post-Dispatch*, February 24, 1997, p. D7B.

44. Marly Harris, "Trophy Kids," *Money*, March 1997, p. 102.

45. For an academic defense of beauty pageants as simply an acting out of community standards, see Michael T. Marsden, "Two Northwestern Ohio Beauty Pageants: A Study in Middle America's Cultural Rituals," in Ray B. Browne and Michael T. Marsden, *The Cultures of Celebration* (Bowling Green, Ohio: Bowling Green State University Press, 1994). Marsden is so intent in focusing on pageants as ritualistic performances that he doesn't notice how ideological his own commentary is when focusing on some of the most sexist aspects of the pageant practices. Hence, for Marsden, bathing-suit competitions simply prove that "beauty can be art." For a more complex analysis, see Robert H. Lavender, "It's Not a Beauty Pageant!' Hybrid Ideology in Minnesota Community Queen Pageants," in Ballerino et al., *Beauty Queens*, pp. 31–46.

46. Stoeltje, "The Snake Charmer Queen Ritual Competition, and Signification in American Festival," p. 13.

47. For a brilliant analysis of the different critical approaches to beauty and the politics of appearance that feminists have taken since the appearance of the first Miss America pageant in 1968, see Annette Corrigan, "Fashion, Beauty and Feminism," *Meanjin* 51, no.1 (1992). What is so interesting about this piece is that nothing is said about child beauty pageants. This is especially relevant since many of the conceptual approaches dealing with the politics of appearance simply don't apply to six-year-olds. For instance, the notion that beauty can be appropriated as an act of resistance and turned against the dominant culture seems a bit far-fetched when talking about children who can barely read.

48. One exception can be found in the collection of essays in Ballerino et al., *Beauty Queens*.

49. While I haven't developed in this paper the implications such depictions have for women, many feminists have provided some excellent analysis. See especially Bordo, *Unbearable Weight*. For a shameful defense of thinness as an aesthetic in the fashion industry, see Rebecca Johnson, "The Body," *Vogue*, September 1997, pp. 653–658. Johnson goes a long way to legitimate some of the most misogynist aspects of the beauty industry but

really reaches into the bottom of the barrel in asserting that resentment is the primary reason that many women criticize the image of waiflike models permeating the media. Declaring that thinness is only an aesthetic and not a morality, Johnson seems to forget that within the dominant invocation of thinness as a standard of beauty there is the suggestion that overweight women are slovenly, older women are ugly, and nonwhite women are not as beautiful as the ever-present blond-hair waif models who populate the media. Sadly, the notion that thinness generates a politically charged discourse in the media teaching young kids that thinness is a principal measure of a woman's worth also seems to have been lost on Ms. Johnson.

50. The classic on this issue is Mary Pipher, *Reviving Ophelia: Saving the Selves of Adolescent Girls* (New York: Ballantine Books, 1994). See also Nicole Peradotto, "Little Women: A New Generation of Girls Growing Up Before Their Time," *Buffalo News*, January 26, 1997.

51. Colleen Ballerino Cohen, Richard Wilk, and Beverly Stoeltje, introduction to Ballerino et al., *Beauty Queens*, p. 10.

52. For a brilliant analysis of how young girls are represented in popular culture and what is learned by them, see Valerie Walkerdine, *Daddy's Girl* (Cambridge: Harvard University Press, 1997).

53. Lawrence Grossberg, "Toward a Genealogy of the State of Cultural Studies," in Cary Nelson and Dilip Parameshwar Gaonkar, eds. *Disciplinarity and Dissent in Cultural Studies* (New York: Routledge, 1996), p. 143.

54. Theodor Adorno cited in Geoffrey Hartman, "Public Memory and Its Discontents," *Raritan* 8, no.4 (spring 1994): 27.

55. Stanley Aronowitz, "A Different Perspective on Inequality," in Henry A. Giroux and Patrick Shannon, eds., *Education and Cultural Studies: Toward a Performative Practice* (New York: Routledge, 1998), p. 193.

Chapter Sixteen

A Credit to Her Mother

Annette Kuhn

My family photograph collection includes two copies of the same studio portrait of myself at four months of age. The baby is naked, lying tummy-down on a blanket, facing camera but looking upwards to a point somewhere above camera level. This, as far as I know, is the earliest photograph taken of me; and one of my copies of it accordingly features on the very first page of the photograph album I began putting together when I was eight, in an effort to make both a family and a life history for myself. The other copy, sent to me by my mother long after I had left home, grown up, and broken contact with her, bears a lengthy inscription on the reverse:

> Thought perhaps you might like this. You were a beautiful baby from the minute you were born. I loved you and you were always immaculate and well cared for. Your hair was very dark and there is a great resemblance to Marion and Samantha. Written in pencil, you may want to erase.

This inscription, pointing up a likeness between my infant self and my two nieces, the only daughters of my two much older half-brothers, was obviously written at the time the picture was sent to an adult and estranged daughter. The copy of the picture which carries this message—my mother's copy—has been trimmed, so that the area of the image which had been background and not baby is cut away.

Two copies of the 'same' photograph, then: but embodying very different uses and meanings at different moments for the various people with investments in it: the parents of the newly born baby, the child herself as a little girl, the mother of the adult daughter, the daughter as an adult. In itself, the image carries meanings outside these immediate contexts, too, revealing a great deal about how infancy is understood in a particular social and cultural situation.

The baby's nakedness, suggesting newness, naturalness, innocence, is set within particular conventions of photographic portraiture, which in turn mimic high art conventions—notably, but not exclusively, those of the (adult, female) nude—suggesting that this is no mere snapshooter's effort, but a professional piece of work. In the process babyhood in general, a particular baby, and a specific image are made special, lifted out of the ordinary, the everyday. My photograph is in these respects no different from the thousands, the millions even, like it: it speaks volumes about the cultural meanings of infancy, the desires our culture invests in the figure of the newborn child. But while such meanings are certainly present in the specific contexts in which images like this are produced and used, every image is special, too: gesturing towards particular pasts, towards memories experienced as personal, it assumes inflections that are all its own. My photograph, then, is the same, and yet it is different.

On the surface, the family photograph functions primarily as a record: it stands as visible evidence that this family exists, that its members have gone through the passages conventionally produced in the family album as properly and necessarily familial. My photograph thus records the fact that a particular child was born and survived. But recording is the very least of it. Why should a moment be recorded, if not for its evanescence? The photograph's seizing of a moment always, even in that very moment, assumes loss. The record looks towards a future time when things will be different, anticipates a need to remember what will soon be past.

Even for outsiders, family photographs often have a poignant quality, perhaps because they speak all too unerringly of the insufficiency, the hopelessness, of the desire they embody. Time has passed, time will pass. The image of the infant, innocent in its nakedness, naked as the day it was born, cannot so much fix that moment of innocence as testify to the inevitability of its slipping away, of a slippage from grace. Hence the sadness, the sense of loss and longing, I read in my mother's words. 'You were beautiful', she says; beautiful, pristinely, 'from the minute you were born'. Her choice of the word 'immaculate' here is telling: I was, she recalls, spotless, unsullied, free from sin or stain; precisely in a state of Edenic innocence.

Perhaps the mother's recollection speaks a degree of identification with the baby—a desire that she, the mother, might partake of the newborn's innocence; that in giving birth she too will have been reborn, granted the gift not just of innocence but of a fresh start. More specifically, the 'immaculate' may be read back to the baby's very conception; as an expression of my mother's wish (which might well have been retrospective—written into the past constructed by her inscription, that is) to have been my only begetter, for me to have been hers alone. The reference to my nieces, my brothers' daughters (one of whom I have never met)—in effect negating the role in my conception of the man I knew as my father, who was not the father of my brothers—would certainly support this reading.

It seems, then, that the mother's love for her baby, not least in its retrospective assertion, is far from unambivalent. 'I loved you', she tells the grownup daughter who has left her. Loved me once, that is, in my immaculate, unspoiled state. Which suggests that this love had a hard time, and very likely failed, to outlive the loss of innocence, to survive the baby's growing older and the mother's learning the hard lesson that life carries on much as before, except that now there is another mouth—and one that talks back, into the bargain—to feed.

In readings which shift back and forth across contexts—from the cultural to the familial to the individual to a specific constellation of family relations—the notion constantly reemerges, in different shapes and forms, of infancy as spot-lessness, innocence; and of the figure, the image, of the newly born child as embodying at once a desire for return to innocence and a knowledge of the absolute impossibility of such a return.

It is also clear, though, that the naked and 'immaculate' body of the newborn Annette figured for my mother as *tabula rasa*, an empty slate, on which her own desires could be written—in an endeavour, perhaps, to repair lacks of her own. Born fourth in a family of seven, the fourth daughter of a man who desperately wanted a son, she felt she had never been wanted, loved, or cared for enough, certainly by her father (in her account a violent man and a poor provider) who despite—or perhaps because of—his absence at war figured overwhelmingly in her childhood memories. (In a book-length memoir written when she was in her sixties, my mother recalls her father's first return home on leave from the war:

> [I]t was in 1915, and our Dad seemed to have been away for ever. But one day during the Summer holidays when we were playing on Moor Mead, a girl came running up to us and said, 'I think your dad's come home. A soldier went in your house'. Without waiting to hear the last of what she was saying, I was on my way home, my bare feet hardly touching the warm pavement. . . . There in the kitchen was my dad, sitting in an armchair near the fireplace. I wanted to climb all over him, but before I could reach him, he said in a very stern voice, 'Where's your shoes? Put them on at once! . . .'.)

It seems clear to me today that my mother's love for the 'immaculate' baby Annette was marked very much by a quest to love the abandoned and unloved child she felt she had been: in other words, that this maternal love involved a work of identification; identification then subjected to threat through that erosion of the ideal that comes with the inevitable loss of the innocence attaching to the figure of the baby. My mother's inscription on, and indeed within, the photo-graph, made when her baby had grown up and to all intents and purposes had decisively separated herself, speaks with some eloquence of these investments, their failure, her disappointment.

In the Eden myth, the moment of the fall from primal innocence is marked by Adam and Eve's covering their nakedness; and, significantly, in the family album nakedness is admissable only in photographs of babies and very young children. My mother tells me that not only was I beautiful in my natural state, from the minute I was born; I was always well cared for, too—well cared for, of course, by her: well turned out, in another favourite phrase of hers. 'Immaculate' here then partakes not only of the natural but also of the cultural: the newborn's primal innocence is overdetermined by—is perhaps even subsumed to—the mother's labour of care for her child.

When my mother says I was well cared for, I know quite well that she is referring as much, if not more, to a public presentation of a 'well turned out' child ('a credit to her mother', she would often say of Marion, the niece whom she maintains I resembled) as to any less outwardly apparent caring or 'maternal love' on her part. Or rather, perhaps, that for her the two things are inseparable: one loves one's baby, of course; and the evidence and the guarantee of that love lie in the labour of care evident in the child's appearance. But there is more to this than mere display. The baby's body is here quite literally a blank canvas, screen of the mother's desire—desire to make good the insufficiencies of her own childhood, desire to transcend these lacks by caring for her deprived self through a love for her baby that takes very particular cultural forms.

In my mother's account, her childhood was deprived materially as well as emotionally, and for her the two types of lack were inseparably intertwined. In this context, loving becomes synonymous with having—or rather with being given—enough to eat and decent clothes to wear (the detail of the unshod feet in her memory of her father's homecoming is, I think, significant). This perhaps explains the enormous investment, in all senses of the word, in my appearance: not just in my clothes, but in my hair, which for special occasions, and with huge effort on her part and much discomfort on mine, my mother would tie in rags to make the ringlets she herself had worn, or would have wanted, as a little girl. As I grew older, she took an interest in my body language as well, trying to get me to stand straight and not slouch: 'Back up, tummy in!' For if I failed to be 'well turned out', that failure would surely be hers, and she would be exposed as a bad person: not just an unloving mother, but—worse, perhaps—an unloved and unlovable little girl.

I am my mother's only daughter, and her youngest child, always to my irritation referred to as her 'baby'. My childhood was none the less punctuated by many births in the family, of the children of my two brothers and of numerous extraordinarily fecund cousins: births of babies and talk about babies were, it seemed, endless. Among the favourite topics of conversation, especially among girls and women in the family, was the sex of a forthcoming baby: will it be a boy or a girl? and which would be preferable? There was a solid, perhaps an overwhelming, body of opinion that girl babies were on the whole the better deal, because 'you can dress a little girl up'.

On this conscious level, at least, a mother's attention to her baby's appearance has everything to do with gender: her love for a girl infant will be legitimately expressed in ways different from her love of a baby boy. Significantly, my mother's description of my niece Marion as 'a credit to her mother' was never applied to Marion's two younger brothers.

In the summer before my fourth birthday, a photograph was taken (possibly by my father) of my mother and me on the front lawn of our ground-floor flat in Chiswick, West London. It is the only picture I have of myself as a small child with my mother. In this one, I am seated on my mother's knee as she grips me firmly in the crook of her left arm and rests her right hand across my ankles. We are both looking at camera; and I am clutching a doll and wearing a tartan dress with puffed sleeves and matching underpants, and a bow in my hair. On the back of this photograph my mother has written: ' . . . Chiswick. She was nearly 4 years old. Dress and knicks by me.' Again the picture has been trimmed, and part of the inscription cut away as a consequence.

This picture disturbs me somewhat: a feeling, I think, which has a lot to do with my mother's uncharacteristic presence in the image. On the surface, it seems a commonplace and happy enough example of family photography. But beneath the sunny facade lurk shadows: the mother-father-daughter triad the picture (assuming it was made by my father) points to was not in fact a 'real' family. The child being held so tightly was an intrusion. If I put myself in the position of my mother as she was at the time this photo was taken, somewhat younger than I am now, all sorts of ambivalences surface.

She holds on firmly to this little girl who is hers, whom she perhaps desires to be hers alone. But children, as she would often remind me, tie you down. When I came along, unintended, her younger son was thirteen and she thought she was finished with childrearing. Life had not been easy with the boys and their father, and now in her late thirties she was hoping, at last, for a good time. If she did find a bit of fun with my father, though, she had been thrown back to square one by its consequences: me. Trapped in a situation she had not bargained for, my mother was tied for the foreseeable future to a child she had neither planned nor wanted to have, and (in days when the concept of the single-parent family had yet to be invented) to a man she would grow to despise.

But if the child was a mistake, she was not entirely a misfortune: she was a beautiful baby from the minute she was born, her mother's only daughter, who would always be her baby. The care and pride that have been lavished on the little girl's appearance are visible in this picture, which is readable—and, I would contend, was certainly read by my mother—as evidence, proof of that care. This is underlined in the statement, seemingly addressed to no one in particular, that the little girl's outfit was of her, the mother's, own making.

Children are a costly commodity: their upbringing calls for hard cash, as well as a good deal of labour of various kinds. This, though (we are told), ought to be a labour of love, entered into freely and without reservation. Counting the cost is not appropriate. Sure enough, the family as it is represented in family albums is characteristically produced as innocent of such material considerations, above price: to this extent, the family album constructs the world of the family as a utopia. And yet I feel sure that my mother, whose own childhood had been so marked by poverty, must have known, or even calculated, the exact cost—to herself, at least—of having and keeping me. Perhaps in my earliest years her economic and her emotional investments measured up to each other, so that her identifications—of her baby with the unloved little girl in herself—could proceed unchecked. In these honeymoon years, being the mother of a well turned out baby must have provided enormous pleasure and emotional reward.

Keeping up appearances could not have been easy, though. From my earliest years, perhaps right from my infancy, both my parents worked outside the home. When I was very small, they shared responsibility for cleaning the public areas of the block of flats where we lived and of which my father was caretaker. They also worked together in my father's photography business, and both had jobs as bus conductors. While I do not know whether these jobs were simultaneous or consecutive, nor indeed whether there were any periods when my mother was actually at home full-time, it seems clear that a lot of hard work was being done to earn the means to keep the household going; and that there would have been little by way of leisure time for my mother to pursue dressmaking as a hobby. Since, however, clothes were still 'on the ration', in common with many other items during the years of postwar austerity, she would simply have had to find the time to 'make do and mend'. In this climate, making clothes for herself and her baby was probably a necessity more than a hobby.

Whatever the case, though, keeping the baby 'immaculate and well cared for', while a source of pride and pleasure, must still have cost a good deal of effort. Hence the ambivalent feelings of a mother whose life and circumstances had been, indeed remained, far from easy towards a baby born into a world which held out the promise of new opportunities for the children of ordinary working people; a baby, moreover, who seemed to be the object of all the love and attention she herself had been denied; a baby, none the less, who would one day grow into a woman in a society still unkind to those of her sex.

Thus may a mother's investments in her baby daughter, inflected by particular circumstances of time, place, culture and class, meld the social with the psychic. This mother's ambivalent identification with her baby daughter already contains the seeds of overidentification, of difficulties of separation. If a daughter figures for her mother as the abandoned, unloved, child that she, the mother, once was, and in some ways remains, how can mother and daughter disengage themselves from these identifications without harm, without forfeiture of love? How can mother and daughter learn to acknowledge that they are separate people, to respect their differences from each other?

Any resolution, it seems, must come with very great difficulty: there will inevitably come a moment when it is no longer possible for the mother to sustain the fantasy of her daughter as *tabula rasa*, of the daughter's body as screen of her own fantasies of plenitude. The child will one day start answering back, refusing the mother's 'gifts', along with the vision of the perfect, immaculate, well turned out little girl. At this point, matters of appearance, including clothes, may well cease to be a source of pleasure for the mother, and even become a site of struggle between mother and daughter.

'You can dress a little girl up' is one of those statements, certainly in the context in which I quote it here, whose truth is assumed to be perfectly self-evident. It points to one of the obvious and most important pluses of having (and not, it should be noted, of being) a baby girl. As a piece of conventional wisdom, it condenses a range of commonplace and generally unremarked cultural associations between dress and gender. But it also asserts a good deal more than that, say, there exist distinct forms and styles of dress which are very much tied to gender. It implies as well that the ways in which we actually relate to clothes and to matters of appearance in general are a ground, as much as an outcome, of sexual difference.

If, for infants themselves, sexual difference is hardly yet an issue, it certainly figures very prominently, and often in unconscious and contradictory ways, in adults' attachments to babies and very young children. 'Dressing a little girl up' is held to be an occasion of rightful and proper pleasure, and reward, for its mother; the unspoken corollary perhaps being that while a boy will obviously have to be clothed, this is more of a functional necessity, and that to dress him up in a way that goes beyond tidiness or smartness might be inappropriate. In this particular social, historical and cultural context, at least, the investments in a mother's dressing a boy baby and dressing up a girl baby are assumed to be quite distinct. In this context it may well be inadmissible for a mother to claim, by word or deed, any pleasure in dressing a little boy up, as opposed to merely dressing him. For this in effect would be a confession that she was disturbing the natural and proper order of gender difference: making a cissy of him.

But even such a forceful prohibition as this cannot account for the *positive* pleasure a mother may take in 'dressing up' her little girl. For the mother, the labour of attending to the appearance of a girl baby is surely of a very particular kind: it is caught up in that series of investments and identifications at play in general in her care of her little daughter. Dressing up a baby girl is a socially sanctioned opportunity for a woman, in caring for the little girl in herself, to love herself; while at the same time providing her with the opportunity to display, for the public gaze, the praiseworthy qualities of an adult who puts the needs of others above her own: a good mother, in other words, and therefore a good woman.

In a number of ways, therefore, having a baby girl she can dress up might be intensely rewarding for a mother. However, the distinctions between dressing and dressing up on the one hand and between having and being a baby girl on the other signal areas of potential contradiction, and are thus perhaps worthy of further exploration. Dressing up as opposed to mere dressing implies, as has been suggested, a more than purely functional attitude towards clothes: it points to the element of display, of performance, inherent in certain relations to dress. Clothes are what you put on and take off, and consequently various identities may—sometimes quite consciously—be created across the surface of dress. This element of performance holds within it the potential of prising apart the gender/dress association, and this in turn can disturb the order of gender difference naturalized in certain clothing styles.

The naturalized order of gender difference rests on more than just the forms and styles of dress, on differences as it were in the *content* of clothing: it is a question of forms of relation to personal appearance more generally, to the entire realm of bodily adornment. Dressing up—like its cognate activities *making* up and *doing* one's hair—suggests a relation of fabrication, construction, production. Herein lies an interesting paradox: dressing up a baby is possible, indeed socially acceptable, provided—and because—the baby is a girl; while (less consciously, perhaps) dressing up will also actually produce any baby, male or female, as feminine. As long as one baby in its clothes could look much like any other, outwardly visible marks of gender (the colour coding of baby clothes, for example) acquire a certain importance. In this context, while dressing up is part of the production of gender, it also gestures towards the very artifice of that production.

A mother's attention to the clothing and general appearance of a baby girl, then, is part of the social, cultural, and undoubtedly also the psychical, construction of gender; specifically, of course, of femininity. It fabricates something we are supposed to believe is natural, already there; and so reminds us that femininity is not in fact a given, but a product of labour. But in the specific instance of a mother's dressing up a baby girl, the labour involved is also imbued with particular investments of desire, fantasy and identification; with the body of the baby figuring as pretext for what will be experienced as an enjoyable creativity. In this sense, the baby girl becomes its mother's muse, its body her canvas, the dressed-up little girl her mother's very own work of art: to be looked at, admired, photographed, and hailed as a credit to her mother.

The often arduous and time-consuming work of producing a well turned out baby girl then becomes an end in itself, its results apparent, its use value palpable. This is visible and unalienated labour, whose product bears, for all the world to see, the signature of its maker: indeed, the most satisfying sort of work. The end product becomes identified with, reflects back on, the worker herself, the mother, just as it constitutes the baby as a little girl. As, through this labour, femininity is produced in and through costume, through masquerade, so a mother's investment accrues to her own credit. Clothes, as they make the little girl, also make the grown woman.

The mother's fantasy of identification (in which she cares for her little daughter as she would be cared for herself, and produces the baby in herself as a beautiful little girl worthy and deserving of love) rests upon a degree of projection, the baby its object, its screen. In the processes of projection and identification, the baby is fantasized as part of the mother—who can then simultaneously have, and be, the baby girl. In both senses, the baby becomes her mother's possession, and the play with femininity involved in dressing her up part of the mother's own involvement with femininity and its paradoxes, its ambiguities and its masquerades.

In this respect, the mother's pleasure in dressing up her baby girl may not be entirely unalloyed. Aside from the possibility that her care for the child could be an attempt to repair, to compensate for, deprivations in her own childhood—in its very nature a highly problematic project—the mother must on some level also be aware that the femininity she is calling forth in the masquerade of the dressed-up little girl is not without its complications and contradictions in the world beyond the mother-baby dyad.

Related to this must be the virtual inevitability of the mother's fantasy of oneness with her baby girl coming unravelled: for as the child grows older the fantasy of the baby as the screen of its mother's desire will become increasingly difficult to sustain. It is here that the distinction between having a baby girl and being a girl child comes into play. What happens when the child herself intervenes in the dressing up process, perhaps to assert her own wishes about her appearance? How, in such a circumstance, can a mother protect her investment?

How can the child continue to be a credit to her mother? And what sort of story might the little girl herself have to tell about all this?

One of the manifestations of my own mother's involvement with her daughter's appearance was a passion for fancy dress. My photograph collection bears witness to the fact that, until I was around eight or nine years old, I took part in numerous fancy dress competitions. This was entirely my mother's idea: she entered me in the contests, made the costumes, and exhorted me to display them to best advantage. A frequently expressed conviction of hers had it that costumes she called 'original' (which for her meant conceptual as opposed to mimetic) stood the greatest chance of winning; and that if an 'original' costume did fail to net a prize, it was still far superior as fancy dress to the obvious, and perhaps more acceptable, sorts of costumes little girls might be dressed in for these occasions—nursery rhyme characters, fairies, princesses, brides and suchlike. While I cannot in truth say I would have preferred any of the more conventionally little girlish costumes, in what I did wear I nevertheless did feel exhibited, exploited, embarrassed. Even if I won, there was little pleasure in competing in this way—in being put on display, scrutinized, weighed up, given points, judged. As I grew older, I grew less willing and no doubt decreasingly compliant.

A photograph of me wearing the costume for what I believe to be the last fancy dress competition I entered shows me, aged about nine, wearing a long shift to which are attached empty cigarette packets, drinks cartons, ice-cream containers, drinking straws, matchboxes; with a head-dress comprised of one waxed Kia-Ora orange juice carton flanked by a pair of ice-cream tubs. On my right arm rests a placard explaining the costume—'Cinema Litter'; and on my left a jigsaw puzzle, presumably my prize. It is difficult to put a precise date to this photograph, partly because, like the others, it has been trimmed down: the background is consequently minimal, offering no clues as to location; and whatever had been written on the back of the picture has been almost completely cut away.

(I find myself extraordinarily, perhaps excessively, troubled by this habit of my mother's of cutting photographs down. The historian in me objects to the tampering with evidence; the critic to the lack of respect for image composition. But the strength of the feeling really has to do with the fact that these acts of my mother's seem to me to be crude gestures of power, at once both creating the evidence that fits in with her version of events and destroying what does not; and also negating the skills and aesthetic choices of the photographer, usually my father. This particular photograph certainly looks like one of my father's efforts: if so, it must be among the last pictures of me he made, for by this time he had more or less given up what was in any case by now no more than a hobby.)

In the context of my own memories, I see this photograph, which I find very painful to look at, as a 'cusp' image, marking a transition. It must have been made around the time of our move away from my first home in Chiswick to live in the house of my recently deceased Granny, my mother's mother. This move was highly traumatic for me, in large part (as I now construe it) because although they remained together, leaving Chiswick marked some decisive rift between my parents.

Our new home was very much my mother's territory: it had been lived in not only by her mother, but before that by one of her brothers. Over the following few years she saw to it that both her sons moved with their families into other houses on the same street. In all this, I believe my father must have felt increasingly marginalized: illness—he suffered from bronchitis which later became emphysema—by now dominated his life and isolated him from those closest to him. This, along with his abandonment of the hobby of photography, which had been a source of such pride and pleasure, must surely be symptomatic. I, too, felt displaced: in my new school, corporal punishment—completely alien and shocking to me—was practised; I was mocked by the other children for my 'posh' accent; I even caught head lice and had to have my plaits chopped off. Desperately unhappy, I started putting on weight.

It was around this time, too, that I started 'answering back', embarking on a lengthy and bitter struggle with my mother over issues of separation—issues which would never finally be resolved. I recall feeling unhappy about being put into this particular costume and into the fancy dress competition, and had doubtless let my objections be known in the various overt and covert ways of the uncompliant child—whining, sulks, refusal to smile and a general 'slouching on parade'. If the photograph itself reveals nothing of all this, neither, though, does it seem to me to present an entirely untroubled surface.

The girl looks neglected and slightly scruffy, a far cry from the 'immaculate' three-year-old. Little effort seems to have been put into her hair, badly cut (could this have been soon after the head lice episode?) and all over the place; her smile seems slightly doubtful; her eyes are closed. The costume is even more illuminating. In itself, it is certainly a clever idea: but more remarkable is the fact that the child wearing it is being displayed as a figure for the detritus, the discarded by-products, of a pursuit whose pleasures hold a distinctly erotic appeal. The implications scarcely need spelling out: it is fortunate, perhaps, that this was to be the last of my fancy dress costumes.

My mother's passion for fancy dress can be regarded in certain respects as an extension of her earlier investment in 'dressing up' her infant daughter: though there is undoubtedly more to it than that. As a cultural form, fancy dress gestures with some urgency towards the performance aspect of clothes. Indeed, it renders this aspects entirely overt: for the whole point of fancy dress is that the masquerade is there, self-evident, on the surface. Fancy dress partakes of the carnivalesque, a turning upside-down of the everyday order of hierarchies of class, status, gender, ethnicity. A bus conductor's daughter can be queen for an hour—or even, indeed, king, for girls can be boys and boys girls, and either can be neither. A fracturing of the clothes/identity link is thus sanctioned—at once permitted and contained, that is—by the cultural conventions of fancy dress.

Also, and relatedly, there is clearly a fantasy component to fancy dress: indeed, the word 'fancy' itself derives from a contraction of 'fantasy'. But whose fantasy? In the case of 'Cinema Litter', as of the other fancy dress costumes my mother made for me, certainly not the little girl's, certainly not the daughter's. Costume which presents itself so unequivocally as performance or masquerade will often—and certainly in the case of 'Cinema Litter'—beg for a symptomatic reading. But while an interpretation of 'Cinema Litter' reveals meanings tied specifically to a particular costume and context, taken together with all the other fancy dress costumes my mother made for me (and certainly if it is accepted that one of the issues at stake here is a mother's identification with her daughter) this can be seen as expressive also of fantasies of a rather different nature: the desire of a working woman, no longer young, to be noticed—seen, applauded, rewarded—as someone special, different from the rest, out of the ordinary, precisely 'an original'. The daughter in fancy dress, attracting attention, winning prizes even, becomes a vehicle for the mother's desire to transcend the limitations, dissatisfactions and disappointments of her own daily life.

But given the 'conceptual' and/or the androgynous quality of the costumes she favoured, it seems to me that at this point my mother's fantasy had little to do with femininity as a site of redemption, and much to do with a wish to overcome the limitations femininity imposes. To this extent, the unconscious aspect of the fancy dress project either runs somewhat counter to the earlier project of producing a 'well turned out' little girl, or underscores the contradictions and ambivalences around femininity that were already, perhaps, lurking in the latter.

While all this might bespeak resistance, or signal the (limited?) liberatory potential of certain cultural practices for individuals and social groups who lack power in the public world, it should not be forgotten whose fantasy it was that drove these particular practices of dressing up and the fancy dress. For the little Annette, her mother *was* all-powerful; and it seems never to have occurred to her, the mother, that her daughter could possibly harbour genuine feelings or wishes or hopes or ambitions that in any way diverged from her own, the mother's.

What, then, of the daughter's story: the daughter put on display, exhibited to the public gaze in a quest for rewards from strangers for costumes, for outward appearances, that by nature and intent cloak, occlude and subvert—as well as create—identities? What if the daughter was not entirely comfortable with such identities, with being the site of another's investments, the vehicle of another's fantasies? What of the daughter who refused to smile prettily at the judges, refused to want to be picked out from all the others as a winner, and yet who found utterly unbearable the humiliation of losing? What of her? That little girl got fat, looked terrible in everything she wore, and answered back. What a disappointment to her mother.

Part III

Child's Play

Chapter Seventeen

Children's Desires/Mothers Dilemmas
The Social Contexts of Consumption

Ellen Seiter

Goods are for mobilizing other people.
—Mary Douglas

Toys, commercials, and animated programs are the lingua franca of young children at babysitters' and grandmothers' houses, day-care centers, and preschools across the United States. Most children leave home long before they enter the public school system, to spend their day away from parents and with other children their own age. At the snack table they admire one another's T-shirts and lunchboxes emblazoned with film and television characters. At show-and-tell or "sharing" time they proudly present the Ninja Turtles, Barbies, Batmen, and My Little Ponies purchased at Toys "R" Us and given them at birthday parties. Most children know the same commercials, television programs, movies, and music. By wearing their media preferences on their sleeves and carrying their most prized possessions everywhere they go, children make visible their identifications with those more ephemeral objects of consumer culture—namely, films, videos, and television programs.

Consumer culture provides children with a shared repository of images, characters, plots, and themes: it provides the basis for small talk and play, and it does this on a national, even global scale. Outside the house, children can bank on finding that nearly every other child they meet will know some of the same things—and probably *have* many of the same things—that they do. Thus very young children are now sufficiently immersed in a consumer culture to be able to strike up a conversation with one another about a character imprinted on a T-shirt or a toy in hand, to spot one of their kind—a fan of My Little Ponies of Ninja Turtles—across the aisles of Safeway or Toys "R" Us. Mass-market commodities are woven into the social fabric of children's lives: they are seen on sleepovers, at show-and-tell in school, on the block or in the apartment building, on the T-shirt. Young children's consumption holds an ambiguous position between domestic space and public space. Young children are only in the process of learning the distinctions between public and private and the activities appropriate to each. In a sense, this is why their consumption activities are so interesting compared with the more restrained and compartmentalized behaviors of adults.

Within the family, children's taste for certain television shows and certain toys can set them apart from their elders. Sometimes young children feel their knowledge and mastery of consumer culture to be a kind of power: something they know, but of which adults are ridiculously ignorant. Young children cannot make purchases or watch television without adult assistance, however, so parents—usually mothers—are implicated in their consumption and often disapprove of their desires. Thus the battle lines between parents and children over toys and media are drawn when the child is very young. Many mothers, and nearly all middle-class intellectuals, view popular toys and children's television as an alien culture with which they are uncomfortable to varying degrees. Adults often perceive TV and toys as dumb and sexist, or depraved and violent. Many parents find the television shows hard to watch, the commercials offensive, and the toys kitschy. Among the upper middle class the conflict between parents and children over toys and television is not based on affordability but on ideological and aesthetic objections. Upper middleclass parents want their children to like things that are "better to like";[1] they struggle to teach them the tastes for classic toys, the aesthetics of natural materials, and the interest in self-improving "educational" materials favored by their class—and to spurn children's consumer culture as mass, TV based, commercial, and plastic.

Mothers may object to children's consumer culture, but they usually give in to it as well, largely because of the usefulness of television programs and toys as convenience goods for caretakers of children. While giving in, adults often harbor profound doubts about the effects of children's consumer culture today and worry that their own children are learning from the mass media an ethic of greed and a proclivity for hedonism.

I believe it is a mistake to judge children's desires for toys and television programs exclusively in terms of greed and individual hedonism. Children's desires are not depraved. In wanting to have toys and see television programs, children are also expressing a desire for a shared culture with their schoolmates and friends and a strong imagination of community. Moreover, observing children's use of consumer goods and popular media can remind adults of the importance of material culture in their own lives. Adults as well as children invest intense feeling in objects and attribute a wealth of personal and idiosyncratic meanings in mass-produced goods.

It is true that young children do not originate any of the symbols of this subculture; rather, a group of professional adults designs toys and TV shows for children that—when their market research tells them it will be appealing to children—deliberately violate the norms and aesthetics of middle-class culture. Market researchers seek children on whom to test their ideas on colors, cuteness, humor, and heroism, but children participate passively in the design process.

Girls may love ponies, but they did not make them a cultural symbol on their own. Toys are made in certain ways using certain materials dictated by the availability of cheap labor, usually in China. Similarly, children's television shows are appropriated into young children's culture on a large scale, but adult scriptwriters devise the stories. What children get is limited by the professional ideologies of advertising and entertainment industry workers, the capabilities of industrial production and design of children's goods and media, and the influence of manufacturers and television producers on governmental regulation and broadcasting policy.

It is a mistake, however, to see marketers as evil brainwashers and children as naive innocents, as they are so often depicted in journalists' accounts of the toy industry. The toy and television industries' defense against their critics is that children are the ones who make or break the toys and television programs offered to them, that they vote with their remote controls and their dollars. This belief must be treated as more than cynical apologism. Children's desire for toys and media is more than the direct fulfillment of the designs of manufacturers and marketers, however attractive this notion may be in its simplicity. The industry's characterization of the children's audience as fickle and discriminating must be taken seriously. We know that children make meanings out of toys that are unanticipated by—perhaps indecipherable to—their adult designers, who are often baffled by the success of toys like Teenage Mutant Ninja Turtles. Children are creative in their appropriation of consumer goods and media, and the meanings they make with these materials are not necessarily and not completely in line with a materialist ethos. Children create their own meanings from the stories and symbols of consumer culture.

By emphasizing the creative processes of consumption, I am also suggesting that a more useful approach to toys and children's television programs is to insist that they *are* culture. As the British anthropologist Daniel Miller argues:

> Mass goods represent culture, not because they are merely there as the environment in which we operate, but because they are an integral part of that process of objectification by which we create ourselves as an industrial society: our identities, our social affiliations, our lived everyday practices. The authenticity of artifacts as culture derives not from their relationship to some historical style or manufacturing process—in other words, there is no truth or falsity immanent in them—but rather from their active participation in a process of social self-creation in which they are directly constitutive of our understanding of ourselves and others.[2]

As cultural objects, toys and children's television deserve much more careful analysis and attention than they are usually granted. They deserve to be studied as complex, hybrid manifestations of adult culture, which are engaged with in various and contradictory ways by different children under different circumstances. To study children's toys in this way demands the suspension of adult judgment for a time. I believe that we need a break from the blanket condemnation of children's consumer culture in order to understand it; we need to identify clearly the resemblances as well as the differences between children's and adults' culture; and we need to clarify the elitist aspects of many critical disparagements of children's mass culture.

Toys and children's television programs are cultural products that mimic adult culture by imitating popular entertainment genres and borrowing from them characters, plots, locales, and costumes. Action-adventure stories, science fiction, musicals, soap operas, and melodramas contribute a store of themes and symbols to children's television. In some cases, children's toys and television characters copy themes of the adult culture but present them in exaggerated versions unacceptable to adults. Gender roles are a notorious example of this. Female characters are marked by exaggerated aesthetic codes: high-pitched voices, pastel colors, frills, endless quantities of hair, and an innate capacity for sympathy. Male characters appear as superheroes with enormous muscles, deep voices, and an earnest and unrelenting capacity for action and bravery. Children's commercial television is also what we may call utopian, universally appealing to children in its subversion of parental values of discipline, seriousness, intellectual achievement, respect for authority, and complexity by celebrating rebellion, disruption, simplicity, freedom, and energy.

Attention to the utopian aspects of popular culture—a type of analysis originated by the Marxist philosopher Ernst Bloch—has been advocated by literary theorist Fredric Jameson as a useful antidote to manipulation theories of the mass media and the tendency to see television as nothing but false consciousness. Film critic Richard Dyer has also identified an element of utopianism in a wide variety of entertainment forms from musicals to comedy to television news: "the image of 'something better' to escape into, or something we want deeply that our day-to-day lives don't provide. Alternatives, hopes, wishes—these are the stuff of utopia, the sense that things could be better, that something other than what is can be imagined and may be realized."[3] In this tradition, certain aspects of mass culture are seen to relate to "specific inadequacies in society": abundance replaces scarcity and the unequal distribution of wealth; boundless energy replaces exhaustion. Dreariness is countered by intensity—"the capacity of entertainment to present either complex or unpleasant feelings in a way that makes them seem uncomplicated, direct and vivid, not 'qualified' or 'ambiguous' as day-to-day life makes them."[4] Transparency replaces manipulation; community replaces fragmentation.

The kind of utopianism found in entertainment is severely restricted, however. Although they see positive sides to utopianism, Jameson notes a "profound identity" between "utopian gratification and ideological manipulation," and Dyer warns that the consideration of problems is typically limited to those for which capitalism itself offers remedies—through consumption. Too often, entertainment "provides alternatives *to* capitalism which will be provided *by* capitalism."[5] Still, the concept of utopian sensibility can help to explain much of the appeal of children's cartoons and commercials. They portray an abundance of the things most prized by children—food and toys; their musical themes and fast action are breathtakingly energetic; they enact a rebellion against adult restriction; they present a version of the world in which good and evil, male and female, are unmistakably coded in ways easily comprehended by a young child; and they celebrate a community of peers. Children's mass culture rejects the instrumental uses of toys and television for teaching and self-improvement preferred by parents.

The contemporary mass culture of childhood can be found in magazine ads and television commercials, toys and toy stores, and television programs aimed at children. How do these reflect differing and conflicting viewpoints between adults and children? How do contemporary advertising, toy sales, and commercial television programming create and reflect the gap between adults and children? How are race, gender, and class differences highlighted or submerged in children's consumer culture? How do children's media borrow and transform popular genres in adult entertainment? How has the market of affluent parents been targeted by "alternative" toy and video makers? . . .

With a clear understanding of the limitations of utopianism in mind, I want to consider how children's consumer culture and the promises it makes grew as big as they are today. The history is complex, involving changes in parents' workloads, the dominance of developmental psychology and the way it has formed our attitudes toward toys, and the impact of television on the nuclear family. I believe it is necessary to place children's popular culture in the contexts of historical changes in households and in the work mothers and fathers do, attitudes toward child rearing encouraged by experts and marketers, and the widespread present perception that television is bad for children.

Household Histories

Children's consumerism is usually discussed in the narrow terms of the relationship between the child as an individual and the advertiser. In that interaction, mothers appear only as shadowy figures of neglect. Mothers presumably are most culpable when they leave their children alone to watch commercial television. But young children's consumption of television and mass-market goods must also be understood in the context of child care, as mothers' work. The growth of the market for toys and children's convenience foods depends as much on the mother's vulnerability as on her children's. The increasing labor and time intensity of mothers' work through the century set the stage for the proliferation of children's consumer goods. Typically, critics of the toy industry attribute its growth since the 1950s to the increasing sophistication of advertising directed at children—especially through the medium of television. This is only one part of the story.

In order for the volume of toy sales to have increased, families had to move to houses with space to keep the toys, and children had to have mothers who were so busy that they needed new ways to keep children entertained. These mothers often did not have traditional child-care support networks in place, as increased mobility meant that more families lived far away from their relatives. A rapid growth in income and the extension of credit in the 1950s and 1960s gave mothers the means to buy toys.

Feminist historians and sociologists argue that mothers now have more work to do than they used to.[6] Such a claim seems counter-intuitive: didn't modernization and the rise of consumerism reduce the workload for each household? The explanation for this paradox lies in the social history of household technology, the increase in consumption as a form of work necessary for the maintenance of households, and the changing standards of child rearing propagated by experts. Each of these factors has played a major role in increasing the work that mothers must do. The rise in consumerism in the twentieth century has coincided with a redistribution of household labor and an increase in the work that adult women living in nuclear families are expected to do.

Throughout the twentieth century, U.S. households experienced an overall improvement of domestic well-being: more clean clothes; more varied diet; cleaner, larger living spaces; more heating. These improvements in the standard of living were brought about by broad-scale economic development initiated in the 1920, and, after a brief but severe hiatus during the Great Depression, were fully realized in the 1950s: the extension of utilities, the diffusion of household appliances, the building of single-family homes (usually in the suburbs), and the availability of mass-produced commodities in supermarkets and shopping malls. Family members expected a greater variety and quantity of goods "in stock" in the pantry and refrigerator. Thus women often felt obliged to make frequent, lengthy trips to a grocery store that was now self-service and located farther from home. Women living in families also faced new kinds of chores, transportation of husbands and children, for instance, became a bigger part of the job, as suburban sprawl required driving to work, stores, schools, playgrounds, and swimming pools.

Changes in household technologies can be divided into three periods.[7] In the early decades of the nineteenth century, some of the domestic work that men traditionally performed for the home, such as chopping wood and raising food, was eliminated for (some) men, freeing them to assume jobs in factories and offices. Some of women's work, such as spinning and weaving, was also eliminated, but women's work in the home—cooking, sewing, laundering, child care, cleaning—was still arduous and time-consuming (notwithstanding the fact that working-class women in larger numbers throughout the century did factory work in addition to these chores, making up 20 percent of the wage labor force by 1910). The second stage began in the 1920s as mass production, retailing, and advertising developed rapidly on a broad scale. At the same time, the home was increasingly mechanized, and municipalities and public service industries laid down sewer lines and gas and electrical supply systems that would determine the locations of future residential building. Historian Ruth Schwartz Cowan has underscored the fact that the planning for these foundations of modern household technology was based on an assumed sexual division of labor: women shouldered the hidden costs of these changes with their household labor.

A third stage extended through the post–World War II period. During this period, domestic standards of living improved on a mass scale, and modern domestic technologies became common to working-class as well as middle-class homes. By 1970, two-thirds of the population owned their own homes: single-family, detached homes in low-density neighborhoods located far from urban centers. These "dream homes" were not available to everyone; single white women, the white elderly working class and lower middle class, minority men and women, and the minority elderly were often excluded from home owner-ship.[8] With soaring real estate prices and mortgage debt, the dream of home ownership has slipped out of reach for increasing numbers of white baby boom-ers as well. Nevertheless, since the 1950s, children have been central to the dream of home ownership; suburban homes—pictured continually in television sitcoms and magazine advertisements—were to be filled with everything the parents had not had. Family and recreation rooms were big enough to accommodate train sets and to provide a place to sit for everyone in the family while watching television or listening to the stereo. Ranch-style houses provided separate chil-dren's bedrooms that could be filled with toys. Driveways, broad sidewalks, and little traffic provided safe places for bicycling and roller skating. The dream houses were located in safe, homogeneous neighborhoods far from the city and were designed to facilitate a new style of child-centered family life. Child care and consumption were to be managed by the mother, now increasingly isolated from urban life and even other relatives.

Cowan argues that the material advantages of the new domestic technologies were such that they produced a kind of social revolution in which women living in families—even the mothers of small children—could enter the paid work force in the 1960s and 1970s without an intolerable decline in material comfort. Between 1950 and 1986, the number of women working outside the home rose from 30 to 55 percent; the number of married women in the paid labor force who also had children under six rose from 23 percent to 54 percent. More mothers have paid jobs (or are seeking work) than childless women.[9] Although the com-fort of children and husbands might not have suffered a blow, another price has had to be paid. The labor cost of the transition to two-income or female-headed households with small children has been borne almost entirely by women, who work a staggeringly long week in the home and on the job outside the home. Surprisingly, women spend about as many hours maintaining the household today as they did in the 1920s (whether they are employed outside the home or not). As feminist scholar Dolores Hayden argues, the work of homemaking has become extremely complex, averaging about sixty hours a week by 1982 and involving complicated negotiations between the commercial sector (stores, banks, credit institutions) and the public sector (hospitals, doctors' offices, welfare of-fices, schools).

> Part of homemaking involves seeing that each family member's myriad personal needs are fully met. The new dress must be the right size; the new fourth grade teacher must understand a child's history of learning difficulties. Sometimes rela-tionships with stores or institutions turn into adversarial ones. If the new car is a lemon; if the grade school isn't teaching reading fast enough, if the hospital offers

an incorrect diagnosis, if the social security benefit check is late, then the stressful nature of the homemaker's brokering work between home, market and state is exacerbated.[10]

Households differ in terms of how much work women do to maintain them. However, the most important factor in predicting the workload is not income, or education, or paid employment, but the presence of children in the home. A time study expert has found, in a breakdown of household tasks, that the addition of an infant increases the total number of tasks done in a household by 412 such tasks per month; when families have children aged two to five, the workload increases by 295 tasks over childless households. When measured in terms of time spent rather than number of tasks performed, a baby adds about ten days' worth of tasks to the household per month; a small child, about five days' worth to the norm for monthly levels of household work. "Any other influence exerted by the characteristics of the home, characteristics of the members, or their preferences pales in comparison with the influence of children on the household."[11] If children increase the amount of housework women do, it is reasonable to assume that a lower birthrate would also reduce women's work. This has not happened, in part because experts advocate more elaborate and time-consuming ways of caring for and entertaining each child, who now has fewer siblings to play with. As one scholar put it, being a working mother in the United States today is "virtually a guarantee of being overworked and perpetually exhausted."[12]

When mothers enter the paid work force, do fathers do more housework and child care? Most studies of men's contribution to housework have answered no. In the 1970s, two major studies concluded that men did no more housework when their wives worked than when they did not and that they often did less work overall because the wife's extra income meant that the husband could put in fewer hours on the job. A study conducted in 1985 found that employed mothers averaged eighty-five hours of work per week, compared to their husbands' sixty-six hours. The "leisure gap" between mothers and fathers has been estimated at eleven to thirty hours per week. Arlie Hochschild averaged the results of several studies to estimate that women worked fifteen hours more each week than men. "Over a year, they worked an *extra month of twenty-four-hour days a year*" (emphasis in original).[13] Hochschild's ethnography of shared housework and child care among working parents found that of the time men spent at home, more of their time was devoted to child care than to housework: "Since most parents prefer to tend to their children than clean house, men do more of what they'd rather do. More men than women take their children on 'fun' outings to the park, the zoo, the movies. Women spend more time on maintenance, feeding and bathing children, enjoyable activities to be sure, but often less leisurely or 'special' than going to the zoo."[14]

Hochschild found no correlation between class position and the likelihood that a father would do a larger share of housework and child care. Interestingly, she noted that working-class fathers—who held traditional notions of women's work—shared the work in practice and underestimated their participation in interviews, while middle-class fathers—who espoused egalitarian notions about housework and child care—shared less and overestimated theirs. The divorce and unmarried pregnancy rates have dramatically increased since the 1970s, in many cases eliminating fathers' participation in child care altogether. A study completed in 1981 found that only 26 percent of divorced fathers had seen their children for three weeks in the past year; only 20 percent of fathers had paid court-ordered child support regularly.[15]

Mothers have fewer helpers than they used to. Throughout the twentieth century, working-class women switched form domestic work for middle-class families to other kinds of work when it became available. In 1870 there had been one servant per eight households; by 1920 there was one per eighteen.[16] Other domestic helpers, such as older children in the family or neighborhood children, were less available, because childhood was increasingly defined as a time of learning and playing, not working. Thus, Cowan argues that since World War I there has been a leveling out of class differences in the kind and amount of domestic work all women do; middle-class women are as likely to scrub their own bathrooms as are working-class women, but working-class women are likely do the chore after an arduous day of wage labor. Phyllis Palmer has described some of the subtle changes in the image of the middle-class housewife that accompanied the loss of domestic servants:

> The years from 1920 to 1945 may be viewed as a transitional period during which middle-class homes changed from being *directed* by a lady-housewife to being *served* by the wife. . . . Both at the beginning and end of the period the housewife's existence was to be devoted to her home and family. By the end of the era, however, she was less able to hire another woman to take over many of the physical tasks such devotion entailed. As a consequence, housewives lost some benefits of the angelic image of the middle-class wife, which derived from their attachment to the home but was enhanced by the contrast between the housewife and the domestic servant. With declining access to servants, the housewife not only did more work, she also felt herself to be a drudge. Without a servant to emphasize her superiority, this wife found her role considerably less tolerable.[17]

From slavery to this day, African American women have routinely worked long hours outside the home *and* cared for their own families. Media and scholarly attention to the plight of the working mother increased only when large numbers of white, middle-class women found themselves working the double shift. Today, increasing numbers of immigrant women—many of them Central American or Southeast Asian—are hired by two-income professional families as housekeepers and nannies. Arlie Hochschild has noted the widening split between "women who do jobs that pay enough to pay a babysitter and the women who baby-sit or tend to other home needs."[18] Hochschild notes the gender dimension of this split as well: "[As] more mothers rely on the work of lower-paid specialists, the value accorded the work of mothering (not the value of children) has declined for women, making it all the harder for men to take it up."[19]

Of course, all mothers do not carry the negative image of their work as drudgery. Helena Z. Lopata found, in a study conducted in the 1970s, that variations in the housewife's role based on race, ethnicity, and class led women to evaluate their labor differently: "While some women are overwhelmed by the isolation, the repetitiveness of tasks, and the double burden of the employed wife, others work out a life style which they find satisfying . . . helping to explain why working-class women may be tempted to leave the labor force—housewifery is creative and autonomous, compared with most jobs which women are likely to fill in the labor force."[20] Although advertising and television denigrate domestic work as something to avoid or do as rapidly as possible, this work carries greater significance for women from strong ethnic traditions. Beatrice Pesquera found that Chicanas working outside the home feel a special responsibility for preserving domestic culture as a part of their cultural heritage, teaching Spanish songs and stories to their children, teaching their daughters to cook traditional foods; but she also noted that this creates tension because it adds on another task to their already crowded schedule.

The enormous demands placed on women's time—exacerbated when mothers work for pay outside the home—make children's goods appealing, even necessary, for mothers. Videos provide tired mothers time to cook dinner, feed the baby, or clean the house. Toys keep children entertained while they tramp along with their mothers on errands to the bank, the doctor's office, the post office—or the welfare office. Snacks and toys and videos make children happy: no matter how fleeting the joy, it is an important goal for mothers in a culture in which childhood means happiness. It is easier to take care of happy children than bored, restless ones. Consumer goods offer mothers what one ad agency researcher called "the chance to be a hero for ten minutes" by buying cereal or candy in the grocery store.[21] Children go shopping because mothers go shopping, and mothers have few alternatives but to take them along. Young children could never have been exploited as a market if they were not already visiting stores with their mothers. Urbanization, the automobile, and a rising crime rate have left few safe public areas where children can play or where children are even allowed. Grocery stores and malls are among the few places where mothers accompanied by their children can go and find they are welcome. The increase in children's consumption of television and toys, then, has been caused in part by the increasing difficulty in the job of caring for children.

Advice about Child Rearing

Ideas about child rearing changed at the same time that mass-market goods were first disseminated and domestic labor patterns shifted. Advice literature defined the job of mothering as complicated, difficult, time-consuming—and serious in the consequences for the child if the mother did not perform well. In her classic analysis of housework, feminist sociologist Ann Oakley observed that "the discovery of the child's importance has affected women more than it has men."[22] While the upgrading of children's lives, the emphasis on early education, and the campaign against physical abuse have brought great improvements to some children's lives, these gains have been won through an increased burden on mothers. Throughout the twentieth century, authoritative knowledge about children has been taken over by specialists—childhood experts, psychologists, psychoanalysts, social workers—thus undermining women's authority as rearers of children.

I use the term "advice literature" for any form of journalism and nonfiction writing that purports to solve the problems of everyday life and proffer a set of behavioral guidelines for women in the roles of wife and mother. These forms share an address to the "average" woman and usually a sympathetic, soothing tone, especially in the hands of women writers. Class differences are normally elided in advice literature, which tends to assume a middle-class or upper middle-class norm. Advice literature includes bestsellers dedicated to these topics (by writers such as Benjamin Spock, Penelope Leach, J. B. Watson); problem columns in magazines that publish letters from readers seeking advice; similar columns by agony aunts such as Ann Landers and Dear Abby in newspapers; expert columns such as the pages written by doctors and psychologists in parenting magazines (*Child, Working Mother, Parents, American Baby*) devoted to children of a particular age; and, most recently, cable television talk shows. These programs— such as *What Every Baby Knows and Growing Up Together* on Lifetime and *Healthy Kids* and *American Baby* on the Family Channel—feature familiar experts such as Penelope Leach and T. Berry Brazelton as either guests or moderators offering advice on parenting problems. The shows are sponsored by companies such as Procter and Gamble—traditional sponsors of daytime soap operas and the makers of Luvs and Pampers disposable diapers. They adopt a developmental perspective on children, emphasizing shared stages in mental, physical, and personality development against a backdrop of dream houses and professional couples. Much academic research on children in the social sciences finds fairly immediate translation into advice literature.

Since the 1920s when J. B. Watson (father of American behaviorism and advertising consultant) published his best-selling book on infant and child care, U.S. advice literature has stressed the paramount importance of early experience and the malleability of the infant through behavioral conditioning. Such beliefs meant that a mother's role (and it was always assumed in this literature that it was the *mother's* role) entailed a grave new responsibility, one much more demanding than the mere hygienic imperatives of early twentieth-century advice literature. Watson and others in the 1920s and 1930s increased demands on mothers' time by stressing not only the need for health and hygiene but also the imposition of strict daily schedules on children's activities and the permanence of psychological formations of early childhood. Expert advice about child rearing picked up momentum after World War II, and book sales soared with the baby boom. Throughout the 1940s and 1950s, Piaget's model of cognitive development was selectively borrowed from in order to emphasize the importance of environment and the child's "active" achievement of growth. Anthropologist Martha Wolfenstein found that the emphasis on parental control in the 1920s and 1930s gave way in the 1940s and 1950s to the equally time-consuming ideal of "fun morality" and the notion that mothers should play with and stimulate their babies.

Accompanying the enormous growth in the numbers of advice manuals sold after the Second World War was the radical change in the kind of advice the new generation of experts offered. Child-rearing "techniques" advocated in the postwar period emphasized intellectual growth:

> The new model baby was warmly affectionate, impulsive, dependent and (preferably) scintillatingly intelligent. Spock talked about the "daily stimulation from loving parents" which was necessary if "emotional depth and a keen intelligence" were to be fostered; Jerome Kagan identified the "two critical concerns" of American parents as "attachment to mother and rate of cognitive development."[23]

The implications of the dissemination of professional advice on child rearing are many. Advice on child rearing now came from experts rather than from family members, neighbors, and friends who would have a more intimate knowledge of the family's cultural and financial situation. Many of the new experts were medical doctors. Thus middle-aged, middle-class men replaced or competed with the advice of older female neighbors and relatives. Experts advised mothers to care not only for the body and its health but for the mind and its rate of development. They increased the demand for nurturing behavior in constant supply. The new child psychology was a child-centered model. Implicit in its proscriptions was a disavowal of maternal authority and an upgrading of the child's own desires as rational and goal directed. Because early life events for the child were of supreme importance, caretaking responsibilities expanded. As historian Christina Hardyment comments: "[B]eing a constant reassuring presence, considering one's child's every need, creating a stimulating environment exactly suited to its current developmental stage—all these take up a great deal of time."[24]

Advice literature's assumptions do not change, even when mothers work outside the home for pay. Media critic Janice Winship has pointed out that such advice encourages women to do it alone, simultaneously acknowledging the insurmountable odds against them, and remaining unremittingly cheerful about women's chances for success. The ways that women's magazines refer to the stress experienced by a working mother while presenting her image as vital, daring, and exciting, rather than as a drudge, are epitomized in *Red-book*'s "juggler," its ideal reader/consumer depicted in ads and referred to in editorial material who enjoys an affluent lifestyle, a rewarding career, and unproblematic relationships with her husband and children.

As experts advocated increased attention to children, product designers moved in to assist mothers in their tasks with new tools. Expert advice about child rearing exists in a complex relationship to marketing. The lines between advice and advertising are blurry. Advice literature in its dedicated form, such as the paperback book or magazine column, cannot be easily distinguished from "advertising" versions, that often include a letter from a mother requesting advice or a discussion of infant nutrition. Advertisements tend to repeat the same advice found in books and proffer the same solutions—often involving the purchase of a commodity or service to ease the woman's workload. As I noted earlier, ad copywriters for everything from baby food to crayons borrow from the unsponsored writing of the experts and do much to popularize and disseminate their work. In toy advertisements from *Parents* magazine, Piaget's ideas about "stages" of development and the separability of skills (cognitive, motor, social) abound. Yet editorial advice about buying things for children can be contradictory: sometimes encouraging restraint and saving; warning parents against spoiling and the use of bribes; encouraging do-it-yourself alternatives to store-bought items.

During the 1920s and 1930s advertisers increasingly forecast and directed the turn that advice literature took. Social historian Roland Marchand found that when advertisements promised that a product would provide a woman with more leisure time, one of the most commonly suggested uses for the product was spending time with children. In contrast to the vision of didacticism and moral guidance common to nineteenth-century ideals of child rearing, parents and children were to spend a new "companionable leisure" together. This leisure had as its goal more than mere pleasure, however; it was a way of fostering the child's personal development. Choosing the right product immediately rewarded the mother with "increased attention and companionship."

Advertising advocated covert forms of parental regulation by suggesting that parents win the child over rather than assert authority punitively. One axiom disseminated through advertising, especially for medicinal and food products, was that "children would inevitably choose the wrong diet or acquire undesirable habits if left to themselves."[25] Yet advertisements encouraged the view of some child experts that children should not be forced or coaxed or nagged into compliance. Marchand uses the example of Campbell's soup advertising campaigns developed during this period—and widely used today: "It's not vegetables to them [which they would naturally reject] it's just good food." Marchand dubs such techniques "the parable of the Captivated Child."[26] In a more negative form, some of these ads portrayed more overt conflict between parent and child. "Drink that milk or go straight to bed," scolds an angry mother towering over her daughter; the addition of Cocomalt can remove such trials. In another ad, a little girl sulks at the kitchen table, flanked by mother coaxing on one side and father reaching into his pocket (for a bribe?) on the other: this under the caption "Must you wheedle your child into eating?" Wheatena offers the "delicious whole wheat cereal" that could answer the parents, problems because "children love Wheatena!" Advertisers offered commodities as the means to achieve the new ideals of child rearing and to banish conflict entirely from the parent-child relationship.

As Marchand suggests, the type of psychological child-rearing advice disseminated in advice literature and in advertising coincided with the "rising enthusiasm for professional 'personnel management' in industry in the 1920s and 1930s," with its attempt "to mold people's behavior and facilitate their 'adjustment' by psychological manipulation rather than authoritarian coercion."[27] Sociologist Nancy Chodorow has noted a similar connection between child-rearing techniques and the needs of an industrial, capitalist society: "Socialization is a particularly psychological affair, since it must lead to the assimilation and internal organization of generalized capacities for participating in a hierarchical and differentiated social world, rather than to training for a specific role. . . . Production, for instance, is more efficient and profitable when workers develop a willing and docile personality."[28] The parental strategy of material rewards and coercions advocated in advertising mimics the adult worker's saving and striving for the material rewards of consumer culture.

During this period, advertising for products to be used for children reproduced ideas from bestsellers on child rearing, probably because the advertisers as an elite, upper middle-class group were themselves early initiates into the new child-rearing philosophies. There were some important emphases, however, added to this material in copywriting:

> For obvious merchandising reasons, the ads advocated parental indulgence with far less qualification than the experts. Sensing that family democracy meant earlier and wider participation in the joys of consumerism, advertisers enthusiastically endorsed the idea of family conferences and shared decision-making. Advertising tableaux surpassed even the child-rearing manuals in placing total responsibilities on the parents for every detail of the child's development, thus magnifying the potential for guilt. And they exaggerated the ease with which children might be manipulated. Psychologists occasionally argued that the mother might need to assert her domination in a direct contest of wills with the child, but the advertising parable portrayed a parent-child relationship in which open conflict was always unnecessary.[29]

These four features of advertising to parents—the encouragement of indulgence in parents; the democratic rights of children in the family; total, exclusive responsibility of mothers for children's development; and the possibility (the promise through consumer goods) of the indefinite deferral of open conflict with the child—are all features that we find present to varying degrees in advice literature, advertising targeted at mothers, and the popular culture of childhood today.

Television

Given the extraordinary amount of unpaid work required of women maintaining households with children, it is unsurprising that television sets—with their potential use as a babysitting machine—were purchased so fast by so many families in the 1950s and that families with children were the first to want them.[30] Television offered mothers a break. Television historian Lynn Spigel has documented the ways that television was at first hailed as a medium of family togetherness, a source of increased domestic harmony and intimacy in the dream home, an alternative to the mother as a source of learning for children at home. But watching television also increased the potential conflicts with children over wanting more than mothers were able or willing to buy for them, and it offered idealized images of the happy housewife and mother fulfilling her job with ease. Worries over television's effects on children—ranging from facial tics to passivity—soon came to the fore, and experts assigned to mothers the job of censoring, monitoring, and accompanying the child's viewing. If a mother heeded the experts' advice, she lost the free time television provided; if she did not, she used television as a babysitter only at the cost of feeling guilty about it.

In social discourse, various portrayals of television compete with one another, each informed by and representing a specific set of interests. In writing about children's television, competing and contradictory positions are advanced by industry producers; consumer protection groups such as Action for Children's Television; academic "childhood professionals," such as educators, pediatricians, psychologists, and social workers; and academic media researchers. Each of these groups contributes to a discourse that allows certain things to be said and rules out other things—or makes them unimaginable. The discourse of child experts usually assumes a certain normative view of what children are like (naive, impressionable, uncritical), of what television should do (help children learn to read and to understand math and science), of what is an appropriate way to spend leisure time (being physically and mentally active, *doing* things), and of what television viewing is (passive and mindless). These ideas derive from larger medical, religious, and social science bodies of thought.

When parents and teachers read about children, toys, and television, they normally rely on journalists' accounts published in newspapers and women's magazines. The tone of such articles has been frequently alarmist, fueling mothers' fears about commercial television's long-term effects on children and inspiring guilt over taking advantage of television's convenience. Warnings from child psychologists about television's effects have been curiously out of step with much mass communications research, which has stressed a view of media consumption as active rather than passive and enumerated the variety of "uses and gratifications" to be gained from the media. Nonetheless, blaming television for everything that's wrong with children is a rhetorical strategy for which the print media seem to have a special attraction. The most quotable and attractive sources for journalists—the story makers—are people who will say in the simplest possible terms that children are unwitting victims of the devil television. It is a satisfying notion: to find a single source with direct, casually observable effects to blame for all that is wrong with children today.

The most widely held belief about television among parents and educators is that television viewing is passive. This notion circulates regularly in media targeted to parents: pediatricians' pamphlets, magazines, agony columns, advice literature. "There is a powerful, idealised image of childhood as a time of activity and doing that reinforces some of my misgivings about television," explains one parent.[31] Complaints about children's TV viewing—such as those voiced by media critics Marie Winn and Neil Postman—are backed by a nostalgic mourning for an idealized vision of a "lost" childhood: a childhood that was a time of doing, of direct experience.[32]

Why is passivity the attribute so often used to condemn children's television viewing? In sharp contrast to eighteenth-and nineteenth-century Anglo-American notions about children, in which submission, obedience, and docility were prized, today passive is about the worst thing a child can be. As I have noted, developmental psychology is now the dominant model of childhood in teaching, psychology, social work, and medicine. Passivity is especially problematic, even pathological, according to this model.[33] The notion of children watching television offends the widely held belief in the importance of the child *actively* achieving developmental tasks. Child experts, television critics, and protectionists are convinced that television deters children from achieving normative agendas of child development: direct interaction with peers and parents, "large motor" skills, socialization, cognitive and physical development. Television is excluded from the list of activities that can "stimulate" growth—and stimulation is something that parents are supposed to provide in endless supply from infancy onward.

Experts regularly advise that the less television viewing, the better; videotapes are preferable to broadcast television because they have no commercials; if you must let your child watch, make it PBS; no viewing is best of all. As one media researcher pointed out: "The amount of television children watch is still quoted in a way which presupposes adult amazement and disapproval. We speak of 'heavy' or 'light' viewers as if there is indeed a measurable 'amount' of the thing called TV viewing which has entered into the child's system and stays there like a dead weight."[34] Child experts can be exacting taskmasters when they advise parents to monitor children's viewing: "Establish ground rules, prevent TV from becoming an addiction," say Dorothy and Jerome Singer in *Parents* magazine: no TV before school, during meals, during daytime hours, or before homework is done. "And don't suggest that the child 'go watch TV' whenever you are feeling overwhelmed or need privacy."[35] Obesity, violence, and poor school performance are continually held up as the threatened results of television viewing.

The first major North American study of children and television, based on data collected between 1958 and 1960, was adamantly neutral about television viewing.[36] Among preschool children, those who watched television started school with larger vocabularies and more knowledge about the world than children who had not watched television. For older children, television was found to be neither particularly beneficial nor harmful. The physical effects of television viewing were negligible, and any correlation between viewing and passivity depended on other factors in the home life of the child. The researchers, Wilbur Schramm, Jack Lyle, and Edwin Parker, noted different attitudes among parents toward television: blue-collar parents were more grateful for television's convenience and less critical of its programs; whereas middle-class parents held stronger reservations about television. In every aspect of the relationship between television viewing and a child's worldview, IQ, social class, and social relations were powerful determinants.

What filtered down to advice literature from this and other early studies was a tendency to urge mothers to work harder at their children's television viewing: by censoring, accompanying viewing, and discussing programming with the child, thus losing the free time that television might offer. Certainly television has changed children's lives. But it has done so in complex—and not necessarily negative ways—demonstrated in a wealth of sophisticated research in the 1970s and 1980s by scholars such as Jennings Bryant, Suzanne Pingree, Ellen Wartella, James Anderson, Daniel Anderson, and Elizabeth Lorch.[37] Recently, a number of mass communications researchers employing qualitative methods to study children's viewing habits have again challenged the notion that children are passive in relation to television. Unfortunately this work has gathered little attention outside academic circles.

Two recent studies based on parents' reports of their children's viewing have sketched a more active—and interactive—picture of children's viewing. Patricia Palmer, in an observational study of Australian children watching TV at home, has charted the great variety of ways children behave when watching television— from intent viewing of a few favorite programs to distracted viewing combined with other activities, such as playing with toys or pets, chatting, drawing. Palmer found that children had a propensity for performing, reenacting, and reinterpreting the material—especially television commercials—often as an affectionate interaction with parents, siblings, and friends. Children spend a lot of time discussing television, arguing about it, and criticizing it, both on the playground with friends and at home with parents and siblings. Palmer's work is important for simply listing the enormous range of children's response to television. Television goes on in the lives of children long after it is seen, and it is constantly subject to discussion and reinterpretation. Palmer reminds us how rich a source of material for social interaction television is, something denied by the persistent image (and I mean this literally, as in magazine and newspaper illustrations) of the child alone before the television set.[38] Far from passive, children, Palmer argues, are a lively audience for television.

The best research on children and television conceives of children's cognitive skills as embedded in a social world and developing at an early age. Dafna Lemish's study of children under two indicates how very early television viewing skills develop, and how babies' experience of television is tied to the everyday world of the family. Lemish's U.S. study, based on parents' recording of their children's behavior, chronicles the rapid changes in babies' attention to and selective perception of television material. Well before the age of two, children were able to monitor television at a glance for interesting material and had mastered a host of audiovisual signs that they used to distinguish among programs and genres. As reported in so many studies of children and television, the toddlers in Lemish's study found television commercials (which *Sesame Street*'s short, dynamic sequences deliberately resemble) especially appealing. Their appreciation of television material progressed rapidly from recognizing familiar objects (children, animals), to selecting favorite animated musical sequences, to attending live-action "story" segments. Young children could distinguish at a glance adult material, such as the news, from children's programming. The children seemed to enjoy teasing parents about their control of the set, manipulating the television as a toy (volume and channel controls) while parents tried to watch adult programs. A study by Paul Messaris found, as did Lemish, that mothers were fascinated by their children's rapid development in relation to television and enjoyed discussing it—but the specter of expert advice hung over them: they wished not to be badly thought of for expressing an interested enthusiasm over their children's viewing.[39] Most adults watch television and most parents let their children watch television, but many mothers feel compelled to apologize for it and see regulating children's consumption of television as part of their job.

The most theoretically sophisticated work on children's television is that of Robert Hodge and David Tripp, who analyze a single episode of an unexceptional 1978 cartoon called *Fangface*.[40] Their project benefits from the contributions of semiotics, structuralism, ideological analysis and post-structuralism; it is a good example of the kind of work currently identified by the term "cultural studies." Cartoons have only occasionally been subject to any kind of literary analysis—and never to the kind of painstaking attention Hodge and Tripp expend on *Fangface*. Instead, child psychologists and media sociologists have tended to use the methods of quantitative content analysis to "measure" the children's cartoon during a fixed block of hours during the broadcasting schedule. Content analysts count how many acts of violence occur, how many males and females there are, how many minority characters appear, how often villains speak with a foreign accent, and so on. The virtue of a structuralist/semiotic analysis is that it focuses on the combinations and structures of meaning. This level of understanding tends to be lost in content analysis, in which the meanings of discrete units of information in a television program are not related to the context in which they appear.

Hodge and Tripp argue that cartoons—widely considered one of the lowest forms of television—are surprisingly complex. Children are fascinated by them not because they have been turned into television zombies but because they are understandably engaged by the complex blend of aesthetic, narrative, visual, verbal, and ideological codes at work in them. Although cartoons are characterized by a great deal of repetition and redundancy, Hodge and Tripp argue that their subject matter, as well as their way of conveying it, is complicated stuff. Children use these cartoons to decipher the most important structures in their culture.

In their analysis, Hodge and Tripp demonstrate "the enormous complexity of what is often taken to be a very simple and straightforward message structure": *Fangface* negotiates the categories of nature and culture, the central myth of society in Lévi-Strauss's terms.[41] Hodge and Tripp grant that the meanings they find in *Fangface* may not be thought of as "residing" in the text at all, but are a product of their own interaction with the text. They allow for the options of chaotic or idiosyncratic meanings in the children's decoding of *Fangface*, as well as the possibility that children will ignore many elements in the cartoon simply because they are irrelevant to them.[42] Hodge and Tripp stop short of relativizing all "decoding" or arguing that "anything goes" in interpreting cartoons. Yet they emphasize the limited and partial nature of the responses that children (and adults) will make about television: how these will be created by the context—the classroom, the home, the laboratory—in which children are speaking; how gender, race and age differences within the group will influence the discussion.[43] Researchers such as Hodge and Tripp, Palmer, and Lemish share my position that children are not passive in their use of television, and their work enumerates the diversity of children's viewing as it is practiced in the living room. The actual behaviors of TV watching can be construed as more active than advice literature normally allows, and I would argue that children's television—even the most banal cartoons—adequately challenges children on a cognitive level.

Despite heavy reliance by mothers on the medium, the middle-class belief in the badness of television content is very firmly entrenched. Complaints and fears often involve its moral reductionism, its lack of reality, its racism and sexism, and its violence. One kind of complaint is based on the types of stories children's television presents, as Peggy Charren of Action for Children's Television put it: "It's all cartoon characters—no real people, no character development. The story is always a simple good-versus-evil, with no complexity and no human emotions: this battle, that crash, this one triumphs, that one fails, and it's all over. History, science, mystery, the arts—these are scarce because they haven't been presold to the 32.5 million children in America's TV households."[44] I agree with critics that the content of children's television warrants serious attention, and I focus on these issues in my discussion of commercials and toy-based programs—the most despised of children's TV genres. The charges directed at children's shows, however, are based on adult attention that is casual and erratic. When adults look more closely at children's television, they will seldom find that it delivers a single, unambiguous message to children. Instead, children's television, borrowing and adapting long-standing adult genres of U.S. popular culture, tends to reproduce familiar stereotypes, settings, and plots.

A more valid basis for faulting children's television is its store of words and images that are loaded with histories of oppression—based on class, gender, race and ethnicity. Children's television—like much of children's literature—places white boys at the center of the action. Children of color and girls of all races are dispersed to the sidelines as mascots, companions, victims. A child's identification with television is at best problematic when that child is Asian American or Black or Latino, or working-class or female—to name just a few examples. What needs to be untangled in the discussion of children's television are the aesthetic norms of high culture from the political critique of race, gender, and class stereotypes. . . .

NOTES

1. The line is Judy Holliday's from the film *Born Yesterday*. Charlotte Brunsdon quotes Holliday and discusses the low status of television viewing in her article "Television:

Aesthetics and Audiences," in *Logics of Television: Essays in Cultural Criticism*, ed. Patricia Mellencamp (Bloomington: Indiana University Press, 1990), 62.

2. Daniel Miller, *Material Culture and Mass Consumption* (Oxford: Basil Blackwell, 1987), 215.

3. Richard Dyer, "Entertainment and Utopia," in *Movies and Methods*, vol. 2, ed. Bill Nichols (Berkeley and Los Angeles: University of California Press, 1985), 222.

4. Ibid., 224–225.

5. Fredric Jameson, *The Political Unconscious: Narrative as a Socially Symbolic Act* (Ithaca, N.Y.: Cornell University Press, 1981), 69. Dyer's argument is familiar from Hans Magnus Enzensberger and Herbert Marcuse; Dyer, "Entertainment," 229.

6. Some useful reviews of this research can be found in Ellen Carol Dubois et al., *Feminist Scholarship: Kindling in the Groves of Academe* (Urbana and Chicago, University of Illinois Press, 1987), 113–125; Stephanie Coontz, *The Social Origins of Private Life: A History of American Families* (London: Verso, 1988), 349–354; and Dolores Hayden, *Redesigning the American Dream: The Future of Housing, Work, and Family Life* (New York: Norton, 1984), 65–95.

7. Ruth Schwartz Cowan, *More Work for Mother* (New York: Basic Books, 1986).

8. Hayden, *Redesigning*, 55–56.

9. Arlie Hochschild, *The Second Shift* (New York: Avon, 1989), 2.

10. Hayden, *Redesigning*, 64–65.

11. Sarah Fenstermaker Berk, *The Gender Factory: The Apportionment of Work in American Households* (New York: Plenum Press, 1985), 197.

12. Cowan, *More Work*, 213; Arlie Hochschild's book *The Second Shift* paints a vivid picture of the fatigue created by what she calls the "leisure gap."

13. Hochschild, *Second Shift*, 3. The summary of the research is included in Hochschild's appendix, "Research on Who Does the Housework and Childcare," 277–279.

14. Ibid., 9.

15. Cited in ibid., 250.

16. Coontz, *Social Origins*, 337.

17. Phyllis Palmer, *Domesticity and Dirt: Housewives and Domestic Servants in the United States, 1920–1945* (Philadelphia: Temple University Press, 1989), 13.

18. Hochschild, *Second Shift*, 246.

19. Ibid., 232.

20. Cited in Nona Glazer-Malbin, "Housework," *Signs* 1, no. 4 (1976): 913.

21. Bert Leiman, associate director of children's research, Leo Burnett Co., interview with author, Chicago, August 1989.

22. Ann Oakley, *Woman's Work: The Housewife, Past and Present* (New York: Vintage Books, 1974), 210.

23. Christina Hardyment, *Dream Babies: Three Centuries of Good Advice on Child Care* (New York: Harper & Row, 1983), 242.

24. Ibid., 226.

25. Roland Marchand, *Advertising the American Dream: Making Way for Modernity, 1920–1940* (Berkeley and Los Angeles: University of California Press, 1985), 230.

26. Ibid., 228–232.

27. Ibid., 232.

28. Nancy Chodorow, *The Reproduction of Mothering: Psychoanalysis and the Sociology of Gender* (Berkeley and Los Angeles: University of California Press, 1978), 232.

29. Marchand, *Advertising*, 232.

30. See Lynn Spigel, "Television and the Family Circle: The Popular Reception of a New Medium," in Mellencamp, *Logics of Television*.

31. Philip Simpson, ed., *Parents Talking Television* (London: Comedia, 1987), 65.

32. Marie Winn, *The Plug-in Drug* (New York: Viking Press, 1977). Neil Postman, *The Disappearance of Childhood* (New York: Delacorte Press, 1982).

33. For an extensive critique of developmental psychology, see Julian Henriques et al., *Changing the Subject: Psychology, Social Regulation, and Subjectivity* (London: Methuen, 1984).

34. Patricia Palmer, *Lively Audience: A Study of Children Around the TV Set* (Sydney: Allen and Unwin, 1986), 135.

35. Quoted in Julius and Zelda Segal, "The Two Sides of Television," *Parents*, March 1990, 186.

36. Wilbur Schramm, Jack Lyle, and Edwin Parker, *Television in the Lives of Our Children* (Palo Alto, Calif.: Stanford University Press, 1961); I have relied on the summary of this research in Shearon Lowery and Melvin L. De Fleur, *Milestones in Mass Communication Research* (New York and London: Longman, 1983), 267–295.

37. Much of this work is summarized in Jennings Bryant and Daniel R. Anderson, eds., *Children's Understanding of Television: Research on Attention and Comprehension* (New York: Academic Press, 1983).

38. Palmer, *Lively Audience*. Television meanings as inextricable from family interactions and the domestic space has been a focus of attention in research by David Morley, James Lull, Jan-Uwe Rogge, and Hermann Bausinger.

39. Dafna Lemish, "Viewers in Diapers: The Early Development of Television Viewing," in *Natural Audiences: Qualitative Research of Media Uses and Effects*, ed. Thomas Lindlof (Norwood, N.J.: Ablex, 1987), 33–57. See also Paul Messaris, "Mothers' Comments to Their Children about the Relationship between Television and Reality," in Lindlof, *Natural Audiences*, 95–108.

40. *Fangface* was an animated series about the adventures of the werewolf Sherman Fangsworth and his teenage companions Kim, Biff, and Pugsie. Generically, the series was based primarily on a comedy-mystery type of story (sometimes called the "Let's get out of here" adventure formula) found in many examples of cartoons, from *Scooby Doo* (1969–1980) to *Slimer and the Real Ghostbusters* (1986–   ).

41. Robert Hodge and David Tripp, *Children and Television: A Semiotic Approach* (Stanford, Calif.: Stanford University Press, 1986), 26.

42. Ibid., 71.

43. David Morley makes this point, which has been increasingly taken up by cultural studies, in *Family Television: Cultural Power and Domestic Leisure* (London: Comedia, 1986), 30.

44. Peggy Charren quoted in Margaret B. Carlson, "Babes in Toyland," *American Film*, January–February 1986, 56.

Chapter Eighteen

Boys and Girls Together . . . But Mostly Apart

Barrie Thorne

The landscape of contemporary childhood includes three major sites—families, neighborhoods, and schools. Each of these worlds contains different people, patterns of time and space, and arrangements of gender. Families and neighborhoods tend to be small, with a relatively even ratio of adults and children. In contrast, schools are crowded and bureaucratic settings in which a few adults organize and continually evaluate the activities of a large number of children.[1] Within schools, the sheer press of numbers in a relatively small space gives a public, witnessed quality to everyday life and makes keeping down noise and maintaining order a constant adult preoccupation. In their quest for order, teachers and aides continually sort students into smaller, more manageable groups (classes, reading groups, hallway lines, shifts in the lunchroom), and they structure the day around routines like lining up and taking turns. In this chapter I trace the basic organizational features of schools as they bear upon, and get worked out through, the daily gender relations of kids. As individuals, we always display or "do" gender, but this dichotomous difference (no one escapes being declared female or male) may be more or less relevant, and relevant in different ways, from one social context to another.

School Routines, Rules, and Groups

On the first day of the Ashton school year I went early so that I could be part of the opening moments in Mrs. Smith's kindergarten. The kids began to arrive, their faces etched with wariness and expectation; each held the hand of a parent (one a father, the rest mothers) and patiently stood in line waiting to meet the teacher. As each pair came up, Mrs. Smith, an energetic teacher in her late twenties, introduced herself to the parent and then kneeled down and warmly greeted the new student, pinning a name tag on the front of each dress or shirt. The teacher then said good-bye to the parent and directed the child, after comforting a few who were tearful, to a predesignated place at one of the five long tables that filled the center of the room.

Above each table, dangling by string from the ceiling, was a piece of cardboard whose color and shape matched its printed name: "Blue Circle," "Brown Triangle," "Red Diamond." Standing above the seated kids and using a loud and deliberate voice that drew the new arrivals together as a group, Mrs. Smith introduced herself and told about her pets. The kids began to talk all at once: "We're gettin' a kitty, a baby kitty"; "My mom won't let me get a kitty"; "I wonder if you're going to give me a book or a pencil to do something." Mrs. Smith broke into the verbal chaos to instruct in a kind but firm voice, "We talk one-at-a-time; you should hold up your hand if you want to talk." Hands flew up, while the chorus of spontaneous comments continued.

Raising her voice to regain their attention, Mrs. Smith asked, "Is there a big boy or girl who would volunteer to be a leader and carry the thermometer outside so we can see how hot it is?" "Me!" "Me!" urgent voices called from around the room of waving hands. "I don't call on me-me's. I'm going to pick one that doesn't say 'me.' Me-me's don't come to school," Mrs. Smith admonished. She chose Jason, and asked him to go to the door and lead the line they were going to form. Tina jumped up at the same time as Jason, and Mrs. Smith told her to sit down. Raising her voice to again instruct the group, Mrs. Smith said, "When we go down the hallway, we have to stop talking. That's a rule: Be quiet in the hallway." She asked the students to repeat the rule, and they chanted together in high sing-song voices, "Be quiet in the hallway." "Now," Mrs. Smith said, "I will choose the quietest table to line up first." She paused, looked around, and then pronounced, "Blue Circle Table," moving over to prod the two boys and three girls at that table to form a single line behind Jason.

After looking around, the teacher made a second pronouncement: "The Red Diamond Table looks ready to push in their chairs." When a short brown-haired boy jumped up and ran helter-skelter ahead of the others, Mrs. Smith admonished, "Todd, you have to walk and push in your chair." He went back to redo his actions in proper form. Mrs. Smith continued to call on tables until all thirty students, with bits of nudging and rearranging, had arrayed themselves in a single line. Admonishing them to be quiet, the teacher motioned the line to move into the hallway. Susie talked noisily, and Mrs. Smith sent her to the back of the line. "Stay in your line," Mrs. Smith called as the students moved along, "this is what you call a line; one at a time." When they passed a water fountain, several kids leaned over to drink until Mrs. Smith stated another rule: "We don't take drinks in the hall; we have a fountain in our room."

Over the next few weeks, Mrs. Smith continued to add to the young students' repertoire of school routines. They learned the named segments that divided each day: "reading time," "center time" (when they went into specialized classroom areas like "house" and "large toys"), "clean-up time," "recess." After instances of "bad behavior," the teacher sometimes threatened to take center time away, which strengthened its allure. During center time and recess the kids were relatively free to structure their own activities within bounded spaces. Mrs. Smith frequently reminded her students to take turns doing everything from sharing toys to going to the bathroom, for which she gave elaborate instructions: "You can go in when the door is open; leave the door open when you're through, but close it when you use it. Big boys and girls have doors shut in the bathroom; that's the grown-up thing to do at school."

Sorting Students into Groups

In managing almost thirty lively children within relatively small spaces, Mrs. Smith, like other teachers and aides, drew on the general power of being an adult, as well as on the more institutionalized authority of her official position. She claimed the right to regulate the students' activities, movement, posture, talking, possessions, access to water, and time and manner of eating. Such collective regulation—or "batch processing"—has a leveling effect; teachers and aides cope with the large number of students by treating them as members of groups.[2] School staff often sort students by characteristics like age, reading or math performance, or by spatial locations like "the Red Diamond Table" or "boys in the large toy area." And, when given the opportunity within classrooms, hallways, lunchrooms, and on the playground, kids also form their own groups. In the process the unique qualities of individuals (the focus of much family interaction) become subordinated to ways in which they are alike.[3]

In any mass of students there are many potential strands of "alikeness" and difference that may be used as a basis for constituting groups. Age is the most institutionalized principle of grouping; before the school year even begins, the staff assign students to first grade or fourth grade, and this sorting has a continuous effect on their activities and the company they keep. All the students in Mrs. Smith's kindergarten class were alike in being five or six years old. They differed by gender, race, ethnicity, social class, and religion, but these differences were to some degree submerged by the fact that the students, placed together because they were similar in age, confronted the same teacher, received the same work assignments, and were governed by the same rules. In both schools age-grading extended from classrooms into the cafeteria and auditorium, where each class was assigned its own space. Ashton School also had age-divided playgrounds: one for the kindergarten, first, and second grades; another for the third and fourth grades; and "the older kids' playground" for fifth-and sixth-graders. The Oceanside playground was not formally segmented by age, but younger and older students went out for recess at different times.

Within their age-homogeneous classrooms, teachers continually establish further divisions, some more or less arbitrary, like "the Red Diamond Table," and others based on differences in perceived talent or performance, like "the Bluebird Reading Group." The social categories and identities of the students—religion, social class, race and ethnicity, and gender—provide additional lines of difference that teachers and students evoke verbally and in their sorting practices, but to strikingly varied degrees.

In my observations in both schools, differences of religion figured into the organization of the school day only when several students from Jehovah's Witnesses families were excused from Halloween and Christmas celebrations. (I am familiar with other public schools that more routinely emphasize religious differences, for example, by allowing Mormon or Christian Covenant students to leave the school for a period of religious instruction elsewhere.)

Oceanside and Ashton teachers never explicitly invoked differences in social class, although subtleties of dress and talk marked variations in the socioeconomic backgrounds of the largely working-class students. Furthermore, class differences in these, as in other schools, were loosely related to "ability grouping" such as the composition of different reading groups.[4] In their everyday practices kids in both schools sometimes drew on and, in effect, marked class differences. For example, the Oceanside fourth-and fifth-graders avoided Rita, whose grooming and clothing displayed signs of poverty, and the emerging core of "popular girls" dressed more expensively than some of the other girls. But apart from side comments about a particular child's family or background, teachers, aides, and students never named or explicitly invoked social-class divisions when they organized groups.

In both schools the race and ethnicity of students was more emphasized than religion or social class, although in eleven months of fieldwork I observed only one classroom situation in which the staff formally sorted students along racial and ethnic lines, and that was for a practical reason. The Oceanside combined fourth-fifth—grade class included two boys, Alejandro and Miguel, who had recently immigrated from Mexico and who spoke little English. These two boys sat at the boundary that divided boys from girls in the U-shaped arrangement of desks, and during part of each school day, they moved to a table at the side of the room to work with a Spanish-speaking aide. Two other boys inthat classroom, Allen and Freddy, spoke both Spanish and English, and severaltimes the teacher asked one of them to translate for Miguel or Alejandro. Otherwise, Allen and Freddy had little contact with the recent immigrants, and the staff never set apart all Chicanos/Latinos as a distinctive group. Three other students were visibly of race and ethnic backgrounds different from the white or Euro-American majority: Jessie, from an African-American family; Rosie, whose parents came from the Philippines; and Neera, whose parents were from India. While adults did not formally draw on race or ethnicity in dealing with these students, ethnic and racial meanings emerged in some encounters.

In the lunchrooms and on the playgrounds of both schools, African-American kids and kids whose main language was Spanish occasionally separated themselves into smaller, ethnically homogeneous groups. These groupings, such as five or six African-American older boys who often ate lunch together and then played basketball on the Ashton playground, were usually homogeneous by gender and, loosely, by age. Like other researchers, I found that students generally separate first by gender and then, if at all, by race or ethnicity.[5]

One regular play group on the Oceanside playground was a notable exception: seven to ten primarily Spanish-speaking girls and boys, including Alejandro and Miguel, regularly got together in a large game of dodgeball. The group, which probably coalesced because of the comfort of speaking the same language in an alien milieu, mixed kids of different ages as well as genders.

Apart from age, of all the social categories of the students, gender was the most formally, and informally, highlighted in the course of each school day. Gender is a highly visible source of individual and social identity, clearly marked by dress and by language; everyone is either a female or a male. In contrast, categories of race, ethnicity, religion, and social class tend to be more ambiguous and complex. Furthermore, recent public policy has set more proscriptions against officially marking race and religion (in the law, both are regarded as "suspect categories"), compared with gender (where, in a tangle of inconsistency, the law both does and does not mark difference).[6]

"Boys and Girls": The Verbal Marking of Gender

In both schools when the public address system crackled an announcement into a classroom or the cafeteria, the voice always opened with, "Boys and girls..." (the word "boys" invariably came first). Teachers and aides often used gender to mark out groups of students, usually for purposes of social control. For example, while the second-graders at Ashton School worked at their desks, the teacher, Mrs. Johnson, often walked around the room, verbally reining in the disruptive and inattentive: "There's three girls need to get busy.... You two boys ought to be busy." Other teachers also peppered their classroom language with gendered terms of address ("You boys be quiet"; "Girls, sit down"; "Ladies, this isn't a tea party"), implying that gender defined both behavior and social ties.

Why are gender terms so appealing as terms of address? Occasionally, the staffs of both schools used words like "people" or "students" to call for general attention. But they much more often used "boys and girls," perhaps because, as one of the principals reflected, "it feels more specific." Indeed, gender categories provide a striking blend of the specific *and* the all-encompassing. Since everyone is assigned to either one or the other gender category, the paired terms, "boys and girls," drop an inclusive net over a group of any size. (Note that "boys and girls" is used as the generic; "boy," unlike the word "man," has never been claimed as a generic, perhaps because children of both genders are subordinated to adults, and boys have less power over girls compared with men over women.)[7] "Boys and girls" may also be an appealing term of address because the words are marked for age, making it clear that children, not adults, are the focus of a comment. The language comes in handy since the structural separation of adults and children is so fundamental to schools.[8] Finally, terms like "the Blue Circle Table" and "fourth-graders" have fleeting connections with individual identities; the words "girls" and "boys" sink more deeply into a person's sense of self.

Spencer Cahill has also noted the centrality of gender categories in the "languages of social identification" used by and toward children. Observing in a preschool, he found that the adult staff used "baby" as a sanctioning term, contrasted with "big girl" and "big boy," which they employed as more positive forms of address. Cahill argues that children pick up the association of gender labels with the praiseworthy state of maturity and begin to claim "big girl" and "big boy" identities to distinguish themselves from "babies."[9]

Use of "big boy" and "big girl" as terms of praise continues in the early years of elementary school. On the first day of kindergarten Mrs. Smith asked for a "big boy or girl" to volunteer to carry the thermometer outside, and she later described the proper bathroom comportment of "big boys and girls." By fourth grade the terms "big girl" and "big boy" have largely disappeared, but teachers continue to equate mature behavior with grown-up gendered identities by using more formal and ironic terms of address, like "ladies and gentlemen." By frequently using gender labels when they interact with kids, adults make being a girl or a boy central to self-definition, and to the ongoing life of schools.

Gender dichotomies ("girl/boy" as basic social categories and as individual identities) provide a continuously available line of difference that can be drawn on at any time in the ongoing life of schools. The manner of drawing, however, varies a great deal. In some situations, gender is highlighted; at other times, it is downplayed. As Gregory Bateson once commented, in the ongoing complexity of social life, a given difference does not always *make* a difference.[10] Individuals enter situations as girls or boys, displaying gender through details like names, dress, and adornment. But gender may or may not be central to the organization and symbolism of an encounter. In some situations, participants mark and ritualize gender boundaries. In other situations, gender may be far less relevant. Note that this line of analysis separates aspects of gender that are always present (individuals never leave aside their membership in the category "girl" or "boy") from those that are more fluctuating (the marking or muting of gender in the organization and symbolism of different social situations).

As my fieldwork progressed, I came to ask: How, when, and why does gender make a difference—or *not* make a difference in everyday interaction in schools? And when gender does make a difference, what sort of difference is it? When they create groups, adults or kids may invoke or ignore gender, thereby separating boys from girls, or drawing them together. I began to think of the patterning as a kind of dance, a choreography of separation and integration, laden with complex and even contradictory meanings. Images of photography also came to mind. I initially thought in snapshot frames, noting patterns setting by setting; then I began to shift to a mental moving camera, tracing the processes by which boys and girls mixed together and pulled apart.

The Choreography of Gender Separation and Integration

A series of snapshots taken in varied school settings would reveal extensive spatial separation between girls and boys. This phenomenon, which has been widely observed by researchers in schools, is often called "sex segregation among children," a term evoking images of legally enforced separation, like purdah in some Islamic societies. But school authorities separate boys and girls only occasionally. Furthermore, girls and boys sometimes interact with one another in relaxed and extended ways, not only in schools but also in families, neighborhoods, churches, and other settings. Gender separation—the word "segregation" suggests too total a pattern—is a variable and complicated process, an intricate choreography aptly summarized by Erving Goffman's phrase "with-then-apart."[11]

Boys and girls separate (or are separated) periodically, with their own spaces, rituals, and groups, but they also come together to become, in crucial ways, part of the same world. In the following verbal snapshots of classrooms, hallways, cafeterias, and school playgrounds, it is crucial to note that although the occasions of gender separation may seem more dramatic, the mixed-gender encounters are also theoretically and practically important. Note also that groups may be formed by teachers, aides, or by kids themselves, and that criteria of group formation may or may not be explicitly mentioned or even in conscious awareness.

The "With-Then-Apart" of Classrooms

In organizing classroom seating, teachers use a variety of plans, some downplaying and others emphasizing the significance of gender. When Mrs. Smith, the kindergarten teacher at Ashton School, assigned seats, she deliberately placed girls and boys at each table, and they interacted a great deal in the formal and informal life of the classroom. Mrs. Johnson, the second-grade teacher at the same school, also assigned seats, but she organized her classroom into pairs of desks aligned in rows. With the layout came a language—"William's row" ... "Monica's row" ... "Amy's row"—for the five desks lined up behind William, Monica, Amy, and the other three students seated at the front. The overall pattern mixed girls and boys, and they participated together in much of the classroom whispering and byplay.

I asked Mrs. Johnson, who was nearing retirement after many years of teaching, what she had in mind when she assigned classroom seats. She responded with weary familiarity: "Everybody is sitting somewhere for a reason—hearing, sight, height. No two in the same reading group sit together, so I make sure they do their own work in their workbook. Or they sit in a particular place because they don't get along, or get along too well, with someone else." Differences of hearing, sight, height, and reading performance cut across the dichotomous division between boys and girls; sorting the students according to these criteria led to largely gender-integrated seating. However, the last of Mrs. Johnson's criteria, the degree to which two children get along, embeds a gender skew. Since friends are usually of the same gender, splitting up close friends tends to mix girls and boys.

Instead of assigning seats, Miss Bailey, the teacher of the combined fourth-fifth grade in Oceanside School, let the students choose their own desks in a U-shaped arrangement open at the front of the room. Over the course of the school year there were three occasions of general choosing. Each time, the students' choices resulted in an almost total cleavage: boys on the left and girls on the right, with the exception of one girl, Jessie, who frequently crossed gender boundaries and who twice chose a desk with the boys and once with the girls. . . . The teacher and students routinely spoke of "a boys' side" and "a girls' side" in the classroom.[12]

Miss Bailey made clear that she saw the arrangement as an indulgence, and when the class was unusually noisy, she threatened to change the seating and "not have a boys' side and a girls' side." "You have chosen that," she said on one such occasion, "you're sitting this way because you chose to do it at the first of the year. I may have to sit you in another way." The class groaned as she spoke, expressing ritualized preference for gender-separated seating. Miss Bailey didn't carry out her threat, and when she reseated individual students in the name of classroom order, she did so within each side. Miss Bailey framed the overall gender separation as a matter of student choice and as a privilege she had granted them, but she also built on and ratified the gender divide by pitting the girls against the boys in classroom spelling and math contests . . .

Physical separation of girls and boys in regular classroom seating affects formal and informal give-and-take among students. One day Miss Bailey wrote sentences on the board and said she would go around the room and give each student a chance to find an error in spelling, grammar, or pronunciation. "We'll start with Beth," she said, gesturing to the right front of the U-shaped layout of the desks. Recognizing that to go around the room meant she would call on all the girls first, Miss Bailey added, "that leaves the hard part for the boys." Picking up the theme of gender opposition, several boys called out, "We're smart!" The divided seating pattern also channeled informal byplay, such as whispering, casual visiting, and collusive exchanges, among boys and among girls, whereas in classrooms with mixed-gender seating, those kinds of interaction more often took place between girls and boys.

When Miss Bailey divided the class into smaller work groups, gender receded in formal organizational importance. On these occasions, the teacher relied on sorting principles like skill at reading or spelling, whether or not someone had finished an earlier task, counting off ("one-two-one-two"), or letting students choose from alternative activities such as practicing for a play or collectively making a map out of papier-mâché. Sometimes Miss Bailey asked the fourth-and fifth-graders to meet separately and work on math or spelling. These varied organizational principles drew girls and boys out of separate halves of the classroom and into groups of varied gender composition standing at the blackboard or sitting on the floor in front or at round tables at the side of the room. When they found places in these smaller groups, girls often scrambled to sit next to girls, and boys to sit next to boys. But if the interaction had a central focus such as taking turns reading aloud or working together to build a contour map, boys and girls participated together in the verbal give-and-take.

Although I did not do systematic counting, I noticed that during formal classroom instruction, for example, when Miss Bailey invited discussion during social studies lessons, boys, taken as a whole, talked more than girls. This pattern fits with an extensive body of research finding that in classroom interaction from the elementary through college levels, male students tend to talk more than female students.[13] It should be emphasized that these are statistical and not absolute differences, and that researchers have found much variation from classroom to classroom in the degree to which boys are more visible than girls, and the degree to which individual teachers treat boys and girls differently. We need further research (my data are too sparse for these purposes) exploring possible relationships between seating practices, and patterns of talk and interaction in classrooms.

Life on the Line

When Mrs. Smith announced to her kindergarten class, "This is what you call a line . . . one at a time," she introduced a social form basic to the handling of congestion and delay in schools. In Ashton School, where classrooms opened onto an indoor hallway, kids rarely moved from the classroom unless they were in carefully regulated lines. The separate lines meandering through the hallways reminded me of caterpillars, or of planes on a runway slowly moving along in readiness to take off. In the layout of the Oceanside School each of the classrooms opened to the outside, an arrangement facilitated by the warm California climate. Although this lessened the problem of noise and thereby relaxed the amount of adult control, the Oceanside teachers still organized students into loose lines when they headed to and from the library and the playground and when they went to the lunchroom.

Gender threaded through the routines of lining up, waiting and moving in a queue, and dispersing in a new place. In Oceanside School it was customary for girls and boys to line up separately, a pattern whose roots in the history of elementary schooling are still evident on old school buildings with separate entrances engraved with the words "Girls" and "Boys."[14] Several adults who have told me their memories of elementary school recall boys and girls lining up separately to go to different bathrooms. One woman remembered waiting in the girls' line several feet away from a row of boys and feeling an urgent need to urinate; she held her legs tightly together and hoped no one—especially the boys—would notice. This experience of bodily shame gave an emotional charge to gender-divided lines.

Like the schools of these adult memories, Oceanside had separate girls' and boys' bathrooms shared by many classrooms. But unlike the remembered schools, Oceanside had no collective expeditions to the bathrooms. Instead individual students asked permission to leave the classrooms and go to either the boys' or girls' bathroom, both of which, like the classrooms, opened to the outside. In Ashton School, as in many contemporary school buildings, each classroom had its own bathroom, used one-at-a-time by both girls and boys. This architectural shift has eliminated separate and centralized boys' and girls' facilities and hence the need to walk down the hall to take turns going to the toilet.

In Oceanside School the custom of separate girls' and boys' lines was taken for granted and rarely commented on. One of the fourth graders told me that they learned to form separate boys' and girls' lines in kindergarten and had done it ever since. A first-grade teacher said that on the first day of school she came out to find the boys and the girls already standing in two different lines. When I asked why girls and boys formed separate lines, the teachers said it was the children's doing. With the ironic detachment that adults often adopt toward children's customs, Miss Bailey told me that she thought the gender-separated lines were "funny." A student teacher who joined the classroom for part of the year rhetorically asked the kids why they had a girls' line and a boys' line. "How come? Will a federal marshal come and get you if you don't?" There was no reply.

Miss Bailey didn't deliberately establish separate lines for boys and girls; she just told the students to line up. It took both attention and effort for the kids to continually create and recreate gender-separated queues. In organizing expeditions out of the classroom, Miss Bailey usually called on students by stages, designating individuals or smaller groups ("everyone at that side table"; "those practicing spelling over in the corner") to move into line as a reward for being quiet. Once they got to the classroom door—unless it was lunchtime, when boys and girls mixed in two lines designated "hot lunch" and "cold lunch"—the students routinely separated by gender. The first boy to reach the door always stood to the left; the first girl stood to the right, and the rest moved into the appropriate queue.

The kids maintained separate boys' and girls' lines through gestures and speech. One day when the class was in the library, Miss Bailey announced, "Line up to go to assembly." Judy and Rosie hurried near the door, marking the start of one line on the right; Freddy and Tony moved to the left of the door. Other girls lined up behind Rosie, who became a sort of traffic director, gesturing a boy who was moving in behind her that he should shift to the other line. Once when the recess bell had rung and they began to line up for the return to class, a boy came over and stood at the end of a row of girls. This evoked widespread teasing—"John's in the girls' line"; "Look at that girl over there"—that quickly sent him to the row of boys. Off-bounds to those of the other gender, the separate lines sometimes became places of sanctuary, as during the close of one recess when Dennis grabbed a ball from Tracy, and she chased after him. He squeezed into line between two boys, chanting, "Boys' line, boys' line," an incantation that indeed kept her away and secured his possession of the ball.

Several years before I arrived at Ashton School, the staff had moved from dual to single lines. This may have been partly a result of Title IX, the 1972 federal legislation mandating that girls and boys should have equal access to all school activities. One teacher told me she used to organize separate boys' and girls' lines, but someone told her that "wasn't the thing to do these days," so she followed her colleagues in shifting to single lines. Although individual girls and boys often stood in front of and behind one another in the single lines, they also had strategies for maneuvering within formal constraints and separating into same-gender clusters.

The front of the line is a desired and contested zone. As a reward, the teachers often let a specific child—the "line leader" or "goodest one," as a kindergartner explained—go first. After that initial selection there is often pushing and shoving for a place near the front. Because of the press to be near the front, kids usually protest attempted cuts in that zone. Farther back, individuals or smaller groups can sometimes tuck in a friend or two; it takes protest to make a cut a cut, and the deed is less likely to be challenged in back than in front. The back of the line is sometimes defined as the least desired space, even a place of punishment as suggested by the much-repeated rule: "If you cut, you have to go to the back of the line."

Although generally a devalued space, the back of the line has its uses. During the process of lining up, socially marginal kids often wait to join the line near the end, thereby avoiding the pushing and maneuvering at the front. Since the end is less tightly surveyed by teachers, aides, and other students, groups of friends may go to the back of the line so they can stand and talk together without having to be vigilant about holding their places. Occasionally when a student leaves a place in line and moves to the end, it appears to be out of a sense of being in the wrong gender territory. For example, in Ashton School after they finished eating lunch, students routinely lined up in the cafeteria waiting for a lunchtime aide to escort them to the playground. In one sequence of actions a girl moved into line behind three boys, then a boy got in line behind her. When she noticed this, a look of discomfort crossed her face, and she shifted farther back in the emerging line, joining three other girls.

Life on the line is time spent waiting. (Educational researchers have found that the time students spend waiting takes up as much as a third of each school day).[15] The process of waiting in line was especially protracted in the Ashton School lunchroom, where lines formed slowly, the time drawn out by the varied speed of the eaters and by waiting for a lunchtime aide to finish wiping tables before she could lead the lines through the hallways and out to the playground. Bored by the delay, the waiting kids created their own forms of entertainment. They often clustered into same-gender groups, sometimes marking their solidarity with shared motions: girls sat on the floor facing one another and played clapping games (I never saw boys do this); a boy jogged shoulders with the next boy in line, starting a chain reaction that stopped when a girl was next. Separate clusters of kids, usually of different genders, marked boundaries between them by leaving a gap of space and/or through physical hassling. In one emerging lunchroom lineup of Ashton third-graders, there was a row of seven boys at the front, then several feet of empty space, then three girls, a few feet of space, then three boys. A girl reached around and leaned across the space to poke the boy behind her; he then pinned down her arms from behind, letting her go after she protested. When everyone had finally finished eating and joined the line, the aide signaled that they could go. There was a lot of pushing as smaller groups eased into the shared motion of one moving line.

The Gender Geography of Lunchroom Tables

Seating in school lunchrooms falls between the more fixed spaces of classroom desks and the arrangements kids improvise each time they sit on the floor of the classroom or the auditorium; an Oceanside teacher once referred to "their strange conglomeration way of sitting," describing the clusters, primarily of either girls or boys, arrayed on the floor. Eating together is a prime emblem of solidarity, and each day at lunchtime there is a fresh scramble as kids deliberately choose where, and with whom, to eat. The scrambling takes place within limits set by adults and defined by age-grading. In both schools, each classroom, in effect an age-grade, had two designated cafeteria tables, placed end to end from the wall.

Table seating takes shape through a predictable process: the first arrivals (who have cold lunches, a reason some children say they prefer to bring lunch from home) stake out territory by sitting and spreading out their possessions, usually at the far ends of each table. The tables fill through invitations, squeezing in, or individuals or groups going to an empty space. The groups who maneuver to eat together are usually friends and mostly of the same gender. The result is a pattern of separated clusters; many of the tables have a mix of girls and boys, but they are divided into smaller same-gender groupings. On the other hand, late-arriving individuals, who have less choice of where to sit, move into leftover spaces and tend to integrate the seating.

The collective table talk often includes both boys and girls, as do some daily rituals, like one that accompanied the opening of plastic bags of cutlery in both schools. As kids pulled out their plastic forks, they looked for and announced the small numbers stamped on the bottom: "I'm twenty-four, how old are you?" "I must have flunked; I'm in the fourth grade and I'm forty-five." "Ninety-three." "You're stupid; you were really held back in school."

Even when boys and girls are seated at the same table, their same-gender clustering may be accompanied by a sense of being on separate turfs. This became apparent when there were temporary changes in the physical ecology at Oceanside School. The combined fourth-fifth-grade class usually had two tables, but one day when the kids arrived for lunch, one of the tables was temporarily designated for another class. The kids began to crowd around the remaining table. Sherry, who had a cold lunch and arrived first, chose her usual seat by the wall; girls usually filled up that end. Scott and Jeremy sat down across from her, while three girls with hot lunches chose seats at the other end of the table. Scott looked around and asked, "Where are all the boys? Where are all the boys?" Four boys arrived and sat across from Scott and Jeremy and next to Sherry, who began to crouch in her corner. In a small anxious voice she asked them, "What are you doing on the girls' side?" "There isn't room," one of the newly arrived boys explained.

Occasionally those who are already seated look around, take the lay of the developing table, and change places, sometimes with a gender-marking pronouncement. In the Ashton School lunchroom when the two second-grade tables were filling, a high-status boy walked by the inside table, which had a scattering of both boys and girls. He said loudly, "Oooo, too many girls," and headed for a seat at the other, nearly empty table. The boys at the inside table picked up their trays and moved to join him. After they left, no other boy sat at that table, which the pronouncement had made effectively taboo. So in the end, girls and boys ate at separate tables that day, although this was not usually the case.

I recorded many inventories of seating in the two lunchroom shifts in Ashton School. There was a great deal of variation from classroom to classroom and day to day, but completely separate boys' and girls' tables were much more frequent in fifth and sixth than in the younger grades. The sixth-graders talked matter-of-factly about "the girls' table" and "the boys' table," spaces so ritualized that they could be deliberately disrupted. A group of sixth-grade girls told me about a day when they plotted ahead, hurried into the lunchroom, and grabbed the boys' table, which was always the one next to the wall. When the boys arrived, they protested, but the girls held out, and on that day, which the girls remembered with humor, the girls and the boys switched territories.

Playground Divisions of Space and Activity

In classrooms, hallways, and lunchrooms boys and girls do the same core activities: working on math or spelling, moving from one area to another, or eating a meal. Same-gender groups might add their own, sometimes collusive agendas, such as a group of girls passing around a tube of lip gloss during a grammar lesson or a group of boys discussing sports or setting up arm wrestling during lunch. But there is no pronounced division of activity by gender.[16] In contrast, on the playground, an area where adults exert minimal control and kids are relatively free to choose their own activities and companions, there is extensive separation by gender. Activities, spaces, and equipment are heavily gender-typed; playgrounds, in short, have a more fixed geography of gender.

My inventories of activities and groups on the playground showed similar patterns in both schools. Boys controlled the large fixed spaces designated for team sports: baseball diamonds, grassy fields used for football or soccer, and basketball courts. In Oceanside School there was also a skateboard area where boys played, with an occasional girl joining in. The fixed spaces where girls predominated—bars and jungle gyms and painted concrete areas for playing foursquare, jump rope, and hopscotch—were closer to the building and much smaller, taking up perhaps a tenth of the territory that boys controlled.[17] In addition, more movable activities—episodes of chasing, groups of younger children playing various kinds of "pretend," and groups milling around and talking—often, although by no means always, divided by gender. Girls and boys most often played together in games of kickball, foursquare, dodgeball, handball, and chasing or tag.

Kids and playground aides pretty much take these gender-divided patterns for granted; indeed, there is a long history in the United States of girls and boys engaging in different types of play, although the favored activities have changed with time.[18] The Ashton School aides openly regarded the space close to the building as girls' territory and the playing fields "out there" as boys' territory. They sometimes shooed away children of the other gender from what they saw as inappropriate turf, especially boys who ventured near the girls' area and seemed to have teasing in mind.

In both schools the transition from the classroom or the lunchroom to the playground began when a teacher or aide allocated equipment. Girls rarely made a bid for footballs, softballs, or basketballs, and boys rarely asked for jump ropes (an Ashton aide once refused a boy's request for a jump rope, saying with a tone of accusation. "You only want it to give rope burns"). Both boys and girls asked for the rubber balls used for kickball, handball, and foursquare. An individual with equipment could gain relatively easy access to designated play space such as a basketball or foursquare court. To indicate that they wanted to join a given activity, kids without equipment went to the routinized space, for example, getting in line to play handball or milling around the court with other would-be basketball players. Then, in games where numbers were limited or sides were essential, negotiations began. Boys rarely sought access to a game of jump rope of hopscotch, or girls to a game of softball, football, soccer, or basketball, although there were important exceptions.

Kids sometimes excluded others by claiming they already had too many players, or simply by saying, "You can't play." Sometimes they used gender as an excuse, drawing on beliefs connecting boys to some activities and girls to others.[19] Day after day on the Ashton playground I noticed that Evan, a first-grade boy, sat on the stairs and avidly watched girls play jump rope, his head and eyes turning around in synchrony with the rope. Once when a group of girls were deciding who would jump and who would "twirl" (the less desirable position). Evan recognized a means of access to the game and offered, "I'll swing it." Julie responded, "No way, you don't know how to do it, to swing it. You gotta be a girl." He left without protest. Although kids sometimes ignored pronouncements about what boys or girls could or could not do, I never heard them directly challenge such claims.

Other Research on Gender Separation Among Children

My observations of extensive separation in the activities and social relations of boys and girls echo a recurring finding in the research literature. In fact, in nearly every study of school situations where kids from age three through junior high are given the opportunity to choose companions of the same age, girls have shown a strong preference to be with girls, and boys with boys. (Because as much as 90 percent of research on children's peer groups has been done in schools, the finding of gender separation among children dominates the literature.[20] Studies of children's social relations in neighborhoods and a study in a children's museum have found much more mixing of girls and boys than is typical in schools.)

To grasp the magnitude of the gender divide, a number of researchers have counted the relative proportions of mixed and same-gender groups in various school settings. For example, Zella Luria and Eleanor Herzog did inventories of the playground groups of fourth-and fifth-graders in two elementary schools in Massachusetts. They found that in a private, upper-middle-class school, 63 percent of the groups were same-gender, compared with 80 percent same-gender groups in a middle-class public school of about the same size and racial composition. In another study on the East Coast, Marlaine Lockheed and Abigail Harris found that in twenty-nine fourth-and fifth-grade classrooms where students constituted their own work groups, 86 percent were same-gender.[21]

In short, there is ample evidence of extensive separation between girls and boys within contemporary coeducational schools. Numerical counts, moreover, may underestimate the degree of separation. Luria and Herzog note that their method of counting all playground clusters regardless of activity may overrate the extent and "quality" of cross-gender activity. For example, in the public school in their study, half of the 20 percent of play groups mixed by gender were integrated by one girl and hence were token situations.[22] The method of simply counting all-boy, all-girl groups also neglects meanings. For example, by these researchers' counting methods, girls-chase-the-boys, a favorite game on both the Ashton and Oceanside playgrounds, would be chalked up as a mixed-gender group or interaction. However, the organization of this activity dramatizes gender boundaries and maintains a sense of separation between the girls and the boys as distinctive groups.

Information not only about the quantity of gender separation, but also about the quality and meaning (e.g., the degree of felt intimacy or social distance) of kids' social relations can be found in their perceptions of friendship. Researchers who have asked kids of different ages to name their best friends have found that in at least 75 percent of the cases, boys name only boys and girls name only girls.[23] Sociometric studies that go beyond "best" friendships to ask about and map broader self-reported patterns of affiliation and avoidance have also documented a deep division by gender. For example, in a study of four fourth-, fifth-, and sixth-grade classrooms, Maureen Hallinan found that all the cliques that the students identified were either of girls or of boys; not one crossed the line of gender.[24] Although she observed, and the students reported, some cross-gender friendships, they were not integrated into the larger, more public and visible groupings or cliques.

In short, although girls and boys *are* together and often interact in classrooms, lunchrooms, and on the playground, these contacts less often deepen into friendship or stable alliances, while same-gender interactions are more likely to solidify into more lasting or acknowledged bonds. Much of the daily contact between girls and boys, as Janet Schofield comments, resembles that of "familiar strangers" who are in repeated physical proximity and recognize one another but have little real knowledge of what one another are like.[25] Some of the students in the middle school where Schofield observed felt that the gulf between boys and girls was so deep that it was fruitless to try to form cross-gender friendships, which they saw as different from romantic liaisons.

Whether painted with narrative or by numbers, the prevalence of gender separation, especially on school playgrounds and in patterns of children's friendship, is quite striking. But separation between boys and girls is far from total. . . .

NOTES

1. Philip W. Jackson, *Life in Classrooms* (New York: Holt, Rinehart and Winston, 1968). Jackson highlights the centrality of *crowds, praise,* and *power* in the organization of schools.

Children who have previously attended day-care centers or preschools have already made the transition from household and neighborhood to a more bureaucratic set of experiences, as ethnographically detailed by Polakow in Valerie Polakow, Paulo Freire, *Erosion of Childhood.* (Chicago: University of Chicago Press, 1992). During the opening weeks of Ashton School, the kindergarten teacher told me that she could tell which children had come from "group" care; they made an easier transition to school than did children coming from home-based care.

2. Philip A. Cusick, *Inside High School* (New York: Holt, Rinehart and Winston, 1973).

3. An observation from Robert Dreeban, *On What Is Learned in School* (Reading, Mass.: Addison, Wesley, 1968).

4. See Jeannie Oakes, *Keeping Track: How Schools Structure Inequality* (New Haven: Yale University Press, 1985), for a thoughtful study of ways in which academic tracking further disadvantages poor and racial minority students.

5. The schools I studied had relatively small numbers of Chicanos/Latinos (around fifty out of four hundred students), African-Americans (twenty-five or thirty in each school), and a scattering from other racial/ethnic groups. Since these children spread across six different grade levels, there were not enough of any age-grade to constitute a critical mass that might separate off.

In contrast, Janet W. Schofield, *Black and White in School* (New York: Praeger, 1982) studied a newly integrated urban middle-school with 1,500 students, two-thirds of them Black, and one-third white. She found that the staff mentioned race only on rare occasions when they urged students to ignore it. When they constructed their own groups, the students often divided along racial lines. These racially homogeneous groups also tended to divide by gender, although Schofield found less gender segregation among Black students than among white students.

6. In an informative history of gender practices in U.S. public schools, *Education in American Schools,* trace complex relationships between official policies and the practices of school staff. Formal practices, which have changed over time, range from the gender-neutral to separating girls and boys into different classes and activities.

7. According to the *Oxford English Dictionary,* in the thirteenth and fourteenth centuries the word "girl" was used as a generic to refer to a child of either gender. Females were called "gay girls," and males were called "knave girls." "Girl" later lost the generic communication and came to refer specifically to young females. The word "boy" appeared slightly later. "Child," a word never marked for gender, goes back to ancient times.

8. Margaret A. Eisenhart and Dorothy C. Holland, who observed fifth-and sixth-grade classrooms in a school in the South, found that teachers continually referred to "boys and girls," especially when directing them to start routines like reciting the Pledge of Allegiance or lining up. The authors observe that this generic usage (teachers were instructing boys and girls to do the same thing) emphasized student more than gender-differentiated identities. See Margaret A. Eisenhart, and Dorothy C. Holland, "Learning Gender from

Peers: The Role of Peer Groups in the Cultural Transmission of Gender," *Human Organization* 42 (1983): pp. 321–332.

9. Spencer E. Cahill, "Language Practices and Self-Definition: The Case of Gender Identity Acquisition," *Sociological Quarterly* 27 (1987): pp. 295–311. Patricia M. Passuth, "Age Hierarchies within Children's Groups," in *Sociological Studies of Child Development*, vol. 2, ed. Patricia A. Adler, Peter Adler, and Nancy Mandell (Greenwich, Conn: JAI Press, 1987), pp. 185–203, observed children in a summer day camp, and found the children were keenly aware of age differences and believed it was better to be older than younger.

10. Gregory Bateson, *Steps to an Ecology of Mind* (New York: Ballantine, 1972), p. 453. Others have also called attention to social processes by which a given category may be rendered more or less salient. For example, Marilynn B. Brewer argues that "which differences are emphasized under what circumstances appears to be flexible and context dependent; this flexibility permits individuals to mobilize different group identities for different purposes." Marilynn B. Brewer, "Ethnocentrism and Its Role in Interpersonal Trust," *Groups and Contact*, ed. Norman Miller and Marilynn B. Brewer, (New York: Academic Press, 1984), p. 350. In the same vein, Sandra Wallman observes that "a cultural or phenotypical difference which counts in one situation does not count in another." Sandra Wallman, "The Boundaries of 'Race': Processes of Ethnicity in England," *Man* 13 (1987): 201. Also see Kay Deaux and Brenda Major, "Putting Gender into Context: An Interactive Model of Gender-Related Behavior," *Psychological Review* 94 (1987): 369–389.

11. Erving Goffman, "The Arrangement between the Sexes," *Theory and Society* 4 (1977): 316.

12. Cynthia A. Cone and Berta E. Perez, "Peer Groups and the Organization of Classroom Space," *Human Organization* 45 (1986): 80–88, observed a similar pattern, including children perceiving a girls' side and a boys' side, in elementary classrooms where teachers allowed students to choose their own seating. Steven T. Bossert, *Tasks and Social Relationships in Classrooms* (New York: Cambridge University Press, 1979), compared the organization of four different classrooms; in those where the teacher let students choose their own seats, friendship groups, usually of the same gender, sat together.

13. See reviews of research in Barrie Thorne et al., eds., *Language, Gender and Society* (New York: Newbury House, 1983), Jere E. Brophy and Thomas L. Good, *Teacher-Student Relations* (New York: Holt, 1974), and in the American Association of University Women Educational Foundation and the Wellesley College Center for Research on Women, *How Schools Shortchange Girls* (Washington, D.C.: AAUW Educational Foundation, 1992). Educational researchers have also found that boys tend to receive more teacher attention, both positive and negative, than do girls, and that some teachers praise and reprimand boys and girls for different things. Several studies have found that boys are more often scolded for misbehavior and praised for their academic work, while girls more often are chastised for poor academic performance and praised for appearance, neatness, and being polite. For reviews of this research, see Marlaine S. Lockheed with Susan S. Klein, "Sex Equity in Classroom Organization and Climate," in *Handbook for Achieving Sex Equity through Education* (Baltimore: John Hopkins University Press, 1985), pp. 189–217, and Louise Cherry Wilkinson and Cora B. Marrett, eds., *Gender Influences in Classroom Interaction* (New York: Academic Press, 1985).

14. See Tyack and Hansot, *Learning Together: A History of Coeducation in American Schools* (New Haven: Yale University Press, 1990) for photographs and floor plans of schools built in the early decades of this century with separate entrances and spaces designated for girls and boys.

15. Robert B. Everhart, *Reading, Writing, and Resistance* (Boston: Routledge & Kegan Paul, 1983), p. 51.

16. Goffman observes that this "parallel organization," in which similar activities were organized in segregated manner, provides a "ready base of elaborating differential treatment," such as having a row of girls file in before a row of boys. Erving Goffman, "The Arrangement between the Sexes," *Theory and Society* 4 (1977): 306.

17. My observations resemble those of Janet Lever, who recovered differences in the playground activities of fifth-graders in Connecticut. She found that boys most often engaged in team sports, whereas girls focused on turn-taking play. See Janet Lever, "Sex Differences in the Games Children Play," *Social Problems* 23 (1976): 478–487, and Janet Lever, "Sex Differences in the Complexity of Children's Play and Games," *American Sociological Review* 43 (1978): 471–483. John Evans, "Gender Differences in Children's Games: A Look at the Team Selection Process," *Canadian Association for Health, Physical Education and Recreation Journal* 52 (1986): 4–9, observed team games during recess in an Illinois public school and found that of 238 team games, 78 percent were played by boys as a group; on only fifty-two occasions (22 percent) did team membership include both boys and girls. Of all team games, 193 (81 percent) were played by fifth-and sixth-graders.

18. While sex differences in children's game preferences are less extreme than in earlier times, Brian Sutton-Smith and B. G. Rosenberg found that between the late 1920s and the late 1950s there were some convergences in the game choices of girls and boys in fourth, fifth, and sixth grades. The change was due mostly to girls adopting interests (swimming, tag, kites) previously limited to boys. On the other hand, boys drew away from some games (hopscotch, jacks, jump rope) that then became more typed as girls' play. The enhanced interest in organized sports for girls that emerged in the 1970s and 1980s has probably further increased the convergence of girls' and boys' game preferences, but the overall separation remains substantial. Brain Sutton-Smith and B. G. Rosenberg, "Sixty Years of Historical Change in the Game Preferences of American Children," *Journal of American Folklore* 74 (1961): 17–46.

19. An early article by Carole Joffe, "As the Twig Is Bent," *And Jill Came Tumbling After*, Judith Stacey, Susan Bereaud, and Joan Daniels, eds., (New York: Dell, 1974), pp. 79–90, first alerted me to children's invocation of gender as an "ideology of control." For a detailed analysis of processes of access and exclusion among children at play in a day-care center, see William Corsaro, "We're Friends, Right? Children's Use of Access Rituals in a Nursery School," *Language in Society* 8 (1979): 315–336.

20. This estimate comes from Willard W. Hartup, "Peer Relations," in *Handbook of Child Psychology, vol. 4: Socialization, Personality and Social Development*, 4th ed., ed. Paul Mussen and E. Mavis Heatherington, (New York: Wiley, 1983), pp. 103–196.

21. Zella Luria and Eleanor W. Herzog, "Gender Segregation across and within Settings," a paper presented at the annual meeting of the Society for Research on Child Development, Toronto, Canada, 1985. Marlaine S. Lockheed and Abigail M. Harris, "Cross-Sex Collaborative Learning in Elementary Classrooms," *American Educational Research Journal* 21 (1984): 275–294. Also reviews of research in Hartup, "Peer Relations," in *Handbook of Child Psychology, vol. 4: Socialization, Personality and Social Development*, 4th ed., ed. Paul Mussen and E. Mavis Heatherington, (New York: Wiley, 1983), pp. 103–196; Marlaine S. Lockheed, "Some Determinants and Consequences of Sex Segregation in the Classroom," ed. Louise Cherry Wilkinson and Cora B. Marrett, *Gender Influences in Classroom Interaction* (New York: Academic Press, 1985), pp. 167–184; and Eleanor E. Maccoby and

Carol Nagy Jacklin, "Gender Segregation in Childhood," ed. E. H. Reese, *Advances in Child Development and Behavior*, vol. 20, (New York: Academic Press, 1987), pp. 239–287.

22. Zella Luria and Eleanor W. Herzog, "Gender Segregation across and with Settings," a paper presented at annual meeting of the Society for Research on Child Development, Toronto, Canada, 1985.

23. For example, when Maureen Hallinan and Nancy B. Tuma, "Classroom Effects on Change in Children's Friendships," *Sociology of Education* 51 (1978): 270–282, asked fourth-, fifth-, and sixth-graders to name their "best friends," 77 percent named someone of the same gender. Elliott A. Medrich, Judith Roizen, Victor Rubin, and Stuart Buckley, in *The Serious Business of Growing Up: A Study of Children's Lives Outside School* (Berkeley: University of California Press, 1982), asked 764 sixth-graders to name their "close friends." The students named a median number of three, and more boys (91 percent) than girls (82 percent) named only people of their own gender; the girls who named at least one boy were more likely than other girls to play team sports.

24. Maureen Hallinan, "Structural Effects of Children's Friendships and Cliques," *Social Psychology Quarterly* 42 (1979): 54–77.

25. Janet W. Schofield, *Black and White in School* (New York: Praeger, 1982). Schofield found that race, as well as gender, was a barrier to the development of friendship; in the racially balanced middle school where she observed, close friendships between students of different genders or races were quite rare.

Chapter Nineteen

Boy Culture

E. Anthony Rotundo

In 1853, a popular etiquette writer called Mrs. Manners launched an angry attack on the boys of America. "Why is it," she asked, "that there must be a period in the lives of boys when they should be spoken of as 'disagreeable cubs'? Why is a gentle, polite boy such a rarity?" She continued her assault in that tone of embattled hauteur so common to etiquette writers: "If your parents are willing for you to be the 'Goths and Vandals' of society, I shall protest against it. You have been outlaws long enough, and now I beg you will observe the rules."[1]

For all her wounded righteousness, Mrs. Manners expressed a widely shared view. Source after source described boys as "wild" and "careless," as "primitive savages" full of "animal spirits." They were commonly compared to Indians and African tribesmen. One writer even called them a race unto themselves—"the race of boys."[2] The literary critic Henry Seidel Canby—reflecting on his own boyhood in the 1880s and 1890s—emphasized the separation of boys' world from the world of adults: "There was plenty of room for our own life, and we took it, so that customs, codes, ideals, and prejudices were absorbed from our elders as by one free nation from another."[3]

This "free nation" of boys was a distinct cultural world with its own rituals and its own symbols and values. As a social sphere, it was separate both from the domestic world of women, girls, and small children, and from the public world of men and commerce. In this space of their own, boys were able to play outside the rules of the home and the marketplace. It was a heady and even liberating experience.

Technically, of course, boy culture was really a subculture—distinct, oppositional, but intimately related to the larger culture of which it was a part. Boys shuttled constantly in and out of this world of theirs, home and then back again. Their experiences with boy culture helped to prepare them in many ways for life in the adult spheres that surrounded them. Boy culture, then, was not the only world that a young male inhabited, nor was it the only one that left its mark on him. Still, within its carefully set boundaries, boy culture was surprisingly free of adult intervention—it gave a youngster his first exhilarating taste of independence and made a lasting imprint on his character.

To be sure, this was not the first time historically that Northern boys had been free from supervision. Perpetual supervision of *any* child is impossible. But the circumstances of boys' lives in the nineteenth century freed them from adult oversight for long periods of time in the company of other boys, and this was different from the colonial experience. In the villages of New England during the 1600s and 1700s, a boy past the age of six was given responsibility for the first time. He began to help his father with farm work, which put him in the company of another generation and not among his male peers. His father did give him independent chores to do, but they tended to be solitary activities like tending livestock or running errands to other farms. Of course, boys did gather and play in colonial New England, but circumstances made it hard for them to come together on a regular basis in the absence of adults. They lacked the independence and cohesion as a group that boys developed in the nineteenth century.[4]

These later generations of the 1800s spent more time in the peer world of schoolhouse and schoolyard. Middle-class boys were needed less to do the work of the family. They were increasingly isolated from males of the older generation. A growing proportion of them lived in large towns and cities, which brought them in contact with a denser mass of peers. And, in a world where autonomy had become a male virtue, there were positive reasons to give boys time and space of their own. In sum, the conditions were ripe in the nineteenth century for a coherent, independent boys' world.

Nineteenth-century boys lived a different sort of life in the years before boy culture opened up to them—a life so different from what came later that it bears special notice here. Until the age of six or so, boys were enmeshed in a domestic world of brothers, sisters, and cousins. They rarely strayed from the presence of watchful adults.[5] Mothers kept an especially keen eye on their children during these early years, for popular thinking held that this was the phase of life when the basis was laid for good character. Thus, for his first five to seven years, a boy's adult companions were female and his environment was one of tender affection and moral rigor.[6] By the time that boys reached the age of three or four, their mothers were beginning to complain about their rowdy, insolent ways.[7] But however much they rebelled, these little boys were still embedded in a feminine world.

The clothing that boys wore during their early years served as a vivid symbol of their feminization: they dressed in the same loose-fitting gowns that their sisters wore. One Ohio man described the small boys' outfit of his childhood as "a sort of Kate Greenaway costume, the upper part of the body covered by a loose blouse, belted in at the waist, allowing the skirt to hang half-way to the knees." Under these gowns, they wore "girllike panties" which "reached the ankles."[8] Such "girllike" clothing gave small boys the message that they were expected to behave like their sisters, and served also as a token of the feminine environment that clothed them socially at this point in life. More than that, boy's gowns and smocks inhibited the running, climbing, and other physical activities that so often made boys a disagreeable addition to the gentle domesticity of women's world. Whether they meekly accepted the way their parents dressed them or rebelled against its confinements, boys were put in a situation where they had to accept or reject a feminine identity in their earliest years.[9]

Finally, at about age six, Northern boys cut loose from these social and physical restraints.[10] Although they would continue to live many years in the woman's world of the home, they were now inhabitants of an alternate world as well.[11] In the cities, middle-class boy culture flourished in backyards, streets, parks, playgrounds, and vacant lots, all of which composed "a series of city states to play in." For those who lived in small towns, the neighboring orchards, fields, and forests provided a natural habitat for boy culture.[12] By contrast, indoors was alien territory. A parlor, a dining room, almost any place with a nice carpet, repelled boy culture. Boys did sometimes carve out their own turf within the house—usually in the attic, where dirt, noise, and physical activity created fewer problems than in the clean, placid lower floors. And the house was not the only indoor space that was alien. Boy culture languished in the school and in the church, and it never even approached the offices and countinghouses where middle-class fathers worked.[13]

How did a small boy enter this new realm at first? One man remembered simply that he "was aware of a great change in [his] world. It was no longer contained within a house bounded by four walls . . . [but] had swelled and expanded into a street."[14] Perhaps the change came for most boys with a similar lack of fanfare. Certainly, the autobiographies and family correspondence of the time reveal no special rite of passage that marked the entry into boy culture. As they broke away from the constant restriction of home, boys also shed forever the gowns and petticoats of younger days. Suddenly, the differences between themselves and their sisters—so long discouraged by the rules and habits of the home—seemed to be encouraged and even underscored.[15] For their sisters were still enveloped by the moral and physical confinements of domesticity and by the gowns and petticoats that were its visible emblems. With great clarity a boy saw that female meant fettered and male meant free.[16]

Boys, of course, were not absolutely free any more than the girls were literally chained. Indeed, their worlds of play and sociability overlapped at many points. At play, girls shared the yard with their brothers, and on rainy days boys cohabited attics and odd rooms with their sisters. Girls and boys enjoyed many of the same games, such as hide-and-seek and tag, and they pursued some of the same outdoor activities, such as sledding and skating. But their social worlds and their peer cultures were distinct. Boys had a freedom to roam that girls lacked. Physical aggression drove boys' activity in a way that was not acceptable for girls. The activities of both sexes mixed competition with collaboration, but the boys placed a stronger emphasis on their rivalries and the girls stressed their cooperation more heavily. Most importantly, the social worlds of boys and girls had different relationships with the world of adults of the same sex. Boy culture was independent of men and often antagonistic toward them. Girls' common culture was interdependent with that of women and even shared much of the same physical space. There was continuity, if not always amity, between the worlds of female generations.[17] The same was not true for men and boys. The nineteenth-century emphasis on male autonomy encouraged a gap between generations of males.

Boy Culture: Games and Pastimes

Boys now enjoyed the liberty of trousers and the independence of the great outdoors. More than that, they were beyond the reach of adult supervision for hours at a time. Boys were suddenly free to pursue a range of activities that would have been difficult if not impossible in the domestic world. The physical activities that had been hindered in early boyhood now became particular passions. Hiking, exploring, swimming, rowing, and horseback riding took on special meaning for boys newly liberated from domestic confinement.[18]

Of course, the boys who grew up in small towns and on farms had the best opportunities to hike and swim, but those who lived in cities had their own chances. Through most of the nineteenth century, urban areas were dotted with patches of scrub woodland where boys could play and explore.[19] Even in the huge cities of the century's later years, rural life could be imported in the form of parks and swimming lessons or improvised in vacant lots and backyards.[20] City and country boys had more or less equal access to the best-loved winter activities of boy culture, such as sledding, skating, or throwing snowballs.

While boys pursued these pastimes for the simple pleasure of exercise, they engaged in many other activities that set them head to head in hostile combat. Friends fought or wrestled for the fun of it, while other boys goaded playmates unwillingly into fights with each other. The varieties of physical punishment that boys inflicted on each other were as numerous as the settings in which they gathered. At boarding schools in the late nineteenth century, new students were forced by older students to run between two lines of boys who tried to bruise them with clubs and well-shod feet; in another variant, new boys ran naked around the inside of a circle while veteran students hit their bare buttocks with paddles. In Hamilton, Ohio, where William Dean Howells spent much of his boyhood, youngsters threw stones at their friends purely for sport or even as a form of greeting. Beneath this violence lay curious veins of casual hostility and sociable sadism. One of the bonds that held boy culture together was the pain that youngsters inflicted on each other.[21]

If boys posed a danger to one another, they were downright lethal to small animals. Boys especially enjoyed hunting birds and squirrels, and they did a good deal of trapping as well. There were several reasons for hunting's great appeal. In the rural North of the nineteenth century, the gun and the rod were still emblems of the male duty to feed one's family. The hunt, in that way, was associated with the power and status of grown men.[22] Yet city boys—given the opportunity to hunt—took the same lusty pleasure in it that their country cousins did. They just liked the challenge of the kill. Another practice that links the hunting habit to the violent tendencies of boy culture is the extravagant sadism that youngsters sometimes showed when they killed their prey. Boys turned woodchuck trapping into woodchuck torture, and they often killed insects simply to inflict suffering. While the boyish interest in hunting and fishing reflected in some part a remnant of earlier manly duties, it was also related to the pleasure that boys took in fighting and even stoning one another.[23]

Not all of boys' play was so openly violent or so freeform. Popular boys' games such as marbles, tag, blindman's buff, leapfrog, and tug-of-war, demanded physical skill, and most involved exercise and competition as well. An informal, prehistoric form of football mixed elements of tag, rugby, soccer, and the modern gridiron game with a large dose of free-for-all mayhem. There were also a number of variants on the current sport of baseball. What united these varied pastimes in contrast to modern games was a lack of elaborate rules and complicated strategies. Spontaneous exercise and excitement were more important than elaborate expertise in boys' games of the nineteenth century.[24] Other pastimes were more personally expressive. Games that developed on the spur of the moment or that grew slowly within the context of a friendship or a gang revealed many of the preoccupations of boy culture. A favorite subject in these improvised games was warfare. Sometimes, the young combatants took on the roles of the knights they read about in books, while during the Civil War they played the soldiers of their own time.[25]

The most popular variant on these war games seemed to be the struggle between settlers and Indians. In this case, the boys were often inspired by the stories of people they knew or by the local folklore about ancestral generations.[26] One revealing aspect of these games involved the choosing of sides. By race and sometimes by ancestry, the boys were kin to the settlers. Yet there is no indication that any stigma attached to playing an Indian. Indeed, the boys relished the role of the Indian—assumed by them all to be more barbarous and aggressive—as much as they did the role of the settler.[27] These settler-and-Indian games allowed boys to enter and imagine roles that were played by real adult males. Such imitative play was a vital part of boy culture, and there were a number of other popular activities that allowed even closer copying of adult men. Some towns, for instance, had junior militia companies just like the ones for grown-ups, and they often staged mock battles. Boys were also enthusiastic spectators at the militia musters for adults, and joined in the action if they could.

There were other settings in which boys could imitate men and even participate in their tasks. During the antebellum era, political parties pressed boys into service for their rallies and parades. Youngsters carried signs and torches and lit victory bonfires; they also generated a certain amount of unassigned activity, such as fighting with young supporters of the other party and lighting victory bonfires even when the opposition won.[28] The boys who lived in antebellum cities followed another exciting man's activity by attaching themselves to volunteer fire companies. Historians have written about the role that these companies played in the cultural life of the artisan and laboring classes.[29] But the work of the volunteer fire units was too dramatic for even the most privileged boys to ignore. Every neighborhood had a fire company and, when the cry of "Fire!"

rang out, each one dragged its engine through the city streets and then pumped as hard as it could to play a stream of water on the fire as quickly as possible. The work was hard but stirring, and the competition between companies was so fierce that it sometimes led to violence. In short, the work of the volunteer fire companies contained almost every element needed to seize the imagination of a nineteenth-century boy.

Most boys took particular interest in imitating—or taking part in—the work of a specially admired man: their father. Opportunities to do this differed considerably for city and country lads. Rural youngsters, after all, lived in closer proximity to their fathers' work, and there was much greater need of their help. Even the businessmen and professionals of the small towns kept farms or farm animals for domestic use, and they needed to rely on menial labor from their sons.[30] On the other hand, affluent city boys were lucky if they could imitate any of their fathers' work activities. Not only were urban boys separated from the work world of their fathers, but most of those middle-class men did work that was too abstract to interest a youngster. Buying, selling, and keeping accounts were not activities that caught a boy's fancy.[31] Beneath this difference, though, lay the essential similarity of urban and rural boy culture, both in values and in purposes. Boys from both settings were drawn to activities that offered excitement and physical exercise. Dirt and noise were often by-products of such pastimes. And certain boys' activities provided special opportunity to enter and imagine the roles of adult males.

Above all, the pastimes favored by Northern boys set their world in sharp contrast to the domestic, female world—the world from which they emerged as little boys and to which they returned every evening. Where women's sphere offered kindness, morality, nurture, and a gentle spirit, the boys' world countered with energy, self-assertion, noise, and a frequent resort to violence. The physical explosiveness and the willingness to inflict pain contrasted so sharply with the values of the home that they suggest a dialogue in actions between the values of the two spheres—as if a boy's aggressive impulses, so relentlessly opposed at home, sought extreme forms of release outside it; then, with stricken consciences, the boys came home for further lessons in self-restraint. The two worlds seemed almost to thrive on their opposition to each other. Boys, though they valued both worlds deeply, often complained about the confinement of home. The world that they created just beyond the reach of domesticity gave them a space for expressive play and a sense of freedom from the women's world that had nurtured them early in boyhood—and that welcomed them home every night.

Boy Culture: Bonds and Fissures

The contrast between boy culture and the domestic sphere extended to the nature and strength of the bonds that cemented each of those two social worlds. The nineteenth-century home was held intact by love and also by adult authority. Its primary purpose was nurture, and this tended to draw its members together in emotional support and in common bonds of conscience and self-sacrifice. By contrast, the world of boy culture was held intact by less enduring ties. The expressive play that gave boy culture its focus was conducive to self-assertion and conflict more than to love or understanding, and this led boys to create a different sort of bond than that which held together the domestic world.

Friendship was certainly the most important relation between boys, and within their world it took on some distinctive qualities. One writer has said that, in boys' world, "friendships formed . . . which [were] fervent if not enduring."[32] Evidently, these fond but shifting ties had as much to do with availability as with deeper affinities. An autobiographer, describing his younger days in Connecticut, said that "in boyhood . . . friendships are determined not more perhaps by similarity of disposition and common likes and dislikes than by propinquity and accidental association."[33] Boys' friendships tended to be superficial and sudden, however passionate they might be for the moment.

Given the ephemeral nature of these bonds, it is not surprising that the strongest and most enduring friendships were forged at home between brothers and cousins. Alphonso Rockwell, who grew up in New Canaan, Connecticut, during the 1820s and 1830s, described the close friendship between himself and his cousin Steve: "We were the same age, and from our sixth to our sixteenth years we were constantly together. Hardly a day passed without our seeing each other."[34] Kin friendships like this one rose on a foundation of love and familiarity that already existed. Of course, a strong friendship could develop across family lines, too. Henry Dwight Sedgwick and Lawrence Godkin, who were cross-street neighbors in New York City during the 1860s and 1870s, enjoyed common activities and shared a deep antipathy to the "muckers" from down the block. They remained devoted friends for several years, but Lawrence is most notable in Henry's autobiography for his steadfast loyalty in times of peril.[35] Good companionship and unshakable fidelity were the keys to friendship between boys, not confiding intimacy. Indeed, the consideration of loyalty was so important in the competitive milieu of boy culture that these youthful relationships often took on the qualities of an alliance.[36]

Loyalty also laid the basis for one of the great passions of nineteenth-century boys—the formation of clubs. Meeting in attics and cellars, these clubs ranged from a small-town cabal that specialized in melon theft to a natural history "museum" established by Theodore Roosevelt. Two common purposes of these boys' clubs were nurture and athletics. Fellow members raided local orchards and gardens, then they cooked and ate their booty together. Boys formed athletic groups that organized extensive competitions among members. The two purposes of nurture and competition were not mutually exclusive, either. One such club in a small Indiana town met in the attic of a local business building to eat pilfered melons and corn together. When the secret meal was finished, the boys retreated to a nearby woods to pummel each other in fierce boxing matches which ended "frequently in bloody noses, blackened eyes, and bruised bodies."[37] This club represented a curious mixture: affection joined with combat; mutual nurture combined with assault and battery. Such mingling of friendship with combat was typical of boy culture.

In point of fact, boy culture was divided as surely as it was united. Club memberships were always limited, which guaranteed the exclusion of some boys. For example, when Theodore Roosevelt started his natural history museum as a boy, he invited two of his cousins to join but pointedly excluded his brother, Elliott. Secret words and codes further isolated outsiders, even as they united those who belonged. Rivalry, division, and conflict were vital elements in the structure of boy culture. Just as friendship between boys bloomed suddenly and with fervor, so, too, did enmity. While good friends often enjoyed combat with each other, hand-to-hand battles did not always take place in a friendly context. Instant hostility frequently arose between boys and was "taken out on the spot," for the youngsters preferred to settle "a personal grievance at once, even if the explanation is made with fists."[38] New boys in town often had to prove themselves by fighting, and older boys amused themselves by forcing the younger boys into combat with each other.[39]

The fiercest fights of all involved youngsters from rival turf. Indeed, such "enemy" groups played a powerful role in unifying local segments of boy culture, and many boys' gangs were really just neighborhood alliances designed to protect members and turf from other gangs. In the countryside, these divisions pitted village against village or the boys from one side of town against boys from the other. In cities, lines were drawn between the youngsters of different neighborhoods. In a large, densely packed metropolis like New York, the crucial rivalries could even develop between boys at opposite ends of the block.[40] Sometimes these geographic battle lines reflected nothing more than the simple accident of residence; but they often coincided with sharp differences of class and ethnicity, adding extra layers of meaning to boyish antagonisms. Reflecting on his own boyhood, Henry Seidel Canby recalled the fierce hostility between Protestant boys from the comfortable neighborhoods of Wilmington, Delaware, and the Irish Catholic boys from the nearby slums. To reach their private schools every day, the youngsters from the "better" families had to cross through enemy turf and pass the public and parochial schools the Irish boys attended. Canby wrote: "Each of us, by one of those tacit agreements made between enemies, had his particular mick, who either chased or was chased . . . on sight . . . It was an awful joy to spot your own mick."[41]

Social differences much less dramatic and vivid could also form the basis for animosity. Henry Dwight Sedgwick described the rivalry between the boys at the Fifth and Sixth avenue ends of New York's Forty-eighth Street in the years around 1870. Henry and the others who lived near Fifth Avenue knew that their houses were larger than those at the other end of the block and that their downstreet neighbors had open-topped garbage cans which sat out in plain sight instead of under the stoop. Sedgwick and his friends were also aware of a less visible difference: "Our fathers' offices and places of business might have interests in common with the offices and places of business of their fathers, but our drawing-rooms, no. Our women folk could not call upon their women folk." At most, the difference between the two groups of Forty-eighth Street boys was the difference between various rungs of the middle class, but this contrast—highlighted by geography—was enough to set them against each other.[42]

While these differences of class and neighborhood carved the boys' world up into large segments, there were finer gradations within boy culture that produced fewer dramatic confrontations but occupied much more of a boy's daily attention. In particular, differences of size and skill became major preoccupations in boy culture. The distinction between bigger and smaller boys expressed itself in a variety of ways. Throughout the century and across the Northeast, bigger boys bullied smaller ones. In Wilmington, Delaware, this custom was so common that Henry Seidel Canby wrote: "Every little boy had a big boy who bullied him."[43] Meanwhile, college and boarding school students during all parts of the century were carrying on that ritualized form of bullying known as hazing.[44] Smaller boys became victims in various kinds of organized games as well. They played the deserters and spies who were shot in games of soldier, and they were the riders who were knocked off their big-boy "horses" in one version of settlers-and-Indians.[45] In some activities, the distinction between age and size blurred: "little" and "young" usually meant the same thing with boys.

Among boys who were close together in age and size, another division existed—a series of informal rankings based on skill. They rated each other by weight, height, "pluck," spirit, appearance, and all sorts of athletic skills from swimming to stone-throwing to ability at various organized games. The frequent fights between boys established a vitally important kind of pecking order. Those urban boys who spent much of their time in school ranked each other's scholastic abilities on a finely graded scale. Although youngsters determined some of these ratings by open contest, they established many others through unceasing observation.[46] While this constant process of comparison did not divide boy culture as deeply as class and geography did, it did provide a basis for elaborate, cross-cutting hierarchies within the group and set the stage for many personal jealousies and conflicts.[47]

In fact, the boys' world was endlessly divided and subdivided. Clearly set apart from the worlds of men, of very small boys, and of the entire female sex, the realm of boyhood was split into groups by residence, ethnicity, and social status. These chunks of boys' world were ordered internally by a shifting series of competitive rankings. Personal animosity created further division. Linking boys across these many fissures were family ties and the loyalty of friendship. But friendships among boys were volatile affairs—intense, short-lived, and constantly shifting. To a great extent, then, boys' realm was—like the grown-up world of their fathers—based on the isolated individual. Although it was a little culture based on constant play and full of exuberance and high spirits, it was also a cruel, competitive, uncertain, and even violent world. How, then, did it hold together? It held together because boys adhered faithfully to a common set of values.

The Values of Boy Culture

Boy culture embraced two different sorts of values. First, there were explicit values, those traits and behaviors that boys openly respected in one another. Then there were implicit values embedded in the structure of boy culture, values youngsters rarely expressed but which they honored constantly through their daily activities and experiences. Both of these layers of value added to the distinctiveness of boy culture, and both formed a part of the legacy of boy culture by leaving a permanent imprint on youngsters' characters.

Boys revealed many of their values in the activities they pursued. In a world that centered on physical play, bodily attributes and physical prowess loomed large. Traits such as size, strength, speed, and endurance earned a boy respect among his peers.[48] More subtle but just as highly valued was the gift of courage. One writer on boyhood called courage "the ethics for ideal conduct in emotional stress," and for most boys behavior under physical stress was just as important.[49] Moments of bravery fell into two different categories, stoicism and daring. Stoicism involved the suppression of "weak" or "tender" feelings that were readily exposed in the feminine world of home—grief, fear, pain. The boys' game of "soak-about" was a classic expression of the demand for stoicism. In this game, a group of boys tried to hit another boy with a hard ball in any vulnerable spot that was available.[50] The victim could not cry out if he was hit—and, just as important, the youngster had to face the possibility of such pain without flinching.

Boys valued the ability to suppress displays of fear as well as of pain. When young Alphonso Rockwell and his cousin Steve were surrounded by five menacing rivals, "it was unquestionably a fact that we were scared." Rockwell remembered that his reaction then was the same as it was many times during his service in the Civil War—"to seem not to fear when I was really very much afraid." Instead of showing fear, young Rockwell's soldierly response was to pick up a stick with one hand and clench the other into a fist. The rival group backed down.[51] This stoic courage, a feat of self-control, contrasted sharply with daring courage, which was an achievement of action.

Like stoicism, daring found ritual expression in boy's games. In the contest called "I Conquer," a boy performed a dangerous feat and as he did so shouted the name of the game to his comrades. The cry challenged the other boys to duplicate the feat or lose the game.[52] Lew Wallace remembered the boyhood compulsion to dare, noting that he and his friends were "given to [this] 'dare' habit; . . . the deeper the water, the thinner the ice, the longer the run, the hotter the blaze, [then] the more certain [was] the challenge."[53] These experiences with the courage of daring may have left a lasting imprint on the boys who underwent them. A number of historians and commentators have noted that the ideal of achievement which grown-ups taught to boys was really the cautious, abstemious ethic of the clerk, rather than the bold and daring code of the entrepreneur.[54] Young males did not learn to be venturesome from the adults who preached hard work and self-denial, but from boy culture with its constant pressure for daring courage. Boldness, like stoicism, was a form of courage that youngsters cultivated in boyhood.

Physical prowess and the various forms of courage were uppermost among the qualities that boys values, but there were also others that they expected of each other. Boys demanded loyalty between friends and loyalty of the individual to the group. Their concept of the faithful friend closely resembled the code of fidelity that links comrades at arms. The true test of this loyalty came at moments when one boy was threatened and the other came to his aid. When an Ohio boy named Frank Beard was in his early teens, he rose to the defense of his cousin and took a thrashing from a much older youth who was larger and stronger than he. This was the ultimate act of loyalty to a friend.[55] Loyalty to the group expressed itself in dealings with outsiders. When boys banded together to defend their turf against rival groups from other towns or neighborhoods, they were performing a vital act of group loyalty.[56] The clubs that boys often formed were also based on loyalty to other members of the club and to its codes and secrets.[57]

There was another group of outsiders to whom boys responded with an exclusive sense of group loyalty—grown-ups. One of boy culture's basic taboos prohibited youngsters from appealing to any adult for help and even from revealing information that would compromise their independent activity. If a boy violated this sanction, his peers repaid him with scorn and abuse. To be labeled a "crybaby" was one of the worst fates for an inhabitant of boy culture.[58]

Together with courage and physical prowess, loyalty was one of the most valued of qualities among boys—and it was the one that they demanded most fiercely of each other. Beneath this layer of values that boys honored consciously, however, there was another layer that developed from the habits and activities of boy culture. The youngsters themselves rarely discussed these implicit values— it seems that they lay just outside of boys' consciousness—but the boys learned some of their most important childhood lessons by learning to practice these valued traits and habits.

Of these implied values, the one that was most pervasive in boy culture was mastery. For one thing, youngsters were constantly learning to master new skills. The boys' many games and pastimes helped them develop a great variety of physical abilities. They also learned a wide range of social skills from their intensive social contact with each other and from the negotiations that threaded in and out of their daily round of activity. Boys' experience in their separate world likewise taught them how to impose their will on other people and on nature itself. Their education in social mastery went on constantly while they were among their peers. Most of their popular pastimes forced boys to seek each other's defeat and thus prove individual mastery. At another level, boys strove for mastery by trying to set the agenda for their group of comrades ("dare" games like "I Conquer" were an extreme version of this impulse). Some boys practiced mastery through bullying.

Boys' attempts to master their environment were often directed at the physical rather than the social world. In a world where people no longer relied on hunting and fishing to feed themselves, the killing of animals taught boys the habit of dominion over their natural environment. Furthermore, there were city boys who hunted to enlarge their collection of stuffed and mounted animals. From this pastime, boys learned to subordinate nature to their own acquisitive impulses. When they named and classified the animals they killed, boys were learning to make nature serve the cause of scientific advance. Other forms of boyhood mastery fed on this same technological drive. The building of toy ships that would actually float, the construction of snow forts, the performance of crude scientific experiments—these common boyhood activities taught youngsters the skills (and the habit) of mastery over nature in the service of human needs and knowledge. The experience of boy culture encouraged a male child to become the master, the conqueror, the owner of what was outside him.

At the same time, boyhood experiences were teaching a youngster to master his inner world of emotions. Games like "soak-about" taught boys to control their fears and to carry on in the face of physical pain. Peer pressure also forced them to control those "weak" feelings, as the fear of being labeled a "crybaby" restrained the impulse to seek comfort in times of stress. As boys learned to master pain, fear, and the need for emotional comfort, they were encouraged to suppress other expressions of vulnerability, such as grief and tender affection. Boy culture, then, was teaching a selective form of impulse control—it was training boys to master those emotions that would make them vulnerable to predatory rivals.

Their activities not only put a premium on self-control, but also created an endless round of competitions. Even activities that were not inherently competitive—swimming, climbing, rock-throwing—yielded countless comparisons. Youngsters were learning to rank their peers, and at the same time they developed the habit of constantly struggling up the ladder of achievement. Moreover, as each boy asserted his will incessantly against the others, he grew accustomed to life as a never ending series of individual combats.

This environment existed in part because boy culture sanctioned certain kinds of impulses. Even as it curbed the expression of tender, vulnerable emotions, boy culture stimulated aggression and encouraged youngsters to vent their physical energy. The prevailing ethos of boys' world not only supported the expression of impulses such as dominance and aggression (which had evident social uses), but also allowed the release of hostile, violent feelings (whose social uses were less evident). By allowing free passage to so many angry or destructive emotions, boy culture sanctioned a good deal of intentional cruelty, like the physical torture of animals and the emotional violence of bullying. Yet much of the cruelty in boys' world was spontaneous and impulsive: as boys' aggressions were given free rein, the sheer exuberance of exercise and the pure joy of play prevailed, and needless cruelty and unthinking meanness often followed. Boys loved to compare themselves to animals, and two animal similes seem apt here. If at times boys acted like a hostile pack of wolves that preyed on its own kind as well as other species, they behaved at other times like a litter of playful pups who enjoy romping, wrestling, and testing new skills. Such play is rarely free of cruelty or violence, and the same can be said of boy culture. Playful spontaneity bred friendly play and rough hostility in equal measure.

The violence that friends inflicted on each other often signified more than the playful assertion of dominance or the unbridled expression of hostility; ironically, some of boys' violence was an expression of their fondness for each other. Since boys worked to restrain their tender impulses in each other's presence, they lacked a direct outlet for the natural affection between friends. This warm feeling sometimes found expression in the bonds of the club and the gang and in the demanding codes of loyalty that bound young comrades together, but another avenue of release for these fond impulses came through constant physical exchanges. Samuel Crothers described boys' world as a place "where the heroes make friends with one another by indulging in everlasting assault and battery, and continually arise 'refreshed with the blows.' "[59] Seen in this light, the boys' stoning of arriving and departing friends in William Dean Howells's hometown becomes a perversely affectionate form of salute. This curious marriage of violence and affection also found ritual expression in the small-town club where the boys fed each other and then beat each other bloody in boxing matches.[60]

The fact that boys expressed affection through mayhem does not mean that violence was merely a channel for fond feeling. Boys held back their deepest reserves of cruelty when they scrapped with friends, saving their fiercest fury for enemies. In their cultural world, where gestures of tenderness were forbidden, physical combat allowed them moments of touch and bouts of intense embrace. By a certain "boy logic," it made sense to pay their affections in the coin of physical combat that served as the social currency of boys' world.

Self-assertion and conflict, in other words, were such dominant modes of expression within boy culture that they could even serve as vehicles for tender feelings. Yet even these were not the most important values of boy culture. There was one value that governed all conduct, that provided a common thread for boys' activities together, that served as boy culture's virtual reason for being. This ultimate value was independence. What made boy culture special in a youngster's experience was that it allowed him a kind of autonomy that he had not enjoyed in early childhood. It gave him an independence that he did not have in any other area of life.

The experience of boy culture did more than simply teach boys to value independence, though. It also taught them how to use it. Boy culture challenged a youngster to master an immense variety of skills; forced him to learn elaborate codes of behavior and complex, layered systems of value; encouraged him to form enjoyable relationships and useful alliances and to organize groups that could function effectively; and demanded that he deal with the vicissitudes of competition and the constant ranking and evaluation of peers. Most of all, the culture of his fellows required a boy to learn all of these tasks independently—without the help of caring adults, with limited assistance from other boys, and without any significant emotional support. At the heart of nineteenth-century boy culture, then, lay an imperative to independent action. Each boy sought his own good in a world of shifting alliances and fierce competition. He learned to assert himself and to stand emotionally alone while away from his family. For the part of each day that he lived among his peers, a boy received a strenuous education in autonomy.

Boy Culture and Adult Authority

One of boy culture's most striking features was its independence from close adult supervision. This autonomy existed, however, within well-defined boundaries of place and time. Many adults tried to influence what went on within boy culture even though they did not supervise it. In order to understand boys' world fully we need to understand certain problems that arose at its boundaries: how boys tried to maintain the boundaries; who tried to penetrate them; and how that penetration—when it did happen—affected boy culture.

Of all the forces that threatened the borders of boy culture, the most pervasive was the community at large. The confrontations between youngsters and their communities came usually over minor acts of vandalism. The reasons for these social collisions varied. Acts of trespass and petty theft often grew out of the blithe disregard that boys had for private property. They refused to recognize the lines that separated one adult's possessions from another's.[61] At other times, it was the very knowledge of possible trouble with adults that led to vandalism. Boys, after all, were constantly daring each other to perform dangerous acts. And since a confrontation with authority was one kind of danger, risking that confrontation was a way to prove one's bravery.[62] Thus, the pleasure in raiding a garden or an orchard came from the adventure as much as the fruit, and youthful mischief-makers made a sport of avoiding officers of the law and irate property owners.

Sometimes an angry private citizen took it upon himself to fight petty youth crime in his community, but doing so made him a handsome target for another form of boyish malfeasance—the prank. One Ohio man—a "strait-laced Presbyterian farmer . . . who often rebuked the boys for their escapades"—paid for his opposition to vandalism when he found a ghastly battered corpse in his barn one morning. Although a frightened inspection showed that the corpse was a carefully prepared dummy, the episode had given the local boys an effective way to express their resentment of the farmer.[63]

Pranks, however, were more than just acts of vengeance. They reversed men's and boy's roles, giving younger males the power to disrupt the lives of older males and forcing the elders to do their boyish bidding. There was, for example, a Connecticut doctor who made a favorite target for the local boys. The "queerest man of the town," he had only one eye, spoke in a high falsetto, and possessed the strange habit of dismounting from his horse every time he saw a stone in the road. This made him an easy victim for pranks, as the boys scattered stones in his path and then watched with delight as he got off his horse to throw them away. The boys had found an exciting way to attack the dignity of an adult.[64]

Pranks resembled petty theft, trespassing, and other forms of vandalism in that they served as skirmishes in a kind of guerrilla warfare that boys waged against the adult world. These youthful raids on adult dignity and property gave boys a chance to assert their own needs and values and lay their claim to the out-of-doors as a world for them to use as they saw fit. Acts of vandalism also provided boys with an opportunity to express their hostility toward adult authority—in other words, toward most grown-up men. It was the men (police, constables, irate property owners) who stood in the way of most boys' adventures.[65] Finally, the guerrilla warfare of pranks and petty theft gave boys a moment of power to foil the intentions of grown men and to gain the property they wanted. Vandalism represented a statement of hostility and resentment by the males of one generation against the males of another, and it served also as an assertion of the needs and values of boy culture against the needs and values of adult (male) authority. Grown men could rarely control vandalism—they could only oppose it enough to make it a more exciting pastime for boys.

Neighbors, teachers, and lawmen fought countless skirmishes with the more troublesome boys of the community. Yet if an enemy of boy culture was one who tried to thwart youthful pleasure or who could compel a boy to do something against his will, then its most potent enemies were fathers and mothers. Parents provided a very different sort of enemy from distant figures of authority. Remote adults could be irked at little emotional cost, but parents were (usually) the two most beloved and powerful people in a boy's life. How did boy culture fare in its conflicts with parents? What happened when the borders of home and boys' world overlapped or the values of those two spheres conflicted?

The situation of fathers presents a simpler picture than that of mothers. Middle-class men had fewer points of contact than their wives did with the boy culture of their sons. While the activities of boys often swirled through the yard and into isolated corners of the home, they rarely approached the offices and counting houses where men spent their days.[66] Of course, fathers did intrude into the world of boy culture. In rural areas, a boy was expected to work on behalf of the family even if his father was a prominent lawyer, storekeeper, or politician. Boys might work at home or elsewhere, but it was fathers who arranged the work, and most fathers oversaw it, punishing failures of duty.[67] Fathers also frustrated boy culture by serving as head disciplinarians in their families. They were responsible for punishing the most serious breaches of household rules and, as a result, usually meted out the harshest discipline. For example, when Lew Wallace, the future novelist and Civil War hero, was banished from his Indiana home after long years of truancy and misbehavior, it was his father, not his mother, who banished him. The father also had the duty of punishing his son when someone from outside the home complained about the boy's behavior. For instance, when a Maine boy named John Barnard was caught stealing fruit from a neighbor's orchard, it was his father who sat him down for a stern lecture.[68] These intrusive duties placed the father in the role of arch-enemy to the hedonism that typified boy culture.

But fathers and other men were only the most visible enemies of boy culture, not the most effective ones. In the role of mother, women had more extensive contact with boys than their husbands did. And it was the mothers—not the fathers—who had the duty of responding immediately to situations that arose in the daily ebb and flow of family life. Women were also more effective opponents of boy culture because of their methods of opposition. They relied less than men on bluster or physical punishment and more on tenderness, guilt, and moral suasion—tactics that seemed to disarm the youthful opposition more effectively than a simple show of power. These contrasts between men's and women's tactics grew partly from the difference in their basic social duty toward boys: men were charged especially with the task of maintaining good order; women were supposed to go beyond that and make boys fit for the sober, responsible world of adults. To be sure, young Daniel Beard and his friends spoke from experience in declaring men as the "enemies of boys, always interfering with our pleasure." But Huck Finn saw deeper when he proclaimed that Aunt Sally wanted to "sivilize" him.[69]

Inevitably, then, the home and the out-of-doors came to stand for much more than just two physical spaces for women and boys—the domestic threshold marked a cultural dividing line of the deepest significance. On one side lay women's sphere, a world of domesticity and civilization; on the other side, boy culture flourished and adult control gave way to the rough pleasures of boyhood. Neither space was exclusive—women entered boys' world to deliver reprimands and reminders of duties at home, while boys sometimes established their distinctive culture in the nether regions of the household. But the home and the out-of-doors had powerful symbolic meaning. When boys tracked mud and dirt across clean floors, they did more than create extra housework—they violated the separation of spheres by bringing fragments of their boy-world into a place where they did not belong. And mothers also viewed their sons' priceless collections of rocks, leaves, and dead animals as invasions of a civilized world by a wild one. Thus, women and boys fought constantly over muddy footprints and other relics of the outdoors that found their way into the house.[70]

But mothers did not just struggle to keep the dirt and hedonism of boy culture out of the house. They also fought to extend their moral dominion into boys' world. Fortunately for women, they had more than one tactical weapon to use in this battle for moral influence. Often mothers attempted to control behavior by maintaining close contact with boy culture. The women who lived in small towns—and in all but the largest of cities—were members of social networks that sent information about their sons back to them quickly. Since they tended to run their errands in the same neighborhoods where their boys played, mothers could even conduct occasional surveillance of boy culture.[71] Most women were able to influence their sons' activities in the world outside the home. For example, mothers often played a direct and active role in curbing the physical violence of boy culture. Mary Howells punished her son William when she caught him fighting. He reported in later years that it was the influence of mothers which sometimes forced the boys to use buckshot instead of bullets in their hunting guns.[72] In a similar vein, mothers kept their sons away from impending "boy-battles" when they had advance knowledge of such events.

Women had other avenues of influence besides immediate surveillance and response. Their moral and spiritual authority seemed immense to their sons. Edward Everett Hale referred reverently to his mother's moral lessons as her "gospels." Ray Stannard Baker, a journalist who grew up in Wisconsin, remembered his aunts' religious teachings with less affection. He described these women, who had raised him in place of his invalid mother, as "veritable gorgons of the faith. They knew all of the shalt-nots in the Bible." He summarized their moral instruction as: "You mustn't, you can't. Remember the Sabbath day."[73]

The dire warnings against boyish behavior, though, came not just from the word of God or even from a mother's pleadings. Most of all, they came from the voice of conscience, that "tyrannical monitor" that condemned in a boy's heart every violation of the moral code he learned at his mother's knee. Daniel Beard, for one, felt this inner influence. His heart sank when his mother told him to stay away from the place where his friends were going to battle the boys from the next town. "This was bad news," wrote Beard, "but I never thought of disobeying her." So confident was Mary Beard of her influence over Daniel that she made no attempt to keep him at home. At the appointed hour, he wandered to a spot overlooking the scene of battle: "I stood disconsolately on the suspension bridge and watched my playmates, feeling like a base deserter." Beard's conscience held fast; with no one there to restrain him, he smothered his own urge to run to the aid of his comrades.[74]

There were other boys like Daniel Beard who loved to plunge into the endless tumult of boys' world but who were held in check by their own consciences. Lew Wallace's habit of truancy from school was restrained only by "the thought of [his] mother's fears" and his memory of her "entreaties and tears."[75] Clearly, mothers had an immense influence which extended beyond their physical presence and stretched as far as a boy could roam. Yet, as the Wallace example shows, maternal influence could not halt the operation of the wayward impulses that drove boy culture—it could only curb them. Boys, in other words, could not subdue their surging desires. They were pulled one way by the power of impulse and tugged another way by the voice of conscience.

In this struggle, the pressures of boy culture supplied a powerful counterforce to maternal influence. The worst fate a youngster could suffer at the hands of his peers was to be labeled a "mama's boy." One man wrote that "the most wicked and wanton song I knew [as a boy] was":

> Does your mother know you're out?
> No, by thunder, no, by thunder!
> Does she know what you're about?
> No, by thunder, no, by thunder!

The boys especially liked to sing this song as they performed feats of daring. The implication was that a mother's control was powerful—but it was delightful to slip beyond her grasp into forbidden pleasures.[76]

A vignette from a midcentury etiquette book suggests the ubiquitous influence of peer values on boys. As a mother earnestly tries to tie a ribbon in her son's collar, he complains that "the boys'll call me 'dandy,' and 'band-box,' and 'Tom Apronstring.'" The author of the book replies that Cousin Horace (the local paragon of good manners) "plays very heartily, too . . . he is no 'girl-boy.'" Even mothers knew the pressures that boys exerted on each other to ignore maternal pleas and abide by the standards of boy culture. It was a painful insult when a boy was accused of being tied to maternal apron strings or was reduced to the early-childhood status of "girl-boy."[77]

Such potent ridicule gave boys a powerful weapon for forcing others to reject their mothers' influence and conform to the hedonistic norms of their own cultural world. Under this kind of pressure, boys did much more than refuse to wear ribbons in their collars. Henry Seidel Canby remembered from his childhood that "breaking windows on Hallow E'en, swearing, pasting a cow with rotten eggs, or lining the horsecar tracks with caps to make the spavined horses run down grade, were protests against being 'goody goody.'" Daniel Beard and his friends scorned boys who "never went barefoot, . . . wasted a lot of time talking to girls, took no hikes, bathed often but seldom went swimming, won prizes at Sunday school but never on the ball field, and bought kites instead of making them."[78] Clearly, boys had a fine-tuned sense of who behaved acceptably and who did not, and nearly all of the unacceptable behaviors were ones encouraged by mothers. Boys employed ridicule, ostracism, and hazing to defend the values and integrity of boy culture from maternal assault.[79]

The boys' world was a culture governed by shame. Male youngsters were constantly watched by the eyes of their youthful community. If they violated the rules of their subculture, boys were subject to name-calling, scornful teasing, and even separation from the group. The threat of such painful treatment usually kept boys in line while they were together. But once away from the presence of their group, boys found it easier to follow along with domestic values. Of course, they misbehaved at home, too, but that was in response to their own impulses, not because of what the other boys would want them to do. Accounts of nineteenth-century boyhood show absolutely no evidence that boy culture affected youthful male behavior at home (unless, of course, it was a matter like dress that would in due time become *visible* to other boys). By contrast, the inner controls implanted largely by women were those of guilt. Boys carried the influence of maternal values out into their own world. Their consciences, as we have seen, made them feel guilty at some of their boyish misdeeds and held them back from committing others. Thus, women's sphere and boy culture differed sharply in the way they exercised social control. In this control, as in so many other aspects of values and behavior, the two different social spaces represented two divergent approaches to life.

Some of the most important lessons that a youngster learned from his experience of boy culture were the lessons about living a life divided between two spheres. He adapted to a constant process of home-leaving and return. And he quickly discovered that this process meant more than just a physical change of scene. It meant a constant adjustment to the clashing values and demands of two different worlds—back and forth from a domestic world of mutual dependence to a public world of independence; from an atmosphere of cooperation and nurture to one of competition and conflict; from a sphere where intimacy was encouraged to one where human relationships were treated instrumentally; from an environment that supported affectionate impulses to one that sanctioned aggressive impulses; from a social space that was seen as female to another that was considered male. At the same time that a boy learned to live in a world divided, he was also learning to live with divided loyalties and a divided heart. It was a conflict that would form a basic part of life for middle-class men.

Outgrowing Boy Culture

Boys defended the boundaries of their world zealously. They waged hit-and-run warfare against adults who tried to stifle their pleasures, and they harassed without mercy those boys who called on grown-ups to intervene in their affairs. But there was one boundary that they could not protect—the boundary of age that separated boyhood from manhood. In time, all boys grew up.

The end of boyhood in the nineteenth century did not come as it comes in the twentieth. There was no sequence of events that marked the progress of boys from childhood to manhood, and there were no key ages at which all youngsters reached important milestones. In earlier times, apprenticeship had marked an end of sorts to the boyhood years (though even the ages of apprenticeship might be indefinite). In the nineteenth century, the ages and events that brought boyhood to a close varied sharply with family and personal circumstances.[80]

In spite of these vague age boundaries, there were a few important events that marked the end of boyhood for many youngsters. These often had to do with leaving home or taking a first clerkship or full-time job. One dramatic example comes from the experience of Lew Wallace. When Lew was in his midteens, his father brought his carefree years of rambling and truancy to an end by turning him out of the house to support himself. Lew took on a clerical job, and, while working at it, conceived the literary ambitions that formed part of his work in manhood.[81] Alphonso Rockwell's boyhood also ended with the start of a clerkship, though his departure from home was more amicable than Wallace's—and in that sense was more typical. Looking back from old age, Rockwell realized that his boyhood stopped on the day he left his home in Connecticut to take his new position in New York City:

> The ties that held me to boyhood days and pleasures along old and familiar lines were to be broken forever. Henceforth there were to be no more trips to "Indian Rock" in the company of boy intimates, where we imagined ourselves wild Indians . . . nor would I ever in the days to come sail [the familiar ponds and streams], or swim in them, or walk their banks with the zest or sense of pleasure I had known.[82]

Alphonso was assuming new statuses now—self-support, a home away from his family—which were acknowledged as distinctive marks of manhood.

But these were not the only changes that signified the end of boyhood. A teenager also brought his time in boy culture to a close when he took his first strides toward another signpost of manhood—marriage. The journey toward marriage began with the dawning interest of pubescent boys in the opposite sex.[83] As boys developed an interest in girls, the customs and habits of boy culture started to lose their luster. Daniel Beard recalled in his autobiography the ways in which his outlook changed when an attractive new girl arrived in town: "Suddenly marbles became a childish game which made knuckles grimy and chapped. . . . Prisoner's base was good enough sport but it mussed one's clothes." The rhymes and rituals of boyhood now "seemed absurd instead of natural" while the services at church took on a new interest. Daniel suddenly began to appear in public with his face clean and his hair neatly combed.[84]

The pubescent boy did not, of course, return to the gowns and petticoats of his earliest years, but he did compromise with the demands of domesticity and restraint. He accepted willingly the confinement of clothing that had once seemed like shackles, and he wiped the once-treasured grime of outdoor activity from his face and hands. As he took his first steps toward marriage, "a life's work, and a home of his own, he clothed himself in the garb of "civilized" manhood and washed off the marks of "savage" boyhood.[85]

The cares and commitments of manhood now loomed up before teenage boys. At first sight, boys approached manhood eagerly; they were impatient to leave behind them the separate world that they had guarded so jealously. For example, when Alphonso Rockwell left his home in Connecticut to start his first clerkship, he did not reflect on the pleasures of boyhood (as he would in later years). Instead, he felt that he "was taking a step up in the world." Swelling with the sense of his own growing importance, he told his carriage driver on the day that he left home to drive fast, "as it would not do for me to miss the train . . . I [have] an important engagement to meet in New York."[86]

Charles Dudley Warner's observations on the end of boyhood ran parallel to those of Rockwell. He, too, was nostalgic about boyhood later in life, complaining that "just as you get used to being a boy, you have to be something else, with a good deal more work to do and not half as much fun." Yet Warner was quick to admit that "every boy is anxious to be a man, and is very uneasy with the restrictions that are put upon him as a boy." Warner also pointed out that, as much as boys liked to "play work," most would gladly trade it for a chance to do "real work"—that is, a man's work. As we noted earlier, some boy-culture pastimes imitated men's activity or offered direct (if token) participation in the work of male adults.[87] Yet, there were important disjunctions between boys' world and the world of men, gaps of duty and expectation that loomed like chasms before a teenage youth. The experience of facing those gaps and then trying to bridge them produced one of the most trying times in the lives of nineteenth-century men: the treacherous and often prolonged passage from boyhood to manhood.

The contrasts between boy culture and the world of men were sharp ones: boy culture emphasized exuberant spontaneity; it allowed free rein to aggressive impulses and reveled in physical prowess and assertion. Boy culture was a world of play, a social space where one evaded the duties and restrictions of adult society. How different this was from the world of manhood. Men were quiet and sober, for theirs was a life of serious business. They had families to support, reputations to earn, responsibilities to meet. Their world was based on work, not play, and their survival in it depended on patient planning, not spontaneous impulse. To prosper, then, a man had to delay gratification and restrain desire. Of course, he also needed to be aggressive and competitive, and he needed an instinct for self-advancement. But he had to channel these assertive impulses in ways that were suitable to the abstract battles and complex issues of middle-class men's work. Finally, a man—unlike a boy—needed a sense of responsible commitment. He could not throw over his family, disregard his business partners, or quit his job on a whim. A man had to have a sense of duty based on enduring loyalty, not on the strongest impulse of the moment. Manhood presented a young male with challenges for which boy culture had not fully prepared him. With the leap from boyhood to adulthood, a young man gave up heedless play for sober responsibility.

The strain of transition from boy culture to the world of men—coming simultaneously with the painful experience of leaving home—created a stressful and uncertain phase of life. Starting usually in the middle to late teens, a boy (often called a youth by now) struggled to make the transition on his own. There was no rite of passage to help him through. Society left him largely on his own to find his way to an adult identity.

NOTES

1. Mrs. Manners, *At Home and Abroad; or How to Behave* (New York, 1853), 40–41.

2. The phrase is from Charles Dudley Warner, *Being a Boy* (Boston, 1897 [1877]), 66–67, but similar imagery appears throughout the source material: Lewis Wallace, *Lew Wallace: An Autobiography* (New York, 1906), 54–55; Daniel Carter Beard, *Hardly a Man Is Now Alive: The Autobiography of Dan Beard* (New York, 1939), 379; Ray Stannard Baker, *Native American: The Book of My Youth* (New York, 1941), 30, 85, 208; Warner, *Being a Boy*, 49, 87, 91, 150–51.

3. Henry Seidel Canby, *The Age of Confidence: Life in the Nineties* (New York, 1934), 46.

4. John Demos, *A Little Commonwealth: Family Life in Plymouth Colony* (New York, 1970), 131–44; Ross Beales, "In Search of the Historical Child: Miniature Adulthood and Youth in Colonial America," *American Quarterly*, 27 (1975).

5. Edward Everett Hale, *A New England Boyhood* (Boston, 1964 [1893]), 22–23, 31.

6. E. Anthony Rotundo, "Manhood in America: The Northern Middle Class, 1770–1920" (Ph.D. diss., Brandeis Univ., 1982), 180–97, 347–56; Nancy F. Cott, *The Bonds of Womanhood: "Woman's Sphere" in New England, 1780–1835* (New Haven, Conn., 1977), 44–47, 57–60, 84–92; Mary Ryan, *The Cradle of the Middle Class: The Family in Oneida County, New York, 1790–1865* (New York, 1981), 157–65.

7. James R. McGovern, *Yankee Family* (New Orleans, 1975), 73; Ryan, *Cradle*, 162; Mrs. Manners, *At Home*, 40.

8. Beard, *Hardly a Man*, 76.

9. Philip Greven, Jr., *The Protestant Temperament: Patterns of Child-Rearing, Religious Experience, and Self in Early America* (New York, 1977), 45–46; Leonard Ellis, "Men among Men: An Exploration of All-Male Relationships in Victorian America" (Ph.D. diss., Columbia Univ., 1982), 395.

10. This approximate age is based on several pieces of evidence: Henry Dwight Sedgwick, *Memoirs of an Epicurean* (New York, 1942), 43; Beard, *Hardly a Man*, 79; Hale, *New England Boyhood*, 16–17; Kenneth S. Lynn, *William Dean Howells: An American Life* (New York, 1970), 43.

11. Gender segregation was not unique to middle-class Victorian children. Psychologists Eleanor Macoby and Carol Jacklin, in their research on group play among children ("Gender Segregation in Childhood," in Hayne W. Reese, ed., *Advances in Child Development and Behavior*, 20 [New York, 1987]), found that boys and girls nearly always segregated themselves when they could. Their findings held true across all cultural boundaries.

The virtual universality of gender-segregated play raises the possibility that this phenomenon has biological roots. However, anthropologist David Gilmore—noting the ubiquity of male self-segregation—has offered a complex explanation (*Manhood in the Making: Cultural Concepts of Masculinity* [New Haven, Conn., 1990]). At least one part of his explanation could account for gender segregation in children's play. Drawing on the theory of several ego psychologists, Gilmore notes that virtually all children are nurtured in infancy by their mothers. When they begin to separate themselves from the primal unity of that nurturing bond, all children face the task of establishing an identity as an independent human. That task is doubly difficult for boys. They must not only separate themselves from their mothers individually, they must also separate themselves as males from females, since virtually all known societies treat social maleness and femaleness as matters of importance. The desire felt by all children to return to primal unity with the mother is thus doubly threatening to boys because it represents not just a surrender of one's independent social identity but a surrender of one's sex-appropriate gender identity as well (Gilmore, *Manhood*, 26–29). Theoretician Nancy Chodorow (*The Reproduction of Mothering: Psychoanalysis and the Sociology of Gender* [Berkeley, Calif., 1978]) has pointed out that one of the many consequences of this regressive threat to male identity is a devaluation of all things female in defense against earlier feminine attachment. This provides boys with a powerful stimulus to segregate themselves from girls. It also leaves the sexes with a tendency to different social needs and styles. As Chodorow notes, this tendency is exacerbated in modern societies by sharp sexual segregation of adults in daytime activity. All of this could account, theoretically, for the farflung custom of separate boys' and girls' play—without resort to biological explanation. Even if there are universal imperatives of psychology or physiology driving sex segregation in children's play, it is crucial to note the powerful role of culture in shaping that play into distinct patterns. In the case at hand, the force of custom suppressed tendencies toward separate play until about age six, then actively encouraged them—except at culturally determined times of the day and the week (for example, the evening, or the Sabbath) when mingling between brothers and sisters would be expected.

12. The "city states" quotation is from Canby, *Age of Confidence*, 35; see also 42–46; Wallace, *Autobiography*, 55; Sedgwick, *Memoirs*, 31; Lynn, *William Dean Howells*, 42; Howard Doughty, *Francis Parkman* (Cambridge, Mass., 1983 [1962]), 14–15.

13. For instance, Hale, *New England Boyhood*, 45, 53–54, 57–59.

14. Sedgwick, *Memoirs*, 31.

15. There is a danger of overstating the similarities between girls' and boys' lives

before age six. They were given different toys to play with (McGovern, *Yankee Family*, 73), and mothers were kept keenly aware of the different worlds for which they were raising their toddlers (James Barnard Blake diary, Aug. 3, 1851 American Antiquarian Society; Kirk Jeffrey, "Family History: The Middle-Class American Family in the Urban Context, 1830–1870" [Ph.D. diss., Stanford Univ., 1972], 202–3), so that they must have treated their children differently according to sex. Still, the early domestic life of boys zealously discouraged basic "male" virtues like aggression and self-assertion in favor of "feminine" kindness and submission.

16. Beard, *Hardly a Man*, 76; Greven, *Protestant Temperament*, 45–46.

17. On girls' play and common culture, see Henrietta Dana Skinner, *An Echo from Parnassus: Being Girlhood Memories of Longfellow and His Friends* (New York, 1928), 87–111, 175–81; Mary Starbuck, *My House and I: A Chronicle of Nantucket* (Boston, 1929), esp. 212, 215; Lucy Larcom, *A New England Girlhood* (New York, 1961 [1889]), 17–117. On the interdependence of girls and women, see Carroll Smith-Rosenberg, "The Female World of Love and Ritual: Relations between Women in Nineteenth-Century America," *Signs*, 1 (1975), 14–19.

18. Alphonso David Rockwell, *Rambling Recollections: An Autobiography* (New York, 1920), 30–31, 56; Wallace, *Autobiography*, 55, 121; Beard, *Hardly a Man*, 203; Baker, *Native American*, 85; Hale, *New England Boyhood*, 40, 88, 151; Warner, *Being a Boy*, 49; Doughty, *Francis Parkman*, 14–15; Wheaton J. Lane, *Commodore Vanderbilt: An Epic of the Steam Age* (New York, 1942), 11, 13, 162.

19. Hale, *New England Boyhood*, 86.

20. Sedgwick, *Memoirs*, 20–21, 28–29; Hale, *New England Boyhood*, 22–23, 40.

21. Thomas Russell to John Brooks, Nov. 9, 1836, Charles Russell Papers, MHS; Wallace, *Autobiography*, 55; Beard, *Hardly a Man*, 78, 92; Lynn, *William Dean Howells*, 54–55; Ellis, "Men among Men," 251–53; Samuel McChord Crothers, "The Ignominy of Being Grown-Up," *Atlantic Monthly*, 98 (1906), 47. It is worth noting that much of the harshest violence seemed to take place in areas of the Midwest that were not many decades removed from frontier status and that were settled by Southern as well as Yankee stock.

22. John Mack Faragher, *Women and Men on the Overland Trail* (New Haven, Conn., 1979), 135–36.

23. Hale, *New England Boyhood*, 55, 151; Warner, *Being a Boy*, 127–28; Doughty, *Francis Parkman*, 14–15; Lynn, *William Dean Howells*, 45.

24. Beard, *Hardly a Man*, 92, 110; Hale, *New England Boyhood*, 23, 200–201; James Lovett, *Old Boston Boys and the Games They Played* (Boston, 1906); William Wells Newell, *Games and Songs of American Children* (New York, 1883).

25. Ellery H. Clark, *Reminiscences of an Athlete: Twenty Years on Track and Field* (Boston, 1911), 6; Beard, *Hardly a Man*, 102–3; Wallace, *Autobiography*, 22.

26. The boys' games of settlers and Indians were inspired not only by folklore but also by their reading. Cooper's *Leatherstocking Tales* was especially important in this regard (see Wallace, *Autobiography*, 54, and Canby, *Age of Confidence*, 192). Cowboys did not enter into these games until the final years of the century—the white men who fought Indians were called "the settlers" in the games of nineteenth-century boys.

27. Warner, *Being a Boy*, 89–91; Beard, *Hardly a Man*, 92; Clark, *Reminiscences*, 6.

28. Beard, *Hardly a Man*, 79; Hale, *New England Boyhood*, 82–83; Lynn, *William Dean Howells*, 45; Joseph Kett, *Rites of Passage: Adolescence in America, 1790 to the Present* (New York, 1977), 91–92.

29. Kett, *Rites of Passage*, 92; Bruce Laurie, *Working People of Philadelphia, 1800–1850* (New York, 1980); on privileged boys, see Hale, *New England Boyhood*, 136–37.

30. Charles Russell to Theodore Russell, Jan. 26, 1830, Russell Papers, MHS. Charles's instructions to Theodore are included in many letters to his wife, Persis. See, for example, letters of Jan. 25 and May 31, 1830, Mar. 14, Dec. 8, and Dec. 16, 1831. See also Baker, *Native American*, 20.

31. Hale, *New England Boyhood*, 36–37.

32. Warner, *Being a Boy*, 50.

33. Rockwell, *Rambling Recollections*, 31.

34. Rockwell, *Rambling Recollections*, 31. Not all kin relationships were as amicable or as apparently lacking in ambivalence as the relationship between Alphonso Rockwell and his cousin. For a loyal but turbulent relationship between two brothers, Theodore and Thomas Russell, see Theodore to Persis Russell, Mar. 25 and Oct. 31, 183[4?], and Theodore Russell to Charles Russell, Sept. 21 and Dec. 14, 183[4?], Russell Papers, MHS.

35. Sedgwick, *Memoirs*, 32–33.

36. An interesting exception to this "nation-state" model of boyhood friendships is the passionate bond between Pierre and his cousin Glen Stanly in Herman Melville's novel *Pierre*. The open devotion and confiding intimacy of their relationship could be readily found in the ties between male youth in their late teens and twenties, but was extremely rare between nineteenth-century boys (Herman Melville, *Pierre, or the Ambiguities* [New York, 1971]).

37. On Roosevelt and his museum, see Kathleen Dalton, "The Early Life of Theodore Roosevelt" (Ph.D. diss., Johns Hopkins Univ., 1979), 171–72. The Indiana club is described in Wallace, *Autobiography*, 55.

38. Warner, *Being a Boy*, 50.

39. Lynn, *William Dean Howells*, 44; Beard, *Hardly a Man*, 78.

40. Lynn, *William Dean Howells*, 43; Sedgwick, *Memoirs*, 32–33; Canby, *Age of Confidence*, 42–45; W. S. Tryon, *Parnassus Corner: A Life of James T. Fields, Publisher to the Victorians* (Boston, 1963), 9. These antagonisms between towns and neighborhoods became the basis for the high school sports rivalries that blossomed late in the century.

41. Canby, *Age of Confidence*, 42–43 and more generally 40–45.

42. Sedgwick, *Memoirs*, 32–33. Sedgwick and his friends also understood their difference from boys further up the social scale: "Boys of Murray Hill, boys of what thirty years later was to be named the Four Hundred . . . would probably have thought us of very little significance."

43. Canby, *Age of Confidence*, 37; see also Stephen Salisbury, Jr., to Betsy Salisbury, Oct. 27, 1810, Salisbury Papers, Box 14, AAS; Beard, *Hardly a Man*, 110–11; Theodore Roosevelt, *The Strenuous Life: Essays and Addresses* (New York, 1902), 162–64.

44. Ellis, "Men among Men," 251–53.

45. Beard, *Hardly a Man*, 92, 103.

46. Canby, *Age of Confidence*, 40; Sedgwick, *Memoirs*, 33; Rockwell, *Rambling Recollections*, 31.

47. Male autobiographers who grew up in the nineteenth century sometimes talked about the democracy that existed among boys. What they meant in modern terms is that their boy culture was a meritocracy in which a boy's demonstrated abilities, not his family's status, determined his standing among his peers. See Canby, *Age of Confidence*, 40, and Hale, *New England Boyhood*, 32–33.

48. See note 46.

49. Canby, *Age of Confidence*, 192.

50. Lynn, *William Dean Howells*, 45.

51. Rockwell, *Rambling Recollections*, 56; John William DeForest, *A Volunteer's Adventures: A Union Captain's Record of the Civil War* (New Haven, Conn., 1946), 57, 93; Beard, *Hardly a Man*, 96.

52. Beard, *Hardly a Man*, 47.

53. Wallace, *Autobiography*, 122. For further instances of boy culture demanding daring behavior, see John Doane Barnard journal, Essex Institute, 3–4; Rockwell, *Rambling Recollections*, 56; Canby, *Age of Confidence*, 44.

54. Ryan, *Cradle*, 161; Canby, *Age of Confidence*, 235 (see also 192–94).

55. Beard, *Hardly a Man*, 74–75; Rockwell, *Rambling Recollections*, 56.

56. For example, Canby, *Age of Confidence*, 45.

57. Wallace, *Autobiography*, 55.

58. See, for instance, Lynn, *William Dean Howells*, 44.

59. Crothers, "Ignominy," 47.

60. Lynn, *William Dean Howells*, 45; Wallace, *Autobiography*, 55; Canby even claimed that bullying, while it represented "primitive sadism," was laced with pleasure because it gave the victims "delicious terrors" (*Age of Confidence*, 37).

61. Hale, *New England Boyhood*, 37; Wallace, *Autobiography*, 55; Barnard, Essex Institute 3–4; Canby, *Age of Confidence*, 43–44.

62. Beard, *Hardly a Man*, 78.

63. Beard, *Hardly a Man*, 73–74.

64. Rockwell, *Rambling Recollections*, 35–36. Younger boys could—and sometimes did—use pranks for the same purposes against older boys (Beard, *Hardly a Man*, 76, 78–79).

65. Beard, *Hardly a Man*, 102.

66. Even in small towns where fathers worked close by, boys found it was their mothers who intervened in their daily activities with friends. See Wallace, *Autobiography*, 22, and Lynn, *William Dean Howells*, 42, 44.

67. Theodore to Charles Russell, Jan. 26, 1830, Russell Papers, MHS; Elisha Whittlesey to William Whittlesey, Dec. 13, 1830, and Elisha Whittlesey to Comfort Whittlesey, Jan. 20, 1840, William W. Whittlesey Papers, Container 1, WRHS; Baker, *Native American*, 20; Warner, *Being a Boy*, 41–43.

68. Wallace, *Autobiography*, 77–79; Barnard, "Essex Institute" 3–4.

69. Beard, *Hardly a Man*, 102; Mark Twain, *The Adventures of Huckleberry Finn* (New York, 1968 [1884]), 346.

70. Sedgwick, *Memoirs*, 23; Warner, *Being a Boy*, 161; Mrs. Manners, *At Home and Abroad*, 42–43.

71. Beard, *Hardly a Man*, 111, 157–58; Lynn, *William Dean Howells*, 44.

72. Lynn, *William Dean Howells*, 44, 42; Beard, *Hardly a Man*, 157–58; Wallace, *Autobiography*, 22.

73. Hale, *New England Boyhood*, 55; Baker, *Native American*, 85.

74. Beard, *Hardly a Man*, 157–58.

75. Sedgwick, *Memoirs*, 20–21; Wallace, *Autobiography*, 27.

76. Beard, *Hardly a Man*, 111.

77. Mrs. Manners, *At Home and Abroad*, 43. See also Warner, *Being a Boy*, 73–74, and the comments in Mark Carnes, "The Making of the Self-made Man: The Emotional Experience of Boyhood in Victorian America," unpub. essay, 11.

78. Beard, *Hardly a Man*, 199.

79. The vituperation heaped on "goody-goodies" not only reflected boys' insecurity about their own tendencies to follow their mothers' advice and their desire to maintain the integrity of their subculture, it may also have represented a way for boys to deflect their own anger from their mothers (who, after all, were trying to frustrate them) onto more acceptable targets.

80. A useful discussion of the indefinite language of age in the early nineteenth century (and the indefinite phases of life which the language indicated) is Kett, *Rites of Passage*, 11–14.

81. Wallace, *Autobiography*, 80–82.

82. Rockwell, *Rambling Recollections*, 63.

83. The average age of puberty for boys in this era was about sixteen (Kett, *Rites of Passage*, 44).

84. Beard, *Hardly a Man*, 199.

85. A squabble between brothers over the use of a suit provides vivid evidence of clothing as a badge of "civilized' manhood." See Theodore Russell to Persis Russell, Oct. 31, 183[4?], Russell Papers, MHS.

86. Rockwell, *Rambling Recollections*, 63.

87. Warner, *Being a Boy*, 1. See notes 28–31.

Chapter Twenty

The Politics of Dollhood in Nineteenth-Century America

Miriam Formanek-Brunell

"Of doll haters I have known quite a few," wrote a contributor to *Babyhood* magazine about the "hoydenish" little girls she had observed swatting their dolls.[1] The observations of this Gilded Age writer stand in sharp contrast to the more pervasive image of the angelic Victorian girl who was, in the words of one nineteenth-century poet, "sugar and spice and all things nice." In this chapter, I challenge the widespread assumption that attributes minimal agency to girls whom we *still* assume slavishly played in socially prescribed ways.

We begin in antebellum America, where the political ideology, class values, and cultural and economic forces of the young nation shaped new attitudes about dolls, play, and girlhood. Mothers, informed by the new domestic advisers, instructed their daughters to be "useful" within the matrix of the family. Dolls, of which there were few, served as training in everything *but* emotional development and expression. Daughters of the evolving middle class made cloth dolls to develop sewing skills that integrated leisure with instruction in domestic economy. Outdoor play, education, and a schedule of daily, weekly (punctuated by the Sabbath), and seasonal responsibilities limited the role that dolls played in girlhood.

In broad terms, utilitarian purposes of dolls and of girls, however, became increasingly obsolete in the Gilded Age as simplicity yielded to splendor among girls of urban middle-class families. Girls' lives, like those of their parents, were affected by the shift from household production to conspicuous consumption. Children's magazines, books, poems, songs, and stereographs revealed that girls were encouraged by adults to develop strong emotional bonds with their numerous dolls, to indulge in fantasy, and to display their elaborately dressed imported European dolls at such ritual occasions as tea parties and social calls.

Although adults, especially parents, perceived dolls as useful vehicles in feminine socialization, this rehearsal for adult womanhood met resistance as it had earlier in the century. At least some daughters with a different agenda from their parents used dolls for purposes other than training in the emotional and practical skills of mothering. Girls' funereal doll play, for example, revealed far more evidence of resistance than of accommodation to newly formulated prescriptions and proscriptions. Memoirs, autobiographies, biographies, oral histories, and the expressive "language" of play reveal that girls—and boys—challenged parental authority, restrictive social customs, and gender roles. Girls in the process of constructing their own notion of girlhood engaged their parents in a precon- scious political struggle to define, decide, and determine the meaning of dolls in their own lives and as representations of their own culture.

Dolls and their clothing, argued Catharine Beecher and Harriet Beecher Stowe in *The American Woman's Home* (1869), provide girls with "another resource . . . to the exercise of mechanical skills." Girls should be "trained to be healthful and industrious." Earlier in the nineteenth century, advice books, "ladies' " maga- zines, and other printed sources similarly urged mothers to apply Christian prin- ciples to the regulation of the bourgeois family, which only recently had become the mothers' domain. Thus, they were to direct their children's play toward use- ful ends. Printed material that offered practical advice and philosophical expla- nations to middle-class mothers standardized methods of antebellum childrearing. In the prescriptive literature published starting in the 1820s, middle- class girls and their mothers were kept informed of genteel manners, bourgeois values, and domestic training.[2]

Girls were urged toward usefulness in their play as natural training in the republican values they would need as future wives and mothers of citizens. New attitudes about girls' play were shaped in part by the political ideology of the young nation. Experts advised mothers to use "gentle nurture" to teach their children to be self-governing and to exercise "self-control" while at play. Eliza Leslie, author of the *Girls' Book*, suggested, as did other prescriptive writers, that making dolls rather than indulging a love of dress and finery would prevent degeneration into godless anarchy. In her moral tracts, Mary Sewell exhorted mothers to inculcate "habitual restraint" by structuring play periods with "ha- bitual regularity."[3]

"In this land of precarious fortunes, every girl should know how to be 'use- ful,' " wrote Lydia Maria Child, one of the best-known writers of the period. A girl's vocation, to which dolls contributed, was to be a domestic one shaped in response to the world beyond the Victorian hearth. A canon of domesticity con- trasted the safety of the home, where women presided, to the restlessness, com- petition, selfishness, and alienation of the masculine world beyond. Although the reality of slipping down the economic ladder was obscured by the mythology of the self-made man whose life of hard work, moderation, and temperance prom- ised untold rewards, young ladies were nevertheless forewarned to make them- selves useful should misfortune strike.[4] *Mothers' Monthly Journal*, one of the leading maternal association periodicals, advised its broad readership that dress- ing dolls provided "a semblance of the sober activities of business." Making dolls, nurturing the family, and taking care of household duties constituted a girl's informal apprenticeship for being a wife and mother. According to such experts as Maria Edgeworth, who "firmly believed in the utility of toys," sewing dolls and doll clothing stressed a pragmatic contribution to the domestic economy of the antebellum household. Popular "ladies" magazines often included directions for making pen-wiper dolls (to clean nibs), sewing dolls (whose pockets held thimbles and other items), and pincushion dolls.[5]

It was from their mothers, who were newly endowed with both the capacity and the social responsibility to determine the fate of their children, that girls were to learn their lessons, both practical and moral. Although the widespread availability of cloth meant that women no longer had to weave the household's supply of fabric, family comfort still depended on skillful use of the needle. Catharine Beecher, who felt "blessed with the example of a most ingenious and industrious mother," suggested that

> when a little girl begins to sew, her mother can promise her a small bed and pillow, as soon as she has sewed a patch quilt for them; and then a bedstead, as soon as she has sewed the sheets and cases for pillows; and then a large doll to dress, as soon as she has made the undergarments; and thus go on till the whole contents of the baby-house are earned by the needle and skill of its little owner. Thus, the task of learning to sew will become a pleasure; and every new toy will be earned by useful exertion.

In their treatise on household management, the nineteenth-century architects of domesticity boasted that they "had not only learned before the age of twelve to make dolls, of various sorts and sizes, but to cut and fit and sew every article that belongs to a doll's wardrobe."[6]

In the absence of mothers, other female kin such as Lucy Larcom's "adopted aunt" provided instruction in how to knot thread and sew clothing for rag dolls. A doll character in one children's story recalled that "there were hours and hours when she [her owner] had to sit quietly beside grandmother, and sew her stint."[7]

In addition to adult women, older sisters often helped younger ones create homemade dolls. "I once knew a little girl who had twelve dolls," wrote Lydia Maria Child. "Some of them were given her; but the greater part she herself made from rags, and her elder sister painted their lips and eyes." One of Lucy Larcom's older sisters outlined faces on her dolls with pen and ink.[8]

Despite the practical suggestions provided to mothers by experts and in turn passed along to girls, the hours during which toys were expected to absorb their attention were limited by genuine household responsibilities.[9] Few matched the ideal as represented in the numerous extant canvases—showing girls leisurely holding dolls—painted by itinerants for socially conscious, middle-class parents. Though the texture of girls' lives was changing, childhood was still neither as precisely demarcated nor as prolonged in the early 1800s as it would be by the end of the century. Instead, a mother of a large rural family was likely to be assisted by the elder children, especially her daughters, as soon as they were able, despite decreasing household productivity and the increasing availability of commercial goods. Thus, the number of hours a girl spent in play would have been circumscribed by immediate familial obligations. Though minding younger siblings combined amusement with training, it was a weighty responsibility nonetheless.

Time spent in doll play was also limited by school attendance, which required an increasing number of girls to spend a portion of their day in decidedly non-leisure activities, and by Sabbath observance. In a children's story from the 1850s, retribution was visited upon two girls who skipped school in order to play with their dolls. Similarly, on Sundays, which were "not like any other day," girls were expected to pray, not play. All middle-class Christian children were expected to observe the Sabbath like adults, even those who were not very religious. "We did not play games nor read the same books," on Sunday as on other days, recalled one girl from the 1850s, and church services and Sunday school seemed to last forever.[10] Consequently, girls were less likely to devote much of their time to doll play.

Though the number of toys had increased since the colonial period, there were still few dolls around in the average middle-class household in the 1850s, a fact of doll demography that would change dramatically only after the Civil War. "Life for children was simple in the extreme [as] there were no array[s] of costly toys," recalled one New England woman in her autobiography. "[My sister and I] had the regulation rag doll with long curls and club feet, very ugly but dear to our hearts," and no others. Harriet Robinson, who grew up a New England mill girl, "had no toys, except a few homemade articles of our own. I had but a single doll, a wooden-jointed thing, with red cheeks and staring black eyes."[11]

Because of the scarcity and cost of dolls, parents and relatives tended to treasure those they purchased far more than did their daughters, granddaughters, and nieces. One father in Petersburg, Virginia, included the two large dolls he had bought for his daughter in his will. With little regard for a doll's economic value, however, girls like Lucy Larcom rejected the "London doll that lay in waxen state in an upper drawer at home." To her, this "fine lady did not wish to be played with but only to be looked at and admired." Larcom, instead, preferred the "absurd creatures of her own invention." Antebellum writer Eliza Leslie similarly observed that cloth dolls "remain longer in favor with their young owners, and continue to give them more real satisfaction, than the handsomest wax doll that can be purchased."[12]

Yet many girls who lived in rural areas preferred to spend their time outdoors instead, largely forgoing the pleasures of even cloth dolls. Lucy Larcom played on farms and in fields, rivers, quarries, and cemeteries; Emily Wilson and Frances Willard (who later led the national temperance movement) preferred skating, sledding, and running to playing with dolls. Carol Ryrie Brink's fictionalized stories about her great-grandmother depict Caddie Woodlawn as an active girl. According to Karin Calvert, girls were more likely to recall rolling hoops, tossing snowballs, and jumping rope to playing with dolls. Hiding in the attic, Harriet Robinson secretly played high-low-jack with the playing cards her brother had made. Little girls lived "as unfettered and vigorous an outdoor life as their brothers."[13]

After the Civil War, doll play absorbed and channeled a number of interrelated changes in the lives of American girls: increased affluence, new consumer outlets, smaller family size, and greater emphasis on imitation of adult social rituals and the formalized play it encouraged. In the country but especially in cities, middle-class girls born in the postwar years amassed quantities of dolls unknown to the previous generation. In contrast to the four decades preceding the Civil War, dolls sold well and widely after 1865 as the traditional moral, utilitarian, and even political functions of dolls were gradually replaced with "needs" based on new middle-class notions.

A rising personal income meant that most middle-class Americans could become consumers of articles formerly available only to the rich whom they admired along with the Europeans that the rich emulated. Nevertheless, buying imported dolls still required a solid bank account. In 1890, when the annual income of an industrial worker was $486, a French jointed kid doll with a composition head cost between $3 and $30. As a result, the majority of dolls remained prohibitively expensive for working-class families. In one doll story, a poor seamstress was unable to purchase a wax doll because she "could not afford to spend her money that way." Her little girl asks, "Does she cost a great deal, mamma?" Her mother answers, "It would be a great deal for us—she costs $10, Lucy."[14]

A revolution in European doll production enabled jobbers, manufacturers' agents, importers, and distributors to channel European toys to American retail stores where mothers and fathers purchased great quantities of dolls made out of china or bisque with open mouths and little teeth or some with closed mouths.[15] Some of the most expensive French fashion dolls in the 1870s and 1880s arrived with fully packed trunks, often tripling the price of the doll alone. French and German dolls—with hourglass figures and *bébés*, idealized and romanticized representations of European bourgeois girlhood—flooded U.S. markets at a time when most Americans began to enjoy increasing affluence.

For those living far from urban centers with financial resources, mail-order catalogues brought the opportunity to shop at home and share in the consumer-goods market for dolls. Seven years after Richard Sears began advertising watches to the rural market, Sears, Roebuck broadened its wares to include dolls. Wholesale suppliers like Butler Brothers provided the small merchant of the rural midwest with dolls and other items.[16]

Beginning in 1865, department stores including R. H. Macy, Jordan Marsh, and Marshall Field dazzled shoppers as spectacular "places of consumption." By 1875, Macy's stock featured dolls and other toys in addition to dry goods and home furnishings. While Macy's was the first to establish a toy department, others soon followed its lead. "Most of us adults can recall the time when the toy shop exhibited but a slim stock," commented one observer. But in the years after the Civil War, toy shops, some of which issued illustrated catalogues, increased in number and size. "Enter one of our big toy shops now and there is really an *embarrass de richesses*," noted one contemporary observer. In fact, "the first impression of the visitor to the big toy shop is . . . apt to be one of bewilderment."[17]

Toy stores also catered to a clientele of urban middle-class women, most of whom did not work outside the home and for whom shopping for self, friends, and family was becoming a central activity. According to an 1881 *Harper's Bazaar*, dolls and other toys were "chosen by mothers with a view to giving their girls correct ideas of symmetry and beauty." In stories from the late nineteenth century, nurturing female shopkeepers patiently assisted leisured female customers. In "A Doll's Story," a jointed bisque doll recalls seeing from inside her glass display case "mostly mothers and young children—sometimes nurses with small children."[18]

Women were the largest group of consumers, but fathers also purchased dolls—some of which said "Papa"—for their daughters at each birthday or homecoming. Bourgeois fathers began at midcentury giving gifts to their children at Christmas, instead of to their employees or to the poor as previously had been the case. One fortunate middle-class daughter of German immigrants recalled that she received gifts only on Christmas and for her birthday, typically in an abundance suitable for several children.[19]

In doll stories, "papas with weary heads" committed to a business ethos were frequently too preoccupied to notice a sick or a sad daughter. Fathers were increasingly separated from the family during the day, especially those who commuted from the sprouting suburbs. Sons might have been more acutely affected by their diminished opportunities to assist fathers, but the relationship of fathers to their daughters was influenced as well. Gift-giving could solace an alienated father and reinforce his belief that he was fulfilling his role as provider. As a result, "most fathers," observed a writer for Doll's Dressmaker, "are inclined to overindulge their daughters." In one story, Pearl's father "bought me a beautiful bedstead," narrated a doll character, "round which were hung some elegant blue silk curtains." In A Doll's Journey, a story written by Louisa May Alcott, one sister reassured another that "papa will give you a new doll."[20]

Generous gift giving, whether on Christmas or at other times of the year, had been a recent consequence of a number of factors, including the increasing emotional distance between parents and children. Busy parents with fewer children provided their daughters with the companionship of dolls, thereby lengthening childhood and prolonging their "dollhood." Middle-class women had become not only increasingly isolated from production but also from their children. Mothers' contact with their children became circumscribed shortly after birth. By the late 1890s, leading pediatrician Luther Emmett Holt observed that "at least three children out of every four born into the homes of the well-to-do-classes" were not fed at the breast. Instead, fashion and etiquette, shopping, and visiting dominated the life of the matron. Fashion magazines, as one indicator, far outnumbered mothers' magazines. Many children probably saw more of "nanny" than their mothers and fathers.[21]

Girls living in urban and newly created suburban areas were given far less productive work, fewer responsibilities, and fewer siblings to look after. Middle-class mothers had successfully limited their number of children, spaced them farther apart, and ceased childbearing earlier than had previous generations. As a result, fewer brothers and sisters to watch increased the amount of time for play but decreased the number of friends and kin with whom to share it. Instead, girls were given many more toys, books, magazines, clothing, and furniture made especially for them. As a single child of well-to-do parents, Margaret Woodbury Strong adored the numerous dolls she received—now the foundation of the museum in Rochester, New York, that bears her name.[22]

In the decades that followed the Civil War, gradually dolls began to serve a more modern and symbolic function than a utilitarian one. Doll play in the post-war era emphasized the display of high fashion rather than the sewing skills emphasized earlier. In one story from the period, Pearl adores the doll she sees in Mrs. Lieb's toy shop though she hesitates to purchase it because it is un-dressed. "You know, dear mother," she says in a whisper, "how badly I sew." The emphasis on sewing for dolls had become obsolete by the 1880s. Instead, organized doll play developed rules that became nearly as formalized as those recently devised for baseball. Pastimes that had made previous generations of well-to-do Protestants uneasy now became increasingly accepted. As with pro-duction and consumption, amusement in general became a more structured activity.[23]

This organized amusement came to be located in the nursery, which for the middle class was the arena where (similar to organized sports), values, attitudes, and standards of behavior were imparted. Changes in the family, childhood, and new marital ideals had given rise to the middle-class nursery by the second half of the nineteenth century, differentiating households as well as the space between family members. The nursery—where the large numbers of dolls, their accoutre-ments, and other toys could be kept—became indispensable. Although Victorian houses were spacious, they were cluttered with possessions too precious to risk around children at play. In the autonomous space of the nursery described by J. M. Barrie in *Peter Pan*, children lived apart from parents and the rest of the household. A room of adorable miniature adult furniture became a standard feature especially of the spacious upper-middle-class Victorian home. Some chairs were stenciled with affectionate names like "My Pet," and miniature tea tables painted to represent marble imitated adult lavishness.[24]

Adults expected girls to imitate the new rituals of high society with their largely imported dolls in their nurseries. Elaborately dressed dolls were thought useful in the instruction of social conventions such as housewarmings. Far more common, however, were dolls' tea parties, frequently depicted in stereographs, tradecards, and books like *The Dolls' Tea Party*. Adults proudly noted that "the children's doll parties of to-day are counterparts of grown-up people's recep-tions."[25]

In addition to tea parties, girls were urged to imitate another adult social ritual of polite society in the Gilded Age, that of visiting. Dolls could be purchased wearing "a stylish visiting dress, and also accompanied by a trunkful of clothes ready for all the demands of fashionable occasions." Miniature calling cards, which were a measure of family standing to neighbors and friends, imitated the mother's *carte de visite* for girls who paid formal visits with their dolls. Now instead of singing, "Here we go round the mulberry bush," girls were encour-aged to sing, "This is the way we carry them . . . when we go visiting." Popular magazines like *The Delineator* advertised instructions for making visiting dresses and even "a stately toilette for Miss Dolly to wear on the promenade." "With their companions or dolls you will hear them imitating the discussion [on fashion] . . . that they daily hear in the parlor or nursery from their mother," observed Mrs. H. W. Beecher in 1873.[26]

Not all the feelings and issues which doll play accommodated were superficial and sweet. Of all the newly constructed middle-class rituals girls were urged to imitate, doll funerals were by far the most common. In a change from sparse and somber colonial funeral customs, late-nineteenth-century Americans (following Queen Victoria's lead) romanticized grief and burial practices. Mourning was demarcated by shades of black dresses, stationery, and other mourning accoutrements. According to Harvey Green, "Visiting ill or dying relatives and friends was an expected and socially required part of women's sphere, part of the broad set of nurturing responsibilities with which she was charged." To middle-class parents in the second half of the nineteenth century, that children devised imaginary and miniaturized funerals was not seen as evidence of a morbid preoccupation with death. As a result, adults encouraged rather than discouraged the doll death ceremonies their daughters conducted. Mourning clothes were even packed in the trunks of French dolls in the 1870s and 1880s. Fathers constructed doll-sized coffins for their daughters' dolls instead of what we consider the more usual dollhouses.[27]

The process of learning about the meanings of grief began early in life, as the etiquette of mourning became an integral part of a girl's upbringing. Young students in private schools learning the decorative arts created countless embroidered mourning pieces filled with new iconographic symbols such as willow trees and morning glories. Even the fictional Rebecca of Sunnybrook Farm routinely staged deaths and funerals with her rural friends. As the ritualization of mourning increased during the course of the century—all maintained within the feminine sphere—it is no wonder that parents encouraged funeral ceremonies meant to properly sanctify the "bodies" and protect the "souls" of those poor, deceased dolls.[28]

Short stories about dying dolls were included in the popular fiction for children and provided them with new ideas about how they should play with dolls. By contrast, earlier in the century so few stories about dolls had been written that one disappointed doll in a story from the 1840s remarked, "I never heard any stories about dolls, and what they thought, or what happened to them!" In the years after the Civil War, however, a conspicuous doll culture unfolded in widely available children's books and popular magazines. Beginning in the late 1860s, colorfully illustrated and miniature books were printed for girls (and their dolls). Nursery shelves were lined with books about dolls, books *for* them such as *The Dolls' Own Book*, which went through numerous editions, and even books *by* dolls. Stories such as "Dolly's Experience, Told by Herself" or doll memoirs were ostensibly written by doll authors.[29]

It was the fictional literature of "doll culture" that broached the more powerful feelings of love and violence. Doll fiction provided girls with both an outlet and a way of playing with their dolls so as to grapple with serious needs. Unlike the antebellum literature for children that stressed the development of skills and morals, doll fiction of the Gilded Age emphasized the exploration of self, interpersonal relationships, and fantasy. Despite the innumerable images of girls washing their dolls and doll clothing, grooming had not yet become a primary justification for doll play because most dolls made out of horsehair or wood shavings had little chance of surviving a good dunking. Instead, it was through her relationship to her female dolls—also portrayed as passive, pretty, enigmatic, domestic, dainty, mute, vain, and delicate—that a girl learned about the essence of "true love" and how to distinguish it from more superficial feelings. While the more elaborate dolls were often portrayed as shallow, one bisque sophisticate observed, "Oh, it's nice to be grand and all that, I suppose/But of late I'm beginning to reap/The Knowledge that happiness isn't fine clothes/And that beauty is only skin deep."[30] Although hopelessly unfashionable, rag dolls were most likely to have insight about interpersonal relationships.

> Lillian Grace is a fine city girl
> I'm but a queer "country cousin,"
> I have one dress of coarse cotton stuff,
> She has silk gowns by the dozen.
> She is so pretty, and dainty and gay
> I am so homely and funny;
> I cost a trifle, I'm but a rag doll,
> She costs a whole heap of money,
> She came from France in a big handsome box,
> I, from a country bazaar,
> Things are more precious I've often been told
> That travel so long and so far.
> Yet it is strange, but Oh! it is true
> We belong to the same little mother
> And though she loves Lillian Grace very much
> It is queer, but somehow or other,
> I have a spot in her dear loving heart
> That Lillian Grace cannot enter;
> She has a hold in the outermost rim,
> But I have a place in the center . . .
> And all the silk dresses and other fine things,
> Though they do look so fair to the eye,
> Are not worth a thought since they cannot win love.
> O a happy rag dollie am I![31]

The portrayal of love between a doll and a girl, which often straddled the boundaries between maternal love and romantic love, was reciprocal, communicative, and passionate. By the early 1890s, the growing importance of mothering and child study had influenced popular ideas about doll play for girls. *Doll's Dressmaker* (a monthly magazine first published in New York City in 1891) reprinted images of girls with their bevies of dolls, which conveyed a new maternal fecundity out of step with actual demographic changes (families were getting smaller) but in step with more scientific notions about mothering. Thereafter, in numerous images girls cradled bébés with maternal sentimentality while contemporaries rhetorically asked, "Is it not the harmless, childish joy that develops and educates the young girl's maternal instinct, and in so doing helps to elevate her to the pinnacle of true womanhood?"[32]

Elsewhere, fictional characters encouraged the pursuit of feminine submission to masculine dominance. In fact, girls' dolls were often portrayed as hapless victims of mischievous boys who taunted girls and tortured dolls. The incorrigible boy was familiar in fiction, art, cartoons, advertisements, and the enormously popular stereographs of the period. One doll in a story recalled that her "little mistress" had a book entitled *Mischievous Tommy*, "about a troublesome, rude boy" who had disgusting manners. As Mary Lynn Stevens Heininger and others have noted, the mischief and manipulation by the boys in *Tom Sawyer* and *Peck's Bad Boy* fulfilled the expectation of stereotypical masculine behavior. Such was the case in another popular story in which a girl named Gladys is portrayed as defenseless against her scheming, scissors-wielding brother who cuts "a great patch of hair out of the poor doll's head."[33]

In addition to bad boys, other threats restricted the boundaries of safety for dolls and, hence, their owners. In numerous stories, birds, cows, and monkeys like "Naughty Jacko" stole, pecked, gnawed, and kicked defenseless dolls unable and unwilling to resist. In *The Dolls' Surprise Party*, a roving mother pig and her piglets attack a group of dolls enjoying their picnic. Although most stories attributed powerful emotional responses to dolls and thus to girls, in fiction both often sat helplessly with "wooden legs" while antagonists hounded them.[34]

Home provided little safety for two dolls in a Beatrix Potter tale in which "two bad mice" destroy their domestic security. In this 1904 children's story, two working-class mice (a foul-tempered husband and his thieving wife, Hunca Munca), ransack the house of two wooden dolls absent from the nursery. Returning from their stroll, the dolls are shocked into victimized passivity. One doll merely "sat upon the upset kitchen stove and stared," while the other "leant against the kitchen dresser and smiled—but neither of them made any remark." Doll policemen and nurses (brought into play by the girl whose dollhouse has been burglarized) set mouse traps. To make a short story even shorter, the repentant mouse husband pays for everything he broke and "very early every morning—before anybody is awake—Hunca Munca comes with her dust pan and her broom to sweep the Dollies' house!"[35]

Stories did not completely siphon off the underlying aggression. Dolls were not necessarily safer in the hands of little girls. In *Little Women* "one forlorn fragment of *dollanity* had belonged to Jo; and, having led a tempestuous life, was left a wreck in the rag-bag." The top of the doll's head was gone, as were her arms and legs. George Eliot's fictional heroine in *The Mill on the Floss*, nine-year-old Maggie Tulliver, expressed her rage by hammering nails into her wooden doll's head, beating it against a wall, and grinding it against a rough brick. In numerous American stereographic images that became a parlor staple by the turn of the century, girls used more typical domestic implements, cutting their dolls with scissors or forcing them through clothes wringers. Like other "Conduct

Stereos," these pictures were probably intended to dramatize proper feminine manners and behavior through humor.[36]

Although a juvenile mass culture was imposed from above by parents and other adults with their own intentions, what about the interactions of girls—and boys, for that matter—with dolls and other toys? Abuse of dolls at the hands of their owners alerts us that adult prescriptions for proper play were often not what girls had in mind. In the last decades of the century stereographs and other images suggest a middle-class ideal of girls, overflowing with metaphors of abundance, yet we know far more about adult expectations than we do about childhood reality. Prescriptive literature tells us little about how ordinary girls actually behaved. Did girls identify with the dolls they heard about in stories? Did they confide in the dolls they cradled in studio portraits? Did they actually prefer dolls to other toys and activities? Were girls who played with dolls more gentle and nurturing than boys or girls who preferred more active play?

There is no disputing that girls in late-nineteenth-century America liked dolls, but not just any doll. According to one study, girls preferred dolls made of wax, paper, rag, and china over those made of rubber, kid, wood, tin, or celluloid. Among the favorite dolls were those made of cloth. Emily Kimbrough disliked the fashionable doll her grandmother gave her but adored her Topsy-turvey rag doll. Adults were often at a loss to understand why their daughters preferred ragged and "countrified" dolls to brightly colored and elaborately dressed ones.[37]

Among rag dolls, black ones were a favorite among white children, observed one contemporary shopper. Both Mary Hunt and her friend favored black dolls over white ones. "My little girl has two such [rag] dolls," commented a mother, "one white and the other black, but her affections are centered on the colored woman . . . never going to bed without Dinah in her arms, and crying for 'di' if the nurse had forgotten to put it in her crib." African-American women played an increasingly significant role in the rearing of middle-class children. Suggesting a relationship born of affection, one four-year-old girl fed everything that tasted good to her black rag doll.[38]

Despite their uniform fictional portrayal as adversaries, boys were also among doll lovers. One contributor to a mother's magazine reported that her son treated the doll he loved with "the greatest care and tenderness." Nor did boys like this one shed their dolls along with their diapers. G. Stanley Hall found that 76 percent of the boys he studied played with dolls to age 12. Not surprising, then, are the numerous examples of boys especially fond of doll play. A boy doll (c. 1875) named "Theodore" became a "chum" to a little boy for eight years. A man who participated in a 1987 doll oral history project recognized a painted cloth boy doll as one similar to his childhood toy.[39]

Boys, like girls, sang to and rocked the dolls they endowed with emotional, intellectual, physiological, moral, political ("democrat"), and religious qualities. They "fed" dolls milk, bread, buttons, or pickles when they were "hungry," occasionally breaking tiny teeth and heads in order to do so. Children succored dolls sick with measles or brain fever with remedies like tapioca and paper pills or dissolved candy. According to one ten year-old girl, "My doll Liz had a head-ache, so I put on her micado and read her some of Longfellow's *Hiawatha*, as she wanted me to."[40]

Girls and boys often played with their dolls in socially prescribed ways. While girls pretended to be little mothers to their dolls, boys often assumed authoritative public roles such as doctor, preacher, and undertaker to sick, dying, and dead dolls. One eight-year-old doll dentist used toothpicks as dental tools. Another boy shot his doll full of holes with a bow and arrow so that he could dress its wounds. Boys' play also included doll crucifixions and executions. Unlike the girl characters in doll stories, however, girls did not always mind. "When my brother proved my doll had no brains by slicing off her head, I felt I had been deluded; I watched him with stoicism and took no more interest in dolls."[41]

Examples of girls like this one—who either always or eventually preferred other activities to doll play—are also numerous. Present expectations that dolls are for girls and not for boys are confounded by the fact that less than one quarter of the girls in T. R. Croswell's study of 2,000 children in Massachusetts considered dolls to be their "favorite" toy. Eleanor Abbott (granddaughter of Jacob Abbott, author of the *Rollo* series) preferred paper dolls, toy soldiers, or fights with her brother to her dolls. As before the Civil War, school-aged girls still largely preferred sledding, jumping rope, or playing tag, hide-and-seek, or any other game to playing with dolls. "In my own immediate family," recalled an aunt, "a canvass through three generations of women shows only two doll-lovers out of fifteen little girls, the rest decidedly preferring rough and tumble, active play in the open air." Someone asked "Wouldn't you rather play with dolls?" of a girl playing horse and driver with her friend. "We'd rather run," replied the pair.[42]

Although Karin Calvert found few girls' diaries from the late nineteenth century that even mentioned dolls, they nevertheless played a prominent role in the lives of many. Surprisingly, however, girls' play behavior was not always submissive nor instinctively maternal; evidence reveals that doll players pushed at the margins of acceptable feminine and genteel behavior. A wide variety of sources suggests that in their doll play, numerous "hoydenish little girls" expressed anger and aggression nearly as frequently as love and affection. "Of doll-haters, I have known a few," wrote the contributor to *Babyhood* magazine in 1905. Punishments were often particularly brutal. One thirteen-year-old girl broke her doll by knocking it against a window for crying. A four-year-old girl disciplined her doll by forcing it to eat dirt, stones, and coal.[43]

Although parents believed doll funerals could be assimilated to proper forms of femininity, girls were often more interested in the unfeminine events that led to these solemn rituals. In the numerous doll funerals that appear with startling consistency in doll stories, memoirs, and questionnaires, it was not the passive grieving that provided doll players with pleasure. Doll funerals probably appealed to girls in part because the domestication of heaven (along with the beautification of cemeteries where families found rest and recreation) made the afterlife sound fun. For others, the staging of doll funerals was an expression of aggressive feelings and hostile fantasies. George Eliot remembered that she "only broke those [dolls] . . . that could not stand the test of being undressed, or that proclaimed their unfleshy substance by falling and breaking their noses."[44] According to an article in the *Pittsburgh Post*, a five-year-old girl purposely broke her doll, then declared with satisfaction, "it was dead." Girls like this one changed the emphasis from ritualized funerals to cathartic executions. Using available kitchen utensils she dug a grave in the backyard and then invited other little girls to do the same. "I have vivid memories of harrowing games with Mary Gordon," wrote Ethel Spencer in her turn-of-the-century memoir, "during which our children [dolls] became desperately ill and died." Though this gruesome scenario bordered on the unacceptable by the end of the nineteenth century, their fascination for girls was not at all unusual. "Funerals were especially popular, with Becky [doll] ever the willing victim," confided one doll player. "No day was too short for a funeral, just so they [my friends] all got home for supper."[45]

For some, a doll's worth was determined by its ability to subvert convention, mock materialism, and undermine restrictions. For example, doll parties, considered entirely too sedate by some girls, were transformed into invigorating activities unlikely to win the approval of adults. Some girls preferred exhilarating "indoor coastings"—sliding down the stairs while sitting on a tea tray—to dull tea parties. Zona Gale and a friend wreaked havoc on their tea party by smashing their unsuspecting dolls to bits. Gale, who became a writer and a feminist, had consciously determined to live life unencumbered by sex roles.[46]

Through their doll play, girls also seemed to enjoy the challenges they posed to patriarchal authority. One autobiographer recalled deliberately sewing clothes for her doll on Sundays, "quite as on other days," until finally sobered by the warning that "every stitch she sewed on Sunday, she would have to rip out with her teeth when she got to Purgatory." Undaunted, she decided to learn how to rip out the stitches that way before she got there. The task, however, proved to be such a difficult one that she gave up sewing on Sundays until her mother purchased a Wilcox and Gibbs chain-stitch sewing machine. "After that, I did all my Sunday sewing on the sewing machine, feeling it would only be an additional pleasure to rip it out [with her teeth] in Purgatory, and with a deep satisfaction at having gotten the best of the Devil."[47]

Girls who played with dolls in late-nineteenth-century America sometimes developed a sense of self that was anything but submissive. Sarah Bixby, who was raised in southern California, skinned, dressed, and boiled rabbit meat for her doll, Isabel. In one story, Lydia smacks a roving pig with her wooden doll, formerly an outcast among her doll peers but thereafter their heroine. Late-nineteenth-century autobiographies similarly reveal that, contrary to the prescribed version, girls whose dolls fell victim to aggressive animals or belligerent boys defended themselves and their dolls instead of seeking male protection. One young girl "burst out" and "flew at" her friend, Harry (who bullied and teased), after he bit a hole in her favorite doll. She "grabbed him by the shoulders, . . . ready to fight to the death for [her] rights, [when] he burst into cries for help . . . I shall never forget my surprise and triumph as I realized that I conquered—conquered in spite of being small, with a strength I could always command. I only had to set [myself] free, to let her come, outside, and she could do anything."[48]

By the turn of the century, dolls with their own wardrobes, literature, and ideology had altered the nature of doll play. Girls born and raised in middle-class antebellum households had few dolls, and those they had were mostly of their own making as prescribed and instructed by a literature directed at mothers and daughters. Making dolls and playing with them had fostered skills useful to character development, self-government, and a domestic economy. In the years after the Civil War, as European imported dolls proliferated and became more splendid, the meaning of dolls in girls' lives changed. Doll stories provided companionship and the seed of fantasies, which brought girls beyond the confines of the material world. Girls were encouraged to display the store-bought dolls they received on holidays and from indulgent relatives. The productive and "useful" activities of their mothers' generation had left the dollhouse as it had the American household, gradually replaced by new values and skills revolving around status (and kin). Previous generations had learned useful household skills, but girls in the Gilded Age were encouraged to play with their china and bisque dolls in ways that increasingly aped the conspicuous display of consumer goods and social status epitomized by the European bourgeoisie their parents emulated.

Although postwar popular culture differed dramatically from the antebellum period, girls revealed obvious continuities over the course of the century. If they played with dolls at all, they rejected elaborate dolls for coarse ones, favored black rag dolls over white ones, resisted rote prescriptions of play rituals by substituting their own earthy versions, and often preferred active "physical culture" to passive doll culture. At times, boys also challenged sex-role stereotyping and at other times reinforced it. Those girls who resisted patriarchal prescriptions in their play displayed confidence, not conformity. Their play, like language, revealed girls' agency in the construction of their own upbringing.[49]

While occasionally victorious in their struggles with parents, girls faced other contenders who claimed it as their right to shape dolls both literally and figuratively. In the years after the Civil War, American businessmen, with no prior experience in dollmaking but eager to make a profit, turned their attention to doll invention and production. How businessmen perceived an American girlhood and how they conceived of the role that dolls would play in girls' lives would have profound consequences for the nature of nineteenth-century doll invention.

NOTES

1. "The Natural Instincts of Boys and Girls," *Babyhood*, April 1905, 143.

2. Mary Lawrence, "Dolls: Logically Considered," *Babyhood*, Oct 1895, 330–331. On conspicuous consumption, see Thorstein Veblen, *Theory of the Leisure Class: An Economic Study in the Evolution of Institutions* (New York: Macmillan, 1899).

3. Catherine E. Beecher and Harriet Beecher Stowe, *American Woman's Home* (1869; rpt. Watkins Glen, N.Y.: Library of Victorian Culture, 1879), 298. On children and the American family, see John Demos, *A Little Commonwealth: The Family in a Plymouth Colony* (New York: Oxford University Press, 1970); Bernard Wishy, *The Child and the Republic: The Dawn of Modern American Child Nurture* (Philadelphia: University of Pennsylvania Press, 1968); Joseph Kett, *The Rites of Passage: Adolescence in America, 1790 to the Present* (New York: Basic Books, 1977); Philip Greven, *The Protestant Temperament: Patterns of Child-Rearing, Religious Experience and the Self in Early America* (New York: New American Library, 1977); Michael Gordon, ed., *The American Family in Social-Historical Perspective* (New York: St. Martin's Press, 1983); N. Ray Hiner and Joseph M. Hawes, eds., *Growing up in America: Children in Historical Perspective* (Urbana: University of Illinois Press, 1985); Steven Mintz and Susan Kellogg, *Domestic Revolutions: A Social History of Family Life* (New York: The Free Press, 1988); Mary Lynn Stevens Heininger, "Children, Childhood, and Change in America, 1820–1920," in Mary Lynn Stevens Heininger et al., eds., *A Century of Childhood, 1820–1920* (Rochester, N.Y.:Margaret Woodbury Strong Museum, 1984), 6. Childrearing literature included Theodore Dwight, *The Father's Book* (1834), Dr. John Abbott, *The Mother's Book* (1844), and Catherine Beecher, *Treatise on Domestic Economy* (1847); see Mary P. Ryan, "The Empire of the Mother: American Writing about Domesticity, 1830–1860," *Women and History*, no. 2–3 (Summer-Fall 1982).

4. Beecher and Stowe, *American Woman's Home*, 299. Eliza Leslie, *The American Girl's Book or Occupations for Play Hours* (New York: C. S. Francis, 1831), intro. This book appeared one year after the very popular *American Boy's Book* and went through 14 editions, the last published in 1849. Mary Sewell quoted in Linda Pollock, *A Lasting Relationship: Parents and Children over Three Centuries* (Hanover, N.H.: University Press of New England, 1987), 103–104.

5. Lydia Maria Child, *Girl's Own Book* (New York: Clark Austin, 1833), iii, iv.

6. Mary Ryan, *Cradle of the Middle Class: The Family in Oneida County, New York, 1790–1865* (Cambridge: Cambridge University Press, 1981), 161; *Mother's Monthly Journal*, July 1837, 127; Richard Meckel, "Educating a Ministry of Mothers: Evangelical Maternal Associations, 1815–1860," *Journal of the Early Republic* 2, no. 4 (Winter 1982): 402–423. Nancy F. Cott, *Bonds of Womanhood: Woman's Sphere in New England, 1780–1835* (New Haven: Yale University Press, 1977), 43. Paula Petrik, "The Paraphernalia of Childhood: New Toys for Old and Selchow & Righter Co., 1830–1870," typescript, 5. "Pincushion," Work Department. *Godey's Lady's Book* 74, Aug. 1867; "Doll Pin-cushion," *Peterson's* 48, Sept. 1965, 209; "The Little Companion," *Peterson's* 47, Jan. 1865. "Fancy Pen Wiper," *Godey's Lady's Book* 60, July 1884, 66, cited in Beverly Gordon, "Victorian Fancywork in the American Home: Fantasy and Accommodation," in Marilyn Ferris Motz and Pat Browne, eds., *Making the American Home: Middle-Class Women and Domestic Material Culture, 1840–1940* (Bowling Green, Ohio: Bowling Green State University Popular Press, 1988), 63.

7. Cott, *Bonds of Womanhood*, 43; Susan Strasser, *Never Done: A History of American Housework* (New York: Pantheon, 1982); Ruth Schwartz Cowan, *More Work for Mother: The Ironies of Household Technology from the Open Hearth to the Microwave* (New York: Basic Books, 1983), 63, 66, 201. Beecher and Stowe, *American Woman's Home*, 298.

8. Lucy Larcom, *A New England Girlhood* (Boston:Northeastern University Press, 1986), 29. Jean M. Thompson, "The Story of Rosamond," *Harper's Bazaar*, May 1906, 474. S. Anne Frost, *The Ladies' Guide to Needlework, Embroidery, Etc.* (New York: Adams & Bishop, 1877), 132–138; Child, *Girl's Own Book*, iii, iv.

9. Paintings in the National Gallery of Art, Smithsonian Institution, Washington, D.C.; Inez McClintock, *Toys in America* (Washington, D.C.: Public Affairs Press, 1961), 68.

10. "Two Sisters," reprinted in *Children's Stories of the 1850s* (Americana Review). Emily Wilson, *The Forgotten Girl* (New York: Alphabet Press, 1937), 7.

11. Wilson, *The Forgotten Girl*, 14–15; Harriet Robinson, *The Loom and the Spindle: or, Life Among the Early Mill Girls* (1898; reprint, Kailua, Hawaii: Press Pacifica, 1976), 23.

12. Suzanne Lebsock, *The Free Women of Petersburg: Status and Culture in a Southern Town, 1794–1860* (New York: W. W. Norton, 1984), 64. Larcom, *New England Girlhood*, 29; Leslie, *American Girls' Book*, 287–288; see also Maria Edgeworth and Richard Lowell Edgeworth, *Practical Education* (New York: Harper, 1835), 16–17.

13. Larcom, *New England Girlhood*, ch. 1; Kathryn Kish Sklar, *Catherine Beecher: A Study of American Domesticity* (New York: W. W. Norton, 1973), 9; Wilson, *Forgotten Girl*, 14–15. In fact, mothers were also advised to permit their middle-class daughters, most of whom still lived in rural areas, to participate in outdoor games. In *The Mother's Assistant and Young Lady's Friend*, Sarah S. Ellis advocated "exercise in open air" as an antidote to "artificial habits" causing a "host of numerous maladies" in genteel daughters. Karin Lee Fishbeck Calvert, *Children in the House: The Material Culture of Early Childhood, 1600–1900* (Boston: Northeastern University Press, 1992); Bernard Mergen, *Play and Playthings: A Reference Guide* (Westport, Conn.: Greenwood Press 1982), 25; Robinson, *Loom and the Spindle*, 23–24; Anne Scott MacLeod, "The Caddie Woodlawn Syndrome: American Girlhood in the Nineteenth Century," in Heininger et al., *A Century of Childhood*, 97–120.

14. *Ridleys' Fashion Magazine*, cited in Jan Foulke, "Dolls of the 1880s," *Doll Reader*, Nov. 1988, 98. "A Doll's Story," *DD*, May 1893, 103.

15. *Ridleys' Fashion Magazine*, cited in Foulke, "Dolls of the 1880s," *Doll Reader*, Nov. 1988, 103.

16. J. E. Jeuck, *Catalogues and Counters: A History of Sears, Roebuck & Co.* (Chicago: University of Chicago Press, 1950); Joseph J. Schroeder, Jr., ed., *The Wonderful World of Toys, Games, and Dolls* (Northfield, Ill.: DBI Books, 1971), intro.

17. Susan Porter Benson, *Counter Cultures* (Urbana and Chicago: University of Illinois Press, 1988), 14. Macy's "was one of the first, if not the first, to sell toys in a department store"; see *Playthings*, Oct. 1903, 6. Philip G. Hubert, Jr., "Some Notes as to Christmas Toys," *Babyhood*, Dec. 1893, 15–16.

18. William Leach, "Transformations in a Culture of Consumption: Women and Department Stores, 1890–1925," *Journal of American History* 71 (Sept. 1984): 319–342; Elaine S. Abelson, *When Ladies Go A-Thieving : Middle-Class Shoplifters in the Victorian Department Store* (New York: Oxford University Press, 1989). *Harper's Bazaar* (1881) cited in Foulke, "Dolls of the 1880s," 94. "A Doll's Story, Told by Herself," *Doll's Dressmaker*, Jan. 1891, 5. *Doll's Dressmaker*, May 1893, 101–102. For other shopping recollections, see Una Atherton Hunt, *Una Mary: The Inner Life of a Child* (New York: Scribner's, 1914), and Meta Lilienthal, *Dear Remembered World: Childhood Memories of an Old New Yorker* (New York: R. R. Smith, 1947).

19. Elizabeth Seelye, "Suggestions Concerning Toys and Amusements," *Babyhood*, Dec. 1890, 17; "Toys for Children," *Doll's Dressmaker* Nov. 1892, 283. Mary Hunt's uncle gave her a French bisque doll (Hunt, *Una Mary*, 161). Lilienthal, *Dear Remembered World*, 43.

20. H. Coyle, "Papa's Weary Head," *Doll's Dressmaker*, May, 1891, 98. Wishy, *Child and the Republic*, 16; Heininger, "Children, Childhood," 19–20. *DD*, May 1891, 100; *Babyhood*, Jan. 1891, 5. Louisa May Alcott, *A Doll's Journey* (Boston: Little, Brown, 1873), 5.

21. One author of a study of Polish children found that doll play ceased at age 10—

earlier than among American children (Madam Anna Grudzinska, "A Study of Dolls Among Polish Children," *Pedagogical Seminary* 14, no. 6 [Sept. 1907]: 385–390). L. Emmett Holt, "Infant Feeding," part of an address given before the Cleveland Medical Society, Oct. 26, 1900, 10, and *The Diseases of Infancy and Childhood* (New York, 1897), 158, cited in Kathleen W. Jones, "Sentiment and Science: The Late Nineteenth-Century Pediatrician as Mother's Advisor," *Journal of Social History* (Fall 1983): 86; Janet Golden, "Trouble in the Nursery: Physicians, Families and Wet Nurses at the End of the Nineteenth Century," in Carol Groneman and Mary Beth Norton, eds., *"To Toil the Livelong Day:" America's Women at Work, 1790–1980* (Ithaca, N.Y.: Cornell University Press, 1987), 126.

22. *Youth's Companion* was founded in 1827, *St. Nicholas* in 1873, *Children's Magazine* in 1879. Other children's magazines include *Harper's Young People* and *Frank Leslie's Chatterbox*. Mintz and Kellogg, *Domestic Revolutions*, xix; Daniel Scott Smith, "Family Limitation, Sexual Control and Domestic Feminism in Victorian America, *Feminist Studies* 1 (Winter-Spring 1973): 40–57. *A Tribute to Margaret Woodbury Strong* Rochester, N.Y.: Margaret Woodbury Strong Museum, 1986), 7.

23. "A Doll's Story, Told By Herself," 5. During the Gilded Age, Americans became participants and spectators of baseball and football as specific forms of leisure and amusement.

24. J. M. Barrie, *Peter Pan* (1911; reprint, Toronto: Bantam, 1985). The Division of Domestic Life of the National Museum of American History (Smithsonian Institution, Washington, D.C.) has an extensive collection of Victorian juvenile furniture.

25. My thanks to John Gillis for bringing out this point.

26. *Pretty Pursuits for Children* (London and New York: Butterick, 1897), 61; *The Doll's Tea Party* (Boston: Lothrop, 1895); "Dressing Dolls," *Doll Reader*, June 1892, 145.

27. "Dressing Dolls," *Doll Reader*, June 1892, 144; Evelyn Jane Coleman, *Carte de Visite; Doll Reader Album de la Poupée*, 1978 reproduction; *Pretty Pursuits*, 78; "Styles for Dolls," *Delineator*, Nov. 1897, 558; Mrs. H. W. Beecher, *Monthly Talks with Young Homemakers* (New York: J. B,. Ford, 1873), 293.

28. Thomas J. Schlereth, *Victorian America: Transformations in Everyday Life, 1876–1915* (New York: Harper Collins, 1991), 290–293; Harvey Green, *The Light of the Home* (New York: Pantheon, 1983), 165; Karen Halttunen, *Confidence Men and Painted Ladies: A Study of Middle-Class Culture in America, 1830–1870* (New Haven: Yale University Press, 1982), ch. 5; Ann Douglas, *The Feminization of American Culture* (New York: Avon, 1978), ch. 5. McClintock, *Toys in America*, 78; Barbara Pickering, "In Loving Memory—Dolls and Death," *Doll Reader*, Nov. 1988, 132.

29. C. Kurt Dewhurst, Betty MacDowell, and Martha MacDowell, *Artists in Aprons* (New York: E. P. Dutton and the Museum of American Folk Art, 1979), 60–62, 66–70; Rozika Parker, *The Subversive Stitch: Embroidery and the Making of the Feminine* (New York: Routledge, 1989). Kate Douglas Wiggin, *Rebecca of Sunny-brook Farm* (1903; rev. ed., Middlesex, U.K.: Puffin, 1985), 63. Mary Alves Long, *High Time to Tell It* (Durham, N.C.: Duke University Press, 1950), 23. Slave children staged funerals as well, according to David K. Wiggins, "The Play of Slave Children in the Plantation Communities of the Old South, 1820–1860," in Hiner and Hawes, eds., *Growing up in America*, 178.

30. Mrs. (Richard Henry Horne) Fairstair, *Memoirs of a London Doll, Written by Herself* (London: 1846; reprint, New York, 1967). R. Gordon Kelly, ed., *Children's Periodicals of the United States* (Westport, Conn.: Greenwood Press, 1984); R. Gordon Kelly, *Mother Was a Lady; Self and Society in Selected American Children's Periodicals* (Westport, Conn.: Greenwood Press, 1974). *The Doll's Own Book* (Ohio, n.p., 1882); many also had large print, such

as, *Twilight Stories* (New York, London, Manchester, Glasgow: n.d.). See issues of *Doll's Dressmaker* for other installments by the same author. Mrs. Jane M. Besset, *Memoirs of a Doll: by Itself* (Philadelphia and New York: American Sunday School Union, 2nd. ed., 1856).

31. Reynale Smith Pickering, "Christmas in Song and Story," and "The New Christmas Doll Complains" (poems) *Ladies Home Journal*, Dec. 1908, 126. See also the poem by Laura Starr, *The Doll Book* (New York: Outing Co., 1908), 199.

32. S. K. Simons, "The Happy Doll," *Doll's Dressmaker*, April 1893, 90.

33. This notion of love also laid the basis for inevitable frustration when girls got older. Among middle-class Americans and the British, love had been "feminized"—caring and loving had become the work of women while support and protection that of men. Gillis, "Ritualization," 15; Fracesca Cancian, *Love in America: Gender and Self Development* (Cambridge: Cambridge University Press, 1987). "Dolls: Logically Considered," *Babyhood*, Oct. 1895, 330–331.

34. In stereographs and illustrations, boys often played the role of doctor as well. Thompson, "Rosamond," 474; Heininger, "Children, Childhood," 26–27; see also: Anita Schorsch, *Images of Childhood: An Illustrated Social History* (Pittstown, N.J.: Main Street Press, 1985), ch. 6; "The Tragical-Comical Tale of Mrs. Kennedy and Punch," *Frank Leslie's Chatterbox*, 1885–1886, 10.

35. For an example of a taunting monkey, see: "Naughty Jacko," in *Dolly in Town* (New York; R. Tuck, 1912). In "The Little Doll," a poem by Charles Kingsley in *The Water Babies* (Philadelphia: J.B. Lippincott, 1917), a wooden doll's arms are "troddened off by cows," See "Kate Douglas Wiggin's Poetry for Children," *Ladie's Home Journal*, Oct. 1907, 50. Aunt Laura (pseud.), *The Dolls' Surprise Party* (Buffalo, N.Y.: Butler, 1863).

36. Beatrix Potter, *The Tale of Two Bad Mice* (New York: F. Warne, 1904), 46, 59.

37. Louisa May Alcott, *Little Women* (1868; reprint, New York: Penguin, 1989), 39. Schlereth, *Victorian America*, 197.

38. Hubert, "Some Notes as to Christmas Toys," *Babyhood*, Dec. 1893, 14. Emily Kimbrough, *How Dear to My Heart* (New York: Dodd, Mead, 1944), 76–77; Lilienthal, *Dear Remembered World*, 20–21;

39. "The Doll of the Colored Children," *Babyhood*, Oct. 1894, 351. Hunt, *Una Mary*, 20. A. C. Ellis and G. Stanley Hall, "Study of Dolls," *Pedagogical Seminary* 1, no. 2 (Dec. 1896): 134. "Home-Made Rag," *Babyhood*, Sept. 1908, 417. David Katzman, *Seven Days a Week* (Urbana: University of Illinois Press, 1981). Ellis and Hall, "Study of Dolls," 141.

40. M. H. Jones, "Dolls for Boys," *Babyhood*, June 1896, 216. "Of average city school children below 6 years, 82% of boys . . . played with dolls; between 6 and 12 yrs., 76% of boys" (Ellis and Hall, "Study of Dolls," 155); For more examples see Calvert, "To Be a Child," 156; *Maiden America & Friends: Parade of Playthings*, Nov. 1984, 51; Dorothy Washburn, "Report: Preliminary Results, Doll Oral History Project," 2, Margaret Woodbury Strong Museum, Rochester, N.Y., doll 79.9962.

41. Ellis and Hall, "Study of Dolls," 145.

42. According to one ten-year-old boy, "My doll used to get angry and I would grab her by the hair and threw her down stairs but afterward give her a nice piece of mud cake wit raspberries on it." Ellis and Hall, "Study of Dolls," 145, 147, 149, 150–151; Jones, "Dolls for Boys," 216.

43. T. R. Croswell, "Amusements" (Worcester, Mass.: J. H. Orpha, 1899), 347. Eleanor Abbott, *Being Little in Cambridge When Everyone Else was Big*, cited in Bernard Mergen, *Play and Playthings: A Reference Guide* (Westport, Conn.: Greenwood Press, 1982), 186–187. Cro-

swell, "Amusements," 5; Brian Sutton-Smith, "The Play of Girls," in Clare B. Knapp and Martha Kirkpatrick, eds., *Becoming Female* (New York: Plenum, 1979), 229–230. "The Natural Instincts of Boys and Girls," *Babyhood*, April 1905, 143.

44. Ellis and Hall, "Study of Dolls," 146–147; "Young Mrs. Wink-et Scolds her Dolly," *Babyhood* 2, 1 (Boston: Lathrop, 1878), 10. Death and burial were the subjects of late-nineteenth-century schoolgirls' ring games; see Brian Sutton-Smith, "Play of Girls," in Knapp and Kirkpatrick, eds., *Becoming Female*, 232; Schlereth, *Victorian America*, 292; "Burying Baby Dolls," *Doll's Dressmaker*, Nov, 1891, 240; Ethel Spencer, *The Spencers of Amberson Avenue: A Turn of the Century Memoir*, ed. Michael P. Weber and Peter N. Stearns (Pittsburgh: University of Pittsburgh Press, 1983), 65; Alice Kent Trimpey, *Becky My First Love* (Baraboo, Wis.: Remington House, 1946), 1–2; According to one nine-year-old, "doll broken, funeral just for fun" (Ellis and Hall, "Study of Dolls," 146).

45. Calvert, "To Be a Child," 153. Lawrence, "Dolls: Logically Considered," 330–331. "The Natural Instincts of Boys and Girls," *Babyhood*, April 1905, 143. Ellis and Hall, "Study of Dolls," 140, 141.

46. James Sully, *Children's Ways* (New York: Appleton, 1897), 492.

47. Hunt, *Una Mary*, 14. Zona Gale, *When I Was a Little Girl* (New York: Macmillan, 1913), 196.

48. Hunt, *Una Mary*, 163–165.

49. Aunt Laura (pseud.), *The Dolls' Surprise Party*. Victoria Bissell Brown, "Female Socialization among the Middle Class of Los Angeles," in Elliott West and Paula Petrik, eds., *Small Worlds: Children and Adolescents in America, 1850–1950* (Lawrence: University of Kansas Press, 1992), 246. Hunt, *Una Mary*, 20.

Chapter Twenty-one

Older Heads on Younger Bodies

Erica Rand

This essay studies adult testimony about childhood Barbie consumption to address several issues. The first concerns the relation between intention and reception in the production of meaning. What meanings do consumers give to Barbie, and to what extent do Mattel-generated meanings accord with consumer-generated meanings? The second concerns resistance. What constitutes resistance to given cultural objects and norms? When does cultural resistance signal social or political resistance? Where, if anywhere, in the relation between intention and reception can resistance be located? Although elsewhere I have used the concept of hegemonic discourse to describe Mattel's strategy,[1] I argue here that, while the opposition between hegemonic and counterhegemonic is valuable, it does not by itself present a model for locating resistance and that resistance cannot always be determined by assessing the degree of fit between intention and reception. . . .

Adult memories of Barbie suggest several general conclusions. First, Mattel has had stunning success at making a doll who is memorable, particularly to women and girls. It's not just that many, many women have approached me with Barbie stories, although the numbers themselves speak to Barbie's memorableness. A more striking indication, however, is that almost everyone I ask has an answer to the question "Did you have a Barbie doll when you were a child?" that is not "I don't know." Most adult women remember whether they had a Barbie. Some remember specific dolls or products: "I had the Barbie camper"; "I had the Barbie perfume factory"; "I had Francie, Barbie's mod friend." Those who did not have Barbie often remember why, the reason often being Mattel's early-identified problem, a reluctant mother. A few had no memory of Barbie specifically, usually attributing this to a general distaste for female dolls: "I only wanted to play with trucks"; "I never got the whole doll thing." But typically people remember the issue of having a Barbie as at least slightly distinct from the issue of having dolls in general; having a Barbie required a separate or additional decision. Most people also remember an attitude toward Barbie in particular: they loved her, hated her, or something in between.

Second, most people remember Barbie as having been of great value and desirability, either to themselves or to others. Barbie's status often depended on the brand name as well as the product. Early Barbie commercials direct viewers to look for the Mattel tag to make sure of getting authentic Barbie products; apparently, however, children did not need a tag to tell the difference. Many people differentiated between official Mattel products and less desirable pretenders. "I only had a fake Barbie," Joleen recounted.[2] Although the similarity between her doll's fate and that of many a real Barbie—"my perverted brothers took needles and poked holes in her breasts"—suggests that knockoff status did not always render a doll ineligible for the Barbie treatment, the distinction between fake and real nonetheless mattered in the assessment of the doll's worth.

In the child's world, too, custom-made originals frequently had less value than clothes off the Mattel rack. As Lise states, "I had a friend whose grandmother sewed her hundreds of matching Barbie outfits. My mother disapproved of this; she thought it was a colossal waste of labor and time. Martha and I secretly knew they were worthless for a different reason: they didn't come in those plastic packages."[3] Nor did they come from official Barbie patterns. It was possible to buy patterns from which to better imitate Barbie's look—which meant that Mattel, via its licensee McCall's, still wound up making money off people trying to avoid the cost of Barbie ready-to-wears in this way.

The Mattel tag, then, conferred value. Barbie was also perceived as valuable for what she represented. From the evidence of many accounts, Mattel was highly successful at creating a doll who was recognized as a model of ideal teenhood: "When I started to feel like I did not measure up to standards of ideal womanhood I compared my image to my sister's Barbie rather than to my Tammy doll because I knew somehow that Barbie had more status." Like many people who remember Barbie as a valued object, the woman who told me this, now an artist in her thirties who makes art about gender issues, was not quite sure how she knew Barbie had great value; she just knew. Others remember sources of value more clearly, citing Mattel and/or the opinions of others. They knew that their friends or people they admired liked Barbie or that their parents wanted them to have Barbie, often despite their apparent disinterest or professed distaste. Or they knew, conversely, that their parents did not want them to have Barbie, adding the appeal of the forbidden to Barbie's charms. Carole Nicksin writes, for instance, that her sense of Barbie's supreme value was constructed through attention to conflicting value-mongers, her mother and "the big girls":

> When I was three years old in 1963 I informed my mother that I was ready for my first Barbie. She obligingly took me to the Shopper's Fair and by that afternoon I was the proud owner of a . . . Tammy. "I couldn't buy that Barbie doll for my three year old," I heard Mom tell Grandma on the phone. "—why, that girl has a . . . a . . . a . . . full bust!" I didn't know what a bust was then but I found out that and many other differences between my Tammy and the Barbie I could not yet have. The older girls spelled it out for me in a way Mom never could—Barbie's Cool!; Tammy? a Nerd![4]

Nicksin's assessment of Barbie's value contains a number of common features. Many people knew that Barbie's value was contested. Virtually everyone knew that in some eyes Barbie was great. Value options might go from good to great or from great to terrible; they never went from bad to worse. Like Nicksin, too, most people remember having taken a position on Barbie, which is remarkable considering how many items are passed over or appropriated routinely, without fanfare, anguish, or conscious decision making. Barbie, in contrast, seemed to demand a stance, which often had to be fought for, or fought over, because more than Barbie was at stake. Taking a position on Barbie meant taking a position about other issues, or defining oneself, or defying authority.

Nicksin's account is also typical in that she remembers locating meanings in the doll itself: she "found out" who Barbie was and what Barbie meant. From adult accounts, Mattel was right to conclude early on that Barbie was not being perceived as a blank slate awaiting the consumer's inscription of meaning. Although no one I encountered remembered having been one of those children Mandeville described who clamored for biographical information about how Barbie became a model etc., his account well registers what seems to have been a prevalent childhood sense that Barbie had an identity and meanings. If you didn't know them, someone else did. Meanings, and consequently the cause of Barbie's value, were to be discerned rather than invented; when unavailable, they were concealed rather than absent. These meanings might be seen to reflect, represent, or inform about meanings external to Barbie; at the same time, however, they inhered in the doll itself.

One of the best textual encapsulations of the complex interplay between artifactual and external sources of Barbie's meaning and value comes, not from a consumer account about Barbie, but from a fictional account about a baby doll. In Toni Morrison's 1970 novel *The Bluest Eye*, nine-year-old Claudia describes initially being "bemused" by the "blue-eyed Baby Doll" that was always "the big, the special, the loving gift" on Christmas, then learning what she was supposed to do with it, "rock it, fabricate storied situations around it, even sleep with it," and finally wanting to do something quite different:

> I had only one desire: to dismember it. To see of what it was made, to discover the dearness, to find the beauty, the desirability that had escaped me, but apparently only me. Adults, older girls, shops, magazines, newspapers, window signs—all the world had agreed that a blue-eyed, yellow-haired, pink-skinned doll was what every girl child treasured. "Here," they said, "this is beautiful, and if you are on this day 'worthy' you may have it." I fingered the face, wondering at the single-stroke eyebrows, picked at the pearly teeth stuck like two piano keys between red bowline lips. Traced the turned-up nose, poked the glassy blue eye-balls, twisted the yellow hair. I could not love it. But I could examine it to see what it was that all the world said was lovable. Break off the tiny fingers, bend the flat feet, loosen the hair, twist the head around. . . .
>
> But the dismembering of dolls was not the true horror. The truly horrifying thing was the transference of the same impulse to little white girls. The indifference with which I could have axed them was shaken only by my desire to do so. To discover what eluded me: the secret of the magic they weaved on others. What made people look at them and say "Awwwww," but not for me?[5]

I return later to why this fictional text, like so many others, bears a striking resemblance to adult Barbie stories labeled nonfiction by the tellers. What concerns me here are the elements of this resemblance, which are many. To begin with, Morrison's text captures in Claudia the imaginative process by which every Barbie consumer identifies human referents for the anthropomorphic artifact. Equations between anthropomorphic artifacts and human beings always, of course, entail imaginative leaps: plastic denotes skin, yarn denotes hair, etc. But Claudia makes other leaps such as age; the baby doll stands for little girls. Her correspondence is also partial and depends on her own sense of identity. Conscious of her own color, Claudia focuses especially on the pink skin, yellow hair, and blue eyes, which she views as being about race. In Claudia's correspondence between white female dolls and white female girls, race matters the most, whereas, in Nicksin's correspondence between Barbie and teenagers, race (being "white") never gets mentioned, and sexuality matters the most. "It is no wonder," Nicksin writes, after lauding Barbie's stiletto-molded feet and firm bust, "that myself and countless other prepubescent girls (if my independent survey is any indication) used this doll in particular to act out budding sexuality."[6]

I do not mean to suggest here that thinking about race is the same as thinking about gender or sexuality or to set up a distinction between Barbie consumers of color who think only about race and white Barbie consumers who think only about gender or sexuality. Although the second characterization has much truth to it, the first has little or none. White Barbie owners from Barbie's prediversity period generally seem to have noticed Barbie's race even less than did the early novelized Barbie, who recognized herself as white for one brief moment. Even if they remember Barbie's blond hair and blue eyes as significant physical features, they do not, as Claudia did, recognize them as ethnic or racial markers. In contrast, Barbie's race seems to have been noticed by most people who lacked the privilege of ignoring their own, whether or not race was not the primary focus. Cheryl, an African American dyke who told me that she "hated that stupid white doll," then proceeded to outline a series of despicable characteristics that were not race oriented: Barbie's hard body; the model-young-lady gender behavior for which she stood and that, Cheryl believes, induced her mother to foist one on her over her protest. (The mother's attempt did not work; Cheryl refused even to open the box.)[7] My point, then, is not that consumers pick one category to think about—race or gender, gender or class, etc.—but that every interpretation, like Claudia's, is based on partial vision in which certain artifactual attributes are transformed and transported into human referents. . . .

The most obvious signs of dyke destiny occur in stories about female sexual desire for females. Not every junior dyke could get off on Barbie: "I hated Barbie; you couldn't spread her legs." But some could. Penny Pollard remembers using Barbie to act out fantasies about her baby-sitter Janet, with help from Janet's mother: "I had a crush on my baby-sitter, Janet (who was also the only person who could get me into a dress). Her mother had turned two Barbies into 'Janet' and 'Carol' dolls, named after her and her sister, dressing girls and dolls in

matching clothes. I got the dolls when they were too old for them and used my
'Janet' doll to act out what I wanted to do with the real Janet."

Here Barbie gets transformed into the object of dyke desire. Penny Lorio
turned Barbie into the agent of dyke desire. Her "Uncloseting Barbie: Get over
It, Ken, It's a New Age" concerns Lorio's attempt to make her unasked-for Barbie
a usable toy—"the last thing I needed when we were hiking through quicksand
was to have her gimping along in high heels"—and her mother's distress that
Barbie was not a socializing tool as she'd hoped:

> "So Barbie should start acting like a young lady," Mom explained, reading the
> dumb expresion on my face. "Because someday she's going to meet someone and
> fall in love. And then she's not going to want to be a tomboy anymore."
>   Oh, right, like falling in love was more fun than climbing trees.
>   "Do you understand what I'm trying to say?" Mom asked.
>   Of course I did. I wasn't born yesterday. I was 7. I knew about life.
>   "Barbie's already been in love," I said, vouching for the heart of a tomboy.
>   Mom smiled eagerly. "Oh, she has? Does she like Freddy's G.I. Joe?"
>   I made a face like a person who's just been served ketchup on pancakes.
>   "Of course not. Barbie loves Midge."
>   And that was a whole different subject.[8]

Not necessarily. In all the stories above, the perception of sexual desire for
women arose in the context of being a gender-role outlaw. The woman who
couldn't spread Barbie's legs (to which she did not attribute dyke content until I
raised my eyebrows) was as much disgusted by getting a girl's toy foisted on
her. Disgust for girls' clothing was a subtext of Pollard's tale of lust, and the two
issues met in her interaction with the same person. Many other dykes told me
stories that indicated, if not a childhood intermesh of sexuality/gender issues,
then a sequential progression from gender outlaw at the Barbie age to sexual
outlaw sometime later.

To many women who later self-identified as dykes, it seems, Barbie did not
provide a role model or suitable imaginary friend. A number just could not see
any potential: they preferred boy's toys, often mentioning trucks. Some found a
different doll in the Barbie line to identify or pal around with. Teresa Ortega,
who spent lots of childhood time playing with Barbies, nonetheless shunned her
as a role model: "I wanted to be Skipper; she had a teenager look, flat feet, and
could do sports." Later, when she got into the Los Angeles punk scene at age
fifteen, she retrieved Skipper from the discard pile, punking her out with tattoos
and other unauthorized accessories. Ortega also related conducting a small survey of the four women in her office that suggested that predyke evidence might
be found in the assessment of Barbie's potential suitors. The two dykes remember
thinking G.I. Joe was too big to date Barbie, while the two straight women made
him Barbie's dream date. What does this mean? Perhaps the woman who identified with Ken has the key. In her eyes, remember, Ken was not really a male but
a cross-dressing female.

Sue also preferred Ken, although she kept asking for Barbie:

Actually, I wanted Ken more, but I was too scared to ask for it. Barbie was a girl, and girls were too girly. I kept asking for one because it seemed like the normal girl thing to have. All my friends [in Limerick, Maine] had one. And asking for Barbie was easy because you were supposed to ask for it; it didn't make you feel ashamed. I asked for Barbie over and over, but I only asked for each of the boy toys I wanted once, and I totally planned it out. I'd wait until a Matchbox car came on a TV commercial and then ask for it like it was a casual idea that had just occurred to me—something generated by the commercial—when really I'd wanted it for a long time. So I kept asking for Barbie, and once I got it I hated it. I never played with it. I think I threw it under the bed. My older sister loved it, though. She crocheted all these little dresses for it; she'd never gotten to have one.[9]

Sue's story underscores how misleading secondhand testimony can be. Did anyone who heard her repeated request for a Barbie know that it camouflaged a desire for Ken and Matchbox cars?

It also underscores how hard it is to draw any broad conclusions about how Barbie rejection relates to future sexual orientation or gender identity. A third dyke present during my conversation with Sue, "T.D.," had also rejected Barbie. When Sue commented, "Now I'm living my second boyhood," T.D. responded, "That's the whole thing about being a young butch dyke—living out your second boyhood." (Sue and T.D. were then, respectively, nineteen and twenty-four.) This comment suggested that Sue had hit on a typical feature of a butch dyke's childhood: rejecting femaleness. But, as the conversation progressed, it turned out that the two women had different ideas about why they had rejected female-coded toys. For T.D. it meant rejecting her own biological gender. After hearing Sue describe a mutual friend's story of burning off Barbie's breasts with matches and then giving her Ken's head, T.D. said, "That sounds like what I would have done with my Barbie if I had ever let anyone give me one. She burned off Barbie's secondary sex characteristics—actually she got rid of all of them, including her female head." Sue, however, had not wanted to be a boy and thought her toy preferences were about something else:

It wasn't about gender as much as it was about going outside. I wanted to play outside and get dirty. Girl toys you used inside; boy toys were for outside. I resented being supposed to do the girl thing all the time. I wanted to do the boy stuff. I think the Barbie thing was also about being treated as too young. I was the youngest of four girls, and my family kept treating me as younger than I was. Throwing out Barbie was related to this. Most girls got Barbie when they were really little, but I didn't get one until fourth grade. I think that, by then, I felt too old for Barbie. It was another example of how my family did not want to let me grow up.

Sue was protesting the gender coding assigned to activities, not the gender assigned to her, and Barbie was just as much about infantilization as about gender.

If the coming-out narrative in particular and habits of narrating the past into the present in general account in part for the dyke destiny verbal nudge, some credit for its prevalence must also belong to Barbie. As has often been noted, Barbie's body signals sexuality to adults. It is a commonplace that Barbie might induce precocious sexual thinking, and adult narratives indicate that Barbie often signaled sexuality to children. From this angle, the dyke destiny verbal nudge can be viewed as an acknowledgement, hypothesis, and/or trace memory that, no matter what is remembered about Barbie, some sexual assessment was or might have been going on, too. That is, if the coming-out narrative overlays my questions with, "Was I a dyke at age seven?" Barbie's body overlays it with, "Was I sexual at age seven?" This lurking question about sexuality is another one that seemed to be present in the minds of many people I talked to. When I asked one of my aerobics instructors whether her daughter had ever "done anything weird" with Barbie, the defensive and panicked haste with which she responded, "Oh, no, she's a very good girl," made me realize that she interpreted my albeit untactful query as necessarily a query about whether her daughter had done anything sexually weird. Dykes don't need Barbie to associate gender with sexuality, but Barbie's sexpot rep certainly helps the cause.

Some credit, too, must belong to Mattel. Barbie would not be so well suited for gender-outlaw rejection if Mattel had not successfully sold her as a model of ideal womanhood and as a proper toy for girls. For some consumers, Mattel's success in this area led to its failure to achieve its other promotional goal of making Barbie a catalyst to fantasize about their own futures: girls who did not like the model threw her out instead. Others, however, found Barbie more adaptable. For Lorio and Pollard, Barbie could be turned into such a fantasy catalyst, although in each case some changes had to be made: Barbie had to be rolled in the dirt or dressed like the hot baby-sitter next door. Thus transformed, she fulfilled *her* dyke destiny. . . .

I have one other reason to distrust the predominance of queer moments, broadly described, in adult Barbie tales: the evidence provided by current children. When I witness contemporary Barbie play by children, I certainly see naked Barbies strewn around, Barbies fucking other Barbies, and Barbies trying to cross-dress. But I also see, in the same children, a huge reverence for Barbie and what she stands for. So, too, do many parents. Three friends recounted to me some version of the following conversation undertaken in a last-ditch effort to talk their children out of Barbie:

> "Why do you want Barbie?"
> "Because she's the most beautiful."
> "Avi's beautiful, and she doesn't look like Barbie; Paula's beautiful, and she doesn't look like Barbie. Aren't they beautiful?"
> "Yes."
> "Then why do you want Barbie?"
> "I want Barbie; she's so beautiful."

Even if the children were not merely assenting that their friends' moms are beautiful for strategic reasons, they certainly seemed to have bought some of Mattel's ideological line, despite, or alongside, heavy counterprogramming.

Now, there's no reason to interpret the phrase "Barbie is so beautiful" as transparent proof that children take what Mattel gives them. For some children, this statement camouflages a sexual fascination that Mattel takes pains not to encourage. I asked one six-year-old girl, for instance, to explain what was beautiful about Barbie. After she named Barbie's hair and clothes, she then pulled down Barbie's dress, touched her breast, saying, "And this," and then quickly pulled the dress back up. She then giggled, looking incredibly embarrassed, and turned away from me, so I didn't pursue the matter; ten minutes later, I noticed her covertly masturbating.[10] Children's statements, like adults', are often opaque. There is no reason to presume that a child who says, "I love Barbie because she is so beautiful," means only "I love her physical appearance" or "I believe that white, skinny, blond women are the best, and I want to trade on my looks to acquire luxury goods when I grow up."

But, while adult and child manifestations of Barbie interpretations may be equally opaque and equally likely to contain queer moments, there seems to be one major difference between them: adults who remember being anti-Barbie or Barbie deviants generally remember or describe themselves as being primarily that; children who manifest negative or deviant stances toward Barbie seem much more often to manifest their actions and criticisms as one set of tendencies embedded in a much more apparently pro-Barbie stance. Hannah certainly did. So, too, did my stepniece Kathryn, whom I interviewed by telephone at her grandparents' house after Grandma (my mother) called to tell me that Kathryn, on arrival, had immediately produced a bunch of Barbies and proceeded to put on a fashion show. Kathryn seemed to go with the Mattel flow in numerous ways. She had a collection with the reigning diversity spectrum: one of her Barbies had red hair, several were black, another "looked like a person from Korea," but most were blond. (She told me that the blond ones looked the same but had different outfits, thus registering a logic of acquisition in accord with Mattel's each-one-is-different marketing strategy, although simultaneously the underlying truth, as it were, is that they are all fundamentally the same.) She described commercial-worthy games in which dolls put on a concert or buy a new house and told me that Barbie was her favorite—in fact, "If you asked all the kids in America that are girls, they'd all probably say Barbie is their favorite. They wouldn't pick other dolls, like baby dolls." She affirmed the child's active role in defining Barbie's personality, which, she said, depended on what the girls who play with her think it is. And, although she described Barbie as having a personality only in order to humor me—"nice and caring . . . if you're asking me"— the one she ventured conforms exactly to the one in Barbie comics. But she also told me that playing with Barbie entailed forgetting about one big negative feature: "Barbie never looks like fat people, that's the bad part. . . . The Barbie company is trying to make Barbie a role model, so if a fat person plays with Barbie, she might feel bad."

This mixture of love and criticism also shows up regularly in the letters column of Barbie comics. Twelve-year-old Jill Monkh combined praise for the "awesome fashions" with a request for a reality check: "I don't intend to be mean, but your comics aren't really based on the real world. . . . In other comics there are rivalries and disagreements." Barbie's response was as evasive as Monkh accused the comics of being: "It's true that the stories . . . do not usually revolve around conflict. We try to show solutions to problems and leave that as our focus. In that way, we hope that our readers will find helpful ways of dealing with problems they may face in their lives."[11] Emely Gonzalez, a "big fan" who wrote, "Can you do something with Barbie talking about prejudice and stereotypes?" registered her recognition that while the comics portray a "multi-ethnic environment," they never address racism. Barbie's answer indirectly admitted as much, although, unlike Emely, Barbie shied away from indelicate terms like *prejudice*: "A very good suggestion, Emely! The issue of how all of us from different races and backgrounds get along is certainly important. We'll pass your suggestion on to our writers, and see what they come up with!"[12] Problems without conflict and diversity without prejudice—exactly the fiction of Barbie comics, which never engage the conflict between Barbie's rightful place on top and the people she must step over to get there.

Preliminary research reveals two conclusions that I'm confident further research would sustain. The first, which backs up the conclusion suggested by adult testimony that virtually everybody seems to have been Barbie's queer accessory in one way or another, is simply that children in general *are* critics and that we condescend to children when we analyze Barbie's content and then presume that it passes untransformed into their minds, where, dwelling beneath the control of consciousness or counterargument, it generates self-image, feelings, and other ideological constructs. I'm not arguing that children either escape the harmful effect of Barbie's dubious messages or function as omniscient critics. Barbie's skinniness still makes Kathryn feel bad, and recognition of this issue does not imply the recognition of other ones; equally important, however, is that she does view critically.

The second, which belies adult testimony that subversion, when it occurred, was the name of the predominant game, is that children's queer and critical moments occur frequently in the context of much straighter, more ordinary, "I love Barbie"—type play. When I look at children with Barbie today, I suspect that my sister must be right to attribute the well-worn condition of our family Barbie doll to me because the contrast between adults and children suggests that this is precisely the kind of forgetting that adults do. We remember deciding that Barbie was bad. We remember queer moments and subversions that made us "different from the other girls." We forget countless other unmemorable, and possibly quietly influential, hours of play.

Conclusion: Hegemonic Barbie, So What?

I have argued elsewhere that Mattel's success at selling Barbie products for over thirty years depends largely on its utilization of hegemonic-discourse content and its increasing mastery of hegemonic-discourse strategies to mask limits, incorporate dominant definitions of freedom, and win the consent of reluctant consumers.[13] Mattel does not actually sell products that abet the wide variety of life choices that it claims to encourage. Nor does it encourage anyone to question whether characteristic features of a just world include the ability of a few to achieve astounding career success or to amass a disproportionate amount of accessories. On capitalism, as on many other topics, Mattel toes the hegemonic-content line so that, when the "anything" that Mattel says we girls can do does not conform to dominant ideologies, Mattel can avoid appearing to have authored it. The line is designed to rope in everyone, progressive to reactionary; the products are designed to avoid challenging the status quo. Mattel's presentation of diversity does not boot blond, white Barbie from center stage. Nor does it address the hard issues—the "rivalries and disagreements" and "prejudice and stereotypes," in the words of Mattel's less euphemistic letter-writing critics—that must be addressed to make societies as just as they are multicolored. Yet, today more than ever, Barbie commentators are invoking Barbie's career freedom and multiethnicity as reasons to love her.

The theory of hegemony, then, helps explain how so many Barbie products have moved from the toy shelves to the cash register and into the hands of millions of children. But what happens then? One might expect that a theoretical model so useful for understanding production and one feature of consumption—purchase—would also offer a model for understanding other features of consumption, such as consumer interpretation of the product. After all, if Mattel's line is hegemonic, shouldn't those consumer interpretations that reject Mattel's line be considered counterhegemonic? Shouldn't those acts and interpretations that seem to follow Mattel's directions—not the directions given in the infinite possibility line but the directions encoded in the actual array of products offered—be considered signs of Mattel's successful promotion of reigning hegemonies?

Only sometimes. The stance of a girl who recognizes Barbie to represent U.S. sanctioned ideal teenage girlhood, despises her for it, and throws her into the fireplace might well be termed *counterhegemonic*. The stance of a girl who loves Barbie, hates her own body, and diets excessively to achieve Barbie's weight might be considered testimony to Mattel's contribution to the maintenance of dominant ideologies. But many acts and artifacts of consumption cannot be so easily classified as one or the other. They cannot be classified at all without studying the consumer and the context of consumption, and they cannot be labeled conforming or resisting on the basis of whether they appear to follow or deviate from Mattel's artistic intention. One person may have put Ken's clothes on Barbie because it "looked funny," implying the underlying dominant presumption that boys should be boys and girls should be girls and that those who aren't should be ridiculed; another might have done so in defiance of precisely the same dominant idea. . . .

This opaqueness of artifacts of consumption—textual, discursive, pictorial, and artifactual—has some important theoretical implications for cultural criticism beyond issues of hegemony and resistance. Central among them is the impossibility of judging how and what cultural products signify by looking at the artifacts apart from the consumers and the (partial) context that they can provide. . . .

There is both a justified thrill and a danger in focusing on deviant or queer Barbie readings. The justified thrill lies in the demarginalization of queer readings and the confirmation that people do not just absorb what is given them. This is crucial to recognize, not just because it authorizes the comforting thought that Barbie can't really steal your sister, but also because so many dubious censorship moves are justified by raising the specter of impressionable children who merely absorb what they see. . . .

There is a danger, then, of overestimating the number of queer moments. More important, however, is a danger of overestimating their significance, and here I return to the subjects of hegemony and resistance. I argued above that hegemony/counterhegemony and conformity/resistance are of limited use partly because so many acts and interpretations cannot be determined to be one or the other or be fixed at some particular point in between. A bigger problem lies in the question of what we would glean from labeling acts of consumption in this way if we could do so. Incidents of anti-Mattel Barbie consumption do not even necessarily signal a consistently or thoroughly resistant stance on the part of those consumers who describe them either toward Barbie or toward what (according to the consumer's perception) she stands for. They reveal less about the adults those children will turn into. Childhood Barbie consumptions do not seem to predict adult cultural or political stances with much accuracy. A childhood Barbie fan once engaged in acquiring as many accessories as possible may now be resolutely and actively anticapitalist. And, if every consumer who cross-dressed Barbie or had queer fantasies about her were now ACT-ing UP, antigay initiatives with a good chance of being passed would not be on ballots all over the United States. . . .

NOTES

1. Erica Rand, *Barbie's Queer Accessories* (Durham: Duke University Press, 1995), chap. 1.

2. Conversation with Joleen, July 1993.

3. Conversation with Lise, 30 July 1993.

4. Carole Nicksin, "Barbie and Tammy: The Real Story!" *Semotext[e]*, (1987): 286 (ellipses in original).

5. Toni Morrison, *The Bluest Eye* (New York: Pocket Books, 1972), 20–22.

6. Nicksin, "Barbie and Tammy," 287.

7. Conversation with Cheryl, spring 1991.

8. Penny Lorio, "Uncloseting Barbie: Get over It, Ken, It's a New Age," *Washington Post*, 2 May 1993, sec. C, p. 5.

9. Conversation with Sue, Auburn, Maine, August 1993.

10. Other adults offer testimony of Barbie's sexual content to children. Vivian Gussin Paley noted that Barbie's sexual taboo status was well known among the girls in her kindergarten class (*Boys and Girls: Superheroes in the Doll Corner* [Chicago: University of Chicago Press, 1984], 11). Carol A. Queen suggests something similar about slightly older children's fascination with Madonna: "Who responds to eroticism more viscerally—and

unconsciously—than a pubescent girl? When I ask my young [ten-year-old] friend and her pals what they like about Madonna, they chorus, 'She's pretty!' " ("Talking about Sex," in *Madonnarama: Essays on Sex and Popular Culture*, ed. Lisa Frank and Paul Smith [Pittsburgh and San Francisco: Cleis, 1993], 148).

11. "Letters to Barbie," *Barbie*, December 1993, 32.

12. "Letters to Barbie," *Barbie*, April 1993, 30.

13. Rand, *Barbie's Queer Accessories*, chap. 1.

Chapter Twenty-two

Confections, Concoctions, and Conceptions

Allison James

This article derives from an incident which took place while I was doing fieldwork in the North East of England, investigating the structure and experience of childhood. An old lady of my acquaintance, remarking on the quality of the paint used by the National Coal Board on properties, grumbled that it was 'all ket—rubbish' and that it would peel off in a few months. Before this I had only encountered the word 'ket' among children who used it as their term for sweets, especially cheaper ones. This difference in use intrigued me, particularly when I remembered that sweets, from the adult perspective, are literally the rubbish which children eat between meals.

Further close attention to conversations revealed that 'ket', or 'kets', was used by adults as a classificatory noun to mean an assortment of useless articles and also as an adjective, 'ketty' meaning rubbishy or useless. Confirmation of this usage comes from Dobson (1974) who defines the word as rubbish. However, Cecil Geeson cites the original meaning as: 'something smelly, stinking, unhealthy or diseased' generally applicable to the 'carcasses of animals dying a natural death and dressed for market without being bled' (1969, p. 116). The Opies (1959) suggested that many old dialect words which have died out in adult language are stored in the child's repertoire but the example of 'kets' casts doubt on an image of passive retention. In this case the semantic content is not stored, but instead undergoes a significant shift. A word which, in the adult world, refers to despised and inedible substances has been transformed; in the world of the child it refers to a revered sweet. In this article I shall explore the seemingly unrelated uses of the term 'kets' in the worlds of adults and children and shall attempt to reveal and explain an inherent and consistent logic in such uses.

To talk about sweets and rubbish inevitably involved discussing the relationship between the worlds of adults and children. I have argued elsewhere (James, 1979) that the social world of children, whilst being separate in relation to the adult world, is nevertheless dependent on it. This dependence is not passive, however. Instead there is a creative process of interdependence: children construct their own ordered system of rules by reinterpreting the social models given to them by adults. [. . .] Hence, the true nature of the culture of childhood frequently remains hidden from adults, for the semantic cues which permit social recognition have been manipulated and disguised by children in terms of their alternative society.

By confusing the adult order children create for themselves considerable room for movement within the limits imposed upon them by adult society. This deflection of adult perception is crucial for both the maintenance and continuation of the child's culture and for the growth of the concept of the self for the individual child. The process of becoming social involves a conceptual separation between 'self' and 'other'. This process is often described in terms of 'socialization', a model which stresses the passive mimicry of others. I would suggest, however, that this process is better seen in terms of an active experience of contradiction, often with the adult world. It is thus of great significance that something which is despised and regarded as diseased and inedible by the adult world should be given great prestige as a particularly desirable form of food by the child. The transformation of 'kets' from rubbish into food is both logical and consistent with the child's culture.

The notion that food might be a subject worthy of discussion in its own right has long been ignored by social anthropologists. Past ethnographers have either made only fleeting references to what people eat or have submerged the topic under more general headings such as agricultural production, economics and ritual.

However, with the publication of *Le Totemisme Aujourd'hui* (1962) and Lévi-Strauss's provocative suggestion that animals are 'good to think with', the subject of food in relation to the social body has become increasingly central in the discipline (see Leach, 1964; Douglas, 1966; Bulmer, 1967; and Tambiah, 1969). In all these analyses it is argued that ideas people hold concerning the edibility of certain types of food are linked logically to other conceptual domains and that, by examining a people's food categories, a more penetrating and incisive explanation of other aspects of the social system can be achieved. Tambiah argues that 'cultures and social systems are, after all, not only thought but also lived' so that particular attention should be given to exactly what people let inside their bodies (1969, p. 165).

More recently Mary Douglas (1975) has directly confronted the subject of food in her analysis of the major food categories in Britain. She identifies the two main categories as meals and drinks. Of the two, meals are more highly ranked and ordered, being internally structured into 'first, second, main [and] sweet' courses, whereas drinks possess no such structuring (1975, p. 255). Meals are also externally structured by a temporal order—breakfast followed by dinner and tea—which parallels the weekly cycle, climaxing in Sunday dinner, a pattern repeated in the annual sequence of ceremonial meals. Drinks, in contrast, are 'not invested with any necessity in their ordering' (ibid., p. 255).

Douglas further suggests that, besides these major categories of food, some 'food can be taken for private nourishment' but it is likely to be condemned if considered 'to interfere with the next meal' (ibid., p. 254). It is here that she locates sweets, but hers is an adult perspective. Sweets, for adults, are regarded as an adjunct to 'real' food and should not usurp the place of meals. For the child, as I hope to show, the reverse is true: it is *meals* which disrupt the eating of sweets.

Sweets—as in 'Ye Olde Sweete Shoppe'—are an entirely British phenomenon. There is no equivalent abroad and the British sweet industry, in its production of a very extensive range of confectionery, seems to be unique. The concept of the sweetmeat is the nearest parallel to the kinds of confections available in other countries, but it is absent from the supermarket shelves and non-specialist sweet shops in this country.

The European sweetmeat dates back to the seventeenth century with the discovery of sugar. During this period sweetmeats were an integral part of the rich man's menu, forming part of the meal, as is often the case in other countries. Today, in Britain, the sweetmeat is best visualized as a home-made confection to be found on Women's Institute stalls or delicately displayed in tiny baking cases in a traditional confectioner's shop. Mass production techniques have replaced the sweetmeat with similar, but not identical, pre-packed products. However, although the sweetmeat has largely disappeared and the traditional sweet shop must now complete with cinemas, newsagents and slot-machines, the sweetmeat's successor strikingly resembles its forerunner in many aspects. In this sense the sweet, for adults, may be closer to the major food categories than Douglas (1975) supposes. 'Kets', the child's sweets, are an entirely different matter.

Kets and Sweets

'Kets' and sweets must not be confused. Although the distinction may seem to be purely linguistic, other more substantive issues indicate that 'kets' are a very distinctive kind of confectionery, belonging exclusively to the world of children.

The analysis presented below is based on observations made whilst working in a youth club in a small North Eastern village. The children referred to range in age from 11 to 17 but age group distinctions are relatively fluid due to the tight-knit nature of the community. A main focus of activity, for children of all ages in the youth club, is the buying and selling of sweets, primarily of the 'ketty' variety, although older children tend more towards other kinds of sweets. However, children almost always use the word 'kets', whilst adults prefer the word 'sweets'; occasionally, adults may jokingly refer to 'kets', especially if they are confections bought for children, but would never use this word for sweets they themselves are going to consume.

It would seem, therefore, that the term 'kets' usually is used for those sweets at the lower end of the price range and it is these sweets which children most often buy. It could be argued therefore that the distinction between 'kets' and other kinds of confectionery rests solely on economic factors. However, before assuming that children buy 'kets' because they are cheap and that children, in general, have less money to spend than adults, certain problems should be considered. Why don't adults buy 'kets'? For 10p, the price of a chocolate bar, they could buy ten pieces of bubble gum. Furthermore, although it is certainly true that children tend to buy the cheaper sweets, it is apparent from field data that the total amount of money spent by a child on sweets *at any one time* may be quite considerable. A typical purchase might be: four 'Fizz Bombs' at 1p each; three 'Liquorice Novelties' at 2p each and two 'Bubble gums' at 1p each. The total outlay, 12p, could buy two small chocolate bars, which are also available at the club. This may be an example of getting more for one's money, but another factor should be taken into account. The spending power of children is obviously an important consideration for manufacturers, but if this were the sole criterion influencing production, why would manufacturers not produce miniature versions of the kinds of confections available in the higher price range? Some years ago it was possible to purchase slim bars of Cadbury's chocolate for one old penny and a slightly larger version for twopence. The equivalent products today are tiny 'Milky Ways' and 'Mars Bars' sold in bags as 'Family Packs'. Why do manufacturers not sell them singly? The answer seems to be that there is no demand for them.

Children, then, do not buy 'kets' simply because they are cheaper or have a lower unit price. 'Kets' have other properties, besides their cheapness, which make them important for the child. Manufacturers may not be exploiting the power of the child's purse directly, but more insidiously, the power inherent in the conceptual gulf between the worlds of the adult and the child.

Junk Food

In order to resolve such problematic issues concerning the attractions of 'kets' I carried out a statistical survey, dividing the range of confectionery into three groups. The term 'kets' was given to all those sweets costing less than 5p. An intermediate group was established for sweets costing between 6p and 10p and a third group contained all sweets costing 11p or more, including the more expensive boxes of chocolates. By isolating 'kets' as a distinct group according to price it was possible to examine further more elusive contrasts between 'kets' and other sweets, an investigation which suggested that the alternative adult meaning of the word 'kets'—rubbish—was indeed a powerful and persuasive metaphor. Much of the attraction of 'kets' seems to lie precisely in the way they stand in contrast to conventional adult sweets and adult eating patterns generally. This is apparent in their names, their colours, the sensations they induce, their presentation and the descriptions of their contents, as well as in the timing and manner of their consumption.

If adults regard 'kets' as rubbish, low in nutritive value and essentially 'junk food', then it is quite logical that manufacturers should label their products in an appropriate manner. 'Kets' are often given names which emphasize their inedibility and rubbishy content in adult terms. Many have names usually reserved for mechanical and utilitarian objects which adults would never dream of eating. Children, however, will gleefully consume them. There are, for example, Syco Discs, Fizzy Bullets, Supersonic Flyers, Robots, Traffic Lights, Coconut Bongos,

Diddy Bags, Telephones, Catherine Wheels, Golf Balls, Pipes, Jelly Wellies, Star Ships and Car Parks. Other kinds of sweets rarely have such names.

Not only do children consume what is inedible, they also ingest many 'animals' whose consumption normally is abhorred by adults and which are surrounded by dietary taboos. Cannibalism, too, ranks highly. Thus children find themselves eating Mr. Marble, Mickey Mouse, Yogi Bear, Mighty Monkey, Snakes, Kangaroos, Spooks, Jelly Footballers, Dinosaurs, Lucky Black Cats, Dormice, Bright Babies, Jelly Gorillas and Fun Faces.

This rubbishy attribute of 'kets' is highlighted when the above names are compared to the names given to other more expensive kinds of sweets. These often describe the actual composition of the confectionery and frequently yield precise and detailed information for the consumer. Adults, it seems, like to know what they are eating. In this range there are names such as Munchie Mints, Butterscotch, Assorted Nut Toffee, Nut Brittle, Coconut Whirls, Rum and Butter Toffee, Caramel, Peppermint Lumps, Toffimallow, Royal Butter Mints, Liquorice Bon Bons and Chocolate Coconut Ice.

Although a few 'kets' possess descriptive names the unfamiliar eater should beware of assuming that the description refers to the taste. The names 'Seafood', 'Shrimps' and 'Jelly Eels' may lead to the expectation of a savoury sweet; they are, however, sweet and sickly. 'Rhubarb and Custard' and 'Fruit Salad' are hard, chewy 'kets' presenting a marked contrast to the sloppy puddings implied by the names. Such inversions and contradictions of the accepted adult order are an essential facet of the child's world so that 'Silly Toffee Banana' and 'Orozo Hard Juice' could only be 'kets'.[1]

'Kets' are mostly brightly coloured, as in the luminous blues and fluorescent oranges of the 'Fizz Bomb' and the vivid yellows and reds of many jellied 'kets'. Some have contrasting stripes, with clashing colours as in the 'Liquorice Novelty'. Here, black strips of liquorice are festooned with shocking greens, reds and blues. All these harsh, saturated colours are absent from the 'real' food of the adult world. Blue, especially, is banned; bright blue belongs to the realm of iced cakes and such concoctions are a highly ceremonial form of food, divorced from the everyday menu.[2] Many sweets, also aimed at the child's market but not classed here as 'kets', are similarly coloured: for example, 'Smarties', 'Jelly Tots', 'Jelly Babies' and 'Liquorice Allsorts'. Such bright and stimulating colours are not normally associated with the dinner plate.

In contrast, the sweets which are aimed primarily at an adult market have a more uniform and duller appearance. Most are coated in chocolate, presenting exteriors of shades of brown, significantly known today as 'natural'—i.e. healthy—colours. In the more expensive boxes of chocolate the highly saturated colours of the 'kets' are present, but they are masked by a coating of chocolate and hidden from sight. Where chocolate is not used, the colours of these sweets tend towards pastel shades, soft, delicate colours inoffensive to the eye, as in 'Sugared Almonds' or 'Mints'. The 'Humbug', with its sedate black and white stripes, is a poor relation of the 'Gob Stopper' and lacks its coat of many colours. For sweets to be suitable for adult consumption, highly saturated colours must be avoided, for such colours are not present in 'real' food, and adults, unlike children, are conservative about what they class as edible.

The eating of this metaphoric rubbish by children is a serious business and adults should be wary of tackling 'kets' for, unlike other sweets, 'kets' are a unique digestive experience. Many of the names given to 'kets' hint at this: 'Fizzy Bullets', 'Fizz Bombs', 'Fizz Balls', 'Festoon Fizzle Sticks', 'Fizzy Lizzies' and 'Fruit Fizzles' all stress the tingling sensation to be gained from eating them. Many 'kets' contain sherbert and 'Sherbits', 'Refreshers', 'Sherbo Dabs', 'Dip Dabs', 'Sherbert Fountains', 'Double Dip Sherbert' and even 'Love Hearts' all make the mouth smart while eating them.

In contrast other sweets provide little in the way of exciting consumption. The nearest rival among these sweets to the explosive taste of many 'kets' is the 'Extra Strong Mint'—a poor rival to the 'Knock Out Lolly'. The stress on citrus fruit flavours and the tangy, often acrid, taste of many 'kets' contrasts radically with the preponderance of sugary or nutty flavours in adult confections. The ferocious taste of a 'Fizz Bomb' is quite distinctive and lingers in the mouth for a long time, temporarily putting the other taste buds out of action.

Chocolate, which is a favoured ingredient in sweets aimed at the adult consumer, is rare among 'kets' but may appear as chocolate flavour. There is a range of 'kets' styled in the shapes of hammers, saws and chisels which, although appearing to be chocolate, are in fact made from a substitute. Similarly, 'Cheroots' look like long sticks of chocolate, but have a gritty texture and are dry and tasteless. They lack the rich, creamy taste and smooth texture so beloved by the advertisers of real chocolate.

This marked difference in taste and texture between 'kets' and other sweets lies naturally in the ingredients used in their manufacture. 'Kets' are frequently unwrapped so that a list of ingredients is difficult to obtain but common substances include: sugar, glucose, edible gum, edible vegetable oil, citric acid and assorted flavourings. Other sweets, in contrast, proudly list their ingredients, frequently stressing their 'natural goodness'. For example a message on the wrapper of a 'Picnic' chocolate bar states in large letters that the bar contains: 'Milk chocolate with peanuts, wafer, toffee and raisin centre'. In much smaller print it admits that the chocolate contains vegetable fat—thus lessening its nutritive properties and desirability—but stresses that there is a minimum of 20 per cent milk solids which must not be overlooked.

It would seem, therefore, that sweets, as opposed to 'kets', are to be valued as a form of food. The 'Picnic', as its name suggests, is to be regarded as a source of nourishment. These kinds of sweets are, like the sweetmeat, closely associated with our major food categories and many can be concocted at home from common household ingredients. Cookery books include recipes for sweets such as truffles, peppermint creams, coconut ice and toffee. 'Kets', on the other hand, are impossible to reproduce in the kitchen.

Thus sweets belong to the realm of 'real' food, to the private world of the kitchen, and are bound to the concept of the meal. They have names indicative of their wholesomeness; their flavours echo the patterns of taste normally associated with the dessert—the sweet course—of the meal. Mary Douglas suggests that it is 'the capacity to recall the whole by the structure of the parts' which has insured the survival of the British biscuit in our diet and similarly it is this mimetic quality of the sweet which has kept it bound to the realm of 'real' food (1975, p. 747). 'Kets', in contrast, are, by their very nature, removed from the adult domestic sphere and belong to the public, social world of children. In name, taste and consumptive experience, 'kets' belong to the disorderly and inverted world of children, for in this alternative world a new order exists which makes the 'ket' an eminently desirable product.

Lévi-Strauss (1975) suggests that the differing culinary modes to be found in a particular culture may reflect its conceptual categories and it is in this light that the adult meaning of the word 'kets' becomes highly significant. If sweets belong to the adult world, the human cultural world of cooked foods as opposed to the natural, raw food of the animal kingdom, then 'kets' belong in a third category. Neither raw nor cooked, according to the adult perspective, 'kets' are a kind of rotten food. These rubbishy, decaying and diseased sweets are the peculiar property of children who are, from the adult perspective, a tainted group. Children are, from the adult point of view, pre-social, in need of training and correction through the process of socialization and thus it is quite consistent that it should be 'kets' which children regard as their most social form of food. Mary Douglas has argued that 'consuming is finding consistent meanings' and that goods are purchased and needed 'for making visible and stable the categories of culture' (1977, pp. 292–3). In this sense the literal consumption of different kinds of confectionery by adults and children reflects the inherent contradiction between their separate worlds.

Metaphoric Meals

Mary Douglas (1975) argues that the eating of meals involves a whole series of rituals concerning both the presentation and consumption of food. Food is served on different kinds of plates according to the kind of meal. It is eaten with cutlery of assorted shapes and sizes, which transfers food from plate to mouth. The use of the fingers for this act is frowned upon by adults and rarely should food enter the mouth by hand. Chicken legs become embarrassing to eat in the company of others and the eating of lobsters entails a battery of dissecting instruments. Finger bowls and serviettes are provided for the eaters of such foods to remove any particles adhering to the hands or lips. As Goffman suggests, 'greasy foods that are not considered to contaminate the mouth can yet be felt to contaminate the hands should contact have to be made without insulation by utensils' (1971, p. 73). The more ceremonial the meal the more crockery and cutlery necessary to facilitate the eating of it.

Those sweets which are to be regarded as belonging to the realm of 'real' food must be similarly distanced from the body, unlike the non-food 'kets'. 'Kets' are usually unwrapped, whereas other sweets tend to be heavily packaged, for the layers of paper provide the necessary separation between the inner and outer body. The phrase 'a hand to mouth existence'—a poor and despised condition—emphasises the necessity for maintaining this purity. As with the eating of meals, the more packaging provided, the more ceremonial the sweet and the further it is removed from the 'ketty' sphere. The ultimate example is the box of chocolates, which is shrouded in paper. Like the eating of meals, these sweets must be insulated against contamination from external sources.

The 'After Eight Mint' is superlative in this respect. The clock face printed on the box is repeated on each tiny envelope which encases the sweet and it registered the time at which this confection should ideally be consumed. Its other name—the 'After Dinner Mint'—secures the place of this chocolate as a highly ordered kind of confection inextricably bound to the concept of the meal. Douglas (1975) suggests that meals are externally ordered by time and that it is the temporal sequence of meals which is used to divide up the day. The 'After Eight Mint' confirms the suspicion that the eating of sweets by adults should be similarly structured.

After the meal has been eaten, the sweets may be passed round. Their tray shaped box and insulating containers recall the crockery and cutlery of the meal and the hand is allowed minimum contact with the sweet. The most criminal of acts, frequently indulged in by children, is to finger the sweets for, as with the meal, food must scarcely be handled. To nibble a sweet and then to replace it in the box, again common practice among children, is never allowed amongst adults for that which has been in the mouth must ideally remain there.

Just as ceremonial meals have a yearly temporal cycle, so do the purchase and consumption of sweets. Boxes of chocolates are bought at Christmas, birthdays and other ritual occasions, as is apparent from television advertising: in the week before Christmas many of the usual sweet adverts are replaced by ones for the more luxurious boxes of chocolates.

One major ceremonial sweet, heavily packed and adorned, is not, however, aimed at adults directly. This is the Easter Egg, given by adults to children. The Easter Egg bears all the characteristics of an acceptable adult sweet and encapsulates the whole ethos of the adult's conception of food. Firstly, it marks a ritual season. The silver-paper covered egg sits resplendent in a highly decorated cardboard box, frequently adorned with ribbon. Under the outer layers the chocolate egg can be found, already separated into two, to avoid much contact with the hand. It is easily pulled apart to reveal a packet of highly-coloured sweets, such as 'Smarties' or 'Jelly Tots', which although ostensibly similar to 'kets' are in fact much less 'ketty'. It is significant that Easter Eggs are never stuffed with 1 p 'Bubble Gums'. The Easter Egg is strictly ordered in both its construction and its consumption and is ultimately representative of the adult's rather than the child's conception of acceptable food.[3]

'Kets', however, are never subject to such constraints. Most 'kets' can be found piled high in a cardboard box on the shop counter, with no respect for variety or flavour, into which children's hands delve and rummage. Few 'kets' are individually wrapped and, if they are, the packaging is minimal. Children do not heed the purity rules of adults. They frequently share their sweets, offering each other bites or sucks of a 'ket'. The absence of wrappers leaves the fingers sticky; dirty hands break off pieces to offer to friends. 'Kets' are fished out of pockets along with other articles and 'Bubble Gum' is stuck to the underside of tables to be reserved for later use.

'Kets' are not distanced from the body. Indeed, many are specifically designed to conflict with the adult's abhorrence of food entering the mouth by hand: 'Gob Stoppers' are removed from the mouth for comparison of colour changes and strings of chewing gum continually pulled out of the mouth. Hands become covered in 'kets' and the normal eating conventions, instilled by parents during early childhood, are flagrantly disregarded.

Indeed some 'kets' seem not to be designed for eating at all: 'Gob Stoppers' fill the mouth totally, not allowing any of the normal digestive processes to begin. 'Chews' produce an aching jaw—reminiscent of eating tough meat—and 'Fizz Bombs' simply have to be endured. 'Bubble Gum' is chewed vigorously but is never swallowed; instead it is expelled from the mouth in a bubble and held at the point of entry until it bursts, spattering the face with particles of sticky gum to be picked off piecemeal later. 'Lollipops' are pulled in and out of the mouth and 'Jelly Footballers' first decapitated. 'Space Dust', perhaps the ultimate 'ket', has no rival. The powder is placed on the tongue where it begins to explode while the mouth remains open and the ears and throat buzz and smart.

The frequent examination of each other's tongues during the process of eating 'kets', together with the other eating techniques required to consume them, manifest a rejection of the mannered and ordered conventions of adult society. The joy with which a dirty finger probes the mouth to extract a wine gum contrasts strongly with the need for a tooth pick to perform a comparable operation at table.

'Kets', therefore, are the antithesis of the adult conception of 'real' food while, for adults, sweets are metonymic meals.[4] 'Kets' involve a rejection of the series of rituals and symbols surrounding the concept of the meal and are regarded as rubbish by adults. Because they are despised by the adult world, they are prized by the child's and become the metaphoric meals of childhood. Although children will consume sweets of any kind, it is 'kets' which the child will most often buy. Adults never buy them. The child's private funds, which are not controlled by adults, are appropriately spent on those sweets symbolic of his world. 'Kets' deemed by the adult world to be rubbish, are under the child's control. [. . .]

The importance of these metaphoric meals for children cannot be overstated. 'Ket' times are in-between meal times and the eating of 'kets' begins almost as soon as the adult meal is over, lasting until the structure of adult society again disrupts their consumption. In our society such continual eating of sweets by adults would be classed as a medical disorder requiring a cure.

Not surprisingly, given the coherent and persistent structure of the child's culture, children have an immense knowledge of the varieties of 'kets' available and are always careful to distinguish between them. 'Chewing Gum' is 'chut' or 'chewy' as opposed to 'Bubble Gum' which is 'bubbly'. A lollipop is rarely simply called a 'lolly', but instead a 'Kojak' or a 'Traffic Light'. Planning one's meal is a serious business.

Conclusion

'Kets', therefore, are the child's food, the food over which he has maximum control. By eating 'kets' rather than other sweets children force confrontations with the adult order, for 'kets' have been despised by adults. The esteem which is attached to 'kets' is emphasised by the ridicule and disgust expressed by the child towards adult food, which is food over which children have little control.

Children are highly articulate in their views on food and school lunches come in for high contempt. The authoritarian structure of the school frequently denies any self-expression by the child so it is significant that it is school dinners which are most abused. Mashed potatoes are known as 'Mashy Arty' or 'shit' when too salty. Mushy peas are likened to 'snot' and school rice pudding looks as if someone has 'hockled' (spat) into it. Semolina is like 'frogspawn'. Thus the foods which children are forced to put inside their bodies by adults are given the status of the excretions which pass out. The most graphic statement of all goes as follows:

> Yellow belly custard, green snot pie,
> Mix them up with a dead dog's eye.
> Mix it thin, mix it thick,
> Swallow it down with a hot cup of sick.

As Charlotte Hardman comments, children perceive the adults' 'weaknesses and responsibilities in connection with food and drink' and much time is spent in reducing 'adult order to humorous disorder' (1974, p. 6). Food is used as weapons by children, but more vehement than the physical attacks with food are the verbal onslaughts directed by children against adults and their control of food:

> Old Mrs. Riley had a fat cow,
> She milked it, she milked it
> She didn't know how.
> She pulled its tail instead of its tit
> Poor Mrs. Riley covered in shit.

The implied sympathy contained in the last line of this rhyme is not genuine, for gales of laughter always accompany the relating of this event.

Finally, if food is equated with harmfulness by the child, it is logical that non-food should be esteemed. 'Kets' are regarded by children as being particularly beneficial but other substances are also considered to be worth investigating. Children frequently dare each other to eat the literally inedible. Sawdust, plant leaves and other natural substances are often consumed, but a particular favorite is the game called 'Fag-Chewing'. A cigarette is passed round with each child taking a draw until all the tobacco is gone. The unfortunate person left with the filter is then made to eat it or, at the very least, to chew it. Such activity is reminiscent of Jimmy Boyle's (1977) memories of a Glasgow childhood, where one child was ostracised until the others discovered that he could eat worms.

This ability to consume metaphoric rubbish is an integral part of the child's culture. Children, by the very nature of their position as a group outside adult society, have sought out an alternative system of meanings through which they can establish their own integrity. Adult order is manipulated so that what adults esteem is made to appear ridiculous; what adults despise is invested with prestige. [. . .]

For children 'kets' are an important vehicle for defining the self. As I have suggested elsewhere (James, 1979) regarding names, adult labels for children are destroyed and a new name—a nickname—is created by children out of the remnants. Similarly the adult, ordered conception of food is thrown into disarray by the child. Adults continually urge their offspring to eat up their food and lament that they are 'fussy eaters', but children are only pernickety in adult terms. Indeed children stuff into their mouths a wide variety of substances; it is just that these are abhorred by adults.

The eating of 'kets' thus represents a metaphoric chewing up of adult order. Food belongs to the adult world and is symbolic of the adult's control over children. By disordering and confusing the conceptual categories of the adult world children erect a new boundary over which adults have no authority. Mary Douglas (1966) has argued that a corollary of the image of dirt as disordering and anomalous is that it can be associated with power. The eating of dirty, decaying 'kets' is condemned by adults and it is this very condemnation which allows the child to assume control over at least one of his orifices. By eating that which is ambiguous in adult terms the child establishes an alternative system of meanings which adults cannot perceive. It is this which allows the culture of childhood to flourish largely unnoticed by adults and, at the same time, to exist largely beyond their control.

NOTES

1. The eating of such disordered food is consistent with the child's culture, but adults abhor such anomalies. On sweet wrappers and other foodstuffs there is a guarantee issued which states that: 'This product should reach you in perfect condition. If it does not, please return it' ('Twix' wrapper). 'Kets', on the other hand, offer no such guarantee.

2. It is important to note that bright, artificial colours do appear in 'real' food but such foods are also classed as 'junk'. Many instant products—e.g. Angel Delight and cake mixes—have extremely bright colours. Bright colours appear often in food at children's parties—e.g. jellies, blancmange and cakes. Such food, like 'kets', is also regarded as being detrimental and essentially rubbishy.

3. There is a smaller, less ceremonial Easter Egg on the market which seems to be aimed at the child market. It has some 'ketty' qualities, for the cream filled egg, although

appearing to contain albumen and yolk, is extremely sweet to eat, and far removed from the taste associated with fried eggs, which it closely resembles.

4. Adverts for sweets for adults fully substantiate this idea and the eating of sweets for adults is portrayed as (1) helping to achieve a desired end—e.g. a 'Flake' gives a girl the world of motor boats and a 'Bounty' provides 'the taste of paradise'; (2) substitute food—e.g. 'A Mars a Day helps you work rest and play'; or (3) an additional, nourishing extra which will not affect normal food intake—e.g. 'A Milky Way is the sweet you can eat between meals without ruining your appetite.' 'Kets' are rarely advertised but one advert for a 'Fizz Bomb' shows cartoon children, with their eyeballs whizzing round in opposite directions. Far from stressing the utilitarian aspects of eating sweets—whether as a source of physical or mental strength—'kets' are to be recommended as an unforgettable gastronomic experience.

REFERENCES

Boyle, J. (1977) *A Sense of Freedom*, Pan, London.

Bulmer, R. (1967) 'Why the Cassowary is Not a Bird', *Man*, n.s., 2 (1), 5–25.

Dobson, S. (1974) *A Geordie Dictionary*, Frank Graham, Newcastle.

Douglas, M. (1966) *Purity and Danger*, Routledge and Kegan Paul, London.

—— (1975) *Implicit Meanings*, Routledge and Kegan Paul, London.

—— (1977) 'Beans' Means 'Thinks', *The Listener*, 8 September, pp. 292–3.

Douglas M., and Nicod, M. (1974) 'Taking the Biscuit', *New Society*, 19 December, pp. 744–7.

Geeson, C. (1969) *A Northumberland and Durham Word Book*, Harold Hill and Sons, Newcastle.

Goffman, E. (1971) *Relations in Public*, Penguin, London.

Hardman, C. (1974) 'Fact and Fantasy in the Playground', *New Society*, 19 September.

James A. (1979) 'When is a Child Not a Child? Nicknames: a Test Case for a Mode of Thought' in A. James and M. Young, Durham University Working Papers in Social Anthropology, No. 3.

Leach, E. (1964) 'Anthropological Aspects of Language: Animal Categories and Verbal Abuse' in E. Lenneberg (ed.), *New Directions in the Study of Language*, MIT Press, Cambridge, Mass.

Lévi-Strauss, C. (1962) *Totemism* (trans. R. Needham 1963), Penguin, London.

—— (1975) *The Raw and the Cooked*, Harper and Row, New York.

Opie, I, and P. (1959) *The Lore and Language of School Children*, Oxford.

Tambiah, S. J. (1969) 'Animals are Good to Think and Good to Prohibit', *Ethnology, 8* (4), 424–59.

Chapter Twenty-three

Living in a World of Words

Shelby Anne Wolf and Shirley Brice Heath

Each morning of her preschool years, my daughter Lindsey and I went through our daily routine of preparing her for the day. We negotiated her outfit, for Lindsey is prone to more outlandish combinations than I, and then brushed her teeth and combed her hair. For the latter, she usually sat perched on the bathroom sink, contemplating her image in the wide mirror as I carefully guided the brush through her hair, smoothing the tangles of a night's sleep.

One morning she requested a pony tail. I swept her hair into a long strand, and then wound it in the grasp of one hand while I searched for an elastic band with the other.

> "Good mother!" she exclaimed. "You're not going to cut it, are you?"
>
> Astonished, I replied, "Of course not. Whatever made you think of that?"
>
> "The witch cut Rapunzel's hair! And when I was a little girl, I had long hair and my mother cut it all off!"
>
> I laughed and said, "No, honey. That was me. When I was little, my mother cut *my* hair."
>
> Lindsey scowled. "No, it was me! *My* mother cut off *my* hair!" (May 28, 1986, 3;6)

Lindsey's story was a personal extension of *Rapunzel*, a book that we had read in recent weeks. My actions, the feel of my hand tightening on her hair, the other hand reaching out, had triggered her entrance into the world of story. She had called me "Good mother," a direct quote from Michael Hague's illustrated edition of the famous Grimm brothers' tale. And the story tells us that the witch *"in her wrath . . . seized Rapunzel's beautiful hair, wound it round and round her left hand, and then grasping a pair of scissors in her right, snip snap, off it came, and the beautiful braids lay on the ground"* (Grimm Brothers / Hague).

Lindsey had also incorporated a tale that I had told her from my own childhood, for as a child I had extremely long hair which I wore in a braid down my back. My mother had ultimately tired of the lengthy routine of braiding such a mass and had cut it when I entered the third grade. These two tales had become internally persuasive to Lindsey, and she had reauthored the Grimm tale by weaving in a narrative of my life and her own. She wove tales from storybooks as well as from her family's history into embellishments of her daily life. Yet her initial interpretations depended less on speech than on actions.[1]

During her first year or so of frequent story-reading times, Lindsey acted on or out of a story more often than she talked about it. One afternoon Lindsey's father, Kenny, told Lindsey that she could read quietly in her room during nap time. He had tucked her in bed with Charlotte Zolotow's *But Not Billy*, the story of a baby boy who is called by every affectionate appellation but his own name. When Kenny passed her room a few minutes later, Lindsey was out of bed and rocking back and forth on her knees in the middle of her bedroom floor.

> "Lindsey," Kenny scolded, "I told you that you could read, not play."
>
> "I am reading!" Lindsey replied indignantly.
>
> She jumped back into her bed and held up the page in the story where Billy is being compared to a rocking horse.
>
> "See!" she exclaimed. "I was being a rocking horse, just like Billy." (May 17, 1986, 3; 6)

To Lindsey, reading was action and each part must be played. The words of story were meant not to lie on the page but to leap off and rock back and forth in life.[2]

Through both talk and action, and later with the addition of her own stage directions to enlist family and friends into sociodramatic play, she created occasions in which she brought literature's scenes, beliefs, and rules for behaving into daily negotiations of time, space, and privilege. She enlisted the characters of storybooks as companions, and sometimes incorporated them into her own character, moving from one imaginary world to another. Lindsey swept the fireplace as Cinderella, lay as Sleeping Beauty to await her handsome prince, dropped off the bed into a pool of tears as Alice in Wonderland, and chased about the house as Max in mischievous pursuit of his dog. In a literate household, living through the stories of sanctioned book characters effectively muffled and evaded direct conflicts between child independence and parental authority.

Lindsey's interpretations were not limited to the larger associations between storybooks and dramatic play complete with props and costumes. There were a thousand smaller, but no less significant, connections made between life and text and back again. These connections often hinged on a sight, a sound, or a movement that sparked the connection between the world of words and the world of the child. The movement of a rocking chair caused a recollection of a baby's lullaby. A word used in conversation by either parent would spark a reminder of a similar word in a text.

One spring day in California, Lindsey went bike riding with her father. It had rained in the afternoon and the wheels of their bicycles splashed a fan of sparkling water up behind them. They toured a bit of our neighborhood before crossing a small forested section of the village to the athletic fields. As they emerged from the trees, a tremendous rainbow greeted them. It hung suspended from the sky, stretching wide, embracing the earth with color.

Lindsey stopped her bike and stared in shocked silence. Since she had lived most of her life in the desert of Saudi Arabia, Lindsey had seen such magnificence only in illustrated text.

> Then she fell to the ground laughing gaily. "Rainbows aren't real! They *aren't* real! They're only in books!"
>
> As she laughed and rolled in the wet grass, soaking up the vision in the sky, her perception changed. Staring up at the rainbow, she cited Kenny a new litany of literary insights. "Giants aren't real. Dragons aren't real. But rainbows *are* real!" (April 24, 1987, 4;5)

What Lindsey saw in the rainbow recalled the words of literary texts to stretch her realizations of categories of meaning in fact and fantasy. Although this connection was more verbally articulated than enacted, the elements of character, plot, and theme came alive in ways similar to the rainbow's evocation of other literary objects possible in the real world: a face summons a character, an action brings plot to mind, a problem evokes a theme, and a new revelation calls for a reshaping of rules.

Literature gave Lindsey the equipment and the process to become an experimenter with her own world. The poet Horace said that literature's purpose was to instruct and delight. Literature, however, does not instruct directly; it provides readers the materials with which to experiment and to test what comes from various settings, characters, and situations. Literature sets up possible worlds to reshuffle for transit and testing in the actual worlds of children. But literature also stands ready to manipulate, and to be manipulated by, the rules within its own texts.[3]

Lindsey often had suggestions for the text that aligned with her personal sense of real-world rules. In the story of *Rapunzel* (Grimm Brothers/Rogasky), the blinded prince wanders in the forest for a year. The illustrator showed the passage of time by turning the prince's clothes into rags and giving him a beard. This transformation did not match Lindsey's vision of the perfect prince.

> "He gots a beard." Lindsey said this last word with distaste.
>
> "I know." Flipping back to the previous page, I said, "He didn't have a beard before, huh? No. Well, he wasn't able to shave himself."
>
> I continued reading, and as the story reached its climax, with Rapunzel weeping into her beloved's eyes, Lindsey stopped me.
>
> "Mama," she said, flipping back to the page before, "I wanna see something. Why does he not have a beard here and he does have a beard there?"
>
> "Because he's wandered in the forest for a long, long time. Even though all we've done is turned the page, *he's* wandered for a long time trying to find Rapunzel. And you know how daddy's beard grows a little bit every day?"
>
> "Uh huh," she replied.
>
> "Well, if he didn't shave it, it would grow to be very long," I explained. "And perhaps the prince wandering in the forest didn't have a razor to cut his beard."
>
> Though I couldn't imagine what the prince would do without his Gillette, Lindsey had an answer. "Well, he could have used a sharp thorn to raze it." (June 24, 1986, 3;7)

Just as a sharp thorn can blind a prince, it can also be used to keep up his appearance. And just as Lindsey adapted an object to the situation, she also turned her familiarity with her father's razor into the verb "raze."

Regardless of the original shape of the children's literature being read—poem, sketch, fairy tale, science fantasy, or catalogue of objects and places—children's memories reshape these into problem-solving narratives. In these, children attribute to animate beings some set of goals, and they place those attempting to achieve these goals in particular types of associations with collections of objects existing over a period of time within spatial limits. Children remember objects most often in their functional roles and especially when they belong to an animate being who has certain goals and intentions for their use. Children can interpret literature because they can locate its stories in their own belief system, which sees the world as inhabited by animate beings who make plans and act on them. In other words, the animate beings within literature also believe that their world contains creatures capable of thinking ahead, building future scenarios, and bringing about subsequent action.[4]

In the most memorable of children's literature, the intentions, goals, and motivations of these agents remain unstated, subject to change, and responsible for surprise endings or outcomes. The fundamental interpretive act of children is to create hopes, fears, and expectations for literature's characters. In fiction and poetry, the author needs to provide only two explicit ingredients—animate actors and arenas for action. Certain literary conventions of genre help move the actors into problem-solving modes, but the fulfillment of these conventions is possible only because children bring to their interpretation the expectation that individuals have intentions, emotions, and motivations.

One night I was listening to a cassette of *King Lear* and following the oral text with the written text from my Shakespeare class. Lindsey wandered in, listened briefly, and asked, "What's the story about?" I gave her a brief accounting of what I'd heard thus far: King Lear had three daughters, two who claimed undying love and a third (the youngest) who claimed a love that matched her duty, no more and no less. Lear, in astonished rage, divided the third child's rightful portion of his kingdom between the other two sisters. Later when he visited his first daughter, she treated him poorly. Disillusioned he cried, *"How sharper than a serpent's tooth it is to have a thankless child!"* (I.iv.295–296).

> When I asked Lindsey what Lear would do next she replied, "He'll go to the second daughter's house but she'll treat him poorly. But then he'll go to the third daughter's house and she'll treat him nicely."
>
> "How do you know?" I asked.
>
> "Because," she explained patiently, knitting her fingers together, "in stories the two oldest daughters often treat their moms and dads poorly. But the third is always nice."
>
> When I asked her for examples she replied, "Well, this is one. Hmmm . . . let's see. *The Fool of the World* [Ransome]. Except his parents treat him poorly and God treats him like He loves him. *Cinderella* [Perrault] . . . the two mean sisters and the mother treat her poorly."

"What about *Beauty and the Beast* [Mayer]?" I suggested.

"Oh, yeah! That would work. Her sisters were real mean 'cause the two older sisters don't really love their father and Beauty does." (November 20, 1988, 6;0)

In literature, children see "rule systems" and common structures that enable prediction of outcome. They see problems work out for characters who must act in situations that others have created and in which they must live. Seeing these simulated problems and their solutions in literature complements children's dramatizations—especially in socio-dramatic play—in which they practice problem resolution without having to encounter direct consequences. The metarules by which they bring in play enable them to announce it as *on* or to *call it off.*

Such supraorganizers and collecting cues come in several forms—genres, predictable scripts or characters, patterned illustrations, and expected modes of description or narration. Here Lindsey recognizes a familiar plot whose characters will replay scripts she knows from other stories. From the very minimal narrative frame that tells of a family made up of father and daughters who lived in an earlier era, Lindsey realizes that the story will be like those she knows in both form and substance. Moreover, some redemptive character will be necessary to the plot, and Lindsey can offer without benefit of direct text examination the descriptions of such characters and situations that motivate them. Added to such organizing principles or metarules, which enable quick comprehension of one literary text and its extension into another, are those that allow transformations of the fantastic of literature to the pragmatics of reality.[5]

Highly conscious that she both knew rules and could make up rules for literature and life, Lindsey often chose to maneuver her preferred outcomes of everyday events through literary interventions. Through fictionalizations of real situations, she adjusted different aspects of characters, settings, times, moods, and degrees of magic to match her own intentions and emotions.

Riding in the car one afternoon, Lindsey was munching on some rice cakes that I had brought for the ride. She happily ate her way through two or three and then dropped the last one. It rolled across the edge of her car seat and fell to the floor.

"Mama. I dropped my rice cake," Lindsey said in dismay.

I had been watching out of the corner of one eye. "Yes, I know. Just a minute."

"Mama. Mama. Can you reach my rice cake?"

Intent on the traffic, I replied, "No, honey. I'm driving. Wait till a stoplight."

"Mama? Mama? . . . Jizo Sama! Have you seen my dumpling?" Unsuccessful with the ordinary language of a four-year-old, she turned to the language of literature.

Laughing at her innovation, I pulled the car over to the side of the road to retrieve her rice cake/dumpling. "Here you are, Little Woman," I replied. (November 5, 1986, 3;11)

Lindsey was paraphrasing a line from *The Funny Little Woman* (Mosel), in which a Japanese woman loses a rice dumpling. The dumpling rolls off her table and falls through a crack in the floor. The woman follows the dumpling, giggling all the way. As she follows, she meets a variety of underground Japanese statues called Jizo Samas. She bows low before every ancient figure and begs the advice of each.

Lindsey's use of the literary reference seemed to be triggered by the visual similarity of her rice cake to the rice dumpling and the motion of the falling cake/dumpling to the floor. But her purpose in re-creating the text was to get my attention. Her conventional pleas received no real response, but by turning to literature and playful language, she had her wish for the return of the rice cake quickly fulfilled. Careful attention to the ways in which she called on literature tells us much about how she formed and recognized patterns, made analogies about the world's scenes, and created metaphors for processes and outcomes.[6]

Her personally internalized metaphors and analogies often made no sense to adults until she gave them some element of the literary reference—the character, plot, or memorable bit of dialogue or scene. Every Easter the girls and I read DuBose Heyward's story *The Country Bunny and the Little Gold Shoes*. According to Heyward, there was not just one Easter Bunny but five, and one of them was Mother Cottontail, the mother of twenty-one perfectly behaved children. Mother Cottontail trained each of her children in the assorted work of the household, and while she was away delivering eggs, the children performed their duties admirably: *"And sure enough, just as she had said, everything was in order. The floors were swept and there were two lovely new pictures painted and hanging on the wall. The dishes were washed and shone in the cupboard. The clothes were washed and mended and nicely hung away"* (Heyward, n.p.). As with past readings of the story, on this Easter the girls seemed less interested in the overriding message of the "well-behaved children" than in the glistening pictures of assorted candy in the Palace of the Easter Eggs. Still, Lindsey managed to take part of the message to heart before the week was out.

The day after Easter was the start of an educational convention in San Francisco, and Kenny and I spent the night in a hotel in the city, leaving Lindsey and Ashley in the care of their grandfather. When we returned late the next evening, the girls were already in bed, but Grandpa said that Lindsey had made a special point of wanting us to notice the two new pictures that were hung in the entryway. Quite frankly, I thought little about them until the next morning, when Lindsey pulled me down the stairs exclaiming:

> "Did you see our pictures? I hung them just the way the Country Bunny's children did!" Sure enough, these were not affixed to the wall with the tape rolls we ordinarily use but were suspended from fishing line hanging from push pins, just like those in the story.
>
> Lindsey's picture was a scene from *The Country Bunny and the Little Gold Shoes* and showed Mother Cottontail returning to her own little cottage after a long Easter night. As Lindsey explained, "You were gone for *soooo* long, and I wanted to make the house pretty for you . . . just like the bunny children." (March 29, 1989, 6;4)

Lindsey's work included no straightening of her room—her clothes were tumbled in her drawer and the remains of a tea party lay unwashed in a corner of the room; but she had never been a literal child. She took what she wanted from the message, and it came, no less, from the heart.

A World of Words

But how did Lindsey come to be able to stretch literature into socio-dramatic play that recast roles and rules of such real-life complexities as bedtime or parental absence? How, in other words, did the interpretive community of Lindsey and Ashley come about and exert influence on them?[7] As they acquired knowledge with and about books, they also learned basic aspects of awareness about oral and written language, sources of information and authority, and gradations of interpretations. Most of this learning came not in blatant directives but in redundant, subtle, often trivial, fleeting but repetitive routines of speech, gesture, or facial expression slipped in among the interstices of everyday family life. Through these rituals, they learned values that surrounded the knowledge and skills we asked them to display. They absorbed from us and their peers notions about what mattered most and least about books, proper and improper ways to handle, read, and think about ideas from print, and ways to judge their behavior and that of others around books. These habits accorded with and mutually reinforced other cultural patterns of space and time use, problem-solving strategies, varying plays of questions and answers, loyalties to certain systems of marking and classification, and preferred ways of spending leisure time. They also learned the limits of ways they could resist and control how books affected and influenced their lives. To reject books out of hand in our household would have been almost as unnatural as to refuse food, sleep, or any other regularly established daily pattern. But both girls were regularly able to negotiate precisely when, how, and what Kenny and I wanted them to read, and to alter interpretations and venture independent thoughts and discoveries. They were anything but a steady, passive, receptive audience: from an early age, they had their own notions of specific rules of illustrating, expanding, enacting, interpreting, and reshaping texts; they found expert ways to derail our agenda for reading, to deflect our line of talk without provoking our absolute refusal to share a bedtime story or take time out for one of their suggested reading tasks. Perhaps most important was the fact that as each girl developed a definition of her self as individual personality, she used books—just as she used other props of her daily environment (such as clothing, hair style, or manner of talking)—to reflect what she did or did not notice, remember, and reuse on other occasions.

Literacy is not acquired in a vacuum. Nor does it spring fully formed from our minds, like Athena from the head of Zeus. It is an evolutionary process changing from generation to generation and from life to life. An analysis of the role of words in our family life is ultimately a personal study of Lindsey's and Ashley's response to literature. Although all people resonate with the values of their community, every life is individual, every action unique, every pattern personalized. And the patterns of life in our literate school-oriented family, like those of many other mainstream families, created an environment steeped in cultural messages. Yet our personal household culture did not just *create* Lindsey or Ashley; they are not only products of our world but extensions. They will take what we give them and change it and shape it into something that is their own. . . .

Lindsey

Lindsey was born on November 8, 1982, in Yanbu, a newly created city in the Kingdom of Saudi Arabia. Once a small fishing village on the Red Sea, Yanbu was turned into a boom town, with many newly constructed oil refineries ready to receive black gold through a pipeline from the Eastern Province. The refined products were then shipped out of Yanbu's highly secretive harbor, up the Red Sea, and out the Suez Canal to the waiting world.

Kenny and I taught in the international school, which provided an American education for the expatriate community in Yanbu. Although most of the students were American, there were also large numbers of children from Europe, India, and the Far East. Lindsey's birth exemplified the international nature of the community: her entry into the world was assisted by Filipino nurses, an Irish midwife, Dutch and Indian obstetricians, and a Swedish pediatrician.

Lindsey was also born into a world of diverse and abundant words. Two weeks prior to her birth, Kenny and I were feted at a surprise shower. "Best wishes to the new cub!" the hand-drawn poster proclaimed, in a wordplay on our last name. A card on one of the gifts said "Welcome Baby Roo," which was a pet name I had already given Lindsey. I chose this appellation after the baby kangaroo in Milne's *The House at Pooh Corner*, which seemed to describe Lindsey's vigorous prenatal kicking.

We received numerous gifts—quilts, booties, small stuffed animals, toys, and baby books, many of which were embroidered, printed, or stuffed with a storybook theme. We played party games, one of which was a "baby crossword" with clues like "Wynken, Blynken, and _____; Little _____ Riding Hood; and _____, two, buckle my shoe."

On the day Lindsey was born, my first-grade class wrote a picture book in her honor entitled "A Short Collection of WISHES and PICTURES on the Birth of Your Daughter." The substitute teacher, who guided its publication, had it delivered to the hospital. The children had written a number of messages:

"I wish your baby would be nice," wrote Anna-Maria.

"I know you are very happy to have your baby and I wish she was called Elizabeth," Kenny suggested.

Todd, however, chose the name "Shelley."

One of the boys in my class, Dengiz, was Turkish and quite new to English. He wrote, "Dear Mrs. Wolf, . . . Hi Wolf. Baby very good."

And Sagar wrote in his neat methodical handwriting, "I wish your baby would never cry." (November 8, 1982)

Friends and family sent notes and cards of congratulations. My father wrote a letter specifically to the newborn:

Dear, dear Lindsey,

How to welcome you into our world? Such a lovely little girl—so wanted and so needed to fill that special place in my heart. How I have waited for you! . . . There is so much to life and I wish I could provide a complete book of instructions instead of these few meager words to protect and help you—but do you know what? I'm sure you will manage and we'll learn from you.

I, too, felt the need to write to Lindsey. Weeks after her homecoming I wrote her a letter about her birth, her arrival home, the way she looked in the crib, and her first bath. Of her birth I wrote: "When you were born, there was an enchanted silence. Minutes before, the room had been filled with cheers of encouragement, 'Come on! Push! This is it!' Dad was holding onto my hand so tight. Then you slipped into our lives like some wondrous fish. Dad bent his face close to mine, and we looked into your eyes for the first time. We didn't need to count fingers and toes. We knew you were perfect."

A physically precocious child, Lindsey seemed to master everything weeks before the date that the baby books predicted. She rolled over at three weeks, crawled at five months, walked at nine months, and could do chin-ups on the dining room table at ten months. Walking soon became passé; she ran everywhere as her first birthday drew near. She did not seem to understand an object fully unless she had either put it in her mouth or climbed on top of it.

Speech progressed at a slower pace and seemed integrally connected to physical movement. Her first distinctive laugh bubbled out with a bouncing rendition of a Mother Goose rhyme:

Ride a cock-horse to Banbury Cross
To see a fine lady upon a white horse;
Rings on her fingers and bells on her toes,
And she shall have music wherever she goes.

At the age of four months, we began to read stories to her. And by ten months we were reading to her every night at bedtime.

"Look at that! What's that?" we would query, pointing to a picture of a baby in a book.

"Ba Ba," Lindsey would answer. At ten months her blanket, her bottle, and any baby were all classified under the rubric "Ba Ba."

But we knew what she meant. "It's a baby!" we encouraged. "Yes, kiss the baby."

Lindsey would lean forward and plant a kiss on the book baby's nose. Actually, any baby would do for this display of affection—the one in the mirror, or on the box of disposable diapers, or even on the cover of Dr. Spock.

"Good! Good!!" we would say, complimenting her on her reading. (Letter to my sister, October 1, 1983, 11 mos.)[8]

Her ability to translate two-dimensional storybook pictures into physical actions and verbal exclamations increased rapidly. She would moo to indicate a cow, swipe at her hair to signify "brush," and say "MMMMMMM" when shown a banana, reaching out for its yellow shape.

Around her first birthday, I wrote to my father to tell him of her progress and thank him for a book that he had given Lindsey:

> Her language skills are really picking up. Naturally, her understanding is way ahead of her vocabulary, but she seems to pick up new words daily. She says Ma Ma, Da Da, hot, yuck, uh-oh, na-na (for banana), wolf, ba ba (for bottle), yeah, night, teeth, more, watszat (what's that?), up, and burp.
>
> "Book" is one of her favorite words and activities. We read to her every night, cuddling on the couch. Her present favorites are *Good-night Moon* [Brown] and *The Runaway Bunny* [Brown]. You should see the latter. It is chewed on all corners and is missing a few pages and its cover! It is definitely a well-loved book, Dad. (Thanksgiving weekend, 1983, 1;0)

Lindsey's favorite book at fourteen months was Harry McNaught's *Animal Babies*. Under the spell of his illustrations and our tutelage, her repertoire of book-related animal sounds increased and she moved from commonplace domestic animals to the more exotic. She would stick out her tongue for the anteater, stand on one leg for the flamingo, roar for the lion, and stretch her neck high for the giraffe. Kenny and I created the original physical labels, but they seemed to strike a chord in Lindsey, who performed them with relish. And the cycle continued as we encouraged the performance.

In addition to the labeling activities which most picture books evoked, Lindsey began, not long after her first birthday, to play out certain parts of books. *Good-night Moon*, read at bedtime, evoked an original dramatic response and her first trip into the imagination. I wrote to my sister: "She has begun to pretend and will fall on the ground and lay still when we say 'Night Night.' When it is truly time to go to bed, she calls 'Ni Ni' to all manner of things. She knows each of her many stuffed animals by name and will pick them up to give them a good-night kiss" (February 4, 1984, 1;3). Books accompanied Lindsey everywhere. We always had a few stuffed into her stroller on short trips around the neighborhood. Several books were essential for long airline trips leading to vacations abroad. While traveling, we bought more books. In Paris it seemed appropriate to buy her *The Red Balloon* (Lamorisse). After our trip to Sri Lanka, we bought several books by Laurent de Brunhoff, for elephants had become a big topic. The cartoon of Babar in suit and bowler could not substitute for the image of the Indian elephant which greeted us outside our hotel: a kingly creature draped in a spangled cloth of a thousand gleaming mirrors. But the sight of the elephants bathing in *Meet Babar and His Family* did remind us all of the real elephant that Lindsey and Kenny rode along a jungle river and then watched being bathed by his Sri Lankan master.

Toward the middle of Lindsey's second year we left labeling activities behind, and, rather than condensing or abridging stories, read them *in toto*. We saw connections between literature and life, and we taught Lindsey to see them as well. Most of the time these connections brought her understanding of life and pleasure in its possibilities, but there were times when she responded with fear. A month prior to her second birthday, I wrote to friends:

> Now she is a big girl, sleeping in a big bed, and Kenny and I still go in two or three times a night to watch our sleeping beauty. We have an every night ritual, which includes brushing away the "bad teeth" and sharing bedtime stories.
>
> Her current favorite is *The Three Little Pigs* [Galdone], and she has a real love-hate relationship with the big, bad wolf. She imitates him by turning the corners of her mouth down in a scowl. With a low, menacing voice she threatens, "Little pig . . . little pig . . . COME IN!!!" Oftentimes, she scares herself, and hugs herself saying, "Wolf. No hurt Lindsey."
>
> Katy, our baby-sitter, told me the other day that she had made a gigantic mistake. It seems that the wind was banging the door, and she casually told Lindsey that maybe it was the Wolf. Lindsey burst into tears and soon had Kara (her childcare playmate) crying too. Katy couldn't believe she'd made such an error. Both girls howled at the door until she convinced them it was safe. Lindsey now understands the word "teasing." (October 1, 1984, 1;11)

Maurice Sendak's *Where the Wild Things Are* rapidly became a favorite and fortified her with the intertextual ammunition to cope with her fears.[9] "Be still!" she would threaten the big, bad wolf as his cheeks filled with air. And she would shout the same words to me when I scolded or denied her something she wanted. By her second birthday she had learned that text provided some answers to life's questions.

The ability to tame "Wild Things" was a theme that carried beyond storybooks and into the narrative of our family life. Shortly after Lindsey's second birthday, we traveled to Tanzania on safari. Borrowing from both reality and fantasy, we developed a narrative that described how Lindsey, a powerful heroine, saves her mother from a hungry lion. In the story, I leave the safety of our van to get a better picture of a nearby giraffe. Concentrating on the photo, I am unaware of the fact that a lion is stalking me. Lindsey is watching, however. She sees the lion and cries out, "Stop, Lion!" The king of the savannah instantly recognizes her power. Staring at her in amazement, he cries, "Queen Lindsey, I didn't know you were in Africa!" After an abject apology, which Lindsey haughtily accepts, he helps me back into the van. I am much shaken, and can only whisper, "Thank you, Sweetheart. You saved my life!" Since its first telling, this story has been refined and embellished. Sometimes Lindsey saves me, and other times she comes to Kenny's rescue. But the compelling theme of her power remains at the heart of the narrative.[10]

Another narrative featuring Lindsey as powerful heroine was created by Lindsey and her baby-sitter. It wove together elements of *Jack and the Beanstalk, The Three Billy Goats Gruff,* and life in our neighborhood. Our playground had swings and a slide, as well as a large climbing structure that incorporated a wooden bridge. In the story, Lindsey saves her small friend Kara from a mean giant, who dominates the bridge. Lindsey orders him off the bridge in no uncertain terms, and then claims it as her own, so that small children are now free to play there.

Lindsey particularly loved this story, since she was able to enter into the narrative physically. She had a magnificent prop (the bridge), a live actress (Kara), and sufficient imagination to supply the giant.

Physical entrée into story was not offered only by books or narrative, but often came from television. Lindsey is an avid fan of television in general, even though she is not allowed to watch cartoons, which Kenny and I call "junk TV." Instead, we are strong advocates of *Sesame Street*, as well as of *Wonderworks* and *Reading Rainbow*, and we often videotape book-related programs so that she can watch them more than once. When Lindsey was well past her second birthday, we made a video tape of Judy Garland in *The Wizard of Oz*, and Lindsey fell in love with it. I wrote to my father detailing her involvement in the story: "She can sing 'Over the Rainbow,' dance like the Tin Man, and shake our broom and threaten, *'I'll get you, my pretty, and your little dog too!'* The other day she began screaming 'Help!' from the bedroom. Kenny and I ran to her aid only to discover her writhing on the floor crying, 'I'm melting!' " (April 21, 1985, 2;5). But playacting for power through anger or diabolical plotting must sometimes shift to plays for strength through other means—also illustrated in literary sources. As a toddler, Lindsey had an all-encompassing temper. Tantrums were tremendous emotional outbursts that tried the entire family. Once, in desperation, I put her in the shower, hoping that the shock of the water would calm her down. As the water pinged against her shoulders and back, she fell to her knees. "I'm melting!" she shrieked. If water had the power to destroy an evil witch, could it destroy Lindsey? To Lindsey's mind, this possibility with props clearly made the metaphor.

In search for more peaceful solutions to rage, Lindsey and I turned to *The Story of Ferdinand* (Leaf), the tale of an ordinarily mild-mannered bull who sat on a bumblebee. His ensuing rage causes him to be sent to fight in the bullfights in Madrid, and only his calm ability to "smell the flowers" brings him home again. On the surface level of text, Lindsey adored his anger. The question *"Well, if you were a bumblebee and a bull sat on you what would you do?"* tickled her at every reading. "Sting him!" Lindsey would crow triumphantly, and then bounce around on the bed holding her bottom in imitation of Ferdinand. But below the climactic surface, Lindsey would visibly calm as Ferdinand found his quiet way home.

Home became a crucial issue for Lindsey during this year, for we left Saudi Arabia and moved back to the States. Everything was new and different; the everyday events of this new setting were exotic to her. I was a university student. Kenny tried his hand at a number of things before settling into a job designing educational software and waiting to hear from graduate schools. Lindsey had a new house, a new bedroom, a new baby-sitter, and new friends. And perhaps most disturbing of all, a physically new mother, for I was pregnant with our second daughter, Ashley.

During this time the story *Who's in Rabbit's House?* (Aardema) became a favorite. It is an African story about a rabbit who returns to his home only to find it has been taken over by a "bad animal." The rabbit undertakes a long and arduous struggle to regain his home, until he is finally assisted by the humor and wisdom of a small frog. Lindsey's adjustment to her new environment was no less arduous. When we read the story for the first time, these connections did not occur to me. But upon reflection, as I think about the number of times she requested it, I realize that the story of the small rabbit struggling to regain his home may have offered comfort in her new world.

Ashley

Ashley was born on December 27, 1985, in Salt Lake City, Utah. Like Lindsey, Ashley joined the world of words at birth. She received gifts of literature and book-related toys from friends and family, as well as the traditional "Welcome to the World" letter from her grandfather. Her grandmother sent a United States Savings Bond to start her college fund.

Above the white wicker bassinet where she slept hung a framed sampler a friend had embroidered with the particulars of her birth—name, date, and "Friday's child" stitched across a parade of baby lambs that Lindsey named "Bo Peep's sheep." Ashley's walls were illustrated with other storybook characters as well: Jack and Jill, Mother Goose, and the cow jumping over the moon. Books waited on the shelves wedged between stuffed-toy versions of Max and the Wild Things. A rocking chair sat in one corner, large enough to hold both Lindsey and Ashley during nighttime story readings.

Unlike Lindsey, Ashley was plunged into the world of school immediately—graduate school. I was a master's student at the time, and Ashley's Christmas birth coincided with winter vacation. And so, at two weeks of age, Ashley accompanied me back to school in her Snugli. At home, she slept in my lap while I sat at the computer and typed out papers and exams. She nursed through stories read to Lindsey and crawled over the books and papers scattered on our study floor.

Ashley matched Lindsey in physical development, but her language skills developed quietly for much of her first three years. Her communication appeared in the raising of an eyebrow, a sigh, the shaking of her shoulders as she giggled at a piece of text, and a few brief words. Unlike Lindsey, who perceived storybooks as social interaction, Ashley would drag a pile of books to a corner of the couch and leaf through them one by one. While Lindsey scurried about the house in search of the right prop to complete a storybook production, Ashley sat on her bed with a favorite book, silently studying the illustrations.

Language came to Ashley with all the speed of a time-lapse film showing the blossoming of a flower. In a few months, single-word utterances became full sentences, and the only thing she confused were the prepositions. "Down, down," she would call, stretching her hands up to be lifted. And "Just shut out!" she would warn her sister when she thought Lindsey was talking too much.

As our Christmas baby, Ashley staked her claim to every children's book in our house concerning the season. She confiscated Lindsey's copy of *How the Grinch Stole Christmas* (Seuss) and monopolized Tomie de Paola's pop-up version of *The First Christmas*. We encouraged her identity with the holiday by buying her *The Polar Express* (Van Allsburg), but when we purchased E. T. A. Hoffmann's *Nutcracker* for Lindsey, Ashley was annoyed. "It's 'bout Christmas. *I'm* the Christmas baby!" she cried.

She also adopted Lindsey's identity with several storybook characters. She slept through her part in Sleeping Beauty and picked flowers as Red Riding Hood, but her muse was Rapunzel. Once, while Ashley was bathing in the tub, I commented that when her hair was wet it was very long. "Yes," she replied, leaning her head back in the water to set the strands afloat, "just like Punzal" (June 26, 1988, 2;6). Ashley was by no means Lindsey's mimic, but she often followed the patterns set by her older sister. I once wrote to the head of my thesis committee: "Like Lindsey, Ashley uses text to get out of trouble. While vacationing at her grandmother's house this summer, Ashley picked the paint off an entire arm of one of the living room chairs. When I discovered the deed, I challenged Ashie in a tone that set her foot to a nervous tap. 'Did you do this?' I demanded. 'No,' she replied meekly. I repeated my question with more vigor. In desperation, Ashley looked up at me with imploring eyes and said, 'How 'bout, Snow White did it?' " (September 5, 1988, 2;9).

Although she could quickly draw on fantasy as an excuse, Ashley often selected nonfiction in her book choices. As an infant she had fewer opportunities than Lindsey to look at books in terms of objects and their labels. There was less time for hours of "What's that?"—"It's a cat, a cow, a fire truck . . . ," for we were reading to two children now and Ashley was often drawn in as a silent partner in Lindsey's storytime. But as she found her voice, she demanded a return to the labeling of objects, the myriad possible answers to the question "What's that?" Richard Scarry's *Best Word Book Ever* (with "more than 1400 objects illustrated in full color") was the book she requested most frequently as a toddler. She called it her "dictionary" and urged us to pore over the illustrations of pig families, fox musicians, and rabbit children playing with their toys. The double-spread illustrations of birds were her favorite, and she tested and retested her knowledge of unusual names—bittern, puffin, toucan—as well as the more common chick, sea gull, and rooster. We played countless requested games of "Find the———," in which Ashley would scan the page and then point to the labeled fowl. Her second most oft-requested pages were those on flowers, and she carried her book knowledge out into the world, often asking me to label flowers we found on our outings, or proudly pronouncing the label herself.

As Ashley grew older she continued to request expository texts, to add to her fantasy favorites. One preferred series of books was on natural phenomena, with each volume prominently labeled "This Is a Let's-Read-and-Find-Out Science Book." Her most requested books included *Germs Make Me Sick* (Berger), *Ducks Don't Get Wet* (Goldin), and *My Visit to the Dinosaurs* (Aliki). As the children grew, we often split the family in two at bedtime, and while Lindsey and I read stories, Ashley and Kenny would often discuss the latest issue of *Zoobook*, a magazine filled with animal facts.

Lindsey and Ashley Together

After her third birthday, Lindsey became fascinated with her clothes. As an infant and toddler growing up in Arabia, she had worn only shorts, but she was now tall enough to reach most clothes in her closet and old enough to make her own decisions. Shorts became passé, and dresses became the mode. And the more dresses the better. Two or three, worn one on top of the other, usually created the desired effect.

Quite often her ensembles originated from storybook heroines. She would sit and study the illustrations of a book and then go to her closet. What she couldn't find there, she would borrow from ours. And what she ultimately couldn't find, she could imagine.

"I'm not Lindsey," became the watchword of her third year. Lindsey was Cinderella, Sleeping Beauty, Red Riding Hood. She was Curious George, Tikki Tikki Tembo, and the Funny Little Woman. She was Alice. She was Una. And she was Ida. Ida is the plucky heroine of Maurice Sendak's *Outside Over There*. Left in charge of her baby sister, Ida fails to watch at a crucial time and the baby is stolen by goblins. Equipped with her mother's yellow rain cloak and her wonderhorn, she must enter "outside over there" to recover her sister.

The combination of pictures and words made Lindsey aware of her own position as a new "big sister," with its incumbent responsibilities. In an initial reading, Lindsey claimed that the crying baby looked "just like Ashley." And later she threatened, "If goblins stole my Ashley, I'd kill them!"

Numerous small plays emerged from this story. In one scene, Lindsey would instruct me to "be the goblins," and while she pretended to stare moodily out the living room window, I would sneak in and take Ashley away. Lindsey would follow, carefully walking backward and playing on her harmonica as if it were a wonderhorn. In another scene, she commanded Ashley to clap hands, and was frustrated by the fact that at three months old, Ashley could not comply.

But with the passage of time Ashley could assume her role, and Lindsey took enormous satisfaction in the vigorous clapping that resulted. Still, there were small frustrations. Sendak writes that the baby *"lay cozy in an eggshell, crooning and clapping as a baby should,"* and I would not allow Lindsey to take eggs from the refrigerator "for Ashley to sit in."

But apart from small denials, Kenny and I constantly encouraged Lindsey's play. It was a continuing cycle. We would borrow books from the library to read. Lindsey would request over and over again those that she liked, and we were eager to read her desired choice. As she became more familiar with a text, she would choose elements to stage, complete with props and actors. We would play parts according to her instructions and help her assemble props. And if a story seemed to be a continuing theme in Lindsey's life, we would purchase the book for her personal library. On her fourth birthday, we bought *Outside Over There* and gave it to Lindsey as a present from Ashley.

In our early storybook productions, the entire family played according to

Lindsey's general instructions, taking up the roles she assigned, interpreting a prop in the same imaginative light, but making extensions of her choices along the way. If we departed too far from Lindsey's vision, she quickly brought us back.[11]

One morning, as Kenny was getting ready for work, the entire family joined him. Ashley was lying on the rug on our bedroom floor and Lindsey was dancing and practicing different faces in the bedroom mirror. With no university classes until later that day, I lounged in a chair, watching this early morning scene. As Kenny began to put on his shoes, Lindsey took off for her room.

"I need my party shoes," she called over her shoulder.

She returned with her black velvet party shoes, a welcome hand-me-down from her cousin. Since she rarely has a need for party shoes, they have become more of a toy than a necessity. She clumped back into the bedroom with both shoes on, but on the threshold kicked off one shoe. It went scuttling toward Kenny.

"Let's play Cinderella!" she cried. Then she reclined on the bed, dangling her shoeless foot over the side. "Now, I'll be one bad sister . . . then the other . . . then Cinderella."

Kenny jumped ahead in the game and addressed Lindsey as though she were Cinderella. "Let's try the shoe on you, Cinderella."

Lindsey sighed, sat up, and explained, "No! I'm the *bad sister!*"

Kenny reversed tack and pushed and shoved and tried to fit the shoe on her foot, but to no avail. He then took the shoe and tried it on Ashley's foot, but pronounced that it was "too big."

Lindsey had no objection to this bit of improvisation, and giggled as Kenny struggled to fit the shoe on her little sister. After he'd given up on Ashley, the timing was right, and he slid the shoe onto Lindsey's foot.

"Will you marry me?" Kenny begged. Lindsey gazed with rapt expression into her father's eyes.

"Yes," she sighed. And the promise was cemented with a kiss. (June 12, 1986, 3;7)

During this play, Kenny introduced two modifications. In one he tried to leap ahead in the action, but when this was not accepted, he quickly reverted to Lindsey's plan. In the second modification, he introduced Ashley as the second ugly stepsister, thus making a change in the object. Although this had not been included in her original instructions, Lindsey accepted and enjoyed the change.

When Kenny and I and other family members entered into Lindsey's play, we would follow Lindsey's lead yet introduce subtle changes. At a tea party of Lindsey and her girlfriends, I played the part of the butler according to Lindsey's instructions. Yet I changed the action by serving tea with a haughty British accent, which the girls rapidly took up and incorporated into their own conversation. Kenny changed the object by introducing an element of reality. He brewed a pot of herbal tea, which then prompted the girls to request real sugar and cream. On another occasion, when Lindsey's grandmother played tea party, she changed the objects as well by bringing down the dress-up box. Then she followed the girls' lead by wearing an elaborate hat, and a boa slung around her neck.

As Lindsey grew older, our role in her play diminished. Lindsey's school friends played more meaningful parts, leaving Kenny and me to play the occasional cameo: Boo Radley to Lindsey's Scout (in Lee's *To Kill a Mocking Bird*) or the parents of Lindsey's Ramona (in Cleary's *Ramona the Pest*). Lindsey still retained the position of director and stage manager, dragging out the broken cardboard dress-up box, assigning roles, and giving stage directions, but she had to negotiate with alternative opinions and vie for the best costuming. Her productions were not limited to storybook interpretation, but extended to other activities as well, as television characters and the movements of her ballet classes were brought into the configuration:

> Lindsey is now in kindergarten. She is bright, happy, and creative and still prefers dress-up to just about any other activity. At Halloween she was the princess from *The Never Ending Story*, with a baubled crown and a flowing white dress. She inherited a plethora of tutus from a neighbor who knew her penchant for brightly colored netting, and Lindsey now hosts neighborhood dancing parties, providing costuming for all. She has also convinced her friends that Jane Fonda is fun and there are many days when I'll come home from work to see the living room filled with twirling, jiving, miniature "Janes" singing "Do it!" (Christmas letter, 1988, 6;1)

As Ashley grew, she joined the play in more significant ways. When Lindsey staged *Peter and the Wolf* (Prokofiev), she still played director, controlling the music on the stereo and pulling out the dining room chairs to get Ashley, cast as the bird, to "climb the tree." But Ashley had her own opinions about her choice of costuming and the movements of the bird. And at one point she leaped down from the "tree" to check her position from the ultimate authority: her book. At first it seemed a dangerous choice, since Lindsey was stalking the living room as the graceful cat. But Lindsey dropped her role to check the picture with Ashley, and waited for Ashley to make her ascent into the tree before continuing the hunt.

In other productions, Lindsey no longer monopolized the star roles, for Ashley made her own needs known. "Why not just have *two* Cinderellas?" Lindsey asked at the end of one argument, and after that most heroines were doubled in play, although Lindsey still managed to convince Ashley to be Beezus and kept the role of Ramona for herself. Besides the Quimbys, there were many games of "sisters," especially those lost in the forest. "Sister! Sister!" I heard Ashley exclaim one night. "Come in the house before the darkness comes." Her tone was dramatically overwrought, her hands clasped together. Lindsey responded in kind, "I'm coming, oh sister," leaping through the door as if pursued by wolves (December 16, 1989, 7;1 and 3;11). They learned to share the mystery and protect each other from the nighttime forest.

Although Ashley's roles increased in importance, her own response to literature did not match the intensity of Lindsey's dramatic play. To Ashley, storybook characters stayed more firmly in the pages of the book—they could be discussed, referred to, and even called upon in the context of everyday events, but their personalities could not be donned with the ease of a costume. Once as she played

Little Red Riding Hood, picking the geraniums that grew like weeds in our California neighborhood, I addressed her as "Little Red." She rolled her eyes in exasperation. "I'm Ashley, Mama! I'm *Ashley!*"

Ashley's emphatic reply served as a reminder that a child's response to literature is highly individual.[12] Although Ashley was often drawn into stories that were specifically selected by and for Lindsey, she quickly developed her own ways of interpreting story, Whereas Lindsey preferred the enactment of story, Ashley more often chose verbal reflection, often making humorous comments, turning original words into risqué remarks:

> When Kenny read the exploits of Max in *Where the Wild Things Are* [Sendak] today, Ashley stopped him after he read the line, *"but Max stepped into his private boat and waved good-bye."*
>
> "No, Dada," she admonished. "Not like that. It's 'and Max stepped onto their private parts and waved good-bye.' Like that."
>
> Kenny laughed so hard at this vision of a vindictive Max that tears came to his eyes, and Ashley laughed right along with him. Even after he explained the difference carefully, Ashley insisted that her way was better " 'cause it's funny." (November, 1989, 3;11)

Ashley's comments on text were often related to humor, and she was able to laugh at her own mispronunciations or reconfigurations of words. Sendak's *In the Night Kitchen* (1970) was a particular favorite, especially the part where the hero, Mickey, stands atop a milk bottle and crows like a rooster. As a young child, Ashley took the familiar rooster call of *"Cock-a-Doodle Doo"* offered by Sendak and transformed it into "Hot Dog Doo Doo Doo." Thereafter, she insisted on substituting her own words for Sendak's, crowing out her own independent rendition.

Ashley's interpretations also centered on the musicality of text. *In the Night Kitchen* is wonderfully musical, filled with rhymes and with bakers and small boys who chant, howl, and sing. Whenever we read the text, Ashley encouraged me to sing a good part of it, and she joined in when we reached her favorite parts, her voice rising loudly over mine. Her interest in the musicality of story language was reflected in her selection of books, for she consistently chose books of poetry over prose and made up original songs and rhymes. One morning, Ashley selected *The Jolly Postman* (Ahlberg and Ahlberg), a story of fairy-tale characters brought together through letters delivered by a local postman.[13]

> When we got to the witch's letter, Ashley took over the reading. The letter is an advertisement for "Hobgoblin Supplies Ltd©" and includes all the necessities of witchhood: *"Cup and SORCERER tea service — it washes itself!" "Easy-clean non-stick Cauldron Set,"* and so on. Ashley asked me if I would like a song and selected the advertisement for *"Little Boy Pie Mix — for those unexpected visitors when the cupboard is bare."* The text is accompanied by an illustration of a witch bringing a smiling-faced pie to her fellow witches seated at table. To the side is a box of the mix which features a little boy standing expectantly in a bowl and underneath are written the words: *"Finest natural ingredients. No preservatives."* Ashley sang:

> Pease porridge hot
> Pease porridge cold
> Bake me a cake as fast as you can.
> Roll it and pat it and put it in the baker.
> And put it in the baker for a Mickey-cake!
> (March 14, 1990, 4;3)

Ashley's creation brought together three poems about food: one about porridge ("Pease Porridge Hot" is a Mother Goose rhyme) and two about cake (Mother Goose's "Pat a Cake" and Sendak's *In the Night Kitchen*). The resulting feast of "little boy pie mix" brought forth images of other nursery-rhyme food, as well as Sendak's illustration of Mickey who was baked in a cake, with one hand rising from the batter. Like Sendak's bakers, Ashley mixed the ingredients from her store of poetry, creating her own concoction.

The blending of multiple verses was a common feature of Ashley's story interpretation and seeped into her day-to-day communication, as well as into her letters to friends and family. One day our family traveled to a local park to see the resting spot for monarch butterflies. Thousands of butterflies hung in thick clusters of bright color, while others flitted through the sun-dappled trees. When we returned home I asked the girls to write to their grandparents and aunts about the adventure:

> Ashley drew a picture of butterflies on most of her postcards, with intricate patterns on the wings to imitate the markings of the monarch. But on her Aunt Martha's card she drew two simple butterflies surrounded by a large expanse of black lines. At first she described her picture as:
>
> > "Two little babies sitting in a tub
> > Jack and Jill went up the . . ."

But as I reached for my pen to write down her words, she changed tack, wanting to start again. She made several attempts and then said "OK, write this:

> Two little babies named Lindsey and Ashley
> Fly away, Ashley
> Fly away, Lindsey
> Come back, Ashley
> Come back, Lindsey
> Come back, Wolf."
> (February 1, 1990, 4;2)

She pronounced the rhyme in sing-song fashion reminiscent of the old jump-rope rhyme—"Johnny and Mary sitting in a tree, K-I-S-S-I-N-G!"—but with the words "fly away" she switched to the rhythm of Mother Goose:

> Ladybird, ladybird,
> Fly away home,
> Your house is on fire
> And your children all gone.

Ashley's first poetic attempt was a description of the picture she drew—two figures "sitting" in a circle of dark lines that might have been the water of a bathtub. The rhythm of the first line, as well as the image of two figures, brought Jack and Jill to mind. But she was not satisfied with this poem, for it said little about the day's adventure. In her final poem, as Ashley connected insect to insect, she linked life events to poetic experience. She knew no butterfly poems, and thus called up a familiar ladybug rhyme, replacing the nameless insect children with herself and her sister, who flew away but ultimately were called back home.

Ashley's love of rhyme combined with her need to reshape texts to match her own rhythms. While Lindsey seldom created her own poetry or sang the poems she knew, Ashley filled the house with her songs. Ashley was the poet and the comic, substituting words, blending rhymes, and creating humorous wordplays, while Lindsey was the dramatist, enacting her interpretations of story.

By the age of seven, however, Lindsey depended less on the movement of her body to express response. At night, as we crowded into bed to read, Lindsey tended to lie still and offer verbal comments about the story. Ashley, however, needed movement to express her humorous response. One night we read *The Five Chinese Brothers* (Bishop), the tale of a family of five boys, all uniquely equipped for survival. The first brother had the power to swallow the sea, and thus acquired a catch to sell at the market each day. In the beginning of the story, he reluctantly agreed to take a small boy fishing, on the condition that the boy obey his every word. When he swallowed the sea, filling up his head like a balloon, the text read:

> *"And all the fish were left high and dry at the bottom of the sea. And all the treasures of the sea lay uncovered.*
>
> *The little boy was delighted. He ran here and there stuffing his pockets with strange pebbles, extraordinary shells and fantastic algae."*
>
> "What would you take home from the sea?" I asked the girls.
>
> "I'd like some starfish and mother of pearl," Lindsey said.
>
> But Ashley leaped from under the covers and began gathering stuffed animals off the bed. "I'd pick teddy bears and this doggie," she said with a droll look in her eye.
>
> "No. No. They're not in the sea!" Lindsey exclaimed. "You know what I'd do? I'd get the gold coins off that pirate ship." (December 12, 1989, 7;1 and 3;11)

Each night, Lindsey and Ashley chose their own treasures from story: shimmering roles, unique dialogue, and iridescent insights into the world of life and literature. They turned the pieces of story over in their heads, assessing the quality, weighing the consequences, judging the beauty. Some pieces they threw back into the sea. But many were stuffed into the pockets of their thoughts, to be brought out at some private pleasurable moment or shared with friends and family. . . .

NOTES

1. Though children—and all speakers—have always respoken the texts of others, this phenomenon drew intensified interest through the rediscovery by Western scholars in the 1980s of the writings of Mikhail Bakhtin, who reminds us: "Internally persuasive discourse . . . tightly interwoven with 'one's own word' [is] gradually and slowly wrought out of others' words that have been acknowledged and assimilated, and the boundaries between the two are at first scarcely perceptible." All internally persuasive words then become creative and productive because they link, organize, and awaken "new and independent words." M. M. Bakhtin, *The Dialogic Imagination* (Austin: University of Texas Press, 1981), p. 345. J. Wertsch, *Voices of the Mind: A Sociocultural Approach to Mediated Action* (Cambridge: Harvard University Press, 1991), explores further the Bakhtinian question, "Who is doing the talking?"

2. Anthropologists and linguists have increasingly emphasized the "ritual of theatre" and sociodramatic play as metacommentaries on the "rules underlying the structures of familiar sociocultural life or experienced social reality." V. Turner, *From Ritual to Theatre: The Human Seriousness of Play* (New York: PAJ Publications, 1982), p. 104. Usually these are dramas that children act out to replay society, but in the case of acting out a scene or adaptation of children's literature spontaneously, children effectively hold up to daily reality not just one mirror—that of play—but two mirrors; they see and enact the play within the literary tale that is itself a play on social experience. The symbolic transformation of objects, people, voices, movements, and relationships is characterized by a meta-communative message which emphasizes that, in play, actions are not what they seem. G. Bateson, "A Theory of Play and Fantasy," *Psychiatric Research Reports*, no. 2 (1955): 39–51, for example, suggests that in a play fight, "the playful nip denotes the bite, but it does not denote what would be denoted by the bite." Lindsey, in explaining to her father her reenactment of Billy as rocking horse, must tell *the story of the story* she reenacts to subvert strictures on her activities. By replaying the story of the work of literature that her father had approved, she ensures acceptance, for she has transformed her own escape from disobedience into obedience. The cognitive complexity and degrees of social sensitivity necessary for such sociodramas receive only scant attention in the scant work on children's spontaneous sociodramas. Yet S. Smilanksy, *The Effects of Sociodramatic Play on Disadvantaged Preschool Children* (New York: Wiley, 1968), in her pioneering training study, recognized the interweaving of role portrayal, situation substitution, and object substitution with the development of cognitive, social, and verbal skills. More recently D. Kelly-Byrne, *A Child's Play Life: An Ethnographic Study* (New York: Teachers College Press, 1989), in her case study of the play of one child, and C. Garvey, "Some Properties of Social Play," in *Play: Its Role in Development and Evolution*, ed. Jerome S. Bruner, Alison Jolly and Kathy Sylvia (New York: Penguin, 1976), in her summary of research on play, have explored the complexity of play and its positive influence on children's development. Garvey, in particular, stresses the relationship between literary play and the acquisition of reading and writing skills.

3. We can understand the "equipment" that texts provide for manipulation through the writings of the philosopher-poet Kenneth Burke. See K. Burke, *Language as Symbolic Action: Essays on Life, Literature and Method* (Berkeley: University of California Press, 1966). His early notions of "dramatism" view the study of language and thought as situated modes of action, motivated in origin and thus dramatic (and dialectic) in form and function. From him, we learn that every text becomes a strategy for encompassing a situation

dramatically as well as referentially; thus, motives and functions, or the goal directions of language use, give meaning far beyond that of the pure naming or referencing role of words. Moreover, the language in verbal performances depends upon kinds of symbolic competence that include movement, action, and emotion and expect the interplay of a dialectic approach to text.

4. The problem-solving powers of narratives in which children explain and interpret are amply illustrated in the evening crib monologues of a two-year-old girl named Emily, who used narratives to take up the puzzles or contradictions of her day. See K. Nelson, ed. *Narratives From the Crib* (Cambridge: Harvard University Press, 1989). Emily's thinking aloud in these narratives enabled her to achieve cognitive goals of logical inference and to qualify her knowledge states by specific linguistic choices such as *but, because, so,* and *probably* or *maybe*. Like Lindsey, Emily shifted propositions around, combined them, and resequenced them in "pragmatically rich, story-like frames." See C. F. Feldman, "Monologue as Problem-Solving Narrative" in *Narratives from the Crib*, ed. K. Nelson (Cambridge: Harvard University Press, 1989), p. 101. For a convincing argument on how stories and theories (the latter often set forth as steps to solutions of problems) intermingle, see R. Coles, *The Call of Stories: Teaching and the Moral Imagination* (Boston: Houghton Mifflin, 1989). Psycholinguists have explored the relative priority of perceptual features (size, shape, texture, and so on) versus functional roles, animacy, and the like in the child's acquisition of vocabulary, but the variety and complexity of categorical organization have made it difficult to construct total theories of semantic development. For a convenient summary of theoretical approaches, see E. V. Clark, "Meaning and Concepts," in *Cognitive Development*, ed. J. H. Flavell and E. M. Markman, vol. 3 of *Handbook of Child Psychology*, 4th ed., ed. P. H. Mussen (New York: Wiley, 1983), pp. 787–840.

5. Within the extensive work on children's perceptions and productions of the genre of "stories," their acquisition of the subtleties of style and particular markers that distinguish one kind of story from another has received surprising little attention from researchers. Yet the few studies available invariably indicate that even very young children achieve awareness of fine distinctions of types of stories much earlier than might be expected and without explicit instruction. The papers collected in Nelson, *op cit.*, tease apart many of the complexities of children's stories, such as dialogue, real-life accounts, hypothetical proposals, reports of mental states, and the role of the listener.

6. Metaphor offers learners the optical, attitudinal, and verbal means to expand that which is within the current instant. The vague, rapidly moving, and frequently indescribable features of the immediate world can often best be captured through metaphor; in addition to their compactness and their immediate encompassing strengths, metaphors are memorable and provide lightweight baggage with which the mind (and verbal expression) can move across highly dissimilar situations and scenes to capture their essence. K. Chukovsky, *From Two to Five*, trans. M. Morton (Berkeley: University of California Press, 1963); E. Winner, *Invented Worlds: The Psychology of the Arts* (Cambridge: Harvard University Press, 1982) and E. Winner, *The Point of Words: Children's Understanding of Metaphor and Irony* (Cambridge: Harvard University Press, 1988) provide numerous examples of the interplays between sound and sense that very young children produce and recognize.

7. The term "interpretive community" refers to the contexts of practice for reading that substantially preconstrain perception—ways of organizing experience that bring individuals to share in distinctions and categories of understanding and relevance. See S. Fish, *Is There a Text in This Class?: The Authority of Interpretive Communities* (Cambridge: Harvard University Press, 1980). Any member of a community-constituted interpreting group (such

as a family, reading club, or class in English literature) is "never individual in the sense of unique or private, but is always the product of the categories of understanding that are his by virtue of his membership in a community of interpretation. It follows, then, that what that experience in turn produces is not open or free, but determinate, constrained by the possibilities that are built into a conventional system of intelligibility." S. Fish, *Doing What Comes Naturally: Change, Rhetoric and the Practice of Theory in Literary and Legal Studies* (Durham: Duke University Press, 1989), p. 83. Research in the late 1980s, especially after the appearance of several works on "reader-response criticism," (see J. P. Tompkins, ed., *Reader-Response Criticism: From Formalism to Post-Structuralism* (Baltimore: Johns Hopkins University Press, 1980); S. Mailloux, *Interpretive Conventions: The Reader in the Study of American Fiction* (Ithaca: Cornell University Press, 1982); E. Freund, *The Return of the Reader: Reader-Response Criticism* (London: Methuen, 1987)) turned to the careful delineation of different types of interpretive communities and their underlying attitudes, frames, and approaches to reading choices, habits, and expectations. See especially the collected papers in C. N. Davidson, ed. *Reading in America: Literature and Social History* (Baltimore: Johns Hopkins University Press, 1989), and the case study by J. Radway, *Reading the Romance: Women, Patriarchy and Popular Literature* (Chapel Hill: University of North Carolina Press, 1984). Though not cast within this theoretical frame or research methodology, earlier case studies of the context for the practice of reading by children in their families provide substantive data on ways these children came to understand their membership in reading families; see, for example, G. Nissex, *Gnys at Wrk: A Child Learns to Write and Read* (Cambridge: Harvard University Press, 1980) and H. Crago and M. Crago, *Prelude to Literacy: A Preschool Child's Encounter with Picture and Story* (Carbondale: Southern Illinois University Press, 1983). These studies were carried out by intimate family members; later, ethnographic studies by long-term participant observers expand the contexts of practice to include as much as possible of the environment of written and oral language development of young children in their communities; see, for example, S. B. Heath, *Ways with Words: Language, Life and Work in Communities and Classrooms* (Cambridge: Cambridge University Press, 1983) and B. B. Schieffelin and M. Cochran-Smith, "Learning to Read Culturally: Literacy Before Schooling," in *Awakening to Literacy*, ed. H. Goelman, A. Oberg, and F. Smith (London: Heinemann, 1984). Several scholars of social cognition urge psychologists interested in cognitive development to extend their interest to studies of the social environment that shapes the acquisition and valuation of knowledge and skills perpetuated in particular institutional communities. See, for example, J. J. Goodnow, "The Socialization of Cognition: What's Involved?" in *Cultural Psychology: Essays on Comparative Human Development*, ed. J. W. Stigler, R. A. Shweder and G. Herdt (Cambridge: Cambridge University Press, 1990), p. 259–286; J. J. Goodnow, "Using Sociology to Extend Psychological Accounts of Cognitive Development," *Human Development*, 1990, 33:81–107; and J. Wertsch and J. Youniss, "Contextualizing the Investigator: The Case of Developmental Psychology," *Human Development* 30 (1987): 18–31.

8. This passage aligns with the pattern of story reading outlined by A. Ninio and J. Bruner, "The Achievement and Antecedents of Labeling," *Journal of Child Language* 5 (1976): 1–15, in which the mother made repeated use of four key utterance types with her child. These are the "ATTENTION VOCATIVE *Look!*, the QUERY *What's that?*, the LABEL *It's an* X, and the FEEDBACK UTTERANCE *Yes.*"

9. "Intertextuality" is a term which signifies relationships among written texts. R. de Beaugrande, *Text, Discourse and Process* (Norwood: Ablex, 1980), suggests that a reader's understanding of one text is dependent on knowledge of other texts. H. Rosen, *Stories and*

Meanings (Winnipeg: National Association for the Teaching of English, 1985), p. 15, further explains that "stories are as they are only because others exist." The word "story" does not define a single narrative confined within the limitations of one combination of setting, character, and plot. Rather, it is the intermingling of texts, where relationships exist among characters, similarities abound among settings, and plots that carry associated themes occur. A story is not one text but many. For a view of intertextuality in children's literature, see M. Meek, *How Texts Teach What Readers Learn* (Exeter, England: Thimble Press, 1988). The notion of intertextuality does not exclude the text (or the narrative) of the reader. The story in print interacts with the story in the mind. A crucial element of this intertextual learning is the "multiplicity of connections" that occurs in reading. See C. Short, "Literacy as a Collaborative Experience" (Ph.D. diss., Indiana University, 1986). New connections are formed with each reading, which in turn transforms new experiences. This presents a kaleidoscope view of intertextual reading with small shimmering bits of experience and text combining and recombining.

10. Throughout D. Kelly-Byrne, *A Child's Play Life: An Ethnographic Study* (New York: Teachers College Press, 1989), a study of a child's play life, she reiterates the power of play (and its dependence on trust, intimacy, and secrecy) by which children can bring adults to their imaginative worlds, points of views, and possibilities of transformation. See also B. Sutton-Smith and D. Kelly-Byrne, "The Masks of Play" in *The Masks of Play*, ed. B. Sutton-Smith and D. Kelly-Byrne (New York: Leisure Press, 1984), especially parts 3 and 5. The issue of power here and in Lindsey's assumption of the role of lion-tamer (as queen) deserves comparison with discussion of what effect reading tales of heroines can have on young female readers. Certain types of heroines enclose or constrict possibilities, while others promote a sense of possibility, a raised consciousness that can liberate a girl from "feeling (and therefore perhaps from being) a victim or a dependent or a drudge, someone of no account." R. M. Brownstein, *Becoming a Heroine: Reading about Women in Novels* (New York: Viking, 1982), p. xix. The paradox of the fiction of the heroine is thus that of "pride and prison" (p. 295) that can carry no final judgements regarding absolute effects. Maturation, individual differences in personality and family circumstances and community norms for age-and gender-appropriate behavior will determine the ultimate transformative potential of the literary heroine on her readers.

11. Theorists of children's play stress three general themes: "(1) play as investigation, (2) experimentation and flexibility in play, and (3) facilitating the transition from concrete to abstract thought through play." D. J. Pepler, "Play and Divergent Thinking," in *The Play of Children: Current Theory and Research*, ed. D. J. Pepler and K. H. Rubin (Basel: S. Karger, 1982), pp. 64–78. These three themes are seen in a developmental light, often as stages through which the child passes. But several important ideas are left out of such a configuration. First and foremost is affect. As L. S. Vygotsky, "Play and Its Role in the Mental Development of the Child," in *Play: Its Role in Development and Evolution*, pp. 540 and 549, explains, "Play is essentially wish fulfillment, not, however, isolated wishes but generalized affects" that are created in an imaginary situation which follows certain rules. In play the rule becomes a source of pleasure: "play gives a child a new form of desires, i.e., teaches him to desire by relating his desires to a fictious 'I'—to his role in the game and its rules. Therefore, a child's greatest achievements are made possible in play—achievements which tomorrow will become his average level of real action and morality." An overriding "rule" is that in play, meaning takes precedence and its social nature guides its internal directions. As Garvey explains, "Social play is defined here as a state of engagement in which the successive, non-literal behaviours of one partner are contin-

gent on the non-literal behaviours of the other partner. Viewed from the standpoint of either partner, this means leaving interstices in one's behaviours for the other's acts and modifying one's successive behaviours as a result of the other's acts." See C. Garvey, "Some Properties of Social Play," p. 570. The varying roles of parents in children's play have been explored in the work of Fein, who suggests that the play of the mothers she studied fell into three categories: (a) *unrelated* play in which the mother played alongside her child, (b) *imitative* playing which the mother basically copied the actions of her child, and (c) *elaborative* play in which the mother introduced subtle changes in the child's play. See G. Fein, "Play with Actions and Objects," in *Play and Learning*, ed. B. Sutton-Smith (New York: Gardner Press, 1979), pp. 69–82.

12. Individual differences in oral language learning have been well documented, but the range of such differences in learning written language far exceeds that of oral language-learning variations. Relative strength of visual over auditory memory and preference for system building over imitation as a learning style, as well as matters of motivation and interactional style, bear strong influence on the development of individual differences in both oral and written language usage. See, for example, essays in C. J. Fillmore, D. Kempler, and W. S. Wang, *Individual Differences in Language Ability and Language Behavior* (New York: Academic Press, 1979). For a discussion of differences in children's preferences for language play (with sound, vocabulary and intonation), see C. A. Ferguson and M. A. Macken, "The Role of Play in Phonological Development," in *Children's Language*, vol. 4, ed. K. E. Nelson (Hillsdale, N.J.: Erlbaum, 1983), pp. 231–254.

13. For an insightful discussion of this particular tale, see M. Meek, *How Texts Teach What Readers Learn*.

Chapter Twenty-four

The Tidy House

Carolyn Steedman

> I ain't a child and I shan't
> be a woman till I'm twenty,
> but I'm past eight, I am. I
> don't know nothing about what
> I earns in a year, I only
> knows how many pennies goes
> to a shilling, and two ha'pence
> goes to a penny. I knows too
> how many fardens goes to
> tuppence—eight.
>
> Watercress seller (eight years), 1850

Introduction: The Narrative

This is an account of three working class eight-year-old girls writing a story. They wrote the story during one week in the summer term of a social priority school classroom, four years ago. The children's first and second drafts were kept, as were the typed and edited versions that were bound and displayed, in three volumes, for classroom use. Drawings and illustrations were also kept. Altogether, the writing produced by the children amounts to about seventeen hundred words. For one day during this week a friend, a lecturer from a local training college who was in the process of collecting material for a course on child language, had a tape recorder running continuously on the table where the three girls were working. There are some four hours of recorded conversation on these tapes, conversation between us and the children, between the children themselves, to accompany the other material. There is a hum of voices in the background, a boy bends down to sing into the microphone, a bell rings, someone comes to the door, there is a class lesson about triangles, a plaster is put on a bleeding finger by one of the three girls, all is suddenly lost in clatter as the rest of the class go out to play. Taping under these conditions, some conversation has been lost. But where we talked to the three girls, and where they, infrequently, only from necessity, talked to each other about their work, there is a remarkable clarity. Later, these tapes were transcribed.

It was a very hot summer, the summer of 1976. The doors and windows of the classroom stood open to the acres of stained concrete houses stretching to the parched hills up behind the rubbish tip. The clatter of the girls' platform soles measured out the time as they moved about the classroom. The heavy air divided us, as it heightened sudden sounds and movement. It is sound and movement that form memories of that week, as well as the pieces of paper, the drawings, the words that trickle like sand from the tape recorder now.

Evidence from that week has been carried around, preserved, as if it bore the seeds of a new life, a way of explaining, a means of understanding. Yet the children's story—*The Tidy House*—is difficult material to interpret, partly because it is so totally without guile. There are no dragons for translation here, no princess sits weeping in her high tower, enchantment is not employed. The tidy house is the house that the three writers will live in one day, the streets that their characters walk to the shops through are the streets of their own decaying urban housing estate, the pattern of life described is one they know they will inhabit, the small children they create (a uniformly irritating, maddening crew) are the children they know they will have, and that their own parents think them to be. In *The Tidy House*, no one is forgiven.

The first part of the three-part story was written by Carla. Her extraordinarily accurate ear for conversation was now, at the end of her eighth year, being directly employed. The confidence and verve of her opening passage arrested me when it was first put into my hands, and still has that power, after several years, and many readings:

> One day a girl and a boy said
> Is it Springtime?
> Yes, I think so, why?
> Because we've got visitors.
> Who?
> Jamie and Jason. Here they come.
> Hello our Toby. I haven't seen you for a long time.
> Polkadot's outside and the sunflowers are bigger than us.
> Carla (eight years) (The Tidy House)

Two married couples meet here in the back garden of a council house, and they are the central characters of the story. Jo and Mark, whose tidy house it is, are childless. The couple who visit, Jamie and Jason, have a small son called Carl.[1] The plot is simple: it is concerned with the getting and regretting of children.

The childless wife Jo spoils the maddening Carl, her friend's little boy, is criticized by his mother Jamie, and gets a child to prove that she does know how to bring up children. 'She's up in competition, see?' said Carla. With grim satisfaction the three authors have Jo produce boy twins, Simon and Scott. They called the last part of *The Tidy House* 'The Tidy House that is no more a Tidy House', for obvious reasons:

The Children:

Carla

Carl

Jeannie

Lindie

Melissa

Lisa

The Characters

Carl

Jeannie

Jo and Mark

Jamie and Jason

Simon and Scott

Darren

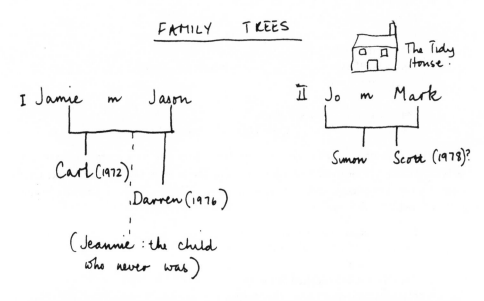

FAMILY TREES

I Jamie m Jason

Carl (1972)

Darren (1976)

(Jeannie: the child who never was)

The Tidy House.

II Jo m Mark

Simon Scott (1978)?

They saw Simon and Scott. They were one and a half, but Carl kept on pushing the twins over and making them cry. So Jamie had to sit him on her lap until it was time for the twins to go to bed, then she would put him down. So it went on like that...

Melissa (eight years) (*The Tidy House*)

Jamie, Carl's mother, produces another boy during the course of the story, and he, as he grows up, fights continually with his brother Carl. All the children produced in the story are boys. Jamie though, longs for a girl:

She wanted a girl because she had thought up a name, the name was Jeannie. Jamie adored that name, she thought it was lovely . . . Melissa (*The Tidy House*)

The extraordinary dark nights of whispering and fumbling in the getting of children, overheard by an eight-year-old girl through the thin walls of her 1930s council house bedroom, were translated into this:

> What time is it?
> Eleven o'clock at night.
> Oh no! Let's get a bed.
> OK. Night sweetheart. See you in the morning.
> Turn the light off Mark.
> I'm going to—
> Sorry.
> Alright.
> I want to get a sleep.
> Don't worry, you'll get a sleep in time.
> Don't let us, really, this time of night.
> Shall I wait till the morning?
> Oh stop it.

(Morning)
> Don't speak
> No you
> No
> Why don't you?
> Look it's all over.
> Thank you Mark.

> Mark kissed Jo. Jo kissed Mark.
>   Carla (*The Tidy House*)

The other two girls, who became co-authors after the first section of part one was written, always sought to make concrete the scenes that Carla constructed entirely by the use of conversation. They made a collage picture of the tidy house, and described it in this way:

> In the back garden there are lots of
> sunflowers. They're bigger than Jo and
> Mark. They also have rose bushes.
> They've got a dog called Toby. He is
> black with a white chest. They've got
> a rabbit called Polkadot. It's white
> and black. Now, outside their house it
> is brown on the walls and has blue
> curtains on the right side and brown
> cord on the left. On the top right
> side is fancy coloured curtains, and in
> the top left corners is brown . . .
>   Melissa (*The Tidy House*)

In the same way, Melissa tried to make visible the bedroom scene that Carla wrote at the beginning of part one. She drew a picture for the cover of the second book, the bedroom of the tidy house. There are hearts everywhere, making the shape of the lamps, the pattern on the rug, the frame of a picture on the wall, the outline of the flowers in the vase. Carla was scathing about this visual interpretation of night's desires:

> *Carla:* Miss, never seen heart flowers.
> *Teacher:* (pointing to a circle covered with hearts) That's the rug, is it?
> *Melissa:* No, that's a nest of babies.
> *Teacher:* Oh, a nest of babies! Of course, in every bedroom a nest of babies!
> *Lindie:* Course there is! (Quotes) 'What is the mother without them.'
> *Teacher:* (to Melissa) But your mum hasn't got a *nest* of children, only two . . .
> *Melissa:* No, not a nest, but she's got this big bed, and she's got all these cuddly toys around it. She's got a teddy that big . . .
>
> (transcribed conversation)

For all three children the writing of *The Tidy House* was a way of trying to understand life's mysteries. The girls knew quite well how babies were conceived and born, and they knew quite well that I knew they knew. The nest of babies was at once a serious physical metaphor, and a serious statement of their feelings about the closed bedroom door, the parental and private place. The doctor's advice to Jo (childless wife at the beginning of the story), to 'try harder' in order to conceive a child, was dealt with in a scene at once furtive and ribald, that Carla and Lindie, who both made attempts at it, knew was dirty enough to necessitate the literary euphemism of the dash, to replace the unsayable, unwriteable word. But this was not really what they were interested in. Procreation was only a means to the emotional relationship between parent and child. Forced to distance themselves from the untidiness, roughness and lack of consideration that is socially disapproved of in little girls, they bestowed these attributes upon the small boys of their story. To write of themselves they had to see themselves as grown women, bearing unbearable children. Yet when they wrote of the boy children they had created for the story, they spoke not precisely of themselves, but rather of how they knew they were often perceived by their parents.

The child Carl (small son of the visitors in the opening scene), caught in an irritated and depressing relationship with his mother, was drawn from life. Six months before *The Tidy House* was started, Carla wrote:

> On Saturday my aunt and uncle and
> my cousin Carl come up my house.
> On Sunday all of us had some ice-cream,
> but Carl would not eat it. After
> my mum cleared up, Carl wanted
> some ice-cream, but there was none
> left, and he started to cry. He
> was after biscuits all the time.
> He ate a whole tin of biscuits.
>
> Carla (diary entry)

From that plain account developed an acute observation of the emotional politics of family life:

> Jamie came over to Jo's house.
> Hello. Happy anniversary.
> Oh, you silly thing. Hang on,
> the doorbell is ringing.
>
> A boy said
>
> Is my mummy here?
> Yes. Jamie, here is Carl.
> Go home. I won't be a minute.
> No, I want to stay here.
> Alright. Stand still and shut up.
> Jamie smacked Carl. Carl started
> to cry.
> Then Mark and Jason came home.
>
> What's this then?
>
> Carl ran up and Jason picked him
> up and stopped him from crying.
> He gave Carl 10p to get an
> ice-cream when the ice-cream man
> came round.
>
> Jo said
>
> Let's have some tea.
>
> Carl said
>
> Can I have a cup of tea.
> Please please aunty Jo.
> No.
>
> So Carl started to cry.
>
> Shut up.
>
> Jason took Carl over his nan's.
> Carla (The Tidy House)

The child Carl cries a lot. A thin, persistent whine fills the pages of *The Tidy House*:

> . . . he didn't want to go home.
> He started to cry.
> > Melissa (*The Tidy House*)

> Carl came in with an ice-cream,
> he was crying.
> What's the matter?
> He dropped his ice-cream.
> > Carla (*The Tidy House*)

> He started to cry.
> Stop it now, boys don't cry
> on their birthdays, do they?
> > Carla (*The Tidy House*)

> . . . that made Carl get in a temper
> and he started to shout and Jamie
> gave him a hard smack which made
> Carl cry all the way home.
> > Melissa (*The Tidy House*)

On Carl's fourth birthday, after three crying bouts, his mother remarks in heartfelt tone:

> Tomorrow he goes to school, thank god.
> > Carla (*The Tidy House*)

The three children were almost entirely without sympathy for their creation, as their recorded commentary revealed:

Melissa: He's babyish, isn't he?
Teacher: Do you think he suspects his mum's glad to get him off to school?
Lindie: Well, in the story she said she's quite glad to get rid of him.
Carla: She probably *is*.
Lindie: His dad pampered him.
All: Yeah.
Melissa: He's spoiled. By his nan and his grandad . . .

> > (transcribed conversation)

They soften towards Carl on only one occasion, when he receives a small car as a birthday present:

> It was a small car. It was small
> as a matchbox. Carl was overjoyed.
> He fell in love with it. He was
> playing every day with it. Jamie
> had trouble in getting him to
> school. She had to let him take
> it with him.
> > Melissa (*The Tidy House*)

They watch his appealing and childish antics with an indulgent but wary eye:

> After dinner they went to Jo and
> Mark's house and had a cup of tea
> up there and a bit of cake and they
> sang happy birthday to him, and he
> got all shy and covered his eyes up
> and hid behind the chair, and when it
> was over Jo put a candle on Carl's
> bit of cake and he blew the candle out
> and they had a good time up Jo's house . . .
> Melissa (*The Tidy House*)

It is with such looks and glances that our bondage is bought. The three authors of *The Tidy House* kept their distance from Carl's pretty tricks, partly because they knew what treachery lay in the relationship forged by them. Dealing with Darren, the boy they had Jamie bear in part three of the story instead of the longed-for girl, Lindie wrote:

> The baby was called Darren and he
> was lovely. When he was four he
> and Carl were always fighting, but
> Darren never got the blame and Carl
> was always sent to bed. Carl hated
> him because he was not spoiled
> anymore, Darren was lucky 'though
> I'm not,' thought Carl.
> Lindie (*The Tidy House*)

At the end of Carl's first day at school, in part two of *The Tidy House*, he refuses to go home (having earlier refused to go into the classroom), and his mother has to carry him screaming out of the building. 'Big lump', remarked Lindie disparagingly, but Carla reached swiftly the heart of the matter, the point of having constructed the scene they were discussing: 'My mum would love us if we didn't want to come home. From school'. Carla remembered quite clearly how glad her own mother had been, four years before, to 'get (her) off to school . . . get rid of (her)'. What she understood of this memory was her mother's aching desire that her children be no longer there. Their absence was to be for no purpose. We asked Carla how many of her own sisters were still under school age:

Teacher: Who's still at home?
Carla: Jeannie.
Teacher: How old's she?
Carla: Three.
Teacher: What will your mum do when she's off to school?
Carla: Go out, I suppose—go out and get rid of us. That's what she says she's gonna do. And she's not gonna come back and she's gonna leave my dad, do all the work and he's got to go up and down to school . . .

(transcribed conversation)

Later, when two of the girls were asked why one of their characters, Mark, husband of the childless Jo, did not want children, Carla replied, 'Probably hates kids', and Lindie continued 'I think all mums do, don't they?' It is mothers who matter, whose bed is the nest of babies, who make decisions and persuade and cajole and negotiate children into life:

> *Carla:* (Jo) met Mark, and they decided to get married. And she wanted a baby from the beginning—
> *Lindie:* But he wouldn't let her—
> *Carla:* And then he sort of liked the idea . . .
>
> (transcribed conversation)

All three children, through a discussion of their own narrative, remembered their first day at school, the admonition they hand onto their own characters: " 'don't cry; if you cry you'll get bad luck" . . . ' Later, they moved to the sociology of their families. Divorces were counted, half-brothers and sisters were listed, the number of children in a family compared. Fathers were dismissed in a short list of variations. They can be flirted with and made ally against a brother. They can be absences—'comes in at eleven, goes out again'—and their sudden and violent anger at the spending of money was related to the daily mystery of their absence and the unknown process that gets money, and brings it home. Parental approval was understood to be most clearly expressed in the spending of this money on the children. Lindie was felt by the others to be the most favoured child:

> *Carla:* She does have presents. Her mum and dad spoils her when it's her birthday . . .
> *Lindie:* Yeah, I know. I get. I get . . .
> *Carla:* She gets gold chain necklaces.
> *Lindie:* Last Easter me and my brother got two whole bags of Easter eggs . . .
>
> (transcribed conversation)

What informed the writing of the three authors of *The Tidy House* was the tension that lay at the root of their life and their existence. They knew that their parents' situation was one of poverty, and that the presence of children only increased that poverty, 'if you never had no children', said Carla towards the end, 'you'd be well off, wouldn't you. You'd have plenty of money.' They knew that children were longed for, materially desired, but that their presence was irritation, regret and resentment. They knew that, in some clear and uncomplicated way, it would have been better had they never been born. But their situation, and the plot they constructed out of that situation, was complex. Carla knew quite well how to prevent children being conceived. She knew that women didn't produce babies as long as they remembered to 'take their pills'. But that wasn't the point: 'they can't help it (having babies) can they?' *The Tidy House* is about this sort of compulsion and necessity. The children's task was urgent: they needed to understand what set of social beliefs had brought them into being.

Reading the Narrative

How can a reader set about understanding a narrative like *The Tidy House*? There
are two sets of problems to consider when we as adults come to read the writings
of children. The first concerns the obvious difficulties that children, as yet imperfectly in command of written language, encounter. Our reaction to spelling mistakes, to errors in syntax, to the distortions in imagery that arise from a child's
incomplete comprehension of the world, is often expressed as a sentimental
delight in her misapprehension. This adult delight in charming childish error is
as irrelevant to an understanding of children's writing as a delight in a little girl's
pretty lisping is to an understanding of her development of spoken language.
The second set of problems is concerned with the *use* young children make of
language, both spoken and written and the part it plays in their growth and
development. It is concerned with real distinctions between the intentions of
adults and children when they come to write (or paint, or draw). The next two
sections attempt to explore our reactions as adults to the reading of children's
writing. If we are not overwhelmed by the *obvious* differences between child and
adult writing, then we will be in a position to understand what function the
child's writing is actually performing for the writer.

Children as Writers

It is easy to construct a dreadful sentimentality of intention around the words
of children, especially their written words. That there is a willing public for the
view that children are naive versions of our better selves is attested to in the sales
of books like *Mr. God, This Is Anna*, and *Children's Letters to God*. The obvious
difficulties encountered by children when they come to write create, in their turn,
problems for adult readers when they come to consider the work of children.
Children may be hampered by poor writing skills, and by an inability to spell,
though truly, in the history of child writing, not many have been hindered in this
way, except when adult strictures upon handwriting and spelling have made
their task impossible. The reaction of adult readers to such errors poses a much
greater problem. When the adolescent Opal Whitely translated the scraps of her
childhood diary into *The Journal of an Understanding Heart* (Whitely, 1918, 1920;
Bede, 1954; Bradburne, 1962) she was careful to leave (and perhaps to create)
many artless and saleable spelling mistakes in her new text: 'the mama where I
live says I am a new sance (sic) I think it is something that grown ups don't like
to have around.' (Whitely, 1920). Later editors have continued to find such errors
'charming' (Boulton 1976a, 1976b)—the editorial equivalent of chucking little
girls under the chin to see them smile. This sentimental reaction sometimes displayed by adults towards the words of children does actually stand in the way
of interpreting the purposes of children when they write. By concentrating on the

surface differences between child and adult writing, readers can, in a warm and naive affection for the deficiencies of child writing, actually trivialize an important means of growth.

Children with extremely limited reading and writing skills can nevertheless use written words in a deliberate and highly structured way. I remember a story written by a nine-year-old boy with a reading age of barely six who had been profoundly influenced by the tale *Tripple-Trapple* (Manning-Sanders, 1973). He disguised his own child and wife-battering father as the devil—the iron pot of the tale—and his mother and sisters as rabbits (echoes of a gentler stimulus than *Tripple-Trapple*). With these simple metaphors he recounted assault, kidnapping, a desperate fear of rejection and hope of rescue. In the end the black iron pot was shot to pieces by a man with a gun, the man who had by then come to live with his mother.

The child who wrote that story could never have *said* what were the limitations placed on his life by others, could not, in any clear way, have *thought* about his family's pathology. He manipulated the symbols of his fears as seriously and as intentionally as children play, and the words provided the means to reflexion, to speculation, the route to conscious thought.

To use the written word in this way, children need to be operating at some level of literary competence. They need to have some understanding of conventional orthography and its relation to the phonological and lexical bases of our language. The child needs to know what it means to write, and that what she has written can be read. She needs to be able to read and write just well enough to operate independently. That we as readers put a wider interpretation on the activity of writing than this, and know that her functioning is (for the time being) minimal, is not the point at all.

When children's writing is to be read by adults and other children, then child writers need editors. In both cases an editor of children's writing needs an acquaintance with the categories of verbal and written linguistic error that children of that age commonly make, and some knowledge of local dialect. The purposes of the editions for children and adults are different, though. When children's writing is corrected in school this is done partly so that other children can use it as reading material, and so that conventional orthography and syntactic structure can be emphasized. This method is also used to help the child writer to spell and structure written language (Goddard, 1974). But the editor who corrects surface errors in child writing (and editing here emphatically does *not* mean cutting) for an adult audience is performing more of a translator's role. Ideally, adult readers should have access to both the child's unedited text and a sympathetic and revealing edition of that text. In this way the reader can be helped over a concentration on the obvious and superficial features of the text and gain easier access to its purpose and meaning.

Children do often, though, have to be asked what they meant by their writing. I typed the final version of part one of *The Tidy House* from Carla's draft, here reproduced:

the tidy houses

One day a girl and a boy

said is it spring-time. Yes!

I think so, why, because

we've got visiter. who!

Jamie and Jason, here thay

I spent a whimsical few minutes interpreting 'pockadots' (sic) (which Carla had told me before the end of school was 'polkadots') as some version of sunspots dancing in the garden around the burgeoning sunflowers. I was told next morning that Polkadot was a rabbit, and I think that Melissa was prompted to write her strictly factual guide to the tidy house as a prophylactic against such romanticism. Yet an editor cannot always seek a child's opinion. I decided to put the conversation between Carla's characters on the page without quotation marks, because she used what they were saying to control and structure events in a way that Lindie and Melissa didn't. She rarely indicated in her text who was speaking, and in some sense this device was deliberately used, for she knew what quotation marks were, and could employ them to some extent. There is meaning here in this manner of writing that is more useful to adults in interpreting children's perceptions of the world than it was to the child who wrote the words. Indeed, for this aspect of Carla's text to have become pedagogically useful to her it would have been best to have put in the speech marks, returned her typed and punctuated text to her, and helped her to learn from it.

come. Hollow! our toby.

I havent seen you for a long

time. Pock adots out Side

and the sun flowers are bigger

than us, mark lets go and

see. ok. look Pockadots

had babys.

Children's Writing As Art

We read children's writing for more than the means to pedagogy, or the fleeting and indulgent smile. We need to read it as well for evidence of individual psychologies in certain social circumstances, and the fact that some child writing offers better evidence than others delineates the second and more difficult problem in reading it. Carla had a fine ear for conversation. Developed, encouraged, well-taught, Carla could come later in life to write very well indeed. Some children do write better than others, and their success and effectiveness depends not on a fast and legible joined hand, nor on a mastery of our spelling system, nor on an ability to maintain continuity over involved linguistic structures (though all these features are of enormous usefulness to young writers, and must be taught). Their success and effectiveness depend rather on their ability to *know* the symbols they are manipulating, to have some understanding of, some control over, their meaning. Our difficulties as readers of children's work must not confuse our appreciation of their writing with the function it actually serves for children. This second problem that adults encounter as readers is similar to the one that Graham Greene encountered when writing about the books of Beatrix Potter (Greene, 1970). What prompted this essay of 1933 was Greene's observation that they are finely wrought, well-written, satisfyingly constructed books. These are the very elements that lead us into believing them to be more than they really are—more than just books for small children. Greene's problem was how to speak of these features. His use of conventional critical terminology—'comedy', 'tragedy', writing intimately of 'the saga' and 'an elusive style, difficult to analyse'—achieved its satiric effect only by wrenching the books away from their contents, and form away from meaning. Greene knew this of course, which is why his essay is at once very informative, and very misleading. But this simple problem can be avoided: when discussing the writing of those who for whatever the reason are outside the mainstream of conventional literary production (children, writers for children) the technical vocabulary of conventional critical terminology can be avoided. Indeed, in the case of children's writing, it must be avoided, for these terms do not relate at all to the actual functions of this writing for the children who produce it. Instead, we must, without literary preconceptions, find out what those functions are.

In their written words children may manipulate and rearrange the symbols of their social circumstances. But if words are the means by which they can act, and become powerful, the world itself remains obdurate. Indeed, children do not write to act upon and change the world, (though they may reveal that they wish the world were different, things not as they are), and a consideration of the precise usefulness of written language to children must take us a long way from conventional ideas derived from adult literary and fictional production. Children do not have an audience in mind when they write, nor a set of assumptions that they share with that audience about the ability of literature to bring about altered states of mind. Children's writing is useful to the children who produce it in a way that it is not useful to the adults who read it (which is not to say at all that it isn't useful to us in other ways). Like a child's first spoken language, written language enables her to do what she would not otherwise be able to do.

Early language development gives young children access to a symbolic representation of the world, a system that they can manipulate and change and restructure in an attempt to take hold of its meaning (Brown, 1976). The errors in English tense structure that most who have had anything to do with young children have noticed are the clearest example of children's use and abandonment of theories within a symbolic structure: the most common verbs in English have irregular past tenses ('I went', 'she saw'), yet young children generalize the rule for 'ed' endings and use constructions like 'ranned' and 'rided', which they have never heard from adults. They do this out of their own reflection on our language system, and it is a helpful though not altogether satisfactory analogy to see child language—their use of rules and meanings—as a kind of foreign language that can be studied and understood in its own right and that must not be confused with our own. It may well be that access to written language allows children to construct and discard theories, and to reflect on form and meaning in much the same way as access to spoken language does.

If this is the case, it becomes clear that it is particularly important not to *equate* child writing (and child art in general) with adult art. As long as we do not see child writing (or drawing, or painting) as the same *order* of production as adult art, then we are free to use it as a window onto child development, free to know that it is not significant that some pieces of work are more appealing, seem better than others. In this way we can view child writing as a means of growth available to all children, work wrought by its own internal rules, as we see a child's first sentences having structure and validity in their own right, and not just as some imperfect version of adult production.

Of course, the second, and most difficult problem still remains: some children do write better than others. It is not enough simply to agree with Berger's point about the differences between child and adult art (in this case, painting): 'A work of art must be born of conscious intention and striving: and the spectator . . . must be able to infer this. A child paints simply to grow up . . . The adult paints in order to create something outside himself in order to add to and . . . alter life' (Berger, 1979). There are two reasons for going beyond this important insight. There lies within it the adult desire for a state of innocence in children and the road to our sentimentality: Berger calls children's paintings 'almost natural objects' and likens them to 'a flower'. Secondly, by seeing in child art only an absence of the intention that informs adult art, it gives us no way of exploring what children are actually up to when they manipulate the symbols of their world in drawings (or words). But when we do understand how children can use the symbolic representation of written language to change and manipulate their experience, then we are free to see that questions of ability, of talent, of writing well, are *our* problems and questions, not the problems of the child writer, and that to create in us these impulses of literary appreciation was nowhere near her intention. Knowing this, it is then possible to talk about *The Tidy House* as a rare piece of child writing, to acknowledge that it is powerful and revealing and important.

The tension in child writing that we adult readers may then perceive—the knowledge that children grow up, that this symbolic representation is of its very nature transitory, that in the end nearly all of us stop saying that 'Goldilocks woked up and ranned away'—will then help us to understand that a child who has chosen to rearrange the pieces of her life, not with a doll, nor a skipping game, nor a smashed tower of bricks, but as *words*, has chosen to rearrange them in a highly deliberate way. Then her writing can be seen as being as serious, and as intentional, and as purposeful as play. Then we, in our different way, through the glass of distance and forgetfulness, half-remembering our own lost childhood, can ask at last, what understanding of social circumstances it was that prompted the writing of *The Tidy House*.

Understanding the Narrative

The Tidy House is unlike much of the writing that children produce in order to think about their condition. Nobody here is represented as dragon, or giant, no dreadful possibility is clothed as black witch. It does not follow the conventional three-part pattern of the folk fairy tale—assault on a given situation, striving, resolution—(Bettelheim, 1978) that many children use as a model for their story writing. Much of the secret and self-exploratory writing produced by girls and women in the past has been in journal form (Moffat and Painter, 1975), and by far the largest category of writing that children in contemporary British primary schools are asked to produce is diary writing. But *The Tidy House* does not proceed step by step through the simple past tense listing of events that is the feature of school diary writing. By constructing a story with no matter what bare bones of their daily life, the children were able to move away from an account of their immediate social reality, to an investigation of what would be the pattern of their future.

By her use of conversation to direct the narrative Carla did actually bring the story of *The Tidy House* directly into the present. It is not so much as if her characters, talking, shouting, quarrelling, smacking, provide an allegory of her own life, or of what she knew her life and the life of other working class girls would be, but rather as if they stand as constant, formless and insistent commentators on what already *is*. The characters are never described; we know nothing of what they wear, nor the colour of their hair, nor what they hand over to each other as anniversary gifts. What the children chose to make visually substantial was the tidy house itself, and the rooms within it.

The writing of children, bearing direct testimony to their daily lives, as *The Tidy House* does, is rarely to be found. It is rarer still from the nineteenth century, yet there are diaries extant, written by children, from this time (Sidgwick, 1934; Creighton, 1967). The voices they transmit are overwhelmingly female voices, for journal keeping was viewed as a suitable pedagogic device for the instruction of small girls. All these female voices are middle class, and to look for continuity in working class girls' perceptions of their society, and their future place in it, it is necessary to look to those nineteenth century social investigators who spoke to children and who took some pains to record their words directly. It is important to do this, not just for the making of neat historical analogies, but because within a historical period when many of the theories that are currently dominant about childhood were created, the metaphors that poor girl children have used to comment on their own socialization and in order to think about their future as women, have remained remarkably consistent.

The tension between the physical desire for babies—the looks, the glances, their pretty ways—and the weariness and burden of their presence that informs every page of *The Tidy House*, is present in the words of the little girls that Henry Mayhew spoke to on the streets of London a century and a half ago. It is important to remember that these children's spoken words, like the written words of

The Tidy House were extracted by means of a relationship within the context of which the children felt able to speak. For the transcribed words of the Victorian street children, the relationship was swiftly made, and soon over. For the middle class investigator the relationship with the children he spoke to was partly built on his fascinated repulsion from their wild hair and broken boots (Mayhew, 1851: 477). Mayhew felt too, though, the charm of his subjects' smiles, the prettiness of their frowns (Mayhew, 1861–62: 506). This genteel paedophilia, soon to set many middle class gentlemen taking photographs of appealing little girls in tumbled clothing (Ovenden and Melville, 1972) may possibly have shaped part of Mayhew's response to the small girls he spoke with; but whatever propelled his warmth, the children felt it, and talked to him not only out of deference and in expectation of the coin to be handed over when the shorthand notebook was shut. The importance of this testimony then, when linked with *The Tidy House* is to show that whilst the material conditions for a childhood of poverty may alter to some degree, children's reactions to such circumstances follow a distinct pattern. Little girls take part in the process of their own socialization, as they have done in the recent past.

All three writers displayed a reluctance to speculate on their story. We talked to the children about their writing, but that conversation, easy on the surface, familiar, friendly, is empty really. Some essential point was not grasped, there was something we did not understand. Was it that like Mayhew, speaking to the watercress seller whose words open this article, we found ourselves undone in the face of experience without knowledge, adulthood without an individual history, a world measured out by restrictions and limitations? 'I did not know how to talk with her', said Mayhew of that nineteenth century eight-year-old. At first I treated her as a child, speaking on childish subjects, (but she) was indeed in thoughts and manner, a woman . . . ' (Mayhew, 1851: 151).

The girls' discussion of *The Tidy House*, even when it centred on aspects of the narrative not yet written, was couched in the present and past tenses:

> *Teacher:* What did Jo do before she got married?
> *Carla:* Dunno.
> *Lindie:* She's a typist. My aunt used to be a typist.
> (transcribed conversation)

Result was confused with intention:

> *Melissa:* We thought . . . um, that, er Jamie would have a boy, and Carl and the boy—the little boy—always used to have fights. And then, and then . . .
> *Teacher:* Why do all these people have these babies?
> *Melissa:* Then Carl won't be pampered then, will he?
> (transcribed conversation)

Their story was not a means of talking about the future, for there was no future. Their lives had already been lived. Yet within this sad certitude—the modern reader turns away, conventional developmental psychology cannot let us see the writers as anything but children, their obsession seems unchildlike, a kind of neurosis—the authors of *The Tidy House* acted upon the story of their life, and the symbol for the greatest restriction, the baby, became the arena for the greatest play of imaginative freedom.

Babies played the largest role in the imaginations of the Victorian street children too. The girls of the 1850s remembered a baby fed and cared for, a badly-missed little sister, the heart-trapping smiles of infancy, feeding a baby—the only work they didn't call work:

> I had to take care of a baby for my
> aunt. No, it wasn't heavy—it was
> two months old; but I minded it
> for ever such a long time, till it could
> walk. It was a very nice little baby,
> not a pretty one; but if I touched it
> under the chin, it would laugh.
>> Watercress seller (8 years) (Mayhew, 1851: 151–153).

> I hadn't to do any work, only just
> clean the room and nuss the child.
> It was a nice little thing.
>> Crossing sweeper (13 years, remembering her eleventh year)
>>> (Mayhew, 1861–162: 506).

> I never had no doll, but I misses
> little sister—she's only two years old.
>> Watercress seller (8 years) (Mayhew, 1851: 151–153).

These ties of affection and responsibility are made early in life, as the writers of *The Tidy House* knew. But in what they wrote there is not only a sad account of the way in which working class girls become working class women. It is not just an account of the tension in which girl children find themselves, the dichotomy of being born, and at the same time able to bear a child. *The Tidy House* had a context in the other writing that the children produced. Carla, especially, frequently touched on the question of freedom in her writing. In one narrative finished a month before *The Tidy House* was started, she dealt at greater length with the possibilities of action for women. In the story *Jack Got the Sack* all the children are girls.

> Jack, Jack, got the sack.
> 'Oh Jack, go to work please
> to get some money for the children.'
> 'Oh, alright.'
> 'Bye.'

> Jack came back soon,
> at half past two.
> Jack got the sack.

> 'Jack, you've got the sack.'
> 'I've got the sack.'

'What are we going to do now?'
'Don't ask me.'

Jack went to every place he could think of.
He got back home at five o'clock.

'I can't get a job now.'

Jeannie his wife said
'I don't care. Just get a job Jack.
We'll starve to death.'

They had a row, and Jeannie left Jack,
the girls came too.

Oh how sad Jeannie was.

She got a job as a barmaid,
it was good money at £20 a week.
Jeannie bought Lindie a bike to ride
and Melissa a doll and their friend
Lisa a dog. They were happy for ever after.
Carla (Jack Got the Sack)

Another story written after *The Tidy House* was completed was the only one in which during that school year she used any image, any metaphor. *Flower Lady* was the only writing she ever produced that did not follow her own life on parallel tracks of commentary:

One day Flower Lady went for a walk.
She was sad because she had no friends.
She sang a sweet song and it went like
this: No friends, no meat, no food to
eat, at least I've got to have some wheat.
That's what she sang going along the road.
Flower Lady lived in a den with chairs
and tables, happily.
One evening when it was very dark,
Flower Lady sang the sweetest song
she'd ever made. It went like this:
My name is Flower Lady. You may like
me. Maybe you like me better than a
bee, and I love trees and bumble bees.
Then she went to bed and had a dream
about songs and laughter.
O, what a night.
Carla (Flower Lady)

Perhaps she remembered here a grandfather who had died the previous autumn. He had been living rough, not allowed into the tidy house by his daughter. Carla's mother. His body had been found in a little den that he had constructed on some waste land. Carla entering the classroom, her face incoherent with weeping, writing what she could not say:

> My grandad is dead he's about 60 or
> 61 he is going to be buried on Tuesday
> at ten o'clock. It makes you feel funny
> when a cat dies and two grandads dead
> actually two cats died one cat we had
> is in the shop it had diahorrea so one
> dog and forty three pigeons I did have
> seven dogs four went to the poodle parlour
> my nan had one . . .
>
> Carla (diary entry)

If her grandfather provided the fleeting image of freedom discernible in her story, then memories of him provided the elegaic self-containment of the song that Flower Lady sang. Image and desire move across children's writing like dreams, as they name imaginary children after their friends, make boy children depositories of all that is disapproved of in themselves, and heap indulgence on their more favoured creations as they long for such indulgence to be extended to them.

It is often the case, as we have seen, that this imagery seems dull and stark, a fantasy constructed out of the workaday, the dull, the uneventful. I think we found it harder to see that Carla's face only really became animated when she spoke of clothes, the unbearableness of flat-heeled sandals (in a summer of platform soles), the appropriate garb for a funeral, the desirability of a velvet top, than did Mayhew to hear how the watercress seller describe how she kept herself clothed:

Carla: She had to go (to a funeral) all in blue, she never had no black shoes. Don't wear black anyway, do you?
Second: No, I went to a funeral the
Teacher: other day, and there was nobody in black.
Carla: Dark blue's next to black, because my mum bought a dark blue top and a dark blue skirt and it came to twenty quid. And my dad went mad—just over a funeral.

(transcribed conversation)

Carla: I'm wearing my blue and white t-shirt, alright; and I was looking for my velvet top; and I couldn't find it, right, and it was underneath this one, but I went past it, the velvet top and my mum went up there, and *she* went past it, so I had to wear this one . . .

(transcribed conversation)

> All my money I puts into a club
> and draws it out to buy clothes
> with. It's better than spending
> it on sweet stuff for them that

has a living to earn.
        Watercress seller (Mayhew, 1851: 152).

Conventional developmental psychology has taught us to expect more than this from children now. Within the context of contemporary theories of childhood, children confound us when they speak, as the watercress seller did, and as the writers of *The Tidy House* do, not of childhood, nor of adulthood, but of some serious preparation for the latter, of some attitudes and beliefs wrought out of material so threadbare and poverty-stricken that they seem no more able to keep a soul warm than did the watercress seller's shawl her body.

What we are left with in this case, are some children's words, and we need some way of interpreting them that is both helpful and uncondescending. When there are no dragons, no frogs to kiss as metaphors, then we must look at the words, and the linguistic and social structures that support those words. The three girls' ability to think about the circumstances of their lives, to speculate and reflect, was rooted in the very restrictions that prompted the writing of *The Tidy House*. The long hours spent in adult female company, the walks to the shops, up and down to the nursery school, visits, cups of tea—'stand still and shut up'—all that listening, gave the children access to a symbolic form of this life, that they could manipulate and change, in written words.

The way in which little girls are taught to be aware of how they look to others, to set themselves at a distance from their own charm and pretty ways (Moers, 1978: 197) can, under certain circumstances, be translated into that most fundamental impulse to creation: the knowledge that whilst we are as we know ourselves, we are also most profoundly as others see us. The children knew that whilst it was their fathers who created many of the conditions of restriction in their lives, it was their mothers who fashioned the chains—they who told them to stand still and shut up, who longed for them only in order to dress them up and because girls' names are so pretty. But out of these circumstances, they were able to find the possibility of power for women.

The long hours of listening had already, long ago, played their part in making the girls' preference for staying in, negotiating the world in an indirect way:

Teacher: What's going to happen to all these people?
Melissa: We're going to have another book. Four books.
Lindie: We're going to try four books. So at playtime can just we three stay in and
    do the next one?
Teacher: Yes, I think so.

                                            (transcribed conversation)

Power had been derived from that listening. The rhythms and cadences of spoken language had been translated and contracted by Carla into the strongly alliterative way in which she wrote. The structure of her particular narrative, propelled not by what people did, nor by what happened next, but by what they said to each other, offers an insight into child development, restricted, altered, made meaningful by precise social and historical circumstances.

The testimony of the three authors of *The Tidy House* rests not just on the enabling interest of a friendly adult (the Victorian street children, briefly, had that), but more importantly on their ability to write. Reflecting on language, they were able to reflect on their own circumstances in a way that the Victorian working class girls could not. What Mayhew noticed in the children he spoke to was their inability to see themselves through other people's eyes (Mayhew, 1851: 480; 481; 487); but what the children who wrote *The Tidy House* were able to understand was that they existed in other people's image of them as well as in their experience of themselves. Knowing this, they could assess their relationship with the world, and find it wanting.

The very narrative of *The Tidy House* is a way of placing events in time, of moving the meaningful symbols into new order. This order may seem to us dull and sad, and we move away, like Mayhew did, in despair and confusion from children who have seen so clearly where they are bound to go. Yet the circumstances of restriction carry within them the means to change: little girls, should the circumstances permit, can work together, and using the very qualities that their lives have taught them—quietness, the ability to listen and to see themselves as they are seen by others—can think about their lives, and deal in terms of change.

> My sister is the youngest
> I am the eldest.
> My mum works in town
> With all my family
> And leaves my little sister
> In the arm
> Of me.
>
> Carla.

NOTES

Carolyn Steedman was born in 1947 and grew up in south London. She studied history at Sussex and Cambridge and has been a primary school teacher for seven years. A book also entitled *The Tidy House* will be published by Virago in 1989. It will include a facsimile of the children's story.

1. The interrelation of names in *The Tidy House* may make this as difficult to read as it was for me to transcribe. Apart from fashion, which dictated the naming of the characters (1976 was the first summer of Jamie Summers, the Bionic Woman) it is important that Carl is the masculine of Carla, and that Jeannie is at once the name of a longed-for girl child, Carla's own younger sister, and the independent woman of *Jack Got the Sack*.

REFERENCES

Bede, Ellery (1954) *Fabulous Opal Whiteley* Portland, Oregon: Binfords and Mort.
Berger, John (1979) *Permanent Red: Essays in Seeing* London: Writers and Readers.

Bettelheim, Bruno (1978) *The Uses of Enchantment* London: Penguin.

Boulton, Jane (1976a) 'Stories for Free Children: The Story of Opal' *MS* 55.

Boulton, Jane (1976b) *Opal* London: Macmillan.

Bradburne, Elizabeth (1962) *Opal Whitely: The Unsolved Mystery* London: Putnam.

Brown, Roger (1976) *A first Language* London: Penguin Education.

Creighton, Ellen R. C. (1967) *Ellen Buxton's Journal* London: Geoffrey Bles.

Goddard, Nora (1974) *Literacy: Language Experience Approaches* London: Macmillan Educational.

Greene, Graham (1970) *Collected Essays* London: Penguin.

Mayhew, Henry (1851) *Life and Labour of the London Poor* Vol. I London: Cass & Co. (1967).

Mayhew, Henry (1861–62) *Life and Labour of the London Poor* Vol. II London: Cass & Co. (1967).

Manning-Sanders, Ruth (1973) *Tripple-Trapple* London: BBC.

Moers, Ellen (1978) *Literary Women* London: The Women's Press.

Moffat, Mary Jane and Painter, Charlotte (1975) *Revelations: Diaries of Women* New York: Random House.

Ovenden, Graham and Melville, Robert (1972) *Victorian Children* London: Academy Editions.

Sidgwick, Frank (1934) *The Complete Marjory Fleming* London: Sidgwick and Jackson.

Whiteley, Opal (1918) *The Fairyland Around Us* Los Angeles: Opal Stanley Whiteley.

Whiteley, Opal (1920) *The Journal of an Understanding Heart* Boston: The Atlantic Monthly Press.

Part IV

Sourcebook

Introduction

The child is often a figment of the adult imagination, a figure of adult desire, a focus of adult anxiety, and the object of adult political struggles. Advice literature aimed at parents often promises the "truth" about the child, telling us what we need to do in order to raise a child who is mentally, physically, psychologically, and socially healthy. The assumptions underlying that advice often draw upon the latest "scientific" understandings, explaining what the experts now "know" about children's needs and development. Yet, advice literature is shaped by larger historical forces. Culturally specific assumptions surface in the ways writers define the problems new parents must confront, describe the desired outcomes of good parenting, and characterize the power relations between children and adults. Often, advice literature embraces specific utopian images of the future—images of social, cultural, or political transformation—that it hopes to facilitate by shaping our children's development. Other times, the literature polices gender or sexual relations within the family according to what is perceived as "best for children." Some of these passages rationalize adult attempts to control and regulate children, to shape their development according to our needs and agendas. Others figure the child through a discourse of freedom and democracy, protecting its innocence from the corruption of adult politics, so that the child may become a figure of cultural transformation—offering a fresh start on solving our most vexing problems and, in some cases, the last hope for human survival.

The Workbook section of *The Children's Culture Reader* is intended to provide concrete illustrations of the role child-rearing texts play in social construction of the child. We want to encourage readers to look closely and critically at what gets taken for granted in our writing about children. What follows will be a series of short, yet suggestive, excerpts from primary documents, mostly from the advice books and magazine essays aimed at young parents. Each of these passages shows how historical forces impact our most banal writing about children. Writing about children permeates twentieth-century culture, and yet, because of its very pervasiveness, it has rarely been scrutinized. My goal here is to "defamiliarize" child-rearing texts, to remove them from their original contexts and to encourage closer attention to their underlying assumptions.

Shaping Children's Desires for Consumer Culture

The rise of consumer culture in the late nineteenth and early twentieth centuries had an enormous impact upon the family. The emerging discipline of child psychology provided invaluable resources for advertisers. Each new insight into the child's development offered them a new pressure point that could be used to encourage the early development of consumption habits. E. Evalyn Grumbine reviews some of the latest discoveries and suggests ways advertisers might use them to sell products. Jess H. Wilson outlines the characteristics associated with boy culture in the modern era, making the boy a figure of the dynamic qualities of early twentieth-century life. If child psychology represented one of the core knowledge bases that advertisers would exploit in marketing goods, it should not be surprising to discover that families also sought to tap into the tools and resources of consumer culture to achieve their own goals. This section from *The Mothers' Own Book* advised parents to employ marketing techniques to improve their children's nutrition.

Chapter Twenty-five

Reaching Juvenile Markets
(1938)

Evalyn Grumbine

Selling to boys and girls has one very great advantage over selling to adults. The natural enthusiasm of youth is an important factor which acts in favor of any manufacturer appealing to boys and girls. The serious business of living does not touch children except in extreme poverty. As a result, all their natural joy of living is put into everything they do and is evidenced in their reactions to their various activities.

An understanding of children, of their physical and mental development, their likes and dislikes, and their reactions to the rapidly changing conditions of living today, will help manufacturers to plan better advertising campaigns to juveniles. . . .

The collecting instinct is almost universal. From about three years of age the child begins to acquire small objects of various kinds. The greatest activity is between eight and fifteen years, with the ten-year-old probably the most intensive collector. Boys will collect such things as cigar bands, stamps, birds' eggs, marbles, shells, buttons, rocks, while girls collect the same objects and add miniature objects, dolls, books, leaves, pressed flowers, bits of ribbon, and feathers. Objects of nature are especially popular with boys and girls.

From about eight until twelve years, the height of the collecting period, the number of collections increase and a genuine interest is apparent. From twelve years on the activity resolves itself chiefly in crazes such as collecting pictures of movie stars, match boxes, and the like. The methods of obtaining change with growth.

The Procter & Gamble Co. enrolled hundreds of thousand of boys and girls in the "Ivory Stamp Club of the Air." A stamp album and 50 assorted stamps were offered separately for 6 wrappers from Ivory soap. Later, special packets of stamps were offered for four wrappers and a 2-cent stamp. The stamp club and offers of stamps continued throughout the entire program over the air despite the fact that special contests giving other prizes were offered at various times. Children enjoy the interesting stories about foreign countries and the fun of collecting stamps and of belonging to the club.

This collecting instinct has prompted boys and girls to insist that mother buy all the cutout packages in the series used for Post Toasties. It is a fundamental appeal which certain advertisers have recognized for many years as evidenced by the series of birds, flags, national heroes, presidents, and many other subjects which have been reproduced in card, circular, or medallion form and packed with manufacturers' products.

There is nothing in a child's environment that escapes his notice. He will imitate everything from the barking of a puppy to the blowing of a steamboat whistle. "Playing house" is developed around the activities he sees in his own home.

"Playing grownup" never ceases to intrigue girls and boys. Girls delight in wearing a discarded evening gown, an old picture hat with trailing plumes, and a pair of high-heeled dancing slippers because it makes them feel that they look just like mother. While boys are not so greatly interested, they are quick to don a cowboy outfit, Indian suit, or fireman's helmet whenever the opportunity presents itself. A stick may serve as a horse and the antics of these juvenile cowboys include the yells and whoops of the rider while the make-believe horse bucks and gallops. . . .

Children do not imitate adults alone. What other boys and girls do is always of great interest. Thousands of packages of prepared chocolate drinks are sold because boys and girls want to do what Betty Jane and Gene are doing in campaigns directed to them through radio, comic strips, and juvenile magazines. Advertisers of many other products have found that an appeal to the imitative impulses of boys and girls has meant increased sales. . . .

Nothing interests a child more than how things are made. He wonders how the stars and moon are made, how stones and birds and flowers are made. Breaking open toys, unscrewing fastenings, opening alarm clocks, experimenting to find out what will happen if this or that is done to a certain object all appear to be destructive activities in the eyes of the average adult.

The true motive is usually overlooked. Such curiosity is a normal outgrowth of intellectual craving and a demand for mental food and may be secured only by personal experiences, questions, and observations. From two to four, little ones taste everything, edible or otherwise. From five to ten, children usually experiment with mixtures of both food and drink.

About a year later the adolescent starts testing and tries all kinds of combinations of foods including anything new that appears on the bill of fare. The natural desire of growing children to test new sensations for themselves is evidenced also in the smoking craze which usually occurs in boys between eight and ten and a year earlier in girls. Bark, seeds, leaves—in fact anything that will burn is tried and unpleasant effects do not daunt their experimenting. . . .

What this offers to the advertiser is obvious—an opportunity to secure the interest of these juveniles by giving them something worth while in the form of real information and interesting facts attractively presented which will capture and hold their attention. The California Fruit Growers Exchange has long recognized the value of furnishing authentic interesting information in the excellent educational material which they have been distributing to children through the schools. Attractive booklets, circulars, and colorful wall charts tell the story of how oranges and lemons are grown and prepared for market. They satisfy the natural curiosity of boys and girls about how familiar objects such as the orange and lemon are brought into their homes. Familiarity with the Sunkist trade-mark is a natural result.

Productive imagination is of the utmost importance. All progress depends on the power of reconstructing something old into something new. Because it is one of the most precious abilities of the human race and should be developed to the highest possible degree, campaigns to boys and girls should be planned in a constructive manner that will not only accomplish the desired results in sales of the advertised product, but will also perform a real service and be the means of creating unlimited and enduring good will for the company. . . .

A good storyteller enjoys having young listeners hanging breathless on every word; children respond with shrieks of joy as the story ends and may play it over and over again. But when they are alone at night in the dark, the joy experienced in the daylight with playmates turns into terror. These facts should be seriously considered by advertisers because the bad effects on children of overly sensational programs, of poor illustration, ungrammatical language, and crime movies have so aroused parents and educators that they are now taking active steps to keep their children from these influences whenever possible. Obviously the advertiser defeats his own purpose if he offends the adult to such an extent that parents will refuse to allow children to have his product because of the antipathy aroused by this type of advertising.

An outstanding example of capitalizing imagination in the right way is shown in the success of one of the programs sponsored by the R. B. Davis Company, manufacturer of Cocomalt, which featured Buck Rogers and his adventures in the twenty-fifth century over the air. It had an educational aspect, and while it included thrilling adventures it did not indulge in disturbing horrors. In line with the educational part of the program, a planetary map was offered so that juvenile listeners could follow the adventures of Buck Rogers, hero, and Wilma Deering, heroine, of the dramatized serial. Thousands of requests for the planetary map were received weekly, each one accompanied by a strip from a can of Cocomalt. . . .

One reason why so many advertisers have resorted to the ultrathrilling themes in air programs is that any other program may fall flat. An advertiser making tests to find a plan for the next year used stories from the classics—which had enough action to hold interest provided they were properly presented. But the test fell flat because too much time was devoted to moralizing.

There has been a great deal of hokum and trickery in some of the campaigns addressed to boys and girls. But it does not pay, as manufacturers have found out. Children are much smarter than adults give them credit for being. They discover when they are being taken advantage of just because they are youngsters and, if they feel that they have been cheated, an advertiser will lose loyalty that can never be replaced.

Chapter Twenty-six

Does Your "Research" Embrace the Boy of Today?

(1922)

Jess H. Wilson

Study the boy of today. He is a tight-mouthed little materialist, "wise" beyond belief, keen enough in his knowledge of human nature to present toward his parents the side that his parents desire, and going so far and no further. . . .

Speed is his keynote. Mediums of speed that we saw develop from the idea to the actuality are the basis from which he begins to think. To him nothing is impossible. He looks forward to 300 miles an hour with confidence, when to us sixty was something to be spoken of with awe. While he may read some of our boyhood literary favorites because it is good policy in his relations with his parents, down in his heart it is "old stuff." New stories have a hold on him, those involving the modern methods of speed, of wireless, flying, even mental telepathy. Fairy tales mean little in his young life, for the actualities he sees exceed them. Because he is a realist and materialist, the boy of today works on the principle of "cause and effect." He analyzes. His mind really thinks, quickly.

Instead of a district school, he attends an institution far, far ahead of the facilities of the district school, and yet, when it is possible to overhear his discussion of the school and his teachers, you will learn that he has a surprisingly keen knowledge of the powers politic, and unerringly places a lot of blame for conditions that do not seem "fair" to him on "politics." . . . He knows that the blind selfishness of his parents permits such conditions to exist. The older folks are a trust for the suppression of youth, but he aims to bust it when he gets older. . . .

Chapter Twenty-seven

"Selling" Food To Children
The Mother's Own Book (1928)

There is no doubt about it, the competition which exists between the corner store and the home for the patronage of the youthful public is just about putting the average parent out of business. Perhaps you have noticed that the demand for spinach tends to fall off despite constant appeals. As for oatmeal, your young customers don't drop in for a dish of it more than once a month.

And while good old-fashioned, wholesome foods are wasting on the shelves of the home shop, the crowd of boys and girls at the corner store grows larger and more enthusiastic each day. Soda water can't be squirted fast enough. There is a constant pop, and clink, and gurgle of busy pop bottles. And the candy which was once sold in tiny bags is now carried away in cartons like so many sacks of flour.

It almost seems as though, what with the chain stores and national advertising against them, the only step left for the parents of the country is to form a merger and get some system into their business.

Getting down to business, let us imagine that you, the parent, are the unsuccessful salesman, while your adolescent child, who is really not a child but a brilliant young man or woman, is the disinterested customer. You have already made several suggestions regarding a valuable dish of spinach you have for sale, but each time your approaches have been turned down. You have even gone so far as to tell your customer that if he or she does not eat his or her spinach, he or she will not grow up to be a healthy boy or girl. (We hope you haven't really said that. If you have, you might just as well stop reading this right now, for not even I can save you.) Or perhaps you have approached your rather stubborn customer with the proposition that if he or she will eat the beautiful spinach, you may be willing to pay as much as five or even ten cents.

How can parents expect to do business with such underselling going on? How can you hope to conduct a successful enterprise by *paying* your customers to patronize your goods?

And just what would you think of a chap who would offer you a "valuable" piece of real estate (not necessarily in Florida), and also agree to pay you to take if off his hands?

The moment you gave your child the ten cents, the spinach lost value. It became a sticky, unpleasant job, only worth ten cents a helping. And as you handed the dime over, your customer raced out of the door and down the street back to the corner store, the very concern with which you are trying to compete.

Or perhaps you are one of those parents who believe in discipline, who *demands* that your customer "remain at the table until every bit of that spinach is eaten." As a rule this method will work and the spinach is usually disposed of. But I can't help wondering just what memories will hang around the transaction. In the child's mind hasn't the spinach become a thing which has kept him from doing something that was much more important, and won't he unconsciously avoid it the next time it is offered?

Perhaps you know the answer.

Examine the Product — Not the Child

But let's not be too pessimistic. Let us suppose you have approached your child simply as a good friend and great admirer and still failed. Usually the first impulse, when he refuses to eat, is to have him examined. Have you ever considered examining not the child, but the product?

Perhaps the article you are trying to sell is neither attractive nor appetizing. Is it made irresistible to your public, so to speak? Remember, your competitors are flooding the market with highly colored sweets and bright colored pop bottles. About the only one of the wholesome foods that can naturally take the attention of the eye from a candy case is bright colored fruit. And even then I have seen more than one green grapefruit or rusty apple passed across the table to a child without an appetite, like so much bad change.

Does your product appeal to the eye and to the taste of your customer?

If it does, and he still refuses to clip the coupon and sign on the dotted line, look over your sales force. Are both of you parents attractive, popular salesmen, who use your own products?

Don't tell me. I know the answer.

The next important phase of your campaign is the publicity. If you doubt my word, step into the corner store and see the placards and stickers which advertise what Babe Ruth, Valentino, Red Grange, Mary Pickford, Jackie Coogan, and the rest of that famous crowd have to say about the sweets for sale in the place. When the product isn't named directly after one of these idols, it is christened with a catch phrase snatched from the great American adolescent vocabulary.

Food Publicity That Appeals

How about the spinach you are trying to sell your customer? Is it presented as highly endorsed by popular heroes? If it isn't, you aren't much of a salesman.

Try this out on your adolescent some time: "One reason Red Grange is always in the pink of condition is because he eats green vegetables."

I'll admit it isn't very clever, but it's better than that one I once heard, which ran: "For heaven's sake, eat your spinach!"

Why not name a few dishes after these heroes? Why not "Babe Ruth's Home Plate" or "Mary Pickford's Beauty Compound"? And incidentally you might let it be known that there is a rumor to the effect that both Babe Ruth and Mary Pickford are very fussy and demand that they have their spinach at least three times a week. If your customer should ask how you know, you can safely say that you read it in a newspaper, which, so far as it goes, is true.

I'll admit that this method sounds rather childish. But no more so than the one employed by a million-dollar railroad of calling its crack train "The Broadway Limited," and allowing the rumor to be broadcast that only millionaires ever travel on it. Just as you do, I like the idea and am quite willing to pay nine dollars extra for such a name, and the opportunity to pretend that all the passengers on board, including myself, are millionaires.

The next step toward interesting your customer in the spinach is your first sales talk, which at the least will be exciting.

Do you really know your child?

Your conversation with this temperamental person must be carefully studied, just as a salesman studies you at least indirectly before he ever calls on you. Remember, your child is no more interested in your club, or business, and the things you like to talk about, than you are in his crowd and the chatter regarding it. But, my friend, you are the salesman. It is your *business* to be interested in all that concerns your customer.

How to Apply Child Psychology

Again, if you doubt my word, slip around to the corner store. I refer to the one where the boys and girls can be found in the greatest number. The clerk, although he never studied the subject, is probably a genius at child psychology. If anything, he is no doubt inclined to be a bit childlike himself. He knows the latest slang, the latest jokes. He knows the kind of people children like and so accordingly takes them as his friends, too. He knows baseball, basketball, football, hockey. And he *listens* to the children from morning to night.

That's why the boys and girls trade there. This big, good-natured fellow, with the wrinkled face, is one of the gang. And so you, too, must adapt yourself to the life of your child, if you hope to win his or her interest and confidence. You must know the adolescent language backward. And, worst of all, you must even laugh at your customer's stories. All good salesmen do. If I am trying to sell a painting to an aristocratic old gentleman, I naturally choose a different style of approach, and talk in another language, from that which I would choose were I trying to convince a mill hand that a certain pair of dollar-fifty overalls is a bargain.

But while you talk to your customer in the adolescent tongue, I warn you to be subtle about it. Let your boy convince himself. Your work is simply to set his mind working and he will do the rest, if any sale at all is going to be made.

Getting Children to Like Spinach

I have heard so many parents, genuinely anxious over the health of their children, explode: "Now I've told you nearly seven times to eat your spinach. I don't want to hear another word out of you. Just keep still and eat it or you'll be even punier than you are."

Supposing the clever fellow who sold you your vaccum cleaner had forced his way into your home and announced in a most unpleasant voice: "I've asked you seven times to buy this cleaner. Now don't argue with me any more. Just keep your mouth shut and buy it or your house will look even dirtier than it does!"

Ever think of your child as a perfectly normal, intelligent human being who responds to flattery and every other form of salesmanship just as you do?

One reason you bought that vacuum cleaner, although you may not want to believe it, is because the salesman slipped in one or two rather charming remarks about the appearance of your home. And he naïvely assured you that any one with as much pride and taste as you have would fully appreciate the benefits of his vacuum cleaner. And after that one you just had to listen to everything he said.

When that agent rang your bell he knew very well you wouldn't want to buy his cleaner. He knew you would make it a point to immediately think up some mighty good reasons for not wanting it. But rather than answer those arguments himself, he let you do it. Yes he did. He first invited you to pour out all the arguments you had as to why you shouldn't buy. After that you were at his mercy. He then proceeded to show you, in a delightfully subtle way, what a marvelous instrument the vacuum cleaner is. He was ready to listen to anything you wanted to talk about. As long as you talked, your door was open. Gradually, by indirect suggestions, he made you rather wish you owned one of the things. He encouraged you to talk about the machine. And, without your knowing it, he helped you yourself to evade every one of your original arguments.

Parents, be patient with your children. Try not to be too eager. As worried as you may be regarding your child's health, be just as indifferent outwardly as possible. You two parents, of course, may enjoy the spinach to your heart's content. Speak about how fresh it tastes. Notice how it melts in the mouth. Somehow the spinach never seemed to taste quite as good as it does this evening. That touch of melted butter is what does it. That slice of yellow egg against the green. . . .

But none of this directly to the child. So much as even a shift of the eyes toward this suspicious customer may upset your entire campaign.

And so it goes. It makes no difference whether you are selling a vacuum cleaner, a dish of spinach, or a bath, the job can easily be done if a real desire is finally created. It may take much careful advance work before your customer even nibbles at the spinach. Perhaps during the entire campaign absolutely no signs of interest will be shown. But if your spinach is tempting, if your publicity is good, and if your sales talk is both appealing and in the language of your customer, then trade will pick up and your hard-earned profits will begin to pour in.

Of course, some innocent parent may try the idea out, and just before closing the contract will let it be known that there is a whole kettle of spinach out in the kitchen which must be eaten so that it won't go to waste. If your customer doesn't dash away after that one, it's only because he's too weak.

No, good friend, we haven't a kettleful going to waste. On the contrary, we have a limited amount. In fact, what you see in the dish before you is all that there is in stock. Even that has been practically promised to somebody else. I'm sorry, because this evening it is unusually delicious.

Must I be so trite as to remind you that when the supply goes down, the demand shoots up.

Of course boys and girls will always love sweets. I like them myself. But we can save the home from bankruptcy and put it on a better paying basis. We can create a desire for the things our children should eat.

And instead of our letting them feel that they are doing us a privilege when they trade with us, we can put such a price on our goods that it will be a privilege when we allow them to patronize our offerings.

The Family in Crisis

The idea of the decline of the family remains a recurrent theme in American thought, one that can be mobilized by social conservatives who want to rein in the processes of cultural change. In this case, however, John R. Watson celebrates the collapse of the family as potentially liberating children from the negative influence of their parents, an attitude consistent with Watson's call for a more professional and scientifically objective approach to child rearing. Watson distrusts "mother's love" as preventing the development of discipline and regularity in children's habits, as making them less suited to the demands of the modern workplace.

Chapter Twenty-eight

After the Family—What?
(1930)

John B. Watson

American family life in large cities is admittedly on the wane. This is shown in many different ways: by the greater number of divorces, fewer marriages, increased age of the men at marriage, fewer children among the well-to-do, the great increase in the number of men who have playmates and in the number of women who are interested in men other than their husbands. Just as surely but along different lines is the same trend shown in the ever-increasing number of boys' and girls' camps which take the children away from the home for the whole of the summer and in the number of children who go to boarding-school while their parents go to Europe. The latest invention is the outdoor winter camp to take the children from Friday afternoon to Sunday night. Parents are becoming ever more willing to shunt the care of the children into well-trained hands. The kindergartens even in great universities now take youngsters at 18 months, and in at least two institutions, infants are taken at or near birth for observation and psychological care.

All this is sensible. I believe the children are enormously better off. Nevertheless it is an open admission that the home is inadequate, unqualified and unwilling to care for children. The movement to take children out of the home is probably one of the swiftest growing movements in the history of social customs. There used to be a saying in Mid-Victorian days which carried over until the World War: "The woman's place is in the home"; one doesn't hear so much of it now. Then too one used to hear: "Home is the place for children"; that trite saying will soon also be looked upon as amusing.

Chapter Twenty-nine

Against the Threat of Mother Love
(1928)

John B. Watson

Once at the close of a lecture before parents, a dear old lady got up and said, "Thank God, my children are grown—and that I had a chance to enjoy them before I met you."

Doesn't she express here the weakness in our modern way of bringing up children? We have children to enjoy them. We need to express our love in some way. The honeymoon period doesn't last forever with all husbands and wives, and we eke it out in a way we think is harmless by loving our children to death. Isn't this especially true of the mother today? No matter how much she may love her husband, he is away all day; her heart is full of love which she must express in some way. She expresses it by showering love and kisses upon her children— and thinks the world should laud her for it. *And it does.*

Not long ago, I went motoring with two boys, aged four and two, their mother, grandmother and nurse. In the course of the two-hour ride, one of the children was kissed thirty-two times—four by his mother, eight by the nurse and twenty times by the grandmother. The other child was almost equally smothered in love.

But there are not many mothers like that, you say—mothers are getting modern, they do not kiss and fondle their children nearly so much as they used to. Unfortunately this is not true. I once let slip in a lecture some of my ideas on the dangers lurking in the mother's kiss. Immediately, thousands of newspapers wrote scathing editorials on "Don't kiss the baby." Hundreds of letters poured in. Judging from them, kissing the baby to death is just about as popular a sport as it ever was, except for a very small part of our population.

Is it just the hard heartedness of the behaviorist—his lack of sentiment—that makes him object to kissing? Not at all. There are serious rocks ahead for the over-kissed child. Before I name them I want to explain how love grows up.

Our laboratory studies show that we can bring out a love response in a new-born child by just one stimulus—*by stroking its skin.* The more sensitive the skin area, the more marked the response. These sensitive areas are the lips, ears, back of the neck, nipples and the sex organs. If the child is crying, stroking these areas will often cause the child to become quiet or even to smile. Nurses and mothers have learned this method of quieting an infant by the trial and error process.

They pick the child up, pat it, soothe it, kiss it, rock it, walk with it, dandle it on the knee, and the like. All of this kind of petting has the result of gently stimulating the skin. Unscrupulous nurses have learned the very direct result which comes from stroking the sex organs. When the child gets older, the fondling, petting, patting, rocking of the body will bring out a gurgle or a coo, open laughter, and extension of the arms for the embrace.

The love life of the child is *at birth* very simple as is all of its other emotional behavior. Touching and stroking of the skin of the young infant brings out a love response. No other stimulus will.

This means that there is no "instinctive" love of the child for the parents, nor for any other person or object. It means that all affection, be it parental, child for parent or love between the sexes, is built up with such bricks and mortar. A great many parents who have much too much sentiment in their makeup, feel that when the behaviorist announces this he is robbing them of all the sacredness and sweetness in the child-parent relationship. Parents feel that it is just natural that they should love their children in this tangible way and that they should be similarly loved by the child in return. Some of the most tortured moments come when the parents have had to be away from their nine-months old baby for a stretch of three weeks. When they part from it, the child gurgles, coos, holds out its arms and shows every evidence of deepest parental love. Three weeks later when they return the child turns to the attendant who has in the interim fondled and petted it and put the bottle to the sensitive lips. The infant child loves anyone who strokes and feeds it.

It is true that parents have got away from rocking their children to sleep. You find the cradle with rockers on it now only in exhibits of early American furniture. You will say that we have made progress in this respect at any rate. This is true. Dr. Holt's book on the care of the infant can take credit for this education. But it is doubtful if mothers would have given it up if home economics had not demanded it. Mothers found that if they started training the infant at birth, it would learn to go to sleep without rocking. This gave the mother more time for household duties, gossiping, bridge and shopping. Dr. Holt suggested it; the economic value of the system was easy to recognize.

But it doesn't take much time to pet and kiss the baby. You can do it when you pick him up from the crib after a nap, when you put him to bed, and especially after his bath. What more delectable to the mother than to kiss her chubby baby from head to foot after the bath! And it takes so little time!

To come back to the mechanics of love and affection. Loves grow up in children just like fears. *Loves* are home made, built in. In other words loves are *conditioned*. You have everything at hand all day long for setting up conditioned love responses. The touch of the skin takes the place of the steel bar, the sight of the mother's face takes the place of the rabbit in the experiments with fear. The child *sees* the mother's face when she pets it. Soon, *the mere sight of the mother's face* calls out the love response. The touch of the skin is no longer necessary to call it out. A conditioned love reaction has been formed. Even if she pats the child in the dark, the *sound* of her voice as she croons soon comes to call out a love response. This is the psychological explanation of child's joyous reactions to the sound of the mother's voice. So with her footsteps, the sight of the mother's clothes, of her photograph. All too soon the child gets shot through with too many of these love reactions. In addition the child gets honeycombed with love responses for the nurse, for the father and for any other constant attendant who fondles it. Love reactions soon dominate the child. It requires no instinct, no "intelligence," no "reasoning" on the child's part for such responses to grow up.

The Adult Effects of Too Much Coddling in Infancy

To understand the end results of too much coddling, let us examine some of our own adult behavior. Nearly all of us have suffered from over-coddling in our infancy. How does it show? It shows as *invalidism*. As adults we have too many aches and pains. I rarely ask anybody with whom I am constantly thrown how he feels or how he slept last night. Almost invariably, if I am a person he doesn't have to keep up a front around, I get the answer, "Not very well." If I give him the chance, he expatiates along one of the following lines—"my digestion is poor; I have a constant headache; my muscles ache like fire; I am all tired out; I don't feel young any more; my liver is bad; I have a bad taste in my mouth"—and so on through the whole gamut of ills. Now these people have nothing wrong with them that the doctors can locate—and with the wonderful technique physicians have developed, the doctor can usually find out if anything is wrong. The individual who was not taught in his youth by his mother to be dependent, is one who comes to adult life too busy with his work to note the tiny mishaps that occur in his bodily makeup. When we are deeply engaged in our work, we never note them. Can you imagine an aviator flying in a fog or making a landing in a difficult field wondering whether his luncheon is going to digest?

We note these ills when our routine of work no longer thrills us. We have been taught from infancy to report every little ill, to talk about our stomach, our elimination processes, and the like. We have been allowed to avoid the doing of boresome duties by reporting them, such as staying away from school and getting relieved from sharing in the household chores. And above all, we have, by reporting them, got the tender solicitude of our parents and the kisses and coddling of our mothers. Mother fights our battles for us and stands between us and the things we try to avoid doing.

But society doesn't do this. We have to stick to our jobs in commercial and professional life regardless of headaches, toothaches, indigestion and other tiny ailments. There is no one there to baby us. If we cannot stand this treatment we have to go back home where love and affection can again be commandeered. If at home we cannot get enough coddling by ordinary means, we take to our armchairs or even to our beds. Thereafter we are in a secure position to demand constant coddling.

You can see invalidism in the making in the majority of American homes.

Here is a picture of a child over-conditioned in love. The child is alone putting his blocks together, doing something with his hands, learning how to control his environment. The mother comes in. Constructive play ceases. The child crawls its way or runs to the mother, takes hold of her, climbs into her lap, puts its arms around her neck. The mother, nothing loath, fondles her child, kisses it, hugs it. I have seen this go on for a two-hour period. If the mother who has so conditioned her child attempts to put it down, a heartbroken wail ensues. Blocks and the rest of the world have lost their pulling power. If the mother attempts to leave the room or the house, a still more heartbroken cry ensues. Many mothers often sneak away from their homes the back way in order to avoid a tearful, wailing parting.

Now over-conditioning in love is the rule. Prove it yourself by counting the number of times your child whines and wails "Mother." All over the house, all day long, the two-year-old, the three-year-old and the four-year-old whine "Mamma, Mamma," "Mother." Now these love responses which the mother or father is building in by over conditioning, in spite of what the poet and the novelist may have to say, are not constructive. They do not fight many battles for the child. They do not help it to conquer the difficulties it must meet in its environment. Hence just to the extent to which you devote time to petting and coddling—and I have seen almost all of the child's waking hours devoted to it— just to that extent do you rob the child of the time which he should be devoting to the manipulation of his universe, acquiring a technique with fingers, hands and arms. He must have time to pull his universe apart and put it together again. Even from this standpoint alone—that of robbing the child of its opportunity for conquering the world, coddling is a dangerous experiment.

The mother coddles the child for two reasons. One, she admits; the other, she doesn't admit because she doesn't know that it is true. The one she admits is that she wants the child to be happy, she wants it to be surrounded by love in order that it may grow up to be a kindly, goodnatured child. The other is that her own whole being cries out for the expression of love. Her mother before her has trained her to give and receive love. She is starved for love—affection, as she prefers to call it. It is at bottom a sex-seeking response in her, else she would never kiss the child on the lips. Certainly, to satisfy her professed reason for coddling, kissing the youngster on the forehead, on the back of the hand, patting it on the head once in a while, would be all the petting needed for a baby to learn that it is growing up in a kindly home.

But even granting that the mother thinks she kisses the child for the perfectly logical reason of implanting the proper amount of affection and kindliness in it, does she succeed? The fact I brought out before, that we rarely see a happy child, is proof to the contrary. The fact that our children are always crying and always whining shows the unhappy, unwholesome state they are in. Their digestion is interfered with and probably their whole glandular system is deranged.

Should the Mother Never Kiss the Baby?

There is a sensible way of treating children. Treat them as though they were young adults. Dress them, bathe them with care and circumspection. Let your behavior always be objective and kindly firm. Never hug and kiss them, never let them sit in your lap. If you must, kiss them once on the forehead when they say good night. Shake hands with them in the morning. Give them a pat on the head if they have made an extraordinarily good job of a difficult task. Try it out. In a week's time you will find how easy it is to be perfectly objective with your child and at the same time kindly. You will be utterly ashamed of the mawkish, sentimental way you have been handling it.

If you expected a dog to grow up and be useful as a watch dog, a bird dog, a fox hound, useful for anything except a lap dog, you wouldn't dare treat it the way you treat your child. When I hear a mother say "Bless its little heart" when it falls down, or stubs its toe, or suffers some other ill, I usually have to walk a block or two to let off steam. Can't the mother train herself when something happens to the child to look at its hurt without saying anything, and if there is a wound to dress it in a matter of fact way? And then as the child grows older, can she not train it to go and find the boracic acid and the bandages and treat its own wounds? Can't she train herself to substitute a kindly word, a smile, in all of her dealings with the child, for the kiss and the hug, the pickup and coddling? Above all, can't she learn to keep away from the child a large part of the day since love conditioning must grow up anyway, even when scrupulously guarded against, through feeding and bathing? I sometimes wish that we could live in a community of homes where each home is supplied with a well-trained nurse so that we could have the babies fed and bathed each week by a different nurse. Not long ago I had opportunity to observe a child who had had an over sympathetic and tender nurse for a year and a half. This nurse had to leave. When a new nurse came, the infant cried for three hours, letting up now and then only long enough to get its breath. This nurse had to leave at the end of a month and a new nurse came. This time the infant cried only half an hour when the new nurse took charge of it. Again, as often happens in well regulated homes, the second nurse stayed only two weeks. When the third nurse came, the child went to her without a murmur. Somehow I can't help wishing that it were possible to rotate the mothers occasionally too! Unless they are very sensible indeed.

Certainly a mother, when necessary, ought to leave her child for a long enough period for over-conditioning to die down. If you haven't a nurse and cannot leave the child, put it out in the backyard a large part of the day. Build a fence around the yard so that you are sure no harm can come to it. Do this from the time it is born. When the child can crawl, give it a sandpile and be sure to dig some small holes in the yard so it has to crawl in and out of them. Let it learn to overcome difficulties almost from the moment of birth. The child should learn to conquer difficulties away from your watchful eye. No child should get commendation and notice and petting every time it does something it ought to be doing anyway. If your heart is too tender and you must watch the child, make yourself a peephole so that you can see it without being seen, or use a periscope. But above all when anything does happen don't let your child see your own trepidation, handle the situation as a trained nurse or a doctor would and, finally, learn not to talk in endearing and coddling terms.

Nest habits, which come from coddling, are really pernicious evils. The boys or girls who have nest habits deeply imbedded suffer torture when they have to leave home to go into business, to enter school, to get married—in general, whenever they have to break away from parents to start life on their own. Inability to break nest habits is probably our most prolific source of divorce and marital disagreements. "Mother's boy" has to talk his married life over with his mother and father, has constantly to bring them into the picture. The bride coddled in her infancy runs home to mother or father taking her trunk every time a disagreement occurs. We have hundreds of pathological cases on record where the mother or father attachment has become so strong that a marital adjustment even after marriage has taken place becomes impossible. To escape the intolerable marriage tie the individual becomes insane or else suicides. In the milder cases, though, the struggle between young married people coddled in infancy shows itself in whines and complaints and the endless recounting of ills. Not enjoying the activities that come with marriage they escape them by tiredness and headaches. If his wife does not give mother's boy the coddling, the commendation and the petting the mother gave him, she doesn't understand him, she is cold, unwifely, unsympathetic. If the young wife does not constantly receive the gentle coddling and admiration her father gave her then the husband is a brute, unsympathetic, un-understanding. Young married couples who do not swear a solemn oath to fight out their own battles between themselves without lugging in the parents soon come upon rocks.

In conclusion won't you then remember when you are tempted to pet your child that mother love is a dangerous instrument? An instrument which may inflict a never healing wound, a wound which may make infancy unhappy, adolescence a nightmare, an instrument which may wreck your adult son or daughter's vocational future and their chances for marital happiness.

C

Children at War

The Second World War posed tremendous challenges to parents who hoped to ensure the "normal" development of their children during "abnormal" times. The absence of the father and the movement of many mothers into the workplace disrupted traditional family structures and created tensions within the home. This selection from the Child Study Association of America sought to reassure parents, yet what it also suggests is that almost all of children's reactions to the war were problematic. The child who whistles with confidence or who takes pleasure in war play may be every bit as much at risk as the child who is overly anxious and cowers. Angelo Patri, one of the pioneers in the progressive education movement in the New York education system, presented a series of radio talks to children and their parents about the war and its impact upon the family. Patri appeals to children's desires to participate actively in the national war effort to shape their behavior, redefining normal household activities in political terms. Children become "citizen soldiers" responsible for maintaining the smooth operation of the family and obligated to do their part to help their community confront the crisis and shortages of the war years. Writing in a Cold War context, André Fontaine urges parents to do their part to prepare their sons, almost from the cradle, for military service. At a time when Benjamin Spock's more "permissive" approach to child rearing is gaining wide acceptance, Fontaine appeals to patriotic duty to promote more discipline-centered methods.

Chapter Thirty

Children in Wartime
Parents' Questions (1942)

Child Study Association of America

Whistling to Keep Up Your Courage

My boy of ten seems almost angrily indifferent to the war. He is impatient with our conversations and constant listening to news reports. Apparently all the instructions given him at school irritate him. He insists there is no danger and that people who think there is are just silly. How can I make him more aware of the seriousness of what is going on?

Don't be fooled. Whistling to keep up your courage is a well-known device. Maybe for this particular boy it is a necessary kind of refuge—each must find his own way. Probably behind all this belligerent indifference there is more anxiety than appears. Don't try to force a more realistic attitude upon him. He probably knows as well as you do what is going on. Maybe some day you'll find a chance to help him admit to more anxiety than he now shows. His discovery that it isn't "sissy" to admit his fears will be a healthy one.

Children manage their fears by different means, and react to danger in a variety of unpredictable ways. Don't be surprised at anything. The child who seems altogether indifferent may be the very one who will show his concealed anxiety in ways that are apparently unrelated. This is true of children, not only in wartime, but in any situation in which they can't admit their *real feelings*. Our experience with young children teaches us that they find ways of masking their feelings. For example, the unacknowledged jealousy of an older child toward a new baby may show itself in recurrences of bed-wetting, thumb sucking, disobedience and other misbehavior even while he apparently "loves" the baby. Similarly the child with whom war-anxiety is largely unconscious and who shows only indifference may now take to bullying the younger child—to demanding extra attention from his parents, or to expressing his hidden fears, in many other indirect ways. Such misbehavior, while it lasts, will call for patience and understanding from both father and mother. In time, these children are likely to get their second wind and quiet down.

The Boy Who Is Thrilled with the War

My eleven-year-old son seems delighted at the war. His walls are full of maps; he gets the news eagerly. He and his friends talk constantly about going out and "blasting" Hitler. "Just my luck", he says, "to live where there's no fighting. Boy! Would I love to have an air-raid!" I find it hard to believe he is really so bloodthirsty. Is there anything I ought to do about it?

Remember that there is invariably a thrill at the thought of real danger. It would be less than human not to be excited and stimulated. In many children the love of adventure is very strong and quite natural and is not as "bloodthirsty" as it seems. The sight of the aggressive primitive male animal, when he happens to be our own son, is likely to shock his mother, though rarely his father. But your son is not abnormal, and the kinds of feeling he is expressing are for very many—both younger and older—certainly natural right now. . . .

Playing at War

The boys on our block play nothing but war these days. Their belts fairly bristle with toy guns and makeshift war-planes are constantly zooming through the air. Isn't the world full enough of this sort of thing without the children having to play at it? How can we stop it?

Don't try to stop this kind of war play. Play is the language of children, their way of working out the matters that concern them deeply at the moment. Boys have always played games that gave release to their war-like feelings. Cops and robbers, Indian and cowboy, Lone Ranger, Superman, or war games have much the same root and much the same meaning for the players.

A certain amount of such play is needed by most normal young males at any time. Their need is even greater today when war surges all about them. Girls too feel this need now. They have to play out their heightened feelings, just as many of us older people need to talk ours out.

Up to a certain point this is perfectly healthy—a real safety-valve. You will probably find that the excitement dies down somewhat as time goes on. If not, some adult help may be needed toward finding other, less exciting substitutes, especially athletic games, dramatics, and other more peaceful or "symbolic" expressions of rivalry and struggle. . . .

The Over-Anxious Child

In spite of all my efforts to "keep calm" (I am not a nervous person), my five-year-old daughter has been terrified ever since war was declared. Even before we went in she asked anxiously if every airplane she heard might not drop bombs. Now she has dreams and night terrors that her baby brother has been killed, that the enemy are coming right into the house. I have forbidden all war discussion, news broadcasts, etc. in her presence but it hasn't helped much. I am afraid that this will leave a permanent impression and upset her nerves for life. Is there anything I can do?

All the testimony of the British psychiatrists and others who have worked with children during the war shows that, like adults, children who are emotionally satisfied and generally well-balanced to begin with stand up well under enormous strain and recover even from what we might consider shattering experiences. Your saying that your child was afraid even before the war started raises the possibility that like many children from the age of two to six or seven, she has had some tendency to fears already. Her present state may be *intensified* by knowledge of real dangers, by hearing news bulletins and reports, but it is not *caused* by these things.

When children are continuously afraid of bombs that *might* come, in terror for the safety of a father who is unlikely to be called, for a baby brother peacefully asleep in his crib, then we must realize that just as children fear giants or wild animals in peacetime, these are not the things which are really frightening them, but are only the symbols with which the real cause has been masked. The real causes are not in the outside world but lie within your child herself. Essentially she is afraid of certain of her own impulses and instincts which she has somehow learned to regard as "bad." She may be afraid, for example, because beneath the surface, she hates the baby, or is jealous of her father, or feels that some of her sex thoughts or acts are "forbidden". Bottling these things up tight within herself—so tight that she no longer knows they are there—she cannot shake off the feeling that punishment must surely follow; she sees it lurking all about her and uses "the war" or other current experiences merely to give it body or justification. Far too briefly and simply stated, this is the psychology of much of the exaggerated anxiety of those people who are forever dying a thousand deaths.

You may help your child by trying to improve all her relationships to members of the family and to outsiders, by raising her self-esteem in every way possible, and by allowing her angry feelings and her natural sex curiosity some expression. Children like these, if their parents will try to be especially reassuring and loving, usually grow out of this phase, and as their general morale improves their "war fears" tend to diminish. Meanwhile, such a child should not of course be subjected to constant reminders of danger, if we can prevent it. But it is important not to stop with such purely negative measures since the real causes lie elsewhere.

If, in spite of all you can do, the child's fears get worse instead of better, it might be well for you to get advice from professional sources.

Chapter Thirty-one

You Are Citizen Soldiers
(1943)

Angelo Patri

Boys and girls of the United States of America, you are enlisted for the duration of the war as citizen soldiers. This is a total war, nobody is left out, and that counts you in, of course.

We are fighting a war for the freedom of the individual, that means your freedom. The Nazis would destroy that freedom so that you would have to work at whatever job the officers gave you, in whatever place they put you, for whatever wages they thought fit to give you.

You would get the education they thought fit to let you have. If that meant none at all, that is what it would be. You would have to believe what the government ordered you to believe, read what they printed for you, eat and wear what they provided for you. The government officers would do your living for you and you would serve them as they decreed.

We say to our enemies, "No, never. We will fight you up and down the world; we will destroy your force; we will make no peace with you until you let go such a stupid idea." We say that for your sake; we fight for your freedom; we battle for your future as free American citizens. And we are not going to cover this up with polite words. We are going at it directly, in the American fashion, with everything we have. We expect you to feel the same way and give your whole strength to the cause, your cause . . .

You are now a soldier in the United States Army. Your duty is to keep well, cheer up your father and mother by doing a good job, help your country by doing the chore appointed you whether it is blowing a bugle, rolling bandages, running errands, or ringing doorbells. Do it to the best of your ability and you will be helping your country.

Don't forget about keeping fit. You can't do that by wishing. Eat your fruit and vegetables, drink your milk, work, play, and sleep according to the rules. That's your duty as a civilian soldier. As such we salute you.

As citizen soldiers you each have a duty to perform. You make yourself useful in whatever situation you find yourself. You do what you can do best to help when help is needed.

We have drills for protection against fire and air raids. You are asked to go to set places and stay there until you are dismissed. You may be asked to stay in the safety room for a period of time. Very well, you stay. But what will you do while you stay? You can't just sit and twiddle your thumbs.

You can play games, tell stories, sing, act, dance. Which of these do you do best? Pick out your bit and practice until you can tell a story or do a dance, or direct a game so well that you can hold the attention and interest of your whole group for the time it takes you to do your job.

Make this a duty. You can't tell a story to a group of children just by knowing the story, having it in your head. A story in your head is not like the one you tell to the group. It is very different.

Take my word for that and begin practicing at home, on your little brothers and sisters, the whole family, until you can tell the story smoothly, nothing left out, no going back to tell the part you left out. Get it down perfectly . . .

When a teacher asks for volunteers be ready to step forward. Don't hold back because you think somebody else can do better. What of it? There is always somebody in the world to better our best, but that does not say our bit is not needed. It is. . . .

Courage begins in the soul, but it must be nourished by a stout body in order to do its work. It is fine to have the spirit of courage, but if the flesh is weak the spiritual courage will be severely strained. Backed by strength of body and bones, it will go farther and do more. Cultivate both kinds of strength by daily practice. Try to face the truth in whatever form it comes. If you have made a mistake, say so. If you do not know what to do or how to do it, say so and ask for help. If you know you should do what you do not like to do, or are afraid to do, do it anyway and strength will come to you as you go about doing your duty. It always does. . . .

You are asking me what you can do to help win the war. Armfuls, dayfuls of things are waiting for you to come along and do them. . . .

If you are a Scout and a Red Cross member, you have made a good start. Now how about home? Are you a homeworker? You'd better be. Home is mighty important. If you don't know it this is the time to learn.

Here is your father working like mad from the dark dawn to the shining evening of wartime. Here is your mother trying to keep the house going, serve three meals, do her bit in the Red Cross, in the voluntary services, and nobody but you to lend a hand.

If you really want to help here's your chance.

Begin in the morning by being up first, making the coffee, getting in the rolls and the milk and the newspaper, getting the baby's bottle ready, walking the dog, feeding him and the cat, attending to your room, tidying the bathroom, helping with the housework.

After school there is time for you to help some more. Get in what is needed for the supper; set the table; cook the meal; and say it all with music too.

You can go to bed on time and get enough sleep to keep you rested and in good shape for growth. Every time a child has to be put to bed and tended some grown person's time and energy have to be used in his service. Try not to be sick and try harder to keep well.

Pick out a job and do it religiously. We have to gather and save waste paper. We have to knit for the Army and Navy; bandages must be rolled and pads made, and the Junior Red Cross members can do these well. School property must be cared for so that there will be less repairing and cleaning to be done.

Children can do a lot by taking care not to break windows, mar woodwork, mark walls, and the like. Needless demands on work, money, or time are waste. No good citizen soldier will waste a penny or a single scrap of anything that can be saved. . . .

Don't forget that you can make Father and Mother smile and be glad just by being on hand, in your place, when you are expected to be there. You have no idea what a help that will be.

You can't do all this? Oh yes, you can, and then some. Just imagine that you are in the jungle with your own army men, an enemy pounding you from the front, another coming in on the right, another zooming over your head, and see how many hands and feet you find on yourself to keep alert and save your side a beating. You'll be surprised how really smart and able you can be if you feel you must. . . .

Chapter Thirty-two

Raise Your Boy to Be a Soldier
(1952)

André Fontaine

Whether you like it or not, the chances are overwhelming that your boy is going to be a soldier, sailor or airman. Universal Military Training is an accomplished fact. You can hate it until the cows come home, but you can't escape it. Once you accept it, however, you'll find there are many things you can do to make your son's inevitable hitch in the service easier and more productive.

Basically there are two things, one psychological and one vocational, that you can do. First, by your handling of your boy from childhood up you can make the psychological adjustment from civilian to military life much easier. It is a job worth doing anyway, of course, since many of the adjustments he will have to make to military training are similar to adjustments he will be making all through life. Second, by learning how to take advantage of educational opportunities the services offer, you can get your boy invaluable training—free—for the job he'll come back to. Since your son is going to have to serve anyway, you'll be helping him if you emphasize the positive, constructive things he can get out of his military training instead of allowing him to feel that the service is the end of everything for him . . .

Building self-reliance in a boy comes hard. Kermit Eby, professor of sociology at the University of Chicago, has two general rules that help: "You have to realize that children are surprisingly indestructible" and "If you give them a chance to do things on their own you'll be amazed at how much they can handle."

When his boys were little, Eby made a practice of giving them responsibilities normally considered far beyond their years. Like letting one boy check coats at a political meeting when he was nine. The kid worked until he was nine. The kid worked until he nearly dropped, and was proud as punch to be helping out his father.

Once when Eby was taking his six-year-old on a trip they lost each other at the station. The boy traveled 750 miles alone, got a cab at the station to take him home, cooked his own dinner and went to bed.

By the time he finished high school the oldest boy had pitched hay on a farm, labored in a highway gang, handled a harvest combine and worked in a steel mill. "Once when he was fourteen we thought we'd overdone it," Eby said. "He had a motor scooter, and one day he disappeared. He was gone three days and two nights, and we were worried sick. But he came back as calm as anything. He'd motored up to the lake, got a job slipping hamburgers in a stand, and slept on the beach. We blistered his ears—not for going, but for not telling us he was leaving."

That boy is in the Army now. He made the adjustment to military life in a breeze.

If you want your son to make a similarly easy adjustment there are a number of things, some major, some minor, that you should do:

Get him away from home. Let him go to summer camps, to visit friends, on hunting, fishing or camping trips with his friends. Encourage him to join the Boy Scouts. He'll not only gain experience in getting along in a strictly male group, but he'll learn practical techniques, such as tenting, fire-building and knot-tying, that will help him when he's in uniform.

Get him accustomed to change. Take him on trips, and let him take them alone. Give him a chance to see new people, adjust to new surroundings, make new friends. And let him handle the situations on his own.

It might even be a good idea to let him have his own gun. All boys are fascinated by guns at some stage. If you don't know how to teach him to use one properly, a Scout leader, schoolteacher or the local gun club can help you out. But by all means insist that he follow all the safety rules.

Give him responsibility. He should have regular chores around the house—and he should be required to do them. Help him get a summer job, a newspaper route, any kind of work where he has a chance to step off on his own and collect the money for his efforts. Then let him do what he wants with his pay.

Tell him what he's going to run into when he's inducted. If he knows about the 27-second haircut the shock will be immeasurably lessened . . .

Popular Culture and the Family

In the 1950s, social reformers, such as Frederic Wertham, warned that popular culture, especially violent comics and radio/television programs, were contributing to the rise of juvenile delinquency. Dorothy Walter Baruch, a prolific writer of child-rearing guides, takes an alternative approach, exploring the psychological reasons that violent entertainment and aggressive play appeal to children and urging parents to provide more direct outlets for expressing oedipal tensions.

Chapter Thirty-three

"Such Trivia As Comic Books"
(1953)

Frederic Wertham

And I verily do suppose that in the braines and hertes
of children, whiche be membres spirituall, whiles they
be tender, and the little slippes of reason begynne in
them to bud, ther may happe by evil custome some
pestiferous dewe of vice to perse the sayde membres,
and infecte and corrupt the softe and tender buddes.
> —Sir Thomas Elyot (1531)

Gardening consists largely in protecting plants from blight and weeds, and the
same is true of attending to the growth of children. If a plant fails to grow
properly because attacked by a pest, only a poor gardener would look for the
cause in that plant alone. The good gardener will think immediately in terms of
general precaution and spray the whole field. But with children we act like the
bad gardener. We often fail to carry out elementary preventive measures, and
we look for the causes in the individual child. A whole high-sounding terminology has been put to use for that purpose, bristling with "deep emotional disorders," "profound psychogenic features" and "hidden motives baffling in their
complexity." And children are arbitrarily classified—usually after the event—as
"abnormal," "unstable" or "predisposed," words that often fit their environment
better than they fit the children. The question is, Can we help the plant without
attending to the garden? . . .

The term *mental hygiene* has been put to such stereotyped use, even though
embellished by psychological profundities, that it has become almost a cliché. It
is apt to be forgotten that its essential meaning has to do with prevention. The
concept of juvenile delinquency has fared similarly since the Colorado Juvenile
Court law of half a century ago: "The delinquent child shall be treated not as a
criminal, but as misdirected and misguided, and needing aid, encouragement,
help and assistance." This was a far-reaching and history-making attitude, but
the great promise of the juvenile-court laws has not been fulfilled. And the early
laws do not even mention the serious acts which bring children routinely to court

nowadays and which juvenile courts now have to contend with. The Colorado law mentions only the delinquent who "habitually wanders around any railroad yards or tracks, or jumps or hooks to any moving train, or enters any car or engine without lawful authority."

The public is apt to be swayed by theories according to which juvenile delinquency is treated as an entirely individual emotional problem, to be handled by individualistic means. This is exemplified by the very definition of juvenile delinquency in a recent psychopathological book on the subject: "We have assigned the generic term of delinquency to all these thoughts, actions, desires and strivings which deviate from moral and ethical principles." Such a definition diffuses the concept to such an extent that no concrete meaning remains. This unsocial way of thinking is unscientific and leads to confused theory and inexpedient practice. For example, one writer stated recently that "too much exposure to horror stories and to violence can be a contributing factor to a child's insecurity or fearfulness," but it could not "make a child of any age a delinquent." Can such a rigid line be drawn between the two? As Hal Ellson has shown again recently in his book *Tomboy*, children who commit serious delinquencies often suffer from "insecurity and fearfulness." And children who are insecure and fearful are certainly in danger of committing a delinquent act. Just as there is such a thing as being predelinquent, so there are conditions where a child is pre-insecure, or prefearful. Would it not be better, for purposes of prevention, instead of making an illogical contrast between a social category like delinquency and a psychological category like fearfulness, to think of *children in trouble*—in trouble with society, in trouble with their families or in trouble with themselves? And is it not likely that "too much exposure to horror stories and to violence" is bad for all of them when they get into trouble, and before they get into trouble?

In the beginning of July, 1950, a middle-aged man was sitting near the bleachers at the Polo Grounds watching a baseball game. He had invited the thirteen-year-old son of a friend, who sat with him excited and radiating enthusiasm. Suddenly the people sitting near by heard a sharp sound. The middle-aged man, scorecard in hand, slumped over and his young friend turned and was startled to see him looking like a typical comic-book illustration. Blood was pouring from his head and ears. He died soon afterwards and was carried away. Spectators rushed to get the vacant seats, not realizing at all what had happened.

In such a spectacular case the police go in for what the headlines like to call a dragnet. This had to be a pretty big one. In the crowded section of the city overlooking the Polo Grounds there were hundreds of apartment buildings in a neighborhood of more than thirty blocks, and from the roof of any of them someone could have fired such a shot. As a matter of fact, at the very beginning of the search detectives confiscated six rifles from different persons. Newspapers and magazines played up the case as the "Mystery Death," the "Ball Park Death" and "The Random Bullet."

Soon the headlines changed to "Hold Negro Youth in Shooting" and the stories told of the "gun-happy fourteen-year-old Negro boy" who was being held by the authorities. Editorials reproached his aunt for being "irresponsible in the care and training of a youngster" and for "being on the delinquent side of the adult ledger."

In the apartment where this boy Willie lived with his great-aunt, and on the roof of the building, the police found "two .22-caliber rifles, a high-powered .22-caliber target pistol, ammunition for all three guns, and a quantity of ammunition for a Luger pistol." This served as sufficient reason to arrest and hold the boy's great-aunt on a Sullivan Law charge (for possession of a gun). She was not released until the boy, who was held in custody all during this time, had signed a confession stating that he had owned and fired a .45-caliber pistol—which, incidentally, was never found. In court the judge stated, "We cannot find you guilty, but I believe you to be guilty." With this statement he sentenced Willie to an indeterminate sentence in the state reformatory.

For the public the case was closed. The authorities had looked for the cause of this extraordinary event, which might have affected anyone in the crowd, in one little boy and took it out on him, along with a public slap at his aunt. They ignored the fact that other random shooting by juveniles had been going on in this as in other sections of the city. Only a few days after the Polo Grounds shooting, a passenger on a Third Avenue elevated train was wounded by a shot that came through the window. But with Willie under lock and key, the community felt that its conscience was clear.

It happened that I had known Willie for some time before all this. He had been referred to the Lafargue Clinic—a free psychiatric clinic in Harlem—by the Reverend Shelton Hale Bishop as a school problem. He was treated at the Clinic. We had studied his earliest development. We knew when he sat up, when he got his first tooth, when he began to talk and walk, how long he was bottle fed, when he was toilet trained. Psychiatrists and social workers had conferences about him.

Willie had been taken care of by his great-aunt since he was nineteen months old. His parents had separated shortly before. This aunt, an intelligent, warm, hard-working woman, had done all she could to give Willie a good upbringing. She worked long hours at domestic work and with her savings sent him (at the age of two) to a private nursery school, where he stayed until he was eight. Then she became ill, could not work so hard and so could not afford his tuition there. He was transferred to a public school where he did not adjust so well, missing the attention he had received in the private school. At that time his aunt took him to the Lafargue Clinic. He had difficulty with his eyes and had to wear glasses which needed changing. According to his aunt he had occasionally suffered from sleepwalking which started when he was six or seven. Once when his great-aunt waked him up from such a somnambulistic state he said, half-awake, that he was "going to look for his mother." He was most affectionate with his aunt, and she had the same affection for him. She helped him to get afternoon jobs at neighborhood grocery stores, delivering packages.

Willie was always a rabid comic-book reader. He "doted" on them. He spent a large part of the money he earned to buy them. Seeing all their pictures of brutality and shooting and their endless glamorous advertisements for guns and knives, his aunt had become alarmed—years before the Polo Grounds shooting—and did not permit him to bring them into the house. She also forbade him to read them. But of course such direct action on the part of a parent has no chance of succeeding in an environment where comic books are all over the place in enormous quantities. She encountered a further obstacle, too. Workers at a public child-guidance agency connected with the schools made her distrust her natural good sense and told her she should let Willie read all the comic books he wanted. She told one of the Lafargue social workers, "I didn't like for him to read these comic books, but I figured they knew better than I did."

The Lafargue Clinic has some of his comic books. They are before me as I am writing this, smudgily printed and well thumbed, just as he used to pore over them with his weak eyes. Here is the lecherous-looking bandit overpowering the attractive girl who is dressed (if that is the word) for very hot weather ("She could come in handy, then! Pretty little spitfire, eh!") in the typical pre-rape position. Later he threatens to kill her:

"Yeah, it's us, you monkeys, and we got an old friend of yours here. . . . Now unless you want to see somp'n FATAL happen to her, u're gonna kiss that gold goodbye and lam out of here!"

Here is violence galore, violence in the beginning, in the middle, at the end:

ZIP! CRASH! SOCK! SPLAT! BAM! SMASH!

(This is an actual sequence of six pictures illustrating brutal fighting, until in the seventh picture: "He's out cold!")

Here, too, is the customary close-up of the surprised and frightened-looking policeman with his hands half-raised saying:

NO—NO! DON'T SHOOT!

as he is threatened by a huge fist holding a gun to his face. This is followed by mild disapproval ("You've gone too far! This is murder!") as the uniformed man lies dead on the ground. This comic book is endorsed by child specialists who are connected with important institutions. No wonder Willie's aunt did not trust her own judgment sufficiently.

The stories have a lot of crime and gunplay and, in addition, alluring advertisements of guns, some of them full-page and in bright colors, with four guns of various sizes and descriptions on a page:

Get a sweet-shootin'——[gun] and get in on the fun!

Here is the repetition of violence and sexiness which no Freud, Krafft-Ebing or Havelock Ellis ever dreamed would be offered to children, and in such profusion. Here is one man mugging another, and graphic pictures of the white man shooting colored natives as though they were animals: "You sure must have treated these beggars rough in that last trip through here!" And so on. This is the sort of thing that Willie's aunt wanted to keep him from reading.

When the Lafargue staff conferred about this case, as we had about so many similar others, we asked ourselves: How does one treat such a boy? How does one help him to emotional balance while emotional excitement is instilled in him in an unceasing stream by these comic books? Can one be satisfied with the explanation that he comes from a broken family and lives in an underprivileged neighborhood? Can one scientifically disregard what occupied this boy's mind for hours every day? Can we say that this kind of literary and pictorial influence had no effect at all, disregarding our clinical experience in many similar cases? Or can we get anywhere by saying that he must have been disordered in the first place or he would not have been so fascinated by comic books?

That would have meant ignoring the countless other children equally fascinated whom we had seen. Evidently in Willie's case there was a constellation of many factors. Which was finally the operative one? What in the last analysis tipped the scales?

Slowly, and at first reluctantly, I have come to the conclusion that this chronic stimulation, temptation and seduction by comic books, both their content and their alluring advertisements of knives and guns, are contributing factors to many children's maladjustment.

All comic books with their words and expletives in balloons are bad for reading, but not every comic book is bad for children's minds and emotions. The trouble is that the "good" comic books are snowed under by those which glorify violence, crime and sadism.

At no time, up to the present, has a single child ever told me as an excuse for a delinquency or for misbehavior that comic books were to blame. Nor do I nor my associates ever question a child in such a way as to suggest that to him. If I find a child with fever I do not ask him, "What is the cause of your fever? Do you have measles?" I examine him and make my own diagnosis. It is our clinical judgment, in all kinds of behavior disorders and personality difficulties of children, that comic books do play a part. Of course they are not in the textbooks. But once alerted to the possibility, we unexpectedly found, in case after case, that comic books were a contributing factor not to be neglected. . . .

Some time after I had become aware of the effects of comic books, a woman visited me. She was a civic leader in the community and invited me to give some lectures on child guidance, education and delinquency. We had a very pleasant conversation. It happened that on that very morning I had been overruled by the Children's Court. I had examined a boy who had threatened a woman teacher with a switchblade knife. Ten years before, that would have been a most unusual case, but now I had seen quite a number of similar ones. This particular boy seemed to me a very good subject for treatment. He was not really a "bad boy," and I do not believe in the philosophy that children have instinctive aggressive urges to commit such acts. In going over his life, I had asked him about his reading. He was enthusiastic about comic books. I looked over some of those he liked best. They were filled with alluring tales of shooting, knifing, hitting and strangling. He was so intelligent, frank and open that I considered him not an inferior child, but a superior one. I know that many people glibly call such a child maladjusted; but in reality he was a child well adjusted to what we had offered him to adjust to. In other words, I felt this was a seduced child. But the Court decided otherwise. They felt that society had to be protected from this menace. So they sent him to a reformatory.

In outlining to the civic leader what I would talk about, I mentioned comic books. The expression of her face was most disappointed. Here she thought she had come to a real psychiatrist. She liked all the other subjects I had mentioned; but about comic books she knew everything herself.

"I have a daughter of eleven," she said. "She reads comic books. Of course only the animal comics. I have heard that there are some others, but I have never seen them. Of course I would never let them come into my home and she would never read them. As for what you said about crime comics, Doctor, they are only read by adults. Even so, these crime comics probably aren't any worse than what children have read all along. You know, dime novels and all that." She looked at me then with a satisfied look, pleased that there was one subject she could really enlighten me about.

I asked her, "In the group that I am to speak to, do you think some of the children of these women have gotten into trouble with stealing or any other delinquency?"

She bent forward confidentially. "You've guessed it," she said. "That's really why we want these lectures. You'd be astonished at what these children from these good middle-class homes do nowadays. You know, you won't believe it, but they break into apartments, and a group of young boys molested several small girls right in our neighborhood! Not to speak of the mugging that goes on after dark."

"What happens to these boys?" I asked her.

"You know how it is," she said. "One has to hush these things up as much as possible, but when it got too bad, of course, they were put away."

There was no doubt that this was an intelligent and well-meaning woman, and yet the unfairness of it all had not occurred to her. Children of eleven do not read only animal comics—whether the parents know it or not. They see all the crime, horror, superman and jungle comics elsewhere if they are not allowed at home. There is a whole machinery to protect adults from seeing anything that is obscene or too rough in the theater, in the movies, in books and even in night clubs. The children are left entirely unprotected. They are shown crime, delinquency and sexual abnormality, but the punishment they get if they succumb to the suggestions is far more severe than what an adult gets if he strays from the path of virtue.

After this conversation, I felt that not only did I have to be a kind of detective to trace some of the roots of the modern mass delinquency, but that I ought to be some kind of defense counsel for the children who were condemned and punished by the very adults who permitted them to be tempted and seduced. As far as children are concerned, the punishment does not fit the crime. I have noticed that a thousand times. Not only is it cruel to take a child away from his family, but what goes on in many reformatories hurts children and does them lasting harm. Cruelty to children is not only what a drunken father does to his son, but what those in high estate, in courts and welfare agencies, do to straying youth.

This civic leader was only one of many who had given me a good idea of what I was up against, but I took courage from the fact that societies for the prevention of cruelty to children were formed many years after societies for the prevention of cruelty to animals. . . .

Some of my psychiatric friends regarded my comics research as a Don Quixotic enterprise. But I gradually learned that the number of comic books is so enormous that the pulp paper industry is vitally interested in their mass production. If anything, I was fighting not windmills, but paper mills. Moreover, a most important part of our research consisted in the reading and analysis of hundreds of comic books. This task was not Quixotic but Herculean—reminiscent, in fact, of the job of trying to clean up the Augean stables.

As our work went on we established the basic ingredients of the most numerous and widely read comic books: violence; sadism and cruelty; the superman philosophy, an offshoot of Nietzsche's superman who said, "When you go to women, don't forget the whip." We also found that what seemed at first a problem in child psychology had much wider implications. Why does our civilization give to the child not its best but its worst, in paper, in language, in art, in ideas? What is the social meaning of these supermen, superwomen, super-lovers, super-boys, supergirls, super-ducks, super-mice, super-magicians, super-safecrackers? How did Nietzsche get into the nursery? . . .

Chapter Thirty-four

The Play's the Thing
(1949)

Dorothy Walter Baruch

Radio Rackets, Movie Murders and Killer Cartoons

"My child has murder on the mind. It's because of those horrible radio programs. I know it is!" . . . "It's because of those dreadful funny books that aren't funny at all but full of killer-dillers!" . . . "It's because of those wild and wooly movies that he insists on seeing every blessed week."

The radio programs, the comic books and the wildest of movies are far from desirable. But they are not the *cause* of the aggression in our youngsters. The aggression, as we know by now, is already there. A child feels himself small and weak next to the adults who tower above him. He desires to be greater and bigger—more powerful. He musters aggression to this end. A child feels resentful and angry of many things as he grows. He wants to be able to let out and get even. He wants to bring out the "murderous" impulses that lie within.

In the radio programs to which he listens, in the comics and movies, other characters bring out and express the aggression which he may not. This feels good to him. He gets a vicarious thrill from it. He identifies himself with the characters who are what he is inside and who do what he would like to do.

"When I see one of those killer pictures," said nine-year-old Wallace, gulping down his excitement, "gee, *I* get to be the man with the gun. I never have any other chance."

To Wallace these pictures mirrored feelings which lay in him and for which he had not had enough outlets in the daily course of his life. So also did the comics that he collected and the radio programs to which he clung. Wallace himself was full of aggression that dated back to his earliest years . . .

The comics and such appealed to him for one strong reason above all else: the people in them could be cruel and vindictive for him. They did what he had no way of doing. He got his satisfaction from them by imagining himself in their boots.

Many people believe that children get an outlet for their aggression through such means. Actually, they don't get enough. For people do not adequately release their aggressions through vicarious participation. The passivity of looking on provides none of the *activity* that is needed to reduce hostile feelings. The outlet for aggression remains the shadow rather than the substance. The child identifies with the bad man, the superman, or the good man who shoots straight and true. But all along he is only the onlooker, the stand-in, the double. He is not actually taking part. . . .

Of themselves, the wildest and wooliest, the cruelest and the sexiest of dramas or picture strips will not make our children into delinquents or criminals. But they do present ways of channeling aggression which are unwholesome ways.

We have to offer strong competition by providing ways that are more wholesome—that carry neither threat nor hurt nor harm. For, in general, the child to whom the killer-dillers appeal most is also the child who has the most aggression to be released. It is for this very reason that he so avidly embraces the aggression in what he sees and hears.

Strange as it may seem, it is far more wholesome to draw pictures of mother and call them ugly and horrid. It is far more wholesome to let out all sorts of hateful feelings on what is recognizably mother than to sit and plot and imagine how one can carry out Crime Number Eight on some substitute female. As we know, unless a child lets out on the person who incurs the anger, he may well continue on and on with a string of substitutes all his life.

Being honestly angry and letting the anger come out honestly against the person who has engendered it, yet channeling it into harmless channels—this, as we've seen, does do good. It is the MOST REALISTIC ANTIDOTE for the appeal of the comics and such.

Wallace's parents tried it. They saw to it that he had many of the active outlets we've been talking of all through this book. They found that as he got his "mean feelings" out in the ways that we've been considering, the pull of the comics automatically lessened. The radio programs he had clung to no longer mattered so much. The whole problem fell into proper place even though nothing had been done to forbid or punish or prevent.

Those parents who have tried forbidding as a way of coping with the problem report over and over that it does no good. The child manages somehow to get his fare on the sly. Moreover, the forbidding generates new hostility. The child feels that his parents are cutting off important mutual interests which he shares with "the other kids." He holds this against them and adds it to a score of other injustices he feels. And this in turn feeds into his hostility and makes it grow.

The flank attack is far better: the solution lies in providing other outlets galore. Other outlets that channel aggression and release it more *actively* and more *directly*. . . .

One Child in His Time Plays Many Parts

We remember well from our own childhood days how we loved dressing up and playing that we were bigger than we were. We've seen the same sort of enjoyment in our children. A paper crown on the top of a child's head can bring him the dignity of a king, a stick in his hand can give him the courage of a conqueror. With a frayed skirt, a child becomes mother; with a stringy tie, he becomes father.

A chest of scraps and discarded clothing is a storehouse that permits of untold variations in playing things out. This is an old and treasured fact born out by our own memories. There are new facts that can be added today, born out of new psychological knowledge.

"You can be any kind of mother you want," says Elsie's mother. "A mean mother, an angry mother, a cross mother, a nasty mother. Any kind that you like!"

"Oh," says eight-year-old Elsie, who up to this point had been putting on an act with her sister of doing everything nice that a mother does. "Oh," she repeats. "I was waiting till you went out of the room for that part."

"But that's the part I'd like most to see."

"So you can see yourself as others see you!" came the answer quick as a flash.

Elsie's mother had come to understand that acting out was not the whole story if Elsie's disciplinary problems were to be helped. Her own presence was needed. Were Elsie to express her resentment and anger surreptitiously, the fear of these feelings might keep on growing because of the anxiety over possible discovery. This fear might only add to Elsie's inner discomfort, pressure and tenseness. It could augment her dissatisfaction with and her anger at the world. On the other hand, by being present and accepting Elsie's feelings, her mother could help her fear to discharge in ways that would not make it boomerang and increase. . . .

E

Freedom and Responsibility

Discussions of discipline in child-rearing guides often depend upon analogies to adult political debates. In the next several selections, we see more or less direct appeals to political ideals to determine the appropriate ways to discipline children. In each case, the writer maps her or his utopian ideals for America's future, ideals that can be achieved only if we appropriately shape children's development. Sidonie Matsner Gruenberg uses a vocabulary of "freedom" and "discipline" to explore the balance of power within the family. Elizabeth F. Boettiger struggles with the need to balance personal liberty and autonomy against the demands placed on the citizen by the community. She promotes the importance of the family as a site for learning about democratic life, while stressing the ways that the family must conform to larger social and cultural norms. Starting with an explicit acknowledgment of the threat posed by nuclear weapons to human survival, Mauree Applegate reminds parents and teachers about the desperate need to develop new forms of relations between the nations of the world. Children, Applegate predicts, will either destroy the world or heal it. Rudolf Dreikurs contrasts the child-rearing practices appropriate to autocratic and to democratic societies, seeing the relations between children and parents as analogous to the relations between citizens and states.

Chapter Thirty-five

New Parents for Old
(1930)

Sidonie Matsner Gruenberg

It is characteristic of the present age to emphasize "freedom" in a way that repudiates all the implications of "discipline." Yet it is obviously absurd to choose between the disciplines that were developed under tyrannies and dominations and coercions, and the freedoms that come from merely letting the child have his way uncontrolled. It is not a question of yielding entirely to the untrained impulses of infants, for that would merely substitute the tyranny of the inexperienced little savage for the autocracy of disappointed and frustrated adults. Whatever meaning one or another group attaches to "freedom," it is necessary today to consider the new demands which the individual makes upon life, upon authority, upon the community.

For the immediate future our disciplines must aim more deliberately at the attaining of freedom and the ability to use it responsibly. Such discipline presents more subtle problems than are attacked by the methods of autocracy, and these problems are not to be solved by mere rules. Furthermore, our methods of discipline must be such as will enable us to make use of the child's spontaneities as indications of his potentialities and needs. The child who is seen but never heard may indeed have nothing of importance to say; but he may also be concealing from his mentors significant truths about himself.

We have to look forward to a time when men and women are able to live together, to coöperate for common ends, to solve common problems not through the restraints and coercions of armies and constables, but through intelligent and self-directed efforts and self-control. We must conceive of the mature person not as one who skillfully evades his responsibilities and escapes the police, but as one who joyously and willingly joins with his fellows in the adventure of promoting common purposes. We must, therefore, learn to train our children not through fear of punishment, through putting a premium upon cunning and avarice, through repressions and impositions. We must seek new techniques that enable the child to assume responsibilities without being overawed, to assert himself without overriding others, to serve without truculence or condescension, to enjoy life without apologizing for it.

Most of us who have attempted to adjust ourselves to the changing conditions and the changing concepts have not abdicated our authority in favor of a reign of lawless freedom. Rather, we have learned that children can obey wise rules and conform willingly to well-ordered routines and even perform disagreeable tasks when they find compensations in doing so. We have simply learned that if undesirable actions can be pleasurable and satisfying to the child, so can desirable ones—and we have set about to make them so. The result has been that we have less of the old-fashioned kinds of disobedience in our homes and at the same time fewer occasions to apply punishments as corrective measures. . . .

Chapter Thirty-six

Families and the World Outside
(1941)

Elizabeth F. Boettiger

In all the recent talk about democracy and its aims, there is a special significance for parents. All people who conscientiously try to define the difference between a democratic and a totalitarian way of living are agreed that fundamentally it is a question of responsibility. In a totalitarian state, individuals are told what to do and how to think; in a democracy, they are expected, within the social framework, to think and act for themselves.

But no one can think and act independently out of thin air. Independence is a state into which one grows. The little boy who wanted to believe what his father believed was going through a natural and very necessary stage of this growth. If family living is a success, the ways of behaving, the habits of thought which are a part of it, will become part of a child's personality as he matures. They form for him a kind of inner regulator, affecting what is done or not done throughout a lifetime, without conscious or reasoned thought. Independent thinking will extend and modify these first attitudes, but by and large they are there to stay.

A democracy relies on people's inner attitudes much more than on the external regulators, laws and forces. Individuals are left as free as possible. Laws are not for regimenting but for assuring to every one the chance to realize his capacities. In modern life, each person's behavior affects many others. The lasting attitudes that begin in family living are therefore of crucial importance. Families are really the center, the core, around which our democratic society is built. In a world which challenges democratic living, then, parents have an added responsibility. The job of setting standards, of developing attitudes, is no mean one—and it can not begin too early. Even the toddler begins to feel the impact of, begins to assimilate, the outside world.

If children are to be helped to develop attitudes consistently, there must be within the family a clearly defined way of doing and thinking which is recognized as *our* way. A little child relies heavily upon this simple acceptance of standards, and it must be firmly there for him to desirable occupations among the parents of a neighborhood. I know of one street in a suburban community where four or five mothers met together for this purpose. Over the tea-cups they had the chance to tell each other the things they wished were different about "the gang's" activities. One mother objected to the large allowance that seemed necessary to meet demands; another was troubled by the neighborhood custom of keeping late bedtime hours; another by the attitude of intolerance which had sprung up against a new arrival.

By talking together, these mothers were able to work out a common ground of agreement in handling all these problems. . . .

Although family standards have to be definite, they can not be exclusive. *Our* way is only the right way because it *is* ours, for a short time. It must stand the test of a wider outlook, too. Accepting standards on faith is a position that is being constantly outgrown. The whys and wherefores of other standards, other ways of doing and thinking, become, as soon as children are aware of them, equally important with their own. It is in attempts to understand these differences that the first uncritical acceptance of *our* way takes on meaning and depth. For it is only by evaluating, by comparing and judging, that any reasoned basis for behavior can be formed. . . .

So it works both ways. First attitudes are important to democratic living; but democracy is also important to first attitudes. For in order that children may continue to grow, the environment roundabout them must be growing, too. It must be one upon which their new enthusiasms, their sturdy ideals, can operate. We do not, as some people seem to think, merely fit children to an existing world. We give them the tools with which to understand it, to be sure; but we also give them, whether we know it or not, an ability that is more than understanding—an ability to change it, to shape it toward their own ends. We have heard a lot recently about the dynamic nature of the totalitarian states. Democracies, too, are dynamic—and for this very reason: they give scope to growing minds. . . .

Chapter Thirty-seven

Time Bombs in Our Homes
(1952)

Mauree Applegate

In every home and in every classroom of the world, parents and teachers are daily putting together ingredients which thirty years hence can blow up the world.

These time bombs being fashioned in our homes and schools are a mixture of ideas, habits, and children—the most highly combustible combination known to man. Twenty-five to thirty years from now these bombs may burst into a new era of creative living for mankind, or they may fizzle out like firecrackers discouraged by competition from atomic weapons . . .

If we want the years ahead to be better than the present years, we must educate our children to know what is good, better than we have known it; to think more clearly than we have thought; and to act better than we, up to now, have acted. For life is becoming more complicated by the day, and the needle of the spirit is in danger of being lost in the haystack of petty affairs.

Only yesterday, we, the nations of this generation, graduated from the nursery school of Isolationism—still youngsters, together in no sense except geographically. Today we are enrolled in the kindergarten of One World. So far we have learned to join forces only when we want the same things or when we are afraid of another and stronger group than ourselves. But we are now, for the first time, trying to work together as nations. Our school is held in a large building called the U.N. When one sees us at work there and hears us shouting at one another in strange tongues, it becomes clear why we do not learn faster how to live well together: we do not even use the same language.

It is hard for the people of one land who have similar backgrounds and a common language through which to communicate with each other to live together in peace. Just try to imagine how great the barriers are that divide men who have been taught from birth only the ways of dissembling. Although this particular branch of education is called diplomacy, it still keeps us from being honest and aboveboard in our dealings with each other.

We, the nations of the world, were long years in nursery school. It may be a still longer time before our teacher, Experience, can help us to learn enough of the skills of living together so that we can pass into grade one. Although our teacher is as old as time, she is very modern in her methods of teaching. She discovered long before John Dewey that children learn most effectively by doing.

In grade one we hope not only to learn how to keep from each other's throats, but also to learn how to read the hearts of men and their hopes and longings so that we may truly build one world together.

During the later years of nursery school, the United States has been a leader among the nations. Perhaps this is due partly to the fact that the United States is larger and better developed than many of the others at this particular school. (I have heard that a rival school to the east has an even larger nation.) Our country's popularity might be due partly to the fact that its pockets are always full of lollipops with which to treat the other youngsters at recess. We would rather think that the other liked the United States because it is a decent sort and really wants to do the right thing, but when one has so many reasons for being flattered, one can never be sure whether one is really liked.

Perhaps it is this vague feeling of dissatisfaction with ourselves that is lately driving us to take a self-inventory to try to find out what we can do to make us more worthy of our position of world leadership. We believe that if all the people of our land could learn the skills of living together at home and at school and in government we would never have to flaunt our size and our riches in order to impress the rest of the world. If it were evident that we had learned how to live well spiritually as well as physically, all nations would naturally turn to us for leadership. For where do men learn to become whole except from those who have themselves learned wholeness and integration?

Surely a nation can work out a curriculum for itself just as a school plans the teaching its children need and just as the shareholders of a corporation meet together to study plans for progress. Surely civilization needs no longer to go forward by the clumsy trial-and-error method. Any alert modern elementary-school teacher knows that social living *can be learned*. And whatever can be learned, parents, teachers, and social agencies can learn to teach. Learning how to live decently together is certainly not easy, but surely the intelligence that has split the atom and worked out the many major inventions of the last century can certainly solve this more important problem. . . .

Chapter Thirty-eight

Democratic and Autocratic Child Rearing
(1964)

Rudolf Dreikurs

Every culture and civilization develops a definite pattern for raising children. Comparative studies of primitive societies offer an excellent opportunity to understand the significance of tradition. Each tribe had its own tradition and raised its children in a different way. Consequently, each tribe developed distinctive behavior patterns, characters, and personalities. Each culture had its own procedures with which to meet life problems and situations. But every man and woman and every child knew exactly what was expected. All behavior was established by tradition.

Our western culture has been more complex than primitive societies, but nonetheless it has had its traditional patterns for child-raising. There were principles such as "children are to be seen and not heard" that were followed in every home. Standards of behavior for children were the same throughout. However, our growing perception of the meaning of democracy and its effects upon interpersonal relationships has profoundly changed this same western culture. From the time of the kings and serfs up through the signing of the Magna Carta, the French and American revolutions, and the Civil War to the present time, mankind has gradually come to realize that man is created equal, not just before the law, but equal in the sight of his fellow man. The implication of this growth is that democracy is not just a political ideal, but *a way of life*. Rapid changes take place, but few are aware of the nature of this change. It is largely the impact of democracy that has transformed our social atmosphere and made the traditional methods of child-raising obsolete. We no longer have rulers such as prevailed in the autocratic society from which we are emerging. In a society of equals we can't rule *over* another. Equality means that each decides for himself. In an autocratic society, the ruler was superior to and had power over the submissive. Regardless of his station in the world, the father of each family ruled over the members, including his wife. Today this is no longer true. Women proclaimed their equality with men; and as the husband lost his power over his wife, both parents lost their power over their children. This was the beginning of a general social upheaval that has been widely felt but little understood. Other areas in our social fabric have been likewise affected. Management and labor are moving toward a closer relationship of equals. The desegregation of the Negro is an urgent social problem spurred by an ever widening understanding of the meaning of democracy. Such major changes in our social structure are more readily perceived than the subtle change wrought by the fact that women and children claim their share in equality.

Adults are usually deeply disturbed at the notion that children are their social equals. They indignantly deny such a possibility. "Don't be ridiculous. I know more than my child does. He can't possibly be my equal." No. Of course not. Not in knowledge or experience or skill. But these things don't indicate equality— even among adults. Equality doesn't mean uniformity! Equality means that people, despite all their individual differences and abilities, have equal claims to dignity and respect. Our conviction that we are superior to our children stems from our cultural heritage: that people are inferior or superior according to their birth, their money, their sex or color, or their age and wisdom. No individual ability or trait can guarantee superiority or the right to dominate.

There is another factor that may play a part in our feeling that we must be superior to our children. We may have a hidden doubt of our own worth, a deep sense of not measuring up to our own ideals. Then a child, in his helplessness, makes a delightful object of comparison by which we can feel grand! But this is a false illusion. In fact, our children are often much more capable than we are and tend to outsmart us on many occasions. This concept of equality has been growing within our culture, although we have not been aware of it and are not quite ready to understand it.

Children are particularly sensitive to a social climate. They have been quick to catch on to the idea that they share in the equal rights of everyone. They sense their equality with adults and no longer tolerate an autocratic dominant-submissive relationship. Parents, too, vaguely realize that their children have become their equals and have lessened the pressures of the you-do-as-I-say form of child-raising. At the same time, they lack new methods based on democratic principles with which to guide and educate their children into democratic social living. Thus, we are faced with our present dilemma.

This change in our social atmosphere from the autocratic relationship of the superior-inferior, of dominance and submission, to the democratic relationship of equals has been recognized by our educators. They sincerely want to be democratic. However, there is a widespread confusion about the application of democratic principles. As a result, we have frequently mistaken license for freedom and anarchy for democracy. To so many, democracy means freedom to do as one pleases. Our children have reached the point where they defy restrictions because they assume their right to do as they please. This is license, not freedom. If each member of the family insists on doing as he pleases, we have a houseful of tyrants with resulting anarchy. When everyone does as he pleases, the result is constant friction. Friction disturbs interpersonal relationships, which in turn intensifies the conflict. In an atmosphere of such constant conflict, stress and strain produce tension, anger, nervousness, and irritability; and all the negative aspects of social living flourish. Freedom *is* part of democracy; but the subtle point that we cannot have freedom unless we respect the freedom of others is seldom recognized. No one can enjoy freedom unless his neighbor has it too. In order for everyone to have freedom, we must have order. And order bears with it certain restrictions and obligations. . . .

The popular practice of letting children have unrestricted freedom has made tyrants of children and slaves of the parents. These children enjoy all the freedom while their parents assume all the responsibilities! This is hardly democracy. Parents have taken the disastrous consequences of the excess freedom assumed by their children; they have covered up for them, taken the brunt of punishment for them, borne their insults, endured their multiple demands, and thereby lost their influence over their children. The children, without knowing what bothers them, sense the loss of order because there are no restrictions to guide them. They become more concerned with getting their own way than with learning the principles and restrictions necessary for group living. As a result, the ever present capacity for social interest, or interest in one's fellow man, remains stunted and underdeveloped. This has resulted in a sense of confusion and has increased the maladjustment of children. Well-defined restrictions give a sense of security and a certainty of function within the social structure. Without this, a child feels at a total loss. His ever renewed efforts to "find himself" take the destructive course we see manifest in our many unhappy, defiant children. Freedom implies order. Without order, there can be no freedom.

To help our children, then, we must turn from the obsolete autocratic method of demanding submission to a new order based on the principles of freedom and responsibility. Our children no longer can be forced into compliance; they must be stimulated and encouraged into voluntarily taking their part in the maintenance of order. We need new principles of child-raising to replace the obsolete traditions. . . .

We must become very much aware of our new role as leaders and give up completely our ideas of authority. We simply do not have authority over our children. They know it, even if we don't. We can no longer demand or impose. We must learn how to lead and how to stimulate. The following chart will indicate the new attitudes which are needed to promote harmony and co-operation in the family. On the left we have listed the autocratic attitudes and on the right those attitudes which must now replace them.

Once the attitudes listed in the right-hand column become more or less our second nature, we will be less vulnerable to getting involved in a power struggle. If our attention is centered upon the needs of the situation rather than upon "making him mind me," we may discover ways to stimulate the child to respond. Whenever we approach a child with determination to "make" him do something, he senses it and immediately stiffens into rebellion. . . .

Autocratic Society	*Democratic Society*
Authority figure	Knowledgeable leader
Power	Influence
Pressure	Stimulation
Demanding	Winning co-operation

Punishment	Logical consequences
Reward	Encouragement
Imposition	Permit self-determination
Domination	Guidance
Children are to be seen and not heard.	Listen! Respect the child.
You do it because *I* said to.	*We* do it because it is necessary.
Prestige-centered	Situation-centered
Personal involvement	Objective detachment

The Permissive Family

If permissiveness sought to grant children more control over their own lives and greater input into the process of decision making within the family, it did not necessarily favor a shift in the balance of power between mothers and fathers. Lilian Jane Martin and Clare deGruchy's book, *The Home in a Democracy* responded to shifting gender roles by reasserting the normative responsibilities that men and women bear in rearing their young. Jules Henry was a harsh critic of permissive child rearing, arguing that it deforms the normal relations between parents and child, and creates a new oedipal conflict. Martha Weinman Lear skewers what she sees as a disproportionate attention placed on children's needs in postwar society.

Chapter Thirty-nine

The Contemporary Mother and Father
(1938)

Lilian Jane Martin and Clare deGruchy

The Mother Must Establish Ideals

In order to develop the ideal home each member in it must assume his appropriate role. The mother is the manager of the whole. She must understand the needs of each, their individual problems, and help them so to budget their lives that each is given opportunity for personal development without sacrificing the others. This is a job for a first class administrator. It is the mother who sets the standard of living physically, intellectually and morally. To do this she must have principles intelligently thought out and well defined, principles that have become habits through being lived daily and expressed with consistency under all the varied conditions of life. Her response sets the example for the children who unconsciously emulate her until they have gained immunity from infection of less desirable response to be found in the community.

The mother must continually fill her mind with world matters and be able to remold her ideas which will have been gained from a past generation and her previous personal life to meet the needs of a new generation as represented by the children. We will then no longer hear the cry from her children that she is out-of-date, old fashioned and non-understanding of their views.

She must be animated by affection that is neither over-possessive nor subjective, but by such affection as considers the welfare and development of each as of greater importance than their individual response to her. Her own expression of love must be sufficiently controlled and reasoning to set before her imitators, the children, a pattern worthy of emulation. She must above all guard herself from that expression of affection that overwhelms the child and renders him incapable.

To her falls the regulation of the time program, the money budget of each, the pleasure periods and that individual guidance each requires for his special needs. If part of this work is delegated to a nurse the mother must train her as to her particular function, and to the standards of social co-operation and the development of such habits as she is desirous of establishing for her household. . . .

The Father Should Broaden Family Life

The role of the father in family life is the one most often displaced. He, being engaged in managing the problem of earning a livelihood for all, should be regarded as manager in charge outside of the home while bringing to the family the interests of the outside world and those experiences that form part of his daily life. Without this the child's development is likely to become one-sided. With such discussion as the father will instigate, suited to the child's comprehension at any age level, the children gain invaluable knowledge for their future functioning. They develop reason and judgment in evaluating the changes taking place in the world outside of the home and school, and will have far greater adaptability in adjusting themselves to these conditions as a result of this early knowledge than if, as adults, they came upon them unprepared.

Also, the father should provide time and opportunity for each child to discuss his personal problems and his future plans, and to these he will give the same attention and respect that he gives to those of his fellow workers and employees. This builds up a relationship that many fathers long for but do not know how to create, and is a safeguard to the child during his years of immaturity. Many fathers hope for such a relation between themselves and their adolescent sons but, having played the role of infallible adults, or commanding parents during the preadolescent period of the child's life, they will find they have built up a barrier between themselves and the youth that is not easy though not impossible to overcome by a swing to a man-to-man attitude toward him now. . . .

Chapter Forty

The New Oedipal Drama of the Permissive Family
(1963)

Jules Henry

Deprived in his work life of personality aspirations, the American father reaches deeply into the emotional resources of his family for gratifications formerly considered womanly—the tenderness and closeness of his children; and his children reach thirstily toward him. Confused by the mass and contradictory character of available values, however, the American father can no longer stand for a Law or for a Social Order he often can neither explain nor defend sensibly against the challenges of his wife and children. So, too, for a man the struggle "in the world" is hard, and often, he thinks, not worth the restraint, the hard work, and the imagination he may have put into it. It seems to him better to relax and have fun. Meanwhile, since fathers cannot abandon their efforts to control children (and even wives), because the consequences of yielding entirely seem too grave, the man is caught between his need for gratifying his tender impulses and the requirement that he be an old-fashioned authority figure, too.

In the past, woman took revenge for her subordination to man and for the condescension with which she was treated by quietly stealing the children. Let her husband have his power and pride; she would have the children's warmth, by gratifying their emotional needs, while their father sat aloof on his ice-cold Super Ego. Now this is changing, and while the not-always-silent tussle for the children goes on day and night, father, too, is learning to fight with the values of the Id. But it is difficult, for it is a new weapon, and he struggles within himself because he knows—or half-knows—that it is wrong to capitulate to impulse and to give the children all the candy they want.

Because nowadays both parents are concerned more and more with the gratification of their own impulses and with a variety of emotional yearnings, father and mother are thrown into collision. This occurs because the old Super Ego values are losing caste; because since father desperately craves gratification he is eager to give it, and because there is pressure to reduce the areas of restraint and the unbearable tension generated by a driven culture, and so to relax and have a good time. It is in this context that we can understand the new role of the American father as feeder, diaperer, and bather of the baby. It is true, of course, that the increased activity of women in economic life tends to reduce the differences between male and female roles, but the cause of the alteration in these roles lies also in the decline of the ancient values and the unshackling and unmasking of a masculine hunger for emotional gratifications. . . .

Egos are almost powerless, for the parent, in his need for love—a need that is greater than his need to train the child to dignity and citizenship—tends more and more to become almost driftwood in the tides of his child's demands. What we see so much in America, then, is that the psychoanalytic metaphor according to which the child introjects the parent (copies the parent, tries to come up to parental expectations) is stood on its head, and the parent copies the child. In America today it is not alone that the child wants to live up to parental expectations, but that the parent wants also—often desperately—to live up to the child's expectations. And just as the traditional child was torn between what he wanted and what his parents wanted, so the contemporary American parent is buffeted between what he thinks he believes to be good for his *child* and what he thinks he knows would gratify him in relation to his child. In these circumstances, the children themselves tend to become more disoriented. . . .

The fact that the American father actively advertises to his children his love for them and courts them through appeals to their primary needs; the fact that he is not a remote but a close and engaging figure; the fact that the mother often punishes as much or more than the father, while the father often diapers, feeds, bathes, and keeps the nocturnal vigils—these must bring about some peculiarly American modulations in the classical Oedipus Complex. . . .

Chapter Forty-one

The Modern Pediocracy
(1963)

Martha Weinman Lear

It has been called, variously, a pediocracy, a filiarchy or, in the stern sociological view, a filio-centric way of life. Hordes of experts and quasi experts have gone into the field to study the phenomenon, and have emerged with the same mournful intelligence: We are living, like it or not—and the fact that we created it does not necessarily mean we like it—in a child-centered society. Having passed more or less unscathed through the bittersweet epoch of Life With Father, and having survived, somehow, the rigors of Momism, we are come upon a time when the child carries the ball. It is a sort of historical triple pass—from Poppa to Momma to Junior—and Junior, at the moment, is out in front and running free. Or so they say. . . .

And, indeed, a preponderance of research suggests that children do control the pattern of family life to an awesome degree. Whole communities are geared largely to their needs. They dominate adult conversation—especially in their absence. Gone are the halcyon days when mothers sat at one end of the room talking about natural childbirth and fathers stood at the other talking turkey. Today they mingle, and they talk—from the heart—about how tough it is to get into a good nursery school.

Children determine, more often than not, where the family will live. They determine what kind of home it will rent or buy; how it will spend its leisure hours; whom it will befriend; when and where it will vacation; what car it will drive; what foods it will eat, and how it will spend its income upon the myriad educational, social, and cultural activities deemed essential to the burgeoning psyche. And their parents—hounded by ghosts of Freud, harassed by bevies of experts, painfully eager to do the right thing by their offspring, to understand him, to relate to him in Meaningful Ways, to win his love, ward off his traumas, and give him every known advantage and some totally unknown beyond our national borders—these parents, almost inevitably, have pushed the child stage center, casting him in a role he never asked to play but which he has learned to play right well.

But is he really running the show? Unlikely. The current mode is to speak, with much wringing of hands, of "child rule," "child tyrants," the "Grand Abdication" of parental authority. It is an expedient fiction, rendering parents helpless before a high command of pre-pubescent tots. The likelier fact is this: Baby is being used. He is a front-runner groomed to show the world what hotshots his parents are.

Striving so passionately to be Good Parents—the ultimate accolade in these child-minded times—many mothers and fathers have turned parenthood into a painfully competitive sport. In an era when traditional status symbols can turn obsolescent overnight, they have discovered that social stature may still be gained by raising the best-dressed, -fed, -educated, -mannered, -medicated, -cultured, and -adjusted child on the block. If he looms discomfortingly large, it is only because they have done their job so well. Exploiting their child, they have created a turning worm, a faithless Galatea—a paragon of such power that he has become the exploiter, and they the victims of their own exploitation.

.These are the parents we call the child worshipers. They are not, as we shall see, always permissive; for competitive parents are generally pediatric trend-followers and they know that permissiveness is a trifle passé nowadays. But they *are* self-conscious, self-doubting, and deeply immersed in the care and psychic feeding of children. Worshipers are compulsive parents. Their rallying cry, although they sometimes wish fervently they could stop shouting it, is "for the sake of the children"; and their goal, although they sometimes wish prayerfully they could forget it, is to be Good Parents in the eyes of the child psychiatrists, the child guidance experts, the Parents' Club membership, and, of course, the neighbors.

Are we talking about all parents? All children? Of course not. There are still plenty of parents who hold the reins taut, who are not afraid of being rejected by their offspring, who can whack misbehavers without feeling guilty, who can say "No" to fancy birthday parties and posh camps and social dancing lessons and organized play and high-fashion wardrobes and child-decorated homes and optional orthodontia and Mothers' Clubs and Ivy League hysteria without fear of traumatizing their young. And there are still plenty of children around who are suffering such quaint deprivations nicely, and may even survive. All American parents are not child worshipers any more than all American adults are joiners, or all American business is big, or all American families eat hot dogs. But we *are* a nation of joiners, of big business, of hot-dog eaters; and in this sense we are a nation of child worshipers. . . .

Contributors

Philippe Ariés (1914–1984) was a French historian who explored Western attitudes toward childhood and death. His works include *Centuries of Childhood: A Social History of Family Life, Images of Man and Death*, and, as general editor, the four-volume work *A History of Private Life*.

Karin Calvert is the author of *Children in the House: Material Culture of Early Childhood, 1600–1900*.

Miriam Formanek-Brunnel is Associate Professor of History at the University of Missouri at Kansas City. She is the author of *Made to Play House: Girls and the Commercialization of American Girlhood, 1830–1930*, and editor of the *The Story of Rose O'Neill: An Autobiography*.

Henry A. Giroux is Waterbury Chair Professor in the Department of Curriculum and Instruction at Penn State University. His books include *Channel Surfing: Race Talk and the Destruction of Today's Youth, Fugitive Cultures: Race, Violence and Youth*, and *Pedagogy and the Politics of Hope*.

Shari Goldin is currently completing her PhD in communication Arts through the University of Wisconsin-Madison. Her dissertation is a social history of childhood and radio from the 1920s through the 1940s. She has taught at both Emerson College and MIT. Currently she is working with the Henry Jenkins at MIT, assisting in the development of a graduate program in Comparative Media Studies.

Shirley Brice Heath is Professor of English and Linguistics at Stanford University. She is the author of, among other works, *Ways with Words* and *Telling Tongues*, and coeditor of *The Braid of Literature: Children's Worlds of Reading*.

Allison James is Senior Lecturer in the Department of Sociology and Anthropology at the University of Hull. She is the author of *Childhood Identities: Self and Social Relationships in the Experience of the Child*, and coeditor of *Constructing and Reconstructing Childhood, Growing Up and Growing Old*, and *After Writing Culture: Epistemology and Praxis in Contemporary Anthropology*.

Henry Jenkins is Professor of Literature at MIT. He is the author of *What Made Pistachio Nuts? Early Sound Comedy and the Vaudeville Aesthetic* and *Textual Poachers: Television Fans and Participatory Culture*, and coeditor of *Classical Hollywood Comedy* and *Science Fiction Audiences*.

James R. Kincaid is Aerol Arnold Professor in the University of Southern California Department of English, where he specializes in Victorian literature and theory. His books include *Child-Loving: The Erotic Child and Victorian Culture* and *Erotic Innocence: The Culture of Child Molesting*.

Joe L. Kincheloe teaches cultural studies and pedagogy at Penn State University. He is the author of *Off to Work We Go: Rethinking the Foundations of Vocational Education*, and the coeditor of *Measured Lives: The Bell Curve Examined* and *Kinderculture: The Corporate Construction of Childhood*.

Stephen Kline is Professor of Communications at Simon Fraser University in British Columbia. He is the author of *Out of the Garden: Toys and Children's Culture in the Age of TV Marketing*, and coauthor of *Social Communication in Advertising*.

Annette Kuhn teaches in the Department of Theatre, Film and Television Studies at the University of Glasgow. She is the author of, among other works, *Family Secrets: Acts of Memory and Imagination* and *Power of the Image: Essays on Representation and Sexuality*, and coeditor of *The Woman's Companion to International Film*.

Erica Rand is Professor of Art at Bates College. She is the author of *Barbie's Queer Accessories*.

Jacqueline S. Rose is Professor of English at Queen Mary and Westfield College, University of London. Her works include *The Haunting of Sylvia Plath, Sexuality in the Field of Vision*, and *The Case of Peter Pan: Or the Impossibility of Children's Fiction*.

E. Anthony Rotundo teaches history at Phillips Exeter Academy in New Hampshire. He is the author of *American Manhood: Transformations in Masculinity from the Revolution to the Modern Era*.

Nancy Scheper-Hughes is Professor of Anthropology at the University of California at Berkeley. She is the author of *Death Without Weeping: The Violence of Everyday Life*, editor of *Child Survival: Anthropological Perspectives on the Treatment and Maltreatment of Children*, and coeditor of the forthcoming *Small Wars: The Cultural Politics of Childhood*.

Eve Kosofsky Sedgwick is Newman Ivey White Professor of English at Duke University. Her books include *Between Men: English Literature and Male Homosocial Desire; Tendencies; Fat Art, Thin Art; Epistemology of the Closet*; and *Novel Gazing: Queer Readings in Fiction*.

Ellen Seiter is Professor of Communications at the University of California, San Diego. She is the author of *Sold Separately: Children and Parents in Consumer Cultures*, and coeditor of *Remote Control: Television, Audiences*, and *Cultural Power*.

Lynn Spigel is Chair of the Division of Critical Studies in the School of Cinema-Television at the University of Southern California. She is the author of *Make*

Room for TV: Television and the Family Ideal in Postwar America, and serves as coeditor of *Camera Obscura*.

Carolyn Steedman is Chair of the Warwick Social History Centre at the University of Warwick in Coventry, England. Her works include *Landscape for a Good Woman; Strange Dislocations: Childhood and the Idea of Human Interiority, 1780–1930*; and *The Tidy House: Little Girls Writing*.

Howard F. Stein is Professor of Family Medicine at the University of Oklahoma Health Sciences Center. He is the author of numerous works, including *American Medicine as Culture, The Psychoanthropology of American Culture*, and *The Ethnic Imperative: The New White Ethnic Movement*.

Barrie Thorne is Professor of Sociology and Women's Studies at the University of California at Berkeley. She is the author of *Girls and Boys in School*, and coeditor of *Rethinking the Family: Some Feminist Questions* and *Feminist Sociology: Life Histories of a Movement*.

Valerie Walkerdine is Professor of Media and Communications at Goldsmith College in London. She is the author of *Daddy's Girl: Young Girls and Popular Culture* and has published widely in developmental, feminist, and critical psychology. She is the recipient of an ESRC Senior Research Fellowship for her work on children and computer games.

Shelby Anne Wolf is Assistant Professor of Education at the University of Colorado, Boulder. She is coeditor of *The Braid of Literature: Children's Worlds of Reading*.

Martha Wolfenstein (1911–1976) authored *Children's Humor: A Psychological Analysis* and *Children and the Death of a President*, and coedited *Childhood in Contemporary Cultures*.

Viviana A. Zelizer is Professor of Sociology at Princeton University. Her works include *Pricing the Priceless Child: The Changing Social Value of Children* and *The Social Meaning of Money*.

Permissions

Every effort has been made to trace or contact copyright holders. The publishers will be pleased to make good in future editions or reprints any omissions or corrections brought to their attention.

pp. 339–358. © 1987 D. Reidel Publishing Company. Reprinted with kind permission from Kluwer Academic Publishers.

Martha Wolfenstein, "Fun Morality: An Analysis of Recent Child-Training Literature." In Margaret Mead and Martha Wolfenstein, eds., *Childhood in Contemporary Cultures,* pp. 168–178. © 1955 The University of Chicago Press. Reprinted by permission.

Eve Kosofsky Sedgwick, "How to Bring Your Kids Up Gay." In Michael Warner, ed., *Fear of a Queer Planet: Queer Politics and Social Theory,* pp. 69–81. Minneapolis: University of Minnesota Press. © 1993 Eve Kosofsky Sedgwick. Reprinted by permission of the author.

James R. Kincaid, "Producing Erotic Children." In Diana Fuss, ed., *Human, All Too Human,* pp. 203–219. © 1996 Routledge. Reprinted by permission.

Valerie Walkerdine, "Popular Culture and the Eroticization of Little Girls." In James Curran, David Morley, and Valerie Walkerdine, eds., *Cultural Studies and Communications,* pp. 323–333. London: Arnold. © 1996 Arnold. Reprinted by permission.

Annette Kuhn, "A Credit to Her Mother." In Kuhn, *Family Secrets: Acts of Memory and Imagination,* pp. 40–58. London: Verso. © 1995 Verso. Reprinted by permission.

Ellen Seiter, "Children's Desires/Mother's Dilemmas: The Social Contexts of Consumption." In Seiter, *Sold Separately: Children and Parents in Consumer Cultures,* pp. 7–26, 31–37. © 1993 Ellen Seiter. Reprinted by permission of Rutgers University Press.

Barrie Thorne, "Boys and Girls Together . . . But Mostly Apart." In Thorne, *Gender Play: Girls and Boys in School,* pp. 29–47. New Brunswick: Rutgers University Press. © 1993 Rutgers University Press. Reprinted by permission.

E. Anthony Rotundo, "Boy Culture." In Rotundo, *American Manhood: Transformations in Masculinity from the Revolution to the Modern Era,* pp. 31–55. New York: Basic Books. © 1993 Basic Books, A Division of HarperCollins Publishers, Inc. Reprinted by permission of Basic Books, a division of HarperCollins Publishers, Inc.

Miriam Formanek-Brunell, "The Politics of Dollhood in Nineteenth-Century America." In Formanek-Brunell, *Made to Play House: Dolls and the Commercialization of American Girlhood, 1830–1930,* pp. 7–34. New Haven: Yale University Press. © 1993 Yale University Press. Reprinted by permission.

Erica Rand, "Older Heads on Younger Bodies." In Rand, *Barbie's Queer Accessories,* pp. 93–101, 114–115, 141–148. Durham: Duke University Press. © 1995 Duke University Press. Reprinted by permission.

Sourcebook Sources

E. Evalyn Grumbine, "Reaching Juvenile Markets," in *Psychology of Juvenile Appeal* (New York: McGraw-Hill, 1938).

Jess H. Wilson, "Does Your Research Embrace the Boy of Today?" in *Printer's Ink*, March 16, 1922.

" 'Selling' Food to Children," in *Mother's Own Book* (New York: Parent's Publishing Association, 1928).

John B. Watson, "After the Family—What?" in V. F. Calverton and Samuel D. Schmalhausen (eds.), *The New Generation* (New York: Macauley, 1930).

John B. Watson, "Against the Threat of Mother Love," in *Psychological Care of Infant and Child* (New York: W. W. Norton, 1928).

Excerpts from Child Study Association of America, in *Children in Wartime: Parents' Questions* (New York: Child Study Association, 1942).

Angelo Patri, "You Are Citizen Soldiers," in *Your Children in Wartime* (Garden City: Doubleday, Doran and Company, 1943).

André Fontaine, "Raise Your Boy to Be a Soldier," in *McCall's*, January 1952.

Frederic Wertham, " 'Such Trivia as Comic Books,' " in *Seduction of the Innocents* (New York: Rinehart & Co., Inc., 1953).

Dorothy Walter Baruch, "Radio Rackets, Movie Murders and Killer Cartoons," in *New Ways to Discipline: You and Your Child Today* (New York: McGraw-Hill, 1949).

Sidonie Matsner Gruenberg, "New Parents for Old," in V. F. Calverton and Samuel D. Schmalhausen (eds.), *The New Generation* (New York: Macauley, 1930).

Elizabeth F. Boettiger, "Families and the World Outside," in *Your Child Meets the World Outside* (New York: D. Appleton-Century, 1941).

Mauree Applegate, "Time Bombs in Our Homes," in *Everybody's Business—Our Children* (Evanston: Roe, Peterson, 1952).

Rudolf Dreikurs, M.D., "Democratic and Autocratic Child Rearing," in *Children: The Challenge* (New York: Hawthorn, 1964).

Lillian Jane Martin and Clare deGruchy, "The Contemporary Mother and Father," *The Home in a Democracy* (San Francisco: Harcourt Wagner, 1938).

Jules Henry, "The New Oedipal Drama of the Permissive Family," in *Culture against Man* (New York: Vintage, 1963).

Martha Weinman Lear, "The Modern Pediocracy," in *The Child Worshipers* (New York: Pocket, 1963).

Index

Abbott, Eleanor, 374
Abbott, Jacob, 374
ABC (television network), 145, 149, 157
action figures. *See* dolls
Action for Children's Television (ACT), 7, 129, 311, 315
Adler, Dr. Felix, 89
Adorno, Theodor, 278
Adventures of Ozzie and Harriet, The (TV), 118
advertising, 102–108, 111, 116, 126–127, 257, 297, 301, 308–310, 458, 459–461, 462, 463–467, 490
Advertising and Selling (magazine), 126
advice literature, 21, 113, 114, 115, 199–208, 209–230, 306–309, 311, 364–365, 457–520
Age of Television, The (book), 116
aggression, 348
Agnew, Spiro, 21, 227
Aid to Families with Dependent Children (AFDC), 181
Alcott, Louisa May, 368, 372
Alice in Wonderland (book), 407, 420
"all deliberate speed," 142
Allen, Woody, 243, 246
American Baby (magazine), 307
American Baby (TV), 307
American Child, The (publication), 89
American Farm Bureau Federation, 86
American Humane Society, 189–190
American Psychiatric Association, 231
American Woman's Home, The (book), 364
Anderson, Daniel, 313
Anderson, James, 313
Angelou, Maya, 154
Animal Babies (book), 415
animation (*see also* cartoons; *specific titles*), 297
Ann Landers, 307
Anne, St., 44
Annie (film), 258
Applegate, Mauree, 496, 501–502
Ariès, Philippe, 15, 16, 23, 41–57, 62, 72, 73, 75, 76, 98, 515
Aristotle, 49
Arlitt, Ada Hart, 213
Assault on Truth (book), 185
Augustine, St., 50

autocratic (child rearing practices), 20, 496, 497, 503–506
autonomy, 350–353

Babar (book), 31, 415. See also *Meet Babar and His Family* (book)
Babette's Pageant and Talent Gazette (magazine), 272
Babyhood (magazine), 374
"back to basics," 153
Bad Seed, The (film), 164, 186
Baker, Ray Stannard, 353
Bakhtin, Mikhail, 426
Barbie, 27, 297, 382–393
Barbie's Queer Accessories (book), 27
Barnard, John, 351
Barney and Friends (TV), 243
Barr, Roseanne, 270
Barrie, J. M., 59–65, 369
Barry, Jack, 125, 126
Barthes, Roland, 15, 107
Bartholomew, Freddie, 245
Baruch, Dorothy Walter, 485, 493–495
Basil, Toni, 255
Bateson, Gregory, 323
Bathrick, Serafina, 122
Batman (toys), 297
Batman (TV), 134, 297
"Battered Child Syndrome," 178
Bazalgette, Cary, 2
Beales, Ross, 73
Beard, Daniel, 352, 353, 354, 356
Beauty and the Beast, 410
Beecher, Catherine, 364, 365
Beecher, Mrs. H. W., 370
behaviorism, 212–213, 307, 470–475
Being There (film), 171
Beisel, David, 184
Bennett, William, 279
Berger, John, 445
Berlant, Lauren, 11
Berle, Milton, 123
"best interests of the child," 179
Best Word Book Ever, The (book), 419
Bettelheim, Bruno, 64, 446

Better Homes and Gardens (magazine), 116, 118, 120

Beveridge, Senator Albert, 86

Birmingham school, 31

Bixby, Sarah, 375

Black America (documentary series), 145

Black History: Lost, Stolen, or Strayed (TV), 146–148, 152

Blake, William, 18

Bloch, Ernst, 300

Bluest Eye, The (book), 384–385

Boettiger, Elizabeth F., 496, 499–500

Bogart, Leo, 116, 119, 122–123, 131

Bowie, David, 171

"boy culture," 29, 30, 337–362, 458, 462

Boy Scouts, 19, 113, 215, 481, 484

boyhood, 26, 76, 147, 337–362, 373, 374

Boyle, Jimmy, 404

boy's books, 27

Brady Bunch, The (TV), 161

Braid of Literature, The (book), 28

Brazelton, T. Berry, 307

Breakfast Club, The (film), 163

Brink, Carol Ryrie, 366

Broderick, Matthew, 248

Brokaw, Tom, 248

"Brown Eyes/Blue Eyes" experiment, 151

Brown v. Board of Education of Topeka, Kansas, 137, 138, 139, 141, 142, 145, 153

Bryant, Jennings, 313

Bubbles (painting), 104

Buck Rogers, 461

Buckingham, David, 2

Bulger, James, 258

Burke, Kenneth, 426

Burns, George, 248

Bush, Barbara, 10

But Not Billy (book), 407

Butler, Nicholas Murray, 88

Cahill, Spencer, 322

California Fruit Growers Exchange, 460

Calvert, Karin, 15, 17, 18, 67–80, 366, 374, 515

Calvin Klein, 23, 276

Canby, Henry Seidel, 337, 344, 345, 354

candy. *See* kets

Candy, John, 161

Capra, Frank, 111

Captain Kangaroo (TV), 121

Captain Video (TV), 119

Carroll, Lewis, 23, 59, 60

Carson, Johnny, 188

cartoons (*see also* animation), 314, 417, 493–495

CBS (television network), 110, 123, 125, 271

CBS Reports Black America (documentary series), 137

census, U.S., 81, 84

Centuries of Childhood (book), 15, 72, 75

Cerf, Phyllis, 120

Champ, The (film), 246

Charin, Peggy, 129, 315

Charities and the Commons (magazine), 90

Chaucer, 244

Chicago News (newspaper), 87

Child (magazine), 307

child abuse, 22, 167, 178–195, 224, 241–253, 257, 259, 267, 269, 276, 436–438

child custody, 7

Child from One to Six, The (book), 213

"Child Is Being Beaten, A" (essay), 189

child labor, 81–94, 97–99, 112, 338, 341

Child, Lydia Maria, 364, 365

child sacrifice, 184–185

Child Study Association of America, 476, 477–479

"Child Study Movement," 19

childhood as freedom, 17, 18, 19, 21

childhood, economic approaches, 81–94

childhood, historical constructions of, 15, 17, 18, 19, 21, 22, 41–57, 67–80, 81–94, 95–109, 337–362, 363–381

childhood illness, 17

childhood innocence, 1, 2, 6, 9, 11, 12, 14, 17, 23, 24, 30, 45, 46, 52, 56, 60, 64, 65, 79, 98, 102, 110, 111, 113, 114, 142, 151, 247, 254, 256, 257, 258, 262, 263, 265–282, 284, 285, 457

childhood, middle ages, 15, 17, 41–57, 73, 96–97

Child-Loving: The Erotic Child and Victorian Culture (book), 251

Children of the Damned (film), 163–164

children's art, 445

Children's Bureau, 113, 199–208

children's clothing, 67, 68, 74, 103–104, 266, 288–290, 338

children's culture: definitions, 4, 24, 25, 28, 95–109; politics, 4

Children's Defense Fund, 10, 12

children's fiction, 23, 58–66, 365, 370–372

Children's Letters to God (book), 440

children's literature, 26, 27, 28, 31, 54, 363, 406–430, 462

children's reading, 406–430

children's rights, 10, 11, 32

children's sexuality, 20, 21, 23, 24, 25, 26, 41–48, 59, 60, 62, 64, 65, 200–203, 210–230, 231–240, 241–253, 254–264, 385–389, 435, 439, 470, 471, 472, 479

children's television (*see also* television), 28, 29, 32, 120–129, 299, 300, 417

children's writing, 431–453

Chodorow, Nancy, 310, 358

Christian Coalition, 279

Cinderella (story), 407, 409, 420, 421, 422

circumcision, 44, 45–46

citizen soldiers, 20, 480–482

civil rights era, 2, 136–158

Civil War, 341, 366, 367, 369, 370, 375, 503
Civilizing Process, The (book), 16, 17
Clark, Kenneth, 141
Cleary, Beverly, 422
Client, The (film), 245, 246
Clift, Montgomery, 244
Clinton, Bill, 8, 10, 14, 153, 250, 266
Clinton, Hillary Rodham, 1, 4, 7, 10, 11, 12, 13
Close Encounters of the Third Kind, 186
clubs, 343, 344, 347
Cocomalt, 461
Codel, April Ella, 116
cold war, 21, 219, 476, 483–484, 501–502
Coles, Robert, 141
Columbia University, 87, 89, 227
comic books, 485, 486–492, 493–495
comic strips, 460
commercials. *See* advertising
Common Sense Book of Baby and Childcare (book), 115
Communications Decency Act, 9, 10
Comstock, Anthony, 114
Conners, Jimmy, 248
conscience, 353
consumption, 297–317, 382–393
Continuing Committee on the Prevention and Control of Delinquency, 115
Coogan, Jackie, 464
Coppertone, 23, 241
Core Gender Identity (CGI), 234, 235
Cosby, Bill, 146–148
Cosby Show, The (TV), 174
Cosmopolitian (magazine), 84
Costner, Kevin, 245
Country Bunny and the Little Gold Shoes, The (book), 411
Cowan, Ruth Schwartz, 302, 303, 305
Crosby, John, 118
Crothers, Samuel, 349
Cruise, Tom, 247
Culkin, Macaulay, 159, 160, 163, 174, 175, 243, 245, 247, 253
Culp, Robert, 148
Curious George, 420
Custis, Martha, 78

Daily Mail, The (newspaper), 251
Dare to Discipline (book), 226
daring, 346–347, 353
Darwin, Charles, 112
darwinism, social, 182, 183
Davis, Dr. Clara, 218
Day, Thomas, 63
daycare, 7
de Brunhof, Laurent, 415
de Dainville, Pere, 43
de Paola, Tomie, 418
de Saussure, Ferdinand, 160

deGruchy, Clare, 507, 508–509
Delineator, The (magazine), 369
deMause, Lloyd, 16, 73, 98, 181–182, 184, 188
democracy, 20, 278, 457, 496, 497–498, 499–500, 501–502, 503
Democracy in the Household (book), 226
democratic child rearing practices, 503–506
Democratic National Convention, 12, 31
Democratic party, 1, 4, 10, 14, 21
Demos, John, 74
Dennis the Menace (comic strip), 21
depression era, 302
desegregation (*see also* segregation), 142, 143, 145
developmental psychology, 2, 451
Devine, Edward T., 90
Dewey, John, 100, 145, 502
Diagnostic and Statistical Manual (DSM-III), 232
Dickens, Charles, 97
digital revolution, 2, 9, 30, 32
Ding Dong School (TV), 121
discipline, 18, 19, 53, 131, 213, 496, 497–498, 505
Disney, 6, 134, 270–271
Disney, Walt, 127
Disneyland (TV), 127
divorce, 159, 160, 305, 469
Dobson, S., 394
Dodson, Fitzhugh, 219
Dole, Bob, 9, 10, 14
dolls, 27, 69, 183, 186, 187, 188, 363–381, 382–393; Barbie, 27, 297, 382–393; Cabbage Patch, 186, 187, 188; G.I. Joe, 183
Doll's Dressmaker (magazine), 368, 371
Doll's Journey, A (book), 368
Doll's Own Book (book), 370
Dolls' Surprise Party, The (book), 372
Doll's Tea Party, The (book), 369
"Dora," 254
Douglas, Mary, 297, 395, 396, 400, 401, 404
Dreikurus, Rudolf, 496, 503–506
Driver, Daniel, 241
Du Bois, W. E. B., 145
Dubroff, Jessica, 269
Ducks Don't Get Wet (book), 419
Dundes, Alan, 188
Dyer, Richard, 300
"dyke destiny," 27, 385–389

Earthling, The (film), 245
Eastwood, Clint, 245
Ebel, Henry, 184
ebonics, 154
Eby, Kermit, 483
Eckert, Charles, 258
Edelman, Marian Wright, 10, 12, 13, 154
Education. *See* pedagogy
Ehrenreich, Barbara, 5, 6, 113
Eisenhower, Dwight David, 29
Elias, Norbert, 16, 17

Eliot, George, 372, 375
Elkind, David, 275
Ellerbee, Linda, 29, 32
Elliott, Jane, 150–153
Ellis, Havelock, 489
Ellson, Hal, 487
Elyot, Sir Thomas, 486
Emile (book), 18, 63
Encino Man (film), 171
English, Deirdre, 113
Engstrom, Harold, 142
Epistemology of the Closet (book), 237
equality vs. uniformity, 504
Erasmus, 48, 50, 53
Escapade (magazine), 220
Esquire (magazine), 115
E.T.: The Extra-Terrestial (film), 186
Ewen, Stuart, 105–106, 108
Exorcist, The (film), 164, 186
Explorers (film), 171
Eye of the Storm, The (TV), 137, 150–153

Fair Labor Standards Act, 86
Family Channel, The (television network), 307
Family Secrets (book), 25, 26
Family Ties (TV), 174
family togetherness, 310
family values, 4, 5, 6, 8, 9, 10, 11, 14, 25, 31, 160, 166, 231, 266, 468, 469
family-wage system, 9
Fangface (TV), 314
fantasies, 259, 260, 261, 262, 290
Fat Albert (TV), 153
fatherhood, 7, 9, 10, 21, 112, 115, 167–168, 304, 305, 342, 351–352, 356–357, 368, 451, 508–509, 510–511, 512–513
Faulkner, William, 155
feminism, 7, 26, 31, 254, 275; domestic, 7
"feminization of poverty," 190
Fireside Theatre (TV), 118
Firestarter (film), 164
First Christmas, The (book), 419
Fisher, David Hackett, 77
Fiske, John, 139, 155
Five Chinese Brothers, The (book), 425
Flintstones, The (TV), 134
Flower Lady (story), 449
Fonda, Jane, 422
Fontaine, Andre, 476, 483–484
food, 394–405, 463–467, 481
Fool of the World, The (book), 409
Forbush, William Buron, 19
Forgotten Children (book), 74
Formanek-Brunnel, Miriam, 27, 363–381, 515
Forrest Gump (film), 248
Forty, Adrian, 103–104
Foster, Jodie, 245
Foucault, Michel, 114, 180, 256

Frailberg, Selma H., 223–224
Free School Act, 99
Freedman, Eric, 8
freedom, 457, 496, 497–498, 504
Freidman, Richard C., 232, 234, 235, 236
Freud, Sigmund, 60, 64, 65, 185–186, 189, 219, 231, 250, 254, 256, 259–260, 489, 512
Freudian psychoanalysis, 20, 60, 64, 65, 185–186, 189, 212, 220, 250
Friday the 13th (film), 162
friendship, 318–336, 343, 344, 345, 347–349
Froebel, Friedrich, 99–101
Full House (TV), 174
fun morality, 199–208, 212, 308
Funny Little Woman, The (book), 410

Gale, Zona, 375
games, 54, 100, 266, 341, 345, 346–349
Garbage Pail Kids, 128
Garland, Judy, 244, 258, 417
Garner, Alan, 64
Gathings, Ezekiel, 117, 123
Geeson, Cecil, 394
gender, 232–239, 283–294, 318–336, 338, 339, 358, 363–381, 508–509
gender construction, 67, 68, 76, 237
gender identification, 26, 68
"Gender Identity Disorder of Childhood," 232, 234
"gender outlaw," 27
General Electric, 116
genre, 409, 410
Germs Make Me Sick (book), 419
Gerson, 46–49, 51
Gesell Institute, 199, 225
Gigi (film), 258
Gilbert, James, 130
Gilmore, David, 358
Ginott, Haim G., 217–218
Girl Scouts, 113, 481
Girl X, 268
girlhood, 27, 254–264, 283–294, 363–381, 406–430, 431–453
Girls' Book (book), 364
girl's books, 27
Giroux, Henry, 4, 265–282, 515
Goetz, Bernhard, 183
Goldin, Claudia, 82
Goldin, Shari, 13, 136–158, 515
Goldstein, Richard, 271
Godey's Lady's Magazine, 78
Godkin, Lawrence, 343
Goffman, Erving, 324, 400
Good Mother, The (book), 209–210, 224
Good Son, The (film), 253
Good-night Moon (book), 415
Gore, Albert, 10
Gould, Jack, 118, 119, 127

Grange, Red, 464
Green, Harvey, 370
Green, Richard, 232, 235, 236–237
Greene, Graham, 259, 444
Greenfield, Jeff, 128
Grimm brothers, 406, 408
Griswold, Robert L., 8, 10, 21
Growing Old in America (book), 77
Growing Up Together (TV), 307
Gruenberg, Sidonie Matsner, 496, 497–498
Grumbine, E. Evalyn, 458, 459–461

Haines, Michael, 82
Hall, G. Stanley, 19, 373
Hall, Stuart, 155
Hallinan, Maureen, 332
Halloween (film), 162, 165
Hard Copy (TV), 242
Harding, Vincent, 137
Hardman, Charlotte, 403
Hardyment, Christina, 307
Harper's Bazaar (magazine), 367
Harris, Abigail, 332
Harris, Marly, 275
Hayden, Dolores, 303
Healthy Kids (TV), 307
Hearts of Men, The (book), 5
Heath, Shirley Brice, 28, 406–430, 515
Heininger, Mary Lynn Stevens, 9, 372
Hendershot, Heather, 7
Henri IV, 41, 47, 49
Henry, Jules, 507, 510–511
Heroard, 41–43, 44, 54, 73
Herzog, Eleanor, 332
Heyward, DuBose, 411
Hiawatha (story), 374
High School (film), 138
History of Sanford and Merton, The (book), 63
Hochschild, Arlie, 304, 305
Hodge, Robert, 314, 315
Hoffmann, E. T. A., 419
Holt, Luther Emmett, 368, 471
Home Alone (film), 159–176, 241, 245
Home Furnishings (magazine), 126
Home in a Democracy, The (book), 507
homosexuality, 5, 6, 26, 27, 215, 222, 225, 231–240, 232, 385–389
Honeymooners, The (TV), 119
Hoole, Charles, 48
Horace, 408
horror films, 162, 163–164, 167–168, 186
Hostess Cupcakes, 124
House at Pooh Corner, The (book), 413
housework, 301–306
How the Grinch Stole Christmas (book), 418
How to Survive Parenthood (book), 226
Howdy Doody (TV), 29, 124, 126, 127
Howells, Mary, 352

Howells, William Dean, 340, 349
Huck Finn, 352
Hunt, David, 73, 76
Hunt, Mary, 373
Hunter College, 87
hunting, 340–341

"I have a Dream" speech, 136
I Spy (TV), 148
imitation, 342
"immaculate," childhood as, 284, 285, 292
impulses, 200, 201, 202, 203, 204, 205, 206, 207, 212, 227
In the Night Kitchen (book), 423, 424
industrialization, 29, 98, 101
Inside the Great House (book), 73
interpretive community, 412, 427–428
intertextuality, 428–429
invalidism, 214, 472–473
Isaacs, Susan, 100
It Takes a Village (book), 11, 13
It's a Wonderful Life (film), 111, 160
It's Alive (film), 164

Jack and the Beanstalk (story), 416
Jack Got the Sack (story), 448
Jackson, Jesse, 154
Jackson, Michael, 241, 243, 246
James, Alison, 28, 394–405, 515
Jameson, Fredric, 300
Jefferson, Thomas, 78
Jenkins, Henry, 1–37, 133, 209–233, 515
Jenks, Chris, 138
Jerome, St., 47
Jesus, 51, 52
Johnny Jupiter (TV), 124
Johnson, Lyndon Baines, 144, 145, 181
Jolly Postman, The (book), 423
Jordan Marsh, 367
Jordan, Michael, 243
Journal of an Understanding Heart, The (book), 440
Jurassic Park (film), 168
juvenile delinquency, 115, 165, 485, 486–492

Kagen, Jerome, 308
Kanka, Megan, 269
Kasson, John, 17
Katz, Jon, 30, 32
Keep Them Human (book), 226
Kefauver, Senator Estes, 115, 117
Kempe, C. Henry, 178
Keniston, Kenneth, 163
Kennedy, Edward, 266
Kennedy, John F., 181
Kennedy, John, Jr., 248
Kerner, Otto, 145
kets, 28, 394–405
Kidnapped (film), 246

Kids Court (TV), 29
Kids Pick the President (TV), 29
Kimbrough, Emily, 373
Kincaid, James R., 1, 2, 4, 5, 9, 18, 23, 24, 136, 211, 241–253, 516
Kincheloe, Joe L., 22, 159–176, 516
Kinder, Marsha, 29
kinderculture, 163, 172, 176
kindergarten, 101
King Lear, 408
King, Martin Luther, 13, 136, 137
Klaas, Polly, 269
Kline, Stephen, 20, 24, 25, 28, 95–109, 516
Kohl, Herbert, 31
Krafft-Ebing, Richard Von, 489
Kuhn, Annette, 25, 283–294, 516
Kukla, Fran and Ollie (TV), 121
Kumer, Shanti, 138
Kuralt, Charles, 242

La Salle, St. Jean-Baptiste de, 53, 55
Lacan, Jacques, 259, 260
LaCour, V. J., 274
Ladies' Home Journal (magazine), 116
Lafargue Clinic, 488–489
Lang, Andrew, 64
Laplanche, Jean, and Pontalis, J.-B., 260, 261, 262
Larcom, Lucy, 365, 366
Lassie (TV), 29
Lasswell, Harold, 204
latchkey kids, 159
Leach, Penelope, 307
Leaf, Monroe, 417,
Lear, Martha Weinman, 507, 512–513
Lears, T. Jackson, 18, 102
Leave it to Beaver (TV), 171
Lee, Harper, 422
Leites, Nathan, 205
Lemish, Dafna, 313, 315
LeShan, Eda J., 212
Leslie, Eliza, 364
Letterman, David, 248
Lévi-Strauss, Claude, 314, 395, 400
Lieberman, Joseph, 14
Life (magazine), 272
Lifetime (television network), 307
Lincoln, Abraham, 87, 150
Little Rascals, The (film series), 245
Little Red Riding Hood (story), 419, 420, 423
Little Rock School Board, 142
Little White Bird, The (book), 61
Little Women (book), 372
Locke, John, 63, 64, 99
Lockheed, Marlaine, 332
Loftus, Elizabeth, 249
Lolita, 254–255, 256, 257, 270, 277
Lonely Crowd, The (book), 205

Longfellow, Henry Wadsworth, 374
Looking Back: A Chronicle of Growing Up Old in the Sixties (book), 128
Lopata, Helena Z., 305
Lorch, Elizabeth, 313
Lorio, Penny, 386
Louis XIII, 41–43, 47, 54, 73
Lowther, T. J., 245
loyalty, 343, 344, 347
Luria, Zella, 332
Lyle, Jack, 128, 312

Macy's, 85, 367
Mad (magazine), 128
Magic Years, The (book), 223
Making of the Modern Family, The (book), 73
"male domesticity," 112
Male Homosexuality: A Contemporary Psychoanalytic Perspective (book), 232
"mama's boy," 353–354
Man Who Fell to Earth, The (film), 171
Man Without a Face, The (film), 246
manhood, 355–357
Mann, Sally, 24, 32
Mapplethorpe, Robert, 24
marasmus, 216
Marchand, Roland, 105–107, 309, 310
Mark, Ellen, 273
Mark, Marky, 248
Marsh, Margaret, 112
Marshall Field, 85, 367
Martin, Lilian Jane, 507, 508–509
Masson, Jeffrey, 185, 254
Masters and Johnson, 217
mastery, 347–348
masturbation, 200, 201, 202, 203, 206, 214, 216–222, 224, 227
material culture, 67–80, 104–105
Mather, Cotton, 77
Mattel, 382–393
Mavor, Carol, 23, 24
Mayhew, Henry, 447–448, 450, 452
Maynard, Joyce, 128
McCarthyism, 21
McHugh, Paul, 249
McMartin trial, 241, 244
McNaught, Harry, 415
Mead, Margaret, 21, 219–220
Meet Babar and His Family (book), 415
Megan's Law, 31
Melville, Herman, 360
Memmi, Albert, 44
Menendez, Lyle and Erik, 241, 244–245, 246
mental hygiene, 486
Messaria, Paul, 314
Meyrowitz, Joshua, 128
Mickey Mouse Club, The (TV), 127

Mill on the Floss, The (book), 372
Millais, Sir John Everett, 104
Miller, Daniel, 299
Miller, Sue, 209–210
Milne, A. A., 413
Minipops (TV), 255, 263
Mischievous Tommy (book), 372
Mod Squad, The (TV), 137
Modell, John, 83
modesty, 49, 53–55
Molinari, Susan, 1, 4, 5, 6, 8
Momism, 512
Money, John, 234
Money (magazine), 274
Montessori, Maria, 99
Moral Majority, 180
Morrison, Toni, 384–385
Mosquito Coast, The (film), 186
Moss, Kate, 273
Mother Goose, 414, 418, 424, 425
Mother Jones, 84
motherhood, 6, 7, 9, 21, 24, 25, 26, 112, 115, 166–
167, 203, 203, 204, 209–210, 219, 235, 283–294,
301–310, 338, 342, 351, 352, 353, 354, 358, 363,
364, 365, 368–369, 413–414, 435, 438, 439, 451,
463–467, 470–475, 500, 508–509, 510–511, 512–
513
Mothers' Monthly Journal (magazine), 364
"mother's movement." *See* National Congress of
Mothers
Mother's Own Book, The (book), 458, 463–467
mourning, 370, 374, 375, 449–450
Movies: A Psychological Study (book), 205
Moynihan, Daniel, 143, 144
Mr. God, This Is Anna (book), 440
Mr. Novak (TV), 137
Mr. Peepers (TV), 137
Mrs. Manners, 337
mud, 215–216, 218
Mulvey, Laura, 259, 260, 261
Murphy Brown (TV), 7, 166
My Fair Lady (film), 258
My Little Pony (toy), 297
My Little Pony (TV), 27
My Three Sons (TV), 173
My Visit to the Dinosaurs (book), 419

Nandy, Ashis, 13
Narratives from the Crib (book), 427
National Advisory Committee on Civil Disor-
ders, 145
National Association of Broadcasters, 117
National Association of Manufacturers, 86
National Center for the Treatment and Preven-
tion of Child Abuse, 178
National Child Labor Committee, 81, 89–90
National Congress of Mothers, 112

National Industrial Recovery Act, 86
NBC (television network), 124
needs vs. wants, 201–202
Neill, Sam, 168
Nesler, Ellie or Willy, 241, 242, 246
Never Ending Story, The (book), 422
New Republic (magazine), 88
New York Times (newspaper), 84, 118, 271
Nicholson, Jack, 168, 248
Nickelodeon (television network), 28, 29, 32, 135
Night and Day (magazine), 259
nineteenth century, 29, 337–362, 363–381
*No Peace, No Place: Excavations along the Genera-
tional Fault* (book), 128
No Sense of Place (book), 128
Norbeck, Edward, 96
North (film), 253
North, Jay, 245
Nutcracker, The (book), 419

Oakley, Ann, 306
object-choice, 233
O'Hara Catherine, 161
"Oh, Mickey" (song), 255
Omen, The (film), 186
On Temperance (book), 49
O'Neal, Tatum, 245
O'Neil, Teddy, 100
Opie, Iona Archibald and Peter, 394
Osterman, Paul, 85
Other, The (film), 164
Outside Over There (book), 420
overstimulation, 216
Owen, Robert, 99

Pageant Life (magazine), 272, 274
pageants, 265–282, 291–293
paintings, 45, 104
Palmer, Patricia, 313
Palmer, Phyllis, 305
parental priorities, 96
Parents and Children in History (book), 73
Parents Deserve to Know (book), 226–227
Parents (magazine), 120, 121, 122, 215, 307, 309,
311
Parker, Edwin B., 128, 312
Pascal, Jacqueline, 43, 52–53
pastoralism, 12
Patri, Angelo, 207, 476, 480–482
Peale, Norman Vincent, 227
Peck's Bad Boy (book), 372
pedagogy, 18, 26, 31, 46–56, 62, 63, 98–101, 103,
138, 144–145, 146–155, 162–163, 172, 176, 206,
231, 256, 258, 276, 278, 318–336, 366, 431, 439–
445, 462, 501–502
pedophilia, 23, 24, 227, 241–253
Pee-wee Herman, 110

Pee-wee's Playhouse (TV), 28, 133
Perfect World, A (film), 245
permissive child-rearing, 20, 21, 22, 210, 217,
     218, 221, 224, 225, 226, 227, 493–495, 497–506,
     507–513
Perrault, Charles, 409
Pesci, Joe, 162, 169
Pesquera, Beatrice, 306
Peter and the Wolf (music), 422
Peter Pan, 58–65, 110, 124, 369
photography, 23, 25, 32, 59, 283–294
Piaget, Jean, 307, 309
Pickford, Mary, 464, 465
Pierre (book), 360
Pingree, Suzanne, 313
Pittsburgh Post (newspaper), 375
Platter, Thomas, 43
play, 27, 28, 29, 30, 100, 107, 113, 121, 199, 202–
     203, 204, 205, 213, 277, 330, 331, 339–342, 346–
     349, 357, 358, 363–381, 382–393, 406–425, 429,
     459–461, 478, 481, 493–495
Playboy (magazine), 167, 244
Plessy v. Ferguson, 140
Plumb, J. H., 96
Plutarch, 50
Polar Express, The (book), 419
Pollock, Linda, 74
popular culture, 14, 20, 186, 254–264, 266; uto-
     pian aspects of, 300
Popular Front Movement, 20
Popular Science (magazine), 115
Post Toasties, 459
Postman, Neil, 265–266, 311
Potter, Beatrix, 372, 444
Powell, Colin, 8
pranks, 350–352
Pretty Baby (film), 23
Price, Vincent, 244
"primal scene," 221
primitivism, 18, 220
Problem Child (film), 164–165
Procter & Gamble Co., 459
Progressive Era, 2, 19, 86, 89, 113, 212
progressivism, 102, 108
Prokofiev, Sergei, 422
psychoanalysis (*see also* Freudian psychoanaly-
     sis), 43, 44, 231, 233, 250, 259, 260, 510
Psychological Care of Infant and Child (book), 213
psychological literature, 26, 185
public sphere, 31
Puritan(s)(ism), 73, 199, 205
purity, 247, 248

Quayle, Dan, 7, 166
Quayle, Marilyn, 10

race, 12, 13, 136–158, 315, 321, 384–385, 389–390,
     503–504

radio, 460, 461, 476, 479, 480–482, 485, 493–495
Radke, Marian J., 141
Raising a Responsible Child (book), 226
Ramona the Pest (book), 422
Ramsey, JonBenet, 268, 269, 270, 271, 273, 274
Rand, Erica, 27, 28, 382–393, 516
Ransome, Arthur, 409
Rapunzel (story), 406, 408, 419
Rather, Dan, 271
Reader's Digest (magazine), 120
Reading Rainbow (TV), 417
Reagan, Ronald, 181, 182
Rebecca of Sunnybrook Farm, 370
Red Balloon, The (film), 415
Red Cross, 481, 482
Redbook (magazine), 308
Redneck (film), 246
religious representations, 45–51
Republican National Convention, 8, 31
Republican party, 1, 4, 10, 11, 14, 21
resistance, 27, 28, 31, 375, 390–393, 394–405
responsibility, 496
Ribble, Margaret A., 216–217
Rich, Frank, 271
Richards, Ellen, 213
Richelieu, 50
Riesman, David, 205
Rights of Infants, The (book), 216
Riis, Jacob, 89
Robinson, Harriet, 366
Rodham, Hillary. *See* Clinton, Hillary Rodham
Room 222 (TV), 137, 149–150
Roosevelt, Franklin, 181
Roosevelt, Theodore, 343–344
Rose, Jacqueline, 13, 23, 58–66, 110, 516
Rosemary's Baby (film), 186
Rotundo, E. Anthony, 29, 30, 337–362, 516
Rousseau, Jean-Jacques, 12, 18, 30, 56, 63, 64, 99
Ruth, Babe, 464, 465
Ryan, Stephen, 184

sacredization, 17, 19, 20, 79, 98
Safer, Morley, 274
Salk, Lee, 225
Sally (TV), 173
Saturday Evening Post (magazine), 87
Saturday Review (magazine), 120
scandal, 250
Scarry, Richard, 419
Scheper-Hughes, Nancy, 22, 178–195, 516
Schmidt, Casper, 184
Schools and schooling. *See* pedagogy
Schramm, Wilbur, 128, 312
Schroeder, Ricky, 245, 247
Scott, Ann, 262
Searching for Bobbie Fisher (film), 246
Sears, Richard, 367
Sears Roebuck, 367

Sedgwick, Eve Kosofsky, 26, 231–240, 516
Sedgwick, Henry Dwight, 343, 344
seduction, 259, 260, 262, 263
Segal, Elizabeth, 26, 27
segregation (*see also* desegregation), 13, 141; *de facto*, 143
Seiter, Ellen, 23, 27, 138, 297–317, 516
Sellers, Peter, 171
Sendak, Maurice, 416, 420, 423, 424
Sensuous Man, The (book), 210
Sensuous Woman, The (book), 210
"separate but equal," 141
Sesame Street (TV), 6, 153, 313, 417
Seuss, Dr., 418
Sewell, Mary, 364
sewing, 364–365, 369, 375
sex play, 224–226
Shakespeare, William, 409
Shane (film), 246
Shayon, Robert Lewis, 119
Shields, Brooke, 245
Shining, The (film), 167–168
Short Circuit (film), 171
Shorter, Edward, 73
Simpson, Bart, 110, 174
Simpson, O. J., 243
Simpsons, The (TV), 110, 129, 174
Singer, Dorothy and Jerome, 312
"Sissy Boy Syndrome" and the Development of Homosexuality, The (book), 232
Sixty Minutes (TV), 274, 275
Sleeping Beauty, 407, 419, 420
Smith, Daniel Blake, 73
Smith, Susan, 165
Snow White, 419
social Darwinism, 19
social engineering, 21
Southern Baptist Convention, 6
Spencer, Ethal, 375
Spigel, Lynn, 14, 29, 110–136, 310, 516
Splash (film), 171
Spock, Benjamin, 20, 21, 115, 120, 131, 132, 209–230, 307, 308, 414, 476
"spoiling the child," 214
Statue of Salt, The (book), 44
Steedman, Carolyn, 25, 431–453, 517
Stein, Howard F., 22, 178–195, 184, 517
Steiner, Rudolph, 99
Stern, Daniel, 162, 169
Stewart, Jimmy, 160
Stewart, Susan, 4
stoicism, 346
Stoller, Robert, 234
Stone, Lawrence, 16
Stop Annoying Your Children (book), 226
Story of Ferdinand, The (book), 417
Stowe, Harriet Beecher, 364
Strawberry Shortcake (TV), 27

Sturges, Jock, 24
subcultural resistance, 2
subculture, 337–362
suicide, 231
Sullivan, Louis W., 231
Sunkist, 461
Suspense (radio), 123

tea parties, 369, 421
Teenage Mutant Ninja Turtles (toy), 297, 299
television (*see also* children's television; *specific shows*), 110–136, 145–155, 171–172, 175, 176, 298, 310–315, 422, 485
Television Broadcasters' Association, 117
Television in the Lives of Our Children (book), 128
Temple, Shirley, 245, 247, 258, 259
Terence, 49
Texaco Star Theater (TV), 123
Thomas, Henry, 245
Thorne, Barrie, 26, 318–336, 517
Three Billy Goats Gruff, The (book), 416
Three Little Pigs, The (book), 416
thumbsucking, 200, 201, 203, 206, 214, 219
Tidy House, The (book), 25, 26, 431–453
Tikki Tikki Tembo, 420
Time (magazine), 9
Times (London) (newspaper), 251
Timmendequas, Jesse, 269
Tin Drum, The (film), 24
Title IX, 327
To Kill a Mockingbird (book), 422
Tolkien, J. R. R., 64
Tom Sawyer, 247, 372
Tomboy (book), 487
Townsend, John Rowe, 65
"Toxic High" stickers, 128
toys, 107, 297, 299, 300, 301, 306, 309, 311. *See also* Barbie; Batman (toys); Dolls; My Little Pony (toy); Teenage Mutant Ninja Turtles (toy)
Toys "R" Us, 297
Trager, Helen G., 141
Treasure Island (film), 245
Tripp, David, 314, 315
Tripple-Trapple (book), 441
Truman, David, 227
Trump, Ivanka, 277
Tyler, Liv, 277

United Nations, 501–502
U.S. Department of Health and Human Services, 231
U.S. Department of Labor, 143
U.S. News and World Report (magazine), 139, 140, 143
usefulness as a virtue, 83, 84, 364
utopian images of childhood, 136, 140, 457
utopianism, 300, 301

Valentino, Rudolph, 464
Van Buren, Abigail, 307
vandalism, 350, 351
Victoria, Queen, 370
Victorian conceptions of childhood, 18, 23, 24, 59, 79, 98–100, 102, 120, 211, 363, 364, 369, 447–448, 452
video games, 24, 28, 114
Village of the Damned (film), 163
Village Voice (newspaper), 271
violence, 24, 117, 172, 184, 258, 340, 344, 345, 346–349, 478, 487–492, 493–495
Vogue (magazine), 273

Walkerdine, Valerie, 25, 254–264, 517
Wallace, Lew, 346, 351, 353, 355
"war on poverty," 144
Warner, Charles Dudley, 356
Wartella, Ellen, 313
Washington, George, 78
Watson, John, 212–216, 218, 307, 468, 469, 470–475
welfare, 178, 180, 181–182, 190, 266
welfare reform, 13
Werthem, Frederick, 141, 485, 486–492
What Every Baby Knows (TV), 307
What Would You Do? (TV), 29
Where the Wild Things Are (book), 416, 418, 423
Whitely, Opal, 440
Wilde, Oscar, 243
"will to orient," 138
Willard, Frances, 366
Willy Wonka and the Chocolate Factory (film), 246
Wilson, Emily, 366

Wilson, Jess H., 458, 462
Winfrey, Oprah, 270
Winky Dink and You (TV), 29, 125, 126
Winn, Marie, 311
Winship, Janice, 308
Wiseman, Frank, 138
Wizard of Oz, The (film), 174, 258, 417
Wolf, Naomi, 273
Wolf, Shelby Ann, 28, 406–430, 517
Wolfenstein, Martha, 20, 199–208, 212, 307, 517
Wolff, Perry, 146
Woman Citizen (magazine), 87
Woman's Day (magazine), 187
Women Against Violence Against Women, 259
Wonderworks (TV), 417
Wood, Elijah, 253
Woodlawn, Caddie, 366
Working Mother (magazine) 307
working-class, 25, 75, 82, 83–85, 88–89, 100, 160, 168–170, 258, 259, 263, 305, 344, 345, 431–453
World War II, 20, 110, 114, 162, 211, 302, 308, 476–482

Yale, 225
Y.M.C.A., 19, 215
You Asked for It (TV), 117
Your Child Is a Person (book), 224
Your Child Makes Sense (book), 226

Zelizer, Viviana A., 19, 22, 81–94, 517
Zolotow, Charlotte, 407
Zoobook (magazine), 419
Zuckerman, Michael, 75